Affective Memories

How Chance and the Theater Saved My Life

an Autobiography by

Laurence Luckinbill

SUNBURY
PRESS

Mechanicsburg, PA USA

Published by Sunbury Press, Inc.
Mechanicsburg, PA USA

SUNBURY
P R E S S
www.sunburypress.com

Copyright © 2024 by Laurence Luckinbill.
Cover Copyright © 2024 by Sunbury Press, Inc.

For information about special discounts for bulk purchases, please contact Sunbury Press Orders Dept. at (855) 338-8359 or orders@sunburypress.com.

To request one of our authors for speaking engagements or book signings, please contact Sunbury Press Publicity Dept. at publicity@sunburypress.com.

FIRST SUNBURY PRESS EDITION: March 2024

Set in Adobe Garamond Pro | Interior design by Crystal Devine | Cover by Lawrence Knorr | Edited by Maresa Whitehead and Elisabeth Edwards.

Publisher's Cataloging-in-Publication Data
Names: Luckinbill, Laurence, author.
Title: Affective memories : how chance and the theater saved my life / Laurence Luckinbill.
Description: First trade paperback edition. | Mechanicsburg, PA : Sunbury Press, 2024.
Summary: This is the brutally honest story of a man's struggle to make something of himself in the theater. Coming from a troubled home, he fights his way to Broadway and Hollywood. He makes mistakes, goes down blind alleys, fails and succeeds, but never quits. It's a portrait of everyone who ever had an impossible dream—full of empathy for all those who strive to rise, to never stop reaching for a goal that is more real than dreams.
Identifiers: ISBN : 978-1-62006-592-1 (paperback) | ISBN : 979-8-88819-095-1 (ePub).
Subjects: BIOGRAPHY & AUTOBIOGRAPHY / General | BIOGRAPHY & AUTOBIOGRAPHY / Entertainment & Performing Arts | PERFORMING ARTS / Theater / Broadway & Musicals.

Designed in the USA
0 1 1 2 3 5 8 13 21 34 55

For the Love of Books!

To my family—
those of you bygone and at rest,
and those of you who are thriving and striving
and still in the game.
You are my inspiration and Spirit Guides—
forever.

ACKNOWLEDGMENTS

Without these Guardian Angels and Mentors, this book would not exist.

Lucie Arnaz Luckinbill, whose love never gave up on me or my finishing this book and who partnered with me for a final edit.

Elisabeth Edwards, who deciphered my hieroglyphics and devoted many years of her life to making a manuscript out of a mess. She is a miracle.

Mark Sendroff, lawyer, but more importantly, a dear friend. His advice has been invaluable.

Charles Scribner, publisher, who said to me, "When you are ready, you will write the book you need to write."

INTRODUCTION

WHY DOES ANYONE ACT? Why would anyone become an actor—actually step away from the ordinary world of what we actors call "civilians" and join a kind of perpetually poor, profane priesthood whose sole function is to become someone else in order to live?

There's only one reason. And I had to discover it for myself.

I was asked to address the graduating class of a fine, prestigious acting studio in New York. I climbed the creaking narrow stairs of a scruffy building, which to me still held faint echoes in many languages of the ghostly immigrants—women and girls mostly—who had trooped up this same stair to work eighteen-hour days at sewing machines, piecing garments together for the carriage trade.

I came into the stuffy, cramped studio smelling of damp winter coats and boots. About twenty-five chairs, all occupied, faced a space where the speaking or acting would happen. There was no stage, just a bare, splintery floor. A couple of floodlights hung from the ceiling for stage light. Bare bones. Good. I had been introduced a minute or so before, but by the time I came in, no one in the audience was looking at me. They were draped over the chairs with attitudes of careless inattention. Some were self-involved, some involved with each other, some cats on a hot tin roof making jokes, challenging, disruptive, on the make. It was like a fifth-grade classroom.

I put my bag down and watched them for a minute. I was a guest speaker from the working world of the New York theater—a place they presumably all wanted to be a part of—so what was this reception? Rudeness? An act? Or something else?

I ditched my prepared remarks and just started to speak very quietly. I said:

"Why did they kill? Not for money, not for spite, not for hate. They killed little Bobby Franks as they might have killed a spider or a fly. For the experience. They killed him because they were made that way . . ."

I spoke slowly, looking at each one of them. I went on with Clarence Darrow's magnificent plea for clemency for the notoriously guilty "thrill-killers" facing the death penalty in Chicago in 1925. Two brilliantly gifted, rich college boys, Nathan Leopold and Richard Loeb—enabled by indulgent and remote parents and drunk with what they thought they had attained: the powers of supermen to do anything they chose (their interpretation of the philosophy of Friedrich Nietzsche). They had used their superpowers to murder heinously a child chosen at random.

For a long moment, the actors were confused. They stopped chatting among themselves. Was this the talk about the theater? Then it dawned on them—I was acting. Oh. This was a show. They began to sit forward and listen. I hadn't grabbed their attention with something dramatic or an announcement of any kind. I had just started talking from within the scene, seizing the moment as it unfolded, and, by the great Darrow's words, fully transformed them into an audience.

I came to the end of the summation:

". . . You may hang these boys. Hang them by the neck until they are dead, dead, dead. But in so doing, you will be turning your face to the past. In so doing, you will be making it harder for every other boy who, in ignorance and darkness, must grope his way through the mazes that only childhood knows . . . I am pleading for a time when hatred and cruelty will not control the hearts of men. I am pleading for a time when we will have learned by reason and judgment and understanding that all life—all life—is worth saving. And that the highest attribute of man is mercy. Mercy. Mercy. Mercy. Mercy. Mercy . . ."

And I knelt before them, head down, begging, my voice almost indistinguishable from the silence in the room. Then, slowly, I stood up and said, "Capital punishment doesn't prevent murders. But it does make more murderers."

They were silent, just looking at me. Then they began to clap, and as they did, they stood up. And as I looked back at them, I realized, saw, what their teachers looked at every day—their true faces. Eager, needy, vulnerable, believing, trusting souls waiting to be led, fed, enlightened. Saved.

Then, for some reason, I said, "Everybody who comes from a dysfunctional family, raise your hand."

A few hands went up, slowly, tentatively, as if each person wondered if he or she dared to say such a shameful thing if it were permissible to admit such a thing in public.

I waited until they began to look around and see who else had raised a hand. When they saw that some of their confreres had done so, the smirks of recognition began to blossom.

Then I said, "And the rest of you are liars."

Everyone laughed. Relief. Truth-telling. Then, every last hand went up until there was a forest of arms raised. And I remembered when I sat in one of those chairs just thirty years before, this would have been unthinkable. You absolutely were not asked and did not speak publicly about your fucked-up family.

A barrier had been crossed. Craft had been demonstrated. And believed. And honored. Trust was in the room. We were brothers and sisters. The truth was plain to see. Now we could talk about what the need to act really is:

Every actor starts there. In dreams . . . of escape.

Escape—Like Houdini—Again and Again

I shall give you hunger
and pain
and sleepless nights
also beauty
and satisfaction known to few
and glimpses of heavenly life

None of these shall you have
continually
and of their coming and going
you shall not be foretold.

—EDWIN BOOTH (1833–1893)
On the God Of All Art
Whispering to Actors

PROLOGUE

KATONAH, NEW YORK. It's dark here at night. The big trees loom over the fragile little wooden cottage and move mysteriously, making ominous shadows under the moon. The moon moves constantly behind the night clouds but stays in the same place in the sky. All is illusion.

The kids are huddled together in a tiny room off the kitchen. Everything creaks like a ship in a storm, and the shadows pass across the single window like creatures trying to get in.

The city kids in the country are spooked. The big ones joke about it nervously, and the little ones look at me like I'm the captain of the ship who can explain every groan and moan and chitter of the house and every dark shadow that wipes out the weak moonlight as if a giant wave has broken over the little boat, swamping it for a terrible second. Big and little, they huddle closer. I am telling a story. It's to become a never-ending tale, which spools out of me as a continual improvisation. It is my own invention of wild events with magic realism and illusion that happen to a very young boy and his companion, an anthropomorphic pigeon who talks. The story naturally includes as characters the four boys and one girl who listen intently because they don't want to go to sleep in this otherworldly old house in the dark woods peopled with friendly giants.

The story has a title: *The Adventures of George and Cucuru*. I will tell this story as a serial for years. My daughter will urge a new episode every night—no matter where we happen to be. She is the greatest example of *E poi?*—*And then?*

John Ciardi, the translator of the best version of *Dante's Inferno*, tells that when he was a boy, his grandma, who spoke only Italian but understood young John's English, would invite him up onto her lap and ask him to tell a story. He would start inventing but ran out of steam and stop. *La Nonna* would gently urge him: *E poi?* And he would find inspiration and tell her the next piece of his story. That was how Ciardi became a writer. All my kids liked the story, but my daughter never stopped asking. "And then what happened, Daddy?"

And that is why I have written this story of my life.

ACT I

Home.

I believed I could fly and decided to try.

I climbed as high as I dared and looked down. The ground was pretty far away. I looked out past the wet, weedy grass, the patches of bare ground, to the chicken coop holding up the leaning barn, and over a broken fence to the alley—the green and shadowed place, No Man's Land.

I would fly that far.

My little sister, Lynne, looked up at me. She looked scared. Did I?

No. I knew I could fly.

I checked to see if my cape was ready to flare out behind me when I soared across the yard. I wanted that effect. I would not go high; this was a test flight.

I stuck out an arm, pointing in the direction of my flight. This would help me level off in a horizontal position. I took a breath. I stepped out into the air.

And fell straight down.

I hit the soft summer earth with one foot in front of the other. It was the pose I wanted, but the pain of the landing spoiled it.

I sprained my ankle so badly that I had to walk with a stick for a week.

My sister, as always, was sympathetic. She didn't laugh.

Neither did I. I was mad. I undid the safety pins, holding the threadbare towel to the collar of my too-large t-shirt. My cape hadn't performed as expected. A design problem.

I had failed.

But what was one failure? What about the Wright brothers? I knew I would try again, like them. Never mind that I didn't have an airplane—I had a strange power. I needed to fly. I had to.

I was nine years old. My sister was five. I had just jumped off the back porch of our little house in Arkansas and dropped about seven feet to the ground.

Some flight, some might say. But it was the first of many tries to fly in many ways, all my life.

I'm eighty-nine years old now. My sister—if only she were still here— would be eighty-four. Before she left, I asked her if she remembered the event that summer day.

She said, "Yes, and I thought you were crazy. And brave. I admired you. I thought if he can do it, so can I!"

Here's what I know now:

If you have to do something you really believe in, do it. Even when it hurts. Just be sure you are the only one it hurts.

And: You can't know if, just by the act of trying, you might inspire someone, even be a mentor.

S C E N E : Four Stories in Fort Smith, Arkansas

We three sat in a triangle. My mother and me, and him. He gave the impression that, seated, he was stumbling. He weaved back and forth to the right and left, slowly and without rhythm. His face was dark red, almost purple, and in his lap, he held his bandaged hand, the white sheeting soaked with drying blood halfway up his forearm.

I could hear the clock. It was tinny sounding, but we had had it a long time, and it still worked. On its face, it said "Big Ben" in curly black letters, and one of my earliest memories—when I was sick for a long time—is connected to that clock. Even before I knew what it was, I identified home with it. Home. Not this place.

The hands pointed straight up and down, six and twelve. Six a.m. In the next room, the shades that had been black all night were now yellow with the age of the night turning to morning, and one beam of light cut through a torn place like a hot knife blade.

No sound. Not even breathing. After a while, I was swinging my legs so that my heels fell against the kitchen chair legs, making a rhythmic thumping sound. One-*two*. One-*two*. One-*two*. *One*-two. *One*-two. My father's head began to sink lower and lower until it rested on my mother's lap where she sat, her hands touching his. I felt her hand on my leg, stopping my kicking. Her hand felt warm and loving as if its quality soaked through the cloth of my Big Buster jeans.

"Shhhh," she said, "Go outside and play now."

Jimmy Cason jumped across from the high rock wall to the roof of the Aristocrat Cleaning plant. It was only four feet across but about twenty down if you misjudged, so we always felt like brave mountaineers when we made it.

We began to throw rooftop gravel at the sparrows on the telephone wires.

"Boy," said Jimmy. "My dad says your dad tried to kill Mr. Christians this morning."

"He did not," I said and threw a rock so hard I almost fell off the roof.

"You better not call my dad a liar," he said. His face was melting into meanness when he said it.

"Shut up," I said. Then I slapped him hard on the back of his neck. He turned away, crying. I was sorry. I was bigger than he was, but I wore his clothes because his mother gave them to my mother since we lived in the apartment they owned, and we were poor, and they weren't.

He jumped across to the wall again and started to walk away.

"I'm sorry," I called. He turned, and his face was very mean.

"My dad says your dad was drunk again this morning, and Mr. Christians locked the store so he couldn't get in, and your dad broke the glass with his fist and went in and chased Mr. Christians with a knife, and your dad was arrested."

I jumped to the wall, but Jimmy backed away in fright.

"He was arrested. And my dad says he can't have it anymore, and you're going to have to move because we can't get any decent roomers because your dad is drunk all the time."

"He is not. He is not!" I screamed, and I took out after Jimmy. Jimmy was faster than me, so I stopped.

"You leave me alone," he panted as he picked up a rock. "My dad says your dad is a goddamned drunkard, and I'm glad you're going to move away, you bastard!" Then he threw the rock at me and ran away. It hit me hard, and I just let it.

When I came in, my mother was wiping the pan she had used to soak my father's bandaged hand.

"Mother," I said. "Where is he?"

She put a finger to her lips and said, "Shhhh. He's sleeping now."

He was lying on his side on a cotton quilt my mother had laid on the linoleum floor. He was long and thin and dark, and he looked dead. I didn't know what to think or feel. So, I didn't.

* * *

My father sat behind the wheel, tapping the dash with his onyx ring. My mother sat in the shotgun seat, arms folded, staring out the side window. On top of our tired, used vehicle, suitcases and boxes were tied to a mattress that Mr. Cason let us keep when he said we must move. Everything we owned was on or in that car.

My older sister Sally was asleep with her knees pulled up to her chest and her frail hands entwined in her thin, damp hair. I sat close to Lynne with my feet up on a suitcase. Lynne looked at the back of my father's neck with her big eyes wide open in the darkness. She didn't seem like she was breathing.

My father said, "Well, what'll it be? Fort Smith or Oklahoma City?"

No one answered. I thought after a while that someone should answer my father. He was the head of the family.

"Let's go home," I said. Home was Fort Smith, from which we had gone two years ago—to the new job, to the big chance—and toward which we now went with all our possessions, going to some other life.

My father turned and looked at me. "No, son, not you. You don't say. This is for us growed-ups." And he stuck his tongue between his teeth like when he thought something was funny. He grinned, looking at my mother, wanting her to laugh.

She looked deeper into the night and didn't laugh, turn to him, or speak.

My father stopped grinning. Then he reached into the back seat and ran his big red hand through Lynne's hair. She stopped sucking her thumb and smiled at him.

"Hi, sugar," he said, "How's my girl?" He sounded confident, but his voice was raspy and strangely quavering. This, I knew, was after he had been drunk for a long time and was just beginning to be normal again.

"Why can't I say?" I complained. "Let's go to Fort Smith, Mother."

My father looked at her.

"How about it, Agnes? Reckon we ought to do what the boy says?"

My mother looked out the window.

Finally, she asked, "Will it be any different, Laurence?"

My father looked sharply out the windshield for a moment. When he turned back to my mother, I could see the annoyance in his eyes.

But he said, "Baby . . . never. Baby, I won't touch another drop as long as I live. It won't happen again. I swear to God, Baby!" He was looking at her all the time he said it, just staring into her.

I watched my mother's face from the side. I saw a tiny light enter her eyes, and I knew she believed my father.

She turned to him and said, "All right, Laurence. I want to go home." She pressed her lips together so she wouldn't let out the cry that was trying to get out.

My father grabbed her, leaned toward her, and kissed her on the mouth. I had never seen him do that before. I could tell how hard he kissed her because their lips were mashed together, and they were tight against each other, and my father had his arms all the way around my mother's back. Then I knew she was crying because her back moved inside her cotton dress in heaves and starts. She didn't make any noise, just heaved. My father put his head on her shoulder and looked toward the back, and I could see the tears in his eyes. They were like burning lights in a cave.

"Goddamnit," he said through his teeth. "May I hope to die if I touch it again."

I felt like crying, too, but I didn't know why. I felt like sucking my thumb like Lynne, with her nammy-nam over her face. But how could I do that? I was The Boy. I looked through the glass and saw a dark green forest. I pretended the forest was moving. I wanted to be in it, in a forest that was going somewhere mysterious, someplace secret. I wished this were a window that opened. What was the use of a car window that didn't open? If it did, I could slide out through it, and the hot night wind would take me right into the dark place. The wind would hold me up, and I wouldn't be me; instead, I would be something in the dark woods that lived there in the air.

Later, the moon came up and made the dusty old car gleam as it descended slowly to the rhythm of the curves of the mountains and down onto the straight road that led to Fort Smith.

The girls were sleeping, even my mother. My father drove like he was a part of the road. He liked to drive. I watched the back of his head. He had his old brown hat on. It was old, but it didn't look old. He always brushed it off, kept it nice. Kept his clothes nice. I liked that.

Finally, I slept too.

* * *

I turned the key in the lock and jammed my shoulder against the door hard.

"He's put the chain lock on."

My mother and Lynne were standing on the porch with their coat collars up around their ears and trying to keep the icy wind off me. I had no coat since I had come directly from work when they said he was at it again. My mother walked to the front bedroom window and scratched on the screen.

"Laurence," she said, "Let us in. Come and open this door. Your son has no coat on."

No sound from inside. No lights on.

"Open this door," I shouted, slamming my shoulder against it again.

Suddenly, it opened wide. I almost fell down at the stockinged feet of my father. He stood there in his undershorts and undershirt, looking vindictive. He smelled of beer, cigarettes, and unwashed socks.

"Watch what the goddamned hell you're doin'," he mumbled. "You bust that lock, and you'll wish you hadn't."

"Let us in," I shouted again, right in his face.

"Laurence, it's cold out here, and the boy has no coat on, so get out of the way so we can get in the house."

He didn't move. He looked bewildered. Then he set his mouth.

"What's he . . . look at what he done to the lock. Look. Listen . . . look . . . here at thish goddamn lock, here."

He leaned toward the door facing and held up the bent chain. He looked at me. Then he pulled back his clenched fist.

"Wash what you done to that good chain, boy. I'm going to beat the livin' daylights out of you."

My mother pushed in front of me.

"Shut up," she said. "Just shut up." She brushed past him into the living room, and he swayed back and started to follow her.

"*Wait* a minute," he said. "Just wait a goddamn minute, you . . ."

My mother turned to him sharply. "Where have you been? Just where in hell have you been tonight?" My mother never cursed.

My father looked surprised, then bewildered, then puzzled. He squinted his eyes and looked at my mother.

"Where have I been? Well," he said, as if he had settled the question, "where do you think I've been?"

She tapped her foot. "Laurence, were you to get paid tonight?"

My father turned and walked into the bedroom, slowly. My mother took her hands out of the pockets of her pale cloth coat and followed him.

"Did you hear me?" she almost screamed. "How much money did you get paid?"

My father rummaged clumsily in the pockets of his new cream-colored pants—a new suit he was set up with at his new job. He pulled out three highway maps and held them out to her.

"Where have I been? Where have I been?" He pointed to each map. "Arkansas, Oklahoma, and Texas."

Huh? He smiled at Lynne and me, but I could not look at him. Lynne looked at the floor.

"That's where I been," he said.

My mother slapped the maps to the floor viciously. "I want to know where in the hell your paycheck is," she said. "We've got to have that money, and we've got to have it now."

The expression on his face turned to cunning. He looked at the floor. "Paycheck?" he said. "Well, hmm, see . . . Ernie said . . . he said . . ." He chuckled.

"Said what?" my mother cut in sharply.

"Well, umm . . . no paychecks till the first is jus' what he told me. Now, you can ask him if you want to."

"I did ask him," my mother said sharply. "I did ask him before I picked up Larry Jr., and you got paid, according to him. Now, what did you get drunk on?"

"I'm not drunk," he said.

My mother looked at him with hatred. Then she grabbed his pants from the bed and started yanking everything out of the pockets. She jerked the last pocket out and flung the pants to the floor. Tears were racing down her cheeks.

"Laurence, if you've taken that money out . . ." she cried. Then she grabbed the double-breasted cream jacket from the bed and pulled out all the pockets. Her hand caught in the last one, and she ripped the entire pocket right out of the jacket. She threw it at the front window.

He watched her, and I could see the meanness start to rise in his eyes. I was ten feet away. His body tensed suddenly, and his legs, with all the purple varicose veins on them, eased into a crouch. His skinny chest trembled with resentment and hate, and his mouth hardened down to a straight line. I stood there. It seemed like a long time. Then she turned and pulled the sheets off the bed. She reached for the roll of bills my father had hidden there, and he jumped at her. He hit her in the chest and fell on top of her, both of them bashing against the foot of the bed and falling to the floor. My mother screamed and scratched his back, tearing away his undershirt with her fingernails and leaving bloody marks down his back.

He grabbed her hand, the one with the bills in it, tore her fingers open, and hit her in the mouth with his fist. I saw blood come from my mother's lips, and then I was behind my father. I pulled the skinny shoulder back hard and hit him in the face as hard as I could with my left fist. He slid back to his knees off my mother's groin and grabbed for me, dropping the money, and I hit him again in the neck. I felt my fist mash into his Adam's apple; then I hit him again in the nose with my right hand. He crumpled to the foot of the bed, and I hit him again. I was crying. Water was pouring down my face, and his blood was on my hands, on my face. Maybe it was my mother's blood, too. There was blood all over—on my shirt, on his shirt, and on my mother's dress, and her mouth was bleeding. Then I hit him again on the head. His eyes were shut and swelling up, and his head bounced off the bed frame, and I hit him. I hit him in the face, in the neck. I hit him, I hit him, I hit him, I hit him, I hit him, I hit him.

My sister was pulling at me, and I heard her crying.

"Larry, please. Larry, please. Please stop."

My mother was trying to talk, but her mouth was already swelling up like a busted piece of sausage. They were both yelling at me. I got off my father. He looked like he was dead, but he wasn't because puke came out of his mouth whenever his chest and stomach heaved. And he laid there at the foot of the bed and puked his guts out, and he didn't even know it. He was out like a light.

My mother and Lynne were both crying hard, and we must have made a sight, the four of us.

Then I turned, went out of the bedroom and through the front door and started walking. I walked until I couldn't see or hear, and when I started to taste the blood I had caused, I started to run. I ran, and I ran, and I ran until the blood was my own coming from my bitten lips. And then I stopped.

It was very cold. The moon was alone in the autumn sky, beautiful as ever. I crawled under some scraggly hydrangea bushes along the west side—the warmer one—of the brick-walled Methodist church and laid there. Later, after the sweat dried up on my body and the blood crusted on my lips, it got much colder.

* * *

The Christmas that Sally and I went home for the last time, we had called from the bus station and got no answer. Sally called Aunt Annie's, and Mother was there, so Sally went to meet her, and I took the bags home.

My father was roaming around the empty house. I put the bags at the front door and said hello to him, thinking this would be a short visit and it might be the only time I could—or would want to—speak to him. All he said was, "Where's your mother?"

I told him, and he sat down and began crying. His hair had turned gray in the last few years, and he looked very old and sick. His hawk's nose was more prominent because the flesh of his face had dropped back and had become a permanent dull crimson. All the blood vessels in his face seemed to have burst and splattered their blood under the skin of his cheeks. His eyes, too, were cloudy, and the whites were yellow. He sat in his favorite chair, surrounded by empty beer cans and full ashtrays. It stank. How could she live like this, I wondered. And I didn't understand why she wasn't there, either, so I asked him.

He said he didn't remember anything but that she had been gone for two days, maybe more, and no one would let him in or tell him anything about her.

"Why did she leave in the first place?" I asked again.

He got up and walked across the room, then smashed his fist into the wall. He turned back, and tears spouted out of his eyes.

"I hit her," he said. "I'm not lying, boy; I hit her. And as God is my witness, I will never do it again. I just . . ."

I sat there trying not to hear. It was never going to end until he was dead. I hated him. I hated him for doing it, and I hated her for letting him. And neither of them could stop. I had been out of it for almost three years. I had tried to forget it, him, even her, and she never mentioned any of this in her letters. The prayers and Mass cards she sent were all about me and my future.

"I'm glad you're home," he said. "You glad to be here?"

"Jesus, Jesus Christ," I must have said out loud, although I only thought it.

"I called Father James. I'm going to go see him Saturday. I'll go to confession. I love your mother. You know that, don't you?"

"Yeah, I know that."

He looked at me. His mouth hardened in self-disgust. "I don't blame you, boy. I'm a failure. But I'm not a goddamned liar."

He got up and went into the kitchen. He opened the icebox, and though I knew what he was doing, I walked to the door and looked. He was drinking from a quart of beer, and his hands were shaking. I looked around the room for the whiskey. He had probably hidden stashes in every room, but I knew he couldn't afford to buy it anymore. Mother kept the purse strings now. She took any checks directly from the mailman and made my father sign them over to her. He put the beer back and sat at the table where he had a half-eaten can of chili with the spoon stuck in it and some saltines.

"Boy, when I was younger than you, I left home and went on the train to Seattle, Washington. I was going to join the Merchant Marine. I wanted to ship out to China. I went with another fellow, but when we got to Seattle, they took Jim but not me. Told me I was underweight and too tall."

"Too tall?" I said.

He stuck his tongue between his teeth and chuckled. "That's what they said, 'too tall.' So, I went home and supported my mother and sister. My brothers took out and left home. I was holdin' the bag. Then, when I met your mother . . ." He slapped himself on the back of his neck. Then, to keep from tears again, he blew his nose loudly two or three times, wiped it, and stuffed his handkerchief back in his pocket.

"Mark run off to Texas, and Harry, Frank, and Dale went to Kansas City right after him. And I stayed. And I met your mother. I kept the same job for twenty-two—no, twenty-three—years. Goddamnit, I was making money when plenty of people were starving, and don't you forget that." He looked at me like he would drill holes through me. "It was tough, then. So goddamn tough, you couldn't . . . Come on, let's arm-wrestle!" And he put his wasted elbow down on the table. "Come on! I can beat you."

I sat down and gripped his hand and smelled the whiskey. He was drunk now. I never knew how to tell. He would be anything but sober, and I couldn't tell until he did something crazy. I don't think he knew he was drunk anymore. But if he couldn't get drunk, he got dangerous.

I pressed his arm to the tabletop. He chuckled and said, "Damn good, boy! Fair and square. You are strong. I'm glad." Then he put his head in his hands and began crying again, great bubbles of grief pouring out through his hands, his shoulders shaking uncontrollably.

"I'm a failure."

I got him some tomato juice, and he drank it all greedily with shaking hands.

"Thanks, son," he said. He got up, went into the bedroom, and laid down on the bed. I followed him to the bedroom door.

"I didn't mean to do nothing . . . I mean anything . . . anything . . . you hear?"

I told him to go to sleep, and I shut the door. I stood by the door, willing myself to stay another minute.

When my mother came in the door, I saw what he was talking about. He had hit her all right. Both her eyes were black and blue and puffed up three days after they fought. There was a big gash in her upper lip where he had broken her upper plate. She looked so frail and hurt I couldn't stand to look at her. It was useless to ask her what happened. She would take half the blame no matter what. She hated him and loved him and would not leave him and would not get help.

"I don't see the point in leaving him. I don't think he can quit. It would probably kill him quicker if he did stop."

Sally asked her to leave with us.

"No, Sally, if this is my cross to bear, then I'll bear it. And I think it will be better if you two go. He generally gets worse when you two are here. It makes him nervous, I guess."

"What about Lynne?" I asked.

"Well, she's not coming this Christmas. She can't get away from that nursing school even for a weekend this year; they are so tough on those girls, and she can't afford it even if she could get away. So, it's fine. Annie and I will be fine. I'm just going to pack a few things and stay with her for Christmas. He will be here by himself, and maybe he can straighten himself out. Father James told me he called him. He will talk to him. Make sure he gets to Mass. So, go. I understand. And I don't blame you. Just write me back when I write to you." And she smiled. It hurt to look at.

I grabbed the luggage, kissed her on the cheek, and said, "We're not leaving for good, for crying out loud. And call me. You know there is such a thing as a telephone."

She didn't laugh, just said gravely, "I know."

She knew I didn't mean it—even though I didn't know it—about coming back, even though I didn't know it myself. She was alone. It was her cross. She would carry it.

When I could, I sent her money. I wrote cards from faraway places.

* * *

These four stories about my family appeared in my typewriter in the fall of 1956 and winter of 1957, many years after the events.

I don't know where any of it came from or what events, if any, kicked it out of my subconscious and into my typewriter. As I finished a page and pulled it out of the tight carriage roller with an audible snap, I saw it in print, and each story became real. The way it was. Like all of history, mythologized but true.

The characters in these stories are all real-ish, although I left out my baby brother Leo entirely. He was two and three, and five when most of those events were played out. He was lucky enough to have been left with our aunts during the fighting, only to be slammed and crushed much worse by his time on the front line than I had been by it all. After I escaped, he and Lynne, too young to get away, had stayed on, living scenes of increasing despair and sorrow in constantly changing settings as the family migrated to California from Arkansas (poor latter-day Arkies). My father got sicker and sicker, and my mother got angrier and more desolate.

Sally had gone to nursing school in St. Louis before our forced evacuation from our Ozark abode. She died young, leaving behind six beautiful children, without truly escaping from the prison of desperation and imitative behavior that was the fate of our family: locked in the dank cell of a madman.

Alcoholism comes in like a cheerful guest at a party who turns out to be a Poe-ish nightmare character who systematically extracts the hearts from the other guests in slow and agonizing ways.

The worst part is that "love" survives it all, but in forms that rival horror movies. In 1957, I described my father's funeral in detail. He didn't actually die for another twenty-four years, but I could not write about him until I killed him. From the moment I imagined him in a coffin, I made him dead in my soul. And then that soul-killer turned on me and killed me, too.

My mother never left my father. She died ten years after he did, deep in dementia, in a state that would have been mortifyingly shameful to her—cursing, stripping herself naked, going into the halls, spouting sexually offensive rants in the lobby of the nice, upscale lockbox where we enlightened boys and girls stuff our betters when they refuse to be seen but not heard.

SCENE: The Family

Mother's family was half-German, half-Irish. She was one of five sisters—two boys had come first and had died of influenza during World War I.

Our family was Catholic on both sides. My father's family was Swiss-descended but called Pennsylvania Dutch. Their ancestors, Johan and Jacob Lugenbühl, had traveled from Switzerland to Philadelphia in a Scottish ship, *The Thistle*, in 1731. They had left the safety of the city and gone into the frontier of Penn's Sylvania to farm. This was before the French and Indian War. They were two brave and intrepid brothers whose families were refugees of Europe's religious wars.

All five Luckinbill brothers were alcoholics. Their father was a shopkeeper in Native American territory before Oklahoma became a state. His store—distinguished by a life-sized silver horse that stood outside on the board sidewalk raised above the muddy street—carried hardware, farm goods, blacksmith goods and coffins. He was the coffin builder and undertaker. One of my father's earliest jobs was tacking the satin covering inside the walls of the coffins.

My grandfather was remote, harsh and violent—an alcoholic. He died young of a heart attack, leaving his wife and six children—five boys and a girl, who was the youngest. His wife, my grandma—we called her Nonnie—had no means of making a living, was too good for trade, and loved to read. By the time I came along in 1934, she was supported by my father and his only sister, who stayed home, never married, worked at the same job in a bank all her life, and who seemed to me to be a very unhappy woman.

The star of the family was the oldest son, who was a Catholic priest; a Benedictine monk who taught Native American children at the Sacred Heart Monastery School in Shawnee, Oklahoma. He died at thirty-six of a heart attack. He was the Luckinbill saint.

I was always curious about him. He was revered. But, considering all the other Luckinbill men, I wondered how—or if—he had extricated himself from the Luckinbill curse, alcoholism.

Mother was pretty, graceful, had nice legs, and loved to dance. A flapper. This 1920s song describes her: "Five foot two, eyes of blue / Oh what those five feet could do . . ."

My father was a good-looking man, an intelligent man, an honest man. Neither cruel nor kind, and ordinary. He was educated only to the seventh grade, but that was very well for the simpler needs of his time and much better than today's seventh graders. He was able but self-disabled.

My mother, Agnes
Nulph Luckinbill.
Fort Smith, Arkansas.

My father, Laurence
Benedict Luckinbill.
Fort Smith, Arkansas.

Although my mother had no chance to act on it, I believe she wanted to escape her family. Her mother and sisters were very judgmental of anyone even a tiny bit different. There was little romance in their lives then. It was toil, toil, and shut up about it. My mother had a need for delight and a sense of humor. She liked to dance and to make a party. The night she met a tall, dark, handsome man who danced well, had a good sense of humor, and had a bit of a wild streak (they whispered that he was a bootlegger, and he didn't deny it), both their fates were sealed.

My mother and father were married in 1926. He was twenty-four; she was twenty-two. They honeymooned in St. Louis and stayed for their first time in a hotel. She was a virgin. So was he. But there was trouble in River City. The marriage was disapproved. Her mother and sisters didn't like him. His mother, sister, and brothers didn't think much of her. They started out married life with two strikes against them.

They loved each other, and they loved their four children who came along about five years apart. But his drinking quickly became a problem. It was a deadly disease.

* * *

There were no heroic models in my family. My engineer grandpa was a hero to me, but he was seventy-four and died when I was five. My monk-uncle was distant and dead. Even though my grandma, Lucy (Nonnie), said I was like him and would be the priest in this generation of Luckinbills, and even though the priesthood was equivalent to sainthood in my grandma's eyes and she favored me, I knew it was not for me. By the fifth grade, I knew I would never be a priest. I liked girls, and I liked being with them. Nonnie was not kind to many, especially her daughter and my father. But she was kind to me. She was content to have me play for hours at her feet while she sat rocking and reading. About once an hour, she would give me a Nehi soda or a Dr Pepper and a Moon Pie or some other Southern diabetes-inducing treat. She'd also have one herself—and she already had diabetes.

I made all my own toys. I created a platoon of two-inch tall American WWII soldiers, drawn on cardboard, colored, cut out, and each fitted with a little paper foldout wing to stand up. I was the leader, of course, and with my paper soldiers, I won the war every day for America. The war was a happy, oblivious time for me.

The great source for heroic models, other than picture shows and Saturday serials, were "funny books" (comic books), which were an important part of my life from ages eight to fifteen. I had graduated from fighting my sister over the black-and-white comic strips—*the Katzenjammer Kids, Krazy Kat, Little Orphan Annie,* and *Dick Tracy*—in the Sunday paper. I became an entrepreneur, a collector of nickel-and-dime 8 x 10 booklets of luridly colored action-adventure stories. As soon as I got my dollar-a-week job, I started assembling sets of these incredibly drawn hero stories: classics, horror, and weird humor. On Saturday mornings, I presided over a brisk trader's market on my porch steps, dealing in these precious items. The most powerful influence on me was Captain Marvel.

Shazam! Solomon, Hercules, Atlas, Zeus, Achilles, Mercury. The lightning bolt gifts of these gods bestowed superhuman strength, speed, stamina, courage, invulnerability, flight, and the power to enact magic lightning of his own upon Billy Batson, a poor, disabled newsboy (me!). *Shazam!* And I was transported to a world of magical adventure and slightly insane, goofy fun. Captain Marvel wore a very cool costume—red, white, and gold. He had a great grin and looked like he was having fun. I didn't like Superman. He never looked like he was having fun when he was saving someone or adjusting a planet's orbit. He was so corporate, all business with Mr. S. A politician doing good deeds with a no-nonsense, no hello, no goodbye, kind of no personality. I liked my heroes with a sense of humor. Batman was creepy. Plastic Man was fun, if way too strange and ugly, but his exploits looked like a possible reality because the properties of plastic were beginning to be understood. He fascinated me. The Torch and Toro were scary weird.

But the Captain was really just little Billy Batson, and I identified with him completely. I was almost totally in my own fantasy. I was the odd one—"disabled" rang a psychic bell. An aunt who lived next door (family members were everywhere) spied on me as I crept through the shrubbery tracking game, being a noble Native American on a buffalo hunt, or getting ready to attack a wagon train (for a good, noble reason, of course). I'd see the lace curtains in my aunt's window twitching as she watched me. It ruined my concentration. My aunts and uncles seemed either amused by my strangeness or irritated and challenged by it. For me, it was not a phase, not a put-on. I was serious. I was who I fantasized I was.

One aunt, the most disapproving of me, the one most like my strict grandmother and the one who slapped my mother when they were both old—my mother, eighty, my aunt, ninety—slapped her hard in the face and knocked her glasses off over some comment my mother made after coming back to Fort Smith from California. This well-to-do aunt felt affronted by my mother's new California attitude, or maybe she still thought she had some ancient power over her younger sister, and she lashed out viciously. My mother was devastated by both the slap and the lack of love—my aunt's inability to accept her as she was even after seventy years.

But this same aunt gave me the most wonderful birthday present imaginable. I was seven. It was the Sunday of my First Holy Communion. She handed me a wrapped present. It was a beautiful book, *The Adventures of Robin Hood*, written by Howard Pyle and illustrated by Lawrence Beall Smith. I opened it at once. The preface began:

> You who so plod amongst serious things that you feel
> it a shame to give yourself up for even a few short
> moments to mirth and joyousness in the land of fancy;
> you who think that life hath not to do with innocent laughter that can
>   harm no one; these pages are not for
> you; clap to the leaves and go no farther . . .

Yes! Oh my God. For an author to say that to a kid like me at age seven / was pure heaven. That rhymes, and it's exactly right. That message was as important to me as knowing the Latin responses when I was an altar boy speaking sacred words.

I stood at the window in our little house in Fort Smith to read these words of Mr. Pyle's, with the crisp new book propped on the sill and our own lace curtains pushed aside so I could get more light (I could not see the words clearly enough—I was twelve before I got my first pair of glasses). Suddenly, I had permission for my feelings from one of my gods—a living author. I wasn't crazy! Some grown-ups felt as I did! I have wondered ever since how it was that my uptight aunt would give me such a book. Didn't she know the sedition she would plant in my heart? Maybe she dismissed Robin Hood as childish. Maybe she thought the pictures were nice, so I could just look at them and be happy. Could it be that she saw me as a poor relation in need of fantasy? The book was a rope ladder lowered to a boy stuck at the bottom of a well. Maybe . . . she loved me?

I ate that book. I smelled it, I tasted it, I kissed it. It slept with me in my bed at night after I read a precious bit of it under the covers with a flashlight. It walked to school in the rain with me, safe in my cheesecloth book bag. It sat beside me at dinner and breakfast. It was my constant friend and the touchstone of my imagination. It was life.

In contrast, what a terror the troll television is! It has the brute power to blank imagination from the hearts of children. It drowns individual thoughts and original images in corrupt and infected committee thinking, assembly-line ideas that induce banality.

I needed only one push into my inner self to believe I could fly. My face must have shone with the light of gratitude. I feel it now, at eighty-nine, still trying to understand life and its amazing surprises and wonders. Ownership of my first book was my first experience of heaven. I saw, behind the paraphernalia of "real" life, something more real. I saw my mind, my imagination. Suddenly, I knew I could trust that more than what was called "real." People dismissed fantasy as unreal, without value. I knew that stories, fantasy, and fiction were more than "real"—they were glimpses of the possibility of all life.

This scared me. I was touching fire. Something in me began to smolder, and the heat challenged all I was being taught about what people had to do to live, and even about right and wrong! I saw that God was much bigger, much more mysterious, and more kind than I was being told. The altar boy in me was terrified. I was being taught hellfire, eternal punishment, and damnation. Sulfurous smoke from the pit would curl around my nostrils! I had to choose. I wanted what I saw in books. And I had to step through the gates of hell to get it: "Abandon all hope, ye who enter here."

SCENE: Fort Smith, Arkansas

I was born and lived for twelve years in an ordinary, affordable, blue-collar house in an unremarkable neighborhood. It could have been a stage set for a George Kelly, William Inge, or Paul Osborn play. The third floor was an attic with two small windows, like tiny eyes on each side. Here, the bones of the house, the roof, were exposed like the head and limbs of a pre-historic skeleton, with spidery nooks and hidey holes everywhere. Dark. Scary, as attics were in stories and picture shows. The unfinished roof joists had a burnt sawmill scent. It was Indian Joe's cave, Penrod's box, and a storehouse of mysterious artifacts of unknown origin. There was an original hand-crank RCA "His Master's Voice" phonograph with a curved horn, a thick turntable, and a heavy phono-arm on a swivel bearing a broad needle waiting to be set into the grooves of the thick wax 78-rpm records that had been left there, undisturbed, for decades.

I cranked up and listened to the Two Black Crows a thousand times. The Two Black Crows performed comedy routines done by two white Negro dialect impersonators, as in the *Amos and Andy Show*, in the unconscious racism of that era. The shows were recordings of vaudeville shtick from burnt cork blackface minstrel shows. My mother saw such shows in our town as a girl, along with KKK cross burnings in the neighbors' backyards. I learned their acts without any judgment. I didn't know why I did this. The energy, the panache,

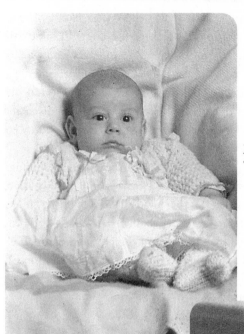

Me, 3 months old already asking, "Who am I?"

Me, 3 years old, my first role, Puck, early optimism and fun.

the slap and shuffle of the words hypnotized me. Show-biz razzmatazz. It had a juice that was new to me, living in a family utterly lacking in that kind of joy. There were opera records—somebody named Caruso—that didn't interest me. There were historic radio casts like "The Hindenburg Disaster." I marveled at the excitement that came to me through the scratchy static of the needle riding around the grooves.

My younger sister believed our drunken father had abused her in that attic as a child. I trusted my sister. If it was true, I hope my father was an unwilling Frankenstein's monster. If it wasn't true, it was her nightmare, which cost her years of pain.

In that attic, I had the feeling of being utterly alone in the universe and liking it, of disappearing, of not being in that family. It felt safe. But I had a nightmare, too, which came many, many nights. I am claustrophobic and acrophobic. The dream was always the same. I am crawling like a bug across a featureless, gray plain toward a tiny opening at the bottom of a towering dark cliff. I have to do this. No reason; I'm just forced to do it. Each time, I crawl into the hole. Once I am all the way in, the walls of the tunnel close slowly around me and squeeze me tighter and tighter. My whole body, head, and face are squeezed by a thick substance, not like flesh or anything ever known before it. It is like taffy, like quicksand, like mucous-filled air, and it moves of its own volition. It's alive! When I cannot move at all—I'm immobilized—I begin to suffocate. There's no air. No light. I'm alone. There's no way out. No help. I can't scream; I can't breathe! Strange to say, I never think about dying. I am utterly, blindly, absolutely determined to get out. Then I wake up soaked in sweat.

One night, I sleepwalked. I was three or four. I woke up suddenly, teetering on the top step into the attic. I had climbed thirteen steep steps and now stood poised to fall backward to the bottom. But this night, I woke up suddenly, surrounded by family: my older sister, mother, father, grandpa. Their hands hold me up; I hear murmured words, see worried faces—then nothing. I passed out.

Around five years old, I was sick in bed for a long time. The family doctor, who had birthed me and presided over every birth and death in our family, visited me often. I knew he was around when I smelled his cigar and heard his stentorian nasal voice saying, "He's very sick. We just have to wait and see." My mother's face bent over me in the bed. I had a high fever, and I was very weak. I couldn't eat or drink anything but goat's milk. That Christmas, it snowed two inches on Christmas Eve—a big snow for Arkansas—and I heard tiny hoof steps on the shingles and Santa's voice, crisp, distant, frozen. I looked out the window and saw the sleigh crossing the sky. And I was utterly happy. Then the fever broke. They said it was my heart—a heart murmur. Rheumatic fever. I knew Santa had cured me.

I was born and brought home to this house. I came out "in a big hurry," my mother said, in the early morning hours of "a dark and stormy night." In spite of the murder-mystery circumstances, I was a happy, optimistic, smiling, quiet, gentle kid—who grew up to be a brooding, depressed, fearful man with a ferocious and frightening temper. I had a dark side that scared and attracted women—damaged, alluring women (think Franz Wedekind's *Lulu*), the self-destructive, sarcastic women who tied me in love knots, fucked me, and left me more screwed up and, paradoxically, more alienated and arrogant than ever.

S C E N E : Fort Smith, Arkansas

I am in the claw-foot bathtub being soaped up. My mother is bathing me. My mother, not our sometime housekeeper. This was before mother went to work. Years later, when I was five, it was always the housekeeper who *warshed* me in the *warshtub* on the kitchen floor. She would heat the water on the stove and pour it over my head, no matter how scalding it was, then scrub the hell out of me with a rough brush. Oh, I was clean then! Skinned! Then she would boil fresh water and warsh my one-year-old sister while I dried myself on a threadbare towel.

But, back to Mom. I am being soaped up, and I am getting an erection, a teenie-weenie erection. It feels good, arising naturally from the warm water and strong, soft hands making the warm bubbles that cover me and that I am turning into soap monsters and laughing about. And I feel the little hardness between my legs. In wonder, I wipe away the bubbles and touch it, then hold it, and that feels good, so I stroke it. It's divine. I laugh. I look up at Mother expecting she will be laughing. She is not! She is the face of wrath! Of horror! She slaps my hand, hurting both my hand and my penis a lot. I start blubbering. Why did she do that? In a shaming voice, she says, "Don't you ever do that again."

Well, good luck with that! The restriction was impossible, making me a lawbreaker practically from birth. The act of "interfering with myself" (thanks, Frank McCourt) had serious, lifelong consequences (and not hair in my palm). Any Catholic—ex, former, or recovering—will know just how *Portnoy's Complaint* is an emotional, spiritual, and ethical problem. Guilt, both for breaking God's law and for disappointing your mama, was set in motion. The extremely repressive idea of sexuality as bad was taught to me by my mother, and to her by her mother, and to all Catholics by nuns and priests in the thrall of the old ideas, which became the main propagation of the faith associated with a Catholic education, smothering any idea of "mercy" or "do unto others" or what "the meek shall inherit." Acting on natural sexual feelings was the unnatural worst sin of all in the huge book of sins we had drilled into our brains, making us suspicious of each other and afraid of life. And we know how that repression turned out for our mental health and for the purity of the priesthood. And our poor parents, charged with saving us from the hell of sex, were looking for hell in the wrong place. It was hiding in the choir loft or the sacristy space where we altar boys dressed all the time.

* * *

Back seat of the girlfriend's father's car, heading downtown. She and I had just been playing sex-find-out in her woodsy backyard, sitting on a log in leafy, piney woods out of sight of the back door. This is pure innocence. Adam and Eve before the snake and the apple. We are stroking each other, she guides with her hand, saying, "No, it's higher; yes, right there!" And I'm wondering what "it" is while leaving her in no doubt as to what my "it" is because it's out and hard, and she is tentatively touching it. Now she is placing my fingers exactly on her "it," and then her eyes close, and she goes somewhere inside her head, and I am scared. Is she dying? What is happening? We could be discovered at any time! My goodness, is this how women are? She has gone into quiet ecstasy. Her face changes, becomes the essence of purity, her sweet lips open, and she exhales, shuddering. I quickly stuff my "it" back into my Levis before it spurts—just in time! And I fill my underwear with heavenly stickiness.

Sweet girl. An innocent, lusty woman at thirteen. And me, a confused child of fourteen trying to be manly and not look as excruciatingly happy, embarrassed, and starkly terrified as I am. I am a good Catholic boy, and she is a good Catholic girl—this is all so wrong. But for an instant, the earth and stars have been upended and are flying, spinning upside down together into eternal space. Morality? This is morality! This is right! But if we are caught, we will both be killed dead, drawn, quartered, and barbecued, and then exiled by parents and priests. But now, she seems beyond happy, having gone into a thoughtful womanly zone that I don't get. Now, seventy-five years later, I get it! She came. She saw. She conquered. Now, with womanly assurance, she makes sure we are both presentable at court and . . . forget the whole thing happened, and . . . butter wouldn't melt in her mouth. And so we ride downtown in her father's car, playing riddle games in the backseat. "Railroad, railroad, look out for the cars. Can you spell that without any *r*'s?"

We had just climbed on the train at the caboose end. It is a train that will snake its way across the landscape of my whole life.

SCENE: Fort Smith, Arkansas

I was crawling in a jungle—the living room rug—when I came upon a grand staircase, a two-shelf bookcase. At the top of it sat a cathedral-shaped temple, the family radio. It gleamed in the gloom, its façade decorated with a tapestry of complex texture and design, which hid its interior and which was framed by three carved arches. I knew that when the one in the high center glowed, it invited me into a place of mystery where the household gods of the temple spoke, chanting of the sacred porcine and bovine creatures that were worshipped here. I memorized the strange chants and, as an acolyte, I repeated them:

> "Good morning, Mr. Farmer,
> Mr. Farmer, hello!
> How's your livestock a-comin'?
> Has your chicks begun to grow?
> If your cows don't give much milk,
> There's somepin' that they need
> It shorely makes a difference
> When you feed 'em OK Feed—
> Buy OK Feed toooo-daaaay!

Now prone in the jungle, I saw two treasure chests—books. One treasure—big, heavy, ornate—was the family Bible. The other was dark red. I slid the treasure off the shelf onto the jungle leaves and opened it. No pictures. Just long words, most of which I couldn't decipher. I was challenged. This was a mystery, and I wanted to crack it.

I must have been four or five and already fascinated by words and sentences. They traveled. They moved. They weren't stuck. They went somewhere I had never been before. I followed the yellow brick words to the cottage of the witch or the queen or the ogre in those rooms of paragraphs where the answer to the mystery of my existence lay.

My mother read to me—and not baby stories. *Grimm's Fairy Tales*, *Moby Dick*. It is the one memory of real closeness I remember having with her. In return, I read to my younger siblings. My mother liked that. I rocked their cradles and played with them in our "jungle." Books and education were important to my mother.

Once when I stole a piece of chalk from school, she made me walk alone in the early winter dark to the nuns' residence next to the school, where I would confess to the crime and pay restitution for the book she was reading to me— *Moby Dick*—by giving it to the nuns. This was giving up my world and my connection to my mother. I still think that was a terrible punishment. And the nuns? The Mother Superior looked at the little boy trembling in front of her with a heavy book outstretched in tearful apology, smiled, and said, "That's a very nice gesture, little Larry, and I'm sure you've learned your lesson. Now take the lovely book back to your mother and thank her for the offer, but it's much too big a punishment for the petty crime of taking a silly piece of broken chalk." And she took an immaculate lace handkerchief from her sleeve and gently wiped my tears away.

Not! This was a Sister of *no* mercy. The book disappeared into her voluminous black habit, and I never saw it again.

The Scarlet Shadow belonged to my grandfather, my mother's father. He was a retired railroad engineer. As I found out much later, this book is a fictional treatment of the great struggle between labor and capital in the West, and its hero was the Scarlet Shadow. Eugene Victor Debs was the great Socialist who had organized the railroad strike that paralyzed the country on behalf of the Pullman workers in 1894. Debs was the Devil Incarnate to Capitalists, and he suffered in federal prison for his pacifism and his crimes of trying to get justice for working men. He was Clarence Darrow's mentor. I never knew if my grandfather was a Socialist, but the book was sympathetic toward Debs, so why would Grandpa have it if he weren't in sympathy?

He was a mild, kind man. I was always welcome to be with him. He would sit in his chair by the window, listen to me talk, and puff on his pipe and tell me, yes, I have Prince Albert in a can on the windowsill. He would tell me stories about driving his great engine, which now sits on a dais at the rodeo grounds in Fort Smith as a monument to the railroad men. More than half a century later, my grandfather's quiet influence on me would dawn on me when I realized why I chose to make a play called *Clarence Darrow Tonight!*, including Darrow's homage to Debs.

SCENE: Fort Smith, Arkansas

I was eight years old. My dad had been spared the draft because of his four children. Two of his brothers were going to invade Europe any day now. There was a gold star in a window on every block in the neighborhood.

Everything was rationed. All the toys were now made of sawdust and glue instead of pot metal or rubber. The barrel of my cowboy six-gun kept falling off. We scoured yards, vacant lots, and roadside ditches for dandelions to harvest for salads. "Poke salad" was a daily staple. Real lard sat on top of the stove in an old gallon coffee can. All the drippings from cooking—all cooking was frying—were poured into it, and the only meat still readily available was local pork. We kept a side of salted pig hanging on the back porch winter and summer and cut our bacon and other goodies to fry up. The drippings can was an icon of the real life of the South.

Life was about my father's increasing inability to stop drinking, and the chaos he caused. We left our little cradle house and moved to Harrison in the Ozarks, where life turned really bad. His business failed—the shrewd guy who sold it to him had failed to inform him the rail spur by which sales goods came to town had been discontinued. A disaster. Drinking followed, and we then crept, diminished, back to Fort Smith, broke and fighting for our lives.

My father went from bad to worse. And my mother went from once-in-a-blue-moon joy and a dance with him—rolling back the rug in the tiny parlor and putting the radio on, the two of them gliding into a foxtrot, smiling, laughing, good at it, enjoying the partnering and graceful together—to always worried and always away from home. She was a working woman, not a good mother in her own estimation. She had to learn the skills she needed to give herself value in the marketplace. Never-ending night study and daily typing exercises made her a first-class secretary, but she regretted the time away from her children. And when we got big, troublesome, and contrary, when we stopped being her babies and became people with attitudes and personalities and plans all our own, she would say, "I loved you when you were babies." She was genuinely sorry that we had to grow up. When she would say that, with a sort of quizzical smile as if questioning her own feelings, I felt bereft. I had to grow up and not be lovable to her anymore. Now I know she was mourning her lost motherhood, her childhood, her life.

Our parents were not ready for the job. They struggled to find unimagined skills of intimacy. They did what they were able. He worked, drank, went to church on Sunday, and prayed to stop drinking. On Monday, he went to work, and on Friday, he was on a "toot" again. My mother went to church with him, knelt by his side, and prayed for him to stop drinking. And by the weekend, she was furious with him (and us). Her anger was like hot ice—it smoked, it smoldered, and it was indiscriminate. This was her life. Her crippling migraines, which must have been like vacations to Miseryville for her, were the only times she could absent herself from work. She would lie flat on the floor beside the bed in the dark with only a cool cloth on her forehead to ease the pain. She lay so still that when I went in one day, I thought she was dead. It scared me so bad it stopped my heart.

We had gone back to Fort Smith from the failed sojourn in the Ozarks, and my father was humiliated and treated with contempt and snickers by the other men in the family. He had four young children to raise and now had to beg all over town for a job. Our lives had broken into two pieces for me: the past, an imagined childhood heaven, the present, hell. We were all being punished for something. We must have somehow deserved this, yes? Our theology mentions Original Sin. Was this it? Or an undeserved punishment?

SCENE: Fort Smith, Arkansas

Growing up Southern

Fort Smith is a thriving mid-sized town on the far western border of Arkansas, midway north and south between Fayetteville and Texarkana, and set right on the weedy edge of the Arkansas River.

When I was a young boy, the Depression was on, and nobody had any money. The town population was German, Irish, Italian, and Black. Everyone lucky enough to have a job worked at a factory, shop, or farm. The neighborhoods emptied of working men before dawn. The stay-at-home women worked at housecleaning and cooking ("frying up") on wood stoves in the kitchens, tending chickens and hogs, and tending the ubiquitous back garden. Gas and electricity in houses were not a novelty anymore, but the days without them were still fresh in memory.

It was quiet. In the South, traffic had yet to be invented, and airplanes were a curiosity until the war.

Milk, with cream on top, came from local dairies in thick bottles that we washed out and returned to the porch for refills. Bread was from local bakeries. Food was unadulterated, no GMOs. Veggies and fruits came directly from the many truck farms close to town, and were brought to the neighborhoods by farm wagons with rubber car tires pulled by horses.

We worked hard in school. We played outside winter and summer. In summer, we never wore shoes, and my feet were so tough I forgot I had shoes. We explored creek bottoms, caves, forests of live oak and white pine, and poison ivy. We turned over rocks in the creeks and gathered good-eating crawdads, ignoring the cottonmouth snakes.

When the war came, metal was scarce, and we made rubber toy guns from pieces of old pine lumber. Dolls were homemade and usually Raggedy Anns.

We played hide-and-seek, rag football, kick-the-can, and broomstick baseball. We raced each other everywhere, and we played rough. Broken bones were a badge of honor with thick, itchy casts—magnets for autograph writers. We had June bugs. We tied a leg by a thread and flew them in circles. We had trees to climb and shooting stars to find. My mother did the wash on an old scrubboard. We jumped on the iceman's truck and swiped shards of broken ice off the back when he was inside a house with a fifty-pound block to put into an icebox. In the evenings, the grown-ups sat and talked on the porches. We kids checked in with the murmur of those voices once in a while. It was mighty sweet. We knew nothing of race riots or injustice. It was an ordered world where everyone fit into his place or else.

My town is famous for a six-man gallows, where Judge Isaac Parker—the "Hanging Judge"—handed down death sentences to about 150 bandits from the territory—mostly, of course, to "bad Indians," as they called them.

SCENE: Fort Smith, Arkansas

Somehow, through his salesman's network of favors, and despite war regulations, my father had gotten a new bicycle—a pre-war one. It was all steel with real rubber tires. He secretly set it aside for a future gift for his eldest son—me—from a shipment to the store he worked for. In the store one day, breathing the heady smells of paint, chemicals, new tires, linseed oil, and kerosene, he let me in on the secret. The bike was parked amid a tangle of farm implements in the warehouse. He told me the bicycle's enormous price, thirty-seven dollars, but said it could be mine if I earned enough to pay fifty percent of it by Christmas. Yes! I can!

I earned one dollar a week delivering free shopping news flyers to every downtown store. Downtown was basically one street. Garrison Avenue ran from the grand Catholic church at the top, one mile downhill past hotels, banks, jewelry stores, clothing stores, five and ten-cent stores, and restaurants, to the Arkansas River and the railroad station at the very bottom. It got increasingly seedy and scary past the brothel and bars and the six-man gallows still left standing from Hanging Judge Parker's court. I remember the smell of that whole street.

I started at the top and put a flyer in some clerk's hand in every store all the way down and all the way back up the other side. There was no question for me—I would get half of the bike's cost by December. No wonder I flunked every arithmetic course in school history.

It was September. My father knew, of course, that the most I could save by Christmas would be twelve dollars, even if I saved every penny and, for the duration, gave up movies (fifteen cents), comic books (ten cents), malts (twenty cents), and twenty-five cent paperback books from the rack at the drugstore on my way home from my job. He stuck the tip of his tongue between his teeth and chuckled—he would be buying at least twenty-five dollars worth of a bike at Christmas.

On Christmas Eve, he wheeled the beauty into the foyer of our small home where the Christmas tree stood, already a glistening mountain of tinseled branches set with real candles to be lit that night. Yes, actual wax candles—the trusting madness of times past. As he brought the bicycle through the door, I saw it again, now washed and polished, a gorgeous blue and yellow fat-tire Monarch bike with fenders, a chain guard, goofy leatherette mud flaps, and lowboy handlebars. It was kind of a grandpa bike, but so sleek and cool to me. I was paralyzed with joy. He was grinning happily and proudly, and I stood awed, afraid to touch the stunning promise of freedom.

Then he stumbled a bit, fell into the doorjamb, and I caught a whiff of a new and unpleasant smell—whiskey. When I turned to look at my mother, her face crumpled from joy to disappointment to sorrow so fast that I got very confused. My hero, my dad, had something wrong with him.

Something changed in me. I was afraid to ask what was wrong with my father. The answers would come as inevitably as in Greek tragedy. Later, in college, when we "actors" were given presents of those geeky Greek comedy and tragedy faces as proud badges of our "profession"—cufflinks, tie pins, brooches—I understood how those two faces, tragedy and comedy, could exist in life, superimposed instantaneously on the same face. It was my mother's crumpling that got me. Her face fell.

I didn't know how or what to feel, but my face must have fallen, too. I had been shot in the heart by something that was barbed and wouldn't come out, and it has not let go and still hurts. It is only now, at eighty-nine, as I brush the dirt from the old arrowheads left on the battlefield, that I can feel the love-hate struggle of the desperate contestants—my parents—who lived, fought, and died in a barren arena acting out their more than five-decade-long murder-suicide pact. And now, ironically, in the thistled greensward of Good Shepherd Cemetery, they lie under a single stone, still together, their dust mingled under a rosebush: "Wed 53 Years."

SCENE: Fort Smith, Arkansas

I was a sweet baby, a happy and cheerful child. I got all my ideas about being manly and heroic from books and movies. But three brothers who lived in the neighborhood chased me home from school every day. They were the three pigs—small, big, biggest. Piglet, pig, and hog, and they had it in for me. No idea why. Every day, I ran from school with them on my heels, or I hid until they got tired of waiting, then went around a long way to get home.

Finally, my father had enough of this. One day, I was being chased, and as I got to my front lawn, my father got out of his car, parked at the curb, and got behind the three pigs. "You! Go!" he said in a hoarse, iron voice. And he herded them toward our backyard garden gate.

The hog-boy opened his fat mouth to try to object, and my father shoved him hard through the gate. My father was livid—ferociously angry. I was herded in with the rest of the convicts. He cornered the three boys. "Dadgum it!" he said. "You've been chasing my boy all year, and it's going to stop now!" He turned to me. "You are going to fight these bums, all three of them. Right now. Take your pick. Who goes first?"

"Mr. Luckinbill, we didn't mean anything . . ." said the hog. "We won't do it anymore!"

"You damn right, boy! Either you fight my boy now, or I'll take you home, and your daddy and me'll fight because first, I'll thrash all three of you!" And he unbuckled his belt and slid it off and wrapped it around his fist. He looked at me. "Which one's first, boy?"

I couldn't believe what I was hearing. "Him," I said, and pointed at the piglet. He was my age and in my class. I thought I had a chance with him. I knew I was going to die this day, anyway, or, if not now, soon, in the rear of the Knights of Columbus Hall at the far end of the schoolyard. I suppose it gave me a certain fatalism because I stopped being afraid and suddenly felt very angry. My dad's anger had opened up room for me to feel what I was really feeling.

I stepped up fast to the piglet and smashed him in the center of his face with my fist. Then I kicked him in the knee and stepped into him and started hitting him with everything I had—knees, elbows, fists. He was bloody in a second and so was I. He cried like a baby and fell down, curled up, and covered his head with his hands. His brothers looked stupefied, then angry. My dad looked like the Avenger—grim. "Next one," he said.

I pointed at the pig and ran at him with the intent of doing the same thing again. But he was bigger than me and shoved me to the ground. I got right up and tried again. Now he hit me side-arm, slamming the side of my face. It paralyzed me and I felt my ear bleeding. It numbed me. I went after him again, arms windmilling, but he grabbed my face and pushed me down again. I resisted this time and took him down with me, kicking and flailing at him. He got off me quickly when I started to cough up my snot on him. My father waited till I got back on my feet and said, "Next."

Hog stepped back. He had had enough of this. I didn't care now. I was ready as a kamikaze. I rushed at him, bleeding, puking up mucus, and flailing. He held me off, pushed me back, grabbed me around my body, and held me so I couldn't do anything. Still, I remember trying to hit him anyway and crying, yelling incoherently out of furious frustration. I really wanted blood or death, or both.

My father opened the gate for the swine and they ran. He warned them he would go to their house next and do it again (promising a rematch with the redoubtable flyweight—me), this time for their father's entertainment. My mother brought a towel; I was cleaned up, fed, and sent to bed with ice on my wounds.

I did well, apparently. My parents were satisfied I had some gumption, which is what they both feared I lacked more than they feared the fight. Now they knew I wasn't yellow, at least. I knew it, too. I also knew for sure there was a deep fury unleashed in me that was uncontrollable and deadly. I was not bothered again by pigs or anyone else in that town, in that way, that is.

SCENE: Harrison, Arkansas

We were ripped out of our fake Fort Smith paradise and moved to the Ozarks to the hamlet of Harrison, population eight thousand, plus one sacred shrine to The Lost Cause of the Confederacy downtown in the square.

Our house was on top of a steep hill. Sledding down that icy hill, we could get six blocks or more of a speedy ride. Our sleds were pieces of thick cardboard ripped from packing boxes that frayed as we slid down, and when they tore away, we slid on our butts. Levi's were tough.

At the bottom of this Ozark hill, I was looking at a fuck book—the property of one of the Joe Bills or Jim Bobs who inhabit these woods. It starred Popeye and Olive Oyl doing it. Popeye had an enormous anaconda of a dick, which was embedded between Olive's legs and accomplishing the anatomically unlikely feat of thrusting its head out of her impossibly wide-open mouth as it comes. As the pages of the little foolscap book were ruffled through with a thumb, Popeye and Olive Oyl gyrated back and forth and up and down and gave a zoetrope-like simulacrum of doing the deed that none of us young panting puppies had ever done. No story. No plot. The act was the whole thing, and the whole thing was the act. As the restroom graffiti says: "To do is to be, to be is to do, Scooby-Dooby-Doo . . ."

Well, needless to say, at twelve, I was fascinated by this interesting artifact and wished to own this first edition for myself. So I traded something valuable for it; I forget what. I stuffed it under my jacket and took it home at the darkening of the day. As lights came on in the few houses up the hill, I trudged upward, wondering where to hide this illicit treasure. I didn't have a room. I slept winter and summer on a bare, screened-in back porch. After deep and canny thought, I hid it in the damp basement on a never-used shelf behind some lye soap and laundry starch.

Wrong. How would I know that Mother used laundry starch every week? I went to the shelf later that evening and the tome was gone! And as when a car is stolen, you think, I know I parked it here, and now it's gone, I began to think I'd lost my mind.

My mother came downstairs to help me find it. She had the shreds of the book in one hand and a thick, heavy-duty, six-foot extension cord in the other. She was weeping raggedly, as if she were trapped in some terrifying happening, a war maybe, a murder, Hell. Her blue eyes were firing electrical bolts at me. I could hear them buzz and crackle in my ear. She yelled in a voice just this side of hysterical, end-of-the-world shrieking—the voice of the desperate citizen in the Orson Welles 1938 radio play, *The War of the Worlds*, in which Martians have landed and attacked New Jersey—"Take down your pants!"

This extremely unorthodox demand was so shocking that, without a word, I did.

"Bend over that chair!"

There was a broken kitchen chair with no back, which I used as a sawhorse. I knelt and bent over it. And she instantly began beating me with the cord, the end of it slamming into my underwear-clad bottom. She was in a fury and distress I'd never seen. She yelled about disgrace, mortal sin, and dirty, dirty, dirty . . . and I agreed with her. I was evil, dirty, and disgraceful. And I endured the worst whipping I'd ever had. I deserved it. Maybe I liked it.

But not at the time.

I knew I was wrong, see, but I didn't know why. It has taken me eighty-plus years of mistakes to realize that the only thing wrong was her perception and mine, led by a misconception taught to all Catholics at the time and maybe still today, that sex is wrong. Any kind of sex, apparently. All I was doing was jacking off, which came with the territory of being me, a human boy. Alive, curious, and by twelve, very aware of the other sex.

Of course, your mother isn't the other sex to a twelve-year-old. She was my *mother*, and she was beating me hysterically, ferociously, banging my butt with the heavy Bakelite square plug end of the cord, which was now cutting into the back of my legs. I took it. I didn't cry.

But I was hurt, bleeding. I don't remember the rest of this scene—a merciful moral blackout ensued, I guess. I probably promised something I shouldn't have, like I would never do this again.

Now I know that the alcohol-poisoned life she was enduring with my father, which she probably blamed herself for, had made her need to beat any disgraceful, dirty, sinful sexuality out of me to purify me, straighten me out before it was too late, get me in line, even if she died trying. Deus vult! God wills it!

Fifty years later, she died, still in her private hell of fear of disgrace. *Semper fidelis Dei gratia*—always faithful to the grace of God. A kind and inoffensive woman, a loving mother, with a hell of an Irish whip arm.

So, I lied.

Is this any way to teach morals and ethics? Like Schrödinger's cat, damned if you do, damned if you don't."

SCENE: Harrison, Arkansas

There was no way out. My brother, sister, and I were locked in a cage with dangerous animals (our parents) without whip, chair, or popgun to control them. I crept from one side to the other, seeking the shadows to hide in.

I survived these terror moments and learned new ways to cope. I was too much of a "good boy" to commit the treason of running away, skipping school, smoking reefer, or being antisocial in any dangerous way. I was the Artful Dodger at home and in all social situations. I turned myself into the class clown. I got low grades——much lower than I knew I could—in every school I attended. I didn't mind if they thought I was dumb. I had a secret, one of the many that marked my life. I knew I was intelligent.

I read, and I understood almost everything I read. I read everything I saw— backs of cereal boxes, labels, instruction booklets, library books from every single stack, letters to the editor, every word in every newspaper. I read the phone book, the encyclopedia, and, best, *National Geographic* magazines.

Our house in Harrison had a damp, native-rock-lined basement. It was a spider cave and a *National Geographic* magazine treasure house. They were piled head-high in every corner. I read every one, always hoping for African stories because they were illustrated with pictures of nude tribeswomen. This was one course in my autodidactic sex education. But it gave me a lifelong interest in every corner of the globe and the universe. I was inspired to research all of it, this incredible Earth, its laws and people, and the strange place in the sky we occupy.

There was one bright strand to this Ozark exile: Puberty!

The advantage I seized was that of being the outsider. I was strange, odd, and eccentric. I talked funny; I read books. I put the role on without even pausing. It became an instant pose. Girls were interested in me because I was "different," and that interested me. Of course, the pose aroused the hostility of the other males, for which I later paid a price.

One girl especially interested me. She was tall and willowy with a heart-shaped face, pretty bow lips, a peaches-and-cream complexion, and curly honey-blonde hair. She had a smart-ass, acerbic, clued-in attitude and a sweet, genuine laugh. I sensed that she liked me, so, *wham-bam*, I was in love. "Love."

Love? Never heard of it before. My older sister mentioned it, I think. It wasn't anything any adult I knew ever spoke of or exhibited. Nothing like in the movies I'd seen and practically thrown up at when they (*phew!*) kissed. But now it meant a local tingling, a romantic aura of moonlit nights, hayrides, and being close to—feeling the heat of, smelling the perfume of—another body not like my own, but female. It lifted me out of my self-absorption.

I stayed on the line to the local radio station for hours until they answered and let me pick a song for the local Top 40 show and dedicate it to my inamorata. On Saturday night, they played the "Coconut Grove" by Harry Owens, dedicated to her by me. Cue ukuleles: "There's a coconut grove where I'll be confessin'/The simple truth that you've been guessin'/yes, sweetheart I'm in love with you/oo-oo-ee-oo/by the light of the South Sea island moon . . ."

Monday, at school, I said, "Did you hear the song?"

"Oh, I never listen to the radio," she said with a smirk.

What? I was confused, deflated. I had gone out on a limb; she just sawed it off. Then she put her face in her hands and ran screaming into a pile of her girlfriends across the schoolyard. I was humiliated, hurt, pissed off. I knew nothing about girls. No one ever told me. I didn't know yet that embarrassment was a sure sign she liked me.

The cool thing was that discovering girls was so powerful. It was like a salve to the frustration and fear in my home life. The problem was I could never invite anyone to visit me at home because of the unpredictable weather there. It was much worse for my mother and sisters, who were much more sociable. I was more like my father, self-alienated, a loner. But unbeknownst to me, a solution was beginning to work its way into my life. Now I began to think that, to get by, I had to be a hero.

Well, I could pretend very well. In fact, I had always pretended. I didn't see a difference between being and pretending. I would be a pretend hero.

Edge of the world map: "Here be dragons."

I was a boiling witch's brew of conflicting and destructive potions that would take years to sort out. All this was loaded onto the happy, joyful, innocent, blank disk of a soul that I was. One inner child was not harmed by the darkness, but his twin was. The question was which would inhabit me permanently? Which one would rule? And why?

I believed I was tough. I felt safe in my illusions—raw experiences, which I interpreted like a novice diver who thinks he knows the ocean because he's wearing scuba gear. I swam in opaque, greasy, green Crooked Creek with cottonmouths and water moccasins next to me that wouldn't bite because I was brave enough to swim with them. I jumped off a limestone rock twenty feet above the green river pool, believing if I jumped out far enough, the giant rock under the surface would drop away just enough so I wouldn't break my legs or die.

I challenged my old nightmare, my claustrophobia, carrying a little carbide lamp and a couple of kitchen matches in my jeans. I headed out to Crooked Creek and slid into the one-foot-high opening under the cave ledge into the dark, knowing there'd be a hole just barely big enough to wriggle through on my belly. Once through, if I dropped into the blackness, there'd be a soft sandy place to land that wouldn't hurt. And then, if I pushed on through a tight tunnel in the wet rock, I'd get to a room where I could stand up, light the tiny lamp, and there'd be a cathedral of stalactites and stalagmites made of dazzling crystal. You weren't tough if you couldn't do this.

I started into the hole under the ledge. It smelled like a tomb, like death. I thought of the corpses I had seen in their caskets at all the funeral masses I served as an altar boy. I got stuck and stopped breathing. I couldn't see. My heartbeat expanded in my chest. It pulsed so hard I thought my chest would explode. I screamed. It sounded like a little dog yelping. Someone yanked at me, pulled me out by my feet. One of my treasured Converse sneakers came off and disappeared into the cave. After that, I wore Li'l Abner boots all day, every day, like a badge of my cowardice. I tried once more to be a spelunker to prove I wasn't a sissy. I couldn't do it—I was a sissy. So much for illusions.

One day after school, two boys followed me as I walked down the Ozark mountain toward town. I knew they were intelligent, shrewd hillbillies-in-training, and I had no beef with them. They crowded me off the path and down the hill below the road. One broke long switches from the trees, and the other ordered me to take down my pants. I said no.

They started beating me with the sticks and laughing. I grabbed a stick and said, "Why are you doing this?" The bigger one said, "You're a smart-ass." I said, "I'm smart, but so are you. So what?"

I yanked the sticks out of their hands. They may have been young DeSades, but I wasn't Masoch. I said, "I'm so smart, I know who is going to win the presidential election!" (It was 1948—Truman versus Dewey).

This long-shot diversion worked. "You don't know that! So, who?"

"Truman," I said. "I'll bet you five dollars"—an indescribably huge sum.

"Okay, dumbbell, I'll bet it's the other guy."

By then I had the sticks and the initiative. I walked up to them and they were flummoxed. They looked at each other and then stuck out their hands. We shook, best buddies now.

Carefully, casually, I asked, "Why did you take after me?" Dr. Frankenstein, the bigger one, said, "We don't like you. You're stuck up. But now you owe us money, and we're going to get it."

"Not until November," I said.

I took the sticks with me back up to the road. I felt like Huck Finn saving Jim the slave with his wits. At thirteen, I thought their behavior was sui generis. Now I know it was learned at home, like racism, which they were also taught.

November came. They welshed on the bet, as I knew they would. Acts of spite are always pyrrhic victories.

SCENE: Harrison, Arkansas

Christmas. My mother and I, she in her nightgown, me in my pj's, not "settled down for a long winter's nap" but crouched down in the tiny center hall of the house in the Ozarks, huddling in the dark around my younger sister and baby brother to protect them while my father raged around the outside of our house. He knew we were there, like the Big Bad Wolf trying to break in. My mother trembled in terror and was hissingly angry with us if we made a sound.

We lived with an unpredictable, terrible, scary monster. I was expected to be the "man of the family." To oppose and beat my father. I knew in my heart that I wasn't up to it and that I was, therefore, a coward. I did not understand, and was repulsed by, the feelings that burned in me like acid. Physically close in nightclothes, my mother and I were co-conspirators. It unmanned me. Repelled me. She was my mother, not my woman. How could I be expected to protect her from her man outside—the crazy horror scrabbling at our cave?

Spring: I'm riding shotgun as she maneuvers the wide car downtown shakily, dangerously, her head barely reaching above the steering wheel. It's near midnight. We are trailing my father as he weaves and staggers from one liquor store to another. No one will sell him any booze. We watch as he cajoles, demands, and grabs at the bottles as a pale, frightened clerk grabs the bottles back, jumps aside as my father trashes a display. He reels out the door and walks away with absurd drunken dignity into the night. The trembling clerk picks up the phone. I look at my mother. She is vibrating like a high-tension wire, in a fury, and scared as a mouse. We hide in the car outside in the dark, waiting to see if the cops come.

Confusingly, I felt sorry for him, not us. We were invading his private life by spying on him. Maybe I was defending myself from—and resenting—my mother's fury at him and her tearful rants. I know now she couldn't help what she did, always so frightened and humiliated. She needed me along for protection and for company. I was her family, the one she could trust. Her sisters were so judgmental. Her humiliation watered his shame, and self-hatred made his fury worse.

We were always one bedroom short in all our houses, and I slept outside all year on the screened-in back porch, usually off the kitchen. One freezing night in the Ozark house, I woke from a nightmare, a frequent event, in which a menacing single blue eye stared unblinkingly at me. I couldn't see the face behind it, but somehow I knew it was the devil (I believed in the devil then). I heard voices, two of them, furious voices. I crept out of the covers and peeked into the kitchen through a gap between the window jamb and the pull-down paper shade covering the window. And I saw the evil blue eye! Then it dawned on me—I was looking at the back of the gas stove in the dark kitchen, and the pilot light was looking at me.

My heart started going again, and the voices returned. My mother was yelling at my staggering, stumbling father. She had been ironing. The iron was the kind you had to heat over an open flame. It was sitting atop a lighted burner on the stove. My father responded to her angry blame by pushing off the wall and lurching toward her. She snatched up the red-hot iron and went at him with her arm out like a battering ram—she was insane. He grabbed a knife and stuck it out before him like a crucifix before Dracula. She hurled the iron at his head. He ducked. His head hit a cabinet and he fell on the floor as the iron slammed into the wall and then to the floor not far from where I stood outside, watching. He started to get up. She turned over the ironing board to stop him. Now she was weeping tragically, hysterically, with great sobs and gasps for breath and deathly moans that were more frightening still.

I knew I should burst through the back door and stop this battle, but I couldn't move. I was paralyzed except for my teeth, which chattered like a skeleton's on Halloween. And now my knees, I realized, were knocking together audibly and hard, painfully banging against each other. It was cold and I was wearing thin pajamas, but that wasn't the reason my knees were knocking. It was terror. The terror I had only read about but was now living.

I was afraid of them both, afraid *for* them both. I was afraid of what would happen if my little brother or sister woke up and came into the kitchen. But I could not move. I didn't have the courage or the faith to confront either of them. I couldn't trust anyone. There was madness, and I could only watch it. What grew in me was the belief that I was a helpless person. My only protection against that feeling was a powerful desire to distance myself, as if I had no family. I would simply step out of the picture. Disappear. I dreamed about it.

Two months later, we departed the Ozarks, as my father's dream of his own small empire was smashed to smithereens, along with his sense of manhood. We headed back to Fort Smith. I needed to get into high school. My father needed a job. Any job.

SCENE: Fort Smith, Arkansas

Mentored: I had a job in a grocery market. It was a grungy place, and I was given the crummiest things to do, like cleaning out the storage cellar filled five feet deep with slimy, rotten potatoes that stunk to high heaven. I stank, too. The place was poorly run by the lethargic, racist scion of the owner. There was only one bright spot: a six-foot, eight-inch skinny Black man whose moniker was Long John Silver. He was the first Black man I had the good karma to know. He was the commander of the vegetable section, and I was assigned to be his flunky assistant. He called me "Luxemberg" with a little Gullah twist to "berg" so it came out "boig."

He was the most knowledgeable about vegetables of anyone I have ever known. He strode up and down the sparkling rows of lettuce, kale, carrots, turnips, onions, and beets as if he were reviewing his troops before sending them into battle. If he saw a tiny brown spot on a leaf or stalk, he would dishonorably discharge that piece and toss it to me for removal from the troop: "Hop to it, Luxemboig!" I would answer like his first sergeant, "Yes, sir!"

The delicate Southern belles shopping with their string bags would take whatever Long John deemed right for their tables, with respect and no questions asked. Whatever those white ladies may have thought of this extraordinary

Black human, if they allowed themselves to think anything at all (doubtful), they kept it secret, and vice-versa. It was the unspoken post-Reconstruction, Jim Crow Southern détente—hide your prejudice, even from yourself, pretend all is well, and fake it until you make it true. But, of course, it wasn't. Black folks had only pretend power.

Long John had a nephew my age, fourteen, who came in to help me one day. We got along, two teenage boys with similar age-related issues. After work, I invited him to come to my house to check out my comic book collection. He was hesitant but willing, and I thought nothing about his ambivalence.

We walked down the street toward my house, and I saw the neighbors' curtains moving. As usual, I was being watched. My new friend refused my invitation to go into the house. I was a guileless, uncorrupted boy. I took no inference from either the moving curtains or my friend's quiet turndown of my offer. I went inside, gathered an armful of my favorite and best comic books, and brought them out to the front porch. He was unwilling even to come up on the porch, so we sat on the steps and looked through the comic books.

Suddenly, my mother appeared, walking down the street toward us. It was mid-afternoon, and she was always at work at that time. I said, "Hi, Mom, how come you're home so early? This is my friend from the market . . ."

Then I noticed her face. My mother was always a courteous, well-mannered woman. But now there was fear in her face. She said hello to the boy, who responded hesitantly. Then she asked to speak to me. That was weird, but okay. I got up and went to where she stood on the sidewalk. Quietly, she said, "You have to walk this boy away from here, now. Walk with him toward where he lives."

I started to ask an innocent question, but she stopped me. "I know you're just making friends, but this boy is in danger. Do you understand?"

Suddenly, I did. I saw my town for what it was, a menace to this Black child. A threat to society, to human life. I didn't get it all at once. But I knew what she meant, and I was afraid of her fear.

I turned to look at the kid. He had the same anxious look on his face as my mother did. I went to him and asked if he wanted to borrow any of my comics. He clearly wanted to but said, "No, thanks, that's all right."

I started to say, "I think we'd better . . ." and he finished the sentence—"Yes, I'll go."

I told him I would walk him back to . . . where? He told me. It was the area on the edge of downtown along the river, behind the roughest part of town and beside the railroad tracks. The houses there were unlike those in the rest of town. We were poor, always counting pennies, but where my friend lived was downright shocking to me. I knew that part of town was there, but it was never referred to by anyone I knew. It was as if it didn't exist.

On the way to his house, we had nothing to say, too self-conscious in the purity of our motives to bring up the result of our separate existences. He had no blame for me. I didn't feel sorry for him so much as stunned that this world existed. I knew about the Civil War, the "Lost Cause," and the unspoken code—now I knew I could never be the same toward this Southern thing again. I could never shut my eyes to it again. I knew my friend couldn't be my friend again. And I knew he had known it from birth. His youth, his sense of humor, and his corresponding innocence were hedged from his lifetime by this "thing," this monster. There is no word strong enough to condemn this inhumanity.

But that day, we parted without a word said about it. We were both infected by this disease—racism—but he was much more likely to die from it than I. This was my sadness from that day forward. Strange friends, to live like this. Strange fruit hanging from trees. He lived with ever-present murder shadowing him. I did not. I now understand that it was not enough to simply know this. And I didn't know what to do about it. I never even knew his name—it seemed superfluous to our chance connection over comic books.

I'm grateful to my mother for saving both of us boys. Even grateful to one of my aunts for warning her that "Larry is doing something stupid."

Stupid, no. Dangerous, yes. It was the beginning of my lifetime course in becoming a human—a pig's ear trying to transform into a silk purse.

I was fired from the market that week, as was Long John, my mentor. I wondered if it was because I saw people as people and didn't understand that way of thinking had consequences in this fucked-up world. I wondered if Long John and his nephew would be able to forgive my ignorance. I have finally forgiven myself for not understanding, but I will never forget.

I wonder if my town and state will ever mature and learn to understand and embrace inclusion, mercy, and compassion. So far, as of this writing, it's still stuck in the old ruts. Sorry, my dear birthplace but it's true. I wonder if you will ever open your hearts and put down your guns.

SCENE: Fort Smith, Arkansas

Mentored: I was given a paper route by the *Southwest Times Record*. A twenty-block circuit, half downhill, half up. Probably eighty houses, most with porches or verandas, as we called them.

I revived my blue fat-tire Monarch bike with new steer horn handlebars. I reinforced an orange crate in two sections with a pine divider nailed across the middle. I fixed it to the carrying platform behind the seat. I sat cross-legged on the sidewalk to fold and pound the afternoon papers into tight rectangles about six inches long, then packed the box very tightly with the papers.

I rode my route fast, hurling a paper toward each porch as I went. I discovered a new fantasy athletic activity: I was my favorite St. Louis Cardinals player, Stan "The Man" Musial, centerfielder.

I threw papers not toward mundane porches, but as Musial, toward home plate to stop the runner from scoring. Now, Enos Slaughter [me]: "Way deep in left, he picks up a ball bounced off the wall and hurls it ninety miles an hour straight as a lance at Red Schoendienst at short [me again], who casually steps on second for the out and whips the ball over to first to Nippy Jones [me] to nail the slow boat runner doing his best to plant a foot on first—in time!—for the double play!"

So, this day, I was folding papers in a good rhythm, absorbing the front-page headlines as I popped the folds, enjoying myself in anticipation of another good day in centerfield being my hero, Stan the Man, when Mr. McKinney pulled up in his wide, spongy, used Chevy Fleetmaster, stopped, and got out. He came straight to me. He was also wide and spongy, and he wore a loose, baggy suit, white shirt, and tie in the Arkansas heat. He was management, my boss, in charge of us lowly paperboys. He was a kind man with a fine, genuine smile, but he was not smiling now. He looked sad and serious, like the priest on Good Friday.

He told me he had had many complaints about me, that my papers ended up in the hydrangeas (where they got soggy in the usual afternoon rain), more often than on the verandas, and that when I did hit the houses, the papers were thrown so hard that they broke front door screens and scared dogs and cats and the elegant ladies who owned the fine, modest homes along my route. These ladies had informed him with their old-fashioned charm and usual tolerant spirit that, although I was a nice boy, I must be replaced.

"So." Mr. McKinney squinted and looked sad and uncomfortable. "You are . . ."

He didn't finish, because my mother, five-foot-two, eyes of blue now blazing like hot ice, had marched across the street from our tiny two-bedroom bedraggled house on the corner in her work uniform of a long, mid-calf skirt and demure collared white blouse. She launched into a determined attack, which set McKinney back instantly as she stepped forward to him, ignoring me except for a sharp finger pointed down at me, making sure McKinney knew I was the son she referred to.

She said, "No, Mr. McKinney, you cannot fire him! You must give him another chance. He's a good boy with his nose in a book half the time, but he can and will do this job right."

McKinney was relieved at this check on the executioner's axe he was about to drop on my young neck. "Mrs. Luckinbill, the folks are complaining . . ."

"I am sure they are, Mr. McKinney. Larry is a good boy [that's two!], but it's my fault for not staying behind him and making sure he knows what doing a good job is. I promise you that is going to change, and right now!" And she turned suddenly and looked at me. It was shocking! It was ominous, like twin .50-caliber machine guns had suddenly rolled out of the blue and pink hydrangeas and were now trained on me. "Isn't it?" she demanded sharply. "And stand up."

I stood up and said, "Yes, ma'am. And yes, sir, Mr. McKinney."

"You can learn to place the newspapers properly on those porches of all those people we know, can't you?"

"Yes, ma'am." And in the "people we know," I heard her humiliation and shame that she hadn't raised me right.

"Can you promise Mr. McKinney to do much better?"

"Yes."

"Do it."

"Mr. McKinney," I fumbled, head down. "I will do much better. I . . . I love this job, sir, and I will do it right." And I really meant it.

Mr. McKinney had been outtalked, outgunned, and stymied—and he was glad of it. I sensed his relief as he gave me a quick reprieve. He lowered the sharp two-bladed axe to the ground, pushed his black mask and hot felt fedora off his brow, wiped the sweat, flicked the moisture onto the grass beside the walk, and said, "Mrs. Luckinbill, thank you! I am giving Larry another chance. He is a good boy [third one!]. He's just a little lazy," he corrected himself as the .50-caliber twin ice-blue machine guns shifted over to him. "I mean, we all get a little lazy from time to time. Me, too. But I'm sure he can do better. Larry, you can do better, can't you?"

"Yes, sir," I said again. Better. I'll do better. I must do better!

"All right, then, Mrs. Luckinbill, nice to see you again," he said, tipping his hat as he climbed back into his steamy Chevy with the napped seat covers that made him move his heavy body inch by inch to the steering position. He drove away on his appointed rounds.

My mother said, "You must keep this job, Larry." She looked at me. I looked at her. I didn't know what she saw. I saw a woman determined to hold her universe together even if she had to tie her apron strings around each and every one of her children so tightly they choked. I saw a small, frail woman whose effort to exude tremendous power and control gave her migraines almost weekly. "Sick headaches," she called them. They felled her as if she were hit by a twelve-pound sledge. But, still, she got up, checked on us, cooked (badly), went to work, and tried to manage (and to love) her drunken, bad-boy fifth child. Who could not love this woman? Who could?

At fourteen, I didn't try. I did as I was told. I would do better. I would place each paper professionally on the porch on the welcome mat. I had to keep this job.

And I did keep it. I ended up doing Mr. McKinney's job a couple of years later, after he moved on. I placed papers delicately, getting off my bike with an armload of papers on each block and racing to place each paper on the porch just so. I saw the lace curtains move slightly as the easy-to-cultivate Southern ladies took note and smiled.

SCENE: Fort Smith, Arkansas

The only theater-like place in Fort Smith was the school auditorium. Is there anything more soul-killing than a school auditorium? But now, memory rewinds and reminds me that I temporarily turned my high school auditorium into a dangerous theater place.

My friend (yes, I had one) and I wrote (*I* wrote) and performed skits for the school assemblies. I don't know how we got permission. The sisters in charge were perhaps the most sophisticated people in town. They were Irish and German and may have seen theater as young girls in their home countries. My skits were brief, one scene, lowbrow, knock-around playlets full of stupid tricks and daring pratfalls. My partner and I threw things at each other and at the audience, and they threw things back at us: food, paper, spitballs, confetti, rolls of toilet tissue. Some of our fellow prisoners were dragged on stage to "volunteer," and there was a surprise ending—anything that wasn't explicitly forbidden by the powers-that-be.

In memory of Charles Moran and George Mack, the white vaudevillians of the Two Black Crows, I wrote a horrible impersonation sketch requiring burnt cork on our faces—blackface. It was absolutely unconscious racism on my part. It was called *The Death of 8-Ball Caesar* based on my deep study of Shakespeare's *Julius Caesar* and *Amos and Andy*, the radio show. In my death scene, I tore down the rear curtain of the stage. The captive audience loved it. The nuns endured it. We were the comical bad boys of the tenth grade. I had ramped it up a notch from my seventh-grade Mario Lanza impersonation.

I begged permission to use the nuns' grand oak library table for my powerful one-scene horror—and horrible—play of *Stankenfrein, Mad Scientist*, in which the surprise ending was my igniting a pile of powdered magnesium "borrowed" from the chemistry lab and laid out on a piece of cardboard on the table. In the scary white shooting flames, I set off an MD-80 Salute firecracker. *Boom!* Ooh! Aah! It made a satisfactory facsimile of a monster-destroying volcano and burned an area about a foot wide on the gleaming, polished surface of the table.

Our show was closed without notice, and we went back to being poor students getting no applause. We were personae non grata on assembly programs. Our shows were banned. Our rocketing comedy careers ended. I had to work to pay for the table, and the good sister who ran the chemistry lab never let me near any supplies from then on. I still felt the laughs we got were worth it.

SCENE: Fort Smith, Arkansas

We were heading downtown to school. He was angry. I didn't look at him. He hit the brakes, and the car abruptly stopped on the busy avenue across from the school.

My father turned and looked at me. His hat was sitting straight and tight on his head. His eyes were hot when I looked at him. They always looked like they were floating in tears.

"What in the nine kinds of hell are you doing in that school?" he said. "You're in trouble. Causing trouble, running with some dumb cluck, making damn shows or something, burning a table. Why can't you get some damn sense, boy?"

I couldn't talk. My tongue was stuck in a dry place in my mouth like it was between two rough-sawed boards. But I was just as mad as he was, maybe madder.

"You're wasting your time with crap. It's crap! You're not going to be an actor or anything. An actor's got to have good looks and talent, and you don't have any of that. You've got about as much talent as a one-legged Indi'n in an ass-kickin' contest."

I wanted to defend myself—my taking time to make stupid shows to make others laugh—even the teachers—if I could. I wanted to say that my friend was not a "dumb cluck." But my father had a way of hitting the nail—me—on the head with his country-made hammer. His bitterness and contempt boiled over like acid on my legs, my hands, and the side of my face. It was burning. I was stuck, awkward, "cheap," too big and too little simultaneously, a pimple, gross. I was paralyzed in the hard, dusty seat of that car that smelled of cigarettes, whiskey, and dust. Dead dust. I couldn't see through the fog of dust. Something in me fought back against being turned into nothing. But I couldn't open my mouth. I couldn't speak to deny this stuff he was saying. Something in him was hurting as he said it. I knew it. I felt it. But feeling it wasn't enough to save him or me. I had to get out. Temporary escape.

I stumbled out of the car, a Frazer. Remember Kaiser-Frazer cars? No? There's a reason. Worst cars ever made. He bought them. He was the one dumb asshole who bought both of them!

I didn't slam the door. It might've fallen off if I had. I stepped across the curb and walked toward the school. I felt his eyes on my skinny back and neck (with a seventy-five-cent GI haircut I hated), and on my wide-collar shirt, which I wore outside of my pants with the collar turned up like someone I'd seen in a movie. I was wearing three-dollar Levi's and a pair of his old, worn-down brown shoes. Who did I think I was? Who was I? What he had said had a ring of absolute hard truth—a basic judgment from the universe. Shame. But I would not, could not, let it be the truth. I didn't know what I was, but I wasn't what he said I was.

I think if he had seen my eyes at that moment, they would have looked just like his: hot, on fire, ferocious, and floating in tears. But I didn't cry. Not for years, not for decades, not for a lifetime.

SCENE: Fort Smith, Arkansas

"Goodbye, Old Paint, I'm a-leavin' Cheyenne."

He walks into the hot, dark street and never looks back. He is taking the 11:00 P.M. Greyhound from Fort Smith, Arkansas, to Oakland, California—a sit-up journey of four days and nights—to start over at forty-eight years of age. He will join my older sister and her husband. Daddy must find a job, get an apartment, furnish it with cadged and giveaway stuff, and send for the family before school starts in September. The family now is only three—Mother, younger sister, and much younger brother. I am to stay behind with my aunt, in her house, and attend Fort Smith Junior College.

He walks with his usual dignity and posture, carrying a small overnight bag, which is all he has. But I know he is quaking like a leaf inside. He is a proven drunk with bus money in his pocket. Can he make this trip without going on a toot and ending up broke again or in jail or the gutter, in some foreign town where they don't know him and where they will treat him like the alien he really is?

We stand at the front door watching him disappear into the August dark. My mother is sniffling. My sister, crying. I hold my seven-year-old brother's hand, and we watch him go. I won't miss him, my mind says. But why are these shaming tears leaping out of my eyes? I wipe them with my shirtsleeve until my eyes are red and hurting. I imagine him walking into the dark through his town where he's lived and worked all his life, a well-known local boy. He got married, sired four children, and now, in middle age, became unemployable here. In penury, shamed to the nth degree, he is now reliant on the charity of his married daughter and her stern and righteous, but kind husband. He is hoping he can pass all the beer joints on the way downtown, get on that bus sober, and make good on his thousands of promises to "never touch another drop again, as God is my witness."

He vanishes into the humidity-heavy dark under the live oak trees. God is his only witness and only help now. But God had never once responded to the pleas on the knees we sent up into the sky. Maybe this time it will work, but I have no hope or sympathy.

My mother closes the door. We are alone together. Now the battle begins.

* * *

He was gone, and my mother and I were having fiery nightly battles over my rebellious attitude and my newspaper job. She needed my salary—all of it. But I bought used books. I had bought a book of plays by George Bernard Shaw, which included *Man and Superman*. I began reading. Shaw's ideas were revolutionary, and I was not ready for them. I struggled to understand this Irish playwright who had shocked and irritated the English establishment, the church fathers, and anyone without a deep sense of humor. But something in him suited my rebellious streak and my anti-authoritarian, bristly razorback backbone (even more now that I'm eighty-nine)—and she was yelling at me.

"Where is the rest of the money?"

That hit a button, and I screamed back at her. I saw red and suddenly began jumping in the air as high as I could, slamming back down onto the floor with both feet as hard as I could like a crazed grasshopper or kangaroo monster. And I was glad I was scaring her with my insane anger. My jumping rattled the doorframes, windows, and kitchen shelves of the crummy little house we lived in. Dishes fell and broke in the sink.

She burst into tears, covered her face and said only, "Look at yourself, look at yourself. You ought to be ashamed!"

I screamed like a banshee, "I am ashamed! All the time!"

And she stood looking at me with whatever expression was left to her until it washed away in her tears. She was beaten. I left the house. What else could I do? It was her fault! Yes. Wasn't it? Just her. All her fault!

That awful moment has never left my mind and heart as one of the lowest, most cowardly things I have ever done. That look, my walkout. I have struggled to understand it ever since. For decades, the shame overwhelmed me. I said to myself at the time that I had no choice. I have since learned I had a choice—it is all about choice. There is constant choice.

My mother . . . I was her favorite in the family. She loved everything about me. But not that ogre who showed up. It must have seemed to her that she was a total failure. How could she understand? For her, too, it was all about choice. Her choice of husband, of life, of beliefs, of stuck-ness.

As for me, I had no idea what I screamed—"I am ashamed! All the time!"— *really* meant. But it was the truth. The source of all my angst. It was the promo ad for the self-show that became my life.

S C E N E : Fort Smith, Arkansas

Tectonic shifts began in me. Unexplored continents burst into existence. In the constant mix of excitement and confusion, sorrow and joy, my soul entered into me. It had been waiting in the wings. I sometimes felt it flutter as it passed. I would catch a burst of feeling, of understanding. Something would pause for an instant at my shoulder, and if I looked directly at it, a glorious light would blind me. It was always there, always hidden, always elusive. I was clueless and increasingly uncomfortable with myself. I hurt all the time but couldn't cry, couldn't feel. I read—novels, science, psychology—to try to find answers. I prayed. I said the ancient Latin prayers to myself. I tried to understand what the rituals and the incense had to do with God. I would get very angry. It seemed like a joke.

The longings had showed up at age fourteen. I had seen few picture shows but zero theater except for one collection of fairy tale stories performed in our grade school auditorium by a company of highly rouged and colorfully costumed over-actors. I remember being excited by their bustling extravagance. They were so unreal that I wondered afterward if it was all a dream. But they were a real troupe, The Clare Tree Major Players.

My first picture show was *Lost Horizon* with my parents when I was five, and then *Gone with the Wind* when I was eight, sitting in the family car with my unhappy mother, outdoors in a drive-in when Daddy was on a toot. I was dazzled by these two experiences. One in a true movie palace in Oklahoma City, with a red carpet, uniformed attendants, velvet hangings, and giant, curving staircases, the other in a hot car under the summer night stars with a giant screen (probably 20 x 20 square feet) and with popcorn brought by a pretty girl in a uniform who hooked a tray to Mother's door for the sodas. At thirteen, I had lived inside the one small movie house on the town square in the Ozarks. It was such a small town I could go on my own. I watched *Fantasia* maybe fifteen times. It was my hideout from home. Later, back in Fort Smith, there were three theaters, The Joie, The Temple, and The New. I saw my first gangster picture, *The Glass Key*, with Alan Ladd as the Hammett hero. Film noir, they call it now. I memorized whole scenes of every movie I saw. Every western, every one of the Johnny Weissmuller *Tarzan* movies, all of the Johnny Sheffield Tarzan, Jr. movies, all serials, and all musicals. The only ones I couldn't stand were the love pictures.

By high school, I began to identify with actors. Olivier, Brando, Clift, Kelly. I saw every movie at least three times. At that time, you could still trade a can of fruit or vegetables for a ticket. I now had two lives—real life and reel life. I didn't know it, but I was developing standards—of good and bad acting, directing, movie making, writing, music—even a moral code. Actors were magical geniuses. Untouchable. The only one I identified with completely was Gene Kelly. I wanted to be Gene Kelly. He was so happy, and he made me happy. He could do everything I couldn't do but wanted to. I dressed in chinos, a loose overshirt, a t-shirt, white socks, and penny loafers, like Gene.

I couldn't have talked sensibly about any of this, but I was intensely aware that this was the "reality" that mattered more and more to me. I would go out of the theater, blinking in the Southern sun, shivering from the twenty degrees cooler inside, sated by the smell and taste of ten-cent popcorn. I came into the stinking, hateful, disgusting light of day like an unwilling butterfly unfurling from its cocoon, failing to get its wings moving. I felt like I had been ripped from life to the non-life that everybody but me believed was real.

And I wanted . . . I wanted . . . something impossible, inconceivable. I couldn't say it. It was too incredibly beautiful, too painful. I wanted . . . to be in that movie screen, in that world. To never have to leave it. To swing through the trees with Tarzan, to wear double-breasted suits and flick cigarettes and punch people and never get hurt, to shoot my glittering six-gun at rustlers and never run out of bullets or have to reload my gun. To sword fight as if those sharp steel blades could never kill. And to dance, to dance like Gene Kelly! I wanted to be there, in that world—or anywhere but where I was.

There was no other place except the no-place of the movies to escape to. There was absolutely no one to share my secret life with. I felt silly, foolish and defiant. And angry at the strange circumstance of the life I dreamed of and the one I was trapped in. There was no live theater where I was. No performing arts. They were impossible shadows. Chimeras.

St. Anne's Academy. One very elderly Sister of Mercy, the geometry teacher, moving as ponderously as an immense black-and-white ocean liner inching into a berth in the harbor, eased her imposing self into her chair. I had tortured her all year, very unfairly. We didn't like each other at all, and I was in the front row where the high-security prisoners were kept. This day, I had put an opened can of sauerkraut in her desk drawer. Her slow discovery of what stunk was wonderful pantomime, and of course, all my friends looked at me as the source of the fun. She closed the drawer, looked in my direction, blew her wimple out, drew the stainless-steel protractor from her desk, and threw it at me point-first. She threw it hard—and expertly—in a side-arm sweep, and it came at me like a Bob Feller fastball, sticking into the top of my desk a few inches from my hand with a shuddering thud. It was followed by the *boing! boing!* sound of the vibrating, sharp-pointed steel shaft now standing upright like a dagger thrown by Zorro. The gasps from a couple of girls filled me with idiotic pride. I smiled at the girls and slid out of my chair to the floor, dead. Sister gave me her basilisk look. She was not amused.

"On your feet, Lookingbill. To the principal. Again!" She pronounced it a-*gain*, as if I had won in the stock market. I loved her.

The principal was a steely woman who improbably continued to like me. That year, she had assigned me to write for the school newspaper with the collaboration of my marvelous English teacher. I didn't know that my mother was conspiring with these two women to get me out of high school and into college in three years by sending me to summer school every summer for make-ups and required courses so I could skip junior year entirely. None of these women believed in my "slacker" pose. I had convinced myself that I would be fine pumping gas, managing the Dairy Queen, working at the post office, or joining the army like so many of my friends were planning to do. But these three women were determined I would make something more of myself. The teachers had glimpsed in me something literary that was worth exploring, maybe as a future professor. My mother saw me in a long, white coat with a stethoscope over my shoulders and one of those reflector mirrors strapped to my forehead: "Dr. Luckinbill will see you now."

I saw no such future. I was in quicksand. This was semi-rural Arkansas, only eight decades out of slavery days and still sorry about it. "Old times there are not forgotten, look away," said the old Confederate song, and it rang true. Sharecroppers still worked the fields; cotton had not yet given way to soybeans.

Me at 14. "Yes, Sister Columba, I did put the sauerkraut in your desk drawer. I'm . . . sorry."

Me, at 16. Hopeless pre-med student. Mom said, "Larry, you've just got to have a chance!"

It was 1951, and Orval Faubus was on the ascendance. This was the state that time forgot, still molded into the poisoned class aspic of the Old South. And I might have eaten the poison and gotten stuck if I had not had three angels prodding me urgently to be something else. They laid out my plan: skip junior year, add summer school, and then transfer into the newly opened Junior College.

Then, the English teacher woke me up. She had assigned me to study a poem by Walt Whitman or Emily Dickinson, and I hadn't read it. When called upon, I parodied it to get a laugh. She instantly came down the aisle to my chair where I sat giggling with my fellow sluggards and slapped me so hard—a right cross—that I flew out of my chair and onto the floor. I looked up at her. There was no anger in her, just a hint of a smile and a permanent Irish twinkle in her eyes. I was so impressed. I loved her. She adjusted the sleeve of her black habit where it had ridden up from the slap. She said, "Don't laugh at the words of poets. Words are very important. Poets are important. This is your language. If you don't know how to communicate, you don't amount to much." Then she turned away and calmly walked back to her desk.

I never ditched an assignment again. Sister and I became lifelong friends. Long after, I heard from people back home that she followed every twist and turn in my career as an actor in New York. I never heard from her. Finally, I wrote her a letter thanking her for all she had done for me. I sent it to the home where she had gone to live outside the convent at the end of her teaching career. The word came back that she had died. That slap and my three angels changed my life forever. They were mentors who thought more of me than I did.

SCENE: Fort Smith, Arkansas

I was 16. My father had been gone a year, and my mother, sister and brother were leaving to join him in California. I would stay behind. High School graduation came and went like birthdays at our house—keep it quiet, let it pass—no celebration. We had learned the hard way that celebrating of any kind was occasion for binge, so I don't remember anything about graduating except sweating in the hot gown and wearing the silly mortarboard with the tassel that was hung from one side, then the other. Get it over with. I was to go across town to the North side where the new Junior College was set up in the ratty, tiny coach's offices underneath the football stadium.

I had moved to my aunt's house. Aunt Annie was my mother's sister—the second oldest (my mother was third)—and was the one who had stayed with grandmother and grandfather until they both died, then lived alone in the little house they had moved to on the South side of town where all the development had gone after the war.

My aunt had taught elementary school for more than thirty years. She was a great teacher. She was now working toward her master's degree in education to keep her job. She was the only one in her family to go to college. I was the first in my family. She was not an intellectual, but she was well informed on matters pertaining to her work. She became my mentor. She was a beautiful woman—sober, thoughtful and always kind. She never criticized me! She gave me amazing freedom. She lent me her car, a mint '39 Chevy four-seater, a beautiful rounded box shape with woven straw upholstery and a floor stick. I learned to drive in it—self-taught—grinding the gears and juddering the clutch like a madman at first. She never said a word. I was so grateful to her. I accepted it all without a thought. She wanted nothing from me. She taught by example, not by preaching. I was expected only to get to college on my old bicycle and let her know if I would be late for dinner.

I worked at the local independent newspaper, the *Southwest Times Record*. I learned a number of jobs because the editor liked me. He was an elegant man, the second Jewish person in town, who had worked for the *Brooklyn Eagle*, a first-class newspaper in New York City. Its early editor had been Walt Whitman in 1846. My boss now tasked me to run the switchboard during elections—a very important job—accurately directing all calls and keeping a call log. He taught me about the advertising side of the paper. He was trying me out. I knew if I wanted to advance in this newspaper work, he would help me.

I loved most of all to go into the pressroom and watch the printers lay out the stories by hand with old lead type, and then I would sit next to the big presses when they ran the day's edition. I loved the noise, the smell of the ink, the heat and the feel of the newspaper as it came out folded and ready to be read. I memorized the names of the reporters at the tops of the stories—AP, UP, Reuters.

One day, I was in the ad department observing when I realized a man was standing behind me quietly. He had been there a while. He introduced himself. He was short with a little potbelly and a round, pleasant face. He had lank, blond-brown hair, which he wore long. It wasn't just long; it was long for the fifties—but not like Elvis. He wore it over his collar in the back, over his ears, and with a forelock that he pushed up whenever it fell across his eyes and brow, which was often. I thought, *That's annoying, why would anyone do that?*

He was the new advertising man. He talked as if he knew what advertising and the news business were about, but there was something off about him, a diffidence, a soft quality punctuated with a slight grin that made him seem younger than he probably was. I thought he was probably eight or ten years older than me, but he seemed like a boy. Strange, too—he didn't look people in the eye. He talked with his face half turned away as if he were shy. But he wasn't shy, I found out. He was even kind of arrogant. The net effect was a man who didn't think much of himself and who talked big, but a man with a secret you would not get. Odd and interesting.

And he was interested in me. A couple hours later that same day, he came to visit me in my concrete cell, my office where I distributed the daily afternoon edition to my small street sales force. One of my jobs was to respond to the kids' complaints and give them advice about their selling location, the competition, their personal problems, etc. These ragamuffin boys out of a Dickens novel liked me, and I liked them. This new guy looked impressed.

"You're good at this!" he said. I felt applauded. Here was a total stranger giving me a compliment. He told me he was directing a play for the Little Theater and that I should come to the tryouts.

It was the first time I'd ever heard of such a thing. A play? A little theater in my town! I really hadn't heard. And what was a tryout? It was like something on the moon. I hid all this flabbergast behind a cool "Oh, I don't think so. I don't know anything about such things." I told him I was just starting a pre-med college course. I would follow my brother-in-law to medical school in St. Louis.

He ducked his head, looked away, smiled a little, and said, "Sure . . . a doctor, huh? Well, if you change your mind, the theater is fun."

* * *

The Junior College was funky, haphazard, populated by seat-of-the-pants teachers making do, making up programs to fill the schedule, borrowing labs in other schools and arranging transportation to them. The students were not exactly dropouts, but we were late finishers, late entries, and late-to-class-ers. We dressed sloppily and were sloppy in our work, but we were enthusiastic. This one-year school was the last chance for many of us—either a beginning or an end to college hopes and dreams of a different life than the one we knew lay in wait like a bushwhacker for those who failed to keep up. We were trying to remake ourselves in some way.

From the first day, I realized just how hard pre-med was going to be. The courses were biology, physics, math, all dark abysses in my experience. What on earth were we thinking? But I had to try.

There was one empty spot in my course load, and for some reason I chose a tough course to fill it—World History. The teacher was from some world other than the one she professed to teach. She was a tall, rangy, brisk, powerful woman with wild gray hair going in every direction but straight. She would slam down the hall, careen into class, throw the book down, and begin the day's challenges. There were no lessons, only challenges. All she cared that you learn was how to think about something, how to analyze. And if you could make sense of it on paper, if you could write it, you were brilliant.

This was very exciting. I jumped in and never climbed out. I did well in history and English—anything where words and stories mattered. I peeked out of my alien role and made a couple of friends. A sense of humor was key. It could be goofy, fresh, smart-ass, seditious, or even malicious, as long as it was intelligent. I knew what it was to play with words, ideas, characterization, personae. To invent stories on the spot.

S C E N E : Fort Smith, Arkansas

The Fort Smith Little Theater "in the round."

Opening night of *One Foot in Heaven*.

Waiting to go on stage in the "vom"—short for vomitorium (Latin for an aisle entrance of a Roman amphitheater)—is "Ronny" (Molly's brother). The antique and graceful program note says:

"Larry Luckinbill (Ronny), now in Junior College, when a student in St. Anne's Academy produced and directed several plays of his own composition. He is looking forward to a career in medicine."

This is my theatrical birth certificate.

I had only a couple of lines to say, and the program note is now wonderfully funny to read. All the "plays of his own composition" were improvisations, notes scribbled on the backs of undone homework assignments ten minutes before jumping on stage in the school assembly and doing them, now upgraded in the lovely, courtly parlance of the day to "plays of his own composition." Plays sadly lost to posterity with the trash, and swept up minutes later by the school janitor. And the medical career was destined to disappear in like manner.

The play: A skinny 16-year-old tyro has been inserted into this amateur show by the director (the odd newspaper guy who invited me).

I wore a bill cap, a horizontal striped jersey sweater, and wide-legged white-flannel knickers as I stood clutching a ukulele and trembling. I remember this young about-to-be actor, but I don't recognize him. He's someone else, doing something I had never seen myself doing. But it's me, all right.

I can't play the uke, but in a second, I would act as if I could as I scrambled toward the in-the-round stage among the serious adult amateur actors.

For them, this acting thing was important—it gave them a super-serious and, therefore, comic specialness. (See *The Torchbearers*, a very funny 1920s play by George Kelly, Grace's uncle).

The cue! And off they all went, in the order directed, up the ramp and onto the stage, as, skidding through them, came a kid shot from a cannon, strumming a ukulele erratically, tunelessly, and way too loud. He launched himself around the circle, smiling at the audience, singing off-key, oblivious to the looks he was getting from the main actors in the scene, and to the fact that the audience was already laughing—at him. He was totally out of order, but intent on his own action, he flung himself at the young actress who was the object of his affection. She sprang back. The audience laughed at this out-of-sequence, interesting happening. Who was this weird kid? He hurled himself onto the floor. Ow! Ouch! He had thrown himself down, knees first, with great force, and landed directly on the broken, jagged edge of a bare floor tile.

He blurted out a mangled clutch of lines directed to the girl and got to his feet. There was a gasp from the audience. He looked down, and the borrowed knickers were quickly filling with bright red blood. Ow! Ouch! He had fractured both kneecaps. Oh, heck!

And . . . scene.

Debut over, bandages applied. Still able to stand, the amateur was in the hotel bathroom rinsing out the wide flannel pants, a donation from a theater-loving man who would not be happy to get back pink-kneed knickers.

I remember the experience was interesting but sort of trivial. The theater was not for me, even as a hobby. I was a serious person. I was going to be Doctor Luckinbill, and I was "looking forward to a career in medicine."

The director of the play, the fellow who invited me that day at my newspaper job to try out for the play, drove me home; I couldn't ride my bicycle. He parked in front of my aunt's house. He wanted to talk. He was amused at my unfortunate but startling debut on stage. It didn't bother him that I had more or less destroyed the one scene I was in. He was sympathetic.

"You are amazing," he murmured with a sidelong look. He pushed his forelock up and behind his ear, then looked at me again, and again away. "I think you have a lot of talent," he said.

What? It wasn't—couldn't be—true. My father had said it definitively. I had *no* talent. But I realized now I hadn't believed him. I felt he had some other reason for saying that. But how could this guy say the exact opposite? It made me feel strange. I didn't know him. Why would he say that?

I limped up the narrow front walk to my aunt's house. He watched me, then drove away. It was dark and cold. My knees really hurt now, but I felt warm. Somebody, a stranger, had praised me, said I was "amazing." Shazam! Billy Batson, lame newsboy, is now Captain Marvel!

SCENE: Fort Smith, Arkansas

I don't remember how it started. I know it wasn't me. The nice man who drove me home became my friend. He was older than I—ten years?—and had graduated with a degree in theater from a university, had a graduate degree, and had been working a few years. I was a freshman in Junior College, just a few months out of high school. He was in advertising at the newspaper where I worked as an upscale errand boy. He was a respected member of the local Little Theater. He knew stuff. He was a director who had put on plays in other cities. He didn't brag about it. He was unassuming, modest, self-deprecating—easy to talk to. He didn't pry into my life, nor did he offer anything about himself. Our conversations were about theater, movies, Broadway musicals, and classical music. He didn't seem to be curious about much else.

My few other friends talked about everything, about their lives and future plans, and they were interested in mine. One was an artist headed to medical school but curious about everything in my world. Another wanted to be a writer, and I was a reader, so we talked for hours at school, on the bus, at the library about Faulkner, Hemingway, and poets like Delmore Schwartz and Ezra Pound. We were all sixteen- or seventeen-year-old Southern college boys just beginning to be intensely curious about everything outside our own small world. We were hungry for a connection with places and ideas, new and old, and with life. For us, time seemed to have begun just today. We were all moving out of our pasts, looking around at the great possibilities everywhere.

But this friend seemed content to have found his place with theater—a place of pretending, of make-believe—which I had been taught was useless, a waste of time, and, worse, a morally dangerous place.

Show biz was seditious and disreputable, sexual, something to fear. My whole family—parents, aunts, uncles, cousins, and even my older sister, now an RN and married, living in California with her new husband—challenged my having any connection to that world and "those sort of people." Their assumptions made me angry. I knew little or nothing, but they were so judgmental, so willingly ignorant—all products of the suffocating small-town attitudes I already instinctively hated, as I was beginning to hate the religious teaching I had endured growing up. I was changing, rebelling, angry, arrogant. I classed all this backward thinking with injustice.

So, I liked talking to this harmless guy. I thought he was worldly. Sophisticated. We talked in his car. He owned a Plymouth convertible. Wow! It was the first one I was ever in, and he let me drive it for little distances. And he never let me pay for the hamburgers and the malted milks I had at the drive-in. I didn't like the charity, but I was grateful and impressed.

I think I earned about fifteen dollars a week as the circulation manager for the street newsboys—not much more than they did. This guy probably made three times what I did, but he treated me like somebody whose opinions mattered. I was challenged by his superior knowledge of the world, even if it was only the theater world. He talked about New York. I knew New York was out there, but it was like Oz or Mars—I would never get there, so don't bother. St. Louis or Kansas City . . . Wow! Those seemed possible, and they were the extent of my known world.

SCENE: Fort Smith, Arkansas

One day, he invited me into his apartment, a spacious, airy place with large rooms and windows. He gave me a lift home from the newspaper offices, and, for some reason, we stopped at his house. He pointed out his state-of-the-art sound system—a turntable with a diamond needle! A warper woofer and tweeter! Outsized speakers! I'd never seen such opulence. My sister had owned a small, portable plug-in 45-rpm player, but she'd taken it to California. I had a small radio. He had a German-made Wollensak reel-to-reel tape machine and audiotapes of shows, lots of new vinyl, and older wax recordings, which were neatly cataloged and stored on shelves. Musicals, recorded plays, spoken poetry, theater books—it was a new world. Ali Baba's hidden cave.

There were magazines on a low table he called a coffee table: *The New Yorker, Theater Arts, Harper's, Variety, LIFE*, and *Time*. It was dazzling. I went to the Carnegie Library in town every week. My friend owned his own special library. It was very comfortable and attractive. An open-minded atmosphere. It felt good. Safe. You could say anything. He was pleased that I was excited.

He asked if I was hungry. I was always hungry. He disappeared into the kitchen, and I looked at the magazines. Shortly, he came back with a huge sandwich: bologna on white bread, lots of mayo, tomatoes and lettuce, and a bottle of Dr Pepper. He moved the magazines and put the food on the coffee table on top of a placemat with a napkin. Wow! It was better than being back with Grandma Luckinbill.

To tell the truth, I was so impressed with everything he did for me that I was beginning to feel like I owed him something because he liked me and was so nice to me. That feeling began to grow over time.

We went to the movies. He gave me rides, bought food, and made sand-wiches. It got to be a regular thing that he would be there, always helpful, friendly, and nice. I had always been alone and okay by myself, but this guy made it easy to hang with him.

We went on little trips, and he would let me drive on the empty Arkansas back roads to parks and wilderness places I knew about and could show him. He was a stranger to Arkansas. There were lakes where we would go and swim, and creeks where I would wade and explore, but he wouldn't. He was a city kind of person.

We would end up at his apartment where he would make sandwiches, and I would sit back and listen to music on his great system and read magazines. I was being educated in the theater and in the glamour and excitement of New York City. He loved everything about it. We studied the lyrics of musicals he loved by playing the records over and over. I liked the melodies, but the stories were mostly just dumb and uninteresting, I thought. By now, I was reading Flannery O'Connor and Truman Capote and Camus and Dostoevsky—they were what I liked. He wasn't interested. He just laughed at that stuff. To him, *Carousel* was the greatest musical work of art of all time.

My mind plunged in many directions during these magical sixteenth and seventeenth years. My family was in California, my aunt treated me like an adult, and now this guy made me feel appreciated, like I had something of value to offer. But it wasn't what I thought about myself.

One day, after months of his talking about the theater, my mentor said, "You have a nice voice, I want to record you." He set up the Wollensak machine and gave me Romeo's speech under the balcony as Juliet appears:

> But, soft! what light through yonder window breaks?
> It is the East, and Juliet is the sun.
> Arise, fair sun, and kill the envious moon,
> Who is already sick and pale with grief,
> That thou her maid art far more fair than she.

I sat in front of the mike on the table and tried my earnest best, and out came:

> Buut, saoft! whut laht thoo yonder winda breaks?
> It euhz the' eas' and Jul-yet is the sun.
> Arahze, fay-er sun, 'n' kill th' invius muun.

I was stunned. I never thought I had an accent. I just sounded like every-body else I knew (*evahbody aelse ah noo*).

The Arkie accent is subtle and hard to discern. It's soft and rahthur pleasing, except when it goes flat on certain words. Then it's just flat . . . flat as a dead bunch-a tars own a ol' Chivalay that's been settin' in the back yord fer abaout twinny years.

I had to laugh. I was listening to recordings of Laurence Olivier, John Gielgud, Charles Laughton, and John Barrymore at the guy's house, and never once had he laughed at my accent. And now, my tyro's attempt at reading Shakespeare. It was meant to help me, and it did.

I did not try this a second time with him. It was a long time of practice to erase the accent before I wanted to hear my Arkie voice or sound again.

Interestingly, Vance Randolph, one of my later teachers, wrote a book, *Down in the Holler*, that proposed that the Ozark sound and dialect came from Shakespeare's time. English, Scottish, and Irish immigrants who went west into the Appalachians and, over time, followed the mountains to the Ozarks used words and phrases I heard all around me growing up. They spoke in a Biblical, sixteenth-century musical way like people in Shakespeare's time.

The atmosphere my mentor created in his nice little house was safe, friendly, and stimulating. If it wasn't musicals we listened to, it was light classical music—Gershwin, Copland, Rimsky-Korsakov, Tchaikovsky, Gordon Jenkins, Chopin, all the romantic composers, and film scores by composers who had been taught by the European masters—dramatic, stirring stuff. I was moved by all of it and would drift with the music into my own world, where feelings of loss, loneliness, sorrow, mistakes, longing, unworthiness—all the sadness of my life—rose to the surface. This music soothed and lifted me to some sort of higher, nobler place. Escape. Before this, music meant mostly hillbilly songs about lost love and getting drunk, which both hurt me and made me laugh. Or the blues and R&B that seeped through the local radio station. Or the music of Mass, which I sang or chanted in the choir or while serving the priest at the altar—requiems, Gregorian chants, *Ave Maria*, and all the Latin prayers which had fixed themselves in my daily life and remain in memory to this day. They were stirring and rigorous reminders of death, the gift of life, and duty to God.

I listened to *Scheherazade* and *Manhattan Tower* over and over. The shades would be drawn, and we would just be with the music. One day, I heard my friend groaning in pain. He always sat about twenty feet away from me in an easy chair on the opposite side of the room. He was rubbing himself, eyes closed, his head back and his legs crossed. The music was rising to its climax. My friend was in his own world. He was masturbating with his clothes on. A bright light went on in my brain. My breath caught. I thought, *I can do that, too*. I felt a sharp challenge: be free, be unafraid! I put my hand on my crotch and saw him hurriedly ripping open his belt and unzipping his pants. My mind went blank. I was drowning in the music. Feelings and sensations overwhelmed me. I unbuttoned my jeans and pulled my underwear down.

I just did what he did. His hand was moving up and down, faster and faster. I matched his pace. Suddenly, he gave an audible gasp, held on until he stopped trembling, took out a handkerchief, and wiped himself. Then I was overwhelmed and released.

He pulled up his underwear, walked across the room, and handed me a new linen handkerchief. That was quick. Did he have it ready for me? That thought was the only one I remember, and then I was overcome with hot shame and instant guilt. This was unthinkable! Wrong! I was headed straight to hell!

He wouldn't meet my eyes. It seemed he was full of guilt, too. We had never touched but had just done something unthinkable to me, and to Gordon Jenkins' *Manhattan Towers*. I tried to laugh, but I couldn't. I felt weird, different.

I couldn't confess this. At Mass on Sunday with my aunt, I mumbled I was too sick to go to communion with her. She was so understanding I felt worse. The truth is, I was glad this thing had happened. I was a physical virgin, but not a mental one. I had imagined making love to girls several million times, but I was the kind of Catholic who took sin very seriously. I believed I had a higher self and that it was the one God wanted me to be. So, God, what do I do with these natural needs? I knew the Catholic answer: don't have them. Ignore, control! I know now how inadequate—impossible—that law was. I had a dilemma—how to change that law—because my body said there was nothing wrong with what I'd done, but the guilt remained. I had no way to deal with it, but I knew it was wrong.

It didn't cross my mind that this man was a homosexual. That was so alien, so remote. I had never seen one, only heard about them at school in bullshit sessions on the playground. I thought there couldn't be any in our town. I thought my mentor was like me—just frustrated that he didn't have a girlfriend, and if he did, that he couldn't bring her to visit him alone in his apartment without the neighbors noticing. Viva Victoria Regina!

So this sex practicing began. It became easier, accepted. Practice made perfect. Sit across the room, jack off together, wipe ourselves, and continue with whatever we were about—lunch, music, work, whatever. I stopped going to confession and Communion. I could think of no way to explain this to any priest in confession (if only I had known!). It sounded gay for sure. But I was not attracted to this man or any man. Men were pretty gross, including me—competitive, sweaty, fartish, bullish. I still thought women were incapable of that. Only a woman could put up with us or find us attractive. What did I know? I was a virgin and would remain so for years yet.

Over time, there was an increase in physical closeness. He would kneel almost between my legs to ask what I wanted to eat or drink and then put his hands on my knees or thighs as a brace to get up. It was always a brief touch, and he was always looking aside or away from me when he did it. It didn't seem like part of a seduction, and, over time, I went from thinking of him as older, to sensing something in him that was so like a little boy—so timid, so lost—that he seemed younger. I began to feel like an older brother.

One of my lifelong friends who knew me then but didn't know of this relationship told me that during that time, he always thought of me as "very assured, very masculine, very certain of yourself and of where you were going, very determined, and very clean." I was a self-centered adolescent with an amazingly pure heart. I remained an altar boy in spite of the dastardly deeds I did in front of this man. I didn't think I was teasing him; I felt somehow I was taking advantage of him.

SCENE: Fort Smith Junior College

A Road Trip

We climbed into our teacher's old car—two boys, two girls, our teacher and his wife. Hours later, we arrived halfway across the state to a 1930s-era college campus. We herded into a high-ceilinged room with seven or eight hundred seats and lacquered wood paneling on walls and ceiling—great acoustics. The curtain was up and the stage was empty, backed by dusty black drapes. A wooden podium was the only piece of furniture.

We didn't want to be there. We knew we were in for some kind of lecture. The audience buzz diminished as the lights went out and others rose on the stage. A pause. Then, suddenly, a man stepped onto the stage. He walked very fast toward the podium to my left. I wondered why he hadn't just come out from the side where the podium was. But I got a good look at him as he walked across the stage. He was not especially tall or imposing, but he walked with great intent. I had never seen a man walk like that, as if we were not in the room with him, as if he was alone. He drew our attention instantly. He was beyond alert; he radiated purpose. His was a predatory kind of walk—a lion beginning its charge, a walk portending danger, a great happening.

He carried an armload of heavy books. He arrived at the podium, still without acknowledging us. He dropped the books onto the podium all at once.

They slammed down onto the bare wood, and he opened the top book in one swipe. There was an electric *snap* as the heavy cover hit the book below. He looked at the open page for a moment, then up toward the ceiling, or to heaven, or to himself, or to God. I was totally caught up in this moment. What was going to happen? I noticed the long, silver hair that flowed below a gleaming white shirt collar. I saw how well his dark blue suit fit him. It enhanced—it made the man. It was a grace of a suit.

All this in a nanosecond. And then the man spoke, a pulsating, powerful undertone, a swift, sibilant whisper:

> In the beginning, God created the heaven and the earth. And the earth was without form and void; and darkness was upon the face of the deep. And the Spirit of God hovered over the face of the waters. And God said, Let there be light, and there was light.

And, to me it seemed literally like there was light. A great light entered my mind and illuminated everything. And from that day to this, I still remember the effect of that light.

I didn't grasp it or know its meaning then. I was aware only of a riveting of my attention on the man and everything he said and recited that night. It was more the words and the way he said them than the stories they told, and the revelations of sound and sense he brought from them effortlessly. He read from the Bible, Shakespeare, American poets, English poets, Melville, Crane, Abraham Lincoln, and even Jefferson and Adams. I didn't know or care. The evening hummed like giant power lines had been strung from this man to us, or maybe just to me!

For two hours I was in a trance, a kind of ecstasy unimaginable before. A new beauty had seized me. Beauty? I had never used the word or thought of the concept before. Now, wild words had torn down the doors of my mind and stormed in, bringing rain squalls, wind, lightning, snow, heat, blazing light.

When I woke up, the man had taken a bow and left the stage. He was as unassuming as a ghost and as powerful as the Pied Piper. He had conjured a chalice filled with a sacrament, and I had sipped from it. It was Arthurian, something holy, like the moment of transubstantiation in Mass. Stupefied, I had become a believer—without knowing what it was I believed.

We climbed back into the car. The teacher and his wife chatted as if the event had been a pleasant diversion. My fellows were polite but unshattered. I was broken into bits, trying to reassemble myself. I was speechless, full of thoughts I could not speak or sort out from the overwhelming emotions that brought me to tears, joy, awe—and even a stunning, inexplicable jealousy—of the power I had witnessed, been moved by, been changed by.

The marvelous reader was Charles Laughton. In the midst of the misery induced by the House Un-American Activities Committee's investigation of Communists in the movie business in the 1950s, Laughton had left Hollywood and barnstormed America using his voice and intelligence to fire arrows of love at us in the hinterlands, reminding us that art—our own great literature and the world's—is rooted in compassion, mercy, justice, liberty, and, above all, love. I just happened to be struck by his arrows that night, and the tectonic plates of my planet shifted. There was a new feeling. I couldn't define it, and I had never felt it before. Now, I call it happiness.

SCENE: California

My aunt and I did not travel first class, so we brought very large lunch boxes and settled in for the four-day, three-night sitting up train trip. At night, I would go to the end of the half-empty train and stand on the back platform, just dreaming as we moved across the moonlit landscape. It was so thrilling. I had never been out of Arkansas but was now click-clacking across the great West. We rocked through Oklahoma to Texas, to New Mexico. The further west we got, the more awesome the mountains became—and we were south of the Rockies.

Then we crossed Arizona, and I wanted to leap off the caboose into the desert and walk toward those flat-topped mountains they called buttes just to see what they were. The breezes off the back platform alternated between blazing hot in the day and freezing cold at night, and these extremes were a character trait of this country I passed through. Me, a young untraveled hick from the sticks about to be let loose on America.

As we came to Los Angeles at Union Station, I saw my first police takedown of a Mexican man. Up against the wall, spread-eagle, rammed here and there by the officer's billy club, the little man winced and cried out with every hit. If he turned his head to say anything, a plea, a curse, he was made to be sorry for it. The billy club beat a tattoo on the flesh of the little human person and turned him into a lump of quiver.

What had he done? The huge cop didn't seem to care. He was the star of the show and enjoyed the gaping crowd of ignoramuses—us—who stood around watching the insane injustice of it all, afraid to say a word of "Excuse me, officer, but . . ." for fear of the swinging head-buster being turned on one of us "innocent bystanders." The Mexican man, too, was certainly innocent enough not to be beaten in Union Station for the edification of the cop's sadism and the audience's cowardice. We didn't want to be interrupted in our journey by testifying on behalf of a fellow human. What was the use of it anyway? The guy was guilty of something, wasn't he? But wasn't he innocent enough not to be beaten like that, no matter what he'd done?

So, I'd been to the big city of the movies and was shocked that there was racism there, too. I stood on the back platform thinking about it, as we rocked and zoomed our way north along the California coast up to Oakland. The injustice had shocked me, and my own silence about it shocked me. When I tried to explain it to my aunt, who, with her infirm leg and hip, had endured this trip in her own magnificent brave silence, she merely changed the subject.

My people were the silent type. They *put up with* rather than rebelling or even allowing a dream of rebellion to cross their pillows. It all just *was*, so what was the use of trying to change it?

And so I came home to my new residence in Oakland, to my family.

SCENE: Oakland, California

I had lived through my first real year in college, never looked up, studied like a drudge, tried hard, flunked my science courses, and was now home for the summer in a strange new city—a college man, broke and jobless, a man of the world.

In my freshman year, now just over, I had developed vanity about my looks. I had a D.A. hairdo—"Duck's Ass"—which was built by letting the hair grow long all over, combing it back and training it to the middle of the center of your head, then overlapping the longest strands together and down, and making a comb line vertically down the center. This (and your pompadour, too) had to be secured in place with liberal amounts of Wildroot Cream-Oil. This was a radical hairstyle, my announcement of rebellion. It was going to shock the home folks. It shocked me when I looked in the mirror! I had evolved into a dangerous radical with a bad boy coif.

From the moment I walked in, my family—my mother, my beautiful, vivacious older sister—crowded around, eyeing me strangely, fearfully. I could see they were all disappointed in me, a nothing, a failure. They hated my haircut. I saw, with chagrin, that my mother was angry with my aunt. She felt my aunt had not taken the right care of me, kept me in line. Why had she let me go wild to humiliate her now with this silly, greasy hairstyle that looked like a gangster or a ne'er-do-well lounge lizard, a bum?

"It's not her fault!" I yelled. "I did it. Get mad at me, not her!"

My sister jumped in, "Well, you have to get it cut."

"Why?" I wanted to know.

"You'll never get a job looking like that."

My mother said, "It's no better than poor white trash."

The mother and the big sister huddled, talking in low voices. I was trapped, feral fury rising. I was ready to walk out the door, walk back to Arkansas. I hated all of them.

I felt betrayed by my sister. She should have been on my side. She was five years to the day older than I was—we had the same birthday. She was the extrovert, the only Luckinbill who could make a party. She taught me to pull taffy and to boogie-woogie and jitterbug in our original home. She could put on a *ba-ba-ba-re-bop* or *choo-choo-choo-boogie* or *shoo-fly-pie* 45-rpm record and do her moves with the door jamb as a partner as I watched, entranced—happy, in heaven, watching her laugh, her long dark hair flying, her big brown eyes sparkling. If it was a romantic ballad, she would grab my hand and turn me into a dancer mid-swing, and I would become a stupid block of wood. I tried my best because I kind of worshipped her. I looked up to her more than any-one—she was a mentor.

Looking into my eyes, she said firmly, "You don't understand. There's such a thing as pachucos out here, and if you look like one, you scare people. You won't get a job anywhere."

"What's a pachuco?" I asked.

"Well, they're bad people. Mexicans. They go in gangs and you'd better stay away from them."

This was calumny. I looked at my mother. "So, they're bad people? Why?"

She said, "They do bad things—rob, steal hubcaps off cars. We can't leave our car on the street. And they hurt people. Even at your sister and brother's school, they hang around the parks and rob the children." Her eyes were filling with tears.

Pachucos? Gangs? Where am I? I didn't yet get that she had gone from being afraid in her home to being afraid outside of it. Back home in Arkansas, she was not afraid to walk in the street, ever. There were no gangs. Black peo-ple—potentially the only "enemies" of us, the Master Race, as was claimed—were subjugated by Jim Crow laws. The Native Americans across the river were reservation-bound and unorganized. Where the heck was I now? My tiny step off the path of total conformity was being challenged, and I was being made to feel ashamed as a means of forcing me back on the path to doom.

My younger sister and brother came home from school full of fun, love, and questions, but found a surly big brother backed against the wall in the alcove in the dining area of the kitchen.

My father would be coming home in the evening, and who knew what kind of dragon the genie of the lamp would conjure then? But, instead of hanging out with my sister and brother, I slammed out of the apartment to take a walk. This raised the anxiety stakes—I was now a loose cannon. Another one.

S C E N E : Oakland, California

My father was not in his cups that night, and was not panicked by the sight of my mutineer's hairstyle. He didn't go into a tizzy and mutter, "What in the nine kinds of hell . . ." as he usually did when startled in a bad way. He had been a young man and probably as seditious as possible back in his day—he had been a bootlegger. He didn't think much of the way I presented, but then, he was also a laissez-faire parent who didn't much give a shit what we did as long as it didn't rile our mother—which this did.

Privately he said, "What the hell are you trying to do?"

"I don't know," I said.

"Uh-huh . . ." There was a long pause. "Well, you couldn't get on with the Navy looking like that," he said. His job was inventory and supply warehouse-man for the US Sixth Fleet at Alameda Naval Airbase.

There was another long pause.

"So, what do you want to do? You going to help out?"

"Yes."

Another pause.

"Lucky's Market is hiring box boys. I saw a sign."

Long pause.

"The box boys have short hair, pretty clean necks."

"Okay."

It was kind of like our famous sex talk on the back porch where I slept in 1946 when I was twelve:

"You know what that thing down there is for, don't you?"

"Uh . . ."

Long pause.

"It's for making babies, all right."

"Uh-huh . . ."

Long pause.

"Okay."

A hand slap on the knee and he was gone.

* * *

The next morning, everybody was gone when I woke up.

I got up, dragged on my jeans and shirt, combed and oiled my pride and joy, walked down to the corner barbershop near Lucky's Market—and had the D.A. consigned to the barber's floor where it was soon swept away.

I had gotten a job at the Lucky Market in Oakland, which was bland and uninteresting—box and carry groceries out to cars, restock shelves, re-stack the stock room, and unload delivery trucks. I worked six days a week for a pittance. I refused tips for loading cars. Life like this was unimaginable. Was this all there is? Yet I could not pity my parents, whose daily lives had always been like this. They were never young. They had always been plodding in place, going nowhere, worrying every single moment of every day that wasn't spent fighting about us kids, money, his drinking, her nattering, or their abusing each other in some way.

And they were not bad people. They were very good people, heroes really. They were both as honest as society allowed them to be, more generous than society allowed them to be, kinder than they had any reason to be. But they were yoked, manacled, until they dropped in place and died. And this was going to be my fate, too? To go to hell and be done with it? I didn't want to work for anyone. My parents, shopkeepers, bosses, and businessmen all said I was lazy, and it was true. Arrogant, too, and angry. I wasn't entitled, not at all. I felt like my life was not for sale. I lived my way, which was definitely not by giving it up to some dreary, uninspiring, Dickensian workhouse job that killed body and spirit and dried up creative juices.

One day, Marvin, my sister's husband's brother-in-law (sounds like the Beverly Hillbillies), came to visit after we had all gone to Mass. He offered me a job in his cannery. He was the manager of a huge fruit cannery further east in Oakland. He told me I had a chance to earn good money. I was to report to the employment office the next day at 7:00 A.M. and fill out an application. He told me not to worry about going back to the Lucky Market. This was my "real lucky day," he said. He was a bright, cheerful, but serious business-oriented man—and so kind. He was a mentor.

I got up Monday at 4:00 A.M. Dressed for work in the cannery, I went toward the kitchen. I heard faint music. I stopped outside the door and looked in. My father sat with his ear close to the radio, intently listening. I heard, *"Volare, oh oh, cantare, oh oh oh oh, nel blu di pinto di blu . . ."* Fly, sing, in the sky painted blue . . . It was the achingly joyful but sad Italian hit song by Domenico Modugno and Franco Migliacci. Love summons us to fly free in the sky painted blue. It's the realization that love is so beautiful but doesn't last long. Even if you don't know the Italian words, the melody opens your heart to the reality. It was my favorite song.

As far as I knew, my father had never cared about music or anything that expressed vulnerable emotions. He never cried unless he was drunk. The song ended. He switched off the radio, pulled out his handkerchief, blew his nose loudly, then turned and saw me at the door. He wiped his face roughly with his hand so I wouldn't see that his eyes and face were wet with tears. But I did.

"How you doin', bud?" he said. "Goin' to work, huh? Good." He got up and poured me a cup of coffee. He was already dressed in his daily outfit: dark denim work pants, rubber-soled shoes, long underwear shirt, thick wool work shirt tucked in, a thick windbreaker jacket, and his old, ever-new, smartly brushed brown fedora hat. (He had two—the brown for every day and the gray for church). He and I drank coffee silently. Then he stood, tucked his cigarettes and tobacco pouch into his jacket pocket, picked up his lunch box, and walked out the door. He always walked like he was on a mission. I always wondered what it was. I never found out.

I sat there thinking about what I'd seen. Judging him. I felt like crap. I couldn't believe it. My buried, smoldering anger against him surfaced, shocking me. It would not allow me to credit him with simple human feelings. My ambivalent ego, like Richard the Third's, was "not in the giving vein today." I buried the incident. It shamed me. I couldn't rise above it.

I had bus fare and my lunch in a brown paper bag in case they wanted to employ me that very day. As I was checking it out, my mother came in, wearing her robe and the snood she slept in tight around her head and brow. Her face, washed clean of any makeup, was prettier than with makeup, but, as always, she was frowning with worry.

"Now," she said, without even a good morning, "You do just as they tell you out there. Don't embarrass Marvin, you hear?" She looked earnestly into my eyes.

"Yeah, sure, of course. Why would I embarrass him?"

"Never mind, just keep to yourself and do what they say."

"Yes, I will."

"All right, this is your chance. It may turn into a real job. Look at what Marvin's done for himself. Why, I believe he must be a part owner of that place. He has certainly done well."

Part owner of a cannery wasn't on my list of goals, but I would check the list.

"Now, you have the fare? You know the bus? Where the stop is? Which stop you get off at coming home?"

I assured her of those things and six or eight others she had on her worry list.

I didn't blame her, but it was debilitating to listen to. She couldn't trust anyone. She was so intent upon helping, so urgent about it all. I suppose she had been let down so badly by my father and blamed for any small thing by her mother and sisters that she just had to assume her son was cut from the same cloth as her husband, and she had to protect us all, even from her blaming clan.

An hour on the bus and I was at the gate of the cannery. It was huge, with multiple buildings in an industrial area close to the bus stop. You could smell cooking fruit syrup in the air. The smokestacks fumed gray smoke skyward. The foreman looked me up and down distastefully. I later learned that was his look. He was like Popeye in gray-striped overalls—squinting, talking out of the side of his mouth, serious, even angry, all the time, probably ate spinach. He was about five feet tall but was strong as a bull. Portuguese American. He told me to follow him.

We walked into the canning factory, a huge shed building propped up by wooden supports that reached a very high roof. Light from the clerestory streamed in from the ceiling but was unable to reach the floor, which was dim and cool, a cathedral of yellow cling peaches.

The smell of boiling fruit, a pleasant smell, increased. The foreman stopped at the end of one of the metal tracks on which hot cans of cooked fruit rolled from the cooker, across the ceiling, and down an incline to a stop at an endpoint where pallets with empty open-sided trays were stacked.

The foreman spoke to a guy who was stacking cans into trays and on pallets as fast as he could. The guy gave me a funny look and walked away. The foreman motioned me to take the guy's place. No one could hear even if you yelled; the noise level was unbelievably loud and continuous.

Cans came rolling toward me fast and stopped. Before the next set rolled by, I had to stack the trays on the pallet. They stacked tight to a tier, six or seven tiers high. I grabbed a can—ow! My fingers were burning. The foreman squinted at me—this time it looked like a smile, genuine, not sadistic. First lesson. He handed me his gloves, miming for me to put them on, use them, and give them back. I mimed back, *okay*.

The Marcel Marceau sideshow over, I licked my blazing hot fingers and then stacked hot cans from 7:00 A.M. to 5:00 P.M., with thirty minutes for lunch. My fingers were blistered by the time I took the gloves off at lunch. A nurse in the first aid cubicle put ointment on them. Then she said, "You ought to wear gloves." Duh!

The stacked pallets were picked up by a fleet of forklift drivers who sped around the huge floor like dragonflies. After almost a day of stacking trays full of hot cans, I had a swollen hand with a red line climbing up my arm.

That night, my brother-in-law looked at it and said I had blood poisoning and needed an antibiotic. These were new medicines, but I had already found out I was highly allergic to penicillin. So I was given a packet of a new kind of antibiotic—some sort of thing ending in "micin." On Friday, the last day of the workweek, my sister's husband's brother-in-law came down from the executive cubicle high above the work floor and took me off the hot can line. I thought I was getting fired again, but, with a great smile, he took me over to a jitney (as they called the small, fast electric forklifts) and patted the seat.

"You know how to drive?"

"Yes, sir!"

"You think you could do this job?"

"Yes, sir!"

"This is your horse, cowboy. Go ahead and climb on and try it."

He smiled so broadly I thought he must be kidding. Maybe it was a bucking jitney, and I would be thrown off to general laughter around the old corral—I had seen too many cowboy movies. But I climbed up, slid onto the contoured metal seat, and turned the key. It was alive under me. I had loved skidding around the backwoods dirt roads of Arkansas in a borrowed car, pretending I was a bad dude bootlegger, so this was heaven! My mentor smiled as I drove backward, turned expertly, and—oops!—narrowly missed knocking down one of the thin pine posts that reached up twenty feet under the joists to keep the roof from falling in.

Yeehaw! I was off on a great adventure. I became proficient at zooming silently around the floor at full speed, grabbing pallets with the fork tines in a flash, tilting them back at just the right angle, and racing away to the loading bays. I was careful not to spill a single can off seven tiers of loose, premium-quality peaches in scalding hot cans.

We stacked pallets eight or ten feet high. The odds for error were enormous, but the team of cowboy jitney drivers was the elite of the factory. I had been given a premier job. I wanted to be worthy of it. I bought better gloves, black jeans, a black shirt that I wore with the collar always turned up, and a cowboy belt with a bright buckle with a bronco on it.

I got my first pay packet at the end of my second week. I was astounded—it was at least five times what I had been paid at Lucky's Market. I would give most to Mother for the family, put some away for me, and keep a little bit for a bus ticket to visit San Francisco across the bay.

I was dazzled. I had never seen so much money in one place, let alone in my own hand. I had a strange thought: *I can make enough money right here at the cannery; I don't need to go back to college.* Remembering this now, I see how desperate and blank I felt at the end of my failed freshman year. Right then I got down to the basic feelings I could not face or admit to myself. Me without money equals worthless. Me with money equals worthy—somebody, a doer, a guy with dough, powerful.

I walked down a bay of stacked, boxed cans ready for shipping when, suddenly, I was grabbed and dragged into the dark space between the stacks. The pay packet I was holding like an Olympic medal was neatly yanked away, and I was slammed up against the back wall by two guys.

"Take it easy, buddy. We're not robbing you, just taking up a collection."

"What?"

"*Sí, hombre*, you a good guy. We see how you work. We like you."

"We want you to join us, pal."

"Who are you?"

They held me by the neck and arms up against the wall. Two guys I'd never seen in the cannery—a lean, hard-muscled short guy and a taller, sleek, handsome Mexican guy.

"We want you in the union, so . . ."

"What union?"

"The Teamsters. You're a driver, friend, and we represent you when you have labor-management problems."

"I don't have any problems."

The short guy laughed.

"We know. That's because of us," the taller guy said. "We know you got friends here, high up"—he jerked his head toward the boss's office—"and that's okay. But you just a worker, boy, like me."

"So, what do you want?"

"We collect the initiation fee and the first month's dues in advance. It's all straight up."

"We just like to be careful," the short guy said. "We agreed?"

I didn't disagree, even if it was a robbery. I had a forearm across my neck, my arms twisted behind me, and a knee in my crotch.

"Sure . . . okay. Okay."

And they let go of me. Slapped me on the back.

"You a good guy, mon." They turned to go.

"Wait," I said. "I'm a Teamster now?"

"That's right, friend."

"And you do this to me every two weeks—take my pay?"

They laughed merrily, teeth flashing in the semi-dark. "No, we said initiation fee and first month's dues, that's it. You're in. Pay your dues and we got no problems." They turned again.

"Wait! Are there meetings?"

That was funny, too.

"Sure. Look us up. Ask Marvin about us. You want to go to a meeting?" The tall guy just closed his eyes and shook his head. Not a good idea.

"Well, okay. Nice to meet you guys," I said, and I meant it. They were gone.

"Oh, wait!" I yelled, "Do I get a receipt?"

There was faint laughter from afar.

It was Friday evening after six. Lucky me, I had bus fare home.

I asked Marvin (my sister's husband's, etc.). He just smiled, a pained crinkle, more of a grimace. "Yeah," he said. "Yeah." That was it. He looked at me straight in the eyes. "Pay your dues, Larry. On time."

And so I was a member of my first union. I was a Teamster. I loved Marvin. I loved those guys.

I got paid fantastically well for an eighteen-year-old with no prior anythings as far as work was concerned. I did my job well, took pride in being a good, maybe the best, driver. I loved it.

* * *

At the cannery, I had met a young, divorced Brazilian woman who worked on the damaged fruit line—women stuffed tins with bits of fruit that had been broken on the premium lines and were canned in a new, and more expensive, way, labeled *Choice*. It was hilarious that damaged fruit, instead of being thrown away, was made more expensive, but it was the same fruit as all the rest, only broken.

This girl was special—intelligent, motivated, and startlingly beautiful. She complimented me on my eyes, my body, my glasses (I wore thick specs), and the way I rode around the factory floor on my forklift feeling like a knight on a charger. After weeks of flirting, we went on a movie date. In the dark theater she took my hand and put it between her thighs. It was hot there. Then she put her hand on my lap. It was hard there. We sat in the theater like that, not going any further, while the movie played. Then she kissed me on my neck and on my mouth. This was the first time I'd met a woman who knew what she wanted and was bold enough to go for it.

She drove us to her house. The television was showing a live broadcast of *Peter Pan* with Mary Martin flying on wires. We watched this for a while, and then my date took my hand and we went to her car. She got in the back seat and invited me to join her.

She laid back and pulled me down on top of her. She was small and vulnerable, unguarded and ready. Our clothes disappeared magically. She was shapely with lovely breasts. She took me in hand and placed me inside her. My imagining of this moment had been completely inadequate to the reality. A rush of feelings, of tenderness, of wanting to please, a glimpse of what love might be like, of wanting to know. This woman overwhelmed me.

She said softly, "No, no, no, go more slow." She seemed to open and take me deeper. I felt right and strong—then I knew I should quit or I would release inside her, and I backed off. It was too late. I was mortified.

She laughed sweetly. "Too quick, too soon," she said. "But you are so big!" She held me in her hand, then licked her fingers.

Oh my God. I had only just learned the word *lascivious* from reading something by Erskine Caldwell: lewd, dirty, smutty, indecent. But this young woman was laughing innocently, joyously. She was fine with whatever had just happened.

Thus did the prurient, lubricious, always guilty altar boy lose his virginity at twenty-one to a nice young lady who meant him no harm and would have—if he was not trapped in an ancient orthodoxy that equated sex with evil—taught him so many good things about women, desire, and how to fulfill it as a man.

I was such a temporary person. Who was I, really? I had nothing to offer this lovely child-woman. I don't give myself credit for having any common sense, but I knew I had nothing to give her. If she got pregnant, would I "do the right thing?" I hadn't given a thought to protection. Why do men assume it's the woman's responsibility? I had been given, freely, a gift from her heart. Where was mine?

SCENE: University of Arkansas at Fayetteville

Veritate Duce Progredi—Go Forward Led by Truth

It took about ten minutes for my aunt to ease her '39 Chevrolet Master 85 on a sharp angle into a parallel space in front of the whitish two-story clapboard house across from the University of Arkansas campus. I unloaded my stuff: a cardboard suitcase with a canvas strap that kept its frayed seams together, a couple of duffels, boxes of books, a black wooden carrying case with my Smith Corona portable typewriter, and a large, fragrant box with a grease spot on top, tied with a string—my dinner for today made back in Fort Smith with a surprise treat in a flat tin.

We went into the pleasant living room where my new landlady, a piano teacher, was teaching a song to a dance and drama class—a small group of children wearing costumes for a show. The lady was a tall, imposing, well-spoken

New Yorker whose husband from Brooklyn had been, she let us know, a player in the pit band of the Golden Theater on Broadway. Wow! I was renting a room from an exotic person from a foreign land.

I was shown my room across from the campus. It was a nice room with big windows on two sides and lots of light and air. There was a bunk bed on one wall, a table, a chair, and a shared bathroom just in the hall outside. No private telephone. That was communal and downstairs. The cost was twenty-five dollars per month, a bit steep. I had a little money saved, and my parents would supplement the rent. The tuition for a semester was thirty-seven dollars. I would get all my food—but no money—by working in the kitchen across the street at Carnall Hall, the women's dorm. I would be the dishwasher for all the meals three times a day, seven days a week.

I was alone in my own room. I will stay here for the next three years. At the end of that time, I will go to medical school and then to an internship in a hospital like my brother-in-law, and then I will be a doctor with my own practice in California. That was the plan.

Breakfast was early for me, about 5:45 A.M. But I was up and ready. I ate what the girls in the dorm were served. It was tasty, plain, lard- and salt-based Southern food, plenty of it. I was a skinny, always hungry, tall kid with short hair, horn-rimmed glasses, one pair of jeans, a pair of shorts, two shirts, regular short-sleeved, one shirt with a collar and long sleeves, one pair of brown leather shoes, and a windbreaker jacket. I didn't have enough socks and underwear. I didn't own a watch or an alarm clock and relied on my accurate internal time-sense.

. I hate being late, but I often am because I am unorganized, not disorganized. I am an improvisatory sort of person, very internal, and always thinking, with an extreme sensitivity to circumstance and an extremely active imagination. I am always scanning my surroundings for signs of danger—from people, mostly, but also from things and other creatures. I make up scenarios about what will happen and, as often as they scare me, they always make me laugh. I don't know where my sense of humor came from, but I've always had it. It's generous, absurd, and a little off. I do not expect to be understood, and often my expectations have come true.

The only thing I didn't like about washing dishes for a living was that most of the young women smoked and ditched their unfinished cigs in their coffee and teacups. The cups would spill the wet cigarettes onto the counter and onto the plates, on top of the scrambled eggs and half waffles and syrup and cups smeared with red lipstick.

It was an unforgettable stink. I held my breath and worked fast. After the first day, I ate my meals before starting work.

I was now an official pre-med student. That was taken very seriously at the university, which was building a fine reputation. There was a tremendous amount of work for the students to do in only three years, and many of the men and women I was with had prepped for this future in high school and had already picked the medical school they hoped to get into. They were already applying. I had bumbled along all through school. I was behind everyone, and having gone to Junior College the first year, I had a lot of work to make up. I was lost from the first class, the first day.

It was physics. There were thirty students. The largest class I had been in before was six. The professor chalked an equation on the enormous blackboard, and everyone wrote it down. Then he began to read aloud from the textbook. I had not found my place yet. I raised my hand.

"Yes?"

"Sir, what does x mean?" Pause. There was a murmur from the crowd around me.

The professor looked over his half-glasses. "What does x . . ." He paused, stumped, I thought, like me. "It's unknown," he said.

"To me, too," I said.

There was a distinct chuckle from my fellow doctors-to-be. The professor just looked at me. "I don't understand."

"Me neither," I said. Now a laugh and some rubbernecking to look at me sitting in the back row.

"X is what we want to find out," he said firmly.

"Yes," I added, just as stoutly. A big laugh. The prof suddenly seemed to think, *I'm losing control here.* I could see he was a little pissed, a little scared. He was not much older than we were. He thought I was doing a number. I wasn't.

"You are . . ." he looked at me over his glasses.

"Luckinbill." I spelled it out for him. I always had to.

He looked down at his class registry, took a pen from the protector in his shirt pocket, and traced the names down to L, I guessed. He squinted and tried again, looked at me.

"You don't seem to be here." Now he got a big laugh. It embarrassed him. He blushed. I laughed myself.

"I'm the unknown, like surprise dessert," I said helpfully. Now the room was rocking. This was fun.

He said, "You're serious? You don't know what x stands for?"

"No, sir," I said.

Instantly the room went silent. Jaws dropped, squints ensued, quizzical looks flew my way. Eyes full of pity and fear turned to me, then slowly turned toward the professor, who now assumed the persona of Sheriff Roy Scheider at the beach as the gigantic dorsal fin slides ominously to the surface (*dun-dun dun-dun dun-dun*).

"Okaaaay!" He breathed out. "See me after class, please."

And he went on with more equations and talk, and my confreres busily wrote down every word and worked their slide rules (the cool, wooden computers of the day), perfectly at home in the scientific milieu they loved. They were excited to be there. I was miserable. No one looked at me again.

After the students had all filed out, the professor gathered his books and papers and climbed up the stadium tiers to where I sat, numb. He looked at me and kindly said, "You're in over your head." I nodded.

"We can fix this. You can drop physics for now. I will recommend you take the advanced math class this semester and you can pick up physics later."

I ventured the thought that if *advanced* were in the title, I wouldn't do well in that class, either.

"Well." He smiled. "It's for the football players."

Oh, I get it. That course. I agreed to do as he said, but suddenly I was very scared. I was off on two wrong feet. I was not ready for this—and wouldn't be in a year or six. I now saw that I was sunk. But I would try. I had to. I had no other options, no other plan, nothing I wanted to do. I felt like a fraud. I had been lying to myself. I felt like crying, but I was The Boy. I couldn't do that.

A version of that class played out in every science course. The organic chemistry professor tried valiantly to make it clear, giving me extra time after class and in lab, but I could still only manage a D. He recommended I retake the course the following year.

The biology teacher, a young escapee from the Nazis and communists in Czechoslovakia, was exasperated with me in a comical way. "Is so simple. But you . . . don't try," and he would hurl the erasers at me from the blackboard one at a time. Once he pulled a real rabbit out of his voluminous pocket and threw it at me. I didn't catch it, and it disappeared.

He was a magician—doves, a goat, turtles, tarantulas appeared—anything he picked up on his way to school. He loved biology so much. Darwin definitely could have used him on the *Beagle*. I loved him and his fabulous gift for teaching. But I couldn't get it. I loved the history of it but didn't get the science. Sometimes I thought I got it, or almost got it, but when the class ended, I couldn't reproduce any of it, and my notes looked like alphabet soup.

My buddies from home tried to help me. We would sit over coffee, and they would take turns explaining and reformulating every shred of my studies and labs, trying to help me catch up. They tried so hard to teach me how to use the slide rule, but I couldn't. I could use an abacus, was pretty good on a push lawn mower or basic carpenter's tools, could count, do multiplication tables, whistle through cupped hands, and stack a dishwasher marvelously. But milliliters and meters and grams and vectors and zygotes and tables of atomic numbers fled my mind the instant they were introduced, like people's names at cocktail parties. Funny thing—I could get the history of each science and the heroes who sacrificed themselves to discover why and how, and who built wondrous machines. All that thrilled me, but the nitty-gritty, the math of learning it and applying it, was a track my mind refused to shunt to.

I got a low D in physics. I took organic chemistry twice and did the labs both times—anyone who has done this should get the *Croix de Guerre* or the Congressional Medal of Honor—and still, I failed, the first time with a D, the second time, well . . .

It was early summer, and I, with a few other hapless combat-weary saps, hung around the campus waiting for the final grades to be posted on the Arts and Sciences bulletin board in the Old Main. My life—and death—hung in the balance.

The eternally lovely old lady at reception came out of her paper house with the grades floating between thumb and forefinger. She held the sheet up to the corkboard and thumbtacked it there, naked and spread-eagle for everyone to see. The flash mob that crowded in was too big to fight, so I hung back until all were gone. Good thing I did. I looked down, across and over to the *L*'s, and there was my D minus etched in pale type for all to see. Failure. I had failed. It wasn't an F, but as far as medical school was concerned, it was as good as one—worse, maybe. If it were a flat-out F, maybe they could have said, "Well, he was sick!" or "It was the war" or something. But the D minus said he doesn't have what it takes. No good. And it's his second try. Sad. Pitiful. Sorry for him . . . but thank God he won't be dropping out of our medical school, mucking up our perfect graduation record with the American Medical Association.

Bitter? No—terrified. My family was counting on me. First one into college and three years of high school summer courses for this?

I was off, running flat out across the campus in the bright morning, running instead of crying, anger replacing terror, then terror beating anger into a blubbery pulp of humiliation. My face burned. I was marked as the dummy, the fool, the worthless wiseass. I blazed across the campus, a falling star, and across the street to the row of graceful old houses where the professors lived. I slowed down and began praying to the God I hadn't needed for years. I was intimidated by the quiet calm of the street and the loveliness of the flowers in the front yards, the neat fences, the old-growth trees that shaded the two-and three-story houses with their chimneys and real shutters and wide, cool verandas with comfortable swings and lounges sitting at ease just waiting for accomplished, well-dressed men and women to walk out with their tall glasses of lemonade in hand and elegant straw hats on their heads. I had watched from afar the yard parties with refined, educated people talking quietly about world affairs after days and lives of study and careers. Careers! Professors of science, history, architecture, the arts—these men and women knew things. Who was I, a confused cracker, a clodhopping Ozark hillbilly, an unworthy dope, to come stomping into their lives, disturbing their peace?

I prayed some more. "Please, God, don't let me fail. I'll do anything. I'll do novenas, recite the rosary every day, be good to my aunt and my parents, send my little sister and brother some pecan pies, I won't jerk off anymore [I made a mental reservation on that one: "As much"], and I'll respect everyone. Please take care of this for me, just this once, and I'll never ask for anything again." It was another lie, but I kind of wanted to mean it.

I was at the porch steps of my chemistry professor's house. D-Day. Do I dare go up the steps and ring the bell?

He was a very distinguished scientist. The story was that he had testified at the Nuremberg trials about the composition and effects of Zyklon B, the cyanide poison the Nazis had used in the gas chambers. He was an awesome man, patient, kind, and calm, with a sense of humor—a lovely teacher. *He will help me,* I thought. And I took that thought as a sign that God had heard me.

I went up onto the porch. There was music playing, some classical piano piece. I looked through the etched glass of his front door. He was at the piano, his bald head shining in the morning sun, focused entirely on the piece he was playing so well. I listened a moment, then rang his doorbell. It was a buzzer, loud, like a dying locust in a tree, rasping, insistent. "Answer me!" it snarled. I almost turned and ran.

His fingers lifted from the keys. He carefully closed the cover over the key-board. I felt he was somehow expecting me. He got up, walked to the door, opened it a bit.

I blubbered, "I got a D minus, sir! I can't get into medical school. What can I do? Help me."

I stopped to wipe my nose on my sleeve like I imagined Oliver Twist might do. It wasn't that I was being fake. This was truly the worst thing that had ever happened to me. But, somehow, a third eye within me was watching me and autocorrecting what I said and did to align with the reaction I felt from the other person—a classic "dysfunction scanner" technique.

Unknown to me at the time, this is the actor's typical reflex as he feels his way along the faces and responses of every member of an audience out there in the dark, spelunking the contours of the emotional cavern he is feeling his way into with the word tools he has been given. There are no coincidences, only an exploration of divine synchronicity.

"Come in, Luckinbill," Dr. Noyce said simply, stepping back. I crept in. I stopped sniveling. It seemed wrong. How can this man help? You failed, not him.

"Sit down," he said, proving by his tone that he agreed totally with my last thought (did I speak it aloud?). My heart stopped for an hour or two as I sat gingerly on a cane-backed chair, and he returned to the piano bench. He was wearing cool seersucker—young, ageless, Olympian.

"I have to get into medical school," I said, "I know I'm a slow learner but I can get it, I promise. This will kill my mother if I . . . help me, sir. What can I do?"

"Luckinbill," he said kindly. "You have entertained the class royally this year, and not only the class, but also me. I doubt you know, but I have eyes in the back of my head, and I think your imitation of me is very good. And your take on the difficulty of learning what I have to teach has made me reflect on the way I have been doing things."

He smiled now and the sun came out. It was going to be okay. Even though I was totally busted for making fun of him behind his back, he was going to help me.

Then he said, "This is what you have taught me about you. You don't belong in the sciences. You should not go on. You have taught me that you belong in show business. You belong in the performing arts. This will hurt you to hear now, but it's the truth. I wish you all success and expect great things from you."

I was stunned. Crushed. I was up against a wall. I didn't hear much of what he said at first. I had to reconstruct it later. I just knew the answer was no. I don't remember leaving the house. I do remember his smile. Angelic. The smile of a true mentor. He changed my life forever with one phrase: "You belong in the theater."

But of course, I didn't—couldn't—believe it. I fled directly to a Quonset hut across from the student union, which housed the special testing department. I knew they gave pretests for dental schools, and there was a good one at Washington University in St. Louis. I asked the guy in charge if I could take the test to enter a dentistry course. I told him I had been in the pre-med course but wanted to change—I loved dentistry.

"Of course," he said. "There is a manual dexterity test, and you can take it now." He seemed eager to give the test. Maybe no one was clamoring for the life of looking in people's mouths, but I had a single thought: *dentistry has to be easier than doctoring, and I could be a children's dentist. That would be okay.* And I thought they must make a lot of money.

Again, my thoughts were read as if I were the electronic news ticker in Times Square.

The guy said, "Dentistry is a difficult profession, and it's really underpaid, so it's great to see someone who seems to have a true vocation for it." And he took a box from a shelf. "Here's your test."

Inside the box, I found a large white cube of chalk, an X-Acto knife, and a detailed picture of a molar.

"Just carve the chalk in accordance with the picture. There is no time limit. But since the time for sending these tests out is right now, do it as soon as possible."

I told him I would do it right then. He thought that was great; he would go get a sandwich across the street and be back.

I looked carefully at the chalk cube, tested my new razor-sharp knife on the edge of a piece of paper, and picked up the cube. What a cinch. I was good with my hands. I drew caricatures, had studied at the Famous Artist's School in Westport, Connecticut—well, by mail, after I answered their matchbook cover ad. Norman Rockwell was my teacher. I hadn't become a famous artist like him, but I knew I could draw and sculpt. Didn't I make great elephants, horses, and cowboys out of soap and clay?

I decided to start at the top and, like Michelangelo, let the molar reveal itself.

I cut into the cube gently. The molar—rather, the chalk cube—instantly split in half in a small cloud of chalk dust. What? No way. I took a half and started again. It crumbled before I could put the knife to it.

I stood there with nothing as the guy breezed in.

"Oh." He examined the skeleton. "Huh," he clarified. "Well, they are old, I think. Here, try this one, it's new," he said, handing me another.

I went to the other room, sat down, and studied the new cube. It seemed sturdier than old, dead, crumbled-to-dust Yorick. I carefully began to whittle a corner off the piece to start the molar shape. Very safely, I cut into the edge . . . and the cube collapsed like a dynamited tenement, spewing chalk dust.

The guy sneezed in his office and came to the door. He gaped at the disaster.

"What'd you do to it?" he demanded.

"Nothing," I said. "It just fell apart."

"Not supposed to," he said. "Well, I'm so sorry, but I can't give you another one. Rules. Too bad. Darn bad luck, son. Anybody who wants to be a dentist as bad as you do should be able to get into school. Try again next year, though."

A failure, and out of ideas, I would go home to California to face the music.

S C E N E : Berkeley, California

University of California, Berkley, Testing Center. My mother followed through, as she always did for each of her children. She had researched and made this appointment for aptitude testing for me. We boarded the Telegraph Avenue bus at 6:45 A.M. and sat silently next to each other for the hour ride to the testing center, where we got off and walked through the university gates.

The gent who opened the door and escorted my mother into the plain room was also plain. He had a temporary smile that came on like a light if he thought he needed it, just for a second, then blinked off again as if he had seen all he needed and was back in power-saving mode before you could smile back. It made for a difficult conversation. My mother explained her worries about me and what I was going to do in life. She spoke clearly and honestly. I knew she was overcoming the fear gripping her, as it almost always did. And it seemed to force a deeper concentration from the young man. I became wallpaper. When he looked at me, it was as if I were an unlit Bunsen burner on a lab table.

The testing explanations and rules confused me. I get confused by complicated instructions involving spatial relationships that involve numbers or written directions. But I can find my way to any location in a Sherlock Holmes story. I see historical places in 4D as I read about a battle, trial, or any event. I can help you picture it exactly and with feeling. But lists, spreadsheets, diagrams, and graphs make my eyes roll upward and my brain blank out.

The tests were handed to me, and I was shown to a smaller room with a chair, a table, and some sharpened pencils. That was it. My future depended on my answers.

"There's no winning and no losing here," said the plain man. "All answers are correct, except on the math part, naturally—then there are right and wrong answers."

"Just mark mine all wrong now. We could save time," I said.

The neon light smile didn't blink on. "We are testing for aptitude, not for excellence in a given subject."

"If I don't know something, should I not answer?"

"It's good to do the whole test. You may guess. You won't fail."

"I'll try my best."

I got the smile. I smiled back. Too late. Darn! It had been there—I had seen it—but it blinked off like a refrigerator light when you shut the door.

"You've got three sections. One-hour time limit on each. Three hours total. Good luck," he said and closed the door.

I had fun with the verbal section. The spatial part was interesting, and I did what I thought was right. When it came to the math, I could only answer a few of the ones I had seen before. And I did some creative guessing.

My mother sat and read her prayers for three hours. As before, we rode back mostly in silence. I thought I had done well and told her so. She smiled and nodded, and I thanked her for doing this.

She said, "Well, it must be done. You've got to get a chance."

This was said with a kind of vehemence I hadn't heard from her before. I got a lump in my throat. She had so much riding on this. I looked out the window at the freeway. She said her rosary.

Two weeks later, we were summoned back for the evaluation. My mother feared the results. I could tell by the way she held her pocketbook flat on her lap, her fingers gripping the handles hard, white-knuckling. Her hands were strong and used to work, and I thought about the years she had spent trying to get my father to stop drinking. It was no use to bring up that subject, I knew.

"Don't worry," I said, and she began to cry.

"You've got to have a chance, Larry. You've just got to."

"I will, Mom, I will."

And she let go of her pocketbook, patted my hand once, wiped her eyes, and said cheerfully, "Well, almost there!"

We entered the plain room again. Mr. Cellophane was in a colorless cardigan today. No smile. We took our seats. The guy looked at his folder and opened it.

"I want to make one general comment before we start." He looked at me. "Mr. Luckinbill, did you take this exercise seriously?"

I was stunned. "What? Yes, I did! I sure did!"

My mother was now looking at me with a deep frown. I had been accused. Accused in my family meant *guilty*. The authority had spoken. The specter of humiliation stood in his shroud at her shoulder to hit her with a frying pan. The coffin was open.

"Did you, Larry?" Her question already answered in the negative.

"Yes!" I yelled. "I tried to answer everything, even the math I didn't know. Just like you said," I turned to the man. "I guessed."

He looked at me sternly. "To guess, yes, but the assumption is that the tester will answer within the realm of the possible correct answer."

"But I didn't know anything and I just . . . I just . . . I . . ." I ran out of thoughts except one: *You failed an aptitude test!*

"Well." The guy shook his head sadly. "There are joke answers."

I don't remember the jokes I wrote between the little ovals I was supposed to "fill in completely using a Number Two pencil provided by Tester." I'm not sorry I can't remember—they were 18-year-old jokes, and I wrote what I wrote from frustration, not smart-aleck-ness.

"Let's turn to the spatial tests. Again, I question the seriousness of the answers. To the point, the shape of numbered sides was to be matched with the lettered sides, and the corresponding holes would have made a three-dimensional box with sides that would have all overlapped. You ignored the problem, drew a three-dimensional birdhouse using most of the page, and made something like an apartment house for birds with many holes for apartments. The number of holes is correct. You can count." He did smile—I saw it. "But then you drew birds flying and singing. I'll say this: you can draw in comic book form pretty well."

My mother was stunned, mouth open, anxiety etching her face.

"Then," he went on. "You answered each of the other spatial questions in a similar way, making up your own shapes that used the problem in your own way. You didn't answer questions except to use them to create your own examination."

"Now, as to the verbal part of the examination, I have great news. 100 percent correct. I would say better than 100 percent. It was so surprising to see this focus and this discipline. That is the report."

"Now, let me give my opinion as to its meaning. I advise you it's only my opinion, and others may have, well . . . other opinions. I have spent years at this testing facility [he was 23] and have seen many, many of these tests. This particular test is improved over the ones that have come before. We have a number of interpretive benchmarks and potential options to give testers based on the results and the analysis."

"In your case"—he spoke to both of us now—"Mr. Luckinbill, Mrs. Luckinbill, I will say with full confidence that Mr. Luckinbill has the oddest—I won't say the worst—the most creative, or, perhaps, most challenging imagination I've come across, and that Mr. Luckinbill belongs in the performing arts. Most likely not in the business or production side, but definitely . . . definitely on the creative side. I can go into more detail in my report to you, or you can come back in a week and we can discuss it. This is a process, not a judgment. An opinion, not iron-clad."

I drifted away.

I don't remember the rest of what he said or how we got on the bus or got home, except that my mother's grim look had subsided by the time we reached the apartment. It was replaced with a calm, almost serene, resignation. Her rosary had moved in her fingers the entire trip home.

When we got home, she went to the bedroom with a headache. I walked to the library, then to the local park. Some boys were shooting hoops. I sat on the sidelines and tried to read my book, but the thoughts kept running through my mind incessantly: The second time—performing arts! What did it mean? I had no idea how to process this. Did I have talent or didn't I? There were conflicting opinions, not least inside of me. And how would I go about finding out the truth? How could I make a living? That was important. That was the most important thing a man had to do in life. I felt very small, and the world felt very big.

What was I going to do? I was standing on a high cliff. Would I jump? If I did, would I fly? Or die?

I noticed the boys had stopped bouncing the basketball. I looked up. Four Latino boys had come onto the scene. Smiling, they surrounded the original boys. One of the originals said something I didn't catch. A new boy took out a switchblade and tossed it up and down in his hand, laughing. It was like a regular high school gathering, except for the switchblade.

I looked at the Mexican boys. They were as clean-cut as any California kids; except they were better dressed. They had great stuff—D.A. haircuts (yes, I noticed), shirts with collars up and in bright colors, and blue denim pants— and the pants were pegged. It was a sleek look, very cool. The cuffs were tiny, half the width of a clumsy khaki chino cuff. The pockets were slashes angled across the front and sides. The belts they wore were a half-inch wide with silver buckles. I made up my mind to get the entire outfit.

I watched the original boys start to leave. I stood up and tucked my book under my arm. I was not afraid. These guys were about fourteen or fifteen. I was a college man. I was taller than any of them and certainly stronger, but there was the knife. I was not their target. I didn't get any vibes from them.

But now, the boy with the knife stood in front of the boy with the ball. He said, "We would like to have your ball. We want to play a game. You give it to me?" This was said with a mixture of bravado and something curiously like an offer of friendship.

The ball kid looked at his friends. They were bigger, but they didn't want to fight. No one looked at me. I was wallpaper in their world. Suddenly, the kid bounced the ball to the other one, who caught it. The kid said, "I want it back, man, tomorrow."

The knife boy said slowly, "I will be here tomorrow." It could have been a threat or a promise.

The two camps turned from each other and split to different corners of the park. This was not the end, but it was a truce for the day.

As I walked away, an odd idea grabbed me. This dangerous moment was a movie-ready scene. I should write it down. I didn't. It was 1952. *West Side Story* opened on Broadway in 1957. The zeitgeist was whispering in my ear. I mistook it for the breeze off the bay. Until now.

SCENE: Learning to Learn, Arkansas & California

Despite being an altar boy and knowing the correct responses to all the sections in the Baltimore Catechism, I knew nothing about faith.

I saw movies and watched faith demonstrated in the Hollywood way, with looks to heaven, washed in the soft, glycerin glow that created the "heaven effect." But none of that reached me. I got it intellectually, and I also got its inadequacy to express anything that would or could change my life or even be real.

But now that I look back, I see three events that were invitations to faith, the real thing: being told a second time, by an expert, that I belonged in the performing arts. My mother, taking hold of her rosary with a serene look on her face, and saying to me, "You've just got to have a chance, Larry." And the Jets and Sharks leaders in the park agreeing to a day's truce with the loan of the basketball.

Each of these events was mine to own, and I didn't see it. I saw the external only. I saw people expressing opinions, trying to influence, saying rote prayers that had no meaning, and asking what was expedient and safe. I couldn't see the interrelation of things. I was unable to articulate more than a vague, thin anger at being in some way manipulated by others.

* * *

I had once found a small, yellow, grungy cur cringing in the alley that was our backyard in Harrison, Arkansas, and fed him. He began to follow me around. I washed him, cleaned him up, and named him Bob. He was a ball of gratitude, and I was flattered by his devoted attention. Animal lovers would say he loved me. I didn't see it that way. I liked him because he was utterly kind and gentle and even funny at times. He was like an avatar that didn't know how to do dog stuff. I would throw a ball or a stick, and he would look at it in confusion or wonder. He really reminded me of me—capable of great fidelity and a klutz.

One day, I was up at bat, batting left-handed as usual. I was a good singles hitter from both sides but couldn't get enough power to hit the long ball. But today, the pitcher was weak, and the ball floated over the plate waist-high, begging to be Babe-Ruthed. I tried to oblige. A giant swing and a giant miss. I came fully around with the bat, my legs tangling, just in time to see the bat connect with the head of my small companion who, naturally, had snuck into the batter's box to be at my heel—his favorite place in his short life. I saw the bat collide with Bob's head, saw him fly into the air, contract into a ball, and hit the ground, where he lay whimpering, crying, his blood spreading from his ear and sprinkling the bare dirt of the batter's box. I dropped the bat and tried to pick him up. But his body wouldn't permit me to touch him. He scrambled and wriggled away. He actually got up and staggered like a drunk—I knew exactly how they teetered. And so Bob moved away from me. I couldn't catch him.

I wouldn't have known what to do if I had. I had no money for a vet and didn't even know what one was. I followed him until dark when he disappeared into the surrounding woods. Days passed. Somebody said they saw him alive but half-blind. He wouldn't let himself be touched; he snarled and threatened. I looked for him every day. Then somebody else said he had wandered into the town square half-blind and looking for food and, while crossing the street, was hit by a car and killed. I did nothing for him except harm. I did nothing to return his love and just sucked up the love he gave. I knew I had never deserved it. And I killed him.

That same summer, I was relegated to catcher. No one else was available. A tall, powerful boy named Joe Bill or Joe Bob or Billy Bob was batting, and the same thing happened—a swing and a miss, the batter pivoting left as his bat carries him around. The catcher (me) leans left to grab the pitch, low and outside, and the bat connects with the back of my head at the base of the skull, just above the atlas bone, C-1, the topmost vertebrae.

I was on the ground, my body spasming. Inside my head, coils of electrical impulses expanded outward. I was out like a light, but I could feel the shock, almost visualize it, since flares and rockets were going off in my brain, making images behind my eyes.

I woke up in the hospital. I had been out for a while, but I felt fine. My head was bandaged like an injured Civil War soldier, with a big, white turban of gauze, and, under it, a blood-caked crack in my skull. I recovered, unlike Bob. I could see, walk, talk, breathe, hear and touch. I could think, speak, read, laugh, dream, and sleep without fear. I was in my bed at home in a darkened room for days, but I wasn't in the woods, hiding from the wolves and bobcats under the leaves, hungry and hurting like Bob. Did I get what I deserved? Did Bob?

If he was my avatar, a bodhisattva from heaven to teach me about the faith that makes unconditional love, it hadn't worked. Had it? Did it? I'm still back in that moment. I have had a few dogs since then, and I loved them in that I took better care of them than I did Bob. And when they died at the vet's office, their inevitable suffering in stoic and heroic silence and patience ended by injection, I vowed never to let myself look for another Bob. I can't forget him.

Was that little dog the first time I knew what love was? Faith, love, the spirit of caring. How many mentors? How many avatars and bodhisattvas does it take? How many died trying to help me? I hadn't given a thought to my family. I was so absorbed in myself. We Luckinbills were closed off from one another, never in hate, often in anger, disappointment, and a sense of loss and hopelessness. So, we marched alone. My obsession wasn't ever about my career. It was always about the fear of being hurt. Now, all are gone.

* * *

I rode the Trailways bus back to Fort Smith. It was the end of summer. I was going back to the University of Arkansas to enroll as a new member of the Speech and Drama Department as a candidate for a Bachelor of Arts degree. I was starting two years behind my new fellow students, years spent in the futile pursuit of a life in medicine. Who would I be at the end of the next two years, assuming I could make up all the lost work? Well, worst-case scenario, I could teach.

SCENE: University of Arkansas at Fayetteville

The spritely professor leaps in a single bound from the floor to the seat of a heavy, wooden chair. "Oh, what a rogue and peasant slave am I," he yells in a reedy tenor. He jumps down, flushed and happy. He is wearing Hush Puppies, brown corduroys, a brown-and-red-checked short-sleeved shirt, a wide orange tie tied too short with a fat knot, and a dark-colored corduroy jacket with leather elbow patches.

He clears his throat—ahem!—every two or three sentences. "Now, you," he says to a girl.

She steps up gingerly and says in a vaporescent wisp of a voice, "Oh, what a . . ."

"Louder, much louder," he says. "Ahem! That won't be heard past the footlights!"

She tries again, to no effect. He turns to me. "You?"

I jump up like a giant grasshopper and yell, "Oh, what a rogue and peasant slave am I," and strike a pose out of a silent movie.

"Ahem, *ahem*! Good. Yes, that's it. Shakespeare is big, directly to the heartbeat of the aroused passion. We have to match that size with our own. Don't think rationally yet. That will come. First, we must get out of our everyday selves. We are going to enter other times when a sharp sword in the gut, death . . ."—suddenly he lunges and thrusts at a student who flinches back from the compact little man with a large head and a continual teasing smile playing on his face—"can solve a ticklish social or political situation."

"Everyone here wears a mask. What kind of masks? Civic roles, courtiers, caste identifications, metaphoric, repetitions of death, the plague, God, the devil, carnival madness. We will explore all this as we go through theater history. Ahem, *ahem*! Hmpf . . . tremendous fun."

This is George Kernodle. Dr. K, as everyone here calls him. The great teacher, the great human being who burst into my life, the mentor I had to have to move out of my own small experiences and persona rooted in time and place. He led me to step forward into the deep, fast-moving river of mimesis, of Greek and Roman plays, of medieval mystery and morality plays enacted by guildsmen on mobile carts, Renaissance masques played at by dilettante kings, queens, and nobles, the *commedia dell'arte* Italian street theater of desperately brilliant improvisatory clowns, Molière's masterful troupe of polished players pricking the pretensions of the royal court right under their own lofted noses, and then Shakespeare, the king! The king of shreds and patches, the king of the base court and the splendor and magic of the enchanted forest and the blasted heath. The magus who would "drive [our] purpose into these delights," presenting the actors, the players, as the universal representation of mankind:

> Suit the action to the word, the word to the action, with special observance that you o'erstep not the modesty of nature. For anything so overdone is from the purpose of playing, whose end, both at the first and now, was and is, to hold, as 'twere, the mirror up to nature, to show virtue her own feature, scorn her own image, and the very age and body of the time his form and pressure. Now this overdone or come tardy off, though it make the unskillful laugh, cannot but make the judicious grieve, the censure of the which, one, must in your allowance, o'erweigh a whole theater of others.   —HAMLET

"Ahem, *ahem*, umpf . . ."

This was exactly what George Kernodle was going to show me, the hick from the sticks. Steve Friedheim, a cool big man on campus, urged me to go to

Kernodle's tryout for his new play. Steve's friendship reassured my fearful self that I wouldn't be harmed but, rather, charmed.

So, I was induced by Dr. K to join his merry band of volunteers armed with coiled copper-wire wigs and French heels, to break into Castle Molière. And we did, and sacking and pillaging had never been such fun as in his translation of *La Malade Imaginaire*, which he called *The Happy Hypochondriac*. The production ran for a week. In that time, I was more observer than actor. I just watched the play unfold, did what I was told on stage, and watched more experienced players go about entertaining the audience every night. I said my words, talked loudly, kept my wig on, and remembered to turn in a slow, unobtrusive circle when speaking to accommodate the in-the-round circular stage we occupied.

Some actors grew more comfortable in their parts and some did not. Some corrected the previous night's mistakes, and some were unable to do that. I tried to keep any laughs I had gotten before, except when my wig fell off and I turned into Jerry Lewis for a few minutes. I tried to understand what the audience was laughing at. Was it the play or me? The situation, the line, or the mugging I was doing? I was the "very robustious, periwig-pated fellow" Hamlet thought ridiculously bad, and I felt it.

In the green room backstage, I saw how some actors were ego-driven and some were not. I watched the interplay of these young people who had joined the guild of theater persons. Did I fit in? Could I fit in? Did I want to? It was an exotic bunch. I felt I was ordinary but different.

Dr. K was a dynamo, an Energizer bunny, with an eternally young but jowly and plump-cheeked burgher's face. His square, perky, enthusiastic, compact self was tireless. He glided, leaped, and bounced. He seemed to be without personal ego. He made us feel equal. He was approachable but not chummy—professional. He seemed trustworthy, a favorite uncle. He was not a fatherly sort of man. He and Portia, his wife, had no children, but it seemed as if we were all their children.

I was invited to join the band that congregated in their house in Fayetteville, close enough to campus to walk to but out of the cozy academic circle where many professors lived. The Kernodles were thus set apart a bit. There was always great food at their house. Portia was a famously good cook and also a formidable intellect like her husband. There were discussions and readings relating to theater subjects.

I don't remember politics being discussed. It was a tense time in Arkansas—school desegregation was coming, and though the storm wasn't yet fully formed, the camps were drawn: White Citizens' Councils, the KKK, rabid segregationists armed with all the old, eternal hates, ideas, and tricks on one side. Moderate whites were on the other, with Black people in the middle. The university seemed an oasis of calm in a sea of prejudice and fear. Loyalty oaths were written and circulated, requiring teachers to state their positions on the issues and sign up on the side of the segregationist Orval Faubus or else. These demands were life-and-death for the teachers. They had to declare themselves, and their jobs were at stake.

At the time, those dilemmas seemed less important to a young student obsessing about becoming an actor. The much bigger question was did I have a chance to make it in the professional world of theater? Which, of course, meant: *New York*!

I first looked for an answer to that question from George Kernodle. He was a mixture of childlike, exuberant scholar and serious theater man. Subtle, acerbic, and zealous. I might have been inclined to think of him and Portia as father and mother replacements, but clearly his real passions were not personal in a way that permitted that sort of attachment. And I would have felt disloyal to my own parents. But I was in awe of him as a guru. He encouraged a person to think for himself. He had a Socratic way of teaching and being. It was always up to us to formulate an answer and even figure out the precise question. He never imposed his solution, even as a director. He wanted brisk playing and clear stage pictures, and he wanted us free to create. He liked excess. He wanted us to go big. To risk. But he gently reminded us to be truthful to our choices. He saw the truth in broader terms than representative reality. His influence was close to supernatural, legendary. No one he taught ever forgot him. And he signed the loyalty oath to Faubus. It shook me. It was my first grown-up moment, to face the dismay of someone in that situation having to give in.

In those days, there was always talk of the dichotomy between representational and presentational acting. Olivier's from-the-teeth-out British style against Brando's from-the-gut American invention. Dr. K liked both and was inclined to teach from the teeth out, so to speak, and, I thought then and think now, this was the right plan for the students he faced at the university. We were all limited by our accents, our prior schooling, our limited imaginations, and our unfamiliarity with the theater itself. Many of us had grown up without any theater, professional or amateur. Those who had, sometimes brought bad habits away from the experience. I, a blank slate, willing and eager to try anything to make myself anew, became Dr. K's favorite kind of experimental crash-test dummy.

Portia was my favorite person. She was a large, beautifully plain woman in form and in heart. She had a superb education and a grand understanding of young people seeking a place in the world, especially in the tenuous world of the theater. She had a great laugh, kind eyes, a kind of Gracie Fields or Mary McGoon sweet, musical burble in her voice, and a genuine interest in us. She cooked brilliantly and loved to see us eat what she made, and then she corrected your idea for a theme paper and gave you, subtly, a better idea. She was mother, aunt, and guide, but she, too, had boundaries. She was not personal at all. You could share your dreams or fears, and she would listen and supply an acerbic Midwestern common sense to your "terrible" student problems as if she were slapping a poultice on a mortal wound, then serve you a great steak lunch and, smiling, shove you out the door and back to work, young man. I loved her as I loved my own aunt, a similar kind of person. I did not commit myself to anyone, but I grew slowly aware of how much I needed the stability of this kind of attention and the rational, scholarly mind that animated it.

So, I had come into different conceptions of families than I had known existed. This new theater family world was wide and deep. I began to think of myself as part of something I could be a success in if I mastered the rules.

I took on every task thrown at me, every single reading, every occasion to improvise, memorize, study, or hurl myself at any and every character anyone needed to have played. I was the on-call apprentice player ready to tear a passion to tatters—have mirror, will hold up to nature.

In the play *Emma*, based on the Jane Austen novel, I played the dodgy suitor Frank Churchill. I was far outmatched by the material, but I understood the bad boy aspect of the character well and did what I could. This was so interesting, to understand a character different from you—an eighteenth-century English country gentleman—and try to be him, to take on his thoughts plus do the technical stuff like accent, vocal tone, way of moving, of inhabiting a room or a suit of clothes. I was beginning to see myself as the future owner of a genuine craft. The art came much later.

Theater mimesis is challenging and impossible to master. I dared to believe I could transform. I began to feel I was born to try this—that I was exactly where I ought to be no matter how scary it was. I was "meant to be in the performing arts."

S C E N E : University of Arkansas at Fayetteville

I was gone—into a world I hadn't imagined before. Ideas could become actions. Actions could become reality. The courses I was now not only showing up for but also eagerly running to, bore no resemblance to any schooling I'd had before. The cliché is that I felt at home. But it was more than that. I had never imagined a home before. Unimaginable confidence gleamed in the dark.

At the time, I could only be faintly aware of these radical potentials spreading through me like the effect of a magic potion. I was aware of myself in a new way. I was becoming a man with a mysterious mission. I was becoming daring, aware that risk was the price of admission to this carnival.

I knew nothing about acting. I only knew how acting affected me when I saw it in movies. I had seen few plays. I knew nothing about great dramatic literature, but now I was confronted with it.

Prometheus gave the gift of fire—knowledge—to mankind, and for that act of disobedience he was condemned by Zeus to be chained naked to a rock on a mountain, where his liver would be eaten from his living body by an eagle every day for eternity. *Prometheus Bound* by Aeschylus leads to a frightening conclusion with dark inevitability when Prometheus denies Zeus' power over him. He isn't a bit sorry he did the crime and is eloquently defiant. He is willing to do the time or be executed. Zeus' flunkies and others show up to sympathize with him, to beg him to relent and save himself, and to bow to Zeus' will. Finally, they threaten him with worse punishment if he persists. Hmm? What's worse than having your liver ripped out of your torso daily for eternity? So why doesn't Prometheus give in? What is the purpose of this heroic stance? This is as good and as melodramatic as any Texas chainsaw movie, and it was written about four or five hundred years before Christ appeared with a very different view of what God is and does. Grande Guignol in metaphysical reality.

This fragment of an ancient tragedy was casually handed to me as my first assigned role as an actor by the professor who would become my most significant mentor. The play goes deeply into every corner of human existence and its meaning. Is Prometheus a hero who created human civilization against the gods' wishes? Or is he a rebellious adolescent who put us behind the eight ball with the Creator from the get-go?

Did Greek doctors know the liver is an organ that regenerates?

We know that injustice—man's doing and God's, too—must be exposed, opposed, and overturned. Does injustice stem from free will?

Are we alone in a hostile universe, and is this the best we can get? Prometheus can't give in if God is a monster. He must stand fast to challenge God's existence. If God is real, Prometheus will be destroyed. If he's the Wizard of Oz, Dorothy gets to go home. Which message does this audience of students and their professor want to send? Which one is true? And how on earth is it to be acted?

I instantly grabbed onto my own simmering stewpot of anger and dumped it into Prometheus' mask. And I screamed, which hurt my throat, and the intensity of my rage was maybe somewhat impressive. It was so raw. I'm sure none of the deeper meanings of the scene got through.

Pick a meaning and act that!

How?

I had no idea. In fact, I had no clue about the possible nuances of meaning. I didn't know enough to even read the text in its simplest meaning.

This is where I had to begin. Fantastic! A mentored moment from heaven.

SCENE: University of Arkansas at Fayetteville

"Put me in! Just give me a chance, Coach!"

Romeo and Juliet. I was dressed in tights that bagged at the knee and crotch over a strange and uncomfortable thing called a dance belt instead of my usual baggy boxer shorts. My regular work shirt was now a many-colored thing they called a jerkin, and on my feet were some sort of slippers instead of cowboy boots. I had a big, floppy beret on and a steel-tipped fencing *épée* in a leather sling around my waist. The *épée* was the only thing I felt comfortable with.

Benvolio was dressed a lot like me, and so was Romeo, but his stuff was prettier—silk tunic, linen shirt with big blousy sleeves, and a brightly colored Ike jacket with a stand-up collar. They both had swords, too.

I had practiced the sword fight a lot. I wanted to look good, heroic, manly before I died on stage. I heard the play out on the stage:

Madam, the guests are come, supper served up, you
called, my young lady asked for, the Nurse cursed in the pantry, and
    every thing in extremity. I must hence
to wait. I beseech you, follow straight.

Oh, God!

In a waking dream, I remember Benvolio and Romeo yanking at my arms. My knees were knocking and I couldn't breathe or see clearly. I was having a heart attack. I had latched onto the edge of the stage wall just offstage, having reasonably decided this was a terrible mistake. I couldn't go out there and speak lines I didn't know, couldn't remember. I didn't even know what play it was or even where I was. I just knew I was wearing ridiculous clothing, and I was going to die if I let go of that wall.

My two friends tried again to break my death grip and hurl me onto the bright hell on the other side.

Benvolio whispered in my ear. "Let go, damn you, it's our cue!"

Romeo tried to be calm. "Please, Larry, you'll be fine."

"No, no, no, I can't!" I—Mercutio—said.

Benvolio said, "We've got to go on without him."

Romeo said, "You're going to be okay, I promise!"

"Shit, man, you're an asshole." Benvolio let go of me. Oh God!

Romeo said, "I have to go out there, too. I'm scared, too. Why can't you?"

"I don't know who I am!" I wailed.

Romeo was exasperated now and loud. "You're Mercutio, the best part!"

"Mercutio? Best part? You think so? You're Romeo!"

I came to. Mercutio was a tough guy, a smart-ass, a prankster. An angry joker who gets killed early in the story. That's a good part.

The Nurse said to Juliet, "Go, girl! Seek happy nights to happy days."

The actors left the stage, coming backstage from the other side. My heart beat like I was running up a steep hill and gasping for breath. I let go of my grip. My friends threw me forward onto the stage like a drunk from a bar. I was in the lights. And there it was, the monster with many heads—the audience. A strange, powerful feeling came from them toward me. I could smell them waiting. They were waiting for . . . me! I had to tame them. I skidded to a stop in my squishy, silly slippers.

"Ah ha!" I yelled, and the audience sat forward a little, startled. Romeo was next to me, unrolling a scroll. Benvolio was on my other side. The three amigos.

Romeo looked at the scroll and said, "Shall this speech be spoke for our excuse?"

The tragedy of Romeo and Juliet—ancient, strange, riveting—was on, and I was part of it. I was no longer me. There was someone named Mercutio in the building.

It was my first real acting job. My first Shakespeare play. The Queen Mab speech—sex jokes, funny guy. I had to ask myself, is this what you want to do? Are you going to do it? Or are you going to fuck it up?

The words came, flowing from somewhere. I was talking too fast, but I got a laugh. It was like walking on air, clouds, a trampoline—pure energy. The end of the scene came too fast. Suddenly, I was offstage, shaking, unable to get a breath, like the only ride I ever took on a roller coaster. I was scared shitless and laughing at the same time. Laughing so hysterically hard that I stopped breathing. The stage manager had to remind us to quiet down. I was so glad to be offstage and safe. I couldn't wait to get back on stage. And next time I would get to die, killed by Tybalt in a sword fight. My life and death in a few minutes, and I get to watch it. To be it. To survive it.

George Kernodle directed *The Madwoman of Chaillot*. He cast me as the Rag Picker, a great part. Then, in another of his unique transliterations, a Chinese classic that he called *Two Wives Under One Roof*, I played the villainous Civil Servant. My model for acting this part was derived from Charlie Chan movies, very slithery, rubbing my hands together, sporting a dripping black mustache whose ends fell below my chin as my words, dripping contempt, fell from my lips. I took my walk from Dr. K's walk, and he never caught on. He walked fast with small steps, leaning forward on precarious tiptoes, yet he was always perfectly in balance, poised to lunge, to leap, to pivot, to prance. He walked as an earthly Puck might walk. There was nothing in his ambulation that was made up or affected. It was pure him.

Portia walked in her own style, too—flat-footed, tall, as bulky as a medieval tower in her long dresses and coats, ubiquitous purse over one arm. She ambled, shambled so comfortably that one wondered why everyone didn't walk that way. The two of them were comfortable in their own skins. I was anything but. I was trying to invent a self and reaching in every direction, hurtling down every blind alley, fed by fury and emotions I was still only faintly aware of: longing and need.

My performance had been noticed favorably in the *Arkansas Traveler*. I was knocked out of my skin by the magic of my name in print, into a kind of Caliban—an angry creature unable to be praised, yet needing to be praised and to stay alive by foolish clowning to get more praise. So, for the next week, I walked through the campus backward everywhere I went, to work, to the union, to class, to town, without explanation. Me, walking backward.

I was noticed all right. Girls giggled, athletes sneered, engineering and math students didn't look up from their own odd perambulations, professors smiled, the campus cops cautioned me cordially against collisions, and my fellow theater students were intrigued. I had found an unusual way to get attention. Maybe stupid attention, but even then, naive as we all were, any attention was better than none.

So, I took the first fun backward steps to being a campus character. The school year ended, and I lurched forward on a Greyhound bus, a sit-up trip of four days to California and back to the cannery.

S C E N E : Back to California

The Fort Smith bus station was downtown in the seedy part. It smelled of diesel fuel and desperation, the quiet kind that Thoreau identified with. There were poor—and very poor—people on the bus: a few students, a couple of evangelists, a grumpy old man, and a woman who talked loudly to herself. I was one of the poor students. I had a large box of food from my aunt meant to last the four days to Oakland, California, and I portioned it out for myself like a survivor on a life raft. Five bucks and a couple of dimes for the phone were in my pocket.

My mind was jammed with images from the year behind me and plans for the next one. I was changing. I thought about my ignorance and the skills I needed as an actor, even as a student, a knowledge seeker. I felt new and raw and unarmored. I was already feeling a new pressure to succeed, to excel. To be the best at something. This allowed me a kind of structure of confidence, and, at the same time, I felt like nothing and no one.

I started as no one, and I was still no one. There was a hole in me that I was only aware of when a wind of shame whistled through me, saying, "Who in the nine kinds of hell do you think you are?" I stoppered that hole the only way I could—with fury. Furious shame when I looked in the mirror and didn't see anything, or rather, didn't see an actor, a hero. I saw a scared, skinny, pretentious yokel with a big happy smile on his face, all the more pitiable because he had big, stupid, completely ridiculous, hopeless dreams. Seeing the ignis fatuus—fool's fire—and following it into the swamp thinking it's love, acclaim, acceptance, proof of existence. That will-o'-the-wisp, a grinning jack-o'-lantern that retreats from you the more you pursue it.

I worked twelve hours a day in the cannery that summer and lived at home. After work, I took the bus to San Francisco. I had spent weeks searching the yellow pages for local theater companies.

I took the streetcar from the Embarcadero and found the Actor's Workshop on the second floor over a judo studio. I went up to a tiny office and a tiny theater behind a curtain. The woman in the office—Priscilla Pointer, actress, wife of Jules Irving and future mother of Amy Irving—asked me what I could do.

I said, "Anything! Sweep out, usher, carry stuff, act . . ."

"Can you draw?" she asked.

"Yes!" I said.

"We need a logo for our stationery. Draw me something theatrical."

I drew a caricature from memory of an actor of the commedia dell'arte bowing. She liked it.

That was my entry into that fabulous world. I began going there on week-end nights after work and doing whatever needed doing. I cleaned the johns, swept the floors, and even ran lines with actors learning parts. I was a self-appointed, self-directed gopher, intern, artist, spear carrier, wardrobe assistant, and janitor. I was invisible to Jules Irving and Herbert Blau, the creators of the impressive off-off-off-off-Broadway theater with the imprint of academia on its existence and product. These guys were university teachers catering to a new kind of theater audience, highly educated, specialized folks who were becoming California's elite. The Workshop gave them classic, modern, and eclectic fare. Its tiny auditorium in a second-floor walk-up above a judo studio was always jammed, every show.

I was finally given a chance to go on stage in a play by J. M. Synge, *Deirdre of the Sorrows*. I had no lines but was one of the brothers of the hero. I stood around on stage looking manly and warriorly in a short tunic and bare legs while Naoise (Nishi), the hero, got to talk love to Deirdre. It's a tragedy and so very Irish. All the main people decide to die rather than live without their illusions of romantic love.

Every night I tried to figure this play out. I never did. I stood around and was stalwart. I couldn't really even pronounce the names of the characters. But I was very excited to be in a world of dim, colored lights, dusty drapes, and seats filled with people willing and happy to be watching a show, even one where all of the basically stupid (but attractive) characters committed suicide. This was Professional Theater! I was at the edge of the frame, just half a face and one bare leg visible. But I was in the picture.

SCENE: Oakland, California

The summer between my junior and senior years went fast. I now had a little earned money to spend. I worked all day at the cannery, went to San Francisco on the bus at night, volunteered at the Actor's Workshop, and hung out in North Beach jazz clubs and ate up Lenny Bruce, Stan Kenton, Dave Brubeck, Lionel Hampton. I hung around the City Lights Bookstore of Lawrence Ferlinghetti. One night I brought a reel-to-reel tape recorder, plugged it into a wall outlet, and recorded parts of a meeting between a hip audience, Jack Kerouac, and Gregory Corso. Allen Ginsberg might have shown up, too. I had heard him read *Howl* there. I was studying to be a beatnik.

On the bus to San Francisco, tired from my day at the cannery, I dreamed. I identified with these dharma bums even as I rejected what I thought was their chaotic way of life because I had begun to realize just how much bourgeois discipline it takes to have a life in the theater. I saw that the search for The Way is both acceptance of chaos—impermanence—and trying to create an artistic life—discipline. In fact, I realized that acceptance of all things—the concept of emptiness, everything is contained in it—seemed impossible. Acting, theater, ran on strife. So, I read Zen koans, confused, fearful, and angry, feeling my way into a dark gulf between the enormity of what I wanted and the reality of what I had, what I could ever get, a dark gulf between what I dreamed of and the mountains I had to climb to get it. I had no idea how not to want, not to need, and live. My mental and physical acrophobia and claustrophobia tied me in knots. My life with my family tightened the knots. The Catholicism I'd been taught and its contradictions doubled the knots. Thomas Aquinas and Thomas Merton or Tom Thumb or Tom and Jerry tied me in philosophical and comic knots. Only the university had helped me glimpse freedom.

The previous year I had played the Rag Picker in *The Madwoman of Chaillot*. That part released something in me that gave me hope that I could one day reach the goal that had been set for me on the first day of my first acting class with George Kernodle when he stood on a chair and yelled, "O, what a rogue and peasant slave am I" with a joy and vitality that imprinted in me forever that acting was fun. It was expressive. You could hit the back wall with your voice, you must leave no stone unturned in exploring who and what a person like Hamlet might be, and you had to dare to be big and foolish and stupid in the pursuit of the giants that Shakespeare saw and made flesh with an intensity that swept paltry life aside and forced attention on the reality of our human subtext.

Dr. K, an oddball egghead—the favorite 1950s putdown of anyone different, intellectual or arty—attacked theater like an animal. A digging, unsubtle, fierce animal like a wolverine tearing at a trapped elk in a snowdrift. The excitement was intense, a cool burning. It was the intellectual challenge. We students buzzed around all the giant talents of the Theater Arts Department like bees to a honeycomb.

So, the Rag Picker: a bum, one of life's castoffs, a commentator, a member of a mad woman's maquis, a cool reasoner. Something in me that I never knew I had come to life—wit?

The mayor—Steve, my buddy to this day—and the police chief sat at a café table together. I picked up a twenty franc note from the street in front of them. They claimed it. I refused to give it to them even though I was supposed to surrender it. The next night I bent to pick it up and found it had been glued to the floor by my enemies. I pulled it up, tore it to pieces, and dumped the useless pieces on their table. They didn't know what to do. And that was the point of the moment—a demonstration of the disconnect between haves and have-nots.

This stuff is not written in the play; it just evolved. The discovery that this is what acting could be astounded me. There were things in me that would do things on a stage that I wouldn't do in real life.

At the end of the school year, the following year's schedule of productions was posted. If you wanted to be cast in one of the shows, you had the summer to read and prepare. You would have to audition at the beginning of the next school year. One of the shows for the next year, my final year, was *Death of a Salesman*. I wanted to play one part: Biff Loman, the salesman's prodigal son. But I was not right for it. Biff was a former high school football star, a chick magnet, a tough guy, now a ranch roustabout out West. He had failed at every good job given to him in New York. He had broken with his father, whose infidelity to his mother had destroyed his belief in his father, in faith, in love and in himself. He had left home, never to return. In the play, he has come back, summoned by his mother—the father's in trouble. The part called for a natural athlete, a strong, well-built guy's guy a few years older than me. A bitter fellow stamped by failure, disillusioned, a chain smoker.

I was none of the above. I was tall, skinny, kind of clumsy, dreamy. Not athletic at all, although I had a decent body. How could I get the part of Biff Loman? I had to do it, somehow. On the first Saturday off from work, I walked to the Oakland YMCA downtown. I knew there was some kind of muscleman trainer there. He had a 15-minute public access TV show in San Francisco where he demonstrated his work on Sunday mornings.

That year, 1954, we had gotten our first television set. A large, brown, fake-mahogany box with glued-on decorative touches. On this set that summer, we watched the golden age of television dawn. It was the only good family activity we had. *Playhouse 90. The US Steel Hour. Omnibus. Armstrong Circle Theater. Ed Sullivan* and, yes, *I Love Lucy*, which I never watched. I was only interested in drama, in stuff that fit my general mood, which was never very light. I was figuring out my life, and since it didn't seem funny, I never watched comedy.

So, I tuned into the muscleman's show. Then I went to see him at the gym at the YMCA. Out came this compact man in a black leotard and black ballet shoes—Charles Atlas conceived by George Balanchine. He spoke in an unimpressive high voice as he showed a couple of clients-to-be his exercises, most of which were gymnastic-based, using your own body as the weight to be manipulated. Isometrics. He went quickly through a routine that was interesting and looked simple. Sit-ups, ab crunches, pull-ups, push-ups, leg lifts, bends, and stretches. He didn't punch a bag or lift giant barbells, although he was surrounded by them. Gradually, I realized this guy was in unbelievable shape, the kind I wanted to be in. I forgot about beefing up like a football player to get a part. I wanted to change my life as this guy had changed his. He told us casually that the next week he would swim the Golden Gate Passage into San Francisco Bay from the city to Marin County—one and a half miles of fierce currents—and that he would be handcuffed and tow five rowboats behind him. His name was Jack LaLanne.

I worked out with Jack LaLanne all summer, every spare hour I had. On weekends I almost lived at the Oakland YMCA. I was never home, never hung out with my brother or sister. I was either at the cannery, in San Francisco hanging out, sweeping out the Actor's Workshop, or at the gym. I burned energy like I had my own endless supply—up late, up early. I had a goal for the first time in my life: to change it. To become . . . something.

LaLanne did everything modestly. He accomplished great physical feats but did not brag, at least not to any of us in his little, unassuming gym. I remember how different he was from the blow-dried super salesmen and women of today's health movement. He ate fruit, seeds, and veggies and had a muscled body, but it was lean, and there were no drugs he pushed. He pushed you to do your best and challenged your view of yourself and your health. By the end of the summer, I had been transformed. I now had muscles I had never heard of—pecs, lats, delts, abs, and psoai. I was lean and hard and looked like a man. But was I?

The Oakland gym had a boxing program. It trained boys for the Golden Gloves. I wandered in one day and watched the guys hitting the speed bag and the heavy bag and sparring. There was a guy there who was training for a middleweight fight.

I was a middleweight, 155 pounds. Without telling LaLanne, I volunteered to spar with this guy. I got outfitted with headgear and sixteen-ounce gloves, big, fat, claustrophobic things. There would be three rounds of sparring. I would give the guy a little game. I looked at him, sweat-stained wife-beater undershirt, old gym trunks from WWII or Korea. Shabby, tired Converse lace-ups. He was poor. I knew the signs and didn't need to hear the story. His face was chipped and whittled out of some kind of weatherworn stone. He didn't look at me but inward, or far away, somewhere. I was like a puppy, young with juice to burn. It would be a play fight. He looked flat-footed and slow. I was fast, fleet, and on my toes. I would break through and hit this guy, give him a run for it.

Somebody rang a bell. Oh shit. I didn't have time to be scared as he lurched out of his corner like the madman in the Abbott and Costello "Pocomoco" skit. On he came, and I danced away, back and forth, corner to corner. He came on, weaving some kind of hypnotic web with his gloves, which moved in constant rhythmic waves, rotating up, down, this side, that. Don't look at them, I warned myself. I decided to attack before I fell into a spell. I ran at him and right through his defenses. I was inside his moving, puffy gloves, peppering him with blows I thought were jabs, hooks, uppercuts. If only I could reach the guy he'd be flattened. I danced and danced until I was sucking air. If it hadn't been for the rubber tooth guard in my mouth, my tongue would be hanging out. I realized that only a few seconds of the first round had clicked by—that clock on the wall must be wrong. Whew, this is hard. Keep on dancing, he can't hit me! I rained blows on him, which somehow never got to him. My arms were tired just from hitting his puffy gloves. I better end this quick, before I run out of steam, before he can get through. I realized he had not touched me, not thrown a punch, but from somewhere—Pittsburgh, maybe—I felt a very hard jolt. A bolt of lightning, a brick wall falling, a rake handle I'd just stepped on, something flew into my jaw. I stopped moving. Nothing hurt. This was odd. I was vibrating . . . my nerve endings were . . . doing some . . .

I woke up smelling the stink of the ring's canvas floor. The guy and the gym manager lifted my head. I sniffed something and it gave me another shock. My eyes stung, my nose burned.

I laid there vibrating. I had been knocked out by the guy's first—only—punch. Me, downed by the sweet science, a one-round pugilistic wannabe. Nobody was laughing but me, inside. I felt so foolish, so stupid, so lame. My life and my opinion of my prowess changed in one blow. It was a long time before I connected this moment to *Salesman*—the moment when Biff sees his idolized father with a prostitute. Later, LaLanne said, "Don't train, don't complain," or something like that. I wasn't complaining. What was one knockout against learning as much in one summer as I'd learned in my previous eighteen?

I got the part of Biff Loman.

SCENE: University of Arkansas at Fayetteville

Agnus Dei, qui tollis peccata mundi . . .
Dona eis requiem . . .
Mea culpa
Mea culpa
Mea maxima culpa

I called the plays *Morality* and *A New Cain*. Oy vey ist mir.

They both had melodramatic leading parts for a young guy about my age, build, temperament, skin tone, and suit size. They were set in a ratty college apartment where the guy lived with colorful, weird roommates. The scene was a party with entertaining female characters interested in the leading character, who was having an existential crisis in each play. Both were my attempt to write a version of myself. Ya think?

I staged each of them with the other students in my classes. I promptly found out that I have a tyrannical bent, a righteous, zealous, obsessive streak. So obsessed was I with my truth that I insisted that others obey it to the letter. I directed—no, I pounded people over the head with directions. The plays have been lost, and so, I hope, has my impulse to browbeat people trying their best to please me by any action. It's not their fault. They just don't get it—so they are talentless, lazy fuckheads unwilling to see, incapable of doing anything right. I operated out of primal fear and thought it was my drive for "Truth." How they all suffered. Sorry, folks. It's late, but sorry.

The dream of social justice held high by American theater workers of the 1930s was a unique thing, born in the social conditions of the time, made by the maturing of the Industrial Revolution. The theater had begun as an attempt to explain the dark forces called gods, which seemed to rule the world of the ancients—and the actions of mankind. They were the forces of what came to be called "evil" and thus objectified. These were challenged by writers who wanted to penetrate the human psyche deeper.

The two one-act plays wrote me in that third year at the university. They were ejected from me by an earthquake of confusion, the effect of the child I still was, a child of unacknowledged repression. An altar boy who still smelled the candles he lit before Mass, who carried the cross with a fierce believer's grip in processions in the churchyard where he was formed. But below the cassock, his sundered-sole flapping old sneakers telegraphed his soul-separated condition at every step.

I had learned that home was a dangerously unstable place and that school offered only emotionally choking, physically gagging peas and carrots that I had to swallow.

So began a succession of mentors, escapes, and confrontations within myself to learn how to cope with the confusions and mental tortures and comedy of what turned out to be my life. In other words, to learn how to act, to reproduce emotions, "to be or not to be" myself in another person, to entertain and enlighten an audience in a safe place.

Theater was open. Acting was pure. Theater was getting off in public, therefore impure, wrong, and condemnable. Alluring. I was confused. What to do?

SCENE: University of Arkansas at Fayetteville

Norman DeMarco was a professor of speech and drama at the university. He was in charge of the media department. He did radio and movies and the fairly new thing, television.

He had been an actor in New York and had played a role in Maxwell Anderson's *Truckline Café* on Broadway with a young actor in his first Broadway appearance—an eccentric kid named Marlon Brando.

It must have been strange for him to go on stage with young Arkansawyers who barely knew stage left from right and dig into the psyche of that giant everyman from Brooklyn, the salesman Willy Loman. I will always be in awe of that play, the role that began the acid wash that shaped me and every single thing I've ever done in the theater. Biff was not me, but the emotional torrent rushing him head over heels through chasms to the drowning pool was exactly me.

How do you attack such a part? The emotion is so thick you could strangle in it, for every word was as if dreamed by me in a repeated nightmare. It all unfolded for Willy in an inexorable straight line of enhanced realism from exhaustion to destruction, aided and abetted by his misguided belief in status and wealth as happiness and his hunger to be somebody, to matter, to the end. Is it a modern tragedy? Some people disagree on classical grounds. Willy's not a king in the old way and not in any way a great man. His fall doesn't bring down a nation or destroy his own family. Oedipus' giant pride brought him down, but wasn't the pride generated by a craving to be someone important?

I believe it is a tragedy. In America, we are taught the dangerous lie that everything we want can be ours if we work hard. Willy certainly believed that. And his self-sacrifice by suicide for his family is the end of a quintessential American king and fool—and dreamer. The man bought the lie that we can be anything we want. We are Americans, we are exceptional. The tragedy is that the family wanted Willy alive and happy. This is clearer today than it was in 1954 or even in 1776 when Jefferson changed "pursuit of Property" to "pursuit of Happiness."

When I showed up at the audition, it was obvious that I had changed physically. I had natural muscles, my posture was straight, and I was California tan and healthy—maybe too fit for Biff, who is now no longer a high school football hero, but a failure at every job he's tried. He's confused, angry, and sad.

I don't remember the audition. It was casual. I remember only that I got the part as if it were no big deal, as if the faculty had agreed beforehand. That would explain the system by which they democratically chose plays for the actors they had, whom they hoped would grow in skill with a part and do something with it. Maybe I was the angry young man in the department.

Biff Loman was a part in a great play, and I felt pressured to come up to the mark. Arthur Miller was to come to speak at the university. I studied Kevin McCarthy's performance in the movie (Willy was played by Fredric March) and decided he wasn't right for the part. I wouldn't do what he did. That was a relief. But now I had to really create my own Biff. It helped that DeMarco played Willy, my father. He was a crusty New York guy, a little unapproachable, intimidating in a brusque way.

My father! Those words give me the heebie-jeebies to write today. I knew that untangling that mess of ganglia, neurons, synapses, and knee jerks was going to be impossible. Well, I didn't know anything—I only felt.

I began to resist any connection with Willy. I couldn't look at DeMarco when we read through the play, and when we got on our feet and started to block the movement of the actors through the play, I avoided contact with him. The other actors may have thought that was weird. I couldn't help it.

I suppose I came off as tight-lipped and cold to hide what I was feeling. I couldn't accept DeMarco as a stand-in for my father in the scene, so I somehow put my father in the scene. This illuminated a problem: an actor must find a role by working with the actors in the play; substitution is tricky. I was left outside the scenes. I felt fake, and it showed. This was intolerable. I still remember the fury that rose in me at being unable to feel what I should. My affective memories of my own father were still an inextricably Gordian knot.

Back at my little dungeon of an apartment below a graveyard on a hill, I practiced football moves while watched by my more athletic roommates, who were sympathetic but unhelpful. I am just not a natural athlete. The moves all the other boys seemed to learn as easily as putting on a stinky t-shirt would just not come to me. After a while, I would take a break and work out in our yard gym using broken concrete blocks for weights and doing a thousand push-ups and hundreds of sit-ups. I got someone to take pictures of me with a Brownie camera in various macho poses, none of which were convincing. I looked like a movie pretty boy with nice eyes showing off his tough-guy persona. I sent these photos to Stella Adler, the legendary acting teacher in New York who had trained Brando (ha!). I knew she would jump at the chance to train this intense, laser-intelligent young actor destined for classical greatness.

I haven't heard from her yet.

In the scenes with Linda Loman, I was at home, having played such scenes with my mother before—especially the ones where she blames me (Biff) for not helping, for being AWOL from the family in her helpless, awful, non-blaming way. And in the scene where Biff and Willy get down to the crux of their disappointment with each other, I was consumed, burned to a crisp, nightly. I had a hard time containing myself to a play and not jumping across the stage and beating Willy until he was bloody and unconscious. I now believe that uncontrolled fury was not the play or even the part. It took stage in a peremptory and obtrusive way. Because I was sensate enough to stay with the play to the end, until Biff's fury is burned down, trying to summon some sympathy—yes, even love—for the man whom he had to call father, I was able to see a glimmer of something I had compassion for and of a knowledge that I had to connect with the man I had to call my father.

At that moment, the bombshell of what real theater is exploded in me for the first time.

The dangerous feelings I was denying and hiding from myself and others, but constantly reacting to, were fully unleashed in this play, and no one died.

The theater was a safe place to be, where I could call up any feelings at all. And these feelings, released into the holy space of the stage, would rise and mingle with the sacrificial fires still smoldering from our ancestors as they struggled with the fear and ecstasy of being alive. What on earth had I gotten myself into? I was baptized in the holy fire now!

No wonder that at the storied first performance of the play in New York, as the stunned audience silently shuffled up the aisle toward Forty-Fifth Street, a man was heard to say to his wife, "That goddamned New England territory was never any good!"

We began to rehearse *Death of a Salesman* scene by scene, methodically, according to a strict timeline governed by opening night's approach.

I was ready, jammed with all the right feelings and memories of a family, of my father and mother. I was toned, looking strong and competent. Now came the actual work of becoming Biff Loman. I was like a rodeo bull wanting to stomp and kick a rider before he is on its back or an untried racehorse wanting to run and win but shying at the unfamiliar gate.

I panicked immediately. I wanted to do it all right so much that I did nothing right. All I had to offer was fury of an undirectable kind. And fury was not all that was demanded.

The genuine emotions I had on tap to bring to the part wouldn't come when I needed them to. I was dry, wooden, overthinking every simple act, and so self-conscious. Just getting out of my bunk in the attic to talk to my brother, Happy, became a whole scene. I was trying to shape how this guy would get out of bed, stand, sit, and light a cigarette. I wasn't present—I was watching a movie I made up. The words came out of my mouth like bricks dumped from a hod.

Searching for my method. University of Arkansas. "Please, God, I *am* Biff Loman. Help me get this part."

I hated myself. I realized I was unprepared, literally unable to do this part that I was so right for—in fact, the most uniquely right in the history of the world. But, unless they kicked me out, in three weeks or so I would be dead, and the world would know I was good for nothing.

The director didn't look worried. He didn't throw me out the door. He continued to work methodically, paying little or no attention to my atrocious inabilities; my stumbling along and scowling, uptight as a steel wire ready to snap at a touch. The other actors seemed fine taking direction casually, writing little blocking notes in their scripts and doing what they were told. I hated them—fucking robots! I couldn't do that. I wanted to tear down the fake walls of the set I had helped designer Mac Magruder build as part of my training.

That night I studied the script for the thousandth time and thought about Mr. DeMarco, my father, Willy Loman. He, too, had seemed uneasy. Maybe nervous because, as a professor, he had a lot riding on this. The only thing I could do, I decided, was to watch all his scenes that I wasn't in. If he was as afraid as I was, maybe it was normal. It was a desperate thought, but the only one I had.

On the second day, the director pushed on fast. The idea was to get the entire play on its feet the first week. At that point, the script had to be completely learned, actors off book.

I got in a spot just offstage where I could watch Willy and not be in anybody's eye line. DeMarco was clutching his script and referring to it a lot. Maybe he was worried about remembering his lines. A few minutes into the scene, he stopped the director and went to talk to him quietly. After a minute or so, they began again from the beginning. This time, DeMarco had changed. He walked much more slowly. He looked different, crunched down, shorter. He seemed confused about where to sit and when or if he should stand or move to the refrigerator. It was tentative, a little scary. But now, I saw, he wasn't holding his script. It was rolled up in his back pocket. It wasn't that he didn't know his lines; he was trying to find who Willy was at that moment. He didn't care about the words or how to speak them. He was focused only on getting into a chair, any chair, or looking into the refrigerator, and he did the actions over and over. Each time he changed, he was somewhere else inside, and I forgot I was watching Mr. DeMarco. I was seeing a man in crisis I had never seen before—Willy Loman.

I didn't know how to analyze it, but it was a punch to my solar plexus: acting is *doing*. Is this the door to my house? How do I open it? How do I go through it? What do I see on the other side? Does seeing something change what I do next? Am I going to sit? Why? Which chair? Do I have a favorite?

First, you *do*. Just do. Nothing else. Forget yourself. Forget how you look. Forget how you will say the words. The words matter, but not yet. You must find your physical body on a stage, and a stage is an alien space at first. There is an audience who must see you and hear you every single moment. There is no camera. Getting it right mentally, physically, and vocally will take hours and days of practice. But the objective is always just to do. Focus on that. You are in a heightened state and pumping adrenaline, but if you have worked right in rehearsal, a doorknob will save you from stage fright. You see objects and "doings" as friends. The set is a friend. Eventually the other actors are friends and the words are friends. You can rely on them.

The words must follow an intention to do something. But just the right doing takes the pressure off the talking and, as in life, creates focus, carves an air sculpture of movement and words. I already knew my words cold. I said them every night like prayers. The first scene with Happy, he's talking, just listen to him and respond. Don't think ahead. Allow the actual reality of your surroundings guide you. You are on stage; people are expecting you to do something. Use that reality to be the reality that Happy expects. Do something about Pop. Transform your stage fright into Biff's fear about himself. Simply be. Really be! It's counterintuitive and uncomfortable until you allow yourself to be Biff. DeMarco's way of rehearsing taught me where I had to begin.

I grew up in a family of six in a house with two bedrooms, one bathroom. We time-shared: *Knock, knock!* I'll be out in a minute! The bathroom was smelly or damp or gray with Lucky Strike smoke.

I slept in the screened-in back porch or a pass-through room. No air conditioning. We were poor; the Lomans were poor.

We had roaches, water bugs, spiders, snakes, ticks, chiggers, and mosquitos in the South. What critters did the Lomans live with? Poverty is the same everywhere. So, I was poor, and we lived on the edge. The Lomans' Brooklyn poverty was like mine. I could smell it. So, in theory, I could be in the play as if it were a real place that I knew intimately.

But I couldn't hold onto these thoughts. I didn't know how to stay with the thread a little at a time in the big blow-up scene with Pop. My personal sorrow and rage broke through. I drowned in my own life and my own father. I could not find a way to be present in the now. I was awful. A huge failure. I was not able to do the one job I was right for. If I had been able, I would have seen that my state of mind—and my emotions—were Biff Loman's.

I remember weeping in every scene. It was uncontrollable. I wiped my eyes constantly, keeping a graying handkerchief in my suit pocket for that purpose, which I made sure was never washed by the costume department.

We had a one-week run. Seven chances to get it right. According to the response, I had gotten enough of Biff to be believed. I even got an award, but I didn't believe I had earned it. I never knew what DeMarco thought, which curled me into a tiny ball of shame every time I ran into him. He never said. He was the god of judgment to me.

I was wasted every night. Every show left me so alone that I ran from the green room after I dressed and walked for hours through the campus and the little town of Fayetteville, which was now my only home. One night I stopped on a railroad bridge. It was two in the morning and moonless with a cold west wind blowing. Streets were empty; no lights were on. I stood at the center of the bridge and looked down. I was forty or fifty feet from the tracks below. I'm an acrophobe, but that night I leaned over and studied the ground below.

I was stone sober. I did not drink, did not smoke, and was naively ascetic, an unhappy, depressed boy-child in a young man's body. I was getting to do what I had learned was the only thing I was passionate about doing in life: acting in the theater. And I was a failure at it. I knew I would be. I was oddly homesick for my family in Oakland, California, and aware of the strangeness of that feeling. I was so alienated from them, but now I longed to be in the midst of the mess again. I did not want to leave the university at the end of the year. I didn't want to stay, either. That would have been an admission of weakness. Those who hung on as graduate students or just stayed, living in town, too weak to leave the sugar titties of the alma mater, were pathetic. And yet, the alma mater was the real thing, my soul mother—the right words to describe what I felt. And I would have to part with her forever. This green oasis in the Ozark Mountains of Arkansas had filled me with wild hope and joy in the three years I had worked there like a person possessed by a dybbuk, first trying, painfully, to become a doctor and then, totally in fantasy land, trying to become an actor, a man of the theater, an artist. Those words were used by my professors unabashedly, unapologetically. They believed we could be artists, and I wanted to believe them.

This thought was swirling in the mix, part of the fog that covered me as I leaned over the parapet thinking, *why not?* I saw myself fall and heard the crunch on the gravel around the tracks. If I fell across the tracks, would the engineer on the 5:00 A.M. freight see me? Or would he run over my dead, neck-broken, worthless self? I didn't want to feel anymore. I wasn't trying to spite anyone. I had no suicide note dramatically blaming anyone. I wasn't playing the hero. No. This was the real me, just wanting out. Not acting.

I stood there, thoughts going a mile a minute, and then they just stopped. Blanked. And I put my hands on the parapet and thought, *I'm going.* Time passed. The wind blew colder. I don't know how long I stood there. I wanted to go but didn't. There was no emotion in it. I'd had enough. At the bridge I had two thoughts: One, *Catholic boys don't do this,* and two, *your mother will cry.* I couldn't stand that. I lifted my hands off the parapet and shoved them into my jacket pockets. I backed away. A decision to reserve. I would try again later. I went back to my room, took off my shoes, and got into bed, jacket and all. I lay there, wide-eyed and shivering with the cold. I felt nothing. I wondered what to do. Who was I?

SCENE: Fayetteville, Arkansas

In the 1950s, homosexuality was not spoken of. I had never heard of pedophilia. Those words seemed forbidden. For anyone in the closet, life was limited and dangerous. In the South, you risked your life if you were "other." Black people were lynched. Gay people were beaten to death, sodomized with broomsticks, or just disappeared, fate unknown.

I was in a summer play. My "friend" from Fort Smith came up to see it. I was ready to leave town and had moved out of my room. We walked around the campus, ate at a restaurant, went to the local lake to swim until sunset, and then went to a cottage near the lake where we would stay overnight. I didn't like the idea but assumed we'd have separate rooms.

He asked me to wait in the car while he checked in. It was dark. We went into a single room with a single bed. He took his things inside. I had just what I had worn all day plus a bathing suit, which was still wet. I did not like this at all, but I didn't want to make a fuss.

I was not afraid of my friend, who had never touched me inappropriately—I didn't count his grabbing my legs—and hadn't done anything to me. He had watched me. I was part of his masturbation routine. I had gone along with it. The guilt was constant.

But in the middle of this night, I woke up. Something was pushing me. I was on the far side of the bed, facing away from him, as far away as I could get on the small bed. I had on my white BVDs. I felt something cautiously but firmly pushing against my butt. After a second, I realized it was him. The head of his naked, hard penis was smack up against my butt, between my cheeks, trying to get in.

I rolled off the bed and stood up. I yelled, "Don't do that! Don't do that!"

He didn't look up at me. He immediately rolled away, pulled up his underwear and the sheet, and didn't move or make another sound the rest of the night. I got up as soon as it was light, dressed, and waited for him outside the cabin. As soon as he got up, he drove us straight back to Fort Smith. We didn't speak the whole trip. That was the end of our friendship. I didn't hate him. I wasn't even angry at him. I just avoided him from that day on.

I now know that my friend may have been a pedophile. I was not a child when it started at sixteen, but I was still a minor, ignorant and oblivious. I was very immature. I had no idea he was committing a crime. I believed for years that the whole episode was my fault, that I was warped and sick for participating. I was guilty as sin. I had encouraged it, given consent. Allowed it. Wanted it. It didn't occur to me that the guy was manipulative or that my need for acceptance and affection was not the same as giving consent. Even now, I don't believe he thought he was doing anything to hurt me. It was his nature. He was driven. If I went along with it and responded to his grooming, I must have wanted what he wanted. Could homosexuality be learned as a way of life? Could it be chosen?

At this point I was eighteen, the legal age of consent. What if he pretended to be my friend to get into my pants? I could not judge him. My heart knew better. He had been good to me. He liked me. He may even have loved me. The thought was repellent then, but it isn't now. He was gay. I'm not. It's not a choice. But it is not as simple as that. For a kid as vulnerable and as needy, as lonely and hungry for escape and—paradoxically—connection, as I was, living in a place and time and belief that held that sex was wrong, that women were sacred flowers, that God was judging every thought and move, what I did with this guy was bound to happen. Sin? No. He thought I "had talent," said I was "amazing." I knew that nobody could love me. How could he? Did he? Why? Confusion!

I could not explain why I did this, so I didn't and hid it. There was so much more guilt and danger in having sex with a woman. So, I froze these sexual events in the deep cold north of my mind. And my anger at myself smoldered deep beneath the tundra. I knew I was not an innocent altar boy anymore. I had been mentored—not for good—and the effect would be something I would deal with for years until I understood it.

SCENE: Fayetteville, Arkansas

I spent the days until graduation drowning myself in music. The turntable was hot, the needle wearing the grooves down incessantly. The sadder and more self-pitying the better. I hugged trees on the grounds surrounding Old Main, laid in the grass and touched the earth. Smelled late spring, early summer, Arkansas, the South, all that I loved and some that I loathed.

My parents came to Fayetteville for my graduation. First one in the family to go to college. I treated them horribly. They were strangers, unwelcome. I was curt. Uncommunicative. They could never understand me, what I wanted, who I was trying to be. We were on different planets.

They came to *Twelfth Night*, the first of the summer plays. I was Feste the clown, one of the great characters in Shakespeare. I was proud of what I was doing in the show. I had learned the rudiments of how to speak the verse in two years as a Speech and Drama student. I had taken every course they offered, crammed them all in—heavy loads of classes and performances—and done well, become a scholar of sorts.

By then I had built sets, stage managed, and played bit parts and leading parts. I had become somewhat comfortable being on stage, but I knew how far I had yet to go. I was wearing the name actor very tentatively, although I was sure this place was where I had to be. I was still unconvinced that I could make a living at it or even be good enough to qualify. I invented a modern dance for Eleanor King, formed a Dramatic Readings Quartet, had done scenes from Greek, medieval, Renaissance, Shakespeare, and Restoration theater—Shaw, Ibsen, O'Casey, O'Neill, Miller, Williams, Odets, and Inge. I was the go-to guy when anyone needed a voice or body to interpret a role. I had worked nonstop and took on every request and challenge.

As Feste I was playing with words and puns, singing, dancing, playing the class clown I had always been, only now wearing laurels for it in Orsino's court.

After the show, my father asked only one question: "Why do you put your foot up on that platform every time you talk?"

He hit the target in the hot button of my fakery as an actor. He knew nothing, but he punctured my balloon. I had gotten into sort of an arched, pretty pose whenever I made a joke, and to illustrate how at ease and familiar I was in the court, I would put one ballet slipper–shod foot up on the riser and lean forward with one hand on my hip and one on my knee. It looked good in the costume, very Shakespearean. And he locked onto it as phony. Indicating. He didn't say that; it just registered as unreal to him. He was curious, looking at it as a layman and the realistic down-to-earth guy he was. It caught his eye as anomalous, not necessary. And it wasn't. I saw it now, too. I hated him for seeing it instantly and for popping my pompous balloon. But not really. I had to laugh: the drama critic, my father, the drunk. He had given me a great directorial note!

He was on his best behavior this trip. He was in unfamiliar territory with educated people. My mother monitored every move, and my aunt was their chaperone and guide to this world of education that neither of them had been lucky enough to have.

They had come a long way to celebrate me. But I wasn't having it. Not from them. They embarrassed me. I had evolved. I was cool. Ha! It hurts me to remember how much I must have hurt them. I was mean and arrogant and ungrateful to these out-of-place people, my folks. I was the one behaving badly in the midst of a happy time, onstage and off. I've never forgotten my father's comment because it went to the heart of what I was doing wrong, what I had not learned, how not cool I was.

Close to the time he died, he asked me in a mystified and hurt way, "Why were you so angry that weekend?" I should have said, "Because I was an asshole."

Years later in New York, I read the advice from Stanislavsky which is the motto of Actors' Equity: "Love the art in yourself, not yourself in the art."

Yes, but first, love yourself. And I didn't.

SCENE: Fayetteville, Arkansas

After graduation, there was a party at Dr. K's house. Our small community of theater folks gathered to celebrate the time together, the work done, and the lives changed in the few years we had worked together. It was an elegy set to the music of Portia's food—down-home, sophisticated cuisine—and quiet laughter and conversation at a level of intelligence, wit, and learning that dazzled me. All of our teachers were accomplished people. They were friends now, not "the adults." Forgotten now was the fact that our mostly progressive professors had been given an ultimatum: the loyalty oath to Governor Faubus' "Segregation now, Segregation tomorrow, Segregation forever" racist, fascist, KKK-inspired regime, and they had signed it. The proof was that they were still there, still allowed to teach—still progressives, but now subjects of King Orval, Emperor Jeff Davis, and the Confederate States of America. They continued to teach their way but stayed out of politics. That way, we had all learned, was the way adults behaved.

We, too, were now part of the adult world. It was up to us to make of it what we could. Some drank and smoked themselves into a daze. Some knew they were done with this theater stuff and would move on to regular lives as civilians. We all had friends outside the Speech and Drama Department who were graduating into ownership of family farms and assuming large debts for big-time farm machines to run them. Some buddies from Fort Smith were going on to medical school. Others would end up in Congress. One friend was moving to New York City to make his art. Brave! And our theater family was breaking up.

I was near tears the whole evening at the Kernodle's ark, the old house burnished and shining with knowledge, scholarship, and so much fun. Portia had taught me to cook steak there, and Dr. K had asked for my opinion on a chapter of his new book, *Invitation to the Theater*. I belonged. I was a member in good standing.

As we were leaving, we were in a raucous, seriocomic conversation on the doorstep, and I was being pompous about myself and my talent. The big questions were: What was talent? Who had it? How did you know if you did? We were all trying to assess ourselves as worthy to go on trying to be actors.

Dr. Kernodle said to me, "Ah, yes, you are unique. One of many unique young men I have known. Twenty-nine unique young men! You are one." It was said in his acerbic, dry way and casually.

Was it meant to puncture pompousness or penetrate the truth? I don't know, but it was a knockout punch. I had no defense, no mental tools to measure such an obvious statement of fact. It drained the blood from me. I felt it pour out into the wet night grass. I walked away.

There was no sidewalk. No guideline. The night smelled of honeysuckle. A cooling, humid breeze traced its way through the live oak trees, the pines, and the maples. The arboreal guards that had protected my time at this house as a guest, then almost as a son. George and Portia had no children of their own. They had us, a continuing round of aspirants working toward a better life. At this point, I had nothing and no one by which to judge myself except them. Of course, unique is unique. Each was one of a kind. No one was special. But twenty-nine? Was I just an unremarkable member of the parade?

I walked away into the dark without a self. A tender, budding sense of self and achievement had been neatly stripped out of me. I was a nobody. Always had been, always would be. The melodrama was not lost on me even then. The walk to my little apartment under the graveyard was a half-hour of amnesia. I don't remember allowing a single thought. I might have gone to the railroad bridge and jumped if I had. Life was over, was a sham, a lie. I was lying to my-self—he said so, or was it him? Was he lying? Why would he? It never occurred to me that he might have been protecting himself from the imminent loss of his students, his children. This man gave 100 percent to me, then cut my heart out in one swipe of his knife.

"Ahem, *ahem*." School was done.

SCENE: Fort Hood, Texas

Out of college forever now, I was on the street. In the wind. On the road. Free. Bereft of home, purpose, and meaning. I left my heavy books and records at my aunt's house in Fort Smith. Carrying one duffel, I walked across the bridge to Oklahoma and stuck out my thumb. I hitchhiked to US Army boot camp. I reported for duty at Fort Hood for my Reserve Officers' Training, six weeks to become a second lieutenant or wash out and go into the draft pool.

Basic Training. The mess hall kitchen—a hundred degrees in the dark, dry outside. I racked up fifty clean, wet trays and wiped out the giant pots and pans of my new life, the words of the WWI song, *You're in the Army Now*, playing in my head. I forgot about the theater. It was over, just a dream anyway.

What did I learn in this six-week introduction to the army? Loyalty, endurance, caution, alertness, a high level of patriotism, a tolerance of other men's way of being under stress, and rough play. I also learned that I was an aggressive son of a bitch with a mean and violent temperament that, when honed as it was now, gave me a swaggering, looking-for-a-fight attitude. I was turned into a junior "bad dude." This was, for me, reversible armor, but for some others, it seemed to be a permanent kind of change. The training played into personality traits that were uncivilized in the extreme.

The army, however, knowing what it was doing, also taught restraint and urged self-control over the impulse to fight, subordinated it to the discipline of obedience to orders. We were being taught how to be officers, the ones in charge, the ones to interpret and give the orders, to take real responsibility for a full company of humans who you may be asked to sacrifice by following superior orders to hold a piece of useless real estate or a crossroads or a gun emplacement. This sobers you up.

Hikes in the July heat. Responding to the deliberately provocative non-commissioned officers' orders and reorders because you didn't do it right. Get it clean. You were five seconds late, had the hat on or off, had the shirt tucked or infinitesimally untucked. The barracks head was not spotless enough to eat from the urinals, and so on. These were all familiar to those of us lucky enough to get to serve. Yes, lucky. Honored. I discovered a high tolerance for bullshit, irrational orders, apparent meanness, and even sadism of a mild sort. This would all stand me in good stead in future theater ventures.

The finale was the field test. Our platoon would fight an imaginary battle over many stations secreted on trails in the broken-up, rough Texas high plains desert, which had a famous history of the great cattle drives of the earlier

Fort Hood, TX. From KP to First Louie in six weeks. I am at parade rest with an invisible mop.

century. We marched with full packs into the wild country, made a camp, set up tents, set out perimeters, hung water bags, and bedded down.

At 3:00 A.M., they woke us up. We were divided into competitive teams. The goal was to accomplish a series of tasks using every skill we had made acquaintance with over the last weeks, from map reading to bridge building. Each station's objective was timed. The pace was a full-out run. Then we had to identify the objective using materials issued to us, materials on site, and materials we had to create on the spot. Make it happen at full speed. We were on our own. The only other people in the area were observers. We didn't speak to them. They were silent, marking their clipboards, checking their watches. The temperature went up as the day wore on. It was over 120 degrees by noon. There was a C-ration break for as long as it took to rip open the packages—the same stuff the GIs ate in WWII and Korea. At one station, we had to kill a large rattlesnake that had coiled under a canvas water bag to enjoy its own personal spa. It met with an entrenching tool and went to rattler heaven.

At the final station at 6:00 P.M., drenched in sweat, we confronted a pile of stacked beams, posts, and building materials. There was no construction plan, no blueprint. The task was to bridge a ravine in front of us, cross it, and race a mile to the final station. As we stopped to look at this massive job, the guy in front of me, a wiry, quiet, tough, and likable Texas boy—the shortest and lightest guy in the platoon—disappeared from my view, collapsing face-first down onto the sand of the clearing. He was frothing at the mouth. What was it? Heat exhaustion, dehydration, a brain seizure, rabies? I didn't reflect. I had a sweat-drenched handkerchief in my upper pocket. I knelt, grabbed his chin, and stuffed it into his mouth, trying to get it between his teeth without being bitten. Somehow I did.

The observer at this final station, the captain, kneeled beside him. He said quietly to me, "Good job." Then he punched his walkie-talkie and said, "Medic team to station blah, blah . . ." followed by, "Good work, Lieutenant."

No one had yet called me, or any of us, that. I straightened up. My face got redder than it already was from the sun and extreme heat. Mentally, I stepped forward to receive my Medal of Honor. Then I looked at the kid. He was twitching uncontrollably now, his legs and arms jerking every which way.

The captain said, "This is epilepsy. Too damn bad."

I realized the kid was toast. He got this far—the last mile—and had just washed out. And so it was. We never saw him again. I felt hollowed out by this. He knew he was epileptic, had to have known. Somehow the army didn't. He wanted so badly to be here and do his job, unlike many of our mates who just wanted to get it over with and get out. Not this kid. His bunk was two up from mine and we had gotten along well, though we had zero in common. He came from a family of farmers. He had studied biology or botany or something related. Like me, he was another Southerner ready to do service, to stand tall at this task. The truth was, the M1 rifle he carried was almost taller than he was. But he has always stood very tall to me.

The bridge was being built without me. I jumped in to lift beams and fetch and carry. Our team finished, and we raced to the finish line. We didn't win, but we finished. There was a graduation in khaki summer dress uniforms. I received a diploma and one little gold bar pinned on my collar. I was very proud. I got a Trailways bus in Killeen and went to California. I was a new shavetail with active duty coming up—a new identity. Who would I be now?

SCENE: Driving to Alabama

In the autumn, the army sent me my call to duty. I was now to spend two years in obligation to the service and, as things stood, would likely be sent to Korea to serve at the DMZ, the embattled dividing line between North and South Korea.

Days before my call-up orders arrived, I visited the president of the small, private California college my brother was set to attend. The job of building a Speech and Drama Department there was mine if I chose to take it. Security. University life. Back into the womb. I was very attracted by this, a chance to build my own theater studio and be close to my brother. Then the orders arrived, and my teaching career faded into a misty future.

I was assigned not to an infantry job in Korea but to a job running a platoon in a Chemical Corps unit now in training at Fort McClellan, Alabama. I drove out of Oakland in my Nash Ambassador in January. I was in the army now. I had to report to Fort McClellan in Anniston, Alabama, on a specific date, and I would be there.

My mother constructed a set of box lunches for the trip. Monday would be meatloaf sandwiches, Tuesday would be ham, Wednesday would be pimento cheese, Thursday would be peanut butter and jelly, and Friday was salami and American cheese. I had a large thermos of black coffee, potato chips, Fritos, pecan pie, and a jar of good old Southern ambrosia, which I had to eat in the first few days. I wouldn't need to spend any money on food. I wore my leather jacket, a striped French polo shirt, pachuco pegged pants, brown hiking shoes with thick soles, and my fatigue hat. I had one black turtleneck sweater and a pea coat. I was Uncle Sam's beatnik.

I took the Southern route straight ahead for almost seven hundred and sixty-four miles. I only stopped to gas up and pee several times, and I was intent on sleeping somewhere in Flagstaff that night, probably in my car with its full-bed interior.

It was early winter. I had a blanket and a pillow in the back. I was sleepy but still excited, only sorry it was night and I was missing the mountain scenery. My thoughts were ranging: Wow! This was a long hill. It must be fifteen miles up a very steep grade. The old Nash was humming along really well, listen to her purr . . .

Blam! Blam! Blam!

I was jarred awake by a shocking noise—three blasts from the air horn of a giant long-haul truck on my left. I woke up fast, from dead asleep to wide awake. I saw the driver above me in his tall cab. He was waving at me, urgently waving his right hand for me to come closer to him. What? Why was he in the wrong lane, right next to me? What?

Then my right front wheel bumped off the concrete of the road, and my steering wheel followed as the Nash began to turn to the right. I looked; there was no guardrail. I was looking down an open cliff that seemed about a thousand feet almost straight down.

I still had the wheel. I had a 21-year-old's reflexes and cool control. I just eased my steering wheel to the left and bounced a little as the right tire climbed back off the narrow verge and onto the blacktop-covered concrete of the highway. Snow and ice were all around, but the road was clear and free of black ice in my headlights.

I started to shake. Now it was hard to hold the wheel straight. The semi blasted past me and into my lane ahead of me just as a car slipped by in the left lane on its way down the hill heading west. The semi pulled over into a wide passing spot and stopped, its air brakes huffing and spitting and the blinkers winking "*Emergency!*"

The driver leaned out and waved me over behind him. I parked and got out, my knees buckling a little. I walked toward him. He stepped down and said, "You all right, kid?" He smelled my breath. "You been drinkin'?"

"No," I said, numb. "I don't drink. Just coffee."

"Bet you gotta pee now, don't ya?" he asked. His round, red face with its gray stubble glowed in my headlights. I nodded and he laughed. "Go ahead, then!"

And I did, over the precipice, looking down where my body would have been. I would have slept in my car that night all right—bloody, dead pulp. The Nash would have come to a stupid bad end. I loved that car, shit! I zipped up and started to laugh. I walked back to the guy. He was a grizzled, tough prospector of a man now banging his hands together against the cold.

"Yeah," he said. "Laughing's good."

"Thank you, sir. You saved my life!"

"Yep," he said. "Now, you ain't driving anymore tonight."

"No, sir!"

"The police is just up to the top, about a mile. You go in there, sleep warm, laid flat. Whir you headed?"

I told him: Alabama. The army.

"Whir you come from?"

I told him San Francisco.

He looked at me, squinting like he was looking at a freak—not unkindly, just like he couldn't credit his eyes and had to be sure of what he thought he saw. "San Francisco? In one jump?" Then he started to laugh again. He pounded me on the back with glee. "You drive almost eight hunnert mile in one jump? You're a dang fool, boy! You gonna make a good soldier. A good got-dang fool, too. Don't do that anymore, you heah?"

"Yes, sir," I said, and the words bounced out of my mouth as he slammed me on the back again like I'd just done something great.

"Got-dang fool. You sleep!" And he climbed back into his cab, put the giant truck into gear, and, with a whoosh of air, eased out of the turnout and was soon just taillights up the road, disappearing fast.

I was cold now—really cold. I thought of looking over the side of that mountain again, but I couldn't, even here in the turnout, where there was a guardrail. I couldn't take a step closer to the edge of that cliff. A mentor, an angel, had steered me away from nonexistence. I was shivering now, teeth chattering.

I climbed into my warm car and very slowly drove in the center of my lane one mile to the lighted police station. I entered, was given shelter, and slept that night in a cell, a free prisoner. A trucker had saved my life. I owed him big time. Sixty-five years later, here I am, owings mounting up. As high as heaven.

S C E N E : Fort McClellan, Alabama

Fort McClellan has been called the most toxic place on earth because of the leakage from various chemical weapons poisoning the air, earth, and water. To add insult to injury, Monsanto has also produced PCBs in their factory there. Depleted uranium has been stored there. The deadly poisons also include mustard gas, sarin (nerve gas), VX (nerve gas), Agent Blue, and Agent Orange.

Of course, Southerners trust the military, which brings tangible goods to life. But the streams, the land, and the aquifers are contaminated. The government has been accused of culpability for turning a deaf ear and a dumb face to veterans' problems.

I was sent to this post for my first assignment as Second Lieutenant, US Army Chemical Corps. It was pretty country in those pine-forested, low hills and winding narrow roads. It was still the Old South there, and the smoke and smell of burned black powder from Civil War muskets still hung in the air. In the town, smoke rose from burning crosses, the weekend fun activities of the KKK. I came upon a white sheet and burning cross party on the evening of my first Saturday leave from the post as I headed downtown to another traditional Southern activity: the boarding house where young officers ate when off post. I watched the hooded figures until I was noticed, then moved on.

I was assigned to lead a Commo Platoon. My unit provided communication services to all other units in the company. This meant I had to overcome a primary fear, acrophobia. I put on climbing gear, long steel spikes strapped to my shins and a thick leather strap with hooks on both ends. I had thick gloves and web belting for carrying coiled telephone wire, wire snips and strippers, tape, a knife, and a screwdriver.

I climbed pine trees and telephone poles by wrapping the strap around the circumference of the vertical object, hooking the strap to my belt on both sides, then sticking my spurs into the bole of the tree, sitting into the strap, and walking up, flipping the belt higher each step up. The telephone poles were about twenty-five feet tall, and the trees were fifty feet up. There was no time to think. I was motivated by a powerful desire not to look like a useless fool, so up I went. I hoped I had made it look easy by acting. I was not going to fall to my doom from some fucking yellow pine tree.

I saw a notice on the company info board. A Fort McClellan swim team was required to compete against other army teams from all over the US in the third Army Olympic Trials at Fort Benning, Georgia, that year. I volunteered to coach the team and swim myself. I was ordered to the Olympic-sized pool to form the team. Three men showed up. No women. The guys were hoping there would be. So was I. I took all three before they could back out.

We would compete in four events: the 400-meter relay and the 100-meter, the 200-meter, and the 1500-meter freestyles. No one wanted the 1500-meter freestyle, so I took that one. Our only qualification for such an enterprise was that we could all swim. We were the very definition of amateurs. Willing we were, competitive we were. Did we have a chance? Not a chance! Did we know that? We did not. Were we losers? Not in the least. We all went in like winners. The problem was we needed a coach. So I coached, and managed, and swam.

We had ninety days to become a top-notch team worthy of representing Fort McClellan. No one cared but us.

When the Olympics rolled around, we met in the faint dawn before the Benning mess hall opened, and I decided to take us off post to a good, healthy Southern breakfast at a famous local diner. We had a grand time slurping up coffee, grits, bacon, sausage, pork rinds, fried green tomatoes, eggs and biscuits with heavy white gravy, and pots of homemade jam. I paid for all.

At the meet, things were set to happen pretty quickly. The bleachers were filling up. Our small contingent got into swimsuits. We didn't match. Other posts had sent athletes and had outfitted them. We didn't even have swim goggles.

At the far end of the men's dressing area was a short, compact Hawaiian. Someone whispered, "That's Ford Konno!" He was the gold medal winner in the 1500-meter freestyle in the 1952 Olympics. His finishing time was eighteen minutes, four seconds. Suddenly, I felt really unprepared. This guy was the real thing. I experienced a familiar tightness and panic: stage fright. I had all the ego in the meet, and it started to fill me up with sick-making butterflies. I actually thought, *I have to beat this famous guy, and I will!*

I had never gone the full distance of this race and had no skill other than my strength of my arms, shoulders, and chest, plus my size. I was six foot one and weighed 155. I was in the best shape of my life. So was he (and probably still is at eighty-nine!).

The event started.

THE 100-METER FREESTYLE.
Last place.

THE BUTTERFLY.
Third place.

THE BACKSTROKE.
Fourth place.

THE RELAY.
Second place! We were gaining on 'em!

The call came for the 1500-meter freestyle, and I lined up on the edge of my block with the other seven swimmers, me on one end, Konno at the far end. We all set in a crouch waiting for the popgun, and it seemed like an interminable wait, and I strained to get out first. And I did! I was in the water and stroking, but . . . no one else was. I had jumped the gun. I came out of the pool and back onto the block so fast it was like reversing a film. Some of the others were laughing or smirking, and I was totally red with humiliation. We were immediately ordered to set again.

This time I waited, heard the small pop of the gun, and saw the others fly off their blocks. I took, it seemed, a long, leisurely dive into the pool after everyone else had begun swimming. Now I had to make up time. And I did! I pulled as I never had before, and I flew to the other wall, did my awkward full-body turn, and flew back, noticing that my competitors were going in the opposite direction. I was *way* ahead of everyone. At this pace, I could win.

I flew back again and again, and then, as I reached the middle of the fifth lap, I suddenly stood up in the pool and threw up my country breakfast—bacon, eggs, biscuits, jam, and I thought I saw a bit of fried green tomato drift sideways in the scrum. The other swimmers were discovering what I had for breakfast second-hand. I don't think they liked my choices much. On the other hand, I regretted only that I had lost such a tasty repast. I mourned its passage, but it was a very large pool and would soon be nothing but fish flakes, and I had a job to do. I had to beat Mr. Konno. I didn't look at anyone. I just stuck my face back in the water and resumed my race. No official stopped me. I raced!

I fought the water and inertia and gravity and proved the laws of thermodynamics to be correct. I spent so much energy, I'm sure I heated up the enormous pool by at least a degree or two as my form devolved into disorder—and I had thirty laps to go. But I had led the pack, including my secret competitor the world record holder, for at least ten laps.

I was passed by all the others, and then I knew how much I should have trained. I wanted to climb out and fall asleep on the concrete for a day or two, but something drove me on. Now the competition was solely between me and my ego. Which was the real me? The one who honorably refused to quit, or the one who would be humiliated if he quit? The one doing this for show, or the one doing it because he had to survive?

The race was over. Everyone was out of the pool but me. I saw my guys waiting at the end, still urging me on. The bleachers were empty, but I struggled on. I was beyond ego now. This was a job I couldn't quit, even though I was now sucking water instead of air after every two strokes. I could barely lift my arms. This was the first time I had reached my physical limits, the first time I knew I had any. I counted every rotation of my arms, every half breath, every flood of bubbles in front of my face. 28 . . . 29 . . . then 30 . . . 31 . . . 32 . . .

Finally I was back with my team, who had stood loyally as I worked my way toward the finish. They lifted my jelly arms up onto the edge of the pool. I heard *clap! clap! clap!* I looked, and in the bleachers sat the major who was the official in charge of the whole meet. And he was applauding me, slowly bringing his hands together, his clipboard on his lap, looking toward me without irony or smile but with genuine respect. It meant something to this guy that I hadn't quit, that I had finished. And it meant something to me, too. It was a foundation stone, a powerful test. And I had passed.

I finished the 1500-meter swim in over twenty minutes. But the army thought we did okay. Our team was commended. We got pieces of paper that said so and notations in our service records. Those things matter in the civics of life and the army. It meant I had gone all the way, through the humiliation of throwing up in the pool and—as a conspicuous loser—on to finish the job. I won by finishing.

* * *

Now we put on rubber suits and tested ourselves against a life-and-death adversary, sarin. Our instruction regarding this horrifying invention was designed to take all emotion out of it, to make using it a dry, technological, logistic, and administrative problem. The process was always defensive: "They came up with that, so we had to come up with this."

This stuff exists, and, of course, "no one wanted to use it," but it was being used by them and by us), and so, we had to learn how to use it and defend against it.

It made sense, but some voice inside was always saying, *but why?* Why don't we outlaw this? How can we stop the tit for tat that actually leads to the next incident? We were taught to respond to violence with greater, more, and better-organized violence. They handed us syringes filled with atropine, the only antidote in case of exposure to sarin. We stuck the needles through our fatigue pants and into our upper thighs and made sure to empty the entire dose into our muscle tissue. It hurt, but not much. I felt protected.

Like tabun and VX, sarin is an organophosphate that kills by interfering with normal bodily processes. Anyone exposed to the gas or liquid has about a minute to live. They will experience intolerable increases in natural functions such as nasal tract secretions, salivation, vomiting, diarrhea, defecation, urination, and, finally and fatally, suffocation—trying to get a breath, jerking in convulsive spasms, then dying. It's a miserable thing to call a weapon of war.

We suited up in an anteroom to the death chamber where the condemned one was having his last meal of sweet lettuce. He was a vegan. We were given bodysuits of some black rubberized material. We were issued gas masks and taught how to seal them and make certain the canisters were up to date and tight. We put on hoods, gloves, and boots. Inside the suit, my body was slick with sweat. This work demonstration would go from 7:00 A.M. to noon. We could not exit the hazard suits for at least five hours, and with the masks on, we could not drink water. We would decontaminate for an hour afterward.

I was twenty-one years old. We had been told that we could die if any suit or mask leaked. At twenty-one, you are never going to die. We laughed a lot, but making good jokes inside a protective suit was hard. It was hard to walk, impossible to sit.

Today, we would kill two victims. They would be monitored throughout the experiment. We would administer the agent—poison gas—after first testing the subject's skin as to results—pain.

This demonstration—murder—was classified. We were sworn to secrecy and silence.

We began the experiments. A nice white rabbit sat in a cage on a wooden table in the quaint, woodsy cabin. He was nervous and had stopped chewing on his lettuce, maybe unused to seeing a large number of animated objects wrapped in black solemnly surrounding it. Whose funeral was it? he might have wondered. A sergeant in a suit and mask explained what he was going to do. He held the rabbit down gently, picked up a small needle dipped into a substance, and touched the rabbit's ear. The rabbit squealed and tried to get away, tried to break out of the man's grasp, but couldn't. We saw a burn appear on the ear. It penetrated. It hurt. It was a blister agent.

We would later do this experiment ourselves in class: We were asked to roll up a sleeve on one arm and touch the arm with a pin coated in a blister agent, sulfur mustard, and observe the result. It hurt. A touch of a pin burned a deep hole in my skin, where it remained for more than fifty years.

The sergeant touched the rabbit's other ear with a microdot of liquid sarin. It began uncontrollably twitching. The sergeant told us to check our masks and hope there was no pinhole in our protective suits. A technician released a tiny volume of nerve gas into the cage. The rabbit fell sideways, its legs trying to run, its paws going rigid then clapping together rapidly, then extending, trembling as it began to leak fluids from its pink nose, genitals, and anus. It never made a sound. How could it, with its mouth opening for air but unable to get any into its lungs? It lasted about forty-five seconds. Then the rabbit laid still. Oh my God. I was glad it was out of its misery.

Our team murdered more rabbits with different stuff. I learned that dogs, goats, pigeons, squirrels, and mice were all used as "laboratory assistants." They were all victims of science, killed to provide men with information on how to build even better weapons with which to kill each other.

But, strangely, I liked the army, the discipline, the crispness of form and focus, the early hours, the strenuousness, the cleanliness of body. And knowing that out of service or off post, you were any man's equal was built in and protected by this system. I was gung ho.

* * *

A letter arrived at mail call just before the bugler played "Taps" in front of Headquarters, when everyone stopped what we were doing, stood at attention, and honored our military brothers and sisters who had died in service for our country. I stood, moved to tears, hand over heart, letter in hand until the last strains faded away.

I read the letter. All reserve officers had received a RIF notice: reduction in force. I thought I would get to stay in the army for the full period of two years. I had gotten used to that idea and had forgotten that I used to be an actor of sorts and a Bachelor of Arts degree man. I went to the proper office and volunteered for the Army Rangers. Immortal me! It would be great to jump out of planes and helicopters, fight snakes in the swamp, climb mountains, learn to speak Korean, Chinese, and Russian, and wear special badges. My family would appreciate me if I joined an elite group and had a regular job with a pension.

They turned me down—not because I wasn't eligible and desirable, but because of myopia. I had 20/400 vision when uncorrected, insufficient for the Rangers. Okay, if I lost my glasses and didn't see the ground coming up at me in a parachute landing and broke a leg, my eyes should still see well enough to identify armed Chinese Communist uniforms coming over the hill in time to keep them from killing us. But, no dice. So now I would be unemployed in a few weeks.

I was entirely without a plan. I would have to go back to the cannery.

SCENE: Oakland, California

I spent my twenty-first birthday alone, standing on North Beach in San Francisco at night, facing a cold Pacific Ocean cyclone, close to the storm surge, wet down to my skivvies, my jacket pockets filling with wet wind-blown sand.

I had been lucky enough to stumble on the doorsill and fall into such a place with such people as those inhabiting the Speech and Drama program at the University of Arkansas in the early and mid-1950s, when the promise of a world change was fresh and new.

Practitioners of all the arts came to the university. They began showing new generations of young men and women that there was another safe world out there called The Arts, where all human expression was not only tolerated but welcomed as the fruit of a new garden in America.

I could not have been happier. So why, one night, coming back to Oakland from San Francisco at 2:00 A.M., did I challenge the California Zephyr train to a race as it barreled toward me on the tracks at the East Bay end of the Bay Bridge? I saw the flashing lights warning that the gate was coming down. There were two cars ahead of me in line. But something compelled me to swing out of the line and charge forward, accelerator to the floorboard, to get under the gate as it swung down. I flashed under it barely ahead of the guillotine scything down, and I was on the tracks. I looked south and there was the Zephyr—huge and beautiful as death—charging forward at sixty miles per hour about thirty yards away, oblivious of me in my Nash turtle. I ground the pedal into the floor. The Zephyr boomed its horn, and I saw the engineer's shocked face high above in the cab as a wild, exultant yell arose from my guts. I jammed my Ambassador over the tracks just as the oncoming train ripped past my taillights, blasting its horn as I sped away, propelled by the hot wake of the double locomotive I had barely beaten in a race against death. I was king of the Court of Fools.

I rocketed away for a mile then pulled over, tucked into a dark street. I shut off the motor, killed the lights, and sat there shaking with my heart blasting in my chest, laughing like a loon, crying like a baby, and wondering where in the nine kinds of hell that insane urge to challenge death had come from.

I waited until I was sure no cops had been called to find the idiot who had done this, then drove home, crept into the apartment, and fell into bed completely dressed and ready for my workday, which started at 4:45 A.M.

The family didn't really get me. I had studied acting and now had a BA in Speech and Drama, but that only meant I had a ticket to a job teaching—I could take care of myself and teach in a high school or grade school, teach speech . . . the drama part got left off. And now that I was out of school, out of the army, shorn of my D.A. haircut and my support system of fellow weirdos who wanted to dress up and make-believe, I began again to think like my family: settle down, teach, get a girlfriend, buy a house. You've already got a car.

My brother-in-law was persuasive. He was a terrific guy, interested in me and my future, and we had some big brother–type conversations. He also took that role on for my little sister and brother. And his opinion was that I should stay in California and partake of the generosity of the life there. Now, between worlds, the magical excitement of my theater adventure fading, I began thinking maybe he was right.

A letter came. I had a place at Catholic University of America's Department of Drama graduate program in September.

My mentor at Arkansas, Dr. K, had stepped in to guide me again. The letter was signed "Fr. Gilbert Hartke, O.P., Chairman of the Department of Drama." Father Hartke—the Dominican priest who ran the professional theater in the great university of Washington, DC.

SCENE: Choices

I had two options now: keep working at the cannery or go to graduate school and continue studying the theater craft that had enchanted me.

The cannery job promised a very good living doing the same tasks every day. The union money was fantastic at the time. The work scholarship at Catholic University promised more poverty and uncertainty, but new places, new friends, and a graduate degree that, if all I ended up doing was teaching, would at least mean a slightly better salary than my bachelor's degree could offer.

My parents were struggling like heroes to keep the family together and give my younger sister and brother educations that would allow them to rise. I was the example—the college man, the success—and I felt the pressure to do well, to make something of myself. They believed I would become a teacher. That was a high calling. My father had a never-quenched drinking problem. My mother never knew from week to week if he would still have a job. She deserved stability, calm, a week, a day without fear. Her religion allowed her no escape. It demanded that you endure until death freed you. If you had followed all the incredible rules and never missed Mass, done your Easter duty, and not eaten meat on Friday, *maybe* you could look forward to purgatory for about a thousand years before the good and kind Jesus would be allowed, by his vengeful, demanding father—God—to invite you to visit Him in heaven. Until, of course, the Last Judgment, when your score would be checked again as you stood naked and trembling with trillions of your fellow sinners waiting to be sent either right or left, to boring heaven or an incredible, sadistic, burning hell, for eternity.

But I was twenty-two years old and immortal. And hungry for more and more knowledge. I knew if I didn't cut it, I could always go back to the cannery. But if I chose to stay at the cannery and not take the chance, I would never have the adventure of going to Washington, of travel, of new weirdos—East Coast–style—with whom I felt such kinship. So, what did I do?

I chose poverty, uncertainty, and weirdos. One week later, I was on the northern route east across America in my trusty turtle, my Nash Ambassador. Halfway across the country, my old turtle friend gave up and broke down. I had to spend a large chunk of my tuition money to get a cheap replacement, which also collapsed forever at the doorstep of my new rooming house in Northeast Washington, DC. I would need a second job to pay my rent.

I walked a mile and a half to the campus in falling snow, as happy a young man as ever could be. What was money anyhow? Nothing compared to new knowledge and a new chance. I would explain to the powers-that-be that I needed a second job. Would they understand? I made a note that my California T-shirt would have to be supplemented with a winter coat and my wet Converse sneakers replaced with snow boots.

SCENE: Catholic University of America, Washington, DC

The smiling gentleman opened the door to the director's office and ushered me in. Sitting behind an old, scarred wooden war surplus desk piled high with scripts and papers was James Cagney, wearing his familiar raised-eyebrow, challenging, grand grin. Or maybe it was Cagney's father. He was, I could see, weatherworn, his Roman collar a little frayed, his black clerical suit well-made but worn and shiny at the elbows. But the man himself was tough looking, streetwise, compact, and completely without pretense or priestly pomp. This was a working man.

He had big, capable hands. He was hastily shaven, with a few unruly silver whiskers left, matching his thick silver mane slicked straight back. He had a regal bearing mitigated by a forbearing sense of humor. The smile-induced crinkles around his eyes and mouth on his wide face gave me all this in half a second. It felt good, homely, welcoming.

"Sit," he said, and waved an arm at the ratty couch in front of the desk. I sat. "So, you have a problem," he said in a raspy, off-hand, kind of street guy growl. "You have a fine recommendation from your Dr. Kernodle in Arkansas." He said Arkansas like it was Timbuktu, a place surprising for its existence, but interesting. "But, you're short of money for tuition?"

"Yes, sir," I said.

"Your old car broke down and you had to spend tuition money to get here, and now you think you'll have to get a job to pay for school?"

"Yes, sir," I said. "I will go out today and . . ."

He stopped me with a look—straight on, a challenge. "You didn't think we were going to let you come here and then not take care of you, did you?"

I shut up. I didn't know what to say. Truthfully, I had thought exactly that.

He knew what I was thinking. He scribbled a couple of words on a memo pad, tore it off, and said, "Take this across the street to the theater. Give it to Jim Waring or Charley Ford. You'll work with them." He stood up and thrust out a blunt, square hand. "You are wanted here, son," he said. "Welcome."

I took his hand, shook it. Gripped it. He was strong. So was I. We connected. I had never felt more welcome in my life. My eyes, my heart, filled up.

This priest, Gilbert V. Hartke, this man, was one of the greatest men in many, many people's lives. He created a highly professional local theater at Catholic University in Washington, DC, which had, before him, almost none. He maintained a sophisticated, nuanced presence in that theater, without any of the old orthodoxy that stunted thought and killed the expression of our common humanity in all our glories and miseries. He was, nevertheless, a thorough Dominican priest-teacher strict in his beliefs. And he practiced those beliefs in a humane way. He was a neutral politician who managed the Washington political game solely for the purpose of furthering the culture of theater. And even though he was not personally gifted with great theater talent, he had something powerful—a genius humanity that gave to all his work every ounce of talent he did possess, the power of flight and of moving mountains. He went to the mountain and then the mountain came to him. He made theater respected in the most self-regarding city in the United States. And all the people who were his team—from Ed Cashman, Joseph Lewis, Bill Graham, Leo Brady, Bill Schulte, Jim Waring, Robert Moore, the faculty, the administration, and even the students—became as powerful as Hartke. I resolved to be his representative. And he became the next great mentor in my life.

I worked as a stage carpenter for designer Jim Waring, supervised and taught by the magic-making Head Carpenter Charley Ford, from the day I started to the day I was awarded my Master of Fine Arts.

I arrived at CUA ready to work but still not knowing how to evaluate the depth of my own place in the theater—or whether it truly existed. I was met by the masters of theatrical art in their full power, and I gave them all I had. I left there in possession of a rubric by which I could pursue the real prize—to be not just an actor content to work, but to fulfill an image of myself as an artist with a plan to make my own imprint on the world. It would be a long game. And now I knew I had to play.

S C E N E : Washington, DC

The pace at CUA Drama was fast and professional, which was both good and bad, depending on the definition of *professional*. One was training for acting, playwriting, designing, directing, and management. Learning your craft and practicing it. At the University of Arkansas, I had a bare two years of full-time working on acting and writing a couple of one-act plays. Now I wanted to learn to become a playwright and a professional actor.

There were two theaters on the CUA campus: the first was the Main Stage, a wonderful pre-fab wooden structure built as a WWII army post theater, which had been transported to the campus after the war, conceivably a "midnight requisition" by Father Hartke. The other was an old, narrow brick building called the Lab Theater. The polished Broadway kind of work was done on the Main Stage. The Lab Theater was the experimental place, and it was there that I was most comfortable, in spite of the fact that to work on the Main Stage meant you were potential Broadway quality.

I made myself available to Lab Theater projects as much as possible. I made the acquaintance of an undergraduate fellow who seemed to share my feelings about theater. He spent time in the Lab's junk-filled back rooms from which sets magically appeared, usually bits and pieces of flats, windows, and door frames, cloth draping, all manner of ragtag props, and stuff that could transform with imagination. This guy was a Southerner from Mississippi. His name was Mart Crowley. Eleven years later in New York, I would act in his daring play about gay men which would, improbably, turn into a smash hit and put me on the map.

I played on the Main Stage in a number of shows that were reviewed by the daily Washington newspapers. That university theater was considered important enough to be reviewed at all was a reflection of Father Hartke's gravitational pull.

I encountered typecasting. I had always seen myself as the hero, but now, when I was cast, it was in character lead roles. That was my type according to the commercial logic of the Drama Department. Looking back at my experience in Arkansas, I could see a similar judgment of who I was—or rather how I presented to people of the theater. I knew I was a "hero," but my persona struck those in charge of making the shows differently. If I had been the best friend type, I think I would have quit on the spot.

Now I took another step toward a life in the theater. I began serious study of what a play is, how it works, what the elements are. How to decide who was

Main Stage production of Herman Melville's *Billy Budd* at Catholic University. Me, typecast as rebellious seaman Jenkins (far right).

right to play a lead. Was there a right combination of actors that could make a play work? I was a step further from the pure amateur love of play and performance to understanding organized and informed judgments of how theater was made. There came with this a sense of greater knowledge and control, but also a feeling of loss of innocence, a loss of pure awe and joy.

At the university, I met the priest who had directed a complete production of G. B. Shaw's *Saint Joan* in Huntsville, Alabama. The play took an entire day to see. The year previous, when I was in the army, this highly courageous production was performed outside in the rural enclave of a local monastery and church. There were horses, cows, pigs, etc. as in the French countryside of Joan of Arc's day. The stage was the old stone steps up to the church doors. The play was spoken by untrained townspeople and monks from the Benedictine monastery. It was authentic, compelling, and terribly moving. *This* was the kind of theater I wanted to do. It was the essence of loving amateurism.

I learned the principles of good vocal work from William Graham, a teacher not much older than I was. Bill was a great teacher. He would grab a book (he always had a passel under an arm), stick it against your diaphragm, and ask you to speak against it using the pressure to feel your diaphragm. It was a brilliant physical reminder that theater-speech requires a constant flow of air that is generated by consciously utilizing your diaphragm to push sound out through your vocal cords—and to get out of the way of the flow by opening your mouth, releasing your jaw, and articulating properly using tongue and teeth and lips.

Easy! Hard to learn. But everyone Bill taught got the book in the gut. And everyone he taught became a good, strong speaker who never lost their voice and who could ping off the back wall of the largest or smallest theater with the greatest of ease.

Bill became my mentor and lifelong friend. His curiosity and openness about the theater and its place and importance in the universe never dimmed a single watt in his life. His own charm was always on hand. His seriousness could bring you up short, but it was always leavened with his great laugh.

His daughter told me that when she was in high school, she was required to write an essay about homosexuality, a subject she knew absolutely nothing about. So, she asked her father, a strict Catholic, what his opinion was. He was rushing out the door, a pile of books under his arm, late for a class, but he stopped dead in his tracks on the stair. And he said, "Love is love," and went up the stair and out the door. In one second, he had given her the essay, his philosophy of life, and enough inspiration for a lifetime.

At the University of Arkansas, I had traveled into Oklahoma with a four-man cast to play Christopher Fry's *A Sleep of Prisoners* in churches and a cathedral. I learned a powerful lesson about the effects of segregation. Our cast was three white actors and one Black actor. The Black man was one of only two Black students admitted to the university that year. Segregation and racism were still everywhere. The two Black men were an anomaly. They knew it. We thought we knew what they suffered. On that tour, we had not been allowed to stay in any hotel in Oklahoma with even one Black cast member in our troupe. None of the white church groups would take us in—they were afraid of what might happen—so we were housed and fed by the Black church community. I was full of joy and gratitude and that naive sense that white people get from being in communion and understanding with the Black community, simply because the community had been so welcoming. I felt as if I belonged to them, too. On the fifty-mile drive back to the university, I jokingly said something in a traditionally Black dialect to my Black friend. He was instantly and furiously angry.

"Stop the car! I'm getting out. I'd rather walk back than ride with you honkies!" He meant me.

I apologized. We stood around the car by the side of the road. Dr. K *ahemmed* his apology on our behalf. Finally, my friend relented. He was deeply offended and hurt and, in spite of all I tried to do, was never easy with me again. He avoided me, in fact. His most revealing comment was, "Don't you take my culture away from me!" He said it in a rage, but I realized he was feeling a terrible loss, and I broke down in tears. He had been betrayed by me, his friend, out of clumsy ignorance. What was easy for me was a lifetime of pain for him. He had been robbed of a crucial element of humanness—his uniqueness as a being, unrelated to color. I couldn't fix it. I knew what he meant and what he was about at that moment, but I could not ever know the depth of it, could never feel it as he did. That was a hard lesson.

Bill Graham's instant answer to his daughter—"love is love"—was similarly deeply felt. Where had this clarity come from? Simply from his true, complex, humble living of the gospel of Jesus, mentoring his daughter as he had me and all others who knew him. It has taken my entire life to understand and apply, even in small measure, the message: "Do unto others as you would have them do unto you."

* * *

I was renting a room in Northeast Washington overlooking a quiet, tree-lined enclave. It was in that room that the four stories at the outset of this tale appeared in my typewriter along with reams of expression that I decided to call poetry, but which stretched that definition beyond recognition. I was very disciplined. I worked. I studied. I read. I took on every task given to me by the Drama Department, tried to conquer each one and win. I began to write my thesis play.

The play took me most of the year. I hitchhiked to California for Christmas and for summer break to work in the cannery, back and forth on my thumb and for nothing. I liked being alone with no ride and then someone taking a chance on me. Some conversation and a hundred or five hundred miles later, I would be dropped back on the side of the road in my leather jacket with my old brown army shoes, my book bag, and my thoughts. I was a dharma bum, for sure.

I finished the play and called it *The Alien*. I turned it in to my advisors. The set-designer professor liked only one line in it: when the landlady in the strange town—the alien's hometown—says to the alien, "The garbage has to be separated from the trash. You know to do that, don't you?" The rest of the play he dismissed with casual contempt, but he passed me. Explain that. I couldn't.

My other advisor had good notes and suggested a path to rewrite. He was encouraging. "Writing is rewriting," he said. "You *can* write, so get on with it!"

I finished my master's degree work. I had an accepted thesis. I was awarded—I like that word—an MFA in drama with a major in playwriting. Was I a playwright? Not yet. I was out of work. Again.

SCENE: Players, Inc.

Father Hartke founded a touring company of student actors called National Players, Inc. This group was nonunion but paid in keeping with the professional standards of the Actors' Equity Association. The company traveled thousands of miles every year to bring classical theater to schools and colleges across the country. In the early days, the regular season was bookended with a tour to military bases in the world wherever US troops were stationed.

I was offered small parts in the two plays set to tour in 1957. This was the company's ninth season. The plays were *The Taming of the Shrew* and *Romeo and Juliet*. My roles were Gremio and Paris. This was a paid acting job. I took it. But before I could get comfortable in the two supporting roles, the actor playing Mercutio in *Romeo and Juliet* and Petruchio in *Shrew* was hospitalized with mononucleosis, and I was thrown—with minimal rehearsal—into these lead character roles, which were just the sort of parts I was vetted to do by the standard-makers of the CUA drama department.

The tour company was minimal, around twelve or thirteen actors. All except the leads played multiple roles, doubling and tripling as stagehands, drivers, and crew. The better drivers rotated the additional duties of driving two station wagons and an eighteen-foot van. The van carried the set, props, and costumes. Load-in and load-out followed a strict pattern. Set pieces were slotted into racks, props compartmentalized in rolling boxes, costumes stashed in bags and hung from wheeled racks. Now, truck fully loaded, actors' luggage was strapped to rooftop racks, actors crowded into favorite seats with coffee cups in hand, and the caravan rolled out of Harewood Road into the bright September light, headed for the first play date.

Kids and playdates they seemed. We were children—very young, very energetic, filled with creativity and a bright desire to conquer our roles in grand plays by the masters: Shakespeare, Molière, Aeschylus, Sophocles, and contemporary writers. We were very competitive, full of juice, ego, and dreams. We were young Quixotes, Sancho Panzas, Juliets, and Dulcineas determined to be the best company of players our audiences had ever seen. And we were dispatched to our mission by a crack team back at the university, brilliant directors and designers. We were booked by the formidable Edith Dappert, and we knew we were eagerly awaited by audiences across the country.

We had our AAA Triptiks in the vehicles—ancient paper GPSs. It was the mid-1950s. Gas was cheap, hotels were cheap, hamburgers were cheap, books were cheap. And we were paid sixty-five dollars per week—a fortune. We would be on the road for ten months. We would play scores of auditoriums, theaters, black boxes, classrooms, hotel ballrooms, and little theaters.

We would arrive, unload actors and truck, carry sets, props, and costumes onto the stage. We would set up dressing areas for men and women, assemble sets on stage, set up two tree light stands, and focus lights. Our rolling boxes doubled as prop tables and sometimes set pieces. We would also distribute programs.

Show time! Sometimes it was 8:00 P.M., sometimes it was 9:00 A.M. Sometimes we had a real curtain, often just a blackout. Sometimes we had actual dressing rooms, sometimes we shared the toilet room or even the back porch of a theater, winter, fall, or spring. Sometimes we carried sets in through an easy ground-floor stage door, sometimes we humped our entire show up five stories on a fire escape, rain, snow, or shine.

After the show we would have a reception. We called them "beadie bags" because the ladies of the school or town who sponsored the shows often carried beaded purses in the reception line. There was usually food; we always ate it all. We played Catholic high schools or colleges where an unattached young actor might find a quick flirtation that, alas, lasted only a few minutes, a few smiles, one kiss, and we were gone. We were nomads and we loved it.

I volunteered to drive the truck because I couldn't stand to sit with a bunch of actors in the cars all day. Also, I had more experience than the others pushing a heavy vehicle since my cannery days. There were two of us in the truck, and we usually left earlier than the actors because we were slower. There were many mishaps and communication problems on the road. There were no cell phones, no GPS. No instant weather info. One situation was potentially fatal: a blizzard struck us as we traveled to a date in Blacksburg, Virginia. The truck was in trouble all the way, sliding sideways, pushed by heavy winds and blinding whiteout snow coming straight at the windshield. It slowed us to a crawl. It was night.

We came to a bridge high above a gorge in the mountains. The road was blocked by a fallen tree. We had to find a detour to our destination. But we went at the problem with what we had—a compass and a flashlight and a AAA map. We found our way to the right road and knew by mileage we were within striking distance of the motel we had booked. But it wasn't there. Just an immensity of drifted snow and total blackness. And silence. Suddenly, my partner yelled, "Stop! Look, up there!" A neon sign blinked on, "No Vacancy."

We were at our motel. Our company was safe in the rooms. There would be coffee and breakfast. We had survived. A company prayer was said, and that night, there was a show at the college that had hired us. The show must go on, and it did. It was a moment from Sol Smith's *Frontier Theater Diary*. We used station wagons instead of covered ones.

* * *

I remember every actor on the tours I did, enough idiosyncrasies for a library of Kaufman and Hart or George Kelly plays about the theater. We acted together and acted out together. Each company was singular, each full of talent and esprit. Many went to work in New York theater and Hollywood television and films after traveling with the Players. One special friend was Saeed Jaffrey, a distinguished actor from India. Our families remained friends for over half a century, until his death in 2015.

I had dreamed of an escape by reading books and acting in classic plays where I was able to become someone else—someone elevated, for a moment—but I still felt I was not good enough, maybe would never be.

I tried with all my might and intelligence and heart to get better as an actor, to unloose the technical and emotional knots that playing the great plays wound about me. I played *Macbeth* for an entire tour season, scores of performances, and never once solved the emotional or the physical challenges. I roared through it, tiptoed through it, sang, crept, and crawled through it, and even though audiences liked it and accepted it, I knew I had not found the man.

The part demands an athlete, an intellect, a complex soul, and a willingness to plunge to a dark side that I could sense and understand I had, but was afraid to approach too closely. I was not a genius, just a hard-working young actor striving to rise to the occasion. What did I learn? I learned that I didn't know enough, hadn't lived enough, could not reach the height I saw above. As the young Edgar says at the end of *King Lear:*

> The weight of this sad time we must obey.
> Speak what we feel, not what we ought to say.
> The oldest hath borne most. We that are young
> Shall never see so much, nor live so long.

This profound understanding and mystery makes me weep. I had no choice but to obey, to try. Or die.

* * *

On my last tour, we brought *Oedipus Rex* to New York City.

"How do you get to Carnegie Hall?"

"Practice."

We had practiced *Oedipus* for ten months on the road. There was a sub-basement in the famous old treasure house of music looming at the intersection of Fifty-Seventh Street and Seventh Avenue. This dark hall had been languishing out of use for a while before someone had the idea of making it into an off-Broadway theater. The Players, Inc., company would be its first occupant with our touring production of *Oedipus Rex* by Sophocles. A play, safe to say, not on the must-see list of many New Yorkers. It was a showcase for the company and its creators and driving spirits—Father Hartke, Josephine Callan, and others. Miss Callan was an important influence on the Drama Department. She was a speech teacher and specialized in choral work. She was a disciplined woman who got amazing sounds from those of us in the Chorus of *Oedipus.*

The Chorus is a main character in classical Greek plays. It represents the polis—the people of the city who have a vital stake in the outcome of the story of every Greek play, tragedy or comedy. This was interesting in the context of American democracy, as our Chorus was composed of townspeople dying of or affected by a plague that had come upon the city from an unknown crime and perpetrator, who had to be discovered and punished so the world could be restored. (Sophocles had written about the plague of Athens, 431 BC). Miss Callan guided us expertly to produce vocal music in the choral passages and make them dramatically sharp and musically beautiful. We, the people, were crucial partners to the protagonist, Oedipus the king, and the other characters.

We worked this play through the season lying cheek to jowl or butt to heel on our tiny, raked platform, wearing distressed ballet slippers and artful rags of burlap. Lots of lake makeup was required to deepen the shadows on faces, under eyes, and between fingers to turn healthy, generally hearty twenty-somethings into dying, miserable plague victims who could sing Sophocles' powerful words in beautiful unison. It is one of the world's best-known—and greatest—plays, and if our participation was serious and intellectually sustained, it was going to work. The situation was compelling and the tight plot had horrifying surprises. Sigmund Freud drew a direct line of human behavior from 400-something BC to AD 1899: the Oedipus Complex.

So, in the depths of Carnegie Hall, we dressed in dank dressing rooms while trying not to breathe the mold infesting the walls. At 8:00 P.M. we went out to play an ancient tale to a mid-century modern American audience.

It was my karma to have two parts: In the first act, I was part of the Chorus, and in the second act, I played the Old Shepherd, a pivotal character. He is the frail old man who saved and raised the young boy left to die in a rubbish heap. Now, that discarded boy is the powerful King Oedipus, who is trying to pin down the source of the plague to an evildoer. The Shepherd's witness in his investigation leads Oedipus to a terrible realization—*he himself is the cause.*

I was twenty-five years old and playing a man in his eighties. I am now eighty-nine, and I know that the old man I created would had to have been about a hundred and twenty to be as decrepit as I thought eighty had to be. But my makeup was good, and I had great sympathy for the old guy—raggedy, poor but proud, clearly heroic in saving the abandoned boy, but wanting none of the praise, just there to tell the truth and help his adopted son, who is king.

As I creakily limped onto the stage, I felt a jolt of electricity flow through me. I felt it when I stepped on *any* stage, but that night the voltage level was much higher. This was the unlikeliest career beginning ever imaginable. *Oedipus* at Carnegie Hall! That night changed my life.

Walter Kerr, a former faculty member of Catholic University's Department of Drama and now the theater critic of the *New York Herald Tribune*, was there to review the play. He reviewed it kindly and saved a few favorable words for my performance. The day after the opening, I got a call at the theater from an agent named Lillian Arnold. She referred to Kerr's notice and asked me to come see her. I went to her apartment on Fifty-Sixth Street, half a block from the staff entrance to Carnegie Hall. She sat tucked up on her simple day bed, surrounded by the *Players' Guide*, the trade newspapers (*Variety, Backstage,* et al.), and two rotary dial telephones. She had a large notepad on her lap and heavy steel braces on her short legs. She told me she had seen our performance and wanted to represent me.

I was stunned. This heroic disabled woman had climbed down three flights of concrete stairs to see the show and climbed back up at the end. I stood there until it dawned on me what she was saying: I had an agent! Someone believed in me. She thought I could belong in the New York theater.

She told me in her iron-inflected voice what I needed to do *right now* so that she could send me out for acting work: Get headshot photos (8 x 10 glossies), a résumé of my acting work (that would be easy—half a paragraph would do) stapled to the back of the photo, an answering service because she would need to reach me at any time, and a contract with her as my sole representative for several years.

I hesitated. I would have to think about it, I told her. She was tough, a yenta (I found out the term pretty quickly), and she argued forcibly that I should move fast after getting a good review. Even though I acted an old man, she could see I had talent. "*Presence*," she called it.

I signed the contract. This brave and intrepid woman had climbed those intimidating stairs down to that moldy room to see a university production of *Oedipus Rex*. I got a picture of the Darwinian way of life in the theater in its world capital. I had been mentored. I was now on a path as an actor. I had been told what it was I really wanted or needed to do—and *I had been chosen*. I belonged in the performing arts. New York City, here I come, ready or not!

I got my pictures made. A moody, intense young man with nice vulnerable, dark eyes appeared. Was that me? I had never thought I was especially attractive. But this serious young man had . . . something.

I had an appointment to meet with a "very high-powered" agent. Someone set this up. Although I was with Lillian, dutifully, I went. He was a florid man in a fine suit with a grand office and lots of office workers. I was a bit intimidated by all the foofaraw, like visiting a raja. He was clearly more important than anyone, including me. That seemed wrong, kind of upside down—the Darwinian version again.

But he was very nice. He had *three* phones on a very high desk. I sat there in a soft chair in front of his desk, my chair lower than his. The phones buzzed constantly. He answered every call. In fact, he was on all three at the same time, talking to clients, producers, his mother? A real macher. Was it to show how hard he worked? It just made me laugh.

A cessation! That toothy grin turned to me. "People say you are a very good actor. You're nice looking. We can do good things for you. But there's a little problem, easily fixed, you agree?"

I started to say something, but it seemed he had already identified the problem.

He went on, "Your name. What is it, anyway?"

Before I could respond, he answered himself. "Doesn't matter. It's too long, that's the problem. Marquees are short, and Laurence Luckinbill is too long. And it's slightly funny-sounding. No offense. May I suggest that you change it?"

Again, before I could open my mouth, he said, "I have a thought. Of course, I want to hear yours. I like this one—short, punchy, sounds like *some-body*. Drumroll . . . (with a toothy smile) Larry York!"

I said, "I'll think about it."

"Good. Great!" he said. Two phones buzzed. He answered both simultaneously, a two-fisted fighter for marquee justice.

Later, I told my mother what he had said. She thought a moment, then said, quietly and modestly, "Well, Larry, if you're going to continue in this business, maybe you *should* change your name."

I was hurt. I thought she meant she would be ashamed to have our family name on a theater marquee. Now I know she meant if you want to be a success, you ought to do what the boss wants. That was her life. Her experience. I thought, *My name is gotdang good enough, dadgum it!*

Lillian represented me for many years. I started with tiny parts in Sunday morning live TV shows for CBS, and then got an "under-five"—five lines or less—doctor role in a soap opera, *Young Doctor Malone*, which starred the fine actor William Prince. My part was four one-word responses to Dr. Malone asking me if the anesthetic was working right during an operation. I was capped, gowned, gloved, masked, and half-hidden by machines. But my mother, older sister, and aunt, watching live in California and Arkansas, called me right after the show aired. They all "recognized me instantly."

"How?" I asked.

"By your eyes."

I had begun. Lillian Arnold had given me a chance.

SCENE: New York!

There are scores of "chances to act" listed in my professional databases since I first walked onto the stage in the Carnegie Hall basement. I remember each of them in detail. They were more than jobs. Each one was an expression of some essential piece of me. Some I did for money to live, but I never did one where I gave less than 100% of everything I had. I couldn't.

I walked around in a dream, looking up at the buildings, wondering who lived there. Why had they come here? If they were here, they must have magic! The rhythm of the city gets into you right away. You start to sing the magic song.

Heaven was New York City. I sang it and danced it. The mean heat, the humid stink of it, the freezing cold, the snow that changed the teeming brutality into a magic white silence, the rain, the swirling gutters, the broken sidewalks, the dramatic steam rising from the vents in the streets, the grime, the noise, the crazed chaos of the subway, the cramped living spaces, the cockroaches, the rats, the garbage strikes, the jazz pouring out of the joints along Fifty-Second Street, the Village, Washington Square, the walking way of getting anywhere, the power infusion that came the day I realized I was a New Yorker.

I could sing a song because I knew that the Bronx was up and my battery was never down in New York City. I didn't have time for relationships, and I didn't have money to date. I lived on the edge, moving my possessions in cardboard boxes each time I changed my address. For eleven years.

I was on the first rung of the ladder, the place from which I would try to do the greatest job a human being could ever imagine—to portray one of our kind in all guises, with all the flummeries and fakeries, all the heroism, all the pain and joy, all the in-between of our lives on this earth. To escape into someone else's life for a time, to look out of someone else's eyes and see the world they see.

It is the pinnacle of empathy. I was a clown standing perilously on the highest peak of the world, seeing the farthest, knowing it all for an untranslatable instant. And then, you fly back down the mountain into the darkness at the bottom—to the jungle of your own life. That's what I did. That's what I have lived to do . . . so much that I could write a book.

. . . For 'tis your thoughts that now must deck our kings,
Carry them here and there, jumping o'er times,
Turning th' accomplishment of many years
Into an hour glass . . .

—WILLIAM SHAKESPEARE, *HENRY V*, PROLOGUE

S C E N E : Washington, DC

It was five years of holy baptism in the fine blue blood of great classic plays of world theater from the time I signed up for the first course in the Speech and Drama Department at the University of Arkansas to my stint with Catholic University's Players, Inc..

I was given massive parts in plays I did not understand and roles I chopped at with a machete hacking through the jungle. My immersion was a secular evangelization. I took it all—big, little, infinitesimal. I worked in my first season of Shakespeare with the Great Lakes Shakespeare Festival, founded by Arthur Lithgow, the wonderful and unique entrepreneur (and the sire of John Lithgow). The first season he cast me in very small parts. The second season I got bigger parts. The third year, I suggested to Arthur that I be his character lead. Because of his incredible loyalty and sense of equity, Arthur instantly agreed.

In the Players, Inc., years, I did three seasons at St. Michael's Playhouse in Winooski, Vermont. I played Bo Decker in *Bus Stop*, Thomas Mendip in *The Lady's Not for Burning,* Captain Fisby in *Teahouse of the August Moon,* and a Russian spy in *The Little World of Don Camillo*. I directed three plays. I helped build sets. I managed the Player's Company and played lead roles in three tours. I traveled with them to Germany and Italy playing in revered ancient theaters, GI mess halls, Quonset huts, and US Army base theaters.

* * *

John Kennedy was inaugurated as president.

> And time, that takes survey of all the world,
> Must have a stop. —*Henry IV*

No one could prophesy, although apparently some were planning, what would ultimately come to this young man who stood there, hatless in the cold January wind, as the living symbol of inspiration to a country and a world hoping for peace.

I was invited by Father Hartke to a bleacher seat at the inauguration, but, instead, I chose to wander far from the pomp and celebration into Northeast Washington in bitter wind and hand- and face-numbing cold. I was, I realize now, in a deep depression, the onset again of a recurring deep sadness and anger, which was the scrim covering a fear as bitter and numbing as the cold. Thoughts—again—of oblivion.

After *Oedipus* closed, the company went back to DC. I stayed in New York. I had exactly five dollars in my pocket. The old fears of the poorhouse haunted me.

I had begun a life in the theater, had been launched headlong into a kind of awkward bounding flight by mentors and muses. I was like a young albatross trying my first take off, learning the use of my floppy feet and amazing wings—bounding, tripping, falling over embarrassingly, and then flailing for a few seconds of satisfactory flight before losing purpose and succumbing to another forced landing.

Nothing I did was good enough, would ever be good enough. I couldn't articulate this; it just swirled like dirty rainwater disappearing down a sewer drain. I could not convert the wind energy of my free-falling thoughts into anything useful. Clearly, I could melodramatize myself, but I was also weighed down by a continuous feeling that I was of no use to my family. Instead of facing that and doing something about it—something simple—I ran, I dodged. I disappeared physically and mentally. I could send home a check for a few bucks now that I actually earned Actors' Equity minimum salaries for acting, but I couldn't connect with my family. And I turned the guilt for this inability back onto the circumstance that I had chosen acting as a life I had to lead no matter what, no matter that it was supremely insecure as a choice, a choice I was defending twenty-four seven in my head.

I had learned a couple of delaying tactics to keep the brain-eating baboons at bay when they started tearing at me. I had learned to drink Irish whiskey and to smoke. Not gross cigarettes. I smoked a pipe, a corncob, like my grandpa. Pipes were cheap, and I experimented with various tobaccos to get one that smelled good enough to be my new aura.

And this started a destructive train. I could blame my grandfather for his pipe, which he smoked with me on his knee while he told me funny little things about the grand engine he drove for the railroad. But this was all my choice. I had begun to fly backward, to look for a steady job—a way to fly from the insecurity of the theater.

Having arrived in New York to act, I immediately put on different armor, picked up my lance, mounted Rocinante, and rode forth to fight the cultural and political windmills in Africa. The glamour of the United States Foreign Service dazzled me. Was this my real chance?

So, I paused the dream of my life for the mirage of serving my country with a two-year contract to fight communism by inventing a national theater in Khartoum, Sudan, and teaching theater in Rome, Italy. But that's a story for another time.

St. Michael's Playhouse. Winooski, Vermont. Dr. Noyce was right. I belonged in the performing arts! I couldn't be happier. Cute socks.

Me, on left, as Bo Decker in *Bus Stop* by William Inge. Players, Inc. "Virge, I just gotta marry Cherry!"

"I dare do all that may become a man. Who dares do more is none." —Macbeth. Players, Inc.

S C E N E : New York

I was back making the rounds. In those days, I would try to get a job in a show by walking into every producer's office in town and seeing the casting person to get an audition for parts in upcoming shows that I read about in *Backstage, Variety, Show Business*—the trades.

I always carried those papers with tantalizing bits of info, even though experience had already taught me that it was either old news, inaccurate, or simply pie-in-the-sky. And I had a thick stack of pictures with my résumé stapled to the back. I had my book with me, too. The book was a photo album with shots of me being all the characters I had ever played: juvenile, leading man, character lead, character—everything from my college triumph as Biff Loman or the Rag Picker to my utilitarian appearances in a Shakespeare festival. All this displayed: my multiple skills, good looks, and charm, which had fueled my rocket rise to this very moment when I needed this job very, very badly.

I carried my junk slung over my back in a bag. It was hot. It was lunchtime and some offices were closed. I was wondering if I had enough cash to buy something to eat. I had a single subway token, which would get me back to my edge-of-Harlem sublet before dark so I could scare the roaches from occupying my day bed. They, by then, were roommates. I had walked downtown that morning from 120th Street to the theater district and had put pictures and résumés in about twenty offices. In the afternoon, I walked further downtown to the Village to leave my stuff in the offices of actual theaters where shows were playing or about to come in, in case anybody needed a sudden cast change. Well, gosh, here I am!

The smaller downtown theaters were collectively known as off-Broadway, a category based on seat capacity. An even smaller seat capacity was called off-off Broadway. My shoes were the same black dress shoes I had worn daily for eight years. I polished them most days because of Arthur Miller's line in *Death of a Salesman* about Willy Loman: "He's out there on a smile and a shoeshine," which made me cry every time I thought of it because it reminded me of my salesman father—who, at that point, I didn't know how to love and didn't even like.

There were holes in the soles of my shoes. I covered them every day by sliding the sports section of *The Daily News*—never the *Times*—into the shoes before I put them on, then tied them carefully, tight around the knots I had made to keep the broken laces together. A poor actor, but always a hopeful one.

That day, I decided I would make one more stop. I went into the ground-floor door of a brownstone building in the 50s east of Sixth Avenue. I climbed the stairs to an office headed by famous producer Herman Shumlin. It was listed as producing a new television show for one of the biggies—*The US Steel Hour, The Philco Television Playhouse, The Hallmark Hall of Fame.* The show was about Irish people and had a lead role for the son, a rebellious young man only a little younger than I was. Well, my mother's side of the family was half-Irish. I could do this part.

The office door on the third floor was standing open to whatever cool air had been left in the dark stairwell. I walked up to this landing and looked in. There was a balding, old man sitting at a receptionist's desk behind an old typewriter. He was two-finger typing, not too well, and cursing under his breath.

I said, "Excuse me, sir." He didn't look up. "Excuse me, but I'd like to leave my picture and résumé for the role of the Irish boy in the new show."

He didn't stop cursing and making a mess of the typing.

"I think, sir, I'd be good for the part. I just did an Irish accent in a show this summer and I'd really like to get a chance to read for this role."

He typed some more, then gave it up. I hadn't gone away. I still stood half in the office, half in the hall. I took a step and gently placed my picture on the desk beside him, then stepped back.

He looked up at me over his half-glasses. He was tired, I could see, but there was a power emanating from him. I thought he was a secretary but looking into his eyes now—which were drilling into mine—I saw he was much more than a secretary.

He stared at me. A chill of hope stirred up my back, or maybe it was just a cool breeze from the stairwell. He was really studying me. Maybe . . . maybe . . .

Then he said, "You're not right. For anything." And he turned back to his typewriter and resumed the hunt, peck, peck, shit! Peck, peck, goddamnit! Fuck! Shit! Peck.

I stepped back, absorbing the shock. "For anything," he'd said. *Anything?*

I turned to leave. On the door, I now saw, was a name painted in black: Herman Shumlin, Producer—the man himself.

I went down the stairs and into the uncaring New York streets. So, I thought, *Herman Shumlin thinks I'm not right for anything.* I looked west toward Broadway, toward the theaters, toward heaven. I have to get there. I *will* get there!

Yes, I am, I thought. *I'm right for something.* Then the absurdity of the turndown hit me. I started to laugh. I thought, *I'll show you, Mr. Shumlin!*

A passing lady stepped aside and gave me a peculiar look. I must have said it out loud. *Anything?*

I shouldered my bag of dreams and headed downtown.

My first time out of the USA. Players, Inc. U.S.O. tour. Germany.
Late 1950s.

SCENE: New York

I had a job. I was the host of O. Henry's Steak House on Sixth Avenue in the Village, just around the corner from cozy, charming Gay Street, the street where the two sisters from Ohio live in *Wonderful Town*. The name became a sure-fire smirk-spawner as gay people asserted themselves to be accepted as humans and homophobic people began losing the argument for hate and resorted to violence.

O. Henry's was a great job. The owner was a Sicilian immigrant, a mysterious guy, vital, ageless, short, compact, and always in dark, well-cut Italian suits with vests and pocket squares. He had a smile that was genuinely warm but instantly appraised you with the long practice of a landlord, an innkeeper, or a beat cop.

He ran a terrifically popular restaurant. The bar was thick with big-assed, big-hipped machers from the city government who were, like my boss, genuinely friendly, gimlet-eyed gentlemen who knew "a hawk from a handsaw."

The joint was pretty mobbed-up, but a couple of gangsters never stopped anybody who wanted to eat there because it was the best steakhouse in Manhattan. Also, for some, the attraction was the fact that the building was the old home of William Henry Porter—O. Henry—the great writer who defined the American short story. And it was a hangout for theater folk.

The owner's son was a lover of the theater, so actors and writers came to hang out just as they had done when O. Henry lived there. The focal point was the open-fire grill with flames a foot high—novel in those days—at the center. Two chefs, both Jamaican, shared the duties. Both were divas to be catered to. As the host, I knew that and made sure everyone who came in got the point that the chefs were the best in the city. That was easy because they were.

The waiters were the entertainment. We had Charley, the method waiter—a tall, handsome former adman with a genuinely nutty, neurotic theatrical air. He once chased a customer who had stiffed him up Sixth Avenue, cursing him in dramatic and probably jingle-worthy profane prose for all the city to see and ridicule the cheapskate. He even threw his straw boater at the guy. All the waiters wore long white butcher's smocks and straw hats—skimmers, boaters.

There was Pierre, the dark, conspiratorial Frenchman who looked like actor Peter Lorre. He was in a constant fuming fury over his customers' manners, parentage, and prospects for future life and love. There was George, the Greek man who was in his eighties but strong like a bull, a man who was a classic New York waiter: thick Greek accent, rude but affectionate, too, like your mother. He had his thumb in the soup but was devil-may-care about it. "My tum' clinner den de bottom you shoe—don' worry 'bout it . . ."

One freezing night, outside, George grabbed me by the throat, shoved me against the brick wall of the joint, showed me a knife, and said he'd cut my throat if I didn't stop playing favorites and giving other waiters more customers than he got. I wasn't scared although George was clearly angry. I was innocent. I told him I was always fair. I had to give the empty tables to whoever came in, even if they wanted to sit in George's station. I was told to seat everybody as quickly as possible, to be smooth about steering them away from their favorite corners, and to put them at empty tables no matter where they were. George knew this. His beef was with the boss's son, not with me. He put the knife away and slapped my cheek too hard, but affectionately, and told me that he knew I understood he was just trying to feed his family.

I did understand. And I kept faith with all the guys, even the chefs. I laughed at their crazy temperaments. If a patron complained and returned a steak, the chef on duty would "accidentally" drop it on the sawdust floor, step on it by "mistake," dust it off, then expertly throw it back on the grill. While cooking it, he would write "Fuck You" in the garnish on the plate, then carefully lay the perfect steak on top of the message.

Famous actors, famous writers, famous drunks, famous ex-bank robbers, famous politicians, famous ex-con politicians, and everyone who lived in Queens, Brooklyn, and Jersey came in. It was a nightly blitz of people who had made it and were flaunting it. I got fifty- and one-hundred-dollar tips pressed into my palm for a better table. There was no such animal. For that reason, and for my fierce pride in my own profession and my determination to make it like all of them, I never once took a tip. I was going to be famous myself one day.

One night, the boss stayed late. So did his son. So did a few heavy guys who sat near the exit onto Sixth Avenue. The emergency door was near the host's station, and I saw a heavy in the corner there, too. Then the butcher came huffing up the narrow, steep stairs from the basement where the meat was stored in refrigerators that were locked every night.

"Hey, the loading door's locked. I gotta climb these fickin' stayahs? What's wit' dat?"

The boss came toward him with open arms. I thought, *He's gonna hug him.* Nice!

The butcher stopped short. He was already short and fat, and in his black overcoat he looked like a piece of wall.

The boss said pleasantly, "Open the coat, Gino."

Gino took a slow look around. He saw the setup. Slowly, one hand in the air in surrender, one hand plucking at his buttons, he unlocked the coat.

Carnegie Hall, New York City.
Players, Inc. *Oedipus Rex*. The
Old Shepherd. He has the key
to the mystery.

As Grumio, insouciant servant to
Petruchio, the wife tamer in *The
Taming of the Shrew*. Great Lakes
Shakespeare Festival.

"Show me, Gino."

The butcher pulled his overcoat open and revealed meat. Raw steaks hung on hooks on his coat, his vest, his belt. It was, to me, like Francis Bacon or Chaim Soutine or Mark Ryden's art studio, the fresh red of the filets, the New York strips, the Chateaubriands brilliant against the black of his undertaker's serge suit. I was awed. So were the heavies. There were murmurs of appreciation for Gino's style and daring, *oh, wows* of shock, and the beginning strains of Verdi's *Requiem Mass* for the dearly departed. Gino. "A nice guy, ya know?"

The boss merely said, "Downstairs, boys!" And the heavies crowded around Gino like pallbearers, lifted him—and his forty or fifty pounds of extra weight—off his feet, and started for the stairs to the basement.

The boss nodded to his son, who showed his meat locker key. "Lock it up, and take Gino out the loading door. Capisce?"

"Son," he said to me, "It's gonna be fine. He's my cousin, but he's gotta know . . . You see what I'm sayin'?"

I said, "I do."

"See you tomorrow?"

"Yes," I said.

I never saw Gino again.

SCENE: New York

In the 1960s, an actor in New York could work in five or six plays a year. There was great excitement, ferment, belief that the American theater was becoming, was nascent, was unique in the world for its internationalism and spanking new history. We were discovering ourselves and the rest of the universe. Regional theaters were starting up, old roadhouses were dusted off, antique movie houses were converted, and empty lofts in NYC were being repurposed into new theaters.

Theatrical producer and director Joseph Papp had a theater in an elderly auditorium in a building built by August Heckscher, a great patron of the arts in New York. It was a shoestring operation. It was currently featuring George Scott and Colleen Dewhurst as Antony and Cleopatra. No set, no costumes, the cast visible, sitting as the characters on a long bench upstage and entering the scene on cue. Joe was fighting battles with the city government to keep it going. It was his obsession and righteous dream, and his timing was good. The country had a new, young president whose wife was strongly for the arts.

It was an uneasy time, but America was the strongest country that had ever existed on the earth. We were complacent in that frame of mind, and the arts were beginning to reflect that complacency. It was time for the master plumber of the human soul—Shakespeare. Joe believed New York needed a permanent company making Shakespeare's works available absolutely free.

Joe Papp cast me in a play! I instantly quit my job at O. Henry's. The boss was thrilled for me. He told me to come back anytime because I was a good boy—"You good boy!" He was a European gent of the old school.

I would play Romeo for the Young Shakespeare Festival in New York City. I was on my way for real. I felt indispensable, worthy, and that I now had an artistic home with this poor but powerful new group of New York players. Arthur Lithgow had given me a chance, too, in Ohio, and I hadn't let him down. I had definitely felt at home with Uncle Arthur. And now, in New York, I was looking to find a home in every company of playmakers. This was paradise found.

I rehearsed with Roy Scheider (Mercutio) and Kathleen Widdoes (Juliet) for three exhilarating days. At the end of the third day, Joe buttonholed me in the lobby. He took the cigar out of his mouth and asked me mildly, "Are you getting enough sleep?"

I said, "Yes, sure."

"You look tired," he said and moved on. What?

A little later, Joe's assistant, a kind lady, appeared in the lobby and told me I was fired. I don't remember her words. I listened and heard but didn't believe. In a fog of emotion, I managed to stutter, "Why?"

She rambled, she preambled, and she said nice nonsense. She finally said, "Joe's concept of the role has changed. He feels maybe you are . . . too old. Your look isn't quite right." There was something about bags under my eyes, blah, blah, blah.

I didn't fight back. I realize now what a pessimist and fatalist lived inside me. People are going to do what they're going to do. They may hurt you or help you. You can't fix it.

"Larry, you've got to have a chance," my mother had said. I expected to be hurt. I was a scanner, hyper-aware of who could or would hurt me. It led me into behavior I didn't like in myself, something to do with running away from loving women who wanted to marry me. I had an internal trapdoor I slammed shut when emotionally threatened in any way.

But this role of Romeo had been a godsend. It challenged those emotions, dared me to open up. Romeo is nothing if he is not open to being hurt, even destroyed, by love, and that's what happened to him. I wanted to find that source in me. This was my *chance*.

Henry V. Fluellen, the Welsh engineer. Great Lakes Shakespeare Festival.

The lady in the lobby was so sympathetic it hurt worse. I looked in her eyes. She truly didn't like what was happening or what she had to do, but she was a messenger.

I stumbled out—rejected. All my pretensions dragging behind me like toilet paper on my shoe in a public place, with everybody laughing at me behind my back.

I went back to my boss at O. Henry's and begged for my job. He didn't laugh at me; he was sympathetic. This man, tough as Sicilian rock, had a big heart. I went back to work, sharing duties with an Italian lawyer my age who was dressed beautifully and knew about ten words of English. This guy, I believe, was a submarine—what they call an illegal immigrant today. In our few broken conversations, I got the essence of desperation he had lived through at home in Italy, and here he had no chance to practice law. He had to start over as a busboy, a restaurant host, anything.

A friend who worked for Joe wrote to tell me that the reason I was fired was that Mr. Papp said I was *overtrained* in Shakespearean acting. I knew too well how to speak verse; I was too quick to attack a scene.

I got it. I get it. Joe liked to mold actors in his own image. He was a kid from the streets. He wanted Shakespeare done the way people spoke where he lived.

I was from Arkansas. I had worked hard not to sound like a cracker, a hick from the sticks, because it wasn't appropriate for Shakespeare's people. But I also worked to sound simply American, not British. I fiercely, obsessively, wanted to find the simple human truth in every role I was ever lucky enough to get.

I had been given only three days to find the truth of Romeo. One day of reading and two of rehearsal. I was on the hunt for that truth from the first moment, using the tools I had then—what actors call technique. I knew how to work and worked hard. I flung myself at Romeo with all I knew to create him in me.

It wasn't enough for Joe. He had given me the role after three arduous audition sessions, then changed his mind—his right, of course—without saying a word to me. Without a chance to try to be what he thought he wanted when he saw me work over the three days. Was I slow to do something he suggested because it didn't feel honest or right? Joe was a great producer, but not a good director. He never learned how to talk to actors effectively. So, I was out. It seemed very strange—until I read a story in the *New York Times* theater page the following week: The heiress daughter of the man who had built an iconic New York City bridge had donated a very large sum to Joseph Papp's fledgling New York Shakespeare Festival. The woman's actor son had just been cast in the coveted role of Romeo in Joe's new production of *Romeo and Juliet* opening at the Heckscher Theater.

SCENE: New York

The difference between then and now in New York is startling. For me, it was a poor existence in terms of money but immensely rich in culture. By that I mean the people and the arts, the aspiration. Everyone I met had a goal. There was hope. America meant hope. And young folks had a place to be, which was like Aladdin's cave. If you knew the "open sesame" password you could find any treasure you were willing to visualize and work to create.

I substitute taught, crafted handmade chess sets, and lived on dough saved from Shakespeare Festival and summer stock work. I lived hand-to-mouth, moving frequently to new digs. A one-hundred-dollar-a-month room on Riverside Drive with a view of the river, a couch in Brooklyn, a borrowed apartment in Queens, a room in Harlem. So did everyone else I knew who was trying to be an actor, a musician, a dancer, or an artist.

Gigs appeared. I danced as Pa Bundren with Valerie Bettis and her company in the marvelous dance rendition of William Faulkner's *As I Lay Dying*, held in the unfinished music and dance theater of Lincoln Center.

I met desirable young women everywhere. I crushed on a dancer from Valerie's company and found my way to Ocean Parkway in Brooklyn to visit. Her father, a doctor, stayed upstairs as we necked like hungry teenagers in her dark living room. But she was looking for a stable business guy to marry and laughed merrily at my heartfelt aspirations to make it as an actor.

I was not a virgin, but somehow, in spirit, I was. In my heart, I was still an altar boy, a guiltless child now living a wonderful dream. By now, I was being hit on by women—and men. I was offered money and opportunities to live better in exchange for—it was unspoken—my body. For time with me. I had rejected love and had been rejected on tour, but now I knew I was attractive to others, and if I wanted only sex, I could take my pick of offers. I skated, always. I wanted a chimera: true love.

SCENE: Ohio, Summer

"Harder," she said. "Is that all you can do?"

They began again, and again she stopped him and demanded that he go harder. "I need it," she said. They went at it again.

This time, the big man hit the woman with a slap that was heard in the last row of the thousand-seat theater.

"Ow!" she yelled, hand to face. She reeled away and screamed a New York scream. "Owwww! What the hell?"

Othello stood quietly as Desdemona left the stage. The director jumped onto the stage to talk urgently to the actor playing Othello. Othello remained calm. He had done what she asked and hit her harder. Was she now going to level charges against him with Actors' Equity?

I, Iago, left the stage while this played out. I went to the dressing room to study my lines. I sat in front of the cloudy mirror in my space at the communal table. My makeup kit, a tackle box, was open on a dirty towel next to a jar of cold cream, some color sticks, the base tubes, and the brushes for details. I took a 3 x 5 card from my Folio Library copy of *Othello,* covered my lines, and continued absorbing the cue lines. I did it mechanically, over and over and over—cue line, my line, cue line, my line. This was how I learned my roles in the Great Lakes Shakespeare Festival.

Desdemona was weeping behind a curtain of the dressing area, and someone was murmuring to her. She was threatening to leave, to sue, to get revenge, to call the Equity Deputy (a member of the cast) or the union representative in New York and make a stink.

Desdemona was a good actress, but she was having a mini-breakdown. Her husband, a college professor, was talking calmly to her as she demanded that Othello be fired. I thought, *This is fear.* She's just afraid she can't do the part right, so she's made it her acting partner's fault.

I understood both sides. She felt she needed a stimulus to kick her into an acting gear that she didn't naturally have and blamed her scene partner for not supplying it to her. If only he'd hit her harder, she would feel what she thought she couldn't. Classic actor projection.

He—Othello—was a natural gentleman and accomplished actor who had performed Shakespeare in Scandinavia in three languages. This calm, experienced fellow had been finally provoked to demonstrate his manhood by slapping an actress too hard. The character Othello would hit Desdemona with a ceremonial kind of tap. It isn't the brutality of the slap that hurts her, but the humiliation in public that reveals that Othello has begun—against his better nature—to believe Iago's lies about her.

As Iago, I was "glad he hit the bitch" and happy to see her cry for real. As Larry, I was sorry for them both. They are tragic characters, good actors, and nice people. Iago was a natural fit for me. I thought I understood most of him. A supremely devious half-man, a masker, a brilliant liar, a woman-hater, an authority hater, a sociopath. It's a great character part, and, again, I wasn't ready.

It was Arthur Lithgow's summer Shakespearean Repertory in Lakewood, Ohio. We would rehearse one week and open the first play, then play the first play and rehearse the second play one week. We'd open the second play and play both shows at night while rehearsing the third play, and so on. Once all six plays were open, the season continued to its end, all plays in rotation. This is repertory.

God bless the people of the state of Ohio! They filled the seats for twelve weeks of Shakespeare. New York has the most challenging, loyal audiences in the world. But Ohio was second. I remember a heavy-set lady in a cotton print dress with three children under the age of twelve who had four seats in the front row for each show. This woman clearly had very little money. The kids were always neat but dressed in old jeans and well-worn T-shirts. She was a great audience, too tired probably to be very demonstrative, but she smiled and stretched herself out in joyful comfort, heavy legs in support hose planted like trees. Those kids watched us cavorting up there with big eyes like it was church.

I played interesting character leads that final year. Arthur Lithgow was fun to work for. He worked so hard himself it was all we could do to try and keep up. I'm a worker; I would rather work than eat, and I was in hog heaven. It's no wonder his fifteen-year-old son John, one of our spear carriers, turned out to be such an eclectic and disciplined actor.

But Shakespeare outmatched me. I had youth, energy, good training, and I loved what I was doing. But did I conquer every one of those characters? No.

I got glimpses of their complexity and tried my best to meet each of them. My imagination is big, my appetite for humanity even bigger. I took on Iago, Feste, Orlando, Bassanio, Hotspur, Justice Shallow, and Oberon—a banquet, a Thanksgiving and Christmas, of roles. I learned, I learned. Thank you, dear Arthur Lithgow!

I reveled in every single moment onstage. There I was—safe—playing an oblivious lover, the King of Fairies, a warrior, an ancient decrepit judge, a psychopath, a studly lover, a clown. I loved them all. But I was most at home with the clown.

No wonder the church fathers wanted to abolish the theater. It was too much fun—not only a huge occasion of sin, but also the best road to hell, listed in all the newspapers, eight shows a week.

The King James version of Matthew 7:13 says "Enter by the narrow gate; for wide *is* the gate, and broad *is* the way that leads to destruction, and there are many who go in by it."

The Broad Way was my goal. I hadn't set foot upon a stage there, yet, but I was already a lost soul. All I dreamed of doing was getting onto that Broadway

"I *am* Iago!" *Othello*. Great Lakes Shakespeare Festival

stage in New York City. I had no idea how near that moment was. All I knew was that when the chance came to run through that wide gate, I would never look back.

As I stepped deeper into the life of a working actor, I began to lose perspective. It was impossible to predict if I'd be working from one day or month to the next. I had to realize that in the theater, that's a permanent condition. The only way to some—but not much—certainty was to become "A Name."

When I first wrote the word *actor* on an application for a driver's license, the bare arrogance of it shocked me. How dare I? Who said? How do you know? When people not in the theater asked, "What do you do?" I equivocated and said I was a student studying for a PhD.

I could not describe myself as an artist until I was recognized as such by directors, producers, and critics who judge such things. I still didn't believe the fact that I had been in many professional plays, been reviewed successfully by New York critics, and had never stopped studying the craft since the first time I stepped on stage.

Why didn't I believe in myself? I didn't ask myself that. I knew deep down. I wasn't enough. Tried, convicted, and sentenced to believe this for life.

S C E N E : CBS Studios, New York

While honing my theater craft, I also worked for a daytime soap opera. This was my first regular, steady employment in the business of show. It felt so good to have a regular job. Acting! It was a good show and I had a really interesting part, a smart newspaper reporter, a bad boy with things in my past—the kind of guy the women fell for. This show was called *The Secret Storm*. The untold story was that the original title had been *The Storm Within*, but the show's first big sustaining sponsor turned out to be a well-known laxative. They changed the name of the show.

The director was powerful, determined, and feared. No one crossed her; they didn't want her wrath. She smoked like she directed, with the lipstick-smeared white stub of a ubiquitous cigarette sticking out between her teeth like the prow of a marauding Viking ship. She twirled the cigarette around and around constantly, talking through her teeth, shooting orders that would be obeyed. She wanted top quality work, and if you were not up to it, you were soon toast—burnt toast. To her, soap operas were a classic American art form.

She worked as if the show were written by Arthur Miller. Her work was never inferior. In fact, soap work was quite difficult, demanding great skill and concentration from all involved. It was taped live, meaning we acted the scenes as if they were a stage play on film.

My love interest on the show was having a difficult time in her own marriage. The character I played may have mirrored characteristics of her husband. I was a bad boy, and I drank. We were heading into a heavy love affair on the show, and both of us were nervous about it. Some may think it's swell to be in show biz and get to romance the gorgeous women and hunky men. It's not. It's uncomfortable and feels like cheating, though it's not. Actors have to use their own real emotions to do what the story says.

Our director, in pursuit of God knows what reality, suddenly strongly suggested that the two of us check into a hotel room in Manhattan to rehearse, and I knew what Ms. Machiavelli—our director—wanted. My acting partner did, too, yet she seemed to listen. I got an inkling that she might be willing to play with Madame's devilish suggestion.

I refused to do it. The director, she who must be obeyed, was surprised. It was her test of my compliance as an actor. Curiously, she was intrigued. I felt a jolt of sexual interest from her, a sense of willingness for daring adventure. But I had a prudish, altar boy thought: immoral, amoral, and self-defeating as an acting technique. A twinge of moral clarity born from my work ethic. My altar boy self was awake and biting my ankles. A good sign. I wasn't dead.

SCENE: Letters from Home

My mother writes that my brother is in trouble for breaking a neighbor's window with a slingshot. And for smoking. He also has a broad view of drinking. He's hanging around with "pachooky-looking" friends and "father thinks he has an undisciplined mind." My sister has received a citation for being "the most outstanding girl in her freshman nursing class." My Aunt Annie is still teaching and going to Boston to get her dysfunctional leg operated on finally, and "Daddy has not had a drink of anything alcoholic since July 4th and says he "always knew he would quit someday." She says I am quite a dreamer—referring to my comment about how she should someday be able to lie in a hammock and not work—and that she has had many such dreams. She says, "the older I get, the more I realize there is very little else in this world but struggle." She tells me not to be disillusioned and that she doesn't know anything that would be nicer than to rest in a hammock.

I'm unable to get home. I am on tour, then heading to Italy and Germany on a USO tour to play for GIs, then to Vermont for summer stock. She hopes

I'll be able to do a small shopping tour in Europe to bring back some toys for my older sister's children and a sweater for Daddy.

My Aunt Annie sends me a Christmas box in New York. She tells me if I go to a department store or a drugstore, I can get bayberry-scented candles to burn at Christmas. "Bayberry candles when burned to the socket bring happiness, health, and gold to the pocket."

My father writes very seldom.

> Hi and a very Merry X-mas to you. Mother has decided to go to Fort Smith. Annie called again, and your mother feels she should go for fear she may never see her again. Nothing serious, just, again, intuition. I am working hard. This automation is really something with the Vietnam orders. Everything is okay. Take care of yourself. God bless you.

My younger sister writes:

> *I guess Mom told you I had my appendix out. I graduate next August from Tulane Nursing School in New Orleans. I wish I could come up to see you, Larry, to New York. Maybe next year I can. I hope you can get the part in the Musketeers [a show I had auditioned for]. You know we'll be watching and praying for you. And don't run around without sending us your address for as long as you did this summer. I wanted to write and didn't know where you were. Love, Lynne.*

My mother says:

> Sally said to tell you hello. She is snowed under with work. She has three children in school now; the twins started kindergarten so she has a big job getting them off every day. However, she always asks about you and reads your letters to us. She was so thrilled when you said you might get a part on TV. I am sure you get pretty lonesome there. Make some connections at church so you can feel like you belong some place.

Aunt Annie sends me a letter after seeing me in *A Man For All Seasons* in St. Louis.

> *I feel like Cinderella, back from the glamorous, fabulous world of Sir Thomas More to 2110 South P Street. I can live a long time on that*

experience. We saw a wonderful play, wonderful cast. I would consider you as one of the best, right along with Roderick [as More] and the Common Man. You really don't know how well you perform and how perfectly hand-some you look. We haven't finished thinking about it yet. Believe me, I have started my novena for you to St. Jude, patron saint of hope and lost causes—I began Sunday—for whatever it is that you want. We want it for you. But right now, as things stand, you have already made it. Who else in this family has ever done as well? Not one! Carolyn called last night from New Orleans. She is really your biggest fan and has been all along. She says you are the only one in the family that amounts to anything. Not a half-year in school, and already dating a rich Dallas boy. What do you think? I say she'll never finish. I hope she picks up a millionaire. We need a few. The only regret I have is that I didn't rent a mink for the play. Then I would have looked like the rest.

After I tell her I didn't get the part in a play, Mother writes:

Keep your chin up and keep right on plowing. I have had many disappoint-ments and hurtles [sic] to go over and I don't know where I ever got strength to go on, but I did. Anyway, I keep trying and praying, and I will rally all the forces here and we will barnstorm heaven for some good luck. If you don't ask, you don't receive, then it was not for the best. Put your best foot forward and keep on trying.

Mother continues about my sister having her appendix out:

Of course, I failed to get Blue Cross on her, so we have the whole bill to take care of. John wrangled everything to get as much done as he could for nothing, but the hospital bill was $225 and of course we only had fifty dollars to put on it, so he paid the whole thing and we are going to pay him back. On top of that, Leo has broken a small bone in his hand and has a cast on it from the end of his little finger almost to his elbow. Blue Cross will pay for part of that, but not all. I had to stop and type a page for Leo's history lesson. I think you should come to Los Angeles and try the movies. Why don't you get on one of those quiz shows and make some quick money that way? I am working hard now. I feel there is some underhand work going on in the department regarding jobs. You know they like sharp-looking, young secretaries to make a good impression so I don't know how this old crow is going to hold out, but

I'll tell you one thing, they will have a fight on their hands if they try to give me the boot. But if it happens, I'll just get something else. Will say bye for now. Will also try to locate the novena to the infant Jesus of Prague. St. Anthony is also a good one to pray to. Write when you can, be good, and keep your chin up. God bless you. Love from all at home.

Father sends a short note:

Will write soon. I am so tired and wore out. I don't have much energy anymore when I get home. I get up at 4:45 A.M. and it's 5:40 at night before I get home. God bless.

Sally writes to tell me about how my father really is.

Well, don't faint! Here I am writing when my beds are unmade and the kids are hungry. First, I want to say I am so proud of you I could really bust. There are always disappointments, but you will get there, I know it! Mother has decided to sell the house and move on without Dad. I feel she should talk it over with you also before she takes this step. Dad is really bad now and only one step above the down road to the end. He is definitely pycotic [sic], and whether the drinking is a result of that pycosis [sic], or it is a result of the drinking, I don't know. Mother and Leo and Lynne have no peace at night or on weekends, and I don't think she can hold up much longer. He still works but Mother doesn't get any money from him or anything. He comes home drunk at night and is fighting and foul. The weekend before Lynne left, they were all over here. John was fishing. (Dad won't come when John is here.) He got steadily drunker and drunker with no apparent reason. Then he was up all night drinking my liquor and left in the morning to get more. This is the way I see it:

Commit him (they will probably not keep him more than seventy-two hours and I have a hard time with that). Then recommit him (he will really be mad at Mother then).

Move out, sell the house, and keep Leo in school—he needs the Brothers there, live closer to her work, keep her good paying job.

Move to Marin where she will feel more security around me, but: 1) no Catholic school for Leo; 2) give up good paying job; 3) higher rent; 4) commute to city for work; 5) still not able to hide from him; 6) cause an embarrassment having to commit him here, but John would rather that than have him hanging around. It would make the local papers here for sure and embarrass Leo since he has a lot of friends here. Whereas, in Oakland, it would not make the papers and less fuss would be made over it.

Mother does not know I am writing all this. But, Larry, I am fed up with him and I am afraid, and I have expected for the last year to be called on the phone that he has murdered her. When he drinks or when he's sober, he blames Mother for everything that ever happens, and I think he is dangerous. Leo broke his hand hitting him when he attacked Mother about three weeks ago. I cannot even look at him anymore.

I am really sorry to burden you with this at a time when you have problems of your own, but I think you should know this and if you can see any solution to this problem that I can't see, please let me know. Leo is a good boy but he has his own problems that are not being helped by all this. He is very insecure . . . my point in even mentioning this is Leo is being forgotten in this shuffle, and it's about time Mother has time to give him without this awful tension.

I am in no way asking that you come home, etc. I know, and Mother knows, your chances are in New York. I am hoping you get an acting part on television soon. I think you are very good. It's a tough nut to crack, and you have gone so far already, and I just know you'll make it . . . don't give up. Love, Sally. P.S. I know how awful it is to get a letter of this sort when you are away and can't see yourself what's going on. I wouldn't have written it if I thought it could be avoided.

But nothing Sally proposed was possible. My mother just kept trying. She would not give up on him. So the nightmare continued.

Where was I? On tour with Players, Inc. We were committed to 180 shows in a territory that covered almost half the US, from the East to the Midwest. We never missed a show.

I had no break time. Unless I quit the company, I could not go home.

I was no help to any of them. I had escaped. Was I flying?

SCENE: Oakland, California

I went home to California after the Shakespeare season. I had been gone two years. I had written a few letters and, when in New York, had called a few times. It didn't seem odd to me to be out of touch with family. I was a solitary kind of person by now. I had few real friends and corresponded with few, and telephoning was rare. I thought only of acting, of making it, of getting better. I was riding a powerful, unpredictable horse I had no control over. And I had not learned how to ride.

I stayed home for a short time. I presented my mother and sisters with the jewelry I had bought from the Khartoum souk and sturdy German sweaters from a stopover in Frankfurt. I gave my brother some interesting knives from the Omdurman battleground.

The family house needed a new roof. I gave them money. My brother needed tuition help. I gave that. He insisted on making it a loan, not a gift. I felt low and ungrateful and distant. I acted the prodigal son pretty well.

My conversations with my father were extremely uncomfortable. My brother's relationship with him was hostile. Years later, I found out Leo had pushed our father out onto a balcony at the apartment and threatened to throw him off if he hit our mother ever again.

My mother took the brunt of all this. Her unwitting martyrdom helped no one. Her children were unready for the world. We were raised in a secretive, violent cave where no one was to know what went on. We knew we shouldn't air our dirty laundry in public, so we walked around in metaphoric dirty clothes feeling shamed and shameful. A life without honesty.

We lived in homes where no friends could ever be invited.

I went back to New York jammed shut. I forced myself to feel nothing for fear that feeling would turn into blame or shame.

But I was functioning, wasn't I? The good-looking clown guy, the moody, sad, attractive guy—the masks were pinching my face and my soul.

SCENE: Princeton, New Jersey

We were working in the famous McCarter Theater. Henry Fonda and Jimmy Stewart had acted on the graceful old stage and were friends and roommates.

I was tasked with three leading character roles: Brutus in *Julius Caesar*, Galileo in Bertolt Brecht's *The Life of Galileo*, and Caligula in the eponymous play by Albert Camus. They were dynamically different men and great in historical memory, myth, and legend.

The Princeton audiences were exactly the kind of folks who loved theatrical treats like these plays.

I didn't audition for these parts. I had worked with Arthur Lithgow in Shakespeare, which gave me street cred with the casting people, the directors, and the producers who served a network of regional theaters that had risen to be a force in the American theater. Communities realized that live theater was good for downtown business just as downtown was showing signs of desuetude. The suburbs were now the place for upwardly mobile families with disposable income.

I lived in a bubble of creativity surrounded by comrades; soldiers of the theater determined to take the objective and scale the mountain that was before us. We had to secure this plot of word, idea, and ground so civilization could be saved and flourish. And so that people could know their own humanity and believe in its essentialness.

Julius Caesar is perhaps the most accessible of Shakespeare's plays. It tells its version of ancient history in the apparent simplicity of forward rushing story yet teems with human complexity. Every main character is complicated and so honest they come at you like a long-lost relative or schoolmate. I knew Brutus. Now, how do I play him?

Choice. A stage manager gave me an opening night present—a piece of plain brown marble engraved with the words "The difficulty is the choice." He was twitting me for my laborious and ferocious way of rehearsing, which gave me much personal angst at every moment of choice, and of my failure to decide how to play a moment.

Is Brutus really an honorable man? Antony casts doubt on this in his famous speech deconstructing the motives of the assassins of Caesar. But Brutus has come to believe his friend and mentor would destroy the republic by becoming emperor. However, he is not certain. He weighs the morality of killing a man who might be a tyrant. The signs are there. So, Brutus, in a burst of emotion, tells himself that to "kill the infant serpent in its shell" is the righteous action. He makes a tortuous choice.

The acting problem is to live the contradiction yet leave a portrait of an actual human, not a noble statue in Roman armor in a museum.

I had to help the audience feel the torture of the contradiction and the awareness of doing wrong for a right reason—to commit murder for righteousness. The moment of inner choice had to be dramatized, discovered now. Dancing in the dark. How would I get there?

We had two weeks of rehearsal. I had to construct a mental and emotional mosaic, each piece different and the right color and shape, while learning the other actors' styles of working, getting used to an unfamiliar style of dress, and speaking verse. I had to learn the director's sense of the play's meaning. What tools did I have? I had learned from Dr. K to attack any part with optimism, good spirits, and full-out energy—the more emphatic, the more athletic, the better—and that applied equally to Hamlet, a folksong, a Greek tragedy, or a Chinese classic adapted in an ironic style. At Catholic University, I had learned from Bill Graham, Father Hartke, and Bob Moore to identify the genius of the playwright's plan and how to play into every problem rather than fight it. I also learned to find the individuality within the type, to speak well and easily, to project while seeming not to, to move gracefully and naturally in concert with my fellows, and to keep a clear stage picture before an audience.

Arthur Lithgow had taught me to go with the flow and to use whatever came up in the playing of the scene to connect my character personally to the audience. For Arthur, every play was an impromptu, a happening, a conversation with friends, a living thing existing only now.

But how do you survive the student matinees when New Jersey's finest young pile into the theater chock-full of juice as a bag of newly picked apples? How do you make a quarrel of cats into a choir of angels? In a quiet moment of a scene with Portia, she showed a self-inflicted cut on her thigh, a little flash of a long, white leg. It was too talky of a scene for hot teen Jersey boys aching for a seduction scene from a Beach Blanket flick. This day, an object whizzed between us, flew past our noses, and hit the rear wall of the theater with a crack like a rifle shot. We jumped apart and looked at each other.

A golf ball rolled quietly down the raked platform of the stage. In my toga, I leaned down and picked it up. Portia went from fear to a smile, then to a chuckle. I walked to the edge of the stage. I held up the ball and looked at it thoughtfully like it was Yorick's skull. Then I leaned back and threw it overhand, as hard as I could, back at the center of the audience. They gasped and ducked as each one thought they were the target. Then I held up the ball I had palmed. Some looked anxious, some laughed a little. I turned and hurled it against the side wall. It hit with a broken, wet noise like a human skull being hit with a bat.

I took Portia's arm and we left the scene. Now there was an empty stage and, in the audience, a deadly quiet, as at a wake when the dead person is removed. Finally, the play went on. It was a great *now* moment. The best-ever audience connection moment. Brutus was a stoic, but a dangerous, interesting one.

Galileo was the production I came to hate. The adaptation was Charles Laughton's. He produced and acted it when Brecht was in Hollywood as a refugee from Hitler. Laughton had turned this pristine, acerbic antihero into a sympathetic character, kind of a beggar for sympathy—contrary to what Brecht wrote.

I loved Charles Laughton as an actor—devious, clever as a fox, authentic, idiosyncratic, surprising. He was everything I treasured. But because he wanted to be liked as the character, the play was turned into sentimental mush. I resisted the weakening of the real story of the church versus science, so I never landed. I was still fascinated by Galileo himself, but our Princeton showing was unsatisfactory, especially to the scientists in our audience who counted Albert Einstein as one of their colleagues. In this version of *Galileo*, we pandered to feelings, not science. I hated that. Not fair to the writer.

Fourteen years later, with my own company, The New York Actors' Theater, I got another chance. More later.

Caligula, by the Nobel Prize–winning existentialist writer Albert Camus, was a challenge. Camus was popular after WWII for two novels, *The Stranger* and *The Plague*. The play confirmed his belief that human life is absurd and meaningless because it means only what we say it does.

I understood the character Caligula as written because I understood the feelings the young, mad emperor had. But he had the power to act out his disgust with life's absurdity in terrible ways. He was a tyrant. I could not give oxygen to such anarchic despair in my own life, but I had grown up with an alcoholic father. This stuff was buried deep inside me and surfaced like glimpses of the monsters in horror movies.

The acting problem was to be in, and sustain, a state of mental chaos, madness, and fear for two hours.

I did my best. But life was beginning to imitate art.

After the show one night, a bunch of us piled into the car and headed back to New York. Someone turned on the radio. We pulled over immediately. The Jersey Turnpike was at a standstill. People were sitting in idling cars and trucks listening as they may have been that night in October 1938 when Orson Welles' Mercury Theater scared America into heart attacks and car crashes, as he and his merry radio players simulated the landing of a spaceship filled with hostile aliens from Mars in *The War of the Worlds*. It had been pretend reality.

The car radio said, "Good evening, my fellow citizens. This government, as promised, has maintained the closest surveillance of the Soviet military build-up on the island of Cuba. Within the past week, unmistakable evidence has established the fact that a series of offensive missile sites is now in preparation on that imprisoned island. The purpose of these bases can be none other than to provide a nuclear strike capability against the Western Hemisphere. Each of the missiles, in short, is capable of striking Washington, DC. In addition, jet bombers capable of carrying nuclear weapons capable of striking any city in North America are now being uncrated and assembled on Cuba." It was President John F. Kennedy.

And it was reality. Nuclear war was here. World War III.

Nikita Khrushchev was like Caligula. They both wielded intense calcula-
tion in their insanity. We were trying to bring life to these insanities onstage,
and now we sat in an icy car, the lovely harvest moon rising, listening to the
tense, staccato words of our young president.

The fear grew like a virus in the car. If Washington, why not New York?
If New York, then Princeton! When? Why? The hate for Russian fear-madness
grew. We all felt . . . what? Felt like volunteering for the army? Not possible. We
were too old, were too gay, or had former Communist Party membership. I was
still an Army Reserve officer, a first lieutenant. If I did all the work, I would be
Captain Luckinbill soon. I would be called up.

As the report ended, cars pulled away, everyone speeding home, grim-
faced, to batten down the hatches. No one who heard that broadcast doubted
that Kennedy had to do this and that this would be the actual war of the
worlds. The actors were sobbing into handkerchiefs, wiping away tears as we
came to Times Square, where people were congregating, watching the TVs in
store windows.

I got out of the car and walked. The moon hung over the silent, silver
Hudson. *Caligula* seemed far away and totally present. Absolutely real and true.
Camus was a prophet. No drama, just life against death, every tick of every
clock.

Nothing to do but play the play as reality. *Vive il teatro*!

By 2022, the Russians were testing the world again. The calculating
Vladimir Putin, acting emperor of Russia, was playing Caligula, inviting the
death of the earth and its people.

SCENE: New York

I saw a notice posted in a newspaper for a position with the US Foreign Service
doing good in those trouble spots in the world. It was a General Service (GS)
job, and the salary bumped up, regular as toast in a toaster. The retirement
benefits were assured. The work seemed valuable, romantic even. Maybe I was
ready—again—to get a real career? The theater was iffy; the movies seemed
impossible. I wanted something safe. I was tired of being good and then being
unemployed. I was tired of the trudging and the inconsistency.

I sat at a desk in the old customs building in the Village off Christopher
Street, wondering if this was the building Herman Melville had worked in as a
Customs Inspector after *Moby Dick* failed to sell. I was waiting for the guy at the
front of the room to say, "Go." There were ten or twelve of us, widely separated

McCarter Theater, Princeton, New Jersey. Playing Caligula by Albert Camus during the Cuban Missile Crisis. Art imitates life.

in the airy room, about to take a timed test as part of our application to join the United States Foreign Service.

I was ready and confident. I had always been interested in US history and politics, and I read a lot. I had worked in the US Embassies in Khartoum and Rome for long periods in the last couple of years, and I thought I could figure out this test. Arms moved in concert, swooping down, swinging open the first page of the virgin USFS exam. Pencils lifted, and we were off.

I failed the test by one point.

I failed Current Events. I hadn't read the daily newspapers cover to cover, all seven NY dailies, because they were all on strike.

Twenty-four-hour cable news channels didn't exist yet.

I could retake it in six months.

I read every newspaper and magazine in existence every day for six months. I read history, civics, and politics. I took the test again.

I passed.

I got a call from an unnamed government bureau (the CIA) requesting an interview at my convenience. I went to the meeting in an anonymous down-town building, just another drab, brown-gray office, gray elevator, gray halls, gray doors.

Inside the office were two men, both, you guessed it, gray. Middle-aged, washed-out, weatherworn gray faces, smiles pasted on like faded flyers on a kiosk for a show already over that you didn't want to see.

They opened folders. The older guy asked questions. The younger guy took notes and maybe ran the reel-to-reel tape machine under the desk with his foot.

"So, you want to work for the US government?"

"The Foreign Service."

"Good. Would you be amenable to any other service or assignments?"

"Well, no. What do you mean?"

"There are parts that may interest you more."

"Like what?"

"The United States Information Agency, for instance. Part of State, but, as you know, USIA runs libraries . . ."

"No, I don't want . . ."

". . . and produces films, shows, radio. That is our main means of informing the world that democracy works. Not our only means, but the most powerful at this time. You don't have to be a diplomat, that's all."

"Okay."

"Good. Now, there's a couple of things: If you are going to be with us, we need to know your vulnerabilities." He proceeded to ask me a series of invasive questions about my personal life. It was outrageous. I declined to answer.

They stood. Smiled. I smiled. And I walked down the gray hall to the gray elevator and outside into the gathering twilight, thinking that I had just given up my chance to work for President John Kennedy.

I called my answering service. "You have an audition," they said.

"With whom?" I asked.

"Whitehead-Stevens."

Oh my God!

Robert Whitehead was in partnership with Roger Stevens, and they were the finest of the American theater. They produced classics and contemporaries and did it right. I didn't know these gentlemen, but I was about to find out why they had their reputation.

I was warmly welcomed into the backstage of the Anta Theater. I was the only actor in sight. Usually, at a casting call, ten or even thirty actors of your type would be lined up, nervously pacing, waiting to show their wares in the dark, anonymous auditorium where the producers and directors sat far enough back to be almost invisible.

I was brought on stage into the light. The auditorium was dark. The stage manager turned to the dark house with a warm smile and said, "Ladies and gentlemen, this is Laurence Luckinbill."

There was a stirring out there. It was palpable, thrilling, as when you really walk out on a stage to face an audience, ready to tell your story, and all eyes turn to you. Programs stop rustling and the silence of attention flows out toward you, enveloping you in a powerful wave of warm expectance.

Just then, a man in a tweed overcoat bounded smartly out of the dark and took the steps in a leap. He was tall, lithe, narrow-faced, sharp-eyed, and intent. He smiled a generous and welcoming smile.

"My name is Noel Willman," he said in a clipped, posh British accent. "We are pleased you're here. Will you please read the part of William Roper with me?"

Oh my God! For the director to read with you . . . !

He stood aside so I could be seen by those in the dark. "We'll begin with your first scene, where you reveal your lifelong contest with your father-in-law over religion and morals."

And he winked. Instantly, I went from apprehension, audition terror, to fun. This is a play. We are playing here; it's a contest. It is indescribable what that twinkle in Willman's eye did for me.

Willman was known as a stern disciplinarian, but he was also an actor, and this play had been one of his great successes as a director. So I was prepared to give him exactly what he demanded—clarity, sharpness, pace, intelligence.

I read Roper. Willman read all the others, projecting his voice effortlessly with a clipped, clear, neutral pattern. I was inspired to create the William Roper I felt he was—sincere, honest, and utterly passionate about God, his marriage, and morality. I was Roper—I am Roper. And I had been given the secret code to the character by the director himself: "A lifelong contest over faith, religion, and morals." A grand direction.

The scene ended.

Willman smiled at me and went back into the dark theater. There was a brief conference. Out of the dark came Robert Whitehead, the producer. He was smiling. He shook my hand and so did Willman. Whitehead said, "You have the part. Welcome to *A Man For All Seasons*."

Oh my God! Oh my God. Oh my God!

My first Broadway show!

The former Foreign Service aspirant went on stage in New York at the Anta Theater on Fifty-Second Street in the late summer. Paul Schofield finished his brilliant run in New York, then reprised it in the magnificent Zinneman film. I was there at the end. He seemed tired. But after doing many long Broadway runs, I understand an actor must reinvent his character for each performance, eight shows a week.

We were the first national touring company. The Broadway show continued, and after playing as an interim cast at the Anta for a week, we began a fourteen-month first class tour.

A few months later, I got a letter from the US Department of State congratulating me for being one of the few who had passed the complicated exam. Apparently, they had approved me despite my lack of answers. I was now vetted and qualified for a position with the USIA. Here was an opportunity to change lives. Freedom was real.

Once again, a choice. I could quit the theater and pursue another interesting occupation. The USIA was staffed with intriguing people—journalists and media people who wrote and produced shows designed to counter Soviet propaganda and to showcase the US as a sane, open society where immigrants are welcome. Here in America, decent life was open to all. But I was already employed in a show that was exactly the type I wanted. I put off making a career-changing decision.

* * *

Traveling across the country and playing great theaters, I began reading American history. The American theater had grown in the eighteenth and nineteenth centuries. I built a show called *The Yankee Vaudeville*. It was a series of monologues taken from the earliest American plays. They featured early archetypes of the nation's characters—the Yankee, the noble savage, the wild riverman, the pioneer, the big-city sophisticates of New York, Boston, and Philadelphia—in plays that were not like the British plays that the early settlers had banned as works of the devil. These new works were expressions of an early innocence and exuberance; we were discovering the challenges of our new land.

Our American Cousin introduced Jonathan, a shrewd, original American bumpkin. This was the play Lincoln was enjoying in Ford's Theater when he was assassinated by a member of the most famous acting family in America—Junius Brutus Booth and his sons, Edwin and John Wilkes. It was a prophetic foreshadowing of the sick, corrupt poison of the diseases called nationalism and populism that threaten to destroy objective truth and the hope of democracy. We still see this in this second decade of the new millennium.

I performed my forty-five-minute show on our off days in the big cities. Edith Dappert, the agent who had booked the Catholic University Players, Inc., knew all the schools and other venues that would pay fees, two to five hundred dollars for forty-five minutes of early American scenes and fast costume changes. I built a theater trunk on wheels with compartments for costume pieces. I added poles I could pull out of the top that became a coat rack or a flagpole with a square piece of white cloth I could disappear behind to change costumes. I thought of my only theater experience growing up, The Clare Tree Major Players. They mentored me for a quarter of a century after seeing them. I was earning three hundred dollars a week in *A Man For All Seasons*, and I added two hundred or more each week that I booked my own show. I was an entrepreneur.

I became bewitched by a woman in the company. I was so in love. She was in love with a mysterious older man she couldn't have, because he was in a bad marriage but wouldn't leave it. She hurt. I hurt.

I pursued her attention in every way I knew how. I pined, I sorrowed, I sent poems and presents. She fled every overture but made love with me and with others when she chose. I spoke of my distress to an older actress in the company, and she spat in contempt. "Propinquity!" she said. "The theater! You're always too close to her in the play, and it turns into this. Forget her. Get away!"

To break the attachment, I had one-night affairs with female fans in the towns we played, and with actresses and movie stars of another era, in other shows playing in town. But I couldn't have the one I thought I wanted. H. L. Mencken wrote, "Democracy is the theory that the common people know what they want, and they deserve to get it, good and hard!" I got it.

My bewitchment—attachment—continued off and on until, one night, her perfidy frustrated me so much that I slapped her. I had never done such a thing before. I shocked myself, apologized instantly, and started to leave. She grabbed me. She cried, "No! It's what I deserve." She threw me off the couch and we made love on the bare floor, burning each other with mutual self-loathing. It was tragic love. Ridiculous. Tears streamed from us both. It was over.

It was the beginning of a real and painful education in love itself. I didn't know then that life is a kaleidoscope, one turn and everything changes. Everything is impermanent, and the imitations of love appear like mirages in the desert. Do mirages know they are not real? It takes karma to find true love, but what the heck is karma?

Like Shakespeare, *A Man for All Seasons* taught me that a classic is a situation, characters, and words that never grow stale or dry of nuance and meaning, scenes that can never be mastered entirely, even if you think you have given the exactly correct interpretation or been fully present. Noel Willman's direction was unfailing, crisp, intelligent, unsentimental—ideas first, emotions follow. Robert Bolt's script is a true realization of the reality of the Spirit at work in human affairs. Thomas More, in Bolt's belief, was a true hero. The story depicts flawed, venal, cruel, confused, loving, furious, all-too-human humans reacting to an incarnation of Spirit in Henry VIII's court. It's not the gospel of Jesus Christ. It's the story of one of his true disciples.

The opening night of this tour was at the outdoor Greek theater in Griffith Park in the Hollywood Hills. We had the Broadway set by Motley, a beautiful stairway that curved down in a single graceful arc from stage left to center stage. My entrance was down that stair into Sir Thomas' home. As Will Roper, I was in high dudgeon (the usual driving gear) and wished to have a dispute with my father-in-law. I launched myself down the stairs and ran into a wall of fog so dense and foul smelling it was as if a wet, dirty horse blanket had been thrown on my face where it stuck. I kept going from sheer inertia, but I lost momentum. I glanced down at the stair glistening with condensation and thought, *Don't slip.* And my mind left the play and vanished into my own present danger. Fog! In Hollywood? Nobody ever mentioned that. Los Angeles was sun and oranges.

I ran down toward my father-in-law yelling "Sir Thomas!" and hit the fog rising off the Hollywood Hills. I couldn't see; I was going on pure nerve as I clattered down. "Sir Thomas!" I yelled again. But my mind was occupied not with the scene I was entering, but with not falling on my face. As I got to the bottom, I stopped short. Sir Thomas was coming toward me, patient and ready for the usual argument with his zealous but loving, earnest son-in-law.

I had no words, no thoughts. I had completely gone up. Bill Roderick, the British actor playing Thomas, looked at me curiously and said his line, and then he said my line for me. Again, nothing. I was frozen to the bottom step, center stage, in full light, in front of six thousand Angelenos and, no doubt, hundreds of movie agents, directors, and producers striking me off their "good actor, must-see" lists.

The panic got worse. Bill said his next line and then my response. I dimly recognized my own line as he said it, but I was someone struck dumb. Unfortunately, not someone invisible. All I knew was I was a complete ass and a total failure at everything I prided myself I had learned.

Bill suddenly moved across the stage in front of me, toward stage right. It was totally unexpected. What? No! My brain screamed, *that's wrong!* He's supposed to move downstage, and I'm supposed to follow him. And with that sudden conscious thought, I returned to the present, to the now of the scene and the play. The be-here-now that is the essence of acting—being here now, in the four walls of Thomas More's house on the Thames River in London with its fog, where now I saw not Bill Roderick, the lovely, kind man, but the Lord Chancellor of Henry VIII's court, my father-in-law. And I had a bone to pick with him. My words came out in a burst as I leaped downstage to where we ought to be. Sir Thomas followed swiftly, smiling his dry smile, and we, and the play, were all right again.

He saved both me and the scene, and I jumped into Roper's story with the renewed energy of fury, as if it were the first time I'd ever said those words. There was no fog, no twelve thousand eyes and ears on me, no Hollywood, and no agents. There was no me. There was Roper and Thomas.

What a splendid lesson. Afterward, I profusely apologized and thanked Bill for saving me. He said simply, "Kinesthetics. We learn our parts by our physical positions, by the blocking of the movements in a scene, willy-nilly, y'see? And if you dry, (the British term for what we call "going up") the antidote is simply to change the blocking and *poof!* The words and thoughts return. They were never gone, y'see, but in the exigencies of playing, sometimes one's brain gets stuck. It's perfectly normal. It was a bloody fog, wasn't it?"

I have been grateful ever since that night for my mentor William Roderick.

All came to a full stop on November 22, 1963. We were in Indianapolis. The stage manager woke me up. He said there would be no performance that night. President John Kennedy had just been shot by an unknown assailant and had died in Dallas. The tour survived as the country mourned. America has felt less safe ever since.

* * *

I had done important leading roles at the McCarter Theater in Princeton. Some people in New York were impressed. I made the rounds as usual. I changed agents. I told my first agent, Lillian Arnold, that I needed someone better connected. She had come to seem out of touch, unable to take me farther up the ladder. My ice-cold decision shamed me. I told her over the phone that I was going with a big agency. She was a disabled woman who sat all day on her daybed like a benevolent and determined queen, with her pad and pen, working her rotary phones. She took my leaving stoically. It shook me. It might have secretly devastated her. I didn't want to find out.

I had stepped far along a particular road—and not the road less taken. Who and what was this person I was becoming? I tried not to hear the last line of Frost's poem: "And that has made all the difference." I was on the road of doing what was best for me. Lillian had spotted me behind a crepe hair beard and old age makeup when I was twenty-five and thought I could be a leading man. Now, I fired her because I was convinced she was too small. I believed the big agency operatives who told me they could move my career into the big time. In some respects, they were right. Lillian was a lone operator who had a hard time getting big casting people on the phone. I was one of her biggest clients and still a non-entity everybody thought would make it. Today, I ask myself, *make what?*

SCENE: New York

I grew up in a place that never felt like home. It was full of fear. We never dared to express ourselves. It was a small town where nothing could ever get bigger.

New York is made up of many small towns inside a vast city, and I had begun to make my own small space within it. The feel of the city had gotten to be second nature. I relied on its energy to give me juice. Looking up into a sky framed by skyscrapers made me want to reach upward for something higher, something better. I wanted to fly.

New York was constant human motion and emotion. For New Yorkers, the chaos had order. Like jungle denizens, they evaluated signs, symbols, and noises as indicators of safety, danger, humor, entertainment, joy, and incredulity. Nothing seemed out of bounds: the almost nude cowboy with a guitar, the guy with the camera who talked young women into letting him film their bare breasts in broad daylight. It was astounding street life. You could break through the bramble of tourists in Times Square and see a couple of guys beating on upturned plastic five-gallon paint buckets—creating a Latin rhythm that makes a grandmother in an old fur coat stop to sway her hips in a tease. The guys on steel pans playing a Caribbean reggae version of Beethoven's "Ode to Joy" during Christmastide on any corner where the cops let them set up. The three-card monte guys. The guy who screamed that the world was ending—every day! The guy who danced waltzes, cha-chas, meringues, and sambas with his tape deck blaring on the sidewalk and his stuffed-cloth girlfriend in his arms with a fixed, pretty smile on her flour bag face and her cloth feet tied to the tops of her partner's shoes.

These were ordinary people in the anonymity of the great hurtling crowds, living their lives in the open, walking in the pulsing mass or stopping in front of you suddenly to argue, or decide where to eat, or what show to go to, or just to talk, or kiss, or threaten each other as if they were absolutely alone. Speaking a hundred languages, wearing

schmattes from ragged jeans and t-shirts to suits and ties, muumuus, dashikis, burkas, or somber, black nineteenth-century gear seen in a shtetl a hundred years ago. Just another New York personage with a dream to open a business, push dresses on a rack in the Garment District, haul a cart loaded with hot dogs and knishes toward a Midtown street corner where you were allowed to sell your goods from daylight to dark, slathering buns with mustard in the humid, stifling heat of summer, or in the Christmastide freezing cold, baking chestnuts on an open fire, and selling scarves, caps, gloves, and umbrellas, Or used books—always books.

To walk through the sounds, the smells, the humming life of the world in microcosm, and arrive at your theater, say hello to the crew guys outside in the street sitting on the red *y's* of the fire department standpipes, smoking, talking union business, kibitzing or kidding each other, and then, to open the stage door, say hello to the old doorman in his niche where he was born and will, no doubt, in another century or two, die, then to step into the dark of the backstage, suddenly blinded, but as your eyes adjust, to realize that you are in your own home, your only true home—it's a feeling so deep that now, even at my age, writing this in my home, I get a pure, not sentimental, frisson. The hair rises on the back of my neck and tears come, stinging my eyes. The best part of my life, a dream realized, gravity defied—*I was flying!*

* * *

After *A Man for All Seasons*, Robert Whitehead hired me again for *Beekman Place*. I was a young swain to the ingénue. Madeline Carroll and Fernand Gravet were the leads—famous, elegant film people from the '30s, now older, but still magical. It was a boulevard play written and directed by the marvelous Samuel Taylor, and I had to learn to be elegant.

Madeline Carroll departed for personal reasons, and the lovely Arlene Francis came in, and I gained a remarkable friend. Another lifelong friend was George Coulouris, the well-known British actor who played the heavy in this light comedy. He told me his reason for doing the play was to update his Hollywood film career and his Screen Actors Guild medical insurance. This was heresy to me, and I told him that. He laughed. He was so good at just being himself on stage or in film. He knew what he was doing and did it expertly, with great élan and zero angst. He knew well that acting is play. If it's not fun, why do it? Another mentor. I had a lot to learn.

I couldn't see then that I was very self-aware. I had become more starkly ambitious about succeeding and less happy-go-lucky. I had actually been willing to quit the theater to become a Foreign Service officer, but I didn't. I had started to give myself a certain number of years to make it or quit. Why was I so lacking in faith but, at the same time, so full of bravado?

This harmed me, as I now see clearly. At the time, I was just a clever guy hedging his bets, but there came a time when it turned on me and turned me inside out.

SCENE: Lincoln Center Repertory, Washington Square

I've learned over much time and many blind decisions that the only thing that stays with you when you know you are close to the effective end of your career is the knowledge that the projects to which you lent your energy and life force as a professional—and your good name or reputation as a performer—were artifacts of social justice, the fair distribution of wealth, opportunity, and privilege within society. The theater is about exposing wrong and promoting right. It seeks truth, elevates individuality, and nurtures community. It is liberal and progressive. In a sense, the entire history of the theater is a moral arc bending toward justice. How wonderful that the theater has always been tagged by the retrogressive right as disreputable and dangerous to morals, possibly seditious to public order, and somehow low class. When in power, the GOP always works to wipe the National Endowment for the Arts off the map, as a certain subset of Americans fears art of all kinds. There are anti-human humans. They take every opportunity to diss art or make it go away. I say, good! Just try to get rid of us. We're the roaches in your cupboards, sinks, beds, and faces, and we'll be here long after you're gone.

Art is holy. I felt it only as a certain Presence when I was at a play that filled me with such high emotion I could barely keep from exploding. Or when I read

My mother.
San Rafael, California.

My father.
San Rafael, California.

Mom and Dad, toasting, "To Life" . . . for a change.

something in a book that made me want to climb into the hero's skin to replace him and be swept away into his adventures. It was a presence that left no room for the petty concerns of local life such as school or dating or any of the lifeless jobs I had to do to earn a few bucks. It was . . . it was . . . I couldn't put it into words. It was consuming.

I finally saw it objectively at *Man of La Mancha*. As Richard Kiley sang "The Impossible Dream," my father put his face into his hands and wept. My mother put her work-worn hand on his shoulder. It was beautiful, the two of them at their first Broadway play, and there was "love among the ruins" somehow. They felt what I have always felt but never knew how to tell them. They had allowed the art into their hearts. They had suspended disbelief and believed. That was the first moment I knew how much I loved my parents. An impossible dream, that's what had always challenged me. Escape to it. Fly!

It was hoped Molière and William Ball could prevent the demise of the original Lincoln Center Repertory Company. Unfortunately, it was just another example of the hit or flop syndrome that affects the American theater.

I had seen Bill's production of *Six Characters in Search of an Author*, Luigi Pirandello's masterpiece. One image has never left me. At the end, the director of the acting troupe, leaving the empty stage after a disrupted rehearsal, reaches up and hits the hanging rehearsal light in irritated disgust, a rejection of a wasted day listening to six strangers—the characters—tell a family horror story that screwed up his "important" rehearsal of a trivial, commercial comedy. He slaps the green-shaded light hard, and it swings across the stage in an arc, lighting up the far wall of the empty set, and then back, to the opposite wall, to reveal the destroyed family—the six characters crouched against the wall, still present, indisputably honest, trapped, and forced forever to search for someone who will believe their story and feel the terror they live with. This revelatory accidental light swing was Bill's penetration to the depth of despair of real people who desperately need to be seen and heard, to connect, but who are denied this by a trivial, busy world. We are the six characters. It was a coup de théâtre that unlocked a piece of the puzzle of life itself, the tragedy of misconnection, humiliation, blame and rejection—a metaphor for human tragedies unseen in our blind pursuit of money, success and status, until revealed by divine synchromysticism. I wanted to work with a man who could illuminate life's pain so brilliantly.

The Lincoln Center Repertory Company had started with extremely high hopes, an impossible dream. It was to represent the best of the legitimate American theater. It would represent New York City, the greatest city on earth. It would represent the United States. And it would prove that, among the great Western civilizations, American theater folks could build a national cultural institution to rival the ancient Globe Theater of Shakespeare's day and its present incarnation in Stratford-upon-Avon, The Royal Shakespeare Theater, and the Royal National Theater in London. We would build a theater to stand shoulder-to-shoulder with La Comédie-Française in Paris, the Berliner Ensemble in Germany, the Moscow Art Theater, even the Kabuki and Noh theaters, the conveyances of the culture of Japan. Lincoln Center would challenge them all.

We had the playwrights, we had the directors, we had . . . Broadway. But Broadway was not a good guide. The world's classic theaters were permanent, subsidized entities protected and funded by governments, private consortia, or foundations. They maintained a repertory of national theatrical literature. The theaters were part of the national and municipal identification of each country. The US had no tradition of subsidy. The theater was a commercial commodity. Productions lived and died by ticket sales. Without support, an otherwise good production of a world classic on an American stage could not survive. No permanence, just product. Please the public, or get lost—the rule of the market.

America is enormous in scale and heterogeneous. The countries with an old and indigenous national literature of theater are composed of populations that largely share similar characteristics and race memories. All had traditions of theater going back hundreds of years. Our government was not obliged to support theater as a part of national identity.

So, the Lincoln Center Repertory Company was meant to prove that an American repertory infused with an international repertory of theater experiences could survive and thrive on private subsidy and ticket sales—a typical American compromise. Success succeeds.

It failed. There were not enough hits to support the flops. Bill Ball was given an impossible mission: revive *Tartuffe*, a classic comedy by Molière, and prove that American audiences would respond and choose to validate the mission.

The cast was terrifically talented with a wide range of acting styles and experience, and we were treated as if we were bound to do something remarkable. Bill trusted his actors' intentions. I was to play Damis, the hotheaded son of Orgon and the first in the family to discover that Tartuffe was not a pious, godly preacher but rather an immoral creature who lusted after my stepmother. I eavesdrop and make a big scene about my discovery.

As the audience was being seated, I crept through an under-stage tunnel and climbed into a coffin-shaped box, which was on stage as a banquette in the salon of my father's house. I had to crouch in the box, legs under me, ready to throw open the box lid and leap out at the cue.

I'm claustrophobic. I can't go into a closed MRI, tight hallway, or elevator. Bill convinced me I could do this. I could become fearless and lose my claustrophobia. It would be worth it, because when I sprang out of the piece of furniture Tartuffe and my stepmother were sitting on, the audience would go nuts. So I lay, choking back the fear that I would die in that box, sweating, holding my sword ready, and . . . *now!*

I came up and out as if I had been hurled by an explosion. I landed on my feet, sword in the attack position, yelling at the top of my voice. I was also yelling with relief that I had survived claustrophobia.

We were too busy in our long rehearsal to consider that the Lincoln Center Repertory (Downtown) had already run into the buzz saws of criticism and a diminution of trust or faith in the project by its backers, who had somehow believed that, with all the best commercial names involved, the giant ark would just float. We didn't know they had already lost the spirit of subsidy. The *Tartuffe* company was the new kid on the block. We opened, and *Tartuffe* was the biggest hit of the inaugural season.

Robert Whitehead, Elia Kazan, Bobby Lewis, and Harold Clurman had respectively done brilliant and dogged work. But the unfamiliar idea of repertory and the particular mix of plays in the first season was already losing traction. And though the same grand, sixteen-acre arts plaza uptown was falling behind on construction, it slowly became apparent that downtown had already lost the game.

Naturalist Alfred Wallace was a generous and moral man who discovered that evolution happens because species adapt to their environments. Where are we now by that metric? Hit? Or flop? In 1856, Wallace wrote, "We are endowed with intellectual and moral powers superfluous to evolutionary requirements." Then why haven't we used them? This will be the last word for our species: Dead and Gone, but with Money in the Bank.

We played six successful months of *Tartuffe*, a joyful time. I believed I was truly an actor in the best New York theater ever. Then, one night, it all dissolved like the Wicked Witch in *The Wizard of Oz*.

I wrote the epitaph for the Lincoln Center Rep company in a piece published in a new, daring newspaper created by actor Ronald Rand, called—fearlessly—*The Soul of the American Actor*.

SCENE: New York

A group of us gathered to read an up-and-coming young writer's new play, a way for a young playwright and his agents to hear the work. It was flattering to be asked. It meant I was an "in" actor.

At the reading was an extraordinary young actress, quite beautiful and very young, maybe eighteen or nineteen. We kept catching each other's eye and laughing for no reason. The play was not particularly holding our interest.

After the reading, for some reason, the young lady and I walked up the block for a drink at the Carnegie Tavern on the backside of the enormous Carnegie Hall building. Her name was Robin Strasser, and I liked her intelligence and sharp wit. She seemed to have the same silly bone I had. We got on very well.

And we parted. I left her on the street to get her own taxi, as she pointed out to me later. Yes, I did. I didn't think a hip, young New York woman needed to be escorted to a cab early on a spring evening on Fifty-Sixth Street. And I had somewhere else I had to be. Uncaring? Ungentlemanly? Ignorant of manners or a warning bell?

SCENE: Pittsburgh, Pennsylvania

Bill Ball refused to give up. He decreed his repertory company would not be in New York. Pittsburgh had agreed to host the new American Conservatory Theater Company (ACT) in the respected Pittsburgh Playhouse complex. The town was vibrant, the company was strong, and Bill's New York reputation was glittering. I was made a charter member of ACT after *Tartuffe* ended at the Anta Theater and the Lincoln Center Repertory Company was dissolved and let out to pasture.

My three roles were The Son in *Six Characters in Search of an Author*, Edmund in *King Lear*, and Biff in *Death of a Salesman*. Robin had also been hired to act with the company. By then, we were a couple.

In the first season at ACT, Bill wanted a forty-five-minute *King Lear*. I was onstage rehearsing the bastard, Edmund. Bill, sinuous as a python and smiling like one with large, innocent blue eyes, was beside me whispering, "Make this the fastest, Lear-est thing you've ever said on any stage. I'll time it. At the end, find yourself upstage at the hanging rope. Climb the rope into the flies. We'll get you off."

I began *King Lear*, act I, scene II:

> Thou, Nature, art my goddess. To thy law
> My services are bound. Wherefore should I
> Stand in the plague of custom, and permit
> The curiosity of nations to deprive me
> For that I am some twelve or fourteen moonshines
> Lag of a brother? why "bastard"?

I draped myself on the stage floor to read the letter that will destroy my brother, Edgar, the legitimate son. I felt raw, ready to fight. Bill's face was beside my ear, a moon in my peripheral vision, smiling a cold, white, enigmatic Mona Lisa smile.

> When my dimensions are as well compact,
> My mind as generous and my shape as true
> As honest madam's issue? Why brand they us
> With "base," with "baseness," "bastardy," "base," "base,"
> Who, in the lusty stealth of nature, take
> More composition and fierce quality
> Than doth within a dull, stale, tired bed
> Go to th' creating a whole tribe of fops
> Got 'tween asleep and wake? Well then,
> Legitimate Edgar, I must have your land.

And Bill whispered, clicking his stopwatch, "Now, up and get ready."

> Our father's love is to the bastard Edmund
> As to th' legitimate. Fine word, "legitimate."

Bill said, "Now! Start now to the rope."

> Well, my legitimate, if this letter speed
> And my invention thrive, Edmund the base
> Shall top th' legitimate. I grow, I prosper.

Bill shouted, "Now!"

I tucked the letter into my tights. I was aroused. I ran my hands up my body in a shiver. I turned and leaped up the stage as I proclaimed the final line in the monologue, "Now, gods, stand up for bastards!"

I seized the swinging rope and mounted it, encircling it with my legs, the thick hemp at my crotch, and, arm over arm, attacked up the rope, ascending like an assassin invading a castle bedroom, as the rope was hauled swiftly up and out of sight.

"Forty seconds," Bill yelled. "Good. Try it again."

* * *

The first season of ACT in Pittsburgh was a big deal. The assembly was composed of a splendid company of actors and directors, all there to make their mark in the American theater and prove Bill Ball's acute eye for finding unusual talent as well as his daring to search out similar spirits who wanted the repertory life.

The first show was *Six Characters in Search of an Author*, a redo of Bill's production I'd seen the year before *Tartuffe*, which made me understand he was a theater genius. I played The Son, a hidden, repressed, traumatized young man who was angry but afraid to speak. I imagined such a person might stutter badly. I found moments in the action when my emotions might block my speech, and I created a painful stutter. In my family's mobile, my psychological place was one of the pieces that got hit most often or was left swinging in the air, helpless. I pushed inhibition to the breaking point. How difficult would it be to get a sentence out? I found brackets, the places in the story where The Son's need to speak is triggered by others in his family and causes him to react violently.

How do you construct the reality of a character like The Son? For me, it leaped from an accidental and seemingly trivial connection with his clothing. I was given a black, long-sleeved, worn turtleneck sweater. I would be anonymous, almost invisible. The garment was from the original New York production. Ah, yes! This shirt had seen, heard, and been a part of terrible doings like I had. At a dress rehearsal, I saw a rip at the end of a sleeve, a ragged place where the threads were hanging loose. Something clicked. I saw myself—poor, neglected, isolated. How ragged my feelings were, and how unfair it was. I had a hot flash of emotion. I was sorry for myself, embarrassed for my family, ashamed for us and of us. And I felt an implosion of fury so powerful that I couldn't speak. I couldn't get a word out.

I held on to that. The tear in my shirt proved I was real, this was honest and terrible, and I had to do something about it. So, I unleashed my terrible version of my misery on my family in the story. It was excruciating, embarrassing, and fury-inducing—for them and for me.

The stutter became organic, not a shtick, but a spontaneous part of me. Its source was behind a red-hot door locked tight to keep me from exploding and killing.

At ACT, I got my second chance to get Biff Loman right. My father in *Salesman*, *Six Characters*, and *Lear* was the same actor, Richard Dysart, a bluff, grouchy nice guy. He was the guy you had to like because even if he did bad stuff, it was a fuck-up, not an evil plan. So, I had to find reasons to dislike my friend.

Acting is really good pretending. Acting is safe, harmless to the actor, the acted upon, the other players, and the audience. But don't mistake the role for yourself. You are just a conduit. The better you do it, the more anonymous you should become. This is the opposite of what the outside world—the strange tribe called fans—wants. They want to subsume themselves in the magic and make the actor into the parts he plays, to make an actor into that golem, a celebrity. This is common. Now, actors are not considered guildsmen who labor to turn a piece of human material into something finished, beautiful, and valuable, but rather they are creatures. Gods or goddesses. Idols to be touched for good luck or self-transformation. Contact is somehow connection.

I did not escape that trap—fame, the lust to be famous, the hope to become a name. I was beginning to think it was essential to success as an artist. It was a notion, if not yet a goal. A step out onto thin ice hiding deep, freezing water. Would it hold me?

* * *

Cecil Smith, the theater and television critic of the *Los Angeles Times*, came to Pittsburgh to look over this ambitious company. He was an avuncular Westerner (and my wife Lucie's uncle) who later became my mentor and a man I loved dearly and wished to be my own real uncle. His presence in Pittsburgh, the stories he filed in the *LA Times*, and the powerful press support he pulled into being for ACT, like Prospero making magic, helped put ACT on the cultural map as a first-class theater. But to make a lasting conservatory theater was a life's work.

Bill Ball was always kind to me, but he was very tactile, always touching, always stroking. And it always seemed possible for it to become sexual. It created an uncomfortable atmosphere. I loved him for his brilliant talent and willingness to abet and applaud creativity. But I was far too much of a lone cactus in my own desert to be comfortable with Bill. So when Robin and I were invited to stay with ACT, we declined and went back to New York to start over.

Ultimately, Pittsburgh's ACT failed. But Bill's theater was very successful in San Francisco. For a long time, it was supported very well, subsidized by San Francisco's merchants and wealthy donors. But exhaustion eventually crept in.

In 1986, I was traveling the US while researching an article for the *New York Times* Arts and Leisure section to find out what a living wage would be for artists. This was an extension of my previous piece on the relevance of actors and theater to society if those actors were consistently undervalued financially. I interviewed Bill in his office in the Geary Theater in San Francisco. He was in trouble with his board—money troubles. Bill seemed utterly exhausted. He said, "All I do now is raise money. I don't direct, act, or think creatively. I've become nothing but a moneyman." I found it hard to believe Bill's vitality had been so sapped. The creative part of him that was truly his life was missing in action.

That year, Bill left his three-decade dream behind and went to Hollywood to work in television. Five years later, he was found dead in his apartment. No cause of death was announced, but I learned from members of ACT that he had taken his own life.

Without Bill, there never would have been an ACT. Is this the price that capitalism exacts in our country?

Art is long, life is short. Hail and farewell, William Ball.

SCENE: New York

I was studying with Uta Hagen at the HB Studio. I went to Uta because she was the best teacher in New York, according to the actors I thought were the best. The credential for *best* to me was simple: actors who I believed in every role they played. They were not all method actors. But Uta's students weren't "indicators," meaning performers who demonstrate only a skin-deep, two-dimensional construct of a person and cannot move you. They can look right and sound right, but they lack soul.

Stanislavsky taught that acting comes from inside. It is alive, simply listening and responding appropriately to other actors in a scene. *Inside* meant using one's own experiences, finding and using all the emotions you felt in your life. Affective memory is the key. You analyze a script by identifying what the character is living through each moment and discovering an analog in your own life. You search for what you have felt and experienced and infuse that feeling into the character in the scene. You find the reality of a character through your own authentic feelings.

It's a tricky process. Uta explained it one day. An actor stood in the arena in Uta's classroom. She was sniffling and wiping tears. She had launched into Lady Macbeth—the "out, damned spot, out" scene in which a mad Lady Macbeth sleepwalks, reliving her part in the murder of the king, Duncan. She is hallucinating, trying to scrub the king's blood from her clean hands. It's a really tough scene in which to find your own experience. This young actress had given up halfway through the scene and burst into self-humiliated tears. The tears were real; her Lady Macbeth was not.

Uta sat at her tiny table in front of the audience of actors on risers. We auditors were experiencing mixed feelings—sympathy and irritation. Maybe some women in the room were thinking, "I could do that better." And the men had a certain fear: "I hope I don't break down like that when I get up there."

No one feared Uta, but everyone feared failure.

Uta yanked her cigarette out and jetted a stream of smoke from the side of her mouth. She stubbed out the butt furiously. "What are you feeling?"

The girl said, too loudly, "Nothing! I can't feel anything. I can't do this scene. I've never killed anyone. I can't imagine killing anyone. Can anyone do this?" She was certain her breakdown was the fault of the impossibility of the scene rather than an inability to find and feel the passion.

"Huh," Uta said abruptly. "Listen." She turned her chair so we could all see. "I got on the bus this morning. I had my notes, books, some scripts, all this crap I carry around every day." She flung a hand at the table piled with manuscripts, books, a carton of her ever-present cigarettes. Her stuff. "I had both arms full. It was raining and I had to run to get the bus. I had forgotten to button my fucking raincoat. I had left the house and forgotten my key. I had to get the spare key. The door locked behind me. I ran. The bus stopped for me. I got on. It was crammed full; every seat was taken. Wet people were standing and looking at me. I'm the one! The one who caused the bus to stop. Yeah, that's me. I managed to get a dollar bill out of the change purse in my pocket." She mimes this with great irritation and difficulty, "I get the buck out and hand it to the driver. He says, 'Exact change, lady.' I say, 'What?' He repeats it. He's mad already, started the day mad. 'Exact change, lady!' I looked at him. 'I don't have change.' Somebody on the bus yelled, 'He said exact change, lady, fa Christ's sake.'

"I said, 'Sir, I don't have exact change. Please take this dollar. It's more than the fare.' The whole bus was yelling 'C'mon, lady, we got to get to work. You're holdin' us up. Stupid! You know you gotta have exact change.'"

Uta does all the voices expertly, and we are in this wet, sweaty, mean bus with her. The girl in the arena hasn't moved. Hasn't dared. Frozen. So are we. Uta is a master. Where the hell is she going with this exact change story?

"I look at them. God! I look at the driver. God! He's not looking at me, just trying to get the bus around some triple-parked cars, and drivers are yelling at him and giving him the finger. I say, 'Please sir, help?' He looks at me, and he is so mean, such a helpless man sitting on his fucking throne, telling me I have to get off the bus. He is going to stop the bus. I will get off and walk. I am so late for this class. And I take out my knife and I stab him in the face. I can't stop stabbing him. He is spouting blood. He dies. And I get off the bus covered in his blood, and I walk here to this stupid class, and now I can't get his fucking blood off of me!"

And she starts scrubbing herself madly, insanely scouring her hands, face, and clothes. It's a sexual orgy of scrubbing. It's a madwoman, a ritual from an ancient sacrifice, a feral-eyed murderer trying to clean up a crime scene. And suddenly she stops, looks at the girl, and says, in a perfectly normal, quiet voice, "See? What you feel every day is useful. Powerful. Think about it. Feel it. Work on the scene."

She turns to her little table, grabs a cigarette from an open pack, lights it, sucks it in, and blows a stream of white smoke into the air, creating the drifting smoke of a battlefield where life and death are as close as not having exact change, or being late to work, or standing in front of a sad, angry, rude bus driver, feeling humiliated.

"Next," she says and sits behind her little fortress of precious words.

We rise as one and applaud this magnificent actress, this remarkable teacher and woman who gives and gives to make artists of cowboys and clods and divas and darlings.

We owe Uta an unpayable debt. She changed my life. One day, she said, "You are extraordinary. You have the technique. Now you have to find yourself. Put yourself in the scene. You. Ordinary. You. Be there." It took me years to understand this simple order. I'm still trying to perfect what Uta commanded.

S C E N E : New York

After ACT, Robin and I returned to my apartment on Sullivan Street. We decided to take some time away from each other to test our feelings about the relationship. I missed her terribly. When she came back, this young girl became my wife.

We were happy together, laughed together. We had two children together, two beautiful boys. And we were bitterly divorced twelve years later. My former wife has striven her entire life to balance her mother's needs with her own life as artist, daughter, wife, and mother.

Robin's mother was not a forgiver, and she passed on to her daughter the same harsh code. This thread of anger, sorrow, and fear was woven into my marriage to a young girl, a brilliant young actress, a girl longing and needing to be taken care of, needing to trust, needing a father. She needed a foundation that was not anger and inherited fear or the distrust of being a victim. She needed an unselfish parent—her father had taken his life—and needed certainty and fearlessness in a partner.

Me, Robin Strasser, and our sons, Nicholas and Benjamin, at home in Brooklyn, New York, with our faithful friend, Mush.

I failed the test.

I had many of the qualities she needed, and I wanted so much to be what she needed. But I, too, as it turned out, was a child in need. It's never fair when grown-ups turn out to be children, but, as we all know too well, we do. Is a twelve-year marriage a starter marriage? A failure? I don't think it's right to take that cop-out. We did so many things right together. We were good for each other and proud of that, and we were proud of each other. It seemed right to be married. I was thirty-two years old. Old enough to know better, as they say.

We had two boys to take care of. I loved being a father. But I didn't understand what it all meant.

A few years after we were married, I was unfaithful. Why? Here's what I know: it was wrong—really wrong—but necessary. I didn't think about it; I just did it. Once. Then I forgot I did it. My working life, my career, consumed me. If it said jump, I asked how high? I thought more about the next job and the next rung of the ladder than I did about maintaining a marriage or a family. I thought it would go on merrily without conscious maintenance and that I could, too. I was a cock-eyed optimist.

A year and a half after the first time, I was away from home and did it again. This time, I needed a lot of alcohol. It wasn't easier because now guilt was present. Raw, looming, true guilt—not Catholic guilt, but a new discovery. Real shame comes from actual wrong actions. Infidelity was not missing Sunday Mass.

Now I understood what actual sin is, and it was tied to my dick like a sandwich board.

> I am in blood
> Stepped in so far that, should I wade no more,
> Returning were as tedious as go o'er.

Macbeth is right. I was in deep. And there were deeper depths to come.

I had begun to like booze—the taste, the comradeship of a warm glass, the loosening. I was insanely determined never to get drunk, never to be drunk. But we know alcohol. It is a sphinx, god and goddess, Cyclops, and chimera—the head of a woman with a goat's head rising out of its lion's back, teats on its belly, breathing fire, with a snake for a tail. A devourer. One day you wake up flat on your back, naked, hollow, eaten to the core, wondering who you used to be. Who are these children? Who was that woman? Who ate my brain?

My life was never out of control, never unmanageable. I did spend nights in my office at home drinking, lying on the floor listening to Doc Watson, calypso, Mozart, Bach, and Puccini, wearing out the grooves on the LPs and rewinding the cassettes over and over to keep rehearsing emotions whose source I didn't understand but whose replays seemed to be the only thing—along with the Irish whiskey—that overpowered and drowned the pain. Then the room would start spinning, and I'd stop the booze, wait, doze, and change the music. In the morning, I'd get up and be normal, be me. But my secret wonder was always whether there was a me out there who was good enough, strong enough, kind enough to be the me I need.

Was there joy? Yes, in my sons and in work. I was successful, young, strong, good at my job—better than good. Nothing was terrible. My life was fine, thanks, and good morning. What's next? Did my agent call?

My wife did not like confrontation. She had quite enough of that in her life. I provided the escape from that. She was Jewish without a connection to the religious practice. There were many such in New York—unorthodox, unreformed Jews aware that they were a "chosen people," a targeted group marked for bigotry and hate. That fact created a super-scanner awareness that gave them a kind of creative power. So many I knew had it, including my wife. I was a self-appointed member of the tribe of scanners, so I fit in.

Who were these women I "connected" with? Anais Nin, the queen of sensual writers, describes men with specific tastes in women as if she accepts the objectification men do without thinking and without owning the principle that objectifying another human is bizarre, wrong, a kind of slavery, a genuine sin. The crime is not the consensual fucking. It is the cruel objectification.

I became that kind of criminal without the slightest inkling that something was wrong. It was the '60s and '70s, after all. Sex was on tap like beer. I was unfailingly nice to the ladies, except for blindly valuing their sexuality above all other things. I wasn't alone. It was the times. We took the wrong message from *Bob & Carol & Ted & Alice*.

Tokens. Charms on a bracelet. Like anyone, I'm attracted to certain kinds of movies, cuisine, or dogs. It's the same thing—not. At eighty-nine, I get it. At thirty, I was a blind man with a cock for a cane. I eventually regained my sight, but how and when? On the road to Damascus? No, actually, on the road to Broadway.

Did I live by a double standard? Yes, the debauched former altar boy Casanova admits. But it's worse. It's holier than thou. The corrupted altar boy demands fidelity from his actual and current beloved. How can that be? Read on, Macduff! It gets deeper.

Among all the women were a couple of men. No ménages. No orgies. No S&M. No minors. I had taboos, but when I looked into the mirror, did any

Actor looking casual on hard rock for my good friend, photographer, Henry Grossman.

principles still look back at me? Are there unforgivable acts in sex? Or in any consensual adult human activity?

Yet, when the monster betrayer—me—was betrayed, he dared feel pain. Dared to retaliate. Dared to moralize. When I was betrayed, I could only react badly and reel in shock. I got what was coming to me. In reliving this story of my life, I've finally arrived at a starting point: my past has caught up with my present.

From that time to now, I've learned that shame is the true problem. When you start out marked with shame, it creates conditions to reproduce itself like a virus. No more, thankfully. I'm left with this aphorism hanging on my mental wall:

All history is myth: It's 3D spacetime, a samsara wheel. Step off, and you are in karma. Myth is real, and reality is myth.

SCENE: New York

It is a cold, dark winter day in the big city. Shoulders hunched against the December chill, my CUA friend Mart Crowley sits across from me in a booth at Jack Delaney's in Sheridan Square, Greenwich Village. Cradled in his arm is a play script, held close to his breast as tenderly and tightly as a baby. He is slight, his large eyes behind big glasses reflecting hope, despair, fear, and courage all at once. He is living on borrowed money and borrowed time. He starts up as the wind-driven rain outside drills a burst of rain bullets at the big window on the street. The sleety rain bounces off the oily black bricks on Seventh Avenue, drenches the legs of passersby, and pools in the gutter. It will be black ice tonight. Everyone hustles, running for shelter in the odd New York manner of motion—bent forward at the waist, leaning into a future destination and willing it to be here! Now! There is in the air the peculiar, daunting, bewitching, hungry tension of New York that promises an adventure ahead that will give you a fantastic orgasm or kill you.

Mart has come to New York from Hollywood after years of struggling without success to find his place in show business, which lately has turned him into a pro tem man of all work for Natalie Wood and her husband, R. J. Wagner. He has been living rent-free in the Bel Air house of a mutual friend in exchange for watching the property and shooing the burglars away—Cinderella, Hollywood style. This is laughable, but he is dead broke. The house larder had been stocked when the good hosts left. Now it's empty. As the food and booze dwindled, Mart, in real desperation, sat down and wrote a play. He wrote fast, the result of which is now in his arms. It's all he has to offer, like the dancers of *A Chorus Line*. "Who am I anyway? . . . What shall I try to be? . . . Oh God, I need this . . ."

It's not just a job. It's his life he is throwing on the table as collateral. His pockets are empty. If his life story is worthless, he is out of options. And his baby is getting a feeble, somnambular reception in the city that never sleeps. Enervated and stunned, people were at a loss, repelled. The play is his life, not so pure and not so simple. It's about nine gay men and how they live in American society. The play is not a social tract. It's a well-written slice-of-life story. It was the 1960s, and as in every other era of American life up until now, homosexuality was considered taboo. Gay men and women hid their sexuality because the penalty for coming out was perilous to social acceptance, careers, and even to life, to actual survival.

Mart is offering New York theater professionals a play that tells the complex truth about the real life of a segment of ordinary urban men who have lived a hidden, dual existence—their public lives and their private lives—and the effect that closeted life has had on them. The play is a party, full of wit, fun, ferocity, shame, sadism, masochism, violence, fear, true love, and enormous bravery. "The love that dare not speak its name" will cry out in full masculine voice for "the two hours' traffic of [the] stage." If it ever gets there. It's new, and it's a shocker.

But New York is not ready. "Come back in five years," an important agent says. Agents don't want to represent it. Actors won't risk it, won't even read it. Producers can't see beyond the risk-to-value metric, only the tsuris in bringing a play about gay people to Broadway or even to that new venue, off-Broadway. Gay producers don't want to take a chance. Even gay actors won't risk it. Gay agents advise their heterosexual clients that it will destroy their careers if they participate in this scandalous event.

* * *

I listened as Mart told me all this on that painfully cold winter day. Close to panic, he almost wept in angry frustration but wiped the tears away. There was one chance: Edward Albee had established the Playwrights Unit off-Broadway with partner Richard Barr. The director of the unit was Charles Gnys (pronounced Guinness), a graduate of Catholic University's Department of Drama and a close friend of Mart Crowley's (and mine). The play had survived Mr. Albee's flinty disapproval. He thought it was déclassé, even trivial. It was cautiously supported by Mr. Barr and Mr. Gyns. They were willing to do an eight-show tryout with available actors who would work for nothing. This idea was as tenuous as Oberon's gossamer fairy wings, but it was the only possible game in town for Mart's script, *The Boys in the Band*.

He had brought the play to me the day before. I had read it once, quickly. He looked at me now, his eyes letting me know he was ready to hear my turn-down speech. "Mart, I'm just so busy right now, I can't . . ." or "I'm sorry, I don't see a part that's right for me," or "Gosh, it's funny and all, but it's just not my cup of tea," or even, "Sorry, I really don't like it . . ." followed by reasons and suggestions for rewrites.

Instead I said, "It's a good play, Mart. I'll do it."

His eyes filled with tears, which he blinked away. "Thank you," he managed.

I told my agent the next day. "All right," she snapped. "But it may be the end of your career."

My next move was to tell my wife what I had let us both in for.

Eight performances. Eight chances to get it right, to transform words into people and scenes into gripping reality. A few days of rehearsal. Nine guys who are supposed to be longtime, intimate friends and frenemies, played by actors who have only met each other for the first time today.

That night I told Robin that I was committing to this workshop. She was very supportive, being an actress and a New Yorker tuned to the issues of the day. She was not bothered by the show's content or the possible fallout from my being in it.

I told no one else. I didn't discuss my work with my parents or siblings. They were all in California, absorbed in their own struggles, although if I had brought it up, I knew they would be disturbed by the idea and extremely cautious about it. My father would not have understood why I'd take such a chance. He probably didn't even know there was such a thing as a gay person. Why did I want to do it?

Mart Crowley was part of a group of young men who were clearly a coterie unspoken of and unacknowledged, a clique of odd men out. No one used the word *gay* then, so they were *homosexual* or worse. At the University of Arkansas, or in the army, for that matter, I had known individuals who were called "nelly," but there didn't seem to be any organization. That was my—and most people's—naiveté. As we learned, the closet was a large and very effective hiding place so the heterosexual world wouldn't have to see or hear or be appalled by or embarrassed by or furious at the existence of such folk.

From my experience as a teen, I already knew about homosexual people but had shut my eyes and mind to that phenomenon since. And at university in the '50s, there were never any open discussions about sexuality in social life. No one was out. But theater people are escape artists, "huddled masses yearning to breathe free." Life's immigrants. We are always arriving at the shores of new countries, always having to become friendly with the native peoples. The theater is a natural land for misfits. I became aware over time that gay men and women were part of every area of the theater. That was fine with me. Although I was a born and bred Southerner, I had somehow been left free of all prejudice. I credit my parents' deep-dyed Catholicism for that. They believed the gospel was inclusive, just as Christ said.

We were all refugees. Mart and I were both from the Deep South, Mississippi and Arkansas. There was a bond between us of shared knowledge about the way things were in that world that no one foreign could know. And we were both born into alcoholic and codependent families. Despite all that, we were still not close friends. There was a slight age difference, which in my twenties seemed much more divisive and important than it does in my eighties.

But Mart called me out of the blue one day when I was visiting my aunt in Arkansas. He was in Mississippi and wanted to know if he could come see me. He flew into Fort Smith, and we spent three days hanging out in my little town. We drove around town in my aunt's car and talked. We dragged the drag, went to the Dairy Queen, drove over the river to Oklahoma for beer and wine, and came back and sat by the railroad tracks above the greasy creek—yes, like a scene from a Tennessee Williams play—watching the water moccasins slide by. We talked about theater and mutual friends and eventually our families and ourselves. He was pale and shaky. He kept looking at me oddly and laughing loudly. He was nervous. He had needed to leave his home. His mother was a dope addict, his father a violent alcoholic. He had to deal with it his whole life. I made some comments about my dysfunctional family. They didn't understand me, and I didn't know how to love them, or anyone.

Suddenly, Mart pulled himself close to me and blurted, "You have no idea how bad things are. I love my parents, but I can't take it anymore. You have a normal family." Then he cried, stopped himself, and said something bitter and funny that I don't remember. I thought, *This kid is tougher than he looks.*

No one knows the undercurrents, the rip tides, the vortices of another's family. He turned to me with his big eyes made even larger by his eyeglasses. He didn't say anything, just looked into my eyes. A moment passed. I knew he needed help, but the look was more than that. Much more. I couldn't respond in the way he might have wished.

A decade passed. I got a call from Mart. Would I read a play he'd written? Yes. I picked up the play from a tiny, grungy downtown theater outside of any known theater circuit and read it.

Thank God for Bob Moore. Robert Moore, the director, was also a Catholic University man. We were all Father Hartke's boys, all his protégés. Bob had kicked around as an actor and was a good, light-comic one. He had only directed The Players, Inc., group in Washington DC, some shows at Arena Stage, summer stock in Olney, Maryland and some regional theater around the New York area. This workshop would be a big test for him. Bob was gay but never seemed troubled by it. He passed easily in society because his aura was neutral. His directorial style was as cool as a banana smoothie. He was a logician of the stage and a superb composer, and he always managed the stage picture marvelously. He did not like Sturm und Drang. Tantrums were tolerated briefly then put down by his fire-extinguishing wit. He would make a joke, the other actors would laugh, and the actor having his Sarah Bernhardt moment would either laugh at himself or be left in the dust to languish for a long break, after which Bob would call, "Okay, let's go to plan B." He was an excellent coach and *team* was extremely important to him. He took charge of the workshop.

Of course, there was storm and stress. The play was about extreme emotions and expressions of individual subjectivity called into being by nine actors, seven of whom were gay men and two who were not but were assuming the position. The producers and crew were all gay people. The theater in New York has been described as dominated by a gay mafia. If that's true, *The Boys in the Band* wasn't yet part of that kind of power axis. It was touching how vulnerable we all were.

Dick Barr was a lovely gentleman who was risking his financial life and his association with Edward Albee if the play proved to be only a well-made but unimportant fake as Eddie assumed it was. Edward's work was totally at odds with the accessible, commercial play Mart had written, but he may have misjudged its accessibility for triviality, because it was about to ring the cathedral bells and vindicate the hunchback hiding in the dovecote.

We opened on a frigid January night. The tiny house—the Vandam Theater then, now the expanded SoHo Playhouse—was full of curious folks, many friends of the participants. The show, like the Playwright's Unit shows, would not be reviewed. If it died, it would be an obscure death, unheralded and unknown, and Mart would crawl back to Hollywood to be a maid of all work for the self-selected elite.

There had been the usual kerfuffle in getting the show up with available tacky furniture and devised entrances in the too-small space. It was a Lab show, a kind of workshop production. One of the actors was violently indisposed toward his part and was replaced smoothly by Mr. Robert Moore, the master of the butter churn. He was able to weather general and specific nuttiness and solve situations without hurting people.

Actors were shifted from part to part. I was not. After wishing a little to be the leading or sharp-tongued part, I shut up and concentrated on Hank, my supposedly squaresville and dull schoolteacher part. But I discovered that the second or third parts, if built as game-changers, are often more fun and even better than the lead parts. I was doing the show for one reason: Mart was my friend. I don't think I was usually so generous, but something in the way Mart had put his trust in me had touched some hidden resource. I knew I had to do this. This play and these boys deserved a voice.

The part fit me like a well-worn, old cardigan. Another surprise: Uta had told me I had technique. Now I had to find myself in the work. Something about Hank was me. And I honored his honesty. I didn't analyze it. It was eight shows for a friend, one week out of my life. Nothing more.

The first show was spotty and unsure. We stepped on each other's cues and laughs, and we were all surprised by how fast everything went. We were flying blind and trusting only instincts and intuition. We hung on each other's words and responses like soldiers in a confused and fast-moving battle. The script seemed long in reading and rehearsal, but playing it was like white water rafting before we had figured out our team positions and equipment or mapped the river. "Bumpy," understated Bob afterward. But we were not able to rehearse anymore. Actors' Equity rules protected actors from management working them more than a few hours once they were open and playing. And in a free workshop, there was zero rehearsal after each show. But after our first performance, we wanted to rehearse to get it right. Actors are willing slaves.

On the crisp, frozen morning after the opening, I walked toward the theater from my apartment just blocks away. I had a check to deposit from my CBS soap opera. It was 10:00 A.M. As I got close to Vandam Street, I saw a huge crowd. I wondered if there'd been a fire in the block. But there were no trucks and there was no noise. No sirens. It was weirdly quiet and ridiculously cold. I walked fast.

As I got closer, I saw something very strange, a line of people extending from the middle of Vandam Street to Sixth Avenue just ahead. It turned north there and extended a very long block up to Houston Street, where it turned west again. People were standing, waiting, deep into the warren of small streets leading into Greenwich Village. The line was composed entirely of men, standing in pairs, talking. Excited. Laughing. Happy. And gay. Our audience!

When I passed our theater, I heard excited talking at the box office—supplication and response.

"Please. Any seat, any day."

"Sorry, no seats left."

"No, not for tomorrow or any other day."

"Sorry, sir, sold out."

Hollywood. My "Sensitive Actor" headshot.

Frank Carver, The Secret Storm, my CBS soap opera role. "I loved my fans, even when one hit me over the head with an umbrella because my character was not being nice to his girlfriend."

"Don't know if it will be extended. Thanks for your interest."

"Would you care to leave your name and number in case the production goes elsewhere?"

A drama had opened in a tiny theater out of any known arts district in New York City and blown the door off the closet forever. It had created an audience overnight. Men and women without a voice or the liberty to be their true selves had just seen themselves on a stage living out their lives in all the sorrow, pity, and comedy they knew was there. They were freed for two hours to laugh and cry, looking at themselves, and looking at the audiences they were a part of looking back at them and seeing them as human beings. Seeing their similarities not as homosexual or heterosexual people but as people trying to build lives, find love, be accepted, and take care of each other. And word-of-mouth was about to make a revolution.

This is the theater, I thought. This is *my* theater. *My* life. I'm here. There's nowhere else to be. This is what it looks like. I didn't think. I just knew. This was Social Justice.

My eyes were wet, and not from the cold. I wiped them on my sleeve, sucked in the freezing air, and went to the bank with my television check.

But, despite the huge human response to the controversial play, getting it to the next level was heavy lifting. It took the producers several months to get capital investments enough—paltry, compared to today—to bring the show uptown to Theater Four on Fifty-Fourth Street west of Ninth Avenue. It was an out-of-the-way, 499-seat off-Broadway house on a dark, undefined street in an area Mart called a "senseless-killing neighborhood." It was owned by film actor Franchot Tone and, originally, by his mother, Gertrude. Franchot was an undervalued film actor capable of greatness on stage. I had seen him play Jamie O'Neill in Eugene O'Neill's *A Moon for the Misbegotten* on Broadway a few years earlier. To my mind, no one could have played the self-destructive boozer better. Tone knew the man intimately since it might have been written about him and his life. He and Colleen Dewhurst—married to another self-destructive drinking man of prodigious talent, George C. Scott—gave performances I have never gotten out of my head.

In a back street, somewhat hidden from the big Broadway world, Theater Four seemed like a natural fit to me. The play that was to live there was about a self-destructive alcoholic, which Mart was (and knew it). He had written about himself and his gay family, many of whom were also drug and alcohol abusers.

The day before the play was to open, I couldn't speak. I went to the famous throat doctor Wilbur Gould, who had also treated John Kennedy and was well-known to all actors as the best throat man in existence. Lyndon Johnson, also a patient, called him "the only legitimate cut-throat in the White House." He diagnosed my problem as globus hystericus, a swelling of part of the voice box caused by panic. I was exhibiting physically what I was feeling emotionally. I, Mr. Tough Guy, was afraid to go on stage and fail. That woke me to the psychic power of an important New York opening night in the life of an actor, which could immobilize him. Being exposed in public as a fraud, a loser, a naked man at a dress-up party.

Why was this opening so scary? It was partly everyone else's fear that had infected me. When I first stepped onto a Broadway stage in *A Man for All Seasons*, everything was new. Anything that happened was exciting and okay with me. I had no idea what the stakes were. I wasn't a leading player. I had no responsibility. Even though I'd opened since in many plays outside of New York, in important shows and leading roles, it seemed now that all those events had been childhood adventures in a forgiving land of elves and play-pretend. Even the important work I'd done with APA, Lincoln Center Repertory, and ACT had been protected somehow. But now I was fledged. I was not a sorcerer's apprentice anymore. I was now known in the world of New York theater. I was on my own in the rough and tumble of success or failure as written by the New York critics. And though I was a member of an ensemble in a symphonic piece where each instrument worked in concert with all the rest to make the music, now I would be judged on how harmoniously I fit in. Was I going to be precisely in tune? Also subconsciously present was the shadow of the possibility the naysayers would be right. I was risking my career. I was determined to do it for my friend, but I knew how insidious and prevalent homophobia was, even in my beloved New York.

The doc gave me some medicine—probably a placebo—and, miraculously, when I showed up to the shared and cramped dressing room, my throat was unimpeded. My voice was clear as always. I loaded up my pipe and put it in my jacket pocket with the matches I would need during the party that night. Two days earlier, I secretly made a hole in the set with my stage carpenter's tool kit, opening a tiny audience viewing station in the stage-right flat that masked the entrance of the partygoers—me, my lover Larry, Emory (the funny and irritatingly one), and Bernard (the token Black guy). I called us the "homosexual *Home of the Brave*" after the clunky WWII movie in which each soldier represented a different ethnic group. The hole gave us a view of the house seats, sixth-row center, so we could check out the audience before going onstage.

Groucho Marx, Jackie Kennedy, and countless other celebrities over the one thousand–performance run of the play in New York—everyone—had to see it, excited voyeurs all. And we could see them seeing our show. One night,

I looked through the keyhole and saw my parents. I had bought the tickets and knew they were there, but it almost stopped my heart that they would now peer into my private world of the theater. "Is *this* what you do?"

Being in a hit show does many things to an actor. There's a New York cachet that is so delicious it's like your favorite dessert being served as a constant surprise. The New York audience is the world's best—they are intelligent, discerning, progressive, tolerant, au courant, and they love good stuff. We were good stuff, for everyone. Maybe not yet in Peoria, but in New York, people knew us, and it wasn't just the gay audience. The play had broken the closet door lock, and the heterosexual audience, eager to be titillated, couldn't get enough of us.

* * *

There was also a negative aspect. I had a side career doing commercials. I had a True cigarette television commercial running in which I sucked on a True in extreme close-up and blew smoke in the viewer's face, as if it were manna from heaven, as I spoke the ad copy. This ad ran several cycles and paid very well. After the play opened, the casting director called me and said I should come in to meet with the clients.

"Is this an audition?" I asked Richard, the casting director.

"Not exactly, Larry. They like you, but, well . . . just come in please."

I went to the Graybar Building across from Grand Central Station. It was a locus for commercial work. Auditioning actors liked to meet there and exchange gossip about the business. I met with the client team, six VIPs in dark suits, ties, and brushed brogans smelling of six different aftershaves and chewing on Sen-Sens to kill the tobacco breath they all had. Maybe it was a company law that they had to smoke. I wonder now how many of those guys died of lung cancer. I hated cigarettes. I smoked a pipe with Dunhill's latakia-laced tobacco for about thirty years. I never smoked cigarettes except for the True commercial, and today, I have asthma and emphysema and use a CPAP machine at night. The pipe made me feel like my grandpa who was never without his corncob and Prince Albert in the can. I loved him and wanted to be like him. He died of a stroke.

The clients asked me to read some new copy for the next cycle. They all lit up and sat back. The room quickly had the blurry atmosphere of a Whistler nocturne. After the reading, there was an awkward pause. Someone said, "Very good, very good." It was odd. The copy was different from my thirty-second spot that had run for a year, but it was the same simple message: We taste good, indulge yourself, you'll like it.

Richard said, "Shall we talk, gentlemen?" I was let out the door.

I was in Grand Central when one of the office people found me. "Larry, Richard needs to talk to you. Would you come back?"

We returned to find Richard waiting for me. "I am so sorry to tell you, but they aren't renewing your contract."

That was okay. Commercials paid well enough to help support a family and helped me keep choosing to do theater projects I thought were important. Some folks I knew became commercial actors and made millions. To me, they were easy come, easy go.

I asked, "Was it something I said?"

He laughed. "Your commercial has been so successful for them, they were talking about putting you on a contract."

"I don't even smoke cigarettes," I said, "I faked it."

"They don't know or care. They go by the quarterly reports. But that's not the problem and why it's so hard for them. But . . ." He giggled.

"What?" I asked.

"They said, and I quote, 'No fags smoke our fags.'"

"Oh God," I said. "That's terrible copy. Who wrote that?"

He laughed. Richard was a quietly flamboyant man, but he had a serious-ness, a depth that enhanced his light touch, comic face, and frizzled long hair a shade too gold to be eighteen karat.

"It's not personal," he said. "They love you. It's just another dead thirty-sec-ond spot." There was, with that, a wry touch of pain. Richard was a gay man in the closet because of his career. Any hint of homosexuality at that time was the third rail of advertising.

"It's nothing personal," Richard said again.

"Yes, it is," I said. "And I know it is." I looked at him. He tried to smile but couldn't. "Thanks, my friend," I said.

SCENE: New York

My parents were in town to visit. We put them up in a Midtown hotel and took them on the subway downtown to my one-room garden Village apartment. The subway had been a shock. The crunching, unrelenting speed of New York was a shock, the jive-walking to get through Times Square crowds was a shock, and now they were about to be exposed to an even greater seismic event: their son playing gay man on stage. A gay man in a hit play that had already been featured in a leering, weird photo essay in *Look* magazine by the unpleasant, super-famous pic-jockey Irving Penn (Arthur's older brother). Irving had done a hit job on the guys of the show, distorting us all just enough to make us look unreal, sad. But it didn't matter. In the world of fashion photography, anything went, and it was the era of Andy Warhol and, soon, the shock of Robert Mapplethorpe. And any publicity is good, see?

Agnes N. and Laurence B. Luckinbill sat in their sixth-row center seats quietly and inconspicuously, as they did everything in life. She was in her small toque and the auburn wig she had taken to wearing as she aged. He wore his white business shirt with a dull blue narrow tie and nondescript gray-brown wool suit. Their spectacles reflected the lights from the stage, their expressions unreadable.

In my family's world, this kind of stuff was scandalous. What would the relatives or coworkers think? It mattered. And publicity itself was a negative force. So, through my spyhole, I watched them watch the first scene with Michael and Donald in which the risqué gay jokes flew off the stage and into the tickled audience. My parents' faces remained impassive as if they were at the wake of a stranger. Not sad, not bored, not happy. Just listening intently.

Was I afraid of their response? No. Would I defend the play if they were scandalized and found it perverse and repellent? I would. I never once doubted the value of what I was doing. The theater was now my church and a source of spiritual sustenance. I knew the message of every play was its own, and if it were written with skill and honesty, it deserved to be heard. Philosophically, that's all I believed at the time.

We party scene people entered the stage, tumbling through the door like a clown car emptying. Right away, I saw my mother and father. Their faces were impassive with no sign of recognition of their son. I thought, *Okay, they hate it*. I put that out of my mind and did the best show I could.

We met in the lobby after. My parents were too shy to come backstage to meet the guys. They were happy to see me but said nothing about the show. We started walking up Ninth Avenue toward Ralph's, an Italian restaurant with the best lasagna and liver and onions in town. Silence.

Finally, I said, "What did you think about the show?"

Mildly, my mother answered, "Well, you did your part very well . . . It was good. The language was . . . a little . . . rough."

I took her arm. "Yes," I said. "I know."

She liked that I had linked arms. We walked on. I could tell my father was pondering something. His head down, he was hiding behind his gray fedora. He slowed and stopped. Looking up the street and not at me, he said, "I knew a fella . . . Jim . . . I was twenty-one and working at the American Express depot at the train station . . ."

"Nights," interrupted my mom. "By yourself. Lifting down coffins and heavy freight."

"Yeah, all night," Dad said. He worked his false teeth as if they hurt. "And my friend, he worked days at the bank."

"City National, where Marie worked."

"Yeah, my sister knew my friend Jim."

My parents exchanged glances. My Aunt Marie was unmarried—a spinster—and was not a happy woman. My father had helped her and his mother for years.

"And Jim would invite me sometimes, on a day off."

"One day off. A Sunday," my mother said. One day a week of the months and years of twelve- and fifteen-hour days and nights he had worked. She was still angry at that injustice.

"Yeah," my father said, dry as a bone. He looked up the street, squinting, remembering maybe that his sister disliked him. My mother looked at him in patient regard with unnameable love and an old exasperation mingled with sorrow and pity.

"And we would go for a walk along the river. And one time, he gave me a book of poetry. It was by some English fella, and it talked about love. And, well, I suppose my friend might have been . . . a homma-seckshul!" He pronounced the unfamiliar word in the flattest, least offensive or communicative way possible, in more of an Arkansas accent than I'd heard him speak in years. He was, I thought, back on that riverbank on a hot Sunday afternoon standing next to someone who had just shocked him profoundly.

"I gave him back the book," he said.

"Did you see him again after that?" I asked.

He looked at me, his liquid eyes burning. "Yes. Yeah. He was my friend. My best friend." He said this with finality, the coda on a piece of life, an unfinished relationship that was both honest and impossible and, still, long after death ended it, a piece of indefensible territory he had nonetheless sworn to defend in a war he could not understand but would, by God, fight.

We walked on. I had my answer. My parents had what they came for. And it had changed them.

I remembered talk of Jim. I'd seen an old picture of him in a small frame, tall and handsome like my father, in a stiff suit, squinting at the old box camera of the day. An inscrutable portrait that told nothing of the man but in the keeping told everything. They had both tried to escape their lives. They went on a train to Seattle together to get work with the Merchant Marine. Jim had been accepted, my father rejected, perhaps because my sister Sally had already been born (and maybe even me, by then). He didn't escape, just came back South. Got a job with Oklahoma Tire and Supply Company and went to work.

He never saw his friend again. But I don't think he ever had a friend again, let alone a best friend. For him, it wasn't about a person's sexual orientation, as we say today. It was truly about acceptance. He had been accepted, maybe even loved (the poems?), and he would return that acceptance, no matter what. I think I understand.

* * *

I walked out of the theater before all of the audience had gone. I had an early call for *The Secret Storm* the next morning and wanted to get home. My Yamaha 750 was chained to the rail outside. I was putting on my helmet as I went out beside some late stragglers who didn't recognize me in street drag— black Henley sweater, leather vest, pegged pants, motorcycle belt with a large silver buckle, and boots. Outside, in the damp chill of upcoming spring, a heavy man clung to the stair rail, bent over and moaning, as a woman in a full-length fur, standing in the street with her arm up, yelled back toward him.

"Sol!" she shrieked. "C'mon, I got a cab." Her voice had a Queens accent freighted with self-admiration for her urban guerrilla skills and barely contained irritation at Sol, who paid no attention to her but hung on the iron banister, trying to get his breath. His heavy face turned to the night sky and twisted in pain.

"Ahhhh," he moaned. Aahhhh . . ."

"Sol!" yelled the wife, angry now. "C'mon! The guy won't wait. We gotta get outta heah."

I put my hand on the man's shoulder. "Sir," I said. "Sir? What's wrong? Are you sick?"

He grabbed my arm and fumbled until he got a good grip, then he let go of the handrail and hung onto me. "What?" he said.

"Are you having a heart attack, sir? I can help. Your wife has a cab. We can get you to Roosevelt." The hospital was only a few blocks away.

"What?" he said again to himself. He pulled at my sleeve and swayed, unable to go farther. In the livid light spilling out of Theater Four's lobby, his face was streaked with tears and twisted beyond pain. It was anguish.

Now he looked at me, pleading. "Those boys?" he said. "Those boys! What's going to happen to them?" The question was urgent.

For a second, I didn't understand what he was saying. Then, I knew. He was talking about us—the boys in the play. He looked into my eyes for an answer to the unanswerable. Then he pulled away, and a darkness covered his face. He was still looking at me but didn't see me, didn't recognize me as an actor in the play he'd just been shocked by. There were no actors in the play, just real people living desperate lives. He had seen something hopeless, beyond sad, past fixing, a sorrow past help. Something he knew well. A son, maybe?

"Sol!" screeched the woman, breaking the spell. She opened the cab door wide, clinging to it to keep the driver from pulling away. Sol turned away, heavy and tragic in his long, bulky winter coat, and stumbled slowly toward his wife.

She helped him in, pushing on his back until he was stowed. She got in, slammed the door, and they were gone. What a profound answer to the question, "Why would you want to be an actor?"

* * *

The original cast was Frederick Combs, Kenneth Nelson, Cliff Gorman, Keith Prentice, Reuben Green, Leonard Frey, Robert La Tourneaux, Peter White, and me. We originated the roles in the workshop and in the off-Broadway production. We took the show to London at Wyndham's Theater in Piccadilly Circus, and we were the cast of the film of the play. We were together from 1967 through 1970. Three years. A lifetime, I now know.

Were we best friends? No. We had separate lives before and after the play. But we were colleagues of the theater who had respect for each other for the entire run of the play. It arose from the quality of the men, their self-respect and strength of character.

None of us dreamed that this would be a permanent marker for our lives in the theater world or that the play would become an iconic standard-bearer of the Gay Revolution. We were a hit show, a mind changer, before the Stonewall police riot that was credited as the revolution's flame. But we were the kindling, the fuel, and the match that ignited it. We were criticized by many militant gay people as demeaning and representing homosexual folk as weak, divided, emotional, hysterical, and bourgeois. Not true. We played human beings, ordinary men of many colors and stripes, who had been kicked to the curb and forced to hide. Men who had made of their lives what they could in society's prison. Men like your brother, your son, your husband who led double lives and, from that conscious and unconscious oppression, had become unique and special in their own world. They were a secret society, self-referential, with all the weaknesses of that. Mart Crowley looked at his world and reported it as it was. And the audience knew it was true. They recognized friends, relatives, and even themselves. As a heterosexual man, I was blessed to see into the depths of the pain and bravery of my friends.

* * *

"Hank? Hank? Hank?" The nasal voice came from behind me. I was heading up the aisle of the concert hall, going backstage after Lucie's symphony performance in Little Rock, Arkansas. I turned to look for the source of the voice.

A guy was making his way up the aisle, holding onto his friend's arm. He looked to be in the throes of a wasting disease, and walking was a challenge. He lurched and dragged himself forward, his legs at odds with each other and with his arms. He had a broad, anxious smile on his bespectacled face and was reaching out toward me.

I stopped. "Are you talking to me? My name's Larry," I said.

"I know," he said in a high, reedy voice. "I know who you are. You're Hank!"

His companion smiled at me. They continued moving forward, slowly, awkwardly, step by step. The companion seemed to be a part of his disabled friend, matching his strong, healthy limbs to his companion's weaker ones as if they were one man walking, half in a nondescript dark suit too large for his shrunken frame and half in an amazingly buoyant, so-Southern tattersall suit with matching vest. They stopped in front of me.

"You saved my life!" the man said.

"Not me," I answered. "Hank did." I knew what the guy meant. He had seen the play, the film, or both, as so many had, and had identified with the characters.

"No, you, *you*! You were Hank, and I saw you, and I believed you, and I wanted to be you. I went home right afterward and told my mother and father that I'm gay."

I absorbed this impassioned speech offered with a nervous smile. That moment had been a life-changing event for this man facing so many challenges already.

I said, "That took great courage. What did your parents say?"

The man looked at his friend, who was beaming now.

"They hugged me!" he said. "Hugged me and told me they loved me. And *you* did that."

"No," I said. "You did it. Like Hank in the play told his wife and children he was gay."

"Thank you," said the man's partner. "We've been together twenty-one years, and what a wonderful thing, you being here today. We've always hoped we could tell you what this meant to us."

He smiled as he took charge of the twinned centaur that was their shared life, and they moved up the aisle toward the open doors letting in the last sunlight. I wondered how they would get down the many marble steps to the street, but I knew they would.

The good effects of this play have ricocheted through the world since its inception. It's not a fancy play. It's a simple story, and it was our fate, guided by geniuses, to do it simply. There was no scene-stealing, upstaging, or me-firsting, and it came from the top. Everyone was taking a chance—Dick Barr, Mart, Bob Moore. All of us. In the film, William Friedkin risked his career on a story with a possibly losing or small niche market appeal. CBS's Cinema Center Films took a risk. The distributor took a chance. And it paid off, both in a groundbreaking social justice context, without ever preaching for anybody's rights, and in financial return over time. But there was an unmentioned danger for the members of the cast. David Susskind, a great producer of quality theater and television work, had a talk show called *Open End*. The cast was invited to appear and express their thoughts about the play. Most agreed to show up. But it got uncomfortable. David was known for stimulating interesting, in-depth conversations on the show. But as a former agent (for Lucille Ball, among others), he also had a nose for celebrity sensation. One question was what is the point of this play about gay people and their love lives? Is it just the sensational aspects of illicit love? Why should we care? I remember defending the idea that the theater was always a place where free speech on any subject was possible. It was uncomfortable but necessary to examine the predominant moral views of society because they were often wrong. And that was the glory of the theater—it was a change agent. It was a heated discussion. Finally, David asked gently whether any of us would be willing to "come out" right there on the show. It was a daring question and well ahead of its time. Cliff Gorman and I were heterosexual. But our fellow cast members clammed up. They were angry. They felt Susskind had bird-dogged them, so the show fizzled out. No Patrick Henry or Nathan Hale speech happened.

The Boys were marks. The actors had volunteered to be in a story about their own lives, but there was still the fact that it was a play. There was still a threat to personal privacy. Careers could be destroyed and lives harmed. It was one thing to play a character, quite another to have a character play you. Gay folks risked their lives by potentially being outed. The guys wanted to live the way they wanted to live. There was plenty of shame, guilt, and fear to go around. It was a long way to Pride Month.

The guys went out almost every night after the show. The baths were very popular. Bette Midler was an obscure, jokey sensation as the only girl at the Ansonia Hotel. Members-only Plato's Retreat, orgy central, was a big deal and welcomed both homosexual and heterosexual people. The smell of sex permeated the Manhattan air.

The theme, if not the reality, was escape. Every night my friends told their harrowing and touching stories in the show, and after, went to live their own stories in very dangerous places, as it turned out.

Twelve years later, our first close friend died from a mysterious malady. It was a lonely, lingering, miserable death that panicked everybody because no one knew what caused it.

SCENE: New York

The first infidelity was a year after we were married with the actress I madly crushed on when I worked with her in the New York Shakespeare Festival. She was unobtainable and mysterious, my cue to go mad for her. But she was the Mona Lisa, "a cold and lonely lovely work of art." Years later, after my opening off-Broadway in a play that became a huge hit, this lady turned up at the stage door after the show and asked if I would have dinner with her. I did. She was in a crisis in her marriage. It seemed to have ended that night, but she made it clear that she wanted me, wanted to give herself. I was pretty sure it was a revenge move against her husband, but I was still entranced by her. It was a crazy, hot proposal. We found an hourly rental hotel, went in, signed Bill and Mary Jones on the register for the clerk whose smirk had been glued on his face for decades, paid a few bucks cash, and went upstairs. It was just what you would expect. It was dark and stinky, the carpet so dirty you couldn't see the faded design. The room was flimsy, and inside was a tiny, dirty sink, a narrow bed against the wall, and a cane chair with a busted bottom. It was Van Gogh's room without art or color.

We giggled and fumbled. Thought—conscience—had shut down. At last I was going to have my fantasy. We were joined, wet, trembling. She fell back on the grimy coverlet and started laughing. I was still in the thrall of mixed emotions—amazed and already fighting the swarm of guilt. I looked up. She pointed at the wall next to us. A cockroach climbed slowly up the wall beside our entwined, sweating bodies. An omen? The bug paused, antennae pointing at us, waving gently as if communicating with us. It clearly was accustomed to this sort of behavior in its domain. A panting, two-backed behemoth disturbing the peace. After this deliberative pause, it continued on its way. It was sobering. We had done it. She'd gotten her revenge on her husband or whatever it was, or maybe she just satisfied her curiosity about me since I had mooned over her. And what had I gained? A few minutes of complete annihilation of memory, marriage, self, obligation, personhood, a blackout of spirit leaving a residue of sensations, tastes, and, yes, ecstasy. I had found a way to be bad, to obliterate the construct, the fake Potemkin village of me!

And now I would have to deal with the fact that I had been unfaithful to my wife, which hitherto I had believed an impossibility.

The actress and I walked onto the crowded night street and looked around, afraid to see someone who might recognize either of us. As we waited for the streetlight to change, she looked at me.

"We should kiss," she said.

"Why?" I asked, ever the Sir Galahad.

"Why? We just made love!" She went up on tiptoe and we kissed with more embarrassment than we had fucked. Then she waved goodbye and stepped into the crowd and was gone.

"Love?" The whole "*Affair to Forget*" had taken only a half-hour to shatter a solemn promise. But the giddy and false sense that I had finally obliterated the sex guilt I carried all my life by reducing myself to burnt ash was still with me. It always will be, smeared on my forehead. Lent. I was guilty of destroying my marriage because I didn't stop there. It became a habit, a necessity. I was "in blood / Stepped in so far that, should I wade no more, / Returning were as tedious as go o'er," or so I reasoned the next time and the next and the time after that . . .

SCENE: New York to London

When you're in a hit show, you start thinking you are just a little bit special. It's an addictive drug. You want more. I know I did.

No one was getting rich acting in an off-Broadway play. I wrote a piece for the *New York Times* Arts and Leisure section about actors' finances that got more mail than any other piece the year it appeared, and it pissed off as many theater people as it edified with its essential truth. A theater actor, even one in a hit, could not live on that salary alone. We had to have supplemental income from some source. Producers like Dick Barr pushed back. He thought he was being attacked. But I was just telling the truth. It's the same—or worse—now as it was in 1970. Most actors experience the extreme difficulty of making a living in theater, so they must subsidize their careers by other means, even if they work regularly.

The actor I wrote about at the end of the piece was Al Pacino. We had talked about his circumstances before he was hired by Francis Coppola for *The Godfather*, a fabulous gift of karma. But it's truly the fantasy side of show biz. None of us in *The Boys in the Band*—"the best ensemble company in America"— had been visited by film stardom. We kept trucking.

In the dressing room, which I shared with my "lover" in the play, we talked about our personal lives. I'm heterosexual, but Keith was skeptical of that. He liked to think everybody is gay and had a good time teasing me about it. The guy playing Cowboy would come in from next door, smiling his lopsided *I'm available* smile, unzip his pants, and thrust his naked cock at Keith's mouth as Keith worked on his makeup. Keith never went anywhere without makeup. He would ignore the dick inches from his ear or mouth and joke about its small size. This was a vaudeville shtick performed with me as the audience. It was done, he said, to get me ready for the show.

Keith was a lovely man with great musical talent. He was unconfident about his acting and treated it like a kid's toy to be tossed aside when he got bored with it. He was somehow untethered to what he was doing at the theater. He had a wicked wit and a deep sadness (I never found out why), which he covered with crazy humor in every part of his life. He was exactly like the character he played in the show. I never got through his armor. He loved to give parties. The guys dressed as women. He invited Robin and me once, and we went. I didn't dress as a woman as Keith wanted. I knew he wanted to sneak a Polaroid shot of me so he could display it to his friends. My wife and I didn't stay long at the party. We couldn't breathe without getting a contact high. We left and no one noticed. All the bedrooms were full of men.

In the summer, the party moved to Fire Island. Again we went out one weekend. The party flowed from someone's house on the beach to the Boatel dance floor to the sex-act assembly line called the Meat Rack along the hedged boardwalk, ocean side. Again, we were out of place, completely out of sync with the permanent orgy atmosphere that had become the be-all and end-all of gay life. It was a frenzied *feijoada*—a Brazilian stew with everything edible in it—of alcohol, sex, drugs, and the continual fucking of anyone and everyone who jumped into the pot. This devolved into the counterculture revolution of the '60s.

It was counter to everything I lived for: work, improvement as a performer, achieving more skill, taking more risks as an actor, getting a name.

* * *

The Boys went to London. We brought the glitter and power of the original cast to Wyndham's Theater on the West End.

On opening night, our very British, no-nonsense stage manager came 'round with cards for the cast officially stamped by the royal government of Her Majesty Queen Elizabeth II. In ceremonious, royal font, the card read: "I am an air raid warden. Please remove your nether garments, lie on the floor, and do exactly as I tell you."

Apparently, our very British stage manager wasn't as no-nonsense as we had thought.

The lift—elevator—from the lobby to the executive office of the resplendent old Victorian theater in the heart of London was polished brass and chamfered glass and mirrors that smashed my image into many faces. The silent gate slid shut. I was told the tale of the lift as I was being pressed from behind by our jolly London producer while standing with my nose practically thrust into the brass gate.

He said, "This is the infamous two-person lift. Believe it or not, it was very effective in intimidating actors as they rose to the second floor with the producer-owner of this theater standing, erect and hard, in intimate contact with their rears. Oh, it set the tone!" The apocryphal story is of a well-known actor, perhaps Sir Ralph Richardson, who endured this one-story ride with Binky Beaumont, and when he stepped out, said, "Binky, I know I'm hetero, but I promise you, it won't show from the front." Ha!

Had I gone down the rabbit hole? London theater was rampantly gay. But in London, this ethos was, if not legal yet, at least quite a lot less shocking to those who worshipped Noel Coward in the past and Shakespeare's cross-dressed characters—men playing women.

The Boys hung out with Princess Margaret and her gay posse, including Danny La Rue (a funny, classy female impersonator), and were invited on Sunday to Tuesday weekends in the country at grand house parties bathed in the fog of sex rising over the early morning city.

The guys often slipped out at intermission to drink at the elegant pub five steps from our stage door in the alley next to another beautiful, ornate theater. They would come back in high spirits for the second act. I felt left out. One night I joined them and bellied up to the bar with my fellow Boys and ordered a Guinness.

I finished my beer and realized my friends were already out the door. It struck me that I was late for the second act. I still had plenty of time to return to the dressing room, where I discovered I was drunk, dizzy. I never ate before the show. I had drunk a thick, dark, tall Guinness, drained it in one draft. The fumes were in my nose. I was due on the stage. My big scenes were waiting for me. There was a sharp knock: "Beginners, second act. Places, please." I got on stage, but the actor playing Larry looked at me funny and started to laugh. He smelled the beer. He smelled of vodka but was so used to it that one drink was nothing to him. I was not in that class.

The scenes rolled by and I seemed all right, but I was slow. Cues seemed to come at me too fast, and I was picking them up late like a third baseman caught on the wrong foot for an infield line drive just a skosh out of reach.

My big scene was now—wasn't it? I was in a magic spell. It didn't feel bad. In fact, when I saw Keith trying to keep from exploding in a laugh, I thought it was funny, too. I smiled. I didn't know what he was laughing at, but I wanted to be part of the fun. Then I saw the rest of the guys looking at me. *That's odd*, I thought. They usually looked elsewhere at this point in the play. The play. Yes, that's what is going on here. A play! Now Keith did break up. Odd, because the words coming out of my mouth were about how I realized I was gay: "I was on a train, heading from New York. And I thought about it . . . and . . ."

I knew I was speaking and walking and thinking in a dream. And then I was telling about the men's room at Grand Central Station. "There was a guy . . ." I stopped, knowing I wasn't actually talking. I was just dreaming. Luckily, I never realized how drunk I was. If I had, I would have panicked. As it was, I walked through a great scene without knowing I was in it, without experiencing it. When it was over, I felt bereft, sad. There were no more nice words to say, nothing more I could think of anyway, so I put the phone down. What? There's a phone in my hand . . . and I got up and left the scene.

Now, in London, the real drinking began, and with it, because of it, maybe, all the rest.

SCENE: London

It was late, near closing time. Alone, I sat at my table at Inigo Jones, a restaurant popular with the theater folk named for a great stage designer of the eighteenth century. Our company was at Wyndham's Theater in Piccadilly. After the show, my castmates ran from the theater to the baths, drag shows, or private parties. I was often invited but never joined them on these excursions. They were all single gay men who went hunting for sex partners every night. I was always alone.

It's incredible to me how able I was to live that way. I had always been secretive and closed off, even from myself. I had been that way from a very young age. I trusted no one. There was a coldness in me, a deep inability to love anyone truly. I didn't love myself. None of this had bothered me much up to then. It was just me, my emotional DNA as an actor, usable on stage or in a film. All I cared about was my acting.

Dinner arrived. I looked around the restaurant. In a dark corner, Ava Gardner was sitting with three gay men dressed to the nines and thrilled to be getting drunk on champagne with—oh my God!—Ava. People said she liked to fuck and wasn't picky. I watched them swan around her and idly thought of being with Ava Gardner. She was truly beautiful, glowing and drunk. But who was I? Nobody.

I ordered another rum toddy, my third. My waiter came to the table. We chatted. He was unusually open, vulnerable, and down-to-earth for an Englishman. I wanted more drinks and asked the waiter if he wanted to join me at a late-hour place to continue our conversation. He was not from London and was lonely here after a divorce. Two nobodies: actor, waiter. He suggested we go to his apartment instead. We would have a drink, and he would call me a car to get me home. I agreed.

As we got out of the cab, the driver made a muttered remark that my friend didn't like, and he got angry with the cabby in a very civilized way. I was pretty drunk. I said, "What was that about?"

He said, "He called us bad names."

"What names?"

"Faggots," he said angrily.

I laughed. "What's his problem?"

He said, "He's a bastard like a lot of Londoners. I just have to get used to it."

We got inside a very simple apartment. He took my coat and poured me a drink, my fourth? Fifth? Then he sat next to me on the most comfortable furniture in the room—the bed. He said, "I am trying to get used to living as a gay."

"I didn't know," I lied.

He laughed. "Really?" Then he asked, "May I kiss you?"

I thought, *Well, this is new!* I had never thought of kissing a man before. I reached out, pulled him to me, and kissed him. It was like kissing a girl. He was a thin boy. And he was a sad boy. He reminded me of me. I thought, *I am going to do this, see what it's like.* So, I went one step further than I had ever gone with "the guy" in Fort Smith.

My head was swimming in booze. But, as always, I was sober inside all the physical sensations. I did not allow "drunk" to take over, ever. But I had dared myself now and would not back down. A line from *Boys* describes, with contempt, exactly what this moment was: "God, was I drunk last night!" A laughable excuse. This crossed my mind. But, the hell with it. I wanted to know what this was about. Another person in me was watching clinically, standing back in a white lab coat, observing Larry's experiment.

Afterward, he grabbed me like I was the gunwale of a lifeboat, held onto me, and cried. Sobbed. I sat there, fully clothed and still in my overcoat, completely removed from the experience. Although I had been driven to try, I felt separated from the event and disconnected from him.

I thought of the boys, out every night, searching for . . . what? There is love, and there is lust. Love gives. Lust takes. I had given, taking nothing and wanting nothing. I realized I liked the physical sensations but had zero interest in men as sex partners or in the gay lifestyle. This was a watershed moment. The question had been there since I was sixteen. I knew that I got a fulfillment from women that just wasn't here, and giving in to the compulsion this night showed me I was not repulsed by any act of sex.

SCENE: London

I became drunk. Stayed drunk. Nobody knew but me. There was a killing fury in me that I had to keep top secret.

It was a long, empty week. I couldn't eat. I couldn't talk to my wife in New York. I can't say I repressed thought; instead, thought repressed me. It was too weird.

The following Sunday, an actor friend showed up at my apartment with two nice, decent, middle-class, non-hippie English women, one for him, one for me. His wife was languishing in the suburbs; mine was back home. We went to Lord's and watched incomprehensible cricket, explained brilliantly by my genius actor friend who was teaching me London tricks. He was making films, working at the BBC, doing a radio show. He got the parts that a bright, handsome, beautifully trained, and too short gentleman from India would get, if you know what I mean.

We all spent the night in my flat. I rolled around inconsequentially with one of the ladies, neither of us into this scene, giggling about how my friend was getting on—and off—with the other. It was Larry and Carol and Mohandas and Suzy. And it was just as uncomfortable. No notches were scored. There were some overs and sticky wickets, some kisses, some self-assisted orgasms, a wet spot, and an English breakfast. We were all so tired, hungover, and civilized. All so uncomfortable. Our pangs were suppressed, consciences pricking hard. Eyes averted and politeness overdone. We all knew this was morally very low. So, we asserted our fake courtesies and bonhomie with each other, having debased something precious with total strangers.

I drank a lot of Tullamore Dew that night. I slept on the floor, not on the bed. I had a license, it seemed. My self-restraint had fled. There were women at the pool and women after the show, and I . . . It seemed I had turned into Mr. Hyde.

My secret potion was Irish whiskey. I began to love drinking. Not yet in need of it, I told myself how much I liked the taste of this one or that, as if there were any difference between one bottle of fermented sugar water and another. *Connoisseur*—the term just made me laugh.

My wife came to visit. There was nothing wrong between us. I didn't know why I was behaving as I was, so I forgot it. I didn't acknowledge it to myself. But inevitably she felt an estrangement.

She said, "You need to see me with new eyes." It was a plea. I didn't get it. Was I distant? I didn't think so. I loved her and especially now. Sex wasn't great between us. Had that started all this? Or was that a result of this?

One movie star visited and was available; another got drunk and was available. Wives of Iranian billionaires beckoned from the pool. And I answered.

Our run in London was coming to its end. I was glad. Life was exhausting—mentally and physically. I could sympathize with the gay men in the company who seemed to have a nightly schedule of assignations to keep. I had already made the move that identified me with them. And I liked it and did not try to hide this fact from myself. I didn't lie to myself. So, my question became, am I gay? Am I bisexual? I didn't know how to answer. I had wondered if that would be my fate someday. I had to find out.

I went to see a psychiatrist on Doctor's Row, Harley Street. His taupe and chocolate office was smallish, suitably paneled, cluttered, fusty, and comfortable. There was no couch. My chair faced his before a small writing desk. The diffuse London daylight in the window behind him gave him a dark halo, an eclipse-like penumbra that suited the weird idea of a psychiatrist for the quester sitting before him.

He looked like the British actor Leo Genn, the personification of the warm-hearted fellow who always stood out by his modesty and trustworthiness. Couldn't ask for better casting, but that made what I had to say to this nice, fatherly fellow even worse. I had to confess that I was a cheater, an adulterer, a pig, and a drinker with a homicidal streak. It wasn't that dramatic, but I was scared.

He was tamping a fresh load of Dunhill's tobacco into his perfectly Jungian pipe (no Freudian cigar). I wished for my own pipe, but that would be presumptuous, wouldn't it? We weren't colleagues. I was the sick one. I had already told him I was an actor and about the show I was in at Wyndham's. He nodded noncommittally through the setup. He didn't seem to know anything about the play, the theater, or actors. That was disconcerting to me. I suppose I thought that "special" information would help him understand. Guess not.

I launched into my story. I blamed the sex act I had done partly on my drinking. But even as I did, I realized how lame and false that was, so I tried to give social reasons. I was around it all the time in the play, so I just thought I'd try it see what all the fuss was about.

"And you liked it, you said," he said.

Did I? "Yes, but that was just . . ."

Original company of *The Boys in the Band* by Mart Crowley. L to R.
Top row: Me, Keith Prentice, Kenneth Nelson. 2nd row: Leonard Frey,
Frederick Combs, Robert La Tourneaux. Bottom row: Reuben Green,
Cliff Gorman, Peter White.

"Just . . . ?" he prompted after my long pause.

"Well, the physical thing." And I told him about "my friend" when I was sixteen.

He listened in a brown study. I love that old-timey literary phrase to describe this man's face as he listened intently and with compassion, with no hint of disgust, horror, or anger. He was not my priest or my friend. Suddenly, I was experiencing tremendous relief. I was near tears of gratitude, but his brown study precluded that easy out, as well. He was onto something.

"What do you feel now?" he murmured.

"Relief," I answered. "Confusion, anger." As I said it, I realized the ragged edges of my fury were almost uncontrollable.

"Yes?" he asked. It was both a mild question and a confirming statement, as if to himself. "What do you want to do?" he asked.

"About . . . ?"

"About anything. Relief, confusion, anger."

I surprised myself and blurted, "I want to leave the play. We have about ten more days here. I want to go home, see my wife. Leave at the end of this week. Get out. Get away."

This all came out in a rush, like vomit. It felt good to get it out, as if I'd already escaped—from London, the play, the Boys, the women, the things I'd started doing, the person I didn't know who'd done them.

Playing the role of psychiatrist, Leo Genn put down his pipe and made a small note on his pad. It was lavender. The pen was exquisite.

"Am I gay?" I asked. It came out more anguished than I'd intended. Not cool.

"Tell me a little about your father," he said. "An alcoholic, you said?"

What? How did he get in here? I began to talk faster and faster, not because I had only paid for one short hour, but because . . . because I had a lot more to say about the old bastard than I ever knew, including that I could call him an old bastard now. This man who, as far as I knew, had never done even one of the scummy things I stood self-accused of doing. As far as I knew. My mother would have known, would have let me know in her way.

I remembered shaking out their front room bed one afternoon after school. I guess my chore was housekeeper that day. As I pulled the covers off to straighten them, a Trojan package fell to the floor. A condom in its original cellophane package. These people were fucking each other! And using contraceptives! They were instantly transformed into rebels, excommunicable rebels and sinners. They had shocked their devoutly Catholic adolescent son, who was doing his chores of cleaning the house and making dinner for the family that prayed together to stay together and to convert godless Russia from communism to Catholicism.

I was shocked. Stunned, disgusted, and really angry. Angry? I remember the fear, too. What was my father if he was a sexual being? Some kind of monster? What was my mother if she let him do that? Unwittingly, I ran through about half of the script of Hamlet. What were their religious beliefs if they defied the church? Hollow. I was as angry as if I were Pope Pius XII, whose framed photo was on the wall in their bedroom, the Nazi sympathizer and contraceptive denier. Are my parents having sex? Eww!

"Leo Genn" listened to my outburst. I spoke without irony. Not cool. He listened in the same way. He relit his pipe and sat back, as calm as ever. "Your mother would let you 'know in her way' that she loved your father and had an active sexual life with him. Would this have made you complicit with her?"

"Yes. No . . . I don't know."

"But it's a troubling thought?"

I was silent, trying not to think.

"Why did you act out sexually with a stranger? Why not pick someone from your company?"

"Oh, God, no! Give them power over me? Let them laugh at me? That would confirm their stupid attitude that I must be gay, too."

He just sat there looking at me. I couldn't stand that.

"And anyway, they're my friends. I like them all. It wasn't even sex, I think. I was just curious."

"Then there's no problem, is there?" He smiled at that, a good smile. "What I mean is that all sexual expression is benign. To your question, I must say, I don't think you are homosexual. It's complex. My guess is that you are working through some very ancient feelings of identification brought on by your choosing to be in this provocative play, possibly with root causes stemming from your father's alcoholism. This is one part of the problem and my very tentative speculation. I recommend that you enter analysis when you get home to America, and in the meantime be easy on yourself." Then he said gently, "You will want to ask yourself why you are willing to risk your marriage by this behavior."

I felt freed, vindicated, told off, and chastised all in one. On impulse, I said, "Would you be willing to write a note to my company saying that I was so strung out by playing this show that I should be released a week early?"

He looked at me sharply, suddenly not Mr. Chips but Ebenezer Scrooge. "No, sir, I would not," he said. "That is not the sort of thing one does."

I felt blamed. "Sorry," I said.

"Good luck," he said. "And cheers."

On my way home from his office, I thought about what he'd said and realized this had been a watershed moment. I saw that I had buried my feelings of weakness and humiliation for being unable to protect my mother, sisters, and little brother from my drunken father. And that my mother's ferocious anger at him had scared and emasculated me. The idea that phallic power is sex in its basest form, power over another human, woman or man—I had no idea *that* had been the problem. Power.

SCENE: St. Thomas, US Virgin Islands

There was a break of four days after closing the London show and before starting the movie. I flew directly from London to the West Indies to meet my wife for some alone time with her. I loved her, missed her, and liked being with her. I had already seamlessly compartmentalized my life in London, and my infidelities had ceased to exist.

I tried to focus on her. On the baby we were having and all the planning and excitement of starting a family, but as I understand now, I was totally engrossed in myself. I was getting to act in a movie. I was nervous. I was wearing hard German-made contact lenses for extreme nearsightedness, and they hurt and were clumsy. I dripped tears all day. I had developed the Londoners' unhealthy pallor, and I had a primal need to get a tan. I needed to get back into the ocean to scuba again. It was critical to get buff and have six-pack abs by the time we started shooting in five days.

I hadn't really been with my wife for three months, and yet as soon as we dropped our bags onto the hotel room floor, I threw myself dramatically onto the four-poster plantation bed with the beautiful mosquito net curtains wafting in the Caribbean lagoon breeze. The trade wind smelled and tasted delicious, but did I care? No. Life was hard.

"My lips are chapped!" I cried.

My wife handed me a fresh-cut aloe leaf, oozing clear balm. "Try this," she said anxiously. We were about to have a baby—but wait—we already had one: *me*.

We had four days in St. Thomas. It was wonderful. We made careful love, talked about the baby, rubbed cocoa butter on her belly, waited for tiny kicks, and tried out various names of both genders. We did not want to know the sex of the baby. It would be like spoiling Christmas if we couldn't contain our childlike curiosity. Robin was splendid in all this—healthy, focused, and happy. We would start Lamaze training in New York. I was actively connected to her and the future now. London seemed like a weird dream. A childhood ago. I was a grown-up now, going to be a father. I had a wife who looked up to me and trusted me. I felt manly and content. I was not a person who drank until I was spinning out of control, who had sex with other women and even with a man. These events didn't happen, wouldn't happen, *couldn't* happen.

Of course, today I know they did, and I feel the shame and the regret of the waste I sowed with my late-blooming wild oats that I couldn't, wouldn't, didn't let myself feel then.

I was thirty-five years old. Finally successful. I could make it. Could support a wife and family. What could go wrong?

We slept, ate healthy Caribbean food, and swam in the luminous, clear sea. New York, London, those things I'd done, the film—all shrank and disappeared like the Wicked Witch. The only reality was this moment. It was the swift onset of island fever.

I went diving. The instructor was a rangy, easy-going ex-Navy diver. He took me from the shallows to the depths. In three dives, I got comfortable with the mask and tanks. I got good enough that I didn't know what I didn't know— just enough to be dangerous. We swam through sunken, sunlit caves alongside painted coral and down the side of deep cliffs where mirror-like blacktip reef sharks flickered in the distance and grinning barracuda longer and thicker than I kept us company in schools, troops, like a faintly menacing police escort.

I had found a world where I forgot who I was and who I hoped to be. Much better than booze. Nepenthe.

We went back to New York, she to her NBC soap, me to do the film iteration of *The Boys in the Band*.

SCENE: New York

In China, it was the Year of the Cock. A good or bad omen? In America, it was the year of the skin flick, of *SCREW* and *PLEASURE* magazines, Andy Warhol's *Blue Movie* and *Dionysus in '69*.

And it was the year of the Hindu Yoni and Lingam.

> Well, my God, if you want to win an Academy Award with a film about faggots, you've got to release it this year. I mean, 1969 is our year!
> —A PRODUCER, *THE BOYS IN THE BAND*

The alarm next to the bed rang at 6:15 A.M. I had been awake for forty-five minutes, afraid I would not hear it. At 6:20, the second alarm rang on the kitchen table, setting off simultaneous vibrations in the nerve springs already coiled in my neck. My sleepyhead pregnant wife did not stir, her lovely belly a big, blue balloon under the summer coverlet in our freezing air-conditioned apartment. I rolled out of bed and put on my track shoes and sweat suit, picked up my basketball, rolled up my house keys in the sleeve of my shirt, and slipped out the door and down to the front desk.

I walked out onto Twenty-Third Street and turned east, jogging toward the river. Nobody was out but the odd hustler creeping homeward under the copper ball hanging in the already steamy haze over Brooklyn across the river. In a car lot, a black limo was occupied by its driver lying slack-jawed in the seat. I wondered if he was sleeping or passed out until I saw a tousled blonde head rising and falling rapidly over his lap. Hmm. Breakfast break?

I jogged east to the river and turned south, paced by a silent tugboat headed for the Battery. I made it around Cooper Union Village twice and returned to my house. I took the basketball across the street to the deserted playground of the junior high school, where for fifteen minutes I practiced dribbling the ball, getting green glass splinters in my fingers from the broken wine bottles on the court. I worked on making jump shots, rebounding, stopping short, passing, and covering my imaginary man. I looked like a goddamned idiot, which is why I did it at this hour. A homeless guy watched hopefully as I missed about twelve baskets in a row and finally turned away in disgust to sleep in the dirty newspapers in the corner of the fence.

I was thirty-five years old and had never played basketball in my life. In one hour, in front of a camera in the gym of the McBurney YMCA, I would be playing a Saturday afternoon scratch game against the Paterson (New Jersey) High School All-American team. Sparking my five, as usual, I would drive hard down the court through those six-foot-four sixteen-year-old heroes, jump, make the shot, and win the game. At home in the dark kitchen, I dressed, drank a cup of coffee, and poured a glass of milk to line my stomach against nerves. I picked up my scripts and left for work. Except for the absence of a brown paper sack smelling of mayonnaise and pickles, it felt exactly the same as it did all those years ago, going to work at the Fruitvale Cannery: Same industrial smog smell to the air. Same skulking, depressed workers waiting for buses. Same hour.

Only now *I was a movie star reporting for my first major motion picture!* (Really?!) I was Hank—"Thirty-two, tall, solid, athletic, attractive"—one of the Boys. Ex-Former college basketball star, high school teacher, formerly married with two kids, now divorced, homosexual. I have my standard equipment in my ever-present airline bag: Excedrin, a bottle of vitamin C, Noxzema, foot powder,

ChapStick, eyewash, deodorant, handkerchief, hairbrush, mirror, toothpaste, and toothbrush. A little more than a purse but less than an overnight bag.

I also had my script, 147 scenes long, which over the next ten weeks I would help translate into more than 120,000 feet of exposed film. It would be edited to one-tenth that length for the final print, mixed with as many as six soundtracks, color coordinated, scored, and released by Cinema Center Films in Los Angeles and New York by Christmas. Under the Academy of Motion Picture Arts and Sciences rules, a picture must play these two cities in a given year to be eligible for an award that year. Although nothing official had been said, we, collectively, were definitely shooting for that award. If our first picture won an award, we were set in the business, right? Or, as one producer said, "You've got a blockbuster here, fellas. This picture is going to make you all stars, and I mean that, kids."

There were nine of us. Nine relatively obscure New York stage actors for whom this was the payoff of two long years of our lives. For some of us, it was the threshold of the thrilling glamour world of the movies. For some, it was only another job, and for one, it was the last step toward prison.

At 7:50 A.M., I arrived at the YMCA and followed the power cables winding upstairs into the gym. Here was a maelstrom of seeming chaos: lights being moved in and out, cables being coiled, sandbags dropping, sound booms hovering like helicopters about to pick up the wounded, and the camera, inscrutable and dangerous as a minotaur, squatting in the center.

An incredibly impressive display of technical skill was happening, but the astonishing thing was the quiet and speed of it. The only sound was a desultory murmuring of the crew and the swish of large, wheeled objects being maneuvered into more precise positions. The director of photography was wandering like a butterfly collector, scooping the light out of the air with a light meter. Using stand-ins, the assistant director was lining up the shot.

A wardrobe man seized me and propelled me firmly into an impromptu dressing room where, together with six or eight of the atmosphere (extras), I dressed rapidly in shorts and a sweatshirt. In seconds, with no makeup and unshaven, I was as ready as your average Saturday jock.

Suddenly, I was called for in a panic-stricken voice by the assistant to the assistant director. I had just arrived. Am I late? Panic is an AD's province, of course, and, poor guy, all upper-echelon insanity burns him as naturally as bacon grease splattering from a hot skillet. It's like the army. No wonder we in this business refer to everyone outside as civilians.

I jogged onto the court and was introduced to my team and its captain.

I had consistently taken the Fifth to the director's casual but insistent inquires as to the status of my hook shot. The AD emerged from the prop room with a basketball, and fired it at me.

"Shoot some," he commanded. "Billy wants to see how you work so we can set up the scene tomorrow."

I shot a few, chasing the ball as it caromed off the rim, hit the nearest 750-watt light stand, and rolled behind sheets of fake brick stacked against the wall. The director appeared, watched noncommittally for a moment, then, taking the ball away, bounced it once and fired it expertly over his shoulder, making a perfect basket.

"Don't worry, baby," he said. "I'll make ya look great." Then, gave me a fist to the bicep, and walked away.

As a result of my impressive performance, they immediately arranged a double for me. "He'll do all the shots and the dribbling. All you have to do is run around," said the AD. "So, no sweat, pal. You're covered."

Sweating, I headed for the court. We were to play five or six half-court games of ten points each. I was assigned a man to guard and told simply to run as hard as I could but not shoot the ball when it came to me, but merely pass it on. The director explained in detail how to throw the ball. We were waiting, ready for the action cue, when someone noticed several septuagenarian sportsmen sidling slowly down the sidelines carrying Indian clubs, medicine balls, and towels. They had arrived for their daily workout and no one had clued them in that we were shooting a movie. Litigiously defending their civil rights, they ensconced themselves at the rear of the room where they remained throughout the shooting, taking no further notice of us, creakingly keeping fit, contributing an accidental verismo to the scene.

The game is dominated by two talented players who performed for the camera delightedly, blocking me with grinning ease and running my ass into the polished floorboards. Once, when I attempted to get in under the basket where the camera is (no fool am I), a very heavy knee crashed into my kidney, stunning me and holding up filming for fifteen minutes while I recovered.

At lunch, one of the boys, a high school star, said, "Man, this is tough, this acting. I'm tired, man. And I'm in shape. I don't see how you're gonna make it at your age!"

Despite this friendly death blow, on the next take, with one of those bursts of adrenaline that creates Congressional Medal of Honor winners, I grabbed the ball, dribbled downcourt behind my teammates, abruptly stopped at the three-point line, lifted the ball in a long shot, and made it. My team was so surprised they applauded. The camera, luckily, had caught it all.

In the afternoon, reduced to a bag of rubber bands and nursing my kidney, I returned to the locker room where I was to do the final shot of the day. I walked to the pay phone that had been installed by our prop man, through teammates and extras showering, dressing, and weighing themselves, where I spoke silently under the hubbub to my roommate, Larry, for whom I had left my wife and children. The take was nearly finished before someone noticed that one of my nude teammates was facing straight into the camera. As oblivious as Eve Harrington, he was eagerly overacting the unfolding of a lavender silk shirt to wear for his movie debut while his unusually well-endowed equipment silently stole the scene. A whispered discussion of whether the sequence could be used prompted the decision to print it pending a release from the lavender-clad lad and ended when some wit makes a bris joke: "Well, it may be possible to cut the piece later."

I was on film. What bit sharply at the edge of my mind was that, for good or for ill, my face would soon be synonymous with homosexuality to millions of filmgoers. I was an unknown film face, and no matter what I may have believed about free expression, I was taking a risk in doing this as my first film. But I had met a great many men like Hank in my life, homosexual and heterosexual, men who stand in the background until they were forced to defend themselves, which they did with dignity and power. I admired Hank.

* * *

I'm not going to say anything about the script. I'm sure you all know more about this little potboiler than I do.

—Mart Crowley, the first day

Thursday, May 15, 1969, was the first day we gathered with the entire cast on the actual set to begin work on this film. It was the eighteenth month since we had come together and the fourth complete restaging of the play since the first workshop. A few days earlier, on May 10th, we had closed in Wyndham's Theatre in London. We had the most challenging run imaginable in England, and everyone was beyond exhaustion. One of us, going through an unhappy love affair, had been openly weeping between lines onstage for the last two weeks. Backstage, at least three of us were not on speaking terms, and this was a group of men who had begun with a great and unusual amount of love and trust for one another, bound in a common cause, taking a risk together. But this had barely survived London. Several, including me, had spent a few intermissions just drunk enough to go back and endure our London audiences again.

English audiences! In New York, our audiences cared more about the play than the display. But London was vanity fair, and we were the grotesques.

Only a month before the film was to begin shooting, we finally learned that our original cast of players was indeed going to be in it. Mart Crowley told us that producer Ray Stark had offered him a ton of dough to replace the original group of "fags" with Hollywood "stars," but Mart had done the impossible—he had hung tough and made it possible for us to recreate in the movie these roles we had lived onstage for so long.

The nine of us had been playing stiff upper lip in London for just over one hundred and fifty dollars a week. We would now be in our first movie. Nobody thought of money. Who cared? Including Mart himself as screenwriter and producer. He deserved it all. He was a mensch. It was a lot bigger than mere money for us. At Hy Brown's film studio on West Twenty-Sixth Street in New York, we nine originals now faced approximately twenty-five film production staff. It was a rooftop terrace set. Around us was the usual battlefield of hammering, shouting, and the sliding of heavy equipment that orchestrates the chaos of any Italian ferryboat sinking. The floor was covered in brown paper, and Krylon was in the air.

The director, William Friedkin, welcomed us and introduced the staff to us. "I just want to say how pleased I am to be working with such a marvelous bunch of actors. You guys don't have to prove anything to me. But there is one thing I will not, cannot, tolerate on a set, and that is any display of temperament. We cannot put up with any temper tantrums from anybody. If anybody has a problem, we'll go to my office and discuss it privately. Okay?" Then, turning to the producers with a wide, boyish grin, he said, "I'm happy!"

There were three producers on the picture. Mart, of course. Then Executive Producer Robert Jiras, a kind, worried, warm, baggy-eyed basset of a man who stood around, hands in pockets, always in a rumpled seersucker jacket and blue cotton work shirt. He usually looked like a visitor watching everything alone from a dark corner of the set, one eye in, one eye out. Perhaps since he commuted from Vermont on weekends to visit his much-loved young son, he was mentally in transit much of the time. The usual half-hourly crises on the set evoked from him a standard shoulders up, hands out Fernandel gesture, and he'd say, "Don't make me the heavy, boys. I tell you, I don't know anything about it."

Dominick Dunne was the other executive producer. He had been around Hollywood for years. His brother was John Gregory Dunne, whose book *The Studio* had done a brilliant axe job on Twentieth Century Fox the year before. Nick was short, suntanned from weekends on Fire Island, and dapper, with the face of a Graham Greene priest. His voice was a shy, barely audible murmur. Nick seemed soft, deprecating, self-effacing, the perfect go-between. Some of the actors felt he was the one in control of the picture. The curious thing was that he nearly always dressed like Mart, whose standard issue uniform was a pair of last season's Gucci loafers, tan chinos, an open-neck polo shirt, and a dark blue blazer. Day after day they dressed the same, except for the fact that Nick's chinos usually bagged around his ankles, and Mart's were always razor-creased and spotless as a German battleship commander's trousers. They pulled so many similar outfits from their respective armoires that some people on the set called them the Gucci Twins.

Jiras and Dunne together dealt with the business of the actors, the unions, and set and studio problems. Mart, as tense and hot as the tungsten wire in an incandescent bulb, was everywhere at once, seemingly controlling all artistic decisions.

Friedkin was a mystery to us. He was twenty-nine years old. His previous pictures included something with Sonny and Cher, *The Birthday Party* with Harold Pinter, and *The Night They Raided Minsky's*. Friedkin was from Chicago, as American as Mayor Daley, you might say, and as violent as cherry pie.

> I'm sure a lot of people are prepared for scenes depicting bizarre and unusual sex practices. Those who are looking for this sort of thing in (the film of *Boys*) are going to be disappointed.
> —WILLIAM FRIEDKIN, *NEW YORK* MAGAZINE, AUGUST 1969

SCENE: The Boys in the Band studio

I'm remembering being in the director's office and William Friedkin is talking about his research for the film. Sitting behind his desk in a fresh, neatly pressed polo shirt, tan chinos, and desert boots, his clothes hang loosely on his tall, thin, gawky frame, even in repose.

Sitting on a couch lower than the desk, I look up at the man sitting in the director's chair—Friedkin—lighting his morning cigar for the second time. He holds it in one hand, away from his mouth, while the other carefully fires it with a butane lighter from the set, and offers, "It gives you cancer, you know, lighting a cigar with it in your mouth," as he slumps soulfully back in his chair, thick, green stogie comfortably lit and nestled gently between long, bony forefinger and thumb. He launches into a story: "So, I went out to Fire Island and stayed a weekend, the Boatel, the beach, the whole bit, and you know what, man? I wanted to find out what it was like, so I told them to take me out to the Meat Rack. You know the Meat Rack? It's fantastic! You go out to the end of the boardwalk, it's pitch dark, you can't see a fucking thing, you dig? It's so spooky, man. I was terrified. All these guys just walk up and down and look at you. Hundreds of guys, walking up and down, looking each other over, and all around, in the bushes, under the boardwalk, in the sand, fucking noises, sucking noises, it's incredible. Man, I was nervous!" He laughs with a gush of air expelled with force. "This first guy came up to me and walked around me several times. Didn't look at me. Nobody looks at your face, man. They look at your crotch. Finally, he just took a step toward me or something, and I jumped a mile. He just shrugged, turned around, and walked off like it wasn't worth the effort. Like, 'Christ, fuck it,' you know?"

Gail, the secretary, pops her head in. "Billy, they're on the phone from California."

Friedkin pulls on his cigar gently, musingly, running through his mental file marked "Homosexual Behavior: Meat Rack." He waves the cigar in the direction of the West Coast. "Fuck 'em. They're too late. I've got a scene to shoot." Light flashes on his glasses as he swivels toward me. "Let's make this film, baby. Ready?" His desert boots carry him out. I follow.

SCENE: A dressing room at Boys in the Band studio

An actor enters a dingy closet with two names stenciled on the door. Scuffing on the filthy rug, he throws an airline bag onto the stained table under the fluorescent-lit mirror, hangs his shirt on one of two nails in the wall, and goes down the dirty hallway. He stops at the open door of the men's room. Rusty water the color of blood stands in the urinals, giving the effect of a clinic specializing in male kidney ailments. The actor turns on the hot water tap. It runs brownish-red for a minute and is only mildly tepid. He shrugs, washes his hands, and inserts contact lenses. He exits and walks a few steps to the makeup room.

Fred, the only custodian for the four floors of the studio, is stashing a hot coffee urn on a shelf. It is full of his excellent brew. Verne Caruso, the latest and best of a series of six hairdressers who resigned or were fired from the film, is waiting with two cups. She hands me a steaming black one and the same to Frederick Combs (Donald)—"Twenty-eight, medium blonde, wholesome American good looks."

He puts down a letter he has been chuckling over. "It's a residual check from a TV run of my first movie," he says. "It's $3.28 for *The King's Pirate*, in which I appeared briefly behind a door and handed Doug McClure some pirate clothes."

Frederick, a mild, friendly chap healthily unconcerned with his super good looks, sips eagerly at one of the many cups of coffee he drinks each day and settles back as Verne repairs his wiry hair, frazzled in a bad straightening job in London. He and I, known as "the hair freaks" have come in an hour earlier than the others to have a coif made up—me (Hank) because my usual method is just to run my hand back and forth through my hair vigorously. The day I showed up on the set with it neatly combed, the hairdresser of the day shrieked that I looked balder than the character Michael, who in the play is worried about his falling hair. Ultimately, however, most of the Boys began getting their hair done because the movie problem of matching the exact same curl or fall of lock from day to day over the whole schedule got to be too much.

Overflowing with Mr. Fish's flamboyance, Kenneth Nelson (Michael)— "thirty, average face, smartly groomed, worried about his vanishing hair"—arrives and falls gracefully into a makeup chair, and opens a book on eccentric Victorian Englishwomen. He is here early to have his own full, curly locks neatly shaved away around the forehead in a weekly ritual that creates the illusion of his encroaching baldness. The room soon fills up with the rest of the cast. Reuben Green (Bernard)—"twenty-eight, negro, nice looking"—sits quietly with a book. Robert La Tourneaux (Cowboy)—"twenty-two, light blond, muscle-bound"—does pull ups from an overhead pipe, shirtless. Peter White (Alan)—"thirty, aristocratic, Anglo-Saxon features"—relaxes in the back of the room in a perfectly fitted off-the-rack tuxedo. This gathering of talented artistes is overseen by our cantankerous clown, John Jiras, brother of the executive producer and head of the makeup department.

The place is a madhouse because John (J.J.) is a madman. He works three chairs at once and oversees the hair and makeup. But his true interest is real estate, and he has deals cooking all over New York, Connecticut, and Long Island. He races from makeup chair to wall phone, powder puff in hand, one shoulder cocked up to hold the phone, pockets full of the pencil stubs and ragged notes with which he keeps his empire together.

Whipping us out of one chair and into another, he declaims, "My empire in Southampton is crumbling, but there's nobody here who knows anything about prosthetics. Nobody understands shading, the delicacy of these hands." He holds out his hands. "My God, I think this is the time to sell. I'm moving from Connecticut to Long Island, and I'll get that houseboat, throw some beer in the box, and rent it out for weekends, fifty dollars a weekend. My God, get Abe Fortas on the phone!"

Back in my dressing room, I find Keith Prentice (Larry)—"twenty-nine with a starkly simple sense of individual style and color in his clothes. Dark eyes,

The film version of *The Boys in the Band*. As Hank, I stop the fight.

"I don't know when it was I started admitting it to myself. For so long I either labeled it something else or denied it completely." —Hank, *The Boys in the Band*

dark hair, mustache, extremely handsome." He is late as usual, barely shaved (he never had a mustache), cursing loudly, and calling for aid in struggling with yet another of his complicated costumes. This is number four in a series of eight blue silk shirts, each costing nearly two hundred dollars, that have been mismeasured, mis-buttoned, shrunk, frayed, lost, or otherwise screwed up. Two of the "best tailors in New York" had been engaged to provide this service, and were responsible for getting leg lengths wrong and making casual chino pants that were purchasable ready-made not two blocks away, from scratch—with darts showing the folded-under material and crotches coming out mysteriously too short.

Leonard Frey (Harold)—"thirty-two, lean, strong limbs, unusual face" is upstairs in the makeup room on the studio floor having plastic pockmarks put on by pockspert Bob O'Bradovich, but later, he will arrive at his birthday party in a Kay Francis–esque outfit—high, wide fedora arched over one brow, long plastic rain cape, umbrella under which is a velvet jacket with a contrasting velvet collar, specially cut so that it can't close and hangs without bunching, raw silk shirt, huge ascot tie, doeskin trousers, and patent-leather pumps.

"I feel like I'm going to a harvest moon ball," Leonard offers, barely moving his lips, his large brown eyes rolling like a drowning squirrel.

"It looks like Halloween," someone says. Billy and Mart stand aghast, and look like Pandora the moment she opened the box. And thus, another exquisitely expensive extravaganza bites the dust. The outfit is replaced with ready-made items off the rack from Ohrbach's. Another accessory—a large green chiffon scarf—and see-through billowing sleeved blouse for Emory, the mintiest guy at the party, is ditched the first day.

> We decided to keep out all easy references to the gay world in the décor and the clothes . . . it would have been a simple matter to camp it all up, dress everyone like Oscar Wilde.
> —WILLIAM FRIEDKIN, *NEW YORK* MAGAZINE, AUGUST 1969

We all had canvas deck chairs with our names painted on them. They were a far cry from the trailers some of us had fantasized about. "I'll be in my trailer" was the standard crisis cry in London, delivered in the best Bette Davis husk. But New York reality was setting in. It was only a little disappointing that our canvas chairs were wedged in between one wall of the set and the toilets, in the only passageway for the carpenters and scene painters. We concentrated fairly well despite breathing in the residue from the odd spray paint job.

This morning, the chair cranny looked like a library, with Ken Nelson drily destroying the *NY Times* crossword puzzle and *The Life That Late He Led* being devoured jointly by Leonard Frey and Bob La Tourneaux. *The Love Machine* was being passed around the stand-ins, who were consigned to wooden benches. One fellow actually read the orchestral score of a symphony for two full weeks lying on a bench, bored out of his skull with the waiting.

"First team!" yells the AD.

The second assistant shouts back, "Flying in!"

Those of us in the first shot go to the set. The set is a fantastically detailed mock-up of Tammy Grimes' East Side apartment. Several daylight B-roll background bits had already been filmed on the terrace of her place to take advantage of the skyline. Inside the studio, where the rest of the picture would be filmed in the evening, a model of the cityscape background had been laboriously built, detail upon detail. There was a miniature skyline with three-dimensional ventilator pipes rising out of rooftops and buildings with cut-out windows, little venetian blinds hanging in them and scaled to be seen as if fifty or more yards away. Some maniacal member of John Robert Lloyd's crew (our set designer who had just completed *Midnight Cowboy*) had even done a minuscule oil painting hanging on the wall of a loft apartment across from the terrace, a still life of red flowers. Plastic moldings of actual bricks and typical brownstone cornice decorations were taken and attached to facades built in perspective like Palladian trompe l'oeil scenes. Finally, a tiny chain of lights was attached to a flat on the east wall of the studio, painted to represent the skyline east of the Fifty-Ninth Street Bridge. As filming commenced, a stagehand stood below this Tinkertoy and played push-pull with an ingenious machine that simulated the moving automobile traffic on the bridge. The crew's fantastic attention to detail, like imitating tiny cracks in brick and rain streaks from a rusty nail in a picket fence, would have delighted the Italian restorers of Giotto's frescos.

The crew is lining up the shot, Harold's entrance at the end of the first act. Hank, assisted by Bernard, has pinned Alan to the floor. Emory, who Alan has just attacked, is bleeding all over the couch and Bernard. Larry is racing for an ice pack past Cowboy, who has just knocked over a table trying to get out of the way. Michael has retreated to the bar, and Donald opens the front door to find Harold, stoned out of his mind, leaning against the jamb.

We will spend the morning on this master shot, which will be seen from one angle. The afternoon will be spent covering it in close-ups from all points of view. Thus, it goes.

The Cowboy has disappeared. He's found behind the set doing pull-ups on his personal chinning bar.

Friedkin calls out, "Glad you are getting some use out of the athletic facilities."

La Tourneaux, who pumped up his biceps each night before going on stage, had used a steam pipe at Theater Four, with gloves for winter.

Friedkin makes marvelous suggestions about the scene. His brilliant technical knowledge of the medium has made complicated split-second shtick effortlessly easy. Now, he takes Leonard aside and gives him a piece of business to do when the door opens that will break Keith (Larry) up.

We are ready to run it through one final time for the camera when Cliff (Emory) screams, "The guy has just been hit in the mouth, right? And there's blood, a lotta blood. Just let me do it for myself, for Chrissake!"

J.J. appears on set, and he and Cliff argue for five minutes. Friedkin makes a decision that solves this. He disappears downstairs to his office.

"Second team!" calls the AD, and stand-ins replace us while our positions are lighted. Hair, costumes, and makeup are fussed over. Half an hour passes. We go back to the set for last-second framing and focus checks. Friedkin continues his quiet, private sessions with each of us, carefully explaining the effects he wants.

The AD says, "Lock it up," meaning the studio doors. Then he says, "Speed." Sound and camera get up to recording speed, the set goes quiet, everything falls away but the moment before us, and Friedkin whispers, "Action."

We recreate the aftermath of the moment when Alan attacks Emory, and we separate them. It ends. Friedkin waits a moment longer for the spontaneous improvisational feeling that follows the action. He says, "Cut! Print that." We go to lunch.

In the afternoon, we do close-ups of the scene, constantly checked by the continuity person for a match. For close-ups to be cut into a master shot, the actors' movements, eye direction, light, clothing—everything, in theory—must match the master. The word *continuity* only barely describes the living record of technical details, notes on the length of the take, the lens used, the kind of shot, any changes in script, the film used, the slate number, and so on.

"Continuity," a young woman informed me. "Formerly, m'dear, I merely point out that you unbuttoned your jacket with your right hand on Michael's line, 'You do know each other,' completing the same on the word 'each,' while at the same instant taking the pipe from your mouth with your left hand and shifting your weight to your left foot. Now, if you do indeed wish to match, and I somewhat plaintively hope you do, then you must not, I repeat, *not* be cleaning your pipe on that line as you just seemed inclined to do."

At first, Friedkin seldom bothered with matching, preferring to cut into extreme close-ups or to let the actors do the master shot over again. He had insisted on shooting in sequence, which was indescribably easier for the actors, and which he did for our benefit, but it kept the pace very slow. In the first week or so, we got an average of five setups a day completed, against television series' records of fifty-six a day.

The brass had desperately wanted Adam Holender as director of photography. He was the hottest guy in the business, having just delivered the huge hit *Midnight Cowboy*. Friedkin and Crowley loved his work. On the day after the showing of the first in-studio terrace scenes, Adam left the picture. Whether he was fired or quit, we never knew. All we knew was that the brass were extremely unhappy over the look of the skyline backdrop, which in dailies came out looking exactly like what it was—plastic and painted cardboard—and the blame had settled most unfairly on Adam. Part of the problem lay with Lloyd's set itself, which came out looking fake even though it was highly detailed and heavily veiled behind a scrim. It was a brave but impossible mission to build and light the set. It didn't work, and had cost lots of time and money. The real issue was the slow pace of shooting, which was now corrected the movie way: by brutally firing one artist and hiring another. Holender worked through that last afternoon, and at 6:00 P.M., on the verge of tears, shook hands with everyone, drank a final round, and quietly slipped out.

Arthur Ornitz, Academy Award nominee at nineteen, now in his fifties and with a reputation for a wild temper, came in like a whirlwind and buckled to his first task: fixing the backdrop stuff. He promptly put the lovely New York miniature into silhouette. No little lights under the bridge, no tiny cars moving over it. No teensy oil painting in an apartment over the way. It was now night in the city. Midnight, cowboy.

The pace moved up terrifically. No more one-hour waits between shots. Ornitz, fierce, with sandy mustache bristling, looking like a Mediterranean tour guide in an ice cream suit and white kid slippers without socks, would shout fifty orders to his crew in seconds. "How much time do you want to spend on this one? Fifteen? You got it! Sal, close that barn door a skosh. Get me a deuce over here and goo-goo it. I need a 750. Gimme an eye light. *Move*, boys!"

We all tried to keep up with his pace. Ten minutes after being handed a complex lighting problem, he would tell the AD to get the director back up on the set, ready to shoot. On his first day, we got seventeen setups. This was our average even through the long dinner scene when Leonard (Harold) had to gobble down a whole plate of lasagna about a hundred times in coverage and retakes. He said he gained forty pounds.

But then the rains came, and order was washed away. The day we all dreaded, the Tennessee Williams turning point—dinner eaten, gifts given, grass inhaled—arrived. Michael turns to face the rising wind on the terrace and says,

"In the end, you are responsible for yourself." At his words, rain splashes on his face, instantly turning into a downpour drenching Hank, Michael, Donald, and Cowboy.

Above the studio-built terrace, a sprinkler system had been installed to provide a massive torrent. Above that, clinging to the grid, three crew guys augment the downpour with fire extinguishers full of cold water, and a seven-foot fan aimed at the terrace turns us all into Sadie Thompsons. Only now has it been discovered that a drain system for the rain has been totally forgotten, and the set is flooded. All work stops. The set is taken down, and a drain system is installed over the weekend. It took only one preplanning error. The result? Overtime for the crew.

Finally, the drain is installed. "Action!" yells Friedkin, and the actors ad-lib through the complicated rain scene perfectly. "Fantastic," said Friedkin. "Now let's get one more right away!"

"Right away" in movieland means at least half an hour, so we stand, shivering in wet clothes from the blast of the air conditioner that someone had forgotten to turn off. When it became obvious that there were many days of wetness ahead, warm robes were provided along with hot soup to keep us on schedule for take after take. And between each take, everything had to be restored completely dry—roses, lasagna, floors, hair, makeup, and costumes. The pressure on Friedkin was now intense.

Efficiency experts—the suits—from Cinema Center Films in Hollywood visited the set to check on delays, and that day, Billy drove everybody: tongue-lashing the slow, joshing the meek, cheering up the downhearted, comforting the sick, supporting the weary—a veritable tower of bagels from which all received sustenance. It was the old army game played by a master. I was in awe of the change in this sincere, brilliantly creative young director, wrought by pressure. He rose like a rocket to conquer all. All the producers had disappeared. Everybody was somewhere else.

Wardrobe phoned the designer—Keith's (Larry's) blue shirt and pants had shrunk in the rain, so he couldn't be filmed from the waist up or knees down. They needed another outfit. The young man who answered the phone at the shop refused to put the call through. The petit-maître was "sketching and couldn't be disturbed." Now everyone was disturbed.

It was like watching a manila rope holding a very heavy weight unravel strand by strand.

* * *

Emotions on the set are boiling over. In the scene, Reuben Greene (Bernard) has been put down savagely by a very drunk Kenny Nelson (Michael), who casually calls him the N-word. Reuben's deep rage and antipathy for a part he—or any Black man—had to hate (because it's a classic Uncle Tom) boils over. He blows take after take, unable to say his lines. Then, at the moment when Bernard rushes at Michael and is restrained by Donald, Reuben overplays and knocks Ken Nelson to the floor. Reuben instantly apologizes, which Ken icily accepts. We stand stunned and embarrassed, aware suddenly of the danger of pressing on the same nerve ends night after night for two years until they are as raw as this. We withdraw, leaving Ken and Reuben to work it out alone on a closed set.

In his big scene, Cliff Gorman (Emory) bursts into hysterical tears and weeps throughout one take. Billy is appalled but lets it play out. The take will end up on the proverbial cutting room floor. Cliff walks away embarrassed. No one can say anything to him.

One director trick is to get an actor to say personal things off-camera to provide a stimulus for the actor being filmed. Sometimes, with comedy, it can work brilliantly. This time, however, it doesn't. Remarks made relating to an affair the actor has not recovered from, as the actor gamely tries to use this very personal hurt in his character's big scene, result only in a breakdown, and the actor has to leave the set.

Cuidado. Affective memories are dynamite. Danger. Use with caution.

SCENE: Boys in the Band Studio: The Kiss

The kiss, in its legal aspect, is a natural application of the ideas which produced handshaking and similar modes of conduct. Medieval knights kissed as modern boxers shake hands before the encounter.
—CHRISTOPHER NYROP, *THE KISS AND ITS HISTORY*

This kiss is a sign that our souls are united and that we banish all remembrance of injury.

—ST. CYRIL

I don't know. The kiss has just got to have . . . despair and comfort.
—MART CROWLEY

What they wanted was a kiss. What was going on in the relationship made a kiss impossible. The Hollywood brass let it be known that a kiss—beautiful,

The Boys in the Band movie, off-camera. As Hank, reacting to the bitter argument with his partner.

hungry, maybe with tongue, no less—would satisfy the vulgar desire to understand the homosexual man. "BS!" I said.

After spending the entire play fighting a lover's duel over Larry's promiscuity, finally, in front of their friends, Hank and Larry take each other apart with razor-edged truth. Hank goes upstairs to deal with his devastating dilemma, and Larry follows, possibly to try to salvage the wreckage of their relationship. In the film script, this scene ensues:

> The room is dark, illuminated only by occasional flashes of lightning. LARRY enters, sees HANK sitting on the edge of the bed, his face buried in his hands. LARRY closes the door, goes over to him, kneeling before him. He reaches up, pushes HANK's hands away, puts his own hands about HANK's face. He rises on his knees, kisses HANK.

This scene was added to the film script. The kiss was not in the play. But it appeared in the film script, and I objected right away. Director Bob Moore had eighty-sixed it from the workshop version and the off-Broadway and London versions and had, ex post facto, decided it was unnecessary. He was absolutely correct.

However, during rehearsals for the film, Mart and I had dinner together at Joe Allen's to discuss the kiss and a couple of line cuts in the roles of Hank and Larry, which I felt should be restored. Amid the flurry of short-jacketed waiters around the table, he vaguely promised that we wouldn't have to do the kiss if we didn't want to. But the gentle intrigue and flimflam flapdoodle that followed would prove otherwise.

There were phone calls at night telling Keith and me how brilliant we were, how our relationship was stealing the picture and, more to the present point, how we needed something, a tag, a real payoff, to walk away with the picture. There were clappings on the back off-set and veiled hints that we would "have to get together for lunch one day and discuss this whole kiss bit."

Friedkin's method was more direct. He grabbed Keith and me separately for interviews in his office to sound us out. He said he knew I probably had psychological reasons, beyond the ones I gave, for not wanting to do it. I was "likely afraid to kiss a man on the lips." With Keith, he argued that refusing to do something demanded by the script and director was the worst, most unprofessional thing an actor could do.

Keith and I refused to do it on four grounds: it was emotionally impossible to justify; given the emotional climate of the time it could only be tasteless and sensational; it had not been done in the play in its twenty-eight-month run and had never been missed; and we had been promised we would not have to do it.

Keith and I compared notes on all these meetings and wondered, since no good reason had been given to us as to why the kiss—never necessary before—was suddenly so important to the film. We came to believe that Hollywood—Cinema Center—was insisting it be included to sell the picture. Simple-minded sensationalism.

There was great shock and consternation at our attitude. The possibility of an actor opposing the brass with his own sense of truth and taste was impossible to accede to. Was it rebellion? Mutiny?

SCENE: Producer's Office at The Boys in the Band Studio

Crowley is behind his desk, Dunne behind his. Jiras is in a chair facing Prentice and me, together on the low couch. Friedkin is behind a table near the door. Foil-covered paper plates of deli food are cooling in front of everyone.

Nick Dunne balances his beer glass in both hands and breathes. "Well, we're here to talk about the kiss. How's that for openers?"

Silence. Friedkin bites on a pickle. Crowley shifts impatiently.

Suddenly, Friedkin says, "Mart feels there should be a kiss, and I must say I agree with him about it. At first, when we met to discuss the script at the Russian Tea Room and he asked me what I thought should happen when the two of you go into the bedroom, my first instinct was nothing. And I told him that. But since then, I've come to believe there can be a kiss. And what's more, there should be a kiss.

"Now, we would like to offer you a compromise because we respect you both so highly as artists and because your work on the film has been brilliant. We just want you to trust us. We will film the scene both ways, your way and our way, and we will look at both ways as fairly as we know how and then decide which one works best. I think that is a reasonable compromise. You're responsible people. But I will tell you this: the kiss will be in the film. It's in the script and it will be in the film."

Keith looked up from picking at his stale, dry hamburger. "Then why do you want to film it both ways, Billy?"

Silence.

Nick Dunne broke in. "Tell us what you want to do, Larry."

"I think since we have done without the kiss for two years, and it has worked brilliantly, that it is better to cut after Keith exits the living room and let the audience imagine what's going on in the bedroom when Michael says, 'What do you suppose they're doing up there, Alan?'"

"No good, man. I don't buy it," says Billy.

"I'm sorry," I said. "Keith and I have to live with what ends up on the screen a lot longer than any of you, and we aren't going to kiss. It makes an ass out of Hank and an idiot out of Larry. How could he think he could save the situation with a kiss? After what he's done to me, I'd knock him downstairs if he tried to kiss me at that point. Why don't we improvise a scene that would happen naturally and you film that? Trust us."

"But Larry," Mart says. "If every actor could refuse to do things he didn't believe in, that would be anarchy."

I said, "Then I guess it's time for a little anarchy."

Keith put aside his paper plate of a half-eaten burger. We both got up.

"Think about it," said Nick.

"We will," I said.

We left and shut the door.

The next day at lunch, Nick, worried, said to me, "Pal, we don't have in mind . . . I don't mean anything like tongues down the throat, anything like that."

I told him that Keith and I had decided that the only way we would do a kiss the way they wanted was if they went to the Screen Actors Guild and forced us to. And then only under protest.

"Pal," he said, "we don't want to get involved with all that SAG mess."

The week wore on. Billy was attentive and warm to us. The night before the kiss scene, whatever it was going to be, was to be shot, Mart called Keith at home and chatted idly for a while, then suddenly said that he had been thinking about the scene and had decided perhaps to go black after Keith entered the bedroom.

Keith asked, "Where are you calling from?"

"Bob Moore's," Mart answered.

Bob, who had not been allowed to direct the film and was understandably hurt badly by that fact, was nevertheless, as was his way, still giving Mart good advice.

The next day, I was sleeping in the unused bedroom set when Mart appeared and sat on the bed beside me. I woke with a start, and he said, with a slight laugh, "Just thought I'd come in and talk to you, find out how you are."

"What's going to happen with the kiss, Mart?" I asked.

He moved nearer. "That's what I thought we'd talk about," he said.

Smiling, I called him a whore. We are forever friends. I think we both hated this standoff.

At lunch there was a "team" meeting. Then all the actors were dismissed except Keith and me. Not one left the building. They all sat around the set, waiting in silent support, as we talked about what we would do if SAG appeared with an order to do the scene the way they wanted.

Finally, Billy appeared and said, "We're going to film it your way. What do you need?" And he proceeded to set up everything so we could improvise a new bedroom scene.

Billy is a fine director and a friend. Maybe he decided he could trust two good actors' instincts in improvisation. We would do something good. But what?

SCENE: Boys in the Band Studio: Finale

The next day, I arrived early at the "dailies" to view the scene we had filmed in two takes the day before. The editors, Carl Lerner and Jerry Greenberg, were also early. I mentioned the scene we were about to see. Carl said, "They won't use it. Mart's taste and judgment are good."

Jerry was listening behind his big glasses. He relit the one-inch stub of a thick cigar. "Friedkin is late," he observed.

The tough-talking young woman in charge of projection said, "Maybe he should have a police escort."

Carl smiled. "Sure," he said. "Police escorts, flags, sirens, crowds, ticker tape!"

The door banged open. The chiefs had arrived. "Roll the film!"

A blank white screen appears and the room goes dark. The words "wide screen common center" appear, bound by vertical and horizontal lines in the center of the white screen. Abruptly the scene begins. We see, from a low angle reflected in the mirror, me entering the bedroom. I step to the window and look out at the rain for a moment. I return to the chair beside the bed and roughly rub my face to push back the emotions. I take off my glasses, throw them down on the bed, and sit. The door opens and Keith enters. He moves to the bed and sits on the edge inches from me. To sit, he has to pick up my glasses. He holds them up to his face in his fist. He presses his fist against his eyes.

"I'm sorry," he says. "I'm sorry. I'm sorry." He starts to cry for real. This is Keith—not Larry, but Keith—in the agony of some old sorrow, crying.

His sobs rise in volume and pitch. Keith reaches to touch my hand and suddenly collapses into my arms. I hold him. I cradle him like a baby. He holds onto me like a child with his daddy or mommy. We stay like this, two men consoling each other through the pain. Time passes. Is it Larry and Hank the characters, or is it Keith and Larry the actors? The scene fades.

The editing room is absolutely silent. The lights come on. A man is weeping. Someone blows his nose. People get up and file into the hall. Silently, we all crowd into the elevator. The elevator descends; no one speaks. We reach the street, step into the usual comforting chaos of New York noise. It's night.

I say to Mart, "What do you think?"

He looks blankly at me. "Well," he says. "I think we'll end with Keith just entering the bedroom and then fade to black. It's beautiful that way."

I smile and put my arm around him. "You schmuck," I say.

At the curb, Billy is saying he will look again at what we gave him, but he feels the scene ends at the point where Keith enters the bedroom. We shake hands all around and separate. Mart gets into a limousine and gives directions to the driver. Billy steps in behind him, closes the door, and leans out the open window.

"I'm happy," he says to us with his appealing, irrepressible, boyish smile.

I believe he believes it. The limo pulls away.

My Arkansas backwoods conservatism still haunted me in my sweet Aunt Annie's gentle drawl. "I don't care what you do in New York, honey, where nobody sees it, but I don't like to think of an indecent picture like that playing downtown, right here at the Joie Theater."

I want to believe that if my dear, loving aunt had seen the picture, she might have changed her mind. Of all my relatives, she was the one who totally believed love is love.

Epilogue

THE PICTURE WAS artistically brilliant and took its good time returning a medium profit. It was no blockbuster but became an enduring cult film, the first of its kind. And like the play before it, it became the igniter of the flame of a desire for social justice for those from a parallel universe claiming their equal rights.

I celebrate Keith Prentiss for his directness, honesty, and charm. I celebrate Leonard Frey for his sweet and wicked wit. I celebrate Reuben Greene for his quiet way of being intensely proud and Black. I celebrate Peter White for his taste in leaving an ambiguous role ambiguous. I celebrate Ken Nelson because he is the most dedicated actor I know and a fantastic trouper. I celebrate Frederick Combs for his spiritual beauty; he is a high priest if only he knew. I celebrate Robert La Tourneaux for his excellent, if obtuse, portrayal of Cowboy. And I salute Cliff Gorman, a genius actor.

I am now the only one left. Everyone else left the scene too soon.

* * *

There was a fifty-year revival of the play, this time *on* Broadway. And a film was also made of that production, both directed by the best man for any theater job, Joe Mantello. I did not want to go to New York for the revival's opening on Broadway. I knew too well the press push and brouhaha that accompanies every opening these days. David Zippel convinced me otherwise with one sentence: "You owe it to the guys, the ones who are gone." That hit me hard.

The only thing missing from the revival was the closet with all its stifling fear. It's a new day. At the Broadway opening of the revival, I got to tell the press what I felt after all these years: that Mart and the original gay cast were the heroes. The gay men of that cast, and Mart, had all risked much more than I had. They came out to the world at a time when it was still poisonous for gay folk. Maybe I risked my career, but they risked their lives.

Before the 2019 Tony Awards, Mart called me. He was trying to pen an acceptance speech in case the play won. He wanted to know how it had been for us, the original Boys. We talked for two hours, then he told me he had been taking notes on all I said. I later wrote him an email recapping what I knew about all of us that he had not known.

Boys won the Tony Award for Best Revival of a Play that year. I saw Mart's speech well after he made it. It was very moving. He gave all the credit to us, the original cast—the people who were the reason he was standing on the Radio City Music Hall stage and accepting an award for a play he wrote in desperation when he was dead broke but had never despaired of getting a hearing for. Heroic. Generous. True Mart. So many lives have been changed by the play. Almost every day, a man tells me how seeing the play had given him hope.

Mart is gone now . . . to Spirit. "*Ave Atque Vale*," as the Romans said. "Hail and farewell." I am at the age when friends leave quickly and quietly. Mart's heart had been a problem for twenty years or more. Finally, it simply said, *Martino, it's time. It will come when it will come.* As Hamlet said, "the readiness is all." I know Mart was ready. He was a tough guy. I miss his presence—my gentle, funny, brilliant little brother. I asked him once why he thought he was still alive when everyone else had gone too soon. He said simply, "I never liked anal sex that much." He was God-blessed.

I remember a saying on a tombstone in an Ozark graveyard that I've kept in my heart all my life: "Another link is broken in the household band / But a chain is forming in a better land."

INTERMISSION

ACT II

Stop! In the name of love!

You can give humanistic value to almost anything by teaching it historically. Geology, economics, mechanics, are humanities when taught with reference to the successive achievements of the geniuses to which these sciences owe their being. Not taught thus, literature remains grammar, art a catalogue, history a list of dates, and natural science a sheet of formulas and weights and measures . . . the Liberal Arts tradition provides a context for what we learn, and for the ethical and moral questions that underlie every field of study.

—WILLIAM JAMES (1842–1910)

SCENE: Brooklyn, New York

On September 12, 1969, a great new wonder came into my life—my first child, a son: Laurence Nicholas Luckinbill. Nick!

Robin was brave, determined, and prepared. We learned the Lamaze method of breathing. I did my best, was in the OR, and saw my firstborn emerge and become. Instantly I knew what was important in life. I was flooded with feelings. I had moved into another role—father, protector, teacher, and guide. Dad.

My old self had been supplanted by this new person. Robin was tired, smiling, triumphant. She had done a wonderful job of helping this boy into life.

It was early evening. I went to the window and looked out across upper Fifth Avenue into darkening Central Park. I was no longer just me. I was a father. I had a new reason for being here. The most interesting question was, *what will we be like together?* Just as I couldn't find words good enough to say what having a son meant to me on the night he came into the world, I'm inadequate to express what it was and still is. I sit here, pen in hand, wishing I could help you and me understand.

He was so beautiful—little squished face, eyes scrunched shut, tiny hands, fingers, toes. Alive . . . my son is alive! Who would he be? He is already more than me.

I don't mean I felt small in his presence. I felt huge, and my whole self was in his service. He was the boss of me now. I could only laugh, suck in my breath, and cry, tears jumping from my eyes. We cried together, my wife and I, tears of joy. Nick! Nick was here!

Robin and I had bought our first house at 231 East Eighteenth Street in Flatbush, Brooklyn, New York—a pleasant area called Midwood. The house was a dream. And for the three of us, the neighborhood had everything—doctors on each corner and a dentist two doors down. And only two blocks away, an Ebinger's Bakery where folks would wait in line on Sundays to buy their famous Blackout Cake. A lifetime early riser, I was triumphant every Sunday and would lord it over the latecomers who had only hope left after I exited the shop carrying my heavy white cake box. It was an ecstatic time for my family, but the country was in trouble.

It was a time of enormous upheaval, protesters everywhere trying to stop the war in Vietnam. I had painted a piece of hardboard with a large, visible skull and crossbones in blue in the center. Beneath that, I wrote the number of dead American soldiers. I put the sign on my front door and updated the number of casualties weekly. I also flew a large American flag above the door. There was to be a protest march on the Capitol. Robin and I decided we had to go.

Five hundred thousand people showed up. Norman Mailer was among the most prominent. Norman became a good friend later. And, as it happened, we ended up in the artists and writers group right next to him, holding hands as we tried to levitate the Capitol of the United States. It didn't work (you'd have heard if it had), but it levitated our spirits.

We faced a line of National Guardsmen barring our way. But it was peaceful and civilized compared to today's militarized police crowd control tools mounted on tanks with .50 caliber machine guns and live ammo.

In my backpack were copies of Senator William J. Fulbright's book, *The Arrogance of Power*. He writes:

> The question that I find intriguing . . . is whether a nation so extraordinarily endowed as the United States can overcome that arrogance of power, which has afflicted, weakened, and in some cases destroyed great nations in the past . . . Power tends to confuse itself with virtue, and a great nation is peculiarly susceptible to the idea that its power is a sign of God's favor, conferring upon it a special responsibility for other nations—to make them richer and happier and wiser, to remake them, that is, in its own shining image.

Fulbright, my senator from Arkansas, was mentoring me in "the patriot's duty of dissent." It was the beginning—a faint dawn—of something new in me.

At the protest, I opened my backpack (today I might be shot for that), took out a copy of *The Arrogance of Power*, and offered it to the young guardsman who stood at parade rest, his rifle across his chest, bayonet fixed, proud, stalwart in duty, and slightly embarrassed to find himself as a leader, an authority figure, an enforcer of the law. He reminded me of myself in the army.

I said, "The book's for you, friend. It's a good look at another way to help our country." He kept his eyes on the horizon, but he couldn't hide the blush rising into his childlike face. "Thanks," I said to him, and his eyes met mine for a nanosecond. He had heard. I placed the thin volume on the ground in front of him and stepped back. Robin and I clasped hands and turned to join our friends, now drifting away from the confrontation.

S C E N E : New York

The war dragged on. Months later, I was cast in a Joe Orton comedy called *What the Butler Saw*. The play is one of the funniest pieces of dramatic literature ever, but *Butler* fit the times—chaotic, revolutionary, insane, countercultural, iconoclastic. The director, Joe Hardy, was life-giving. He encouraged the cast to go with the emotion in the way you do when you hit your elbow and vibrate with pain and pleasure as you jump two feet in the air and come down laughing, crying, and cursing.

I was commuting to Manhattan from Brooklyn daily, driving through the tunnel. One spring day in 1970, four Kent State students were shot dead by National Guardsmen on their Ohio campus. Some were protesting the continuation of the Vietnam War into Cambodia, ordered by President Nixon. Some were simply walking across campus. National Guardsmen, ill-trained and afraid, shot indiscriminately into this group of students, killing four unarmed and unthreatening kids. They wounded nine. One, shot in the spine, lived but was paralyzed for life from the chest down.

This horrendous incident was still going on when I drove my car to the Brooklyn–Battery Tunnel on my way to do the Orton show that night. The usual obscene and rude scrum was happening as cars inched toward the tunnel in ever-narrowing lanes. Courtesy was called for but AWOL. A guy behind me kept pushing in and trying to cut me off when he had no business doing that. He was behind me. I was going to get into the tunnel before him simply because I was better positioned. I was in the right lane, and I was right.

He jammed me on the next minor shift of all the cars pointed toward Manhattan, and I swung my wheel and nosed him by a few inches. He would have to hit me to get by. He threw me the finger and mouthed, "motherfucker." I smiled and gave him a sarcastically innocent "V for Victory" peace sign. He cursed me silently, wrenched his wheel a fraction over and forced his muscle car far enough across my right fender to be touching. The tables were turned. He grinned and gave me the finger again.

I went red. By that, I mean it was as if a blood vessel broke in my head and filled my eyes with red, and my head was bursting with burning blood. Time stopped. Everything went silent. Without knowing it, I reached down and grabbed the tire iron on the floor of the passenger side of my Jeep. I kept it there just in case. New York was a violent place to live in those days.

In one roll I exited the car, iron in my fist. I remember running the few steps to his car—it felt like I leaped over the front end of my Jeep in one bound—and ended in a crouch at his side window. He turned and saw me at his left shoulder, and his whole face changed. His smile disappeared and his mouth opened as I raised the tire iron.

There was nothing in my mind. It was all in my body, the swing, the smash, his window giving way in a shower of safety glass. If I had a thought it was, *Punch through the plastic shit in the safety glass and kill this motherfucker.*

I saw me beating him to death and his brains splashing his driver's seat upholstery, the way I'd seen when I was twelve, a headless soldier's brains on his dashboard after he drove at full speed into the rear of a truck carrying steel I-beams. And I saw this fucker's eyes open wide and his mouth silently yelling, "No, no!" His anger and smart-ass attitude turned to satisfying fear, terror—pants-shitting fear. I heard loud noises in my head now. Was I going crazy? Car horns honking, all kinds, blaring. And I looked up and people were hitting their horn buttons in all the cars surrounding us and waving at me. I wondered, *What are they waving at? What are they worried about?* And then I saw the tire iron in my left hand, and it was above my head, and the guy was slumped down in his car. Was he dead? Had I killed him?

I lowered the tire iron.

And I saw that the lanes into the tunnel were open, that all the cars trying to jam their way in had stopped, quit their stupid competition to be first, to honk their horns at me, to stop me from murder. Our two cars were now in the first position.

And they saw me wake up, and they slowly began to drive forward around us into the tunnel one by one like a funeral cortege. Now they took care to give their neighbors room, and an orderly parade was moving into the tunnel. I stepped away from the guy's car and went back to my own. I threw the tire iron into the backseat, got in, took my car out of park, and sat there, draining wrath like an hourglass, the sands of fury draining down and leaving the upper chamber of my brain still, empty and calm.

The guy straightened up. He looked over his shoulder, but not at me, as if waiting for me to make a move. But I waited, just breathing, and he checked over his shoulder again, still not moving. I flicked a finger at him from my hand on the wheel, a one-finger salute meaning, "You go ahead."

He rolled forward into the stream and went into the tunnel, and after a second or two, I rolled forward and took my turn in the parade of humans headed for Manhattan madness. At the time, I thought this kind of killing fury was just me. I didn't notice it was as dangerous as it was. I assumed it was related only to the proximate causes. I had safely buried infidelity, drinking, and my whole family life before now. I was fine.

When I got to the theater, I told the stage manager I wanted to make a speech about Kent State and Nixon and the Cambodia invasion at the curtain call. Word came from the producer immediately: "No, you won't!" And so I waited.

In the first scene, when I had my unfaithful stage wife, almost stark naked in her teddy, bent over my consulting desk in a compromising position, and my new secretarial applicant naked behind the patient's dressing screen, waiting to be seduced, suddenly the audience began to murmur and gasp. We looked up to see an actress we all knew weaving down the center aisle. She was stoned out of her mind, yelling at us about violence, the war, and women's rights. She reached the front of the stage, held up a flower in her hand, and collapsed in a pile of scarves and fringes like someone had knocked over a mannequin in an East Fourth Street head shop. She was out like a light. There was confusion until she was removed by the staff. The show, as shows always do, went on.

At the end, we assembled for the curtain call. Before we could bow, I stepped out and said, "Thank you for being here. This play is perfect for these times, because it is about lunacy. We have lunacy in our government this week with the killings of student protestors of the war at Kent State. The students were killed by the very boys of the National Guard they were protesting for, trying to save them from being sent to a war now made worse by President Nixon's invasion of Cambodia after he promised to give us peace. He said it to get elected! We actors acknowledge these tragic events and honor the dead who only wanted a better nation and peace. Our play is about madness. We could not let this madness affecting our country and others pass without saying to you, as the young lady who broke into the play wanted to say, help! Can we please help each other now to get out of this? To quote Joe Orton's wonderful play that you have just seen, "an olive branch may also be used as an offensive weapon."

Management hated that I made this speech. But the audience was generous and relieved to have an acknowledgment of the horrendous turn of events and to know that actors were also citizens who shared their thoughts relevant to the issues of the time.

On the Sunday following, I came out of my house in Brooklyn very early and found FBI men in my driveway and by my back door. I had caught them on my property. They showed ID and we stood in a stalemate at my Jeep, parked in the grassy driveway. I told them off. I was loud and scared. What did they want?

They wanted to question me about my opinions about the president. How did I feel about him? I told them I was a reserve officer in the US Army and was totally on the side of my country, but that I reserved the right to dissent with my government and not to have schmucks like them messing around in my yard. I had a child and a wife inside and told them they were trespassing and if they didn't scram, I'd call the NYPD. They didn't like my attitude, but they were in the wrong and had been caught without reason or warrant on my property. They left, and I did not hear from them again. But I now knew just how nutty Nixon was—and Hoover—to sic these guys on someone who criticized them at a curtain speech. It was a tense time.

SCENE: New York

I wrote a piece for the *New York Times* Sunday Arts & Leisure section and sent it to the editor, Seymour Peck. Sy, as everyone called him, was a truly great man, a natural mentor—the kindest man I have ever met and a fine editor. Amazingly, he published my piece with no editing. I didn't know then how rare this is. It was about the economics of the American theater from an actor's perspective. I felt I had some small right to comment on things I knew well.

I called the piece "The Irrelevance of Being an Actor." It was published in 1970 and drew about five hundred letters to the *Times*, which Sy invited me to answer if I chose. That was another astonishment: All the letters from the public were very positive toward my thesis. But some folks were downright pissy and rude about it, and all of those letters came from a few of my fellow actors who thought I had denigrated our profession by pointing out that actors in the "legitimate" theater were so underpaid that our labor was basically a subsidy of the theater and the producers to whom all profits flowed.

Sy Peck was killed when a drunk driver going the wrong way smashed into him as he was headed home for Christmas. Sy, I miss you still.

The *Times* piece and the unpublished (thank God) essay about the filming of *Boys in the Band* convinced *Esquire* magazine editor Don Erickson to ask me to interview Robert Redford. The profile was meant to be a survey of his work and a portrait of the man. As I found out, an assignment from *Esquire* was a choice one in the world of magazine journalism. And so I started by talking to Redford's press representative, Lois Smith, a very pleasant, down-to-earth woman and the classiest PR person in the business.

It was, I realized, an audition. Lois wanted to know me, how I thought, what I thought, my feelings. And she was refreshingly candid and straightforward about it. She wanted her boy taken care of by any writer assigned to him, but she wasn't saying, "Don't go there, go here," which would have been useless with me anyway. She just wanted like-minded folk to genuinely try to communicate. I passed scrutiny, since that was my whole intent anyway. And so I went to Bob's apartment on East Eighty-Sixth Street and met Lola, his wife. Bob was getting dressed, she said. Ten minutes later, he entered from another part of his comfortable, but not grand or pretentious, apartment. He wore faded jeans and a western shirt and was hopping on one sock-foot, carrying his other cowboy boot in one hand, his hair, like gold strands, flung in many directions. Grinning, he said, "Sorry, I'm always late."

I said, "You've got a book in your case that I have at home—*40 Miles a Day on Beans and Hay*." The book was about a Black cavalry unit in the Indian Wars in the American West, circa 1870–90.

He was delighted; the smile grew. "Yeah, thinking about making a film out of it. You like it?" he asked as he sat down, pulling at his boot, and poured some cream into his coffee on the tray that Lola had laid out. He stirred it with a quick whisk of a ballpoint pen he then stowed between his teeth as he used both hands to finish getting the boot on.

"I've got a meeting downtown later, but we've got plenty of time," he said around the ballpoint.

"Yeah, I've been working on a story about the Indian Wars or massacres. I've been calling it *The Red and the Black*, like . . ."

". . . Stendhal?" he asked and cocked an interested eye at me. "The French writer."

"Yeah, a story about a guy like Julien Sorel, used and killed by his society, the wrong class. A lot of the soldiers who fought Indians were Black. It struck me that we consciously used one subject race to subdue another one."

"Yeah," he said. "Who taught us that?"

And we were off to the races, protocol mutuality established.

I visited off and on with Redford for a few weeks and asked him about every project he had done. We had a mutual friend in Robert Jiras, the producer of the *Boys in the Band* movie who had helped Bob get a personal film, *Downhill Racer*, made.

My angle in the piece was his take on the more personal films he had made but which had not done as well as he had wanted. How did he take on a project and why? What kind of man was he and what were his values? What was his long-term goal?

Redford had a stubborn anti-authority streak and a powerful sense of social justice. I liked this guy. We got along. He was curious, committed (to his work, wife, and kids), and determined to be a kind of secret outsider in Hollywood. He didn't live there; he wouldn't live there. His wife was raised Mormon and they had roots in Utah and the West. We were nearly the same age, but I had just broken through with my first film. I felt no envy or competitiveness with him, which made our talks easy. The interview was supposed to be no more than four thousand words—it went to eight. It was published in *Esquire* in 1970.

The *New York Times* piece got me a meeting with the distinguished publisher Charles Scribner to discuss my writing a book on the theater, with an advance of $4,000! I was over the moon but then began to feel strange. I'd never had an advance before, money paid for work yet to be completed, creative work I was always uncertain about. So, was I really a writer? I still could barely think of myself as an actor, and I'd been doing that in New York for eleven years. But success was always the leprechaun's pot of gold at the root of the next tree, not the one you thought. I began to feel like I'd taken the cash on false pretenses and that I couldn't guarantee Mr. Scribner a book, much less a good one. I didn't want to let him down.

At *Esquire*, it had seemed like a lark. I wrote a piece, they liked it or they didn't, they paid me or not, and I was free. I was paid very well for the Redford piece. I was getting what Gay Talese got in those days, I was told. If true, that was the absolute top of the scale. The advance from Scribner's was not in that category, but why should it be? I'd never written a book. But I thought I could write a bombshell book about the art I loved as much as anything. I was a real writer!

SCENE: Brooklyn, New York

On my office wall was a Czech poster, white with blue words: "We Will Fight To The Last Drop Of Ink." It was the battle flag of Czech writers and artists flown in the face of the USSR. The Prague Spring Revolution of 1968 had been crushed by Soviet tanks and 200,000 soldiers. It put an end to "socialism with a human face."

This poster was my personal mantra. More and more, I thought of myself as a writer-manqué. A wannabe. I had written plays, poems, newspaper articles, and magazine pieces, but never anything that exposed my real self.

I went to see Mr. Scribner again. He was a gracious man, elegant, courteous, and thoughtful. His father had published Hemingway and Wolfe. He sat at his galley-laden desk and listened to my fears. I told him that if I wrote the book, I knew I must make a case for a fully subsidized national theater. I would be cutting into the arteries of Broadway's commercial culture by challenging our failures to live up to our ideas of social justice. I found myself articulating personal feelings to America's premiere publisher that I had only been dimly aware of until now. He listened with care and interest. He had already told me he loved my writing. He quoted from the *New York Times* piece, one line about actors: "Plowing back 50 percent of our incomes each year into an occupation as peripheral as a company making plastic candy for display purposes only," which had convinced him I was the man to write the book he wanted to read.

I said that if I did write the book, it would take me a couple of years to research, to follow the money, to pry open producers' accountings to find out why the average theater actor's earnings were too low to support a family living in New York. To grasp the currents of public taste and why it lagged in serious drama. To understand the impact of television, movies, and sports on the theater audience. It was a monumental task. And I believed I would never get another acting job in the New York theater if I wrote it. Therefore, I must return the advance and hope he would forgive me.

To his credit, he didn't laugh. Like Dr. Noyce, my chemistry teacher at the University of Arkansas, I saw a depth of compassion in his eyes that I had not asked for or expected. He smiled as I laid his check on the desk before him, forgave me with his look, and said, "Thank you, Mr. Luckinbill. When you are ready, you will write the book you need to write. Good luck!" We shook hands.

I was relieved. I regretted it. But embarrassing yourself is better than lying and never doing the right thing. If you must do something, do it, even if it hurts. Just make sure you are the only one it hurts!

I wrote a lot more magazine journalism in the '70s. After the Redford piece, *Esquire* commissioned an examination of Francis Ford Coppola and his American Zoetrope company in San Francisco.

Francis had taken his creative crew, which included young George Lucas and Walter Murch, out of Hollywood as Moses took his tribe out of Egypt—the place of corruption—to supposedly purer creative environs in San Francisco and Marin County.

I wrote the Coppola piece after hanging for weeks with all these folks who were to become the vanguard of the new cinema for the next decades. I called it "The Teddy Bear's Picnic." The men were all bearded, and the men and women dressed as farmers and laborers.

Don Erickson read the story, which I knew captured the essence of Francis and the others accurately and with great affection. These new writers, directors, and tech geniuses were discovering the new American landscape shaped by an awareness of the shocking and immense torque of forces that were shredding trust and blind belief in American goodness and exceptionalism. Nixonian lies, the destruction of the Great Society, loss of faith in the government and religious institutions, Vietnam, corporate thievery, urban blight and neglect, and racism so deep and hidden—we were drowning in it and didn't know it. The Zoetropers were expressing the PTSD of a failing society.

Don paid me but turned the piece down. The reason? I ended it with a news squib in the *Hollywood Reporter* saying that Francis had signed a contract with producer Al Ruddy to write and direct a film made from Mario Puzo's novel, *The Godfather*. Don decreed that this was a downward step by Francis, a money move to a mediocre, cheesy B-level gangster picture. Francis had sold out. *Esquire* lost faith in Francis's promise as an A-list original filmmaker. I lost faith in *Esquire*.

Cosmopolitan's editor, Roberta Ashley, hired me to write a piece on Raquel Welch. I spent a day in New York trying to get acquainted with Raquel and find an angle for a story, which was impossible because she insisted on wading in the shallowest tide pool at the edge of the ocean of her experience in Hollywood. I told Ms. Ashley that there was no doubt a tale there, but Raquel wasn't ready for *Cosmo* to plunge into her personal story.

Roberta then handed me a plum pudding assignment: write a big piece on Jack Nicholson. This became a fantastic chase story to find the real Jack. He was charming and willing but insisted on turning the story into Fantasy Jack, New Jersey Jack, Roger Corman Jack, a Yesterday, Today, and Tomorrow Jack who changed personas, venues, and stories into a fabulous kaleidoscope that was fascinating, but would have been the length of *War and Peace*.

I turned in the one story that seemed most accurate to the "now" (the 1970s), that told of Jack, the Master of His Soul—but his soul of the moment was a mirror, a chimera of self-indulgence. An ego/id trip. I ended with a scene of Jack talking on the phone to me about his next movie while getting head from a woman. I liked the man, Mr. Jack Nicholson, a fine actor who insisted on playing games when I was trying to write a deeper story about him, one that *Cosmo* had hoped for. Now I think Jack had been playing me.

Ms. Ashley paid me and began looking for some other celebrity profiles for me to do. She then asked me if I would be their next nude male cover after the coy one Burt Reynolds had done. I said no. I was confused at first. My Scorpio self said why not? But I'd learned two things: One, I wanted to be an actor sought after for his work, not the one who chased after the big names. Two, I was beginning to think I could write something more important than "celebrity journalism."

I bowed out. I admired Roberta Ashley. She superbly edited a magazine headed by my fellow Arkansawyer, Helen Gurley Brown. Helen had made *Cosmo* a sophisticated women's emancipation magazine out of one formerly about styles and trivia. Helen was a true rebel and wrote so well about female sexuality in such an entertaining, but to-be-taken-seriously, way that she had lifted sexual expression out of the men's self-grope of *Playboy* and turned it into an instruction manual to free women. *That was a serious writer,* I thought. And for that reason, I thought my piece about Jack was okay.

I wrote seriously about a guy who was trivializing his own sexuality. And what was I doing? It was an effect of the times. The '70s were raunchier than the '60s. The '60s were about kids rebelling against war and parents, teachers, preachers, and cops trying to put them in jail for protesting and smoking an innocuous weed. The '70s were about parents rebelling against being grown-up and having to take responsibility for the kids they birthed. The '60s ended at Woodstock, a love fest in the mud. The '70s ended with nine hundred members of the Jonestown cult committing mass suicide together by drinking Jim Jones' cyanide-percolated Kool-Aid. It was prophetic of our era of mass confusion, anti-Victorian mores, anti-capitalism, and anti-war chaos.

Both eras showed where America was headed: into feckless, indulgent irresponsibility toward being clear-eyed citizens of the only democracy that has survived for over two hundred years. Litterers—literally—in the farm field at Woodstock and with their own dead bodies in the compound in Guyana. America was headed to the trash pit. Now, in 2024, the GOP lives there and is trying to drag the rest of us down with it.

I wrote another screenplay called *Roy Brightsword,* based on a news story in the *Arkansas Gazette* about a young hillbilly who kidnapped his even-younger girlfriend—Romeo and Juliet in the Ozark mountains. I wrote and rewrote this story, trying to get it into a tight film script. My agent at the time was an ambitious kid who went on to head Creative Artists Agency. He got me a meeting with Pat Kelly at First Artists, which was Paul Newman, Barbra Streisand, Sidney Poitier, Dustin Hoffman, and Steve McQueen.

I pitched the story of the wild outlaw in the Arkansas Ozark Mountains to Pat. He said, "Bring it." I changed the title to *Roy Hurd* after Pat mentioned that Paul had a name fetish. He thought names beginning with *h* were lucky— Hurd, Harper, etc.

I went to work to rebuild the movie for Newman and Streisand, who wanted to do something together. I created two fabulous parts for them: an ignorant hillbilly woodsman and a Jewish social worker from Brooklyn working with the Works Progress Administration to try to improve the way Ozark people lived. The unlikely love affair between Roy and the woman is the great heart of the story. They team up to fight the absentee landowning, sharecropper-exploiting capitalists.

I took the script, 138 pages, to Pat Kelly. It was a great, poetic story. I placed the script in Pat's hands. He weighed it in his hand and said, "Too long! Bring it back thirty pages lighter and I'll bring it to the stars."

I was mortified. The script was perfect! What to do? My agent grabbed the script from me. "Here's how you cut a movie script." He tore out thirty pages and tossed them away.

I was aghast, hurt. "I can't do that," I told him.

He said, "Take thirty pages out and I'll get this script made into a movie."

I couldn't. I couldn't do things that way. I took the script back and left.

I could not understand Hollywood. I had accepted option money from First Artists before reworking the script into its present form—vastly different from my first inspiration, and better. Maybe I could take out ten pages or even twelve. But thirty? I didn't know how to abandon characters, color, and detail that made a movie a real event, not just a movie. My young agent was ruthless. He wanted to succeed at any cost. I could not go in that direction.

Was I stubborn? Bull-headed? Antiauthoritarian? Yes. All of the above. But not stupid. I tried to cut out whole scenes, whole events that told a complete story of two vastly different human beings learning to know, accept, and love each other against all the odds. It didn't work. This was the story I could tell. I could not thin it down.

I gave back the option money on a turnaround clause. I loved Pat. He was a mensch. He killed the deal, but left us both alive and still friends. I never saw that agent again. It had been a transactional Hollywood friendship dependent totally on success. I realized much later that I had repeated this same action when I turned down an agent's pitch to sell my script *Trolley Rider's Blues* in my twenties and Charles Scribner's advance to write a book in my thirties. Apparently, I wasn't ready to sell the writing I did from my heart.

SCENE: New York to Hollywood

I went straight from *What the Butler Saw* to the American West in *Bonanza*.

I hadn't worked in Hollywood yet. I was invited there in the '60s to audition for Revue Studios at Warner Brothers. I had been in the running to play Maxwell Smart in *Get Smart*. The New York people were excited about my chances, but it went to Don Adams, a better choice in my opinion. Not that I felt that magnanimous when they said, "We went the other way."

I was screen-tested and offered a three-year standard contract as a Revue studio player. It was a lot more money per week than I was getting as a host at

O. Henry's Steak House, but they got testy when I asked questions about the contract.

"Yes, if you get popular, we can loan you out. Yes, you would still get the same salary as in this contract. Yes, we can loan you out for more money. No, you don't get any of it." I passed on the offer. Hollywood!

Now, I was at Warner Brothers to play an obnoxious investigative reporter from a San Francisco daily. The candidate for governor in the territory, Dean Jagger, was a racist who hated Native Americans, and I intended to prove it. Hoss, the Boss, and Little Joe were mistakenly backing this bad guy, and I intended to set them straight.

I reported to makeup at 5:30 A.M. There was nothing to do for my face. I am naturally olive-tan, so I was off to wardrobe. Wardrobe (they were human, but they referred to themselves by their job description) was in a flurry to get me costumed. But the clothes they laid out were wrong for the character. They threw on the counter, tagged with my character's name, a standard ranch hand's outfit that a cowpoke would have worn—blue jeans, work shirt, handkerchief, belt, scuffed brown boots, and a black, flat cowboy hat. Well, I was a New York guy, a New York *actor*, mind you, and fresh from a socially significant, bona fide off-Broadway hit. Little did I know how little—how less than nothing—a theater show meant in movieland. But I had studied my Bonanza script and applied my actor's intuition, my Uta Hagen training, and my very own method to it, and I had in my own mind's eye what this dandy, smart-ass reporter from the big city would wear. I refused to try on their idea of me as a reporter. You'd have thought I had refused a direct order from God or a superior officer in battle. They were nonplussed: "This is what's been chosen for you. Try it on for size." They gave curt orders. I smiled back curtly.

"No," said I. "But how about if I find my own stuff in the stacks?"

They didn't even begin to reply or look me in the eye. The chief "wardrobe" went immediately to the emergency Red Line—the wall phone direct to the executive branch. He looked sideways at me. He murmured into the mouthpiece. Did I hear the words "mutiny," "going rogue," and "wants to pick out his own costume"?

"Yes, yes, he's the guy from New York . . . yessir!"

In seconds, the door opened and in came David Dortort, the producer and writer—lean, pale, with a shock of hair falling over his forehead, young-old, a wise man, sanguine, handsome, focused. He was mildly amused and bemused.

"Larry?" he asked.

"Yes, sir!" I said.

"Welcome to *Bonanza!*"

"Thank you."

"I hear you have some thoughts on your wardrobe?"

"Yes, this guy is strictly city. He has a certain contempt for these ranch types. He's got the goods on one of their favorites and plans to put this town's corruption on the front page. I'd wear a reporter's derby hat, a shabby frock coat, maybe a snazzy vest, shiny city britches, probably pinstripe, and a white shirt with a formal collar. Half boots, low heels made for city streets. This guy's not a hick!"

Dave smiled—a real smile—at me. "Sounds good to me!" he said. "Got that, guys? Get that stuff. This guy's read the script." And he laughed.

The atmosphere cleared. The king had spoken. No one would be fired for acting like a human. They scurried.

Dave said, "Get to it, Larry. I'll be looking for you on set." And he was out the door in less than a minute.

I got exactly what I wanted in spades. In about two minutes, wardrobe handed me a stack of city-slicker stuff to wear, which I quickly tried on. It all fit. Fabulous!

I was driven to the set about two blocks away. In Hollywood, only "unimportant" people walk. The rest—and now me—were too important (and late) to walk. So, I learned that the first step on the rung to self-importance and to a caste system as embedded in Hollywood as it is in England or India, is to accept *all* perks. They are like life—impermanent. And, of course, another tip of the hat to the Teamsters Union at the apex of the pyramid. As in the cannery, wheels ruled. Lucky me!

After a wait of about two hours, I was brought onto the set. It was the exterior of the ranch house—veranda and front door, front yard with appropriate corral dirt, and some scattered plants. The house front looked inviting and shady like the paradise *Bonanza* emulated.

I felt great. The welcome by Dave Dortort was the kind of tonic an actor needs: You are wanted, expected, and respected. You are the best for this role. "Go to it Larry, do what you do best!"

Lorne, Dan, and Michael came out one by one to listen as I stood in the yard below the veranda steps, telling them their pick for governor was a no-good racist bum. In the first shot I would be off-camera. Their reactions were being photographed over my shoulder. We would shoot my speech facing them later. Almost all movies and some television shows are shot out of sequence.

In the first rehearsal, the guys were in their stocking feet. All except Blocker were normal-sized guys. I was given an eyeline on the porch behind the boys so the height of the porch would register. I memorized it, a notch on the veranda post.

Now, the take. My first in Hollywood. I was as eager as a kid on his first visit to the fair, as ready as Hotspur to battle the king. I gave it a lot of juice off-camera. The boys were pleasantly surprised. I gave them something they could respond to, get insulted by, laugh at, wonder at, and they responded. But I noticed that my eyeline had risen by about six inches. Each of them had gained height, even Blocker. Then I saw that all three had put on a pair of boots, each of which was higher than the next. The heels—tall, taller, and tallest—had been adapted to the egos and competitive spirit of the Great American West. It was a Bonanza of Boot Heels! Hilarious. I loved it.

There was camaraderie and laughter, but always tension. Everyone—cast, crew, and especially the director—was under pressure to get more set-ups, shot sequences that tell the story.

The director was Leo Penn, an actor of repute and the father of Sean Penn. He was gruff, tough, a hard driver and hard-driven by management. At the end of this fast, long, long working day, he was hurrying and snapping orders. Suddenly, he broke off, walked fast to the far wall of the studio, and faced a bare corner. I thought he was really pissed off. Then he opened his fly and actually pissed against the studio wall, stepped back, zipped up, and returned to the set. Nobody was surprised but me. My jaw was on the floor. I picked it up and put it back on my face. In the theater, there is a lot of screaming, storming off, and coming back, but you never pissed on a theater wall. That would have been sacrilege.

Mr. Penn may have seen my shock. He growled, "If they want to get the work done right, they ought to bring the fucking restrooms closer!"

The following morning, I was picked up at 4:00 A.M. and limoed out to the first location shot. It was some place called the Vasquez Rocks in the mountains of the San Fernando Valley northeast of Hollywood.

On the way out, the elderly limo driver said, "You ride?"

"Oh, sure," I said. "You know . . . um . . . English saddle."

He asked if I was from New York. "Yep, I'm a New York actor." I looked at his eyes in the rearview mirror. He was amused. He was trying to tell me something. My only time on a horse and actually riding—not counting when I was five, photographed in Beaumont, Texas, sitting on a Shetland pony wearing wooly little boy chaps, a giant sombrero, and brandishing a shiny cap gun—was when I sat in a line of sad horses, noses to tails, for an hour through Rock Creek Park in Washington, D.C., in aid of a one-shot hot date with a Georgetown debutante. And the time in Sudan when a French diplomat, angry that his wife was flirting with me, had tried to kill me by making me ride a wild Arabian stallion. *Une liaison dangereuse.*

It was a long ride to the location, and the driver told me a hair-raising story about the making of *The Charge of the Light Brigade* at the same location back in 1936. The actors playing cavalrymen were warned not to unsheathe their swords. The only people allowed to ride with unsheathed swords were the few principals.

"But, naturally," the driver said. "Being actors, they disobeyed." They had all lied about being experienced riders when they were hired. Some died that day because they knew nothing about being on a horse, much less a running horse, much less a "movie horse," much less with a sword raised high. I wondered what a movie horse was. I was about to find out.

The driver gave a grisly account of the dead and dying men he had carted to the hospital that day. The blood, the screams. The eyes put out, saber cuts, broken necks, horses destroyed by bad riders. As he told me all this, he looked at me in the rearview mirror. Then, he said, "And, of course, all the actors who died were New York actors."

I sat there, numb. Of course I had lied to everybody. I said I could ride. What was riding a horse, anyway? Nothing. Kids do it. I'd seen monkeys do it on television.

I looked out the window. There were these enormous rocks above the mountains—in reality, precipices, cliffs, twisted, distorted shapes and deadly-looking rocks, thousands and millions of feet high. The Himalayas without snow.

"Where are we?" I asked.

"We're here," announced my Tiresias, the ominous doomsayer, and he turned onto a bumpy desert track.

I looked over my scenes for the day, searching for riding moments. What? How could I have missed this? Oh my God! Oh, God . . . In the black type, I saw that Little Joe and I gallop side by side across a ravine and up a slope to the top, where we pull up our trusty steeds at the very edge of a cliff, just in time to see the villain racing away across the desert below.

* * *

It was the first scene after lunch.

Everybody is sleepy and grumpy. Why not? The crew has been awake and hustling continuously since about 3:30 A.M. Actors like me have been going over their lines alone in their mobile dressing rooms. There is a high state of tension in each setup. Each new technical problem in the first long day of exterior shooting is rushing toward the inevitable call of "We're losing the light!"

at which point tension ratchets up to peaks of lost tempers, especially with our volatile director.

Our scene has been foreshortened. Eighty-six the long ride up to the cliff's edge. Little Joe and I will sit on parked horses, do some of the dialogue, and then spur the beasts forward to the edge of the cliff for the climactic reveal scene.

I'm very relieved all I have to do is sit on the horse like it's a couch, do the dialogue, then just walk Thunderhead and Flicka up to the camera, which is set on the cliff's edge. Then we pretend to look down at the abyss—sorry, the desert below.

Little Joe (Michael) is entirely at ease on his cayuse, which is, in fact, a family friend. It's the horse Little Joe has grown up with. They talk horsey-talk together.

I'm on a nag that doesn't like me. She's irritated that I don't hold the reins right or something. She shifts her weight continuously from one set of hooves to the other. Clump . . . clump . . . like a Macy's clerk relieving her feet at the end of a long Black Thursday sale. But if I shift my weight, she looks around at me as if to say, "Are you going to keep doing that? You know you're hurting me? You're sitting on my damn back!"

I'm acutely aware that I don't belong here. But to his immense credit, Little Joe used my discomfort to feed him in the scene. It gave him something to amuse himself with. Our relationship in the episode is one of mutual distrust. My job is to prove that their candidate is a fraud and that my character is sure of himself, so it's funny that I'm scared of Old Nelly, the movie horse. Wait! What's a "movie horse?"

Our dialogue's done. I hear the director say, "Action!" Simultaneously, a loud horn brays. I mean *loud!* And my horse takes off at the jump and attains warp speed in three leaps, headed straight for the camera crew. Luckily, I still have the reins around my fingers. I try to pull on the reins gently, but Nelly pays no attention. Doesn't she know there's a 200,000-foot-high cliff just thirty yards ahead? Out of the corner of my eye, Little Joe's horse comes up on the left and pulls up even. My crazed horse thinks it's the stretch of the Run for the Roses, and she surges into the lead. I have no control whatsoever.

I am dimly aware that the horse wrangler is running toward us on my right. At the same time, the focus puller on the camera crew dives to his left out of our way. The heroic cameraman hunkers behind the dolly like the captain of a doomed ship white-knuckling the helm. The director is roaring, "That's good! Now. Pull her up!" Then he's screaming, "Pull her up! *Now!*"

Desperate, I yank the reins with both hands. I pull the sucker back from the chasm of death, saving the cameraman and the stupid horse. By sheer strength (and cruelty), I pull the reins right up to my chest. She rears like you've seen horses do—up on her haunches, noble head fighting the bit, wanting to really kill me, throw me and stomp on me, neighing, "I hate actors!" I managed to stay on her.

I have stopped the horse, miraculously, right on its marks. She comes down with a thud. Little Joe comes to a stop beside me. He is looking over the cliff. He points. I remember that I'm in a scene! I follow his gaze, look down (I'm seeing the top of the cameraman's head), and turn to Little Joe with a supercilious grin as if to say, "See, I was right!" We finish the scene.

Afterward, no one criticizes me except the wrangler, who tells me about the horse. "She's a real movie horse and responds like an actor to the horn. It surprised you, didn't it? Yeah, and you pulled her up too hard. You could've really hurt her mouth. She's a good girl, not at all dangerous, you know. She knew exactly where that cliff was. Horses are smarter than humans sometimes."

I got it. I said, "I'm so sorry. I've learned something today. Thanks."

I'm not meant to be a cowboy star. In the show, the scene is a nano-second. The horse looked great, and made me look okay. Now I felt sorrier for the horse than ever. I should have sent flowers—or hay.

SCENE: New York

After the 1970 release of the *Boys in the Band* film, producer-director Otto Preminger put me under contract for two films. The first was *Such Good Friends*, based on the popular roman à clef by Lois Gould. Dyan Cannon would play the Gould character; I played her husband, based on a famous magazine editor, whose adultery was memorialized in his little black book—so I was the bad guy. The cast was a tiara of sparkly New York actors—Jimmy Coco, Ken Howard, Burgess Meredith.

The second film I signed for interested me more than the character in the Gould story. It was based on a spy novel that involved climbing a famous mountain in the Swiss Alps. I would finally play the hero. I hoped all the climbing would be in a studio where I was never more than two feet off the ground. But I was excited at the prospect.

Otto was exactly as his reputation promised: exacting, imperious, charming, knowledgeable, sure, angry, unfair, contentious, a too-too Teutonic director, and, finally, a sadist.

Like all bullies, he had nicknames for his favorite whipping actors, and they changed daily. One day, Jimmy Coco was "Coconut," the next day, something even more denigrating. Dyan was horribly labeled, with dripping contempt,

"Mrs. Cary Grant." From day to day, we never knew who would get it next. But he was relentless with Dyan. She was a good actress. She had good instincts, was prepared, and was not in any way a prima donna. But Preminger seemed to hate her. He ridiculed her senselessly and ceaselessly for no apparent reason. She was doing her job very well. And she had the right quality of cheerful naiveté tempered by a deep understanding of the world. But Otto's contemptuous attacks would begin the moment she walked in the door. "Ah, Mrs. Cary Grant is here!" She bore all this, tried to ignore it, and showed all the grace the bullying tyrant lacked. Something about her infuriated him. Maybe it was that she was not the actress he had wanted, or perhaps it was her simple modesty and grace.

The rest of us received his meanness, too, but not as much. We were not upholding a Hollywood reputation as Dyan was. Some of us were not afraid to talk back or to let Otto know we were pissed, a lot of the time at his treatment of her. But she handled it all with the aplomb that perhaps she had taken from Mr. Grant, a man with a sterling and well-deserved good reputation. Dyan was no longer married to him, but they had a daughter together whom they both loved very much. Dyan, like Mr. Grant, was a class act.

Otto had asked me to grow my hair long, '70s style, so I did, down to my shoulders. I looked like an olive-skinned Prince Valiant. But then, Otto decided I liked my long hair and told me that he would soon "cot" it! "We are going to cot your beautiful hair, Lugenbiel, that you love so much!"

I didn't love it so much. I had never liked Prince Valiant. I just thought Otto was nuts. He tried to rag me, but I laughed at him.

Finally, I had enough. I told his brother, Ingo, the associate producer, that I didn't intend to take his insults to me or the other cast members any longer. Since my contract was still unsigned, though we were already shooting, I considered myself free to walk—and I did, out of his office and home. It was the end of a workweek, and I told the brother I would not be back at work on Monday.

This was a big no-no. I called my agent and told him the news. He didn't panic. He said he would get on this. Someone at William Morris could talk to Otto.

In those days, your agent was powerful and invaluable for finding work, making connections, showing up for your work, and troubleshooting. The thing was, I meant what I had said. My feelings went back to my dad forcing me to fight the hog family—if you don't intend to kill someone, don't get into the fight. I intended to stop Otto Preminger from behaving badly. I knew it would cost me this and maybe many movie jobs. They could and did blacklist troublemakers quietly. You never found out, you just stopped getting hired.

CBS had blacklisted me a few years before for the second soap I was the star of. I couldn't take the useless and stupid pre-rehearsal, so I led a revolt—wrote a manifesto, signed it, got a couple more coconspirators who promised to sign but didn't, and gave it to management. I was a revolution of one, which refused to honor a contract that locked in stupidity, so it was a five-year blacklist from CBS for me, which I endured.

Over the weekend, something was worked out, and I went back to work on Monday. Otto was now Amazing Otto. He was as charming as he could be, but it seemed genuine. He even seemed to like me. Otto was a bully. I fought back. He liked it!

When we got to the part in the script when my character was young and buzz-cut military, I threw a party—just come and watch my locks get shorn. I didn't invite Otto. It was quick, and during it, Otto walked in. I guess he hoped I'd be a vain actor and mourn my youth—that I'd be hurt to lose my gorgeous hair. I wasn't. It was just hair and took too much washing in filthy, lovely old New York. We were all laughing. I offered to save some of my hair for Otto's bald head. He almost smiled. I looked like my old Army self. I liked that self. I was at my most macho then.

I had to rape Dyan in the next scene. The character was the sort of guy who could go home from a one-night stand, fuck his wife immediately, and feel nothing for either encounter. What a sad, inexplicable, irredeemable monster. Hmmmm . . .

On my last day, I "died," a victim of the misdiagnosis of a mole on my neck. A petty, trivial tragedy for Richard, but he deserved it.

Shooting day. The critical care nurses in the ICU at Flower-Fifth Avenue Hospital were shocked, outraged, and helpless. Their critically ill patients had been moved out of the ICU and were parked like valet-driven cars at an expensive Hollywood A-list party. Some said Preminger had promised the hospital board of directors a donation to be allowed to rent the ICU for one shooting day. The patients were in the hall (this is all true, even if they deny it at a distance of almost fifty years), and inside the ICU/OR, all the indispensable, expensive, and photogenic machines required were in place. The walls were lined with beds filled with fake patients, very old actors who looked the part of desperately sick patients. They were culled from God-knows-where, maybe the Retired Actors Home in New Jersey. They were put into hospital gowns and rolling beds; plastic curtains surrounded the beds. It looked like a ward in Thomas Mann's *The Magic Mountain*—spare, pristine, and brightly lit. The crew had worked all night to create this. The old extras had been wheeled in at dawn and given a film set breakfast in bed: a paper plate with a burrito and coffee in a Styrofoam cup.

I, as Richard, was already on a gurney, hooked up to the cardioversion machine. I was happy it was my last day on this job. Otto had eased off on me, but not Dyan. He harassed her at every opportunity, and she still took it like the pro she was. The rest of us could do nothing. My rebellion had been small potatoes. Nothing could stop Otto's need to insult and diminish his leading lady. It was stupid and unfair and ungentlemanly and sad. But it was movieland—everyone was smiling through gritted teeth. God forbid you get a reputation for being difficult, producers and directors excepted. Their piggish behavior was considered "eccentric genius." Dyan was now resisting Otto's crude cruelty like a Zen master. But he could still get to her.

My job for the day was to be dying, then dead.

The desperate doctors are trying to revive me. Dyan has come to the OR to see me, having found my little black book listing the names of all my sex partners, my many infidelities. She is devastated by this and afraid I might die.

This is a climactic moment in the film and a difficult emotional task for any actor. The camera will move 360 degrees around my supine body as Dyan moves around the gurney and expresses her anger, her love, her shock at my infidelity.

This is it. The whole day has been given to this one setup. I am hoping no actual patients are dying in the hall.

Dyan is late to the set. It's not her fault, maybe makeup, maybe something else. She is apologetic. Otto is livid. He screams. The sound cans he wears to eavesdrop on the camera crew's chatter are hurled to the floor.

I hear all the commotion and sit up. Otto yells at me, "You must lie down. It's critical." It certainly is.

He yells at Dyan. She turns and leaves the set. He follows her, screaming into the hall. The ICU patients are getting a free show from a sociopath. It's not funny—it's very dark comedy like our movie script. I hope Otto's yelling fury doesn't shock a critical patient to death.

Dyan walks into the ladies' room and shuts the door in Otto's face. He bangs on the door with his fist and *goes in after her*! He rages at her, then exits the ladies' room and returns to the set. No Dyan. He demands a new set of sound cans. I note the soundman marking a number on his invoice pad. This will be an expensive day for earpiece replacements, and they will bill for it.

Otto demands a rehearsal of the 360-degree camera move. I lie down and play dead. It's a tricky move, but it goes smoothly for the dolly operator. The cameraman asks for another go. They go back to first marks. Otto says, "Action." They start the move. There's a terrible crash! One of the lights attached the night before to the ancient plaster ceiling of the old hospital has given way and smashes to the floor. Otto yells and starts to throw the cans from his ears to the floor, then thinks better of it.

Dyan has come back. Her face is red, and she's clearly in pain. That's actually good for this moment. Otto yells, "Action." She speaks to me on the bed, an anguished speech about my betrayal of her and that she still loves me. Halfway through, she starts to laugh. Her personal defense mechanisms are kicking in from the sadistic treatment she is enduring from Otto, which mirrors in a way what I, her husband, have done to her. And she is reacting and going with it. The absurdity of the story and this day is getting to her. "*Cot!*" yells Herr Director.

Wham! The cans go to the floor. The soundman pulls out a new pair. Otto curses aloud. He doesn't look at Dyan. Again he yells, "Action!" Dyan begins her long speech again, and I can feel the camera moving with her perfectly.

A nurse, a real one, comes to the gurney I'm on. She turns on the defibrillator and removes the paddles. I look sidewise. The needles are jumping on the machine.

I say calmly, "What the fuck is going on here?"

The assistant director tells me, "Otto wants us to see the needles working in real time as Dyan comes around the bed."

"Then what?" I ask.

"Then, the nurse here—a professional—will step up to you with the paddles and . . ."

"No!" I say. "No, it's dangerous."

"You're in no danger, Larry," says Mr. Assistant Director.

"No," I say again. "Tell Otto I'm not up for this."

The nurse speaks to the AD. "It is dangerous, sir. The paddles can kill a healthy man. If there's a mistake . . ."

"Okay," says the AD. "What can you give us that'll look like you are going to shock him?"

The nurse says, "How about if, when the camera is in front of me, I take the paddles out and lift them like I'm going to shock him, but I won't be close to him."

The AD confers with Otto. Otto urges him on. The AD says, "Let's try it."

They are going to try it! This is crazy. Otto is nuts! Maybe he planned this to get back at me for telling him off. I start to laugh. It'll make a hell of a story in *Variety*: "Actor Dies in Bizarre Paddling with Dyan Cannon."

Dyan begins again. Otto is angry. He doesn't have many more of these takes before he has to give the room back to the desperately sick and the dying.

The AD yells, "Quiet!" I think, *it's as quiet as the grave*, as I lie there helpless, pretending to be dead, when, in a few seconds, I could be.

Dyan starts. The camera moves with her, and I hear her catch her breath. She slows, moving in sync with the camera. What she is saying to me is moving, true, and beautiful, and this will be a great scene, and . . .

"*Pfaw, ptui!* Help! Let me out, help!" A weak cry comes from the far wall where the forgotten background patients have been unbelievably quiet and patient for about twelve hours. But now the plastic curtain on a bed is pushed at, pulled at, slapped. There is another cry. "I've got to get out. Got to . . . *help!*" And the plastic parts like the Red Sea. A very old man thrusts a knobby, white leg off the bed and leans out, almost falls, grabs the plastic drape, turns, and slides down till his feet touch the floor. His hospital gown is open in the back, and his skinny white ass wobbles as he turns to us.

"Please," he croaks. "Please, help me. I've got to . . . go to the bathroom. I've got to go . . . please." His arm is taken by the second assistant director, a woman who does not laugh at the old gentleman but walks him toward the restrooms in the hall.

Wham! Another set of expensive earpieces hits the floor and disintegrates. Otto is beyond-words angry—angry at the old gentleman, Dyan, the actors, the crew, the earth, the spring day, New York, and the universe. He roars the only thought he can get out. "I ask for extras," he snarls, "and you send me *sick* people!" And he stalks off the set.

The silence is broken by Dyan's giggle, my laugh, and then the roar of the whole crew. They're getting the first relief they've had since this miserable, tyrannical travesty began. It doesn't have to be this way, folks.

* * *

On the weekend after wrapping *Such Good Friends*, I appeared on *The David Frost Show* in New York. I told the truth about Mr. Preminger, and repeated two or three stories of his negative exploits, enough to give ordinary people shingles. I got lots of laughs from Frost and his audience. It was funny, sort of, in the retrospect of even a couple of days, but I wasn't proud of my part in it or my chosen world and profession that tolerates someone like that because he is, as a producer, a job creator. When people in charge behave badly, it's crucial to stop them and model a better, more humane way to create jobs. That's what humans do, isn't it? I wasn't happy that I had let Otto behave that way to Dyan. But she was a grown-up—more than the rest of us—so hats off to her.

That night when I got home to Brooklyn, Robin and Nick were sleeping. I was in the kitchen with a double West Indian rum when the phone rang. I grabbed it on the first ring. It was Otto.

He said in a cold, iron voice, "Ve are done, Lugenbiel. The picture we discussed? Forget it. I've torn up the contract." *Good*, I thought.

I wanted to ask, "Can you legally do that? Don't you have an obligation to me under the contract?" But I said, "Thank you—very much, Mr. Preminger," and hung up. I slept very well.

SCENE: New York

I was running around the oval track built above the gym floor at the West Side YMCA. The number of laps for a full mile was posted on the wall. It was a severely banked track to allow for speed, so running it was an exhilarating series of steep rises and descents. I felt like I was zooming.

This day, it was just me and one other guy whose face I never saw. He was ahead of me and running fast when I entered the track. I usually went around as I pleased, to feel my legs and breath, responding to my demands without hesitation.

But this guy was lapping me mercilessly. Suddenly, the competitor in me awoke and I surged forward to catch him. He sped up. So did I. Now we were toe to heel. I matched his speed, going faster than I ever had and doing well, loving the pounding of our feet, looking forward to the sweep up the bank on the turns and coming down immediately, only to sweep up again after a few yards of straightaway.

The guy never looked back and never connected with me. He kept a steady speed, and I began to think of him as my pacer. The hypnosis of running took over. I had always liked the zone-out aspect. I laughed out loud at the exaltation of putting my body to this test.

But now I began to feel pissed off. I couldn't pass this guy, couldn't beat him. I challenged him a few times, moving to my left and increasing my stride. He always instantly felt the different pressure and, effortlessly it seemed, moved a little faster. I began to feel something unrelated—that my life as an actor had failed me, that I had failed it somehow. I had not flown as I had dreamed of doing. I wasn't good enough; I could not match it. The great ones could run me down and I couldn't keep up the pace. I was fated not to fly but to run in a circle and never win. Without conscious choice, suddenly I saw my life as tawdry, small, petty, and this turned to anger, then fury. It scared me so much. Anger is fear, and I was a classic example of that, always in second place or worse, and that was too terrible to articulate, to think.

I moved myself to the guy's left into the next lane and poured on the speed. I stretched, lengthened, and gave it all I had. I didn't care if I blew myself out and faltered—I had to get ahead of this son of a bitch. He was now the enemy!

And I gained on him, about a half step. There was a tumbled rhythm of feet hitting the boards of the track now as I went faster, out of sync with his constant speed. And then we came around the exit turn, the finish mark of a mile, which led right to the door of the track. And the guy simply sped up like the demigod Mercury, like the sudden attack of an undersea predator, and he ran away from me instantly, up the bank of the turn and out the door of the track, and vanished into the hall.

I was beaten by a ghost. Beaten to hell and back as if I weren't even in the race. I could never have caught him. He was just toying with me. I didn't quit now. I kept running. I couldn't stop. But the impetus, my rage to win the game, was over. It was just me running in a circle, going nowhere special, not flying, not free—never had been. Not fast enough. Not good enough. Stupid, stupid! I realized I was only six laps short of my own mile, so I kept on at the pace I had run for the whole distance in the untouchable wake of a real runner. The pace set by this anonymous trickster, this arrogant bastard who'd led me and fooled me. I peeled off six laps in that one thought, and I hit the mile marker and ran up the ramp and into the hall, realizing I was not even breathing hard. I could have actually run another mile right then. Strange. I looked at my watch, and it told me I had just run a mile in five minutes and ten seconds. Not a four-minute mile, not a three-minute-and-change mile that the best milers were running, but a mile run I could never have imagined: 5:10.

I knew I had done my personal best, paced by a mirage. I never ran a 5:10 mile again. I had been mentored. It revealed emotional currents in me that would take me years to confront and begin to accept or use positively.

I was on the *samsara* wheel going in a circle, still believing there was something to win.

SCENE: Los Angeles, California

Polish filmmaker Krzysztof Zanussi met with me at a restaurant in LA and asked me if I would go to Poland to play the lead in the film he intended to make. I had to be willing to submit references to the hyper-paranoid Polish government, which was then part of the Soviet system of oppression in the countries on the other side of the Iron Curtain.

The script was terrific, but the filmmaker warned that it hadn't yet passed the censors. This director was very popular in his country, so you might expect he'd have some say about the script's contents. Not true. He had to be clever.

We talked about freedom one day over bowls of steaming latte at Orso. "In America," Zanussi said, "you see freedom as freedom from. We see freedom as freedom to."

"What does that mean?" I asked.

"Americans want to be free of all restraints. That will make them happy, they think. Freedom from all rules, except the ones you make up as an individual. This is a false idea of order. It is ultimately just chaos. The professor is an ultra-liberal and believes no State has a right to tell him what to do with his life, his ambition, and his love. The young woman he falls in love with has lived all her life accepting that she belongs to the State. The professor wants her to go to America with him. The State goes after them."

"So, what's freedom to?" I asked him.

He said, "In my country, a bus conductor can dream that he's the conductor of a symphony orchestra." He sipped his coffee.

"But can he literally become an orchestra conductor?" I asked.

"It would be theoretically possible but very difficult," said Krzysztof. "He would have to have a singular musical talent at a very early age. He would have to overcome our rigid education system, which sets people in categories of class or status very early."

"So, how is that freedom?" I asked.

"Even if you can't rise, you can dream," he answered.

"I can dream in my country, too," I retorted. "But I can also actually make the dream reality."

"If you have money," he said.

I said, "So, your way, the State pays for the bus conductor to express his dream—and owns him. Here, he somehow raises the money?"

Krzysztof interrupted with a smile. "Here, he takes on massive debt, which he must repay to someone for whom he must work. So how is that freedom?"

I said, "Either way, the man with the dream is owned. Then, it depends on what kind of owner he is willing to work for."

"Yes! Socialism or capitalism, there is a worker—a dreamer—and an owner. It depends on which owner you choose."

"And which do you choose?" I asked.

Krzysztof relit his pipe. A smoke cloud rose around his head. "I'm here at Orso talking to you, so what do you think?"

"But you're going back to Poland to make a movie—or conduct your orchestra—on socialist terms."

"It depends."

"On what?"

"On how clever a bus conductor I am," he answered.

I lit my pipe and puffed. We were now both enveloped in smoke, sweet and pungent. "I like your story, no matter who pays," I said.

The check came. I paid. We both laughed.

His film never happened. It was sidetracked by the Polish government censors. They didn't want him to use an American actor. *Really,* I thought, *they wanted to censor Krzysztof's dream?* What was mine? Did I still have one?

SCENE: Brooklyn, New York

Nick Luckinbill, in his bouncy chair in the backyard of our Brooklyn house, would get traction by slamming his hands down on the little plastic table in front of him and use his strong little legs to try to go somewhere, anywhere. He would start yelling, "Bulsi, Bulsi!" And often, 90-year-old Mr. Trabulsi, our next-door neighbor, would come slowly out of his kitchen door, down the stoop, and over to the wooden fence that separated our houses. He would smile at Nick and talk to him. He always addressed him as Nicholas, never Nick. Trabulsi was an antique carpet merchant, and a wonderful, kind man. I could see him from our kitchen window chatting with Nick over the fence, and Nick would answer him by saying "Bulsi" again and again, laughing and smiling and being serious. Nick's first friend.

When he was not quite two, there were many nights that I held Nick in my arms in my old orange and yellow terrycloth bathrobe and danced with him to Aretha's music in front of the fireplace in our lovely Brooklyn house. We both loved "Respect." Nick loved to dance. So did I. We were R & B fans.

One Christmas, I went searching for a toy Nick wanted—Rock 'Em, Sock 'Em Robot. I couldn't find it in any store. I looked everywhere they were sold in Manhattan and Brooklyn, from FAO Schwarz to tiny mom-and-pop stores. Sold out! So, on Christmas Eve, I was running up Flatbush Avenue toward the beach, trying every store that was still open. I wanted to get him that boxing robot toy. You could knock its block off. The kids all loved it. Nick giggled every time he saw one get knocked apart in the ads on TV and did his best to say, "Rock 'Em, Sock 'Em!"

I found one in a ratty little candy store near the beach. It was in a dusty window nobody had cleaned in years, and the box looked a little beat up. I ran inside and yelled, "Is this for sale?" A man with a scruffy beard appeared from the back. He looked unfriendly as if I were intruding. I was pointing at the Rock 'Em box in the window.

"It's for display," the guy said.

I said, "My son loves this toy. This is my only chance. It's Christmas Eve. Please sell it to me."

He looked at me sourly, "We're closed," he said.

"I'll pay cash," I said.

A light came in his good eye. "How much?"

"On TV they charge $49.95," I said.

He laughed.

I didn't know what kind of storekeeper he was, but when I looked around, I saw, piled like trash in one dusty cabinet, racing forms. Suddenly, I thought, *This is a money laundry, a bookie joint.* I knew I had to disregard the guy's attitude and deal with the anti-Santa.

"One hundred bucks, cash," I said. "And keep it off the books. If my boss knew I was paying this much, he'd be mad."

"Who's yer boss?" the guy asked. By now I'm thinking *this is Brooklyn.* The five families, the Mafia. Out of nowhere, I said the name of my boss at the restaurant I worked at. The guy's head swiveled away, and I laid the bill on the dirty glass counter.

He took it, went to the window, yanked the box up, and stuck it in my hand. I felt a surge of joy. "Thanks! And Merry Christmas!" The guy didn't answer or look at me. He shut the door in my face.

I felt like Bob Cratchit. I had met the Brooklyn Scrooge—far worse than the London version. I ran all the way home, stopping only to grab a bottle of Bushmills Irish whiskey. This coup deserved a drink.

When I got home, Nick and his mother were asleep. It was midnight. I sat on the stairs in the living room, drinking whiskey and thinking about my family and the obsession that drove me to find this toy for Nick or die trying. I had paid double for it, but I didn't even know if the toy was actually in the box. The way the guy acted, there could have been a dead rat in it. But Rock 'Em was there, and I wrapped the box in the pages of the *New York Times* and wrote, "To Nick, From Santa" on the front.

I was successful, but I felt endless guilt. It peeked through my heart's holes every holiday, with every song I heard. I wasn't good enough. I had left my family in the lurch. My younger brother and sister were stuck in the Minotaur's labyrinth, and I had done nothing about it. My mother was neglected, and no one helped her. My heart cracked. I was not a good son or brother. Or father or husband. I was too hungry for success, fame—for myself. I took another swig of the Irish. I didn't know it never worked that way.

My son and his mother slept. It was bitterly cold outside. Suddenly, it was bitterly cold inside. I sat on the stairs that led up to the bedrooms and drank, unable to go up. I had been unfaithful. I was no good. A scene from *Long Day's Journey Into Night* reeled through my mind. Was I Edmund or Jamie? I sat there, replaying the past, rationalizing the present, miserable in both, unable to see through my dark mirror to a future different from this. I sat there, like my father, and drank, solitary, by choice, I thought.

I remembered another Christmas Eve: my father wheeling my beautiful bike into our foyer where the tree was. He was stinking drunk. I took another belt of Bushmills. I wasn't him. *No!* I wasn't drunk—*ever!*

My dad had tried hard that night, mixing joy and his actual sacrifice to buy that bike when we were always poor, and letting me believe I had helped him buy it. His drinking wrecked the whole holiday again, setting us ablaze as if the Christmas tree had exploded in flames.

I was replaying my tape in solitary—all the feelings of inadequacy, rage, and sorrow I had always accepted as normal. I was so sad for my parents, brother, and sisters.

Was raising children a goal, a sacred mission? Or just a haphazard, dumb job? "They're here, I love 'em, good luck to 'em." That was a stance some people took. And their kids, some of them, turned out just fine. And some parents helicoptered to every sports game and school report day and PTA meeting, every class or school event, and their kids were screwed up. Every parent has to give TLC and personal attention at least. Real love. Where was I on that scale? I always tried. But did I even know what real love was?

Each of my children has unique strengths and unique troubles with life. Any ideas about life and how to live it that you impart to your kids are subject to constant change. The fixed stars we call reality—morality, ethics, belief in God, in connecting—are shaky now. Who today accepts ideas about God just because their parents are believers?

SCENE: New York

I had eleven years of apprenticeship in the New York theater, taking any theatrical work that came my way. I always chose the one I thought was the most noble, the classiest turn, even if it paid less or paid nothing. I worked at non-theater jobs that let me eat and sleep—barely. I almost never had money in my pocket.

Eleven years of moving my cardboard treasure chests from borrowed couch to walk-up furnished room. From Harlem to Manhattan to Brooklyn to Queens, to actors' digs in summer stock companies, and finally to extended daytime TV work and my apartment. I always studied the craft and art of acting with various teachers. Those years went by in a flash.

It was "token living." If I had two tokens, I could traverse the city underground. The subway was a cheap and rewarding people-watching opportunity.

It was a climb from one line in a CBS Sunday morning live TV show to a tiny part in the original production of *The Fantastiks* (plus understudying three roles), to five lines of dialogue in a TV soap opera, to summer Shakespeare and winter regional repertory, playing small, medium, and eventually leading parts. There was a Broadway national tour, an off-Broadway success, the first movie, the second movie, and an ABC series starring in the lead role.

By 1973, I was known. I had succeeded in working in all venues where actors sought to excel and I had a good reputation. Now came the hard part, the choices. How do you build a "careen" into a career? Can it actually even be done? Many actors, it seemed, had done it. I still had to learn that it was an illusion.

I had good, diligent agents, but they were not enough to guide me to fulfill my dream: to be a hero and express the best in humankind. This dream I had to manifest alone. For this, I needed great purpose and common sense. I had to maintain my vision and search for positive ways to make it come true. I didn't yet know that to be an A-list actor in Hollywood, I had to find material that expressed me—my persona—on my own and then find a way to turn it into a successful movie.

I had the vision and the intensity and the work ethic, but I needed something more—an overall plan of action. I do not think strategically. I am, by nature, a tactician. I tended to take a short-term situation over a long-term plan. And I am not a cool head. Antiauthoritarian impulses are ancient in me, from being eager to get out of the womb (as my mother described my birth, it was a dark and stormy dawn, and I was in a big hurry) to my nightmares as a child, trying to escape from a gray tunnel I had entered, whose soft, dark walls were slowly, inexorably smothering me. My impulse was to rebel, to respond to the immediate stimulus, to scan my biome constantly for potential threats. This gift of nature was not very helpful in making cool-headed decisions.

So, I made emotional ones. I didn't know what to believe, so I zigged and zagged between resistance and going along to get along. A zig was brilliant, a zag was just dumb. I didn't know how to step back and look objectively at what I was doing.

As I understand it now, karma is to take action with the intent that whatever life brings you, you will accept it completely. To resist, defend, and regret with outrage fate's fickle finger choosing you is to hurl into space and time a spiritual boomerang that will come right back at you. If, on the other hand, you accept what happens to you and respond with mindfulness and compassion for all who must endure what life brings, you will be instrumental in creating good in the world. Narcissism and hubris need not apply.

Yet, I had too much of both. In this unconscious *push me, pull you* state, I married and had a child. I made a reputation in New York as an interesting actor and someone to watch. As a result of the first and second New York-based movies I was featured in, I had cultivated a small reputation in class A films. But with a family to support, my priorities shifted. As I see it now, this was the moment I got confused about my basic goal—to raise myself to be the best actor I could be. I began to drift sideways and put more value on earning a better and better living.

Imprinted memories I didn't even know I had were now driving me. My earliest memories growing up were of poverty, blue-collar poverty. My parents scraped their entire lives for every dollar. When I was a kid, my father's pay packet was parsed out to pay bills, and sometimes there would be two dollars left for extras. My mother's change purse was supplemental, apart from her secretary's salary, and that change purse held pennies, nickels, dimes, and quarters. No half-dollar coins and no dollar bills. That change purse was for discretionary funds. They lived in fear of real poverty—as Black people lived it across the railroad tracks, as the local farmers lived it, dependent on "the shame of the government dole" and "going to the poorhouse."

"If your husband keeps on the way he's going, Agnes, you'll end up in the poorhouse," my aunt told my mother acidly. And the acid burned her.

The poorhouse was a farm four miles south of Fort Smith, where white and Black paupers were allowed to live separately as long as they worked the farm. They grew their food and sold the produce to help out. The county gave a small charity stipend to keep the place going. My parents knew people who had "ended up" there. People who died there were buried in a large, bare potter's field south of the farm. It was the depth of shame and disgrace to end up there.

My earliest model of a heroic working person was our family's only outside help when we were kids, Mrs. Channing. We called her Channy. Her bosom was ample and down to her waist. Her lap and her kindness were, to a little boy, gigantic. Her cooking was atrocious. Her accent was a kind of soft, slurred, sing-song Southern sound that, as a boy, I loved to hear. It arose out of the mud of the creeks, the stink of the swamp, and the absence of all things I now call culture. Channy washed us in the "warsh tub" and made us "porched eggs" for breakfast after our parents had gone to their dreary jobs. Channy cleaned negligently and made beds by pulling the covers up and walking away, but she taught me how to tie my shoes. Endlessly. As a left-handed little boy, I could not get the higher math of that task. One day after school, she took us upstairs to a tiny bedroom looking out over the alley beyond the barn and chicken coop, locked the door, and made us get down on the floor because her crazy drunk consort was in the yard waving a gun and yelling to the house, and cursing her, and vowing to "kill yore ass when you come home!" We kids thought this terror, reminiscent of a scene from Faulkner, was a great adventure and even scary fun. Then Channy made us sugar and margarine sandwiches on white bread. Yum! When Mom and Pop returned, Channy walked seven miles home in the early winter dark.

I have always wondered if Channy ended up in the poorhouse. She was poorer than we were.

* * **

While I was working in the Lincoln Center Repertory Company in *Tartuffe*, I began auditioning for commercial work, two kinds: voice-over (announcers) and on camera (spokesman). A commercial agent offered it as an easy way to make good money and not be committed to the substance (or content) of the work. That alone should have warned me that this road led away from truth and passion. Ads are always pleasant lies that mimic hopeful truths. Nothing advertised is ever as good as promised and, in fact, may be destructively wrong.

I made a huge hit in the ad biz. My first on-camera commercial for a bank "went viral," as they say today. I was selling a bank with pieces of my soul. This sounds melodramatic, but melodrama begins as truth. People (consumers?) liked me—my authority (truth?), my sincerity (acting), my looks, and my deftness (competency). The ads proliferated for many cycles of thirteen weeks. Other commercial work flooded in—on camera and voice-over—and then my commercial agent sold me to an airline—TWA—for five years. I got the part because I knew how to say "double-u."

Two things happened: I went to see Sydney Lumet at Silvercup Studios in Queens, where he was casting a new movie. I revered Sydney. We had a great conversation. He told me he had seen my work onstage and was very complimentary. I told him how much I would like to work with him.

Then he said, "I've seen you a lot on television in those airline commercials, and I think you might be overexposed to the public. You are a very effective spokesman and an excellent actor, but the part I'm looking to cast has to be someone the public must be surprised by—it's fundamental to the story. So, I'm sorry, but I have to say I can't cast you."

It was devastating to hear this. I wondered why he had even asked me to come in to see him. Maybe he truly thought I was a good actor who was overexposing himself. He was giving me a friendly, avuncular warning. I don't know, but my respect for him only grew.

The film was *Dog Day Afternoon*, and the role was the transgender partner of Al Pacino's character, which Chris Sarandon played brilliantly.

* * *

I stepped out of the commercial world and never did another one. Have I missed the easy money? Yes, once in a while. But I am free of it now.

It was then that I took the first step away from wealth and the luxe life and back toward my childhood dream of being a hero. By pleasant serendipity, a play was offered.

Gordon Davidson, my friend and the artistic director of the Mark Taper Forum at the Music Center in Los Angeles, sent me *A Meeting by the River*, a new play by Christopher Isherwood. I was invited to meet with Isherwood and his partner, artist Don Bachardi, at the Polo Lounge at the Beverly Hills Hotel.

Isherwood was quiet and humble in a way I understood as Buddhist. We talked about his play, which was intensely personal to his life—a conversation with his brother. The brother was a big-time publisher and film producer, and Chris was written as a Buddhist monk. The meat of the play was the extreme difference in the way of life each had chosen. The difficulty would be making the long conversations dramatic. In fact, they were, but only for people deeply interested in philosophy. Sam Waterston, whom I had known for years, would play the monk.

Other people in our theater business often wondered about my connection to *The Boys in the Band*. How could I play a gay man so well and be straight? Chris saw into this. Somehow, he knew my empathetic nature as if he had known me as an adolescent boy. He clearly was happy that I would play his brother, who loved and envied his Buddhist self and, at the same time, was having an affair with a young man. He hoped his wife would see that he loved her and had no compunction presenting her with the dilemma of endorsing his childlike need to "play," to be himself. It was as if Chris knew by intuition the sort of life I was then leading with women outside of marriage and understood it for what it was.

The play was not a commercial success, nor was it ever meant to be. It was Gordon Davidson's homage to a great writer—and that was also Gordon's greatness as a man, producer, and director.

SCENE: Hollywood

Six-foot-five Sam Rolfe strides along at a fast clip just above the tide line on fabled Malibu Beach. He doesn't fit in. He is pale, has a Marine haircut, and is wearing work clothes—dull black cotton pants, an unchic, worn-out polo shirt, and brown street shoes with white socks. He looks like a farmer, which he had been in the way back. He's uncomfortable with this kind of meeting, and so am I.

I walk with him, aware that this beach stroll is my audition for the lead in Sam's new ABC series, *The Delphi Bureau*. He side-glances me often, and I focus on not trying too hard to impress him. It's an uneasy feeling, but there's no end of stuff to talk about. Sam's pilot script is a two-hour TV movie, and I love it. The script and the character of Glenn Garth Gregory, the reluctant spy, has intelligence and wit and is very believable. Sam's other work is impressive. *The Man from U.N.C.L.E.* and *Have Gun—Will Travel* had Sam's signature simple reality and breezy tone. This new show is fun, and I want to be a part of it.

He stops walking suddenly. Looks at me. "You're the guy," he says.

"Really?"

"Yep."

"Thank you, sir!"

"Let's walk back and get your people to talk to my people."

I thrust out my hand and he grips it. "I won't let you down, Sam."

He squints and says, "I like you. I think you've got the real goods."

"Just like that?"

"Yep, just like that."

In Hollywood, you don't encounter many men like Sam. His word was his bond. He meant what he said. He wrote and produced every bit of his work, and it had integrity. He was a tough, strong guy and a fierce competitor. And he worked full-out. He was a success in Hollywood—an incredible feat. And yet he maintained a deep part of himself that was pure country. He was a guy who could order sarsaparilla or buttermilk in a saloon, and it would be delivered, respectfully, in a nice glass. Now I was Sam's guy.

What kind of guy was I? I was not easily pigeonholed. I got the job purely on Sam Rolfe's trust. What could I offer him?

Nick was three years old when *The Delphi Bureau* began. We were in California renting a Frank Lloyd Wright house owned by my agent and good friend, Hal Gefsky. The house was a block or two from Sunset Boulevard, on Sunset Plaza Drive, right in the heart of the strip. Robin was between soaps and trying to get a career going in Hollywood.

Hal had bought the house from Anne Baxter after her husband, actor John Hodiak, died of a heart attack. Anne was Frank Lloyd Wright's niece, so the house was just as her uncle conceived and built it. And it was haunted by John, 'twas said. He had appeared several times, standing outside the kitchen window, looking in in a longing, loving way. What scared people who saw him outside the kitchen window, just standing there in the dark, was that the kitchen window was on the second floor, twenty feet above the ground. Hal told us this story casually after we had agreed to rent the house. The master bedroom also had some peculiarities in the dressing room, which had been John's. The built-in shelves behaved oddly, and the door opened mysteriously after it was shut.

Our son, Nick, was a sunny boy, a *boy*-boy, curious about everything in his surroundings and unafraid. He slept in that dressing room. Several nights, I woke up with a hair-raising feeling that something was strange in the house. I would hear the click of the magnetic latch and then the door would pop open. When I went in, Nick was sleeping with a smile on his face, but . . . *but* . . . the drawers next to his little bed were all pulled out in different ways! This happened for many nights, then, for no reason, it stopped. No bad vibes, just a deep mystery.

The drawers were beautifully fitted into the wall in a cool geometric pattern. With the drawers open, that order was disturbed, but in a whimsical way. It looked like the way a bureau would be left if someone were late for an appointment and had pulled out a shirt, socks, a belt, and a tie. Maybe Hodiak was late for an appointment with St. Peter in heaven. Or was he reliving a part of his life on earth that had been rudely interrupted by his heart attack, and he wanted to visit his house, now occupied by the pure goodness of the happy little boy sleeping? We never felt a malign presence. Nick was safe. I believed in the spirit of John Hodiak and considered him a family friend.

One night, at 3:00 A.M., muted voices woke me up. The dressing room door was ajar again, but the voices came from outside, twenty feet below where we slept at the side of the house in a dark grove of eucalyptus trees. They were speaking Spanish and English. A drug deal was in progress. I called LAPD and was told not to approach or speak to these folks. Three minutes later, a patrol car silently eased up to the dark corner in the trees and made arrests very civilly, very politely, very quietly. I got the feeling these folks all knew each other and accepted the rules. Welcome to LA!

* * *

After *The Delphi Bureau* was picked up, we moved to Malibu. I worked twelve to fifteen hours a day, not counting two more hours of driving time in LA traffic to Warner Brothers Studio in Burbank in "the Valley." I was consumed by my work life. I was so new to filming—how to do it, and learning how to be present and alive on camera. The character I played was the most interesting one I had ever played in series television. And now I was trying to find a footing, solid ground, to walk in Hollywood, a most interesting and dangerous landscape. I had gone to New York as a naive twenty-six-year-old, having left Fort Smith as a nineteen-year-old mewling and puking baby. I had gone to the Army as a pubescent commissioned officer and to Africa as a wide-eyed rube. As an adult, I had found a place to set my feet and dig in—in the streets of my homeland, New York. But at thirty-six, I found myself on safari, tracking the jungles, the swamps, and the sunny heights of Hollywood.

I worked constantly in the company of coworkers who were attracted to me. I didn't pursue them. If someone, once in a while, connected with me in a sexual way, I was flattered and responded. I had no shame, no guilt, no thoughts, just sensations. My moral compass was askew. No one seemed to have any inhibition anymore. I won't say the encounters meant nothing—they were anodyne, like a rum toddy. It was the '70s, open season all the time. My depth of focus was on one thing: the work—doing it right and climbing the ladder to the top.

At the same time, I made decisions that contradicted that superego goal. I undercut my own supposed ideals. As a new boy in town, I was observed for signs that I had "the real goods." A bottle of tequila in your trailer at 7:00 A.M. indicates bad character. I was not an alcoholic or even a heavy drinker, but it sure could have looked like it to the well-meaning gossipy folks who were the heart of Hollywood.

* * *

We walked into the restaurant Scandia at the top of the Sunset Strip. Hal, who had been leading our way to the table, suddenly and subtly changed places with me. Now I was in front and unsure which table we were headed for. I turned to ask him, but he just whispered through unmoving lips, "Corner table, facing the room!" I turned and saw it. It was in full sunlight, open to the entire room, totally exposed. I got it, and I didn't like it.

"Take the seat in the corner," Hal hissed. I did, trying to look casual. I felt like a rebel prisoner facing the hard eyes of the politburo or the parole board. The restaurant was a base for producers and casting directors who gathered to lunch and schmooze and check out the fresh meat coming in on the hoof. They were assessing me. Was I a sirloin hamburger or a patty melt?

In the theater in those days, your stage work was seen, judged, and noted. The word about you—your appeal, skill, charisma—would slowly creep up through the theater community, and, one day, you would get a call from a producer who had seen you prove your skill and value in some show, large or small. It could be on Broadway, off-Broadway, off-off-Broadway, or in one of the many regional theaters that were coming to life across the country. Your work would be known, judged objectively, and if you got a call, you knew that someone had made at least a preliminary assumption that you were right and ready for their project. You could proceed to try to prove it in an audition.

In my experience, the first step into the swim of movie acting was not skill or expertise. It was your look. If you got past the physical judgment, you might proceed to a casting call at a studio. "Rounds" meant you spent the day in your car driving to a studio gate and being checked out by armed guards, given a pass to display, and told exactly where to park. Once parked, you walked to a bungalow where the production company offices were located and joined a few actors waiting to see the casting director.

If you passed muster, based on no criteria that seemed relevant to talent, skill, or experience, you would stand in a room in front of a camera and read some lines from a script (not necessarily the script of the project you were up for). On occasion, you might be asked to meet with the actual director. The process was more or less to decide what "type" you were, based on your look.

This was disconcerting. I looked okay, I thought, but I relied on my ability to cold-read a script and on my belief that my previous work had gotten me to this point. Now I was in a system that didn't care much about past work unless you were prominent in a current film—and one that was doing well. In Hollywood, the trade papers' news was focused on the film grosses and the "overnights" of television ratings. This was the news that mattered. At that time, in New York, success or failure was analyzed more substantively, more traditionally. In Hollywood, if the film you were in did well at the box office, you got some credit by association, and assuming a base competency, a career could be built on a shrewd choice of "vehicles."

SCENE: Hollywood

7:00 A.M., *The Delphi Bureau* set. The far end of Burbank Airport. A small plane lay smashed to bits by a crash landing. One wing was sheared off, the propeller blades stuck out at odd angles, and the cabin was a mess of metal and plastic. I, Glenn Garth Gregory, a reluctant and mildly venal spy, was investigating this wreck. It would turn out to be trouble for me, I had no doubt, and Sybil, my blithe boss in Washington, would, as usual, be unavailable if I needed help.

A pink girl was on the set. Her teeth were chattering in the cold. Everybody was cold at this hour in Southern California. "It's cold and it's damp," but this lady was not "a tramp." She was my love interest of the week, the proximate lure that would get me deeper into danger, the damsel in distress whom I must help. The first AD looked around. The girl was shivering and snuffling, her knees practically knocking from the cold. By noon, it would be hot in the sun, cool in the shade. It was winter in Hollywood.

The AD yelled, "Hot set!" The camera crew practiced a small dolly move toward the actress, which revealed the smashed plane over her shoulder. She was a pale, spindly young woman of about twenty-two, dressed in a light pink sweater and a thin cotton jumper. She was submitting to the hairdresser and the makeup artist who were fussing over her face, which would become the entire landscape of this camera shot of the show.

I hadn't yet met her, but I would be locking lips in a tender kiss with her in just a few minutes. This was the first shot of the first episode of my very own series. I hadn't met the director or the crew either. I was picked up in Malibu at 5:00 A.M. and driven to Warner Brothers Studio in Burbank. I arrived at 6:00 and was escorted to my dressing quarters by a staffer and shown the suite of rooms I would have at my disposal during the run of the season of eight shows.

The staffer opened the bungalow door in a large park-like area with old shade trees and subtropical plantings. The grinning young fellow waved me in with a cheery, "Good morning, Mr. Bogart!" I walked into a large three-room apartment. It had a full bedroom and an en suite bathroom with Spanish tile counters and a shower. The second bedroom/office had paneled walls and doors in the dark Craftsman look of the '30s. The living room was enormous and comfortably furnished with couches, easy chairs, and a coffee table. In the corner was a makeup and hairdressing area with a chair that could tilt flat.

"This was Humphrey Bogart's dressing room?"

"Yup," said the young man. "He practically lived here."

Oh my God. I was dreaming.

I grew up in *houses* smaller than this place, in homes with only one basic little bathroom for the six people in my family. We had to make an appointment, and it was too bad for whoever had to follow Dad, who used the bathroom as a smoking room and never liked to open the tiny window. Some Peeping Tom might be out there, he told my sisters, or you'll catch your death of cold.

Bogey smoked, too, as everyone knew from the movies, and the bungalow walls were permeated with the smoky residue of "coffin nails." I thought because I smoked a pipe, it was a step up. I keep that in mind now, at eighty-nine, with shortness of breath, asthma-induced emphysema and COPD, and an atrial fibrillating heart.

I loved this dressing room. I'm not the guy who "takes on," as they say in the South. I don't have "airs." I don't desire fabulous cars, yachts, or first-class treatment. I regard it all from a distance, with no desire to fight to get such things. Still, I did want money. I wanted a buffer between me and the poverty that had stalked my family. I wanted to be safe and make my own family safe. After eleven years of constantly working at least two jobs in New York—being in some show or workshop or as an extra in a live-on-tape television show taped in New York and my restaurant host gig at O. Henry's Steak House that gave me the one good meal I got in a day—there I was in this bounty, this gossamer connection with a great film actor, as I embarked as the star of my own television series.

I threw my stuff on the makeup counter and walked outside to be given the keys to my studio car, a maroon 1972 Buick Riviera—one of the finest cars Buick ever made. Not flashy, but solid and dependable. And I thought, *Wow!*

I was driven to the Burbank Airport by a ubiquitous teamster. And now, I was off-camera, speaking my first lines of the series to the young actress.

I finished my line and . . .

"Cut!" Said the director. "Good one. New deal!"

The actress was taken aside for more hair and makeup, fluffing and puffing.

Now the AD yelled so that all Burbank could hear, "Roundy-roundy on the stiff!"

The crew laughed. They began turning the camera around 180 degrees. The director introduced himself to me. He was very pleasant, very nice. He said, "Have you looked over the scene?"

I laughed. "Yes, sir."

He looked confused. "Ah," he said.

"I've studied it."

"Ready to do it?"

"Yes, sir."

"God, you're polite." He grinned, turned to the AD and said, "Okay, get whatshername in. I'll be a minute." And he walked to his trailer and went inside.

I asked the cameraman, "What does 'roundy-roundy on the stiff' mean?"

The cameraman laughed. "That's you," he said. "Jimmy's been top AD for about a century. He's done a million shows. He was even on the *I Love Lucy* show for a while. He has the old slang. The stiff is the guy in the suit and tie, the hero, the lead. So, the stiff—that's you."

"Ah," I said.

The young woman was brought to her mark on the ground where she was to stand. They had laid a sandbag there. I still had not met her.

"I'm Larry," I said. "Welcome."

She smiled, "Thanks, nice to meet you."

The director interrupted. "Okay, Larry, this is simple. You step in, you talk, then you kiss her. We'll cover that, so just remember how you did it."

"Stiff," I said.

"Huh?"

I just laughed. The cameraman smiled. The director looked confused but then he brightened. "Ah," he muttered. Then he yelled, "Let's shoot this!"

I stepped to my mark. This was the last scene of this episode, the end of our little flirtation. I said the now-forgotten line. I leaned in and tenderly brushed her hair out of her eyes. I kissed her.

"Cut! Okay, let's go again, and Larry, this time don't do that thing with the hair."

"Why?" I asked.

Now he was genuinely stumped. "I . . . it looks bad, that's all."

The young woman looked at me, embarrassed. She said, "It, uh, messes up my hair is all."

"Ah," I said.

We did it again. This time I felt different, out of it. My simple human impulse was taboo—it resulted in "messed up hair" and "looked bad." Maybe all that was true. I knew I didn't yet know much about acting on film. I went on my intuition, which was questionable at the time. Maybe there was a reason all those male actors were called stiffs.

We filmed on location, and it was exciting. The high slopes of Mount Hood in Oregon. A logjam full of leeches (really!) in the American River. In a pit full of rattlesnakes. On a steep roof à la *To Catch a Thief*. I had to learn how to act on film. I wasn't seeing the dailies (also called the rushes), meaning the bits of film shot that day, which were rushed from the set to the developer and the editing rooms. Producers and directors saw the stuff every day after shooting and made immediate decisions about each take, which the editors assembled into a rough cut of the show.

Exciting. Exhausting. Every scene was crucial. Every shot demanded total concentration. There was no rehearsal of scenes except for camera and light placement. The actors rehearsed alone or together in their trailers, and during blocking for the camera on the set. We had to go on guts and whatever technique we had and try to be spontaneous and free in every moment.

I studied lines every night for the next day's shoot and tried to remain loose, keep my imagination fresh, and continue developing Glenn Garth Gregory into a real person. The directors, too, were on the roller coaster. They were shooting *The Delphi Bureau* this week while reading and prepping notes for another gig on a different show the following week. It was like summer stock.

I loved every second of it. Sam Rolfe was a solid, incisive writer. His plots worked. There was the deliberate sense of a superior, intelligent comic book story being told. He created a universe where extra-bright, sharply drawn people lived, schemed, and/or loved and fought the good fight against the odds. I was finally playing my kind of reluctant hero.

After discussing the character with Sam, I took the logical position based on his writing. My character would not carry a weapon. His only defensive tool was his photographic memory, which got him into and out of trouble. But weapons kept turning up in the scripts for me to use somehow. And I kept saying to Sam, I—he, Glenn—wouldn't do that. And Sam would squint and grimace and agree and eliminate it. It made the show distinctive and it made me a different kind of hero. A mind guy. A book guy. I was in good shape. I could shoot, could handle a gun, could rough and tumble. But when I asked to do my own stunts, I was turned down flat: "Actors act. Stunt people do dangerous things. If actors get hurt, the show shuts down."

I saw what my stunt double—a swell guy and very brave—did in the pilot. It was very dangerous. He broke out in a sweat when he had to climb out an eleventh-floor hotel window and inch along a narrow ledge. I broke out in a sweat, too, standing on level ground watching "me" do this. There was an invisible but untested safety line if he slipped and fell. "It should work," he said before he slid out the window.

People die making movies. Electrocutions, falls, mishandled firearms, vehicles going out of control, and actors ignoring safety rules. Or acting—as in *The Charge of the Light Brigade*—by stabbing themselves or someone else with an unsheathed sword when horses collide and dump riders.

I had a lot to learn, and I had to learn fast.

* * *

No matter how many movies I have seen, it's still hard to believe how sensitive a camera is to thought. Simple thought. It's also a detector of no thought. I believe the best film actors think on camera. A specific thought or emotion can be read into a still face. In 1910–20, experiments by Russian filmmaker Lev Kuleshov proved that viewers brought their own ideas and feelings while observing an actor's face while he watched a montage of random pictures: a bowl of soup, a little girl in a coffin, and a woman lying on a couch. The actor's face stayed the same in each instance, but viewers believed the actor was feeling hunger, grief or desire. Emotion is perception.

I progressed easily with the camera and the peculiar distractions of shooting a movie. It's easy to get trapped in the mechanics, the awareness of the camera, the marks, the surprising lack of physical movement needed in a talking scene, and the trick of not seeing the camera as your eyes move past the lens. The secret to ignoring bad direction is just to agree and then do what you know is right. Good directors are not traffic cops but psychologists. Not-so-good directors succumb to the *hurry up* syndrome and are afraid to dig into the script's reality. Go through every scene to find active, positive subtext. Build a thought stream for every moment. If actors don't do this, they will play scenes just making faces that badly approximate thought. This is fake. This marks an actor as an "indicator"—the worst of actors.

I had begun to learn this while filming *The Boys in the Band* and *Such Good Friends* (Billy Friedkin was a fine director; Otto Preminger, a traffic cop), but television work was much, much faster. However, Sam Rolfe's scripts had logic and clear feeling. Most episodic television scripts are plot heavy and light on logic and motivation, over- and underwritten at the same time. For an actor, it's a defensive minefield. The text can be something unplayable, and the subtext nonexistent. So, actors develop shticks—brands that identify them to audiences who have learned what to expect from them.

They try to cultivate originality and a spark of character that's amusing, moving, and pleasing to audiences. These actors work steadily, make reputations and careers, and can become stars, even in bad shows. But without some protective device, like a strong subtext, they could quickly turn into hacks.

I gave *The Delphi Bureau* all I had as a performer and as a person. I loved the show and Sam. I don't think I solved the character completely or that my film acting technique progressed to perfection. I do think I learned how to project my natural self pretty well. I am a naturally cheerful, courteous person. I have an always-functioning sense of humor and a tendency to look for the funny parts of life in every situation. God alone knows where that came from. It's paired with a dark anger that also inhabits the Laurence Luckinbill mind/body experiment from time to time. My sense of injustice is high—not for me, but for others. I hate authority—all authority—yet I submit myself gladly to being mentored. I am a grateful person now, but then I was too busy to be so. Is that why I had an empty feeling that something had passed me by, and I hadn't even experienced it?

After the pilot and eight episodes of *The Delphi Bureau* aired, the series was not renewed. ABC had programmed a schedule they called "The Wheel." It consisted of three shows under a generic title—"The Men"—that rotated in the same slot on the same night each week. The idea was that one, or ideally all, of the shows would become a hit. Sam Rolfe was a hitmaker with a great history. He knew The Wheel was an impossible way to get an audience to stay with any show, but that was the game that season, so he played, and I with him.

We stood in front of Len Goldenson's desk at ABC, making our case for staying on the air. Mr. Goldenson was a pleasant guy in the great position of bringing ABC back to life. Sam knew him well, so it was odd that we stood before him like peons begging the patron for a favor. All I knew to say was that I loved the show and would work even harder. Sam quoted some good reviews and ratings numbers but said little more. It ended quickly. Mr. Goldenson had no hope for any of the shows in The Wheel. It was a done deal. Canceled. He was sorry, and it wasn't our fault.

We went back to the set to finish the day's shooting. Sam was in a state of contained misery. We finished. It was the end of the week. I walked back to Bogart's bungalow to change (the golf cart rides seemed to have vanished) and found my stuff—all the items I had collected over several months of living there—in a box at the end of the walkway where my car, a gift from Sam, was still parked where I'd left it. My name had been painted on the curb. It was my space, but my name had already been erased. I had been eliminated as if I had never existed. I saw Bogart laugh at me. I heard my father in his smoky car telling me I had "about as much talent as a one-legged Indian in an ass-kickin' contest." I heard the mavens at college telling me I was not the hero type; I was a second or third character-lead type. I heard Herman Shumlin tell me in his uninflected hard voice, "You aren't right for anything!"

No one said goodbye. I should have walked over to Sam's office and said, "Let's go to the Sportsman's Lodge"—the unofficial Warner Brother's drinking establishment on Barham Boulevard, across the road—"and get a drink or two. You are the best goddamned boss I've ever had." But I didn't. I was too ashamed. I had failed him.

Sam survived the loss. But he died of a heart attack a few years later. He hated to fail. I miss him still. I did not go to his funeral. I don't do that.

* * *

I'm watching *The Delphi Bureau* pilot in its first run on ABC television with my four-year-old son, Nick. We are watching the big, climactic action scene in the episode. My character has (almost) figured out who the real villains are and is trying to escape from their murderous henchman, played by Cameron Mitchell, by hiding in a dense cornfield. But Cameron has a fiendish plan. He gets aboard a tall combine harvester and comes after me, following the broken cornstalk path I've made for myself and the girl (the female lead, a different one each week). I know he's coming, so I make the young woman slip away in another direction and then I run, making a wider trail for the bad guy to follow. Eventually, he runs me down and I fall under the combine. Underneath it is a rotary cutting blade and razor pincers that direct the material—in this case, me—to be sliced to ribbons underneath.

Suddenly, Nick bursts into tears. He doesn't wail, but his face is absolutely miserable and his tears are pouring down. I hug him. "What's the matter?" I ask.

He manages to say, "They're going to hurt you, Daddy!"

Oh my God. It never occurred to me that he would have this response. Am I an idiot? "No, son, it's just a show. I'm here. You see me here, don't you?"

"Yes," Snuffleupagus says, hugging me closer.

"So, it's a show. And wait until you see how I get out of that machine's clutches!"

On-screen, I cling to the machine's undercarriage, just out of reach of the big rotary blade and the pincers. My photographic memory shows me a design manual for the deadly machine, which I speed-read as I cling there desperately. There's no escape if I weaken. I see the schematic of the gasoline line that feeds the carburetor. I yank it loose. Voilà! The machine slows and stops. The bad guy, irritated, pulls a gun and climbs down to finish me off the old-fashioned way, but I pop up from his blind side and knock the gun away. We grapple, and in the melee, I punch him in the jaw, knock him cold, and hurt my punching hand. That'll learn me! The girl and I are reunited, and the bad guy is felled. After about four more surprise twists—good ones—I am victorious. The girl and I say goodbye, only to meet again in Washington for a delicious kiss in the Hall of Justice before I'm off (in another twist) on another reluctant mission.

Nick is happy. He stayed at my side the entire day and all was well. I was happy. Me and my son.

SCENE: Hollywood

I got a call from Robert Brustein, the esteemed liberal critic and founder of a theater company at Harvard called the American Repertory Theater. He offered me a place in his company in Boston for a season and a juicy, serious lead part, in *Danton's Death* by Georg Büchner, a German tale of the excesses of the French Revolution. I thought about it, waffled, and turned him down. I think the coincidental timing involved a contract for a guest-starring role in an episode of the cop show, *The Rookies*. Brustein flew off the handle, crawled through the telephone line, and tried to strangle me. He called me a traitor to the theater, a weakling stuck on money and bullshit, a coward who was afraid to test myself as an actor in his company. If he's alive, I hope he doesn't remember his foaming-at-the-mouth tirade because it demeaned him as he tried to demean and shame me. It was funny, but I did feel ashamed. He got to me.

Brustein was partly right. It was too easy to stay in Hollywood. He cursed me and hung up. He was right on the merits but wrong on human understanding. Life is not an ideology, and as karma, always trying to help me save myself, would have it, my next job in Hollywood would be a two-play repertory season with the Center Theatre Group at the Mark Taper Forum in downtown LA. I landed leading roles in *The Shadow Box* and *Too Much Johnson*, working for my mentor, the wonderful Gordon Davidson, my friend for life.

Gordon was one of the new masters of twentieth-century American theater. He had inherited the artistic directorship of the Mark Taper Forum, the best theater in Los Angeles and the prize of the Center Theatre Group, from John Houseman, the old master who had worked with Orson Welles in the Mercury Theatre Group and who believed that theater could live in LA, even in the glass house environment of the dominant species in town—the movies. Houseman trusted Gordon, his former stage manager, to carry on the growth of West Coast *legitimate* theater. Gordon did much more—he brought it to world recognition and created a unique legacy. He heard a different drum. He worked in Hollywood in the theater. He understood the actor's nakedness in the marketplace. He knew the lure of the movies. And he was unique, a unicorn. In LA, there are many fake exotic creatures: cows with cone-shaped cardboard horns pasted on their heads, bulls with plastic pizzles standing erect on their faces, and real rhinos with killer horns. But Gordon was the real thing, a consummate theater man who worked alongside the monster movie business and carved out a space for the theater's coexistence on its own terms. He made the space respected and sacred.

Gordon was a Renaissance man who knew how to negotiate both worlds. He had superb taste in literature, a hunger for social justice, and a tuning fork for the tenor of the times. As the '60s gave way to the '70s and America turned inward and began examining its humanity, Gordon was there to explore how the living stage could explain, elevate, and protect the world. He thought deeply and read widely but remained humble, proportionate, and honorable. He was the kind of man we used to consider a real American, unafraid of the future or the challenges to creativity. He trusted that he could keep his theater relevant and popular. And if an actor had a dire problem in rehearsal and hurled his potential solution into the arena, challenging Gordon to come up with a better one, he would scratch his gray, curly locks, screw up his benign, humorous face, and say, "Well, I don't know . . ."

But you knew he did know, and you knew his opinion of your idea just by the gentle response, which put all the onus back on you. Gordon was the king of doubt, of "I don't know, but . . . try it." And you tried it your way until you realized that your way was wrong, that the problem was more straightforward than it seemed and didn't require a solution that was a Unified Theory of the Universe. Gordon had shaved it into a simple solution. He was a barber who had borrowed Occam's Razor.

I had just been cut to pieces on the phone by Robert Brustein, who mentored me by telling me I was a cowardly disgrace to the theater. Almost immediately, Gordon offered me a season of repertory at the Taper. We worked together on four shows: *Too Much Johnson*, *The Shadow Box*, *A Meeting by the River*, and *Unfinished Stories*. Theater in Los Angeles was the place where an agent didn't want to know an actor was working. Plays were no longer the source. The theater paid *bubkes*, so the agent's commission was *gornisht*. But Gordon made it the place to be and work.

This was the Mark Taper Forum's first attempt at repertory. *Too Much Johnson*, a farce, and *The Shadow Box*, a drama, would be seen alternately throughout the season. It was a gamble. The same actors were cast in both shows. The company included Simon Oakland, Marge Redmond, Rose Gregorio, David Huffman, Cynthia Harris, Tom Rosqui, me, and a few others. In *Johnson*, I played Johnson, a horny businessman; in *Shadow Box*, I played Brian, a gay writer with terminal cancer.

Too Much Johnson is a venerable comedy by William Gillette, an American actor of the nineteenth and early twentieth centuries who wrote his own vehicles—*Sherlock Holmes* and *Secret Service*. *Johnson* is a good old-fashioned farce with lots of expository scenes, but when Bert Shevelove—librettist of *A Funny Thing Happened on the Way to the Forum*—adapted it, the exposition was eliminated, and the play turned into hilarious one-liners and a brilliant story that moved with dizzying speed. It was a thoroughly satisfying smart-ass romp about male randiness. *The Shadow Box* is a somber, humane take on the occupants of three units of a terminal cancer hospice and the folks who temporarily inhabit them. Michael Cristofer, another Catholic University colleague a generation younger than I, wrote the piece and was honored with the Pulitzer Prize.

We rehearsed in a plain concrete box of a building called the Annex on a featureless street across from the theater. In LA, it seemed as if all streets were wide, all days sunny—the ambience of all existence in the present, white, light, and bland. Getting that New York rehearsal hall feeling—dirty, cold, and drafty or hot and humid; flights of narrow, sagging stairs and elevators that were joltingly scary and unreliable; small rooms, noise, and poor ventilation, the feeling was that life was a tough go, nip and tuck, uncertain and dangerous, an impetus to retreat to or dig into your psyche, was jarringly inadmissible in cheery, have-a-good-rest-of-your-day LA.

At first, in Hollywood, I allowed these feelings to lock me out of the real work of an actor, which is to imagine yourself in the circumstances of the play and to find harsh, affective memories analogous to the character you are to inhabit. To be able to imagine yourself hot in a cold winter or poor when you drove to rehearsal in a fine car. In New York, there was a cabal that helped actors to believe in their myth, that they were a band of guerrillas advancing on the capitol armed only with imagination and indomitable spirit, facing overwhelming odds, and certain only of one thing—that they would die trying.

This is not hyperbole.

Gordon brought all sorts of folks to rehearsal. It was like a seminar. For *Shadow Box*, there were psychologists, speakers, and videos about the medical challenges in hospice care. For *Johnson*, we listened to Irving Berlin's "I'll See You in C-U-B-A," an infectious, saucy, fun Tin Pan Alley song, to put us in the mood for silliness, and we played theater games to warm up. I worked on learning the cha-cha—that innocuous turn was as lascivious as we would get—and I eventually did the dance on my knees around a fountain in the finca patio in pursuit of too many girls, which was Johnson's problem. And mine, too.

By that time in my life, I was riding on my libido. Women were more casually aggressive about sex than I had experienced growing up. Their assertiveness must have seemed very rebellious to them and like a step forward for the female nation. And I joined the rebellion:

> Not so far from here
> There's a very lively atmosphere
> Ev'rybody's going there this year
> And there's a reason . . .
>
> Cuba, where wine is flowing
> And where dark-eyed Stellas
> Light their fellas' panatelas . . .
>
> —IRVING BERLIN

How far had I devolved? My trysts weren't utterly meaningless. There was a lot of deep conversation about freedom of expression and equality. Now, it sounds empty and sad and schizoid. But then, I didn't know that "some things are in fact irrevocable" (Joan Didion, "Goodbye to All That"). I was headed down the path to find out.

Johnson was a farce. Fast, loud, and real. Real. Your mother-in-law heaves into view of your telescope on the deck, and as you spot her, she's so mean and ugly that you throw the telescope in the air, leap across the stage, and hide. Big laugh. But the timing and the action had to be truthful, so you had to find a substitution for the moment that allowed—forced—such an extreme reaction. The audience will laugh only if it seems natural. And the humor was good only if the mother-in-law was a real Gorgon.

Our company of actors was so generous that the give-and-take of such moments was continuous and contagious. I was using the name Johnson to hide from my wife and mother-in-law. The owner of the tobacco plantation in Cuba was named Johnson. His overseer was also named Johnson, hence "too much" Johnson. And Johnson is a slang term for male sexual equipment. We have too much testosterone. The owner was a huge man, dangerous, and ferocious, and his confused rage was the foil for my Johnson, who was a slick and sly playboy determined to have every woman he encountered. Was it perfect casting? Our real Johnson, the actor, was a kind and civilized man, and I was really an altar boy, not a Casanova. That's acting!

The Shadow Box was putting myself into the heart, mind, and soul of a man dying of terminal cancer. Having to interact with contentious and fearful family members and alternately opening my character's fear to an unseen therapist (a quiet, amplified voice behind and above the audience) was akin to an acrobat trying the triple somersault without a net. It felt personally dangerous to be alone on stage with a persistent, calm, kind voice prying gently into my psyche in the play's words. But it also was the voice in my head trying to get me face-to-face with my own fears of death and failure. Psychologically, I was naked and defenseless out there, my own shaky, repressed life crowded into my character's life on stage.

Gordon mounted three productions of this play: The Mark Taper Forum in LA, The Long Wharf Theater in New Haven, Connecticut, and finally, The Morosco Theater in New York City. Each production has a story.

SCENE: Hollywood

I had left something behind in New York—a sense of belonging to a rare breed, crucial to the evolution of man, upward, onward, higher.

In Hollywood, I felt like an outsider who didn't know the rules of the game and was already losing a step. Had I sold out for a mess of pottage? In films, if I were thought of at all, it was in the role of the interesting villain in

Sam Rolfe's *The Delphi Bureau*, ABC-TV. 1973–74. I have a photographic memory. It's going to get me in big trouble.

Gordon Davidson's production of *Too Much Johnson* at The Mark Taper Forum, Los Angeles. Me, as Johnson, doing the cha-cha. My wife and mother-in-law are not amused.

the piece. In TV, I was considered for the secondary roles, the husband of the "Woman in Jeopardy." This was the networks' phrase du jour for products with content that would attract a female audience who were then sold other kinds of products by the attractiveness of the talent involved. The show was the come-on, the loss leader.

I realized that in the insanely violent and explicit movie ethos, I would be required to have a gun, or worse, to threaten or kill some or all of the other talent. We were flattened, one-dimensional types, and the talent's job was to inject into the content of the product the colors, quirks, and heartbeats of actual, real people.

My opinion of myself as an actor could not withstand the confusion of fighting for these products to sustain a lifestyle—a bigger house, better cars, swimming pools. I was in the soup. I drank, smoked, was unfaithful, and neglected my family, all in pursuit of shiny objects that had no meaning for me. This life had no relation to the reason I had escaped into acting.

"Does thirty pieces of silver sound about right?" asked my agent, Mephistopheles, adding that the billing would be either "second above the title or last on a separate card." Both would display my magnanimity and increasing importance. But actually, it was just a retreat to less and less importance or interest.

My wife was pregnant a second time, so I did the right thing: I escaped back to New York. I forced the move in a classical "geographic" straight out of the AA handbook. And you know the response, don't you? "Wherever you go, there you are." My wife arranged a meeting in Malibu with an actor named Anthony Hopkins, a recovering alcoholic. I blew him off.

And I was not an alcoholic, but I behaved like one, which is the same thing. Not a codependent, but I sure looked like one. And not a sex addict, but I took targets of opportunity, shot my Cupid's arrow, and took the intoxicating rewards as if they were shots of rum. I had no inkling of the free fall coming.

SCENE: New York

Robin and I were living temporarily in René and Judith Auberjonois' apartment on Seventy-Ninth and Columbus. They were friends from our days in the American Conservatory Theater. I had bought our house at 152 East Eighty-Second Street and had worked to renovate it. It was a Federal-style brownstone built in 1852 by a sea captain who had two daughters, so he built three contiguous houses exactly alike. The first house was immediately east of Lascoff's famous old pharmacy, an excellent example of city life in the nineteenth century.

Lascoff's windows were decorated with large old-fashioned beakers filled with red and green liquids. Whether or not they represented some kind of medicine of the era, they were festive and cheery. The store was a landmark at Lexington Avenue and Eighty-Second Street. Across from Lascoff's was Pascal's, a tiny French restaurant below street level, which was Jackie Kennedy's favorite bistro for a time. This meant that at night, the narrow street outside our house was filled end to end with double-parked big black limos awaiting the satiety of society. The presence of the haut monde also attracted the coyote class of paparazzi, who skulked about and then attacked en masse anyone of note who entered or left.

Before we could move into this graceful house, we were waiting for Benjamin, our second son, to arrive. We were in the mezzanine section at Radio City Music Hall—not quite the nosebleed section, but what we could afford. It was the Fourth of July celebration show, and we were there as a distraction during the last tough days of a pregnancy in the hot, humid city. The Rockettes were high kicking to "Three Cheers for the Red, White, and Blue" when Robin's water broke. We ran to the ladies' room, which was empty, and went in. I managed to get paper napkins to wipe up the flow. On the nearest pay phone, I called our doctor. He asked about the contractions, which were not close and not yet uncomfortable. He told us to go home and relax. No hot bath now— that would be risky. Just keep checking on the contractions, and when they get closer together and heavier, go to the hospital. "I'll meet you there whatever time it is," he said.

The next morning there was no doubt that Benjamin Joseph Luckinbill was on his way to change the world. He was a beautiful child and is a beautiful man. Ben is a peaceful addition to the world. He is kind, compassionate, mindful, and intensely curious about the world and everything in it. He is self-educated on more subjects than I can count.

His curiosity got him into a jam early when he was playing outside the front door of our house in the well where the basement door was, which was enclosed with an elegant wrought-iron fence. Ben wanted to know what it would feel like to stick his head through the vertical iron bars into the street side. He did. And got stuck. I was not home when it happened, but I got home in time to see the good gentlemen of the fire department lever my son's head out of the fence. He had been locked in for hours, like a prisoner in the stocks. He had tested a law of the universe, proving that the head of a sweet-faced, fresh boy of three can be inserted through iron fence palings six inches apart but cannot be withdrawn. Ben's experiment was accomplished with the assistance of two large firemen and one giant red truck blocking eastbound traffic. Conclusion: don't do that again.

Ben's temperament is that of a second child: a peacekeeper. Yet, he has a healthy temper derived from the sibling rivalry with his older brother. Nick is athletic; Ben, not so much. But their rivalry was intense, with Ben trying to prove he could best his brother. Nick, in the early days, wondered what this strange new obstacle to his supremacy and dominance of the family was. They are the best of friends now, many decades later.

Ben liked school until he was bullied, and then he fought back with enormous anger. It was unjust, not right, he said. He enjoyed putting things together. At that time, toys were robots made of interlocking pieces. Ben was fascinated by these things and still is. If asked what art he has taken as his own, I would say patience. He is determined to do things his way and takes his time.

SCENE: New York

In the HB Studio, I sat facing Herbert Berghof across a tiny table. We had been working hours, days, weeks, and months to translate the Czech writer Pavel Kohout's play, *Armer Mörder*, from German to English. *Poor Murderer* is a weak translation for the title. Maybe the Czech word for *poor* conveys the double meaning. Poor: in lack or need, in poverty, but also powerless, inept, not capable. The German word *armer* may have both meanings, but in English, *poor*, unless qualified, is taken primarily to mean without money or means of support. The English title should have been clear—an incapable murderer. Even more precisely, someone *unable* to kill.

So, the title is the title. My contribution to the project was mainly to Americanize Herbert's somewhat stilted, laborious English translation. I had studied German for a year at New York University and liked the language. I just wanted to help Herbert. I needed a mentor, and he was one, but he was also a complex personality. I loved him. He was tormented by feelings that nothing was good enough in the theater. He, a Viennese, wanted perfection. I was in tune with that myself, but I had a sense of humor about it. Herbert was humorless. He was also a kind of genius and a very determined man. The HB Studio was by far the best acting school in New York. Herbert Berghof and Uta Hagen were my most honored teachers.

He had invited me to act in an HB Studio production of a play by the brilliant Romulus Linney (Laura Linney's father), *The Love Suicide at Schofield Barracks*. I came late to the project, which was also unpaid under Equity rules, which allowed waiver productions to further theater and gave actors more chances to show what they could do. I took a radical approach to my role, which was a witness in a trial, a professor. I made him into an unpredict-able, wild, flamboyant, "unclosetable" gay man. I had recently met Tennessee Williams and lunched with him with actors from the Taper in LA. At that late part of his life, he was an astounding caricature of himself, both hilariously funny and toxically fearful. I had seen him often in the West Side YMCA gym in New York, a small, hunched, vulnerable nude figure on the way to and from old Al's massage table. Tennessee would not look at anyone or touch another person—he dramatically shrank from human contact. This affective memory of Tennessee inspired the character I created. My take delighted Herbert, who trusted me and loved my acting work. The production of *Love Suicide* was brilliant. Rom Linney loved it.

Poor Murderer was mounted for Broadway by producer Kermit Bloomgarden, with Herbert directing. He asked me to play the lead, Anton Kerzhentsev, an actor confined to an insane asylum. Kerzhentsev plays Hamlet in the asylum, but like Hamlet, he's "only mad north-northwest. When the wind is southerly, I know a hawk from a handsaw." The play is a vivisection of the splintered, paranoid society the Czech people lived in under Soviet occupation. It is simultaneously subtle, cynical, hopeful, funny, and bitter—a difficult, complex situation. This was a starring role on Broadway in a role my life had written for me. I was antiauthoritarian, angry, insubordinate, indecisive, obsessed with my work, confused about my life, and had a mordant sense of humor about it all. I wasn't clinically insane like Kerzhentsev, but was I close enough to the edge? The young Czechs had put flowers into the gun barrels of Soviet tanks. I thought of the poster on my home office wall.

The play was a successful failure. It was praised and damned and didn't stay long at the Ethel Barrymore Theatre. It was misunderstood: either overpro-duced and ham-handed or intellectually dazzling and intriguing, depending on who you read. Rex Reed was mystified and thought I shouldn't be acting at all because I didn't look the way he wanted his leading men to look. I took off my shirt in the play to be examined by a doctor, and Rex found my slight lack of six-pack abs underwhelming and scandalous, maybe as disastrous as the Soviet occupation of Eastern Europe.

The play also starred Maria Schell, the alluring Austrian-Swiss actress who played the character I was obsessively in love with. Maria became a friend and somewhat more than that. She informed me with absolute certainty that Luckinbill is a Swiss name and not German. Her mother confirmed it. The head of the Swiss Bank in New York confirmed it. There was no doubt. This was all so different from my father's assurances that we were Pennsylvania Dutch that I felt compelled to prove it.

Years later, I went to Bern, Switzerland. I walked off the train from Zurich into the great Bahnhofplatz in the Swiss capital. I hailed a cab, and as I got in, I saw a gigantic black train engine suspended on its nose as if it had fallen from the sky. It had bits of metal dangling from it—a frozen train wreck, a muscular statement of chaos. It was both imposing and uniquely interesting.

I asked the taxi driver, "Whose sculpture is that?"

With a slightly sour expression, he flung a word over his shoulder: "Luginbühl's!" He pronounced the name like "Luckinbill's."

Oh my God! Luckinbill's? I asked, "Is he well known here?"

Another suspicious look. He said, "Lives here. Famous around here. Has a *fondacion!* He almost spit.

A foundation, I thought. "Is this good?" I asked innocently.

He looked at me again. Was I a cop? Nah. Tourist. He said, "It's a tax dodge," and now he did spit out the window.

Hmmm . . . not a popular artist with the hoi polloi, or else I got a cab driver with a chip on his shoulder that he was trying to shrug off onto me.

I walked into the Grand Hotel in the old town of Bern. I checked in and asked the concierge if he knew of a Luginbühl Foundation.

"Oh yes, it's not far!"

I asked if he could put me in touch with the folks there.

"Oh yes, Herr Bernhard Luginbühl lives there."

I was handed a phone. Someone on the other end of the line was speaking French. I returned it to the concierge saying, "Sorry, no French. Italian? English? My name is Luckinbill."

He looked at me for a moment, brightened, and then spoke into the phone in rapid French and then Schweizerdeutsch. Amazingly, this country's language facility puts us, speaking only "Murkin" in the US, to shame.

The concierge said, "Oh yes, I spoke with Frau Luginbühl, told her you are our guest, and your name is . . . so similar, and you would like to visit tomorrow at noon. May I arrange transport for you?"

"Yes!" In seconds, it seemed, all was done. I would visit the *Fondacion*—or tax dodge—and see a Luginbühl! Switzerland, the land of minor miracles? Oh, yes!

I had a late breakfast (*frühstück*), and the lovely young lady who served me refused to let me leave the table until I finished my cheese plate. I asked politely, "Why?"

She answered politely (and charmingly), "It is what we make here, and we are very proud of our cheeses."

I asked what they were. She delicately touched each piece with the cheese knife—"Emmental, Gruyère, Tilsit, Tête de Moine."

I said, "Do I have to eat all of them?"

She said, "Oh, yes, please!"

I said, "I will then, since it's very important."

She asked, "Are you *Américain*?"

"I am."

"Oh, yes, lovely!" she said with an angelic smile and disappeared.

Flirting? No. It was about cheese. I ate all my breakfast like a good boy. Oh, yes!

The car, a limo, showed up. The driver, Italian, spoke five languages. On the way, we chatted in my schoolboy Italian as we drove deep into a magnificent green landscape. Very rural, only minutes and kilometers from the town center. All of Switzerland was like this, it seemed. The pleasant landscape was so well cared for and not done to impress. Simple. The mountains all around were the stars, but also simply simple.

We pulled up to a field with no gate, and beyond the road was a lane shaded by enormous blocks of metal—pieces of ships, airplanes, and factory machines, all upended like the train engine but clearly set as a sort of wrecked foyer, not sculpture. The effect was startling, imposing—a work of art in situ, but seemingly made not as art to impress but as the only arrangement that could exist.

A woman approached us carrying a tiny dog and teetering on very high spiked heels in the fresh grass. She extended a hand and a smile straight from Paris to me. She spoke in rapid French. The driver translated: "You are very welcome. My husband is angry today, but not to worry. All is well."

Her language, combined with the place and time, reminded me of Jean Renoir's light fantasy of sudden love and doom in a beautiful estate house, *La Règle du jeu* (*The Rules of the Game*). We followed her to the end of the alleé filled with broken works of men and came out at the veranda of a graceful dacha.

Out from the house came my uncle! A big, broad man, heavy, wearing no shirt, no visible underwear, and denim overalls with the sides unbuttoned, revealing his substantial belly flesh. He was my Uncle Mark to a T. He lumbered to me and stuck out a hand. I gripped it—it was like grabbing a piece of rough granite. He turned to his wife and said something in guttural Schweizerdeutsch. Angry.

Another family member appeared on the horizon. A young fellow made by the same divine sculptor, tall, heavy, angry. He waited for Pop to finish greeting me. Pop turned and yelled at him, and the two came together like two Goth warriors, but no war occurred. Just an angry exchange as the two men went to a site in a field where a railroad siding had been laid. A railcar awaited. The job was to pull it onto the siding track—heavy work entailing much necessary anger and red-faced *push me, pull you*.

The incongruous and yet fully in charge wife watched this for a moment, then turned to me with a bright smile and said, *"Thé? Pour vous?"*

I said, "Oui," and we were communicating.

My driver went back to the car. I followed Fifi—not her name, but irresistible—to the long table. Tea and some sort of pastries were brought. No cheese. We talked as best we could, total strangers sharing a few words of each other's language. The men in the distance heaved and groaned. I brought out my book with pictures of me in my work as an actor—*"Un artiste!"* (her word)—and a VHS tape reel of my career so far.

In my book, she recognized someone. She let go of the dog and touched the picture with one delicate white hand. *"C'est vous? Le président?"*

"Oui," I responded. "Lyndon Johnson."

She was suddenly interested. She knew something about me.

We watched the men who had gotten the car onto the siding. I took note of the railcar. It was definitely of WWII vintage, smaller and frailer compared to today's shipping containers, great blank golems. But this railcar might have carried Jews to their death at Buchenwald or Dachau. I asked her what was in it.

She said simply, "L'art de Jean Tinguely." A Swiss sculptor, an ingenious neo-Dadaist and Constructivist who made art from parts of machines, radios, etc. He thought the tech revolution of the '30s, '40s, and '50s was civilization gone mad. The lady said in English, "He was . . . my husband's friend."

I climbed into the car. It was very spooky—tables full of machine parts delicately made into partial human shapes. There was an innocence to it all, and also a feeling of pain, as if machines had replaced the people. I climbed down. This day was turning into a scene from the Book of Revelation.

Back at the table, Herr Luginbühl, much more amenable now that the work was done, sat with a drink of some kind and looked at my book. He flipped through, occasionally looking at me like Uncle Mark did—with grudging respect. Hard to tell. Finally, he saw a picture he recognized: Lyndon Johnson. He looked at me, then at the picture. "Him?" he asked his wife. She smiled. Yes. Now he got who I was. A fellow artiste.

Abruptly, he got up, went to the house, and returned with a very old book wrapped up with string.

Fifi said, "He wants you to have it. Be careful to open it." She placed it gently on the table.

I flipped through the sculptor's book—incredible pictures of metal mechanical monsters, stuff that had broken loose from its mundane purpose and gone into strange, purposeful chaos. I came to the last section, structures made of fitted precious woods, all colors fitted as seamlessly as the blocks of pyramids or Mayan temples, and as strangely imposing and mysterious and beautiful. I turned to the last page. The sculptures were now sitting on barges in the river Aare, which wound like a turbulent serpent around Bern. The barges were anchored and the sculptures were afire, flames reaching up fifty feet in the air, burning to death.

Ah! My heart stopped. I said, "Why? What happened? Accident?"

Luginbühl snorted like a rhinoceros and stood as if to charge. "*No!*" he yelled and slammed his ham of a fist down on the table. In his broken, guttural English, he burst out, "This is Europe! We build beautiful things—*and then we burn them down!*" Oh my God.

Fifi hugged me. The sculptor growled at me, but it meant *you're alright, kid.* Maybe. I like to think so.

At the hotel, I opened the book he gave me. In fading ink and an impossibly delicate hand were chronologies of the Luginbühl family going back two centuries, and many of the first names of these people were the same as those I had unearthed of my own family. The anarchic spirit of the Luginbühls transformed by art!

* * *

On my second trip to Switzerland, Lucie was with me. In Zurich, in a chapel off the nave of the cathedral, we found the incised names of two Luginbühl boys who had fought and died in the religious wars. They were fifteen and eighteen.

They build beautiful things—and burn them down! My ancestors escaped to Pennsylvania. Could they have brought with them a Luginbühl artistic gene? A longing for art that would survive the chaos? I like to think so.

* * *

Herbert Berghof and I parted company forever during the Broadway run of *Poor Murderer.* I admired him. I believe Uta Hagen to be the best actor and teacher of acting. But I could not ever be a disciple, a groupie. A follower or member of a coterie or cult that raised anyone to guru or diva status.

Without even thinking of payment, I worked with Herbert and had fun doing it, but I saw pretty clearly that he was an autocrat and not always nice to people. I worked well with him translating *Poor Murderer* and acting in *Love Suicide* at HB Studio. But I did not expect anything from him as a result of spending months helping the translation process of *Poor Murderer.* I was not promised a leading role in a production of it. I never discussed or even thought of it. I was right for the leading role, but it was Broadway, and at that point, I had not yet had a starring part on the Big Street. I still had to prove myself. I knew that. So his offering the leading part to me was surprising and pleasing.

I had just acted a role that delighted him. I got no direction from him then—I did exactly what my intuition told me to do, and the audience liked it. So, I thought we could work well together in the Czech play.

I failed to take into account the Broadway panic factor. Kermit Bloomgarden had okayed me to play Kerzhentsev. Bloomgarden was a legend and a very nice man. The rehearsals were okay for a while, but Herbert grew increasingly autocratic. The tension of carrying through the success of a Broadway play made him sweat. And naturally, his fears and worries communicated to the really unusual and excellent cast.

The set by Boris Aronson was huge and overpowering as if the architecture of the Austro-Hungarian Empire had been dropped upon the stage of the Ethel Barrymore Theatre. Kevin McCarthy, who had inspired me as Biff in the movie version of *Death of a Salesman*, was the heavy and became a forever friend. Peter Maloney, a friend from the Open Theater, did a wonderful turn, and I was the crazy/sane hero/antihero Hamlet character.

I tried hard to take Herbert's direction. He wanted a cliché Teutonic way of being—loud, fast, and angry. He didn't like the way I approached the part, which was exactly the way I worked in *Love Suicide*: stay loose, use rehearsal to find out all of the character's impulses, and express them. My research told me the multifaceted ways Czechs invented to live under Soviet occupation, and the metaphor of being in the insane asylum. The play was subtle and supple, but Herbert insisted it must be rigid, strained, and angry. The witty, whimsical, passive-aggressive Czech sense of humor was being ironed out of the play. It was all wrong. It didn't fit me or the play. I was in a double bind. Herbert and I had gotten along so well. How had this happened?

I knew something was wrong when, at a matinee performance, I accidentally looked into the wings and saw an actor I knew very slightly from Hollywood. He was standing in the shadows, observing me intently. It was Anthony Hopkins. Again! He was known, had a film name already. And it hit me like a subway train—Hopkins was here *to replace me*! And this was how I found out?

I went to Herbert to get the truth. He couldn't or wouldn't tell me. He didn't admit that Hopkins was even there. I decided to level with him. I told him straight out that I needed room to find my own character of Kerzhentsev, that I felt straitjacketed by his fear-inducing way of trying to lock all of us into a rigid format. I said I didn't understand why this was happening. We had a great time working on *Love Suicide*. I trusted him, I said. He should trust me. I was puredee honest with him. I never said anything nasty or stupid. I didn't feel that. I felt confident in myself. I was surprised that he didn't seem to trust me—or himself—anymore. He looked disgusted and angry. He took off his white knit beanie and rubbed his large bald head. He growled, literally, and gnashed his teeth. He called what I was doing anarchy. I think he was Broadway scared. It's a virus that is sometimes fatal for plays.

As it turned out, he was done with me as a person. But I was not replaced. Mr. Hopkins disappeared. Maybe Kermit Bloomgarden thought I was doing okay. If not, I would have been replaced. But Herbert never spoke to me again. Nor did his faithful assistant, nor did Uta. As Kerzhentsev, I had sent roses to the woman Maria Schell played. It was a grand, touching moment. For years, I sent Herbert and Uta flowers—roses—on the anniversary of our work together. No response. Ever.

The play got mixed notices. We didn't last long, but we were not a disaster. Pavel Kohout's subtle humor about living in a Soviet-imposed dictatorship missed the mark with our New York audience. Our heavy-handed production didn't help. This was so disheartening, so disappointing, so hurtful. The whole thing shocked me. Was this Broadway? What a way to live!

I began to question my great dreams that seemed to be going sour. Some force was trying to teach me, but I didn't want to listen. I had gotten to a place where I'd rather sit in a bar and drink, always alone.

SCENE: New York

In my theater world, there was a sense that what we did mattered to the world we knew. The talk in the coffee shops of Bleecker Street, or at the Cedar Tavern near Washington Square Park, or at Toffenetti on Forty-Second or the Polish Tea Room in the Edison Hotel on Forty-Seventh, was of the work and art of the country we lived in, the society we were responsible for. There was a body of evidence to support the value of serious inquiries into human existence.

We were students in an academy of American life, but soon, as a few advisors were sent into Southeast Asia by our idol, John F. Kennedy, we started to understand that World War II was misnamed. We were being dragged into World War Everlasting. World War Until-Hell-Freezes-Over. And so it was.

We showed up on stages lit by one bulb to audition for juicy plays from the British, French, Belgian, and Italian theaters and from Africa, Asia, and South

America. Unbeknownst to us, the earth was shrinking, even before the existence of cell phones.

But, as I gained prominence as a professional, I lost something—my amateur virginity. I considered the money with each new job and discussed the salary with my agent. This was the Name Game. I believed it was necessary, and I hated it, but I also hated when my agent couldn't get better billing for me. It reminded me of how high I had yet to climb. It was so extraneous to what I felt. And it was never really about money—I had never cared about that before. It was about the competition and status, being paid and billed less than someone on the same track I was on.

But, gradually, the whole star bullshit took hold of me. The more I obsessed over it, the less of a star I made myself. In truth, I was just grateful that I was even a part of the theater world, thankful I was allowed to do this, to be worthy. To think about how to play a part, to work with other actors, to help get the whole unwieldy machine up and running. To be one of the functioning parts and not wanting to let down the group.

* * *

Each company I was in became my family, closer than my flesh and blood family.

I struggle with choice. I always ask why. I challenge authority. I never think I am good enough to reach my own standards. My emotions run hot. I flail in anger at myself for my stupidity and for my inability to master a phrase of dialogue or a complex set of moves to an objective or to find and feel an emotion demanded by the scene. But once I realize I am holding up the other actors, I cut the shit and try again. I don't waste the time and energy of others.

In our system, the tactical plan of getting a production up to performance speed in a one- or two-week schedule must lose the strategic depth of context and knowledge. The audience gets the razzle-dazzle of adrenaline-fueled performances, but the sense of social purpose is lost. The truth is, we are not just putting on a show, we are illuminating the human condition—holding a mirror up to nature.

The theater is the story of humans, humanity, and humanness. It isn't made by efficiency experts or folks with planned obsolescence in mind. Serious theater can be *Antigone* or *All in the Family*, and it always starts and ends by engaging the audience as partners in a quest to understand ourselves, to lead our hearts to reach for something higher, something better than we have known before. The audience is always willing to suspend disbelief and join us. It's a high-wire act with no net.

* * *

So, *Othello*, the end of Act I—I am Iago, off to Cyprus to defend Venice. I am alone on the vast Piazza San Marco in Venice or the broad stage of a high school auditorium in Lakewood, Ohio. I begin a soliloquy, setting the scene for my hatred of my friend and military superior, Othello, and my plan to destroy him. It's opening night, jam-packed house. Two thousand eyes on me. I'm laying out for myself a plan to destroy Othello. I have so many reasons. Are any of them true?

The question hangs in my mind unresolved and is now a troubling bit in my preparation. I should have chosen before now whether Iago might have a reason. Is he worse than a sociopath? I should know by now. And am I telling an audience something? Am I trying to justify to these people what I plan to do to the Moor? And who are these people? Or am I verbalizing the plan to myself to see if it sounds believable?

I can't decide any of this now! It's too late! In the darkness, they are waiting to hear, to see, what's next. They are hushed in an active tension of attention. Their willing expectancy has a smell, an allure, a tactile power. It's catnip. It's apple pie à la mode. I'm on! My dream is working! And . . .

. . . this celebratory thought lasts only a nanosecond and I've gone up! Shakespeare's words have vanished in a moment of self-regard. What the heck comes next? I'm blank. I have now been grabbed by terror, alone on this vast, empty stage. I look offstage—about a mile and a half away—for help and I see the stage manager at his podium, earphones on, script open before him. He doesn't look up, not even at the deadly silence on stage, which has now stretched to about half an hour. I look hard at him, willing him to cue me. He looks up, sees me, and smiles beautifully. Oh my God! He's drunk. Again. He usually is, but he gets the job done. Now, he's just happy at the sudden quiet, looking at me so sweetly.

I eject myself off stage left and confront the stage manager. "What page?" I demand. He points to it. It's wrong. I flip forward three pages. There! There's an important speech coming up. I eject myself stageward. I start speaking as I plunge toward center stage. I've been gone for a week and a half while the audience has amazingly sat quietly in my absence.

I start talking, and everything is suddenly crystal clear. I'm Iago, and I have a problem. I rip through the speech and the rest of the play, urged on by Edwin Booth's *On the God of All Arts*.

Years later, someone who had been in that audience said, "You remember that terrific moment when you just walked off the stage? It was so strange! And when you came back, you looked like you'd just killed somebody! It was so Iago!"

I said, "How long was I gone?"

"Maybe two seconds. Nothing, no time at all. Very mysterious. Riveting! A great theater moment."

Yeah.

I learned to add to my preparation a keyword for each scene, a layer of concentration that triggers warnings to stop any stray thoughts that screw up being totally in the emotion of the scene.

Now, I try to solve every question of the play and the character beforehand. As I enter the theater, dress, make up, and go to my entrance at *Places, please,* I step out into the light and leave everything behind but the story I am telling.

SCENE: New York

Robin and I founded a nonprofit called The New York Actor's Theater. I had a commitment from Schuyler Chapin, then the chancellor of Columbia University, to host our first production—Bertolt Brecht's *Galileo*—on the Columbia campus at 116th Street and Broadway. Schuyler was a swell guy who had the nerve to give space to an underfunded fledgling company of actors with a dream of adding forgotten classics to New York's cornucopia of theater companies.

I wrote a piece for the *New York Times* announcing our season of plays at Columbia: *Galileo, Mandragola* by Niccolo Machiavelli, and Jean Kerr's *Poor Richard,* the full version which didn't make it to Broadway but which was much superior to the cut version that did. I took a lot of heat from the press about the selections. What was our company's purpose, our mission statement? And why include a commercial Broadway play with two classic gems like *Galileo* and *Mandragola*?

We had assembled a fabulous company of actors, dedicated folks who would work for the off-off-Broadway pittance the Equity contract allowed in the Columbia situation. I looked for works of significance to our day and that had solid parts for all actors. I wanted to revive *Poor Richard* because it was really good, but also because her husband, Walter Kerr, insisted she publish the first draft, which was better than the commercial version. Walter had taught at Catholic University but was now the distinguished critic of the *New York Herald Tribune,* and he had mentored me when he reviewed me in the Players, Inc., production of *Oedipus Rex* we'd done at Carnegie Hall almost two decades earlier. The Players had survived a long time by mixing classics like *The Merchant of Venice* with *Charley's Aunt*, a commercial farce whose primary cultural value was that it made the audience laugh hysterically. We were following the pattern.

Havemeyer Hall was centrally located on the campus, an easy walk from the Broadway subway stop and well lit at night. Its problems as a theater, however, were mind-blowing. It was a nineteenth-century chemistry auditorium, a vast, high-domed room with rows of tall glass windows and no stage. There was an extended crescent-shaped platform with a high desk and an array of Bunsen burners fixed to it. The acoustics were seemingly impossible. Sound—speech—bounced from the walls and high dome to the expanse of glass windows, and produced a ringing sound of overlapping atonal, unmusical echoes. The words of Galileo sounded like a garbled alien language, a conversation onboard a Klingon starship in *Star Trek*.

I went to see Cyril Harris, the genius of acoustics who had fixed the Vivian Beaumont Theater's severe acoustical problems. Cyril was so helpful and generous. He told us exactly how to fix our problem with panels and drapes against the walls and windows and baffles hanging from the ceiling. We painted very large flags with the Italian and Vatican insignias. We made these sound aids part of the ambiance of the play. An elegant solution. It cost $700. All labor was voluntary.

I had played *Galileo* before at Princeton's McCarter Theater in a dull production using Charles Laughton's Hollywood version, which softened the whole tone and gave Laughton a heroic edge. That was not the Brecht text. Brecht had been sponsored by Laughton but chased out of Hollywood by the House Un-American Activities Committee. I wanted to use the strong and unsentimental translation by Ralph Manheim. But we were a tiny, untried company filled with talents, the spirit of creativity, and little or no money. Brecht's agent was a legend and a tough negotiator for authors. I had to talk my way into her office, but she liked my attitude and that Columbia was mentoring us. We got the rights.

The production was done in the chemistry auditorium as if it were an academic examination. The programs were printed in the actual exam blue books used at that time. The cast wore long gray lab coats and were all on stage throughout—a trick I loved. Joe Papp had done it in *Antony and Cleopatra* with his poor, fledgling Shakespeare festival. It made the play a contest among the players, which *Galileo* certainly was. A life and death struggle between the scientist and the purveyors of religious orthodoxy—the Pope and cardinals of the Catholic Church.

The actors were that special breed I call New York Actors, the cream of the crop, artists who dug into the roles, subtext, social implications, and ambient reality of every play's context. These were actors who challenged the status quo, and carried on from the Group Theater, the idea of an American theater of social justice. Havemeyer Hall was where physicist Harold Urey announced the discovery of heavy water in 1931. This was crucial to the Manhattan Project and the process that led to the first atomic bomb. Urey was still alive. I asked him to speak to the company or write an insert for our program. He turned me down flat with a contemptuous sneer. "I don't have anything to do with jugglers or actors." Ah ha! We'll show him!

We supplied our own costumes. The set was the chemistry auditorium's moveable classroom blackboards. The designer was Bob Gale, a cartoonist for the *New York Times*. He drew a metaphoric or symbolic representation of each new scene in colored chalk in a blur of speed and pastel dust.

Gordon Davidson's father, a marvel of cheerful energy and former Brooklyn College drama teacher, played a part. Jo Davidson was a sprite, a leprechaun— the soul of the production and a touchstone of spontaneity and life, our spirit guide. A legendary teacher, he was in the early stages of forgetfulness and unable to remember his lines. But he laughed joyously and improvised along with us. One day, as I was walking up the steps, Jo danced down to me in his usual good-spirited, effervescent way, stopped, and looked into my eyes. He said, "You're a fine man. The show's great. It's time for you to be happy, to *kvell* for what you've accomplished." Then he looked at me deeper—into my soul. He put a hand on my shoulder. "It's time for you now. You will find happiness. It's right here, all around you. It's yours, son."

He saw right through me.

After my TV series was canceled, I had stayed in Hollywood for another two years, trying to become a respected part of the film community. But I couldn't make peace with the fact that work in television—with all the poor writing, the hack stuff—was just what one did to pay for the house, the car, the pool, the personal trainer and the public relations maven who kept your name in the mythical eye of the A-list gatekeepers.

I had returned to my true home—the theater. And this show was superb. I was good. The whole project had class and intelligence. New York loved it. Columbia loved it. We never had a bad audience, and we sold out. This was the show I had wanted to bring to my adopted home of New York. This was the ultimate prize of a long climb of allegiance to the theater. So, why was I still so unhappy?

SCENE: New York

A young actor named Mandy Patinkin came into *The Shadow Box* to play my dying character's lover for the New Haven production, and went on with us for the New York production at the storied Morosco Theater, where it became a hit.

Mandy and I became friends. Six days a week for months, we rode together with a group of actors in my Jeep from New York to the Long Wharf Theater in New Haven, Connecticut. Mandy's father was very ill at the time, and on his days off, Mandy flew to Chicago to be with him. I was impressed with his sorrow and love and need for his father. Under the pressure of time before his father died, he was trying to resolve his relationship with him. I was older and had almost no relationship with my father, but I felt a fatherly connection with Mandy. We went to New York with the play under Gordon's direction, and it became a hit and had a decent run.

I was terrified of death and fled from it. But now, I had to go on stage every night and deal with it as Brian, a brave, self-mocking, not-great writer whose terror was overwhelming. When I walked out with only my journal in hand, my stage fright was so intense that I stuttered and talked so fast to the hidden therapist—out there as an invisible, quiet voice—that I would lose my ability to make sense.

I began to hate going into our theater. Me, who had loved every theater. As our run continued, something would force me to leave right after the curtain calls, run to my dressing room, throw on my street clothes, and escape from the cast, friends, and fans, usually to a bar to drink, alone. I would escape the theater before anyone could climb the stairs to the dressing rooms.

One night, my agent came to the show. He had brought people to see me, but I was gone. He was shocked, angry. I had not waited. Good friends were treated the same way. This was something subconscious. I couldn't stand the compliments. Everything said was a lie.

Dr. K and Portia came from Arkansas to see me on Broadway, and I drove them to another event they wanted to attend. In the car, George told me he had Parkinson's disease.

Without a beat, I said, "It may kill you, but it won't make your handwriting any worse!"

There was a pause, and then he said quietly, "Ahem, *ahem*, no, I suppose not."

Portia let me know how hurtful my spiteful comment had been. She just sighed, "Ooh!"

These were my best friends, my guides. I was getting him back for lying to me that I was special to him. He told me I was just one of twenty-nine unique young men he had mentored.

George and Portia had been my mainstays at the university. They had stayed in touch every year since I graduated. Now they were old. He was sick. They came backstage and applauded my work as Brian. I cringed. I didn't want to hear it. I couldn't stand to take any applause, celebration, or joy about me or my work. So, I hurt them.

I didn't know I had such hatred, such malice, in me. I didn't want to know. I hated myself. A need to hurt myself was now driving me.

Night after night, I would drink a bottle of Irish whiskey alone, sitting up with my yellow pad and pen, trying to write, my head spinning from too much whiskey, and cry.

I spoke to no one about this. This was the behavior of an alcoholic, but I was sure I was not one because I did not drink every day, every week, or even every month. But when I did, I had an enormous capacity to drink and not be drunk. Brendan Behan's *Richard's Cork Leg* was a deadly example—the play put Behan into a deathly binge. Or Dylan Thomas, the great Welsh poet, who died drunk in the street outside the White Horse Tavern, minutes from my Village apartment. The urge to die, as when I stood on the bridge over the railroad tracks in Arkansas, was abetted by a stupid sense of immortality. Was I turning into my father? *God, no!* Did he want to die, too? No. Really?

I thought I was failing to grow as an artist. My inability to write was so frightening that I swilled it away. I poured good Irish whiskey on the wounds. Lucky I was that no one lit a match when I was drinking—the fumes would have blown me up. I smoked my pipe and looked and sounded wise, calm, and Jung-like. Fake. Fraud.

My journals of the time enlighten me today. After gathering dust for decades, I have now opened and faced them. I see that I have been dastardly hard on myself all my life. All my life, I've tried to write. Poetry first, just blank verse or ill-rhyming stuff, almost all asking the universe for love. I filled pages with raw anguish for the pale women who would fulfill my heart's need. Women I scared away with my emotions, with my recurring religiosity and spiritual need. Women I remade in my imagination to be "The One." None were. They, being women, knew it. Women who told me they couldn't fall in love with an actor. They could play at it and were fascinated by it, but common sense told them no. Stability. Less passion. This guy is not going to settle for a nice home and children. He's a wild heart. Poetry, indeed. Reading my long ago words is embarrassing, but I'm old enough now to forgive both of us—him, and me.

I was nominated for a Tony for *Shadow Box*. I was embarrassed by it because I knew I would come to believe I deserved it. But I did not believe in awards that pitted actor against actor for "best," when any fool could see that every role was different and that one actor could act well and another be brilliantly inspired by a role. So how could there be a *best* choice? Based on what?

And yet, as I knew I would, once nominated, I burned with greed to get the statue or whatever-it-was that marked me as the chosen one. I burned to be *the one*. My spiritual balance was already drowning in the mucus of jealousy, envy, pride, ambition, and secret vice. The nomination took me straight to rapacious hunger, and I could believe without believing that I was now *special, unique*, goddamnit! Finally proved!

I lost. High-larious! All my intellectual and spiritual pretensions were stripped away by my vainglorious need for sensation and, worse, for *winning* in a test I truly despised. I was demoted publicly at the outset. At the Tony rehearsal in the Broadway theater, Alexander Cohen, a good producer and a ruthless but kind mix of a man whom I couldn't help but like, took the stage with a booming handheld mic to rearrange the final seating for the evening. My originally assigned seat was on the aisle. I was sitting there, so close to that beautiful stage, that place I had given my life to stand on, and was now so close—*so close*—to being elevated to Winner. To Hero!

I was working on my humility, on my humble . . . when I heard Alex call out: "Larry Luckinbill?" He searched for me over his half-glasses as Herman Shumlin had looked at me two decades prior when he told me, "You're not right. For anything." And Alex found me where he knew I was sitting, and he said, "Larry, you move to seat blah, blah, blah . . ."

I listened but didn't hear. I got up from my aisle seat in the third row and moved like a dead man walking to my new assignment—tenth row, extreme house right, far from glory.

I was the only one who knew the depth of my disgrace and self-loathing as I realized I was not to win anything, and that the assembled nominees, all savvy to the meaning of seat reassignment, knew that, too. They were all quaking in their boots, and many were chosen to move as I was, but a few stayed in winner's seats.

When the winner in my category was announced, he wasn't even there.

I was still in the struggle. I was ashamed of my being. I failed to be faithful to a wife who had done me no wrong. I neglected to learn the maps of two un-discovered countries—my sons. I had procrastinated and hung back from my real life, believing my ignorance to be wisdom. I both under- and overestimated myself. I drank to stop the steady stream of bitter self-criticism. I looked great. I acted well and was well-liked. I progressed. I was a star on Broadway and in the movies. And I was a hollow log rotting in a beautiful sunlit forest.

SCENE: New York

I sat next to Robin on the small Victorian love seat, which faced the garden of our townhouse on the Upper East Side. My wife was angry and scared. She had heard from friends that I had French-kissed an actress in the play we had produced together and that I was acting in. And she asked if I had had an affair with a woman I had worked with on commercials a few years back.

The time had come. I knew I had to tell her the truth.

I confessed all my sins, but not in specifics. I told her that I did not understand myself. I had been unfaithful with a number of women and even with two men—one I had touched and one I had let touch me.

She said, "You are a homosexual."

I said, "No."

I didn't mention the person who had groomed me (in today's unenlightened words) when I was sixteen and seventeen—the man who had stamped something on my soul, which had not gone away.

But now I wanted her to know how sorry I was for *all* of it. It was over, and I wanted to fix it. To rebuild our marriage. I would go to a psychiatrist to sort this out. And if she would go to counseling with me, maybe she could begin to see that none of this had anything to do with her. She was not the cause of it. I believed, I hoped, we were good parents, good partners. Despite my disastrous behavior, we could fix this.

It was an impossible plea for such crimes.

It was horrible for her. I hadn't understood the depth of her need to trust me. I was her hero, and I had betrayed every belief she had. And now, I needed her to trust me. Again.

The real truth was I was incapable of understanding the catastrophe of pain I had dumped on her without any intention of doing such a thing. I cared for her, didn't I? Loved her?

"Yes!" I screamed furiously. "But I deserve forgiveness, don't I? Just let's get over it and start again."

Oh my God.

I had no way of knowing then that I had buried another me so deep in an icy prison that it would take a 10.0 earthquake, a cataclysm, or a karmic blessing—a light ray from some far-away sun—to release the other me—the good twin?—and, like someone's Neolithic child fallen into a glacier's crevasse and buried for eons, be resurrected to new life.

I see now the fifteen-year-old me jumping violently up and down on the floor of our little house, breaking crockery in the kitchen. I see my mother's heart as she stood there in shocked silence while I screamed, "Yes! I am ashamed! I am ashamed all the time!"

That night with Robin was the end of our twelve-year marriage. It could not recover from my blind attempts to repair it.

She retreated. Called lawyers, got writs. Forced my removal from our house and began divorce proceedings.

What else could she do, trapped in her own past? I had begged for forgiveness she couldn't give. Forgiving, for her, would be the final insult. The fury for hurt radiated with a half-life of no measurable end.

It was clear that the causes that tore us apart were there from both of our beginnings. We were both immature. Robin could not let go of the false conviction that I was, in her words, a "faggot." That was the worst humiliation for her. Now, I wonder, why that?

We gave our sons cause to trust no one ever again. They live as good, trustworthy, honest men because of their character, not our example.

I did not, and do not, excuse or deny anything I did or have done. I cop to the many instances when I forgot or had not yet learned that I am good. And by that aphasia and neglect, I have harmed others.

It took decades more before I understood I had not abandoned right and wrong or the purity of the altar boy I was. I had buried my true self under a cloud of unforgiveness and revenge against old ghosts.

"I am what I am," wrote Jerry Herman in a song for all humanity in *La Cage aux Folles*. It's an anthem for each of us to become our whole selves.

I now forgive that kid because I must. But in this confused life we live, how could I expect anyone else to do so?

SCENE: US Interstate 4, Florida

I'm driving a rented van. The boys are still damp from a day at a waterpark back at Disney World. It's late afternoon. The purple, black, and orange horizon in the west is gigantic with thunderhead clouds running before the wind—galleons under full sail, an armada on the attack—coming straight at us and booming with cannonades of thunder and flashes of icy lightning, which zap the ground ahead, all backlit by the torch of a setting sun. A Biblical epic land-scape in Technicolor.

The lightning is traveling toward us. I can smell the ozone in the air after each crackling strike.

Nick, in front with me, sits forward, his just-forming face pressed hungrily to the window, vibrating with the awesome storm. I believe he is willing himself to be in it, of it. Ben is in the back, seatbelt fastened, watching the display qui-etly, his cherub's face innocent, his eyes big. He is taking the storm's measure. I turn on the radio to get the weather, but Debby Boone is singing, for the ninety-nine millionth time, "You Light Up My Life."

Suddenly, I am insanely happy—a feeling I've never known before. I've been happy, but never this kind of happy. These are my sons. My sons! And I feel like I barely know them, nor they me. But we are here together now.

I start to sing with Debby loudly, kidding with the song but getting into it in spite of myself. "You light up my life!" Now both boys get into the spirit. We are Debby's backup boys. We're not trying to sing but to make fun of the song. But it feels so good to sing it. It's impossible to make fun of it. You can't satirize something already so goofy, so saccharine, so grating on the nerves. So irresistible.

We start to laugh together—really laugh. The laughter means something different to each of us, but makes us equals. We laugh till we hurt. Till we cry.

I drive the car at the storm. We will get through it. I shout, "We're going into the whale's mouth! Will we make it through?"

"Yes!" they yell, trusting in me, the omnipotent father.

My marriage is ending. The boys suspect and fear but don't know. I don't either. Is there a way out of the mess I seem to have made? There is a hollowness in my heart. I gasp for breath at it.

We three press on through Florida's sudden blinding rain, thunder, and lightning. It's a blasted heath in Scotland, and Macbeth, bloody and ferocious, has come upon the old hags stirring a glowing pot. They can tell his future, but they can't kill him.

Suddenly, I realize my future: I am a father! The father of these spritely, strong boys. They are mine! I must not, will not, let them down.

The hags fragment and disappear, vaporize, as we burst through the rain clouds. Suddenly the rain eases as it does in the tropics, and up ahead we see the shining span of the Tampa–St. Petersburg bridge—The Sunshine Skyway! Yes!

I drive the wet road, streaming, steaming, curving with it until it points straight south. We will cross the bridge. And on the other side, I tell my boys, we will see alligators. And panthers will cross the road, and we will look for

them roaring at speed in an airboat, floating inches above the Everglades. Their
eyes glisten.

* * *

weekends with the boys

thumb inside fist at last
the little one lets go his soft
clinging tug of me
and drifts off to sleep
to dream of monsters who don't exist
and dinosaurs who lived when we were dead

the big one tied like Houdini in his
blanket
the dirty hair indistinguishable
from the beige wool
foot over the edge of the upper bunk
the electric crackle as he stripped off
his polyester-fire-hazard Superman pajama top
and threw it down still plays around the bed
like St. Andrew's fire of young frustration

six books—no, eight—lie with him
secret glee: "Books!"
Books!

the little one sleeps stunned where he
fell two yawns and one snore into sleep
but the big one twirls and kicks
karate-ing his life into shape in dream
as he cannot in life

divorce
separation
and four red perfect lips
part
in sleep and cries
issue forth that break the heart

of the daylight's sullen coping
and cheerful understanding
and a thousand fragments catch
the light and fly into imprinted history

the dirty toenails the unwashed teeth
the stupidness of bags packed with six shirts
but no pants
no extra shoes
so don't get those sneakers wet this
weekend
please

weekends
I know the time frame well
sleep late
cartoons
a matinee
a half-assed football game
hide-and-seek
the *Times*
wrestle on the floor
with the couch cushions
story time

and into bed alongside the little one
who with clutching a thumb will make do
"until I go to sleep"
the big one eyes me over the side
of the top bunk
mute survivor of the sinking
looking over the rail
into the crowded lifeboat
hoping for a spot

in the top, the alone
the isolated bunk
The Boy now
the coper, "nothing's wrong at school, Dad"

nervous teller of endless Polish jokes
a little overweight magician
now merges head with rumpled sheet

and drowns in raging sleep

I touch his hair
gently cup his head
and wish him silently (it seems best)
all the love I have
in the world
I get back vibrations of such need that I stand
in the dark, hand tingling
knees weak

hoping

a father

of two sons

I disengage
Feet, hips turn, hands follow
into the lighted hall
the body goes

the head hand
the heart
remain behind

the body in the hall
the soul in two bunks at once
thumb clutched
touching tangled hair
forever

SCENE: New York

The divorce papers have been filed. My ex-wife has left *Chapter Two*, the Neil Simon play we worked in together for months. She has been replaced. The new "Jennie Malone," the bright and talented Marilyn Redfield, is nervous about her role and wants my coaching help. Simon has been known to fire actors he loses confidence in—those who overplay the jokes, or assume his reality is always a joke or a set up for one, and who play in a blatant, in-your-face way.

Chapter Two is a remarkable play, maybe Simon's best. It's a deeply serious tale from his life, and he needed actors who could not only create a grounded reality that would underpin long, painful exchanges between Jennie and George but also have the skills to deal with Simon's ever-present sharp sense of the human comedy. The funny stuff arises organically within the serious stuff so naturally that the actor's task is to constantly and instantaneously identify, separate, and justify—motivate—the thoughts as they are spoken. All the strands must be clearly thought, felt, and expressed—played—in the right rhythm. This has always been the difficulty and the joy in playing Simon's work.

The play is the apex of his brilliance. Being able at this demanding multi-task requires an actor to be both fully emotional—lost in the situation—and fully objective—aware of the stream of character, plot, and humor. It requires intelligence and emotional maturity. It requires belief in one's competence and ability. It requires a light touch that lets the audience know it's safe to trust the writing and the actor. And it requires the gravitas, the actor-power, to be able to stop the whole train with a look or a way of speaking a line. Playing Neil Simon requires its own method.

I went into the show not knowing any of this. I simply believed the producer knew what I could do and trusted me to do it. At that time, Emmanuel Azenberg, Chief of Iron Mountain Productions, was the best producer in the New York theater—and maybe the country. Maybe the world. He produced all of Simon's comedies. He also took on many of the most somber stage plays of his time—for example, *Whose Life Is It Anyway?*

Manny had also been recently divorced and knew how it was with me. He came upstairs to my dressing room, put a hand on my shoulder, and simply said, "You gotta forgive yourself the forty-nine percent, pal."

This shook me. Forgive myself? How? I beat myself up twenty-four hours a day, did my show, and slept a few hours a night, only to wake up to another day of self-disgust. I starved myself and started running three, four, five miles a day, punishing myself like a good Catholic must do. I went into therapy immediately. I rented a dark, crummy apartment so I could be within walking distance of our house, available to the boys after school.

* * *

I'm kneeling with my back against the brick wall of a tenement with a baseball mitt on my hand. Nick is pitching to me, practicing for his school team. He is a strong, athletic boy, and he is throwing hard. In fact, he's hurting my hand. And every pitch is harder and hurts worse. And then I see the tears in his eyes, spilling over and streaming down his cheeks.

He is punishing me, hurting me as he is hurting. The kid is telling me I fucked up and he hates it. He doesn't hate *me*, but he wants to tell me and can't form the words. He loves us both and so has no one to blame. So maybe he blames himself, and that's a lie. This broke my heart as I had broken his.

He's a full-grown man as I write this and still doesn't put it into words. He hugs me like a bear and cuddles like a babe. But he still hurts. I know it. Neither of us wants to voice it all over again.

Now, I walk him home, my hand still stinging and swollen from our game of catch. I leave him at the doorstep of the house that was my home.

SCENE: New York

I was divorced. My children were hurting. My life had crashed and burned. I was in emotional and moral free fall. I couldn't sleep. I had developed migraine headaches like my mother. I remembered the torture she lived in. I quit drinking cold and completely. I quit eating. I starved myself and lost twenty pounds. I went to an old turnverein in Yorkville—Germantown. I beat myself up using the old leather gym balls stinking of sweat, knockwurst, and sauerkraut. I hit the pendulous heavy bag as if it were me I was punching.

Primal needs overcome promises to honor. Having someone means winning something, and winning props up self-esteem. But you always know you won a rigged race. If you dare look in the mirror right after, you will see a squandered, atrophied, vain, *so what?* face looking at you with eyes as shallow as black Mylar—a portrait of a Dorian Gray, one who knows "the price of everything and the value of nothing."

My after-divorce adventures in the jungle: eyes meeting in cafes, bodies meeting skin to skin. I encountered every variety of female pulchritude—every skin tone and every occupation, from neurotic actress to kindly ticket mistress. It was anodyne and panacea. And like pharmaceuticals, it treated the pain, the

George in Neil Simon's *Chapter Two* on Broadway. Am I calling Jenny, my leading lady, or my new lady friend, Lucie Arnaz?

symptom, but not the cause or the disease. What was the disease? I didn't know, but it was aided and abetted by objectivization. Even the one actress I got a serious crush on was a capsule, a tablet, or a spoonful of sugar to make the medicine go down.

Finally, I lost interest in the pursuit of painkillers and began to focus solely on my sons. And, through hard, zero-sum bargaining by my lawyer, I was fighting for equal custody of them. I fought to care for and raise my boys every other week and trade off the big holidays. I rejected my wife's lawyer's original bitter-fruit-of-divorce offer to see them only a few weekends and one holiday per year. I absolutely refused to give up my sons. We would just have to figure it out together.

SCENE: New York

Just after we were divorced, I was offered a stunning career change.

In an attempt to right a wrong and get some justice for American workers, I had arranged to air an interview I had taped with a representative of a shoe manufacturer about the decline of his industry due to foreign imports. Reese Schonfeld, a media talent scout, had seen it and contacted me. He told me I was the person he was looking for to anchor CNN's first production of twenty-four-hour news.

I was thrilled. A regular job. I saw myself in a safari jacket on a rooftop in Africa or the Middle East, gunfire and bombs in the background, or in a ghetto in the Bronx, microphone in hand, explaining and dramatizing the news. In other words, it was another role. A part to play, but one with real-life consequences. I would no longer be a pretend hero, but a real live one.

The job came with steady and fantastic money. I would be doing what my family considered "success." I knew I would grab hold of the rules of the game and win it. But . . . I would have to fly to Atlanta three days a week. Commute from New York.

Suddenly, I realized this was impossible. I had equal custody of my two boys. I was committed to them. In my previous life, I had grabbed every job that appeared. I had assumed all would go well with my sons. But it couldn't be like that anymore.

I passed on reality and went back to insecure pretend. Years later, I understand that the news business is also show business. I don't regret, for one second, passing on this glittering distraction.

SCENE: New York

Marilyn says she will meet me between shows at Joe Allen restaurant, a fabled actor's hang in New York on Forty-Sixth Street. She has nervously asked what I can tell her about acting in this Neil Simon play in which she has been cast. I don't have my sons with me this week, so I have the time. I walk from the theater to Joe's. It's September, and already the crisp cold of autumn that makes even New York smell good has arrived. The chill of winter is in the air. I step through the door.

Inside, there's a long bar on one wall and a few four-tops along the opposite wall, crammed into the spaces between brick arches that open into the dining room. At those tables, you eat and drink with butts at the bar overhanging your table. In winter, overcoats brush your face and jar your elbows as drinkers push their way to the restrooms and back. The jam is part of New York's DNA—it's why you love it, the crush and rush of bodies, attitudes, voices, and ideas. The constant frisson gives tsuris, hope, and energy all at the same time. My dark mood of the day is lightened by the trek to this iconic actors' clubhouse. And right now, the joint is empty.

I see Marilyn at the last table near the end of the bar. This conversation is not going to be easy. It is the stage manager's divine right to give notes and I could be jeopardizing my relationship with Manny and Neil by giving any advice on playing this play. I'm going to choose my words carefully. I can see that she's talking with another person, a woman with a corona of dark, curly hair sitting straight as a dancer in her chair and looking at me.

Marilyn greets me and says, "Larry Luckinbill, Lucie Arnaz."

I recognize Lucie from the picture in the *Times* review of her performance as Annie Oakley in *Annie Get Your Gun* at Jones Beach. And also from the opening night of Manny's production of *They're Playing Our Song*. I saw the charisma and charm of this young woman. She impressed me as an actor, but I knew nothing else about her.

Marilyn is talking. I have the impression from her tone that the women are close friends. Lucie is smiling as she listens but looking directly at me. My new co-star's voice fades . . .

I look at Lucie. We are alone together. I sit down facing her.

There is something in her face that is very beautiful, but it isn't only beauty that I see. There is in her eyes a readiness, a fullness, a ripeness, as of a human first arising into her being. And this readiness, this ripeness of womanhood, reached out to me. Me, a broken man who had only just faced the fact that his blind, childish behavior had caused grave harm to his newly broken and lost family. A man who is living with the full realization of that—the sorrow of divorce and the shame that threatens to overwhelm him. Reaching back into his childhood faith that he is still somehow a good person is his only hope.

I talked, and she laughed. I was funny, but her laughter was not a cocktail party laugh. It was real. She was listening for real. She searched my face for . . . me. And I found me. Not a new me. The real me.

Strangers. Connecting. There are many songs about it—"Some Enchanted Evening" and "Strangers in the Night," are just two that say it beautifully. They assume that sudden love can be real and forever. But, as Hemingway's Jake says bitterly, "Isn't it pretty to think so?"

All my life, I've been a romantic looking for love from the universe. And there I was, caught by a sturdier hook: reality. Lucie was also caught. Truly. But, as her nature demanded, she was also processing this man's potential as a partner.

What did she want? She was twenty-eight. I was forty-five. What did I want? I was in no shape for a romance, for a relationship. I wasn't looking for that. I was, I thought, barely alive and unfit for connection. As I learned later, Lucie had had some recent nasty shocks in her own personal life, but was, nevertheless—because of her charming, honest self—the centerpiece of a swirl of swains of all kinds, manners, and shapes. Her social life was that of the new kid in town. The star of a new and fabulous musical, and she and it were taking the town by storm, as the cliché has it down pat.

I was also starring in a wonderful and popular play in a theater a few blocks away from hers. I was at the apex of a long climb up to a hard-won, first-rate peak: Broadway stardom. She had arrived in Cinderella's coach almost overnight. I had built a solid reputation in New York theater; she was a starburst. I was focused solely—aside from playing George Schneider on stage—on becoming a better father to my two sons, and negotiating a calmer life for them after the storm of divorce. And yet . . .

I realize now that I had come face-to-face with something so unexpected and shocking that I knew it had to be unbelievable. That ancient cherubic baby deity with the bow and arrow had shot a bolt of lightning, and the light was Lucie. Luz . . . Lucia . . . Light.

Was the *chance* of this event the same for her?

The other night, after dinner, we were washing up the dishes and pondering our lives together after more than forty years. I joked, "And they said it wouldn't last." And Lucie said, "Yeah, well, something out there knew better!"

At that moment when everything in our lives changed, right there in Joe Allen's, nothing changed. We talked and we parted. There was no pursuit, no flirt, no tease, no promise. It was a polite introduction. But it was, then, for each of us, the beginning of a cautious friendship. Cautious because we are both intelligent people. Such things as love at first sight don't—can't—happen. Can they?

I invited her to my show, but on the day of, I was sick. I missed the only show I've ever missed in my life. Lucie showed up but gave back her ticket. She had come to see me.

SCENE: New York

Was it a date? Lucie Arnaz sits in the passenger seat of my Jeep. I know her name, know her acting, and that's about all. I look at her profile. Her insouciant curly frizz-do for *They're Playing Our Song* bounces when she laughs, which is often. Her profile is clean with an aristocratic nose. She is animated. Everything is bright and exciting to her.

It was autumn, and we both wanted to see the glory of the leaves changing. Although this trip will become a landmark, a crucial test, it's just an interesting, casual date, the first I've had since separation and divorce. It feels strange but right. Nothing is expected other than an extension of friendship. We both agree on that without it being mentioned.

I am thinking about history, about a remarkable woman named Adah Isaacs Menken who played a male role in a play called *Mazeppa* in the nineteenth century. Something about Lucie reminds me of Adah, so I tell her the story of a self-determined woman who made herself into an actress, then a celebrity, then a bona fide star in an era when actors had yet to be cultural icons. Adah scandalized the world by portraying the hero of Ukrainian-Polish independence—a fighter who was caught, stripped naked, tied to the back of a wild horse, and released into the frozen steppes to die. Adah devised a shocking costume, a naked-looking, flesh-colored body suit. Mark Twain saw her show in a Nevada mining camp and wrote a hilarious review. Neither the novelty of a comely, full-bosomed woman playing a rugged warrior nor the acting impressed Twain, but I think Sam Clemens enjoyed the mild frisson of female nudity and the daring of it all.

Lucie really listens. She asks real questions. She's eager for these stories. She tells me if history had been taught like this in school, she would have learned some.

We stop at Lake Minnewaska, a deep, icy crater lake in upstate New York. It's a glorious fall day. We walk in the woods. We laugh about show business and the theater. We are both in love with the theater. We get along well.

Back in the city, we stop for a bite to eat. Standing in front of the restaurant, unwilling to end the day, I look at her smile. She has had a good time. I say, "You are very tall and very wise."

It's a strange comment and I don't know what I even mean. We are barely friends, and yet, from the exact moment that we met, something within this person asserted itself to me, without notice or sound, without grabbing me with a specific part of her woman self, without blinding me to her person (a twenty-first century *Mazeppa?*).

She is genuine. Her frankness, enthusiasm, and openness are freely given. She is present and accounted for. Self-reliant, not needy. And yet, there is something else . . . a depth unseeable, a sense of something undiscovered in her, something wild and untamed, maybe untamable, something she knows and doesn't know, something . . . lost, yet to be found.

In an earlier conversation, she had mentioned something about a character in one of the *I Love Lucy* shows. I didn't know what she was talking about and said so. She was astonished. I had never seen the show. I knew, in a glancing way, that her father and mother were Desi Arnaz and Lucille Ball, but I was a tabula rasa on them. It wasn't a choice. I wasn't a snob. I love comedy, but I didn't have a television habit, then or now. So I did not know her parents or their shows. I wasn't interested in her parents or a TV show. I was only interested to know her. This seemed fantastic, almost impossible, to her. I wasn't sure she believed me then, but it was true. As karma would have it, this simple fact made all the difference.

SCENE: New York

Lucie called me. I had a phone in my dressing room. I had not asked for one, didn't use it. It was a workroom—no time for personal BS. The phone rang. Huh? I answered. This bright person invited me to join her and other actors between shows on Saturdays to something she called The Matinee Idles—a group of actors who typically might have eaten alone between the matinee and evening shows but who could now join an eclectic group from several shows. I loved the pun of the title she invented, but I knew I could not join such a clubby thing. Between shows on Wednesdays and Saturdays, I was dedicated to making dinner for Nick and Ben. So I took in the info but knew I would not be part of it.

She kept calling.

How does love grow? How does love progress? These two separate and vital questions might seem the same at first glance. But words matter.

I admired Lucie, whose verve and joie de vivre made her an equal companion to all and different, because she was the organizer. That year, the Matinee Idles was her free gift to the New York theater world. Conviviality, collegiality, and generosity. I observed her, fascinated. She was so different from me. We were so unlike each other, yet *like* had somehow taken root between us. She liked me. I liked her. Cool. It would stay that way, I felt. Neither of us exhibited any need to go steady. So, I asked her to dinner.

One night after our shows, we went to Gallagher's Steakhouse close to both our theaters. We talked; I don't know what we said. There was definitely something going on though. It was odd. Usually in a boy-meets-girl scenario, when *like* occurs, a structure manifests itself: pursuit, flight to others (which can be manifold), catch, connect, sex. Maybe love follows and maybe not, although love is usually the first word introduced if the pursuit turns serious.

That simply was not the case here.

She had a thing going, I eventually learned, with two other actors, both swains to her in the old-fashioned sense and, as she eventually learned, also to each other. Very '70s New York. I had been entangled with a young actress I'd just worked with in a film.

Lucie told me things about her life as if she were a traveler in a fascinating and strange land. She was making discoveries from moment to moment about life and people with a combination of delight and shock, like a young child in a bubble bath watching each bubble float up in a wondrous flight of all colors of the spectrum, only to burst in her face, getting a soapy mess all over her. She took life as kind of a pie-in-the-face joke.

She was amazing. Her spirit never flagged. I could feel her genuine theatrical joy in life, raising my comic spirit from the depths. I felt lighter with her. She wanted to know more about me, my story. I, a person who had no interest in her family and that glittering world but who was genuinely interested in her, was a phenomenon she was eager to explore.

Each time we parted after these exploratory but tethered space walks, the sense of her connection to me deepened. And yet, sex was not a vector of the equation.

What is friendship? How does it work, man-to-woman and vice versa? I had discovered a woman I did not objectify. I did not think of her as a sex object but as a friend-female. Despite my current circumstances, I found myself wanting—willing—to know her deeply. And yet, and yet . . .

One day, walking with a friend on Ninth Avenue between shows, I saw Lucie walking with one of her friends. We stopped and had a small conversation, then they turned and started away. Lucie was wearing purple pants. They were cotton. They weren't tight. They were casual workwear. The statement of those pants was matter-of-fact, clear, and simple: "I am real." I wanted to test the statement she made wearing those pants. I wanted to know that it was true, absolutely true.

And something else. I wanted to know who was inside those pants. Lucie did not walk as a provocation. I had seen her act and knew she knew all that stuff. She just walked. And I just stared. I memorized the straightforward, dancer-like way she moved. I suddenly knew I wanted her. Impossible—we were so unalike. Pepper and salt. Grits and guacamole. Tiramisu and pecan pie. But now, I could taste her, smell her, like favorite foods, blankets, or old shirts or negligees. Like wood fires and California sun. Like tall and wise, like intense and intellectual and bookwormy, like us. The history man really wanted to kiss the California girl. Now what?

Put it aside. Rationalize. I truly was happy with my sons even though the horrible furor was still going on with Robin. It was awful, both of us screaming on the phone, tearing the tatters of the relationship to tinier shreds to justify the failure, with the boys in the middle. I refused to make them bargaining chips. Robin was desperately hurting, and I was the cause. The phone became a weapon to hit each other with. We acted like monsters—two people who had shared twelve years of working and living together. It was awful.

I'd have such a conversation, then go to work and do the best job I could to fulfill Neil Simon's complex character of George Schneider. And I was trying to cook for my boys. I had my hands full.

There was a place called Ted Hook's Backstage, a restaurant popular with actors and run by a kind of genie, Ted Hook. He was slight in stature but enormous in generosity and a perfect innkeeper. He loved all things and folks theatrical. If an actor went in twice, the third time he was seated at a table where a little lamp had his name imprinted on the shade. This was the kind of Broadway I had been unable to imagine when I was a kid in Arkansas, but which, when it was an actuality, said this was exactly right.

After a couple months of friendship, Lucie invited me to join her at Ted's. We sat across the little table with the little lamp with our names on it and looked at each other. Two actors living the biggest dream either of them had ever had. Two accomplished people taking a turn in life that astounded them. We looked at each other. What we felt had to be unreal, didn't it?

I said, "I've been thinking I'm not your type."

She said, "I've been thinking I'm not *your* type."

"Really?"

"Really?"

She said she was tired of "twinkies"—the kind of guys who were not serious. Who said they would call and then didn't.

I said, "You want to be courted."

"What?" she said. Then, "Yes."

The next day, a huge basket of every kind of flower the florist had in stock arrived at her dressing room. It smelled like Hawaii. And the card said, simply, "Courting."

And the world turned upside down.

SCENE: New York

There's a Kurt Weill song about the end of autumn, of the year, and the coming of the onset of winter. The song is lovely, about rue and endings, aging, and how things "dwindle down to a precious few"—days, life, love . . .

That year, that brief period, was just the opposite. That year, a new kind of love was planted in me, and I began to change.

I observed Lucie do her star walk into a room of partygoers. It was special—a fast walk to the center of the power and then holding forth in the room, an assumption that she belonged at the center. Had she learned this as a child as she followed her mother and father through crowds of fans in Hollywood? Later, as a young woman of seventeen or eighteen, she had already gathered remarkable experience in show business. She had a quick wit and an open, friendly personality, and everyone welcomed her.

Lucie made me an instant part of her inner circle by introducing and connecting me. I accepted this although I did not seek it. I'd worked intensely as an actor to become the best artist I could be. I had had bouts with the "fame clap" and had lost some and won a few. I was working inwardly, even now, to stifle—to kill—the ego that urged comparison with and envy of others. I was in a long battle with that amygdalin ogre. I didn't have a clue yet that there was a higher self, which now I recognize as my part of the "I Am" spoken by God to Abraham in Genesis. I was at the beginning of a long struggle with little Larry's little ego, and the change in me by what happened with Lucie was the preparation for me to do battle to the finish with the sad little monster.

Lucie liked to party, but she was utterly not a party girl. She had a dignity and a sense of responsibility to herself that simply precluded her from being taken cheaply in any way by anyone. She had had it drilled into her by her mother that she was a mark. Con men could see a mark coming a mile away, and her behavior needed to be exemplary, not only because it was becoming to her as a young woman, but also because any bad behavior on her part would reflect poorly on her family. This was huge in her mind—don't do anything that disgraces or even discomfits her parents. Avoid the con men. Be careful with the press. Remain on the qui vive. *Cuidado*. Maintain inbred, effortless class.

And so, natural niceness was hedged with this stricture. She carried it well. I hadn't yet realized it was a part of Lucie's long struggle to create herself completely, to step out of the shadow of Lucille Ball, to stop thinking for two and just rest easy as herself.

I'd never met anyone before who actually believed that thinking and acting positively could change any dire situation. My alcoholic family certainly didn't. As it happened, neither did hers. We shared the alcoholism of a father, and my way of coping was silence and escape. Hers was trying reason and common sense—and escape! We had both escaped into the theater.

I don't remember a lot of "erotic wrestling" (I'll return to that phrase—hers—in time) during this glorious autumn of getting to be friends. I know I liked very much being close to her. She was easy with her body but not in the least licentious. There was a refreshing sense of time and place and the rhythm of "leading up," as she liked to say.

SCENE: New York

Soon after the Hawaiian flowers, I invited Lucie to a supper club on the Upper East Side. The band was hot. It was a Latin rhythm. I'm not a good dancer, but I offered her my hand and led her onto the dance floor. For once, my feet found the rhythm. I held this woman in my arms, and we moved together for the first time. Lucie's a superb dancer, but that night I was a superb dancer, too. I was inspired by Pan himself—and by this woman moving with me.

Music. Dance. Restraint. Cool. The night was cold. We got into *her* car—her *Song* contract gave her transportation to and from home to the theater. I told her driver to take us to my address. Two hazel eyes and a smile in the dark of the limo. I put my arm around her to keep her warm. She snuggled. We pulled up to my building at 163 West Eighty-Third Street. She didn't hesitate; she just told her driver not to wait.

We went inside. My boys were at their mother's house that week. We went straight to the bedroom. My bed was large with a French blue coverlet. We sat on the bed. Lucie liked to be kissed, and I liked to kiss her. After a while, she lay back. The night was cold. The streetlight through the shutters was the only light in the room.

I took off my clothes and stood naked in front of her. I said, "This is what I look like. I want to see you."

Looking at me the whole time, she slowly disrobed without any pretense. She lay back. Her nude body was long with just-right curves. I saw her eyes, really, and she mine.

We didn't have sex that night. We made love. It was mutual. It was utter. Total. Full-out. Uninhibited. And so tender.

A new land. A new map. A new geography. I didn't know then, but I should have—I would spend the rest of my life exploring it. All the curves, the nooks, the coasts, the bays, the hills and forests of her. New-mown hay. Sweet, salty, sea foam moisture, long arms around me. Her eyes growing larger in the dark. Her tender lips and demure tongue.

We lie together, complete for now. Both realizing even if we don't yet say: We fit! We fit, hand to glove, like to like. Body and each part of each body, we fit.

This had never happened before in the history of the world! Sure, sure, you say. But no. Love—true love—had crashed the party and taken over the joint. Nothing could stand in our way.

* * *

I brought my sons to meet Lucie, who was shooting a TV commercial for her show. Nick was ten and Ben was four. I was so proud of my boys and very protective of them, like a new father. Yet, I don't remember feeling the least bit uneasy about them meeting Lucie. I was confident in her and in them. They would get along fine. What I did feel was trepidation about the boys meeting a new woman-person in their Dad's life so soon after the lightning strike of divorce and my leaving the house as a result of a court order—a letter sent from Robin's attorney to mine: "Get out or go to jail" was the subtext.

The boys had sat on the two-step ancient stone entry that was the architectural signature of the row of Federal houses on the block. They were helpless as I carried my stuff out of the house past them. Suitcases, boxes, paper bags, my clothes on hangers—they watched me speed-load my Jeep, double-parked in the street. I had boxed up my books to pick up later.

My confession to my wife had put me totally on death row. I was a convicted felon. I deserved nothing but a murderer's fate. I kind of agreed with that myself. My boys were uncomprehending, just miserable. Years after, Ben, wrote a marvelous account of his and his older brother's feelings as they sat on the stoop. Nick was in shock, speechless, his head down. Ben wanted to hug him, to take care of him. He knew somehow that he understood less of what was happening than Nick did, but at four, he had one hundred percent empathy. It would take them many years to make peace with their feelings at the time, against which they had no defense.

* * *

On the set, Lucie is wearing her costume from the title song scene, a short red dress with fringe. Nick wants to toss her his football, and Ben is absorbed by her makeup table—all the color sticks, the pots of cream, the brushes, the eyelashes. He will become an artist. His brother will never stop matching himself against every grueling, challenging individual sport he can find.

Lucie likes them! They like her! And they get along fabulously. The buried emotions in that room, like St. Elmo's fire or heat lightning, electrify each of us. This is a huge deal. Personal feelings have been stowed under the bed for the time being.

The pain was there, but hopefully not forever. No guarantees. Two helpless, brave young men hurting secretly. And a brave young woman confronting her new now, if she is sticking with me, if this lasts, if this is the *right* she had always dreamed of. And I—a reprieved, un-innocent, condemned man walking the streets now made new by an unexpected mercy, dropping "as the gentle rain from Heaven," looking in on that dressing room as those I love and those who love me pour urns of kindness on my beaten and bloody self—I discover simple gratitude.

* * *

A gaggle of actors is being served lunch at Sardi's, the iconic theater restaurant. I enter with Lucie and my sons. Counter to her own rule that actors can't bring outsiders to the Matinee Idles gatherings, she has caused my sons to be included. Walking to her seat, she says *sotto voce* to the others, "I made the rule, I can break it." So there.

And here we are. My boys are nicely dressed for a school day, and they are hungry. They shake hands all around and get down to the important business of eating. They've been around. They've met dozens of top actors and have been as unimpressed as fairly polite young men are with anyone old. They're not worried, nor am I. Nor is Lucie. The other actors are probably a little nonplussed at Lucie's dictatorial edict smashing, but they're tolerant folks, as actors are. I like this high-handed girl very much, and I love that this group instantly accepts my kids just as they are. It's cool. They're cool! Lucie is proud and glad. Is she looking ahead? Rehearsing a new role? Auditioning?

* * *

The four of us are walking on Columbus Avenue after dinner at a restaurant in the neighborhood. It's a casual-seeming walk but is really anything but casual. This is the first time this new family group has spent the whole day together. Nick, Ben, Lucie, and me. It's a Sunday night, and like many New Yorkers, we have just eaten supper at a local Chinese restaurant (as ubiquitous in New York then as Starbucks is now, and always good). We have read each other's fortunes and laughed at their inane pronouncements.

Ben has taken his prediction seriously: "Your wisdom will help the world." Someone asks him, "How will you do that?"

And Ben says, "I'd take all our nuclear bombs"—he has trouble pronouncing nuclear so it comes out *nukalar*—"and put them in space beyond the moon where they couldn't hurt anyone." Oh. Ah! Yes!

He stops walking beside me and says simply in his sweet, clarion voice, "Carry me, Daddy." I lift him to my shoulders, and his arms surround my neck. He gets a grip as we jog down Columbus, crowded as always with the New York version of every human group in the world. We have gotten ahead of Nick and Lucie. I stop and look back. They are coming side-by-side like old pals. She is laughing at something Nick said. He's a witty child already, fending off the sadness and anger that sometimes overcomes him with surprising quips and corny jokes that he hears at his school, St. Ignatius Loyola. His current favorite is, "You know how Staten Island got its name? A guy on the ferry boat looked at it and said, 'S'dat an island?'" He tells it with a true New York intonation, a mixture of accents and "tawk" that perfectly mimics Queens, Brooklyn, and Bronx street sounds.

Whatever Nick just said to Lucie, she liked and responds to this ten-year-old boy she has admitted into her life with the same verve and natural good humor that charms everyone she meets. Nick is charmed, I can see, as he walks along with this tall, beautiful woman who likes him. He is not charging ahead, or challenging his brother to race so he can beat him, or swinging on a street lamp pedestal, or dribbling the basketball he's carrying—yes, even to a restaurant, always a token of the latest sport he's trying to master. Lucie is giving him something he needs now: an adult person's full attention.

"Oh, God," I think. "Can this be?" I turn around with my precious burden on my shoulders and say, "Hold on, Ben, this horse is going to gallop now," and

I run a few jogging steps. I hear Lucie and Nick laughing. We stop and wait for them. This is so new, so . . .

My heart is so full. Will it burst, or heal?

SCENE: New York

It's Monday, early evening. Lucie, the boys and I have been apple picking in South Salem, Westchester County, New York. We roll down the Saw Mill River Parkway, go through the toll over the Hudson River where it curls around the northern tip of Manhattan and becomes the East River at Spuyten Duyvil, and speed down the Henry Hudson Parkway toward our exit at Seventy-Ninth Street. Suddenly, my used Jeep Wagoneer decides it needs to stop at the turnout at 158th Street, so it does. A total breakdown. Something wrong with the carburetor. (I love Jeeps, but, for a time, they were lousy for minor breakdowns. I kept buying them out of loyalty.) Now, this is embarrassing.

I pull over. The traffic, like all New York traffic, is fierce, merciless. Horns blare at me as I try to cross a right lane to get into the turnout, curses and middle fingers en passant as I try. I am angry and humiliated.

But suddenly, I have a corps of helpers. Out of the car pop three pushers. Two smallish boys and a tall, long-legged, curly-haired woman. They put their shoulders on the rear of the Jeep and push. My children and my Beverly Hills girlfriend save my ass. I jam the car into neutral and steer toward the exit. The vehicles behind enjoy a view of a manly ten-year-old, a hard-pushing four-year-old, and a leggy dame helping out a dumb hick driver. I hear whoops and whistles now instead of curses. New York is rooting for Nick and Ben—and offering to date Lucie.

I love my town! When you're up, they love ya. When you're a schlemiel, get outta da way! Finally, the cops saved us. They called AAA. It's the last year of the '70s and my Beverly Hills girlfriend is now part of the Luckinbill gang.

SCENE: New York

Lucille Ball and Gary Morton are in town!

Lucie's mother and stepfather have come to New York to visit her. For some reason, I offered to cook dinner for them at my apartment. I am not a cook.

My apartment had a door that swung shut as you left the place, like a hotel door. It had a German-made lock with a four-inch ratcheted key. I always knew I had that key in my pocket when I went out—unless I did so under great stress.

I decided to cook something down-home, a little soul food for Lucille Ball. I bought eggplant—to be fried, of course—and other stuff, potato salad and smoked ham, at Zabar's.

I got home early from my show and laid the table. Previously, I had owned only three of everything, so I bought more from Conran's. They still had the same stuff on permanent sale. I got out the silverware, plates, napkins, and condiments, including, I am pretty sure, Tabasco sauce. I used my two serving bowls for the potato salad and green beans. I had a cake from the Erotic Bakery across the street from my house—not one of their famous penis or vagina cakes, just a plain chocolate one. That should be good. I had no dessert plates, but I figured I could wash the dinner plates and silverware and reuse them.

As I write this, I wonder what the heck I was thinking. What kind of crazy peckerwood yokel nut would serve such a dinner in New York City to Lucille Ball?

Well, a clodhopper from the Ozarks who insisted on being himself, that's who. A guy who wouldn't cater to his girlfriend's mother because, well, just because. That's all. "This is me!" I wanted to say.

I could have said it better, maybe, at Le Cirque or Ristorante Raphael or l'Alpi. I knew a lot of excellent and easy restaurants, but something in me said, I would like this woman, Lucie's mother, to know what I'm really like. How much I feel for her daughter, and how it's just me, a poor boy from Arkansas, feeling it.

I put on the eggplant to fry. I made the first plate of perfectly golden-brown circles. I made the second platter. I had one eggplant left. What the hell, maybe Lucille would be hungry. I put it in the frying pan on low. They were due in fifteen minutes.

What had I missed? I checked the table. I thought it looked good. Kind of picnicky. Maybe a watermelon—no, I have chocolate cake. Oh my God—wine! I'd forgotten the wine. Oh my God! There was a liquor store on the corner, just fifty steps away.

I ran out the door. I ran down the single flight to the corner and into the store. "White wine!" I yelled to Sam.

"What kind?" he yelled back.

"I don't know!"

"Who's it for?"

I didn't say Lucille Ball. No way. "A lady!"

"Take this. One or two?"

"Two!" I yelled.

He handed me bottles. I handed him cash. I could have been buying raspberry slurp wine for all I knew. But I knew Sam.

I ran out the door. The street was filled with a fire truck, a huge one. Where's the fire?

A firefighter came down my stairs and out my open street door. I ran up to him.

"What's happening?"

"Kitchen fire. The guy left the door locked. We have to break the door."

"Which apartment?"

"That one." He pointed up one flight to my apartment.

I could smell eggplant. Burning. Pan. Burning. The truck siren was blaring. A crowd gathering. Oh, Jesus.

My next-door neighbor—same building, next apartment—opened my door and stepped out. Smoke followed him. The fireman had returned with an axe. A huge axe, Paul Bunyan size.

My neighbor held up my key. "You left your key, Larry," he said mildly. "And I turned off your eggplant. It's pretty burnt."

"My God," I said. "How did you get in?"

"I smelled the eggplant burning so I went out on my balcony. I stepped over to yours and opened your kitchen door. It was unlocked. I turned off the pan, saw your key, and figured you had forgotten it. Right?"

"Yeah, Jesus, man. Thanks!"

"Looks like a nice picnic up there for you and Lucie."

"Yeah, nice," I said. "I forgot the wine."

"Okay, here's your key. Don't you hate these things?"

The firemen were stomping around checking the walls for heat. Looking at the ham and potato salad. Should I invite them and my neighbor, too? To meet Lucille Ball, the biggest star in the world?

I looked at the time. It was time.

My apartment was a haze of smoke. I could barely see across the room. But the fire was out. The pan was burned. There would be less eggplant for everyone, but it was okay. I wouldn't eat any.

The firemen clomped down the stairs. I'd make a picnic for them another day. My neighbor had been so kind (and pushy), but I had to escort him out the door. How did he know I was going out with Lucie? He was, I later learned, a Broadway dancer. They know everything in the theater.

I swung my front door open to clear the smoke. I could almost see across my kitchen when the downstairs street door opened and Lucie ushered in her mother and stepfather. I saw the top of a tousled red head. Lucille Ball was climbing the stairs to my apartment.

She coughed loudly in the smoke. "What the hell is going on here," she growled.

Challenging. This was my impression of Lucille Ball's first look at me and mine at her. This woman had seen everything and done a lot and was not impressed with much, if anything, at that stage of her life. She gave the impression of a person waiting. For what? To be charmed, surprised?

She looked a little like "Lucy," but more like the woman carrying around the legend of "Lucy." She was older (at that moment, sixty-eight), and—aside from her henna-rinsed, carefully coiffed hair; her application of lipstick, which created a slightly different lip line than the one she was born with; and her drawn-on, too-real-to-be-real, perfect eyebrows—she didn't bother to disguise her aging skin. I liked that. She had a smoker's prematurely old and scratchy voice, which she often used to command. And she gave the impression of someone who felt she had to be in charge or the world she inhabited would collapse.

She was huffing and puffing from the climb, and I sympathized with her.

Lucille sniffed the air. "What's burning?"

"Nothing now," I answered. "I was cooking eggplant for—"

"Eggplant?!" she demanded.

"Yes," I said. I finished my previous sentence. "For dinner."

"Huh," she said. "Gary?"

Gary Morton made it up the stairs with Lucie, who introduced us all.

I didn't look at Lucie. Her mother sounded angry about eggplant, even the idea of eggplant. Suddenly eggplant seemed to be one of the worst vegetables and the worst idea I'd ever had. Okay, I'm not a cook, just trying to please.

Gary said, "Lucy, this smoke is bad. We should get out of here."

"Yeah," said Lucille. Maybe she was allergic. Okay.

So, the brief conversation turned to what restaurant we could all get into and where we could get a proper dinner.

I wished for a tarp to throw over all the food I'd laid out. Let's just forget the whole event.

What a messed-up introduction. High-larious!

I might have thought I'd made a horrible mistake, but I didn't and I hadn't, and I didn't feel like I had. Later, I learned this was Lucille's reaction to almost everything. Anything new startled her, so she responded like someone jabbed with a pin. Anything new was not a good thing, couldn't be, had to be challenged: "Halt, who goes there?" Lucille was a sentry in her own life.

Later, Lucie described working with her mother as an art. Lucille Ball rejected manuscripts at the first read-through and couldn't understand how the "black type"—the description of the sometimes bizarre action she would have to perform in a scene that would end in a brilliant comic shtick for her—could possibly work.

In the original *I Love Lucy* show, Desi would get the writers' intention very quickly and be able to explain (*'splain?*) it to Lucy. Working with her mother in *Here's Lucy*, Lucie would experience the startle effect on her mother and watch the director and writers try valiantly to explicate.

As disconcerting as it could be, it was, in a way, a good thing. Lucille demanded excellence—instant excellence. She would not spare herself in that quest until she achieved it. And she came to want, even expect, that of everyone else. I understood that totally. The desire to perfect—that's how great things are made, but perfection never comes ready-made. That's what, for me, made conversation with her like rolling doubles the hard way in a craps game.

I didn't want to play games with her, neither mind games nor backgammon, her favorite. So, I had no idea how to communicate with her. I thought it was my problem. Later I learned it was hers, too. I watched Gary do her bidding and wondered how their relationship worked. He told me later that the "key to a good marriage is two words: yes, dear." I laughed but cringed. I knew I couldn't do that.

In fact, at this point in my forty-four-year marriage to Lucie, I understand these two words in a different way (more about that later). And I understand Gary and Lucille in a different way. (I am writing this on the eve of the anniversary of Lucy's death—over thirty years ago—and it is no accident that I picked up my pen that day to begin trying to write for myself the relationship I had, or didn't have, with "Big Red." I was, in some way, maybe just hearing what she wanted to tell me.)

Gary wanted to get out of my apartment right away. He knew Lucy would want that, and it fell to him to insist. So, we all trooped out, leaving my burnt repast in the fridge and the trash can, and went, in their limo, to the 21 Club speakeasy for dinner. Control of the meeting was taken from Lucie and Larry and given to Lucy and, nominally, Gary. We were off to a strange start.

It was always hard for me to talk to Lucille. We didn't live in the same world. I knew nobody from hers, and it didn't seem like she had the slightest interest in mine. It wasn't a hostile disinterest, just lack of interest. How could I bridge the gap? I never did. I never fit into her frame of reference. I tried. It seemed every thought I had, every conversation gambit I had, was met with a challenge. Lucie could talk to her mother. She tried her best to explain our marriage to her.

I talked occasionally to Gary. Even though his life before Lucy (there's a show title!) had been nightclubs and working "in one," as he said, all his grown-up life, it was not as remote as Lucille's. I understood the Bronx and being a Jewish comedian and working in the Catskills. He seemed younger when he talked about the Big Apple Rest in Tuxedo, New York, where all the comics hung out. "If those walls could talk," he'd say. I knew guys who had clued me in on that stuff—the all-night clubs and diners and crummy hotels, Vegas, opening for Sinatra or whoever.

I knew Lucille's early life had been plenty hard, but she didn't want to talk about it with me. "Huh," she'd say if I tried to go that way. "You had to be tough." And then she'd change the subject. It was like cross-country skiing on sand.

Her daughter loved me, so she tried to accept me, but not very hard. I was way older than Lucie and had two children—all challenges. *Older? Two kids?* I got the feeling that Lucy would have been happier if her daughter had married one of her gay male friends who could speak Lucy's own language. I understood all that. I understood I was different, and she was different. She had won the biggest craps game in show business—against awful odds, even worse than throwing a double the hard way ten times in a row. Impossible odds. She was a legitimate Queen of Comedy. And she was a legitimate actress. She had played that game fair and square and won it all. I had and have enormous admiration for her. She wasn't any kind of snob. She just didn't know how to relate to someone who didn't do the dance for her. I was an alien.

Having never seen an *I Love Lucy* episode until just before meeting Lucille was a good thing for me. I was old enough and experienced enough in playing comedy by then to understand and appreciate her enormous skill—genius, really—in keeping the innocence and reality of her memories of her child-self, which she recreated as the eternally optimistic, forever believing she could do the impossible, "Lucy."

Television Lucy is forever pure of heart, chaste, ardent, innocent, and in-genuous. She glows. She shines still, even in black and white. She is candid and an icon representing to generations their desires to be like that—to retain childlike beliefs and have them come true. She is proof it can happen, and she had the absolutely perfect partner in Desi Arnaz, a man who was like her in childlike innocence and charm and who eternally respected and honored her for those qualities.

On the show, they created unconditional love. In life, that was, tragically, just beyond the reach of either.

I think about Lucille—how she worked like a plowhorse and drove everyone nuts trying to be perfect in her comedy. How unhappy she became in retirement. How she tried to scare unhappiness away with her Billy Goat Gruff manner. And I wonder, had she lost the child's impulse she had to make us laugh, to express the wild joy she felt at being able to do this? Did life or age take from her the amateur spirit, which is the actor's soul?

I love creating for nothing. I discovered I could make happiness by my own spirit. But the process of becoming a professional, of selling my love and my joy in order to live, to scramble for fame, money, billing, status—all that was a time and life waster. Lucille lived an entire lifetime coping with that. She lived in flashbulb light. But she had no equal when she escaped to her beloved set on the studio lot and created a copy of her childhood joy-person. Joy made her. Did the effort of holding on to all that success had given her, take something vital from her and leave her, at last, alone?

* * *

Lucie wanted unconditional love. She might not have articulated that, but there was in her a tremendous, fearful need for someone who would see her. Hear her. Believe in her. Because of her, I had love to give and have it to this day. Our lovemaking was magnificent—open, free, original, honest, like we were the first people on earth to discover each other's bodies. For me, she preceded all others in time, space, and degree. It was—I was—truly made new.

It was a charmed time. Everything was more real, more vivid. But not like a fairytale. Lucie had been married at twenty and separated at twenty-one. Not the guy's problem—hers. She had been too young. And I was recently divorced. If there was a problem, it was mine. I accepted that. Lucie and I had in common the feeling of gratitude that life had offered up—oh my God—another chance.

Slouching Toward Dharma

Let me not to the marriage of true minds
Admit impediments. Love is not love
Which alters when it alteration finds . . .

—WILLIAM SHAKESPEARE, SONNET 116

We have made love again, fully. Heart to heartbeat, eyes to eyes. Laughing at the end, again. We sleep in our big blue bed. Later, in the dark hours, I turn over to look at her and find her looking at me. Eyes bright, lights shining on me.

What's happening? In my closet are her clothes. Not much, just a feather's trace across skin, a blouse, a pair of jeans, the purple pants. Part of the *something* that clicks us together like a latch. One touch and it's open, another and it's joined. "Only Connect." It's happening.

I look at her. I say, "I want to make a baby with you."

I reach for her, draw her closer. Her eyes are like stars but moist and on earth; not distant in the black sky, but right here in my bed. We kiss. She likes to kiss. I have another thought, like a schoolboy remembering his lesson in bits. It comes out.

"And I want to marry you."

She laughs, a merry burst. I laugh, relieved. I've said something so radical. We've been together not yet three months. She is not laughing at my foolish heart.

She takes me in her arms. "Yes," she says. "Yes."

And again, something so powerful was offered and accepted. And it begins.

This was my situation. Forty-six years of age after a difficult divorce. My two innocent sons are with me for real now. I have found the love of my life and offered her this man, this child-man, to walk with into a new Eden. Crazy? Foolhardy? No. Daring? Yes. The right thing. Finally.

I was in *Chapter Two* on Broadway and had entered chapter two of my life. I opened the door and stepped in.

* * *

I went to Chicago to make a film called *Prelude* for public television, playing an alcoholic doctor who wrecks his family. I was staying with my younger sister, Lynne, my closest friend growing up. Lynne heard me talking on the phone to Lucie in New York. With my sister's shamanic powers of intuition, she said simply, "You're in love with her. Don't lose her."

Lynne knew me. I was not a committer. I had thought I was committed to Robin, but I learned through the sorrow and misery I made that I was not. I was not in love with any of the women I had connected with. But it was never for trivial sex. Then what was it?

It was me. My rope-a-dope with other women, like a temporary high, had made me think I was attractive. But I would have to drink a lot to be with another woman. Each time was the same distant out-of-body, out-of-mind feeling. I was not with a person but with a sex object.

My dreams of women were hopelessly romantic. I felt they were all goddesses and the most interesting humans in existence, and I wanted them all. I wanted to penetrate the hot place and gaze at their naked bodies for a lifetime. When I was young, it seemed to be a harmless, pleasant dream.

Then ambition stepped in to save me, or so I thought. I didn't want a lascivious life as my fate. I wanted the spartan life of work and art. I wanted to be the best actor who ever lived.

The theater had saved me, given me the chance my mother hoped for me—the chance to reach for something higher, something finer in myself. It had awakened a sense of honor and ethics, a genuine heroism I could actually have. I could really be Captain Marvel, couldn't I? In this next act of my life, I would be forced to find out.

* * *

Lucie was suddenly cast in a blockbuster-to-be film starring Neil Diamond and Laurence Olivier, another remake of *The Jazz Singer*. She would have to leave *They're Playing Our Song* to play opposite Neil, as the girl he loved. Her agent's way of thinking was, "You've been there a year and a half, got all you can get out of this Broadway show. The movie will be huge, so move on!" Lucie was torn. She loved doing the play, but she trusted her agent. She was no stranger to showbiz. She knew the odds. So she gave notice and prepared to move back to her lovely little house in Los Angeles to star in a hot film.

I finished my film in Chicago. It was a work of love produced by Joan Croc, Ray Croc's wife. Ray had founded McDonald's restaurants, made a fortune's fortune, and, along the way, become an incurable alcoholic. After he died, Joan wanted to warn people of liquor's dangers, particularly for people who were ambitious, intelligent, highly motivated, and seemingly impervious to addiction. It was written and directed by a brilliant man who was a recovering alcoholic. I had no idea of karma then, but now I see it in the luck of my playing this successful, brilliant doctor caught by alcohol. The denials, the omissions, the lies, the affair with a woman who tolerated his drinking, the confession to his wife, the misery of telling his daughter he was a drunk—there was a synchronicity that asked me to consider the possibility of the Divine.

Now I was in the final days of the run of *Chapter Two*, and Lucie was preparing to leave town. I was busy with my children and my show. I had loved it with all the intensity Neil Simon had put into my character, his alter ego. My best friend, Richard Zavaglia, a fine actor, was playing my brother, Leo. Richie and I were a great team. We played together so well that we anticipated each other's moods, irritations, and tiniest responses.

To celebrate the closing of the play, I asked Manny Azenberg if I could throw an onstage party. He agreed. I called Joe's Clam Bar in Sheepshead Bay and ordered a feast for the entire O'Neill Theater workforce—actors, management, crew, ushers, and janitors.

Seasons turn, and actors—in a permanent striving to express human truths—move on to new challenges, where each moment seems supremely important, when the inflection of a word is a laugh gained or lost, where a line stepped on is a tragedy within a tragedy, and memories ultimately fade to a meet at Joe Allen's, where the Broadway flop posters hang on the wall to remind you that plays are play, and even the flops were fun.

SCENE: Los Angeles

I went to LA to visit Lucie who was working on the movie. We went to a pretty restaurant called Four Oaks. It was a fine moment. We made each other laugh. Life together would be fun and, we secretly hoped and prayed, lasting. I drew us a picture on a napkin, me as an oak tree and she as a gorgeous palm. The two trees embraced each other and their branches combined. It meant we would grow together and strengthen each other as long as we had life. And, like trees, we would bear fruit. It was impossibly romantic. And, right then, a child's name came to Lucie: Simon. If we had a boy, he would be called Simon, for Neil, who had brought us together. And so it was.

I went back to New York and my sons, and suddenly had an attack of piety. I had caused chaos in my first family's life, and it now seemed an act of God had changed my life and needed to be met by a reconsecration to my abandoned creed. Strange? It seemed right at the time. I started going to church to pray in the empty rows of pews, to try to find my way back into the old veneration I had felt all my life, the rules of faith I had embraced with the pure love of a seven-year-old with a need to love something, to be dedicated to something, to God. I had held this church belief until I couldn't abide by its contradictions and institutional pettiness anymore. This was before the sexual abuse scandals. I would live as the rebels—the Berrigan brothers and others—did. Faith by action, not by rules. Thomas Merton was more germane than Thomas Aquinas. Pope John XXIII's sense of a renewed church was the key.

I wrote Lucie missives and tomes, litigating my newfound faith. I scared the hell out of her. I didn't know. I was trying out a new self, born from self-blame and self-shame, and trying to make up a new religion of faith, morality, good-ness, and love without Catholic guilt. I would be a good man by living up to my own self-creed, my own self-rule. I was trying to find a way to love myself for the first time in my life.

I rededicated to my children and to making *pax post matrimonio* with my former wife. This was a time when women offered themselves to me, but I did not want or need such ego boosts. My ego had been burned in a cold fire that came from somewhere. Heaven? Was there a Heaven? Was it already here?

Lucie shrank from this kind of fervor. She had no idea of this type of reli-gious drama. I pulled back, tempered by her needs. She wrapped her picture, energized by the promise of a new phase of her life—movie star—and returned to New York, to me.

And she was pregnant! Our lovemaking was, as always, free. Were we crazy? Yes, crazy in love. She had let me know about the baby as soon as she found out—on the same day she was to play a scene in the film discovering she was pregnant. The synchronicity was amazing. Our lives had conjoined, I believed forever.

But now, something arose that could turn the romantic dreams and the future of our love affair and life together into a pile of smoking embers. She had a brief affair with her acting partner during the filming of the movie. I don't remember how or why she told me. Maybe I had a suspicion, and somehow it came out. Did I grill her? Why would I? I think somehow she wanted me to know the truth.

I had trusted her, but now I was in the position of my former wife: be-trayed. Cheated on. How else to say it? How could this be? Was everything suddenly a lie? No. It couldn't be. Lucie knew it wasn't. She had been honest with me. I suddenly realized that I didn't know her at all, or I did, but not any of the depths or currents of her. Or I knew some—surely I did—but how? Why? What? Where? And what was I supposed to do now?

She was sitting on our big blue bed, looking at me, eyes large, hands clasped around her knees. She wasn't crying, but she was miserable. I said something like, "I can't do this. I can't believe you could do this." I remember I couldn't breathe. I had to think, to cry, to mourn. It was over, this fantastic dream—a lie. Or not a lie. No, she wasn't a liar. And I wasn't a liar either, but somehow I had lied to my wife for years by omission. But Lucie had told me the truth straight out.

I had asked, "Is the baby mine?" I honestly did not know.

She said, "Yes."

Somehow that was worse. I said, "I have to leave."

All she said was, "What about the baby?"

I walked out and down the stairs into Eighty-Third Street like a blind man who knows his way without a cane. I turned left onto Columbus and headed downtown. Why downtown? I don't know. My theater was there, now dark. The show I had loved had closed. If I had a thought it was *I'll get a hotel room. I can't go home anymore.*

I had to get away from the reality, the imagery. Scenes filled my mind of the flirting, the seduction, the kiss, the deeper kissing, the hands on her, the assent, the undressing, the opening to the—all the same things we do—did— now done with a passing stranger. No—a powerful star in the music world, a world-famous songwriter, an attractive man who described himself to her as "one of the walking wounded." Was that his come-on? I understood it, all right. Who the fuck wasn't? I had never used those words but had also played that role in seducing. And now, he had taken my woman, my sacred person.

I closed my eyes and stopped walking. I must have looked like a drunk or sick man. I remember leaning against a building. I moved on downtown, block after block, crossing streets, empty it seemed, but maybe teeming with walkers. I wouldn't have noticed. The ugly thoughts had blown a hole in my psyche and my new life with Lucie. Oh my God. It was hardly lost on me that this was exactly what I deserved. In the cynical scheme of things, "turnabout's fair play" and "do unto others before they do unto you."

I accepted that, as I accepted that I was the villain in my first marriage. I realized it was a symptom of my unmanaged anger, which I wanted to blame on Robin, but couldn't. What rationality I had left pointed inexorably at me. "You're the problem!" What I did *not* know was that the "problem" lay much deeper, buried in long-ago, unexpressed fury at my father and even, unfairly, at my mother for her codependence, that I thought had made a hash of her four beloved children. The confusion I still felt had given me the fire to become an effective actor but mightily impeded my growth.

I stood on the street corner, blank except for stabs of pain such as I had never experienced. "The walking wounded?" For real. There was a child on the way. She had asked, "What about the baby?" Yeah, what about the baby?

I was completely immobile. I was blasted to a hell I had never imagined. Was this how Robin had felt? She probably felt worse than this. We had been married almost twelve years and had two children. No wonder there could be no forgiveness for me.

What should I do? What could I do now?

A thought came from nowhere: *Forgive. You must forgive.* And more: *You must go back. You must live this story that has come to you, this love you never imagined or conceived. It is real. You know it. You must live it. Go back. If you don't you will lose your soul completely.*

These inchoate thoughts came to me as if written on sheets of ice from a white place in my mind. A place I didn't know existed and had never visited. Completely incredible, completely new, and completely compelling.

In a dream state, I walked to a coin telephone on the wall of a nearby building. I called my apartment. She answered. I said, "I'm coming home." And I turned and went back to my apartment, to Lucie, to begin the process of becoming.

Together we began to make sense of life in a way entirely new for us both. To become truly lovers, truly partners, truly parents, truly humans. It has been the most challenging thing either of us has ever done. And the best.

This is not the end of that story of forgiveness and transformation of two humans that has lasted over forty years and continues. It has enveloped our relations with all others, requiring as much love as we can muster, each in our own way. It has forced hard truths on both of us. When I say hard, I mean pain. I mean sorrow. I mean the discovery of things in ourselves we didn't like but fiercely resisted changing. I mean fight and flight. I mean paying the price for real love—which is a very high price.

SCENE: The Wilderness, North Carolina

And now, we are making a movie together—*The Mating Season*. Apropos. It was a clever, genuinely funny comedy. But backstage, in the rented condo we were staying in, we weren't having a fun time. Our wedding was coming, the date was set, and yet, this was the time when it seemed as if Lucie was determined to drive me away. She was on an unseen border between us, panicking, furious with me for being me, and afraid of the commitment she had made to us.

I had pulled myself through the *Jazz Singer* incident by confronting her costar with what happened to Lucie and me as a result of their tryst. He was honestly embarrassed and apologetic. I had accepted what happened, but now my new potential partner was so scared that it seemed she was unconsciously replaying the misery she had seen her parents go through at home during the last days of their marriage. She was nine years old then.

We were going to our set in the North Carolina woods every day and playing a fun story, but back home with the cameras off, she was wildly unhappy and blaming me for it. I didn't know what to do. I was bewitched, bothered, and bewildered. But I hung on. I tried to respond without anger—to support a person I loved but who I believed was a terrified girl. She had run from her first marriage and maybe now believed this one would be another trap for her, as she saw it. And she was pregnant.

In our movie, I was an ordinary dry cleaner, a widower with a young daughter, and I was an authentic man whose role with his daughter was to fill in the gap the young girl was feeling after losing her mother. And now, her father has met a woman whom he liked. I had one line to my daughter, which meant everything to me. I explained my own feelings by saying, "Geese mate for life, you know?" I meant that line. If I married Lucie, it would be for life.

Lucie's character in the film was confused and unhappy and struggled to find out who she was supposed to be. And the mysterious synchronicity between this role in a light comic movie and her actual life may have started the long process by which she was able to come to a reckoning with her "ugga-buggas" (as she calls them), which caused unhappiness to her and to others. Affective memories can do more than help actors create reality; they can help heal pain carried for generations.

Nick came to North Carolina to visit us. I think it helped Lucie. Nick had accepted her with a sweetness that moved me, and maybe Lucie, very deeply. He made it real. Our mentor was eleven.

SCENE: Kingston, New York

What is a wedding? For the main actors, it's a happy blur. It's being wrapped in a warm blanket on a cold day or cooled by an ocean breeze that lets them fly. It's being hyperaware of precious moments that rush past at nanospeed or suddenly slow down, to be reconstructed pixel by pixel, framed, and hung on memory's wall for a lifetime.

Lucille Ball and Gary Morton; Desi and Edie Arnaz; Desi Jr., and Linda Purl, his then-wife; Laurence and Agnes Luckinbill; my sister, Lynne Wachowski, her husband, Ron, and their four children, Julie, Laura, Larry (named for me) and Andy; and my two sons, Nick and Ben, all together, all interacting, each in their own way. And all of our best friends from the circle of theater that has warmed both of us and kept us safe. This is the one time all these folks will ever be together, and Lucie and I are the occasion. Lucie needs family.

She has imagined this wedding beautifully. The ceremony, the food, the time in which all will happen. She had arranged a simple picnic in an apple orchard. Our guests would arrive in a school bus, each with an Arkansas crazy quilt to sit on the ground with under the apple trees. Lucie's best friend, Judy

The Mating Season. CBS-TV. It truly was the mating season for us.
We were married the following June.

Gibson, would cater it with delicious, picnic-style food and drink. It was an impressionistic painting—Monet's *The Luncheon On The Grass*. It's the happiness of a day in the country for city folks. It's not meant to be complicated; it's meant to celebrate. Yet the complexities of all the lives intertwining on this day insert themselves.

I thought of Lucy and Desi coming together after all the years apart to see their daughter get married. I thought of the lives that have come and gone, leaving little and large wakes on the surface of life that diminish but never entirely disappear in the swirl and detritus of life's unresolved bits and pieces. Most of those present then are gone now. And Larry and Andy Wachowski are now Lilly and Lana. Desi Jr., and Linda are long parted. All the children are grown. My older sister, Sally, is long since gone, far too young. My brother Leo, also gone. And Lynne and Ron have left us as well. Connecting, unconnecting. Impermanence.

I don't go to wakes. Not since my grandfather and grandmother died, and I had to kiss cold, dead faces before the coffins were closed. Or when I served Requiem Mass for people I didn't know and heard "Dies Irae" sung, and watched families cry and be comforted and helped out of the church on someone's arm: "Day of wrath, day that will dissolve the world into burning coals and ashes . . . What can a wretch like me say then? What pardon can I beg for when even the just are not safe?" Scary stuff! But today is a day of joy.

As I waited next to my best friend, Richie Z., for the ceremony to start, my mind drifted through the pain I had caused my family. My mother and father had been put through it by my divorce. My mother had tried to help Robin deal with her misery. She refused to let Robin's accusations define me. I had no idea what my father felt. Maybe he was thinking of how much he had disappointed my mother. He did not excuse his own life. He was a fair man. My mother was a tigress in defense of all her kids. Her love was all action, all doing for her family. She constantly worried about us—and now me. I was her golden boy. She would fight the Catholic Church for me.

Lucie came out of the farmhouse on her father's arm, behind her maid of honor, Madeline Stone, and walked toward the place between two big trees where I stood. The marriage meister was a local justice of the peace who looked exactly like the screwball comedy version—slightly disheveled, carelessly shaven, in a suit that had seen a thousand couples standing before it, holding hands in hope, with the stub of a chewed-on cigar cupped in one hand behind his back while the other held the state's required reading.

Nick was the ring bearer, and Ben the flower boy. Nick's eleven-year-old face was a study in determination to do it right. Also to hide what he was feeling. I knew he had to be hurting. He couldn't have absorbed the hurt of the divorce so quickly. It had been a little less than a year since I set up a new house at 62 West Eighty-Third Street. Nick was at a precarious age, the edge of puberty. He was computing the loss of one family and all the seeming stability that broke like an eggshell just when he needed stability most. He walked down the green path toward me, preceding Lucie and her father, his sweet face a mask of somber control. My heart cracked to see it. He was followed by Ben, who was about to turn five. Both boys had nice jackets. Nick wore a tie. Ben had a young boy's open-collar shirt and, as the flower boy, was taking his job very seriously. He delivered each rose petal to the ground very deliberately, placing each one where his artist's eye told him that petal was meant to be. It was funny and so moving to watch his lovely little face, unaware of anyone or anything other than doing this job as well as he could. Nick, focused on task, aware of everything, intent, serious, not fucking up, doing right. And Ben, going inward to a well of beauty that is his natural soul, unimpaired and trusting that to protect him. Pure Nick. Pure Ben. People watching my beautiful boys chuckled, smiled, and understood. They knew the history.

And Grandpa Desi, ever the showman, the great director and creator of a vast theatrical empire, trying to get down the aisle behind this Little Boy Blue who forgot his cows were in the corn, muttering, "Go faster, boy!" to no avail as he and my wife-to-be adjusted their walk down the aisle to the flower boy's rhythm.

Nick stood beside me between the trees. I put my hand on his head with the tousled blond pageboy haircut. He vibrated with seriousness. He leaned against me a little. I had two sons who loved me despite everything. And a woman who loved me was coming straight at me to tell me so.

I was a man blessed beyond reason and beyond any deserving or possibility of paying forward. I was ignorant of anything called karma. But the hourglass of my karma was tipped over in the spirit world and began running at this moment.

We are taught that Spirit is always with us. That, in fact, we are nothing but Spirit. Nothing, that is, but soul, which is "a piece of the whole, of the main." We proceed in life as in a wedding march—step, pause, step, pause. For some, the steps seem backward, but it is all progress toward the ultimate end when the body melts away from the soul and reveals the soul in its brightness. We two apostates took our place among the believing and began our progression together.

I had my paper in hand. My promises to my wife-to-be, carefully pondered, and yet a mess of notes and changed lines and thoughts not to be trusted to memory in the crush of the day. Lucie had hers somewhere. Where could she have put them in her perfectly *soignée* ensemble?

She held a bouquet before her like a flower girl in a school pageant. Her expression was questioning, yet also with a sense of wonder, as her father, accompanied by a mustachioed, comically intent concertina player, sang one of his signature tunes.

> *Forever darling*
> *While other hearts go wandering*
> *You'll find mine as faithful as can be*
> *I'll be your true love forever and forever*
> *I'll care for you eternally.*
> *I've known your kiss*
> > *And I've been close to heaven*
> *The thrill of this will last me*
> *Till my life is through,*
> *I've made this promise*
> *And willingly, I'll keep it*
> *Forever, forever darling*
> *You will find me true.*

> —SAMMY CAHN AND BRONISŁAW KAPER,
> "FOREVER DARLING"

It was perfect! It was the song Lucie had requested he sing. A long, old-fashioned lyric, delivered in a leisurely tempo, the concertina wheezing out a thin sound in the heavy summer air. Desi, in a cream-colored tropical suit, the jacket tight over a now-large belly, turned toward his daughter, singing full out that lovely melody and the words that were for lovers only—impossible sentiments for an era when The Doors and The Sex Pistols screamed a different vibe for love: "Come on, baby, light my fire."

The faces of the guests reflected love mixed with ambivalence. And Lucille, for her own reasons, listened, with compressed lips and distanced eyes, to her man, now Edie's man, sing out fully, giving his all for his daughter—a romantic story that had to have been true for Lucy and Desi in their lives, too, but which had been obscured, smudged by his many infidelities and her humiliation. Nevertheless, he sang, meaning every word, and Lucy listened, her feelings hidden behind a carefully constructed mask.

Such is life. Such is art.

Desi was a complete man. He did not stint in life. Generous to a fault, he was almost completely broke when he died. Lucy was a saver, very cautious.

Also very generous, but protected better by a suite of advisors, accountants, and lawyers. She was, like Desi, a worker bee, tireless in seeking perfection in her work. Lucy supported most of her birth family and, of course, her own. She was not rich, not even wealthy by today's standards. What she built was enough for her. A clock-puncher who invented her own factory. Somewhere, the fun had gone from it all. She could be twitted by her court jesters, but not much, nor for too long, before she lost patience with them and cut them out of her life. I was never one of her court. I wanted nothing from her. But I understood her because I understood how joy in life could be lost.

Her daughter never took money from her. She wanted something else, but that is the subject of Lucie's life, the motor, perhaps, that powers it. She will tell it beautifully when she decides it has intrinsic value for her to write it for herself. Or not.

Lucie approached me, looking at me as if for the first time. Was she thinking, *who is this guy and what the heck am I doing here?* I saw these things, but in my eternal optimism (God knows where it came from), I saw only a woman whose essence I had tasted and found to be the stuff of real life, which is love. I was willing to go the distance with her, to be patient, to be kind, to hope, to believe, to endure all things.

My parents stood next to Lucy, Gary, Desi, and Edie. My mother was full of love for the music and words of "Forever Darling." My father, standing shoulder to shoulder with her, looked faintly distracted, half listening to Desi sing and half maybe thinking, *I'm stuck here on this farm, dependent on others, and I don't see a bar. Are they going to serve liquor today? At least can I get a few beers without Agnes knowing?*

I was thinking of our firstborn-to-come, already residing in Lucie's womb at that very moment, missing all this family fun and glory, just a few months away from being in and of this world. Maybe he would hear the love being exchanged and be happy he is joining it. We didn't know yet that he was a he.

I said what I needed to say to my wife. I relied on First Corinthians, chapter thirteen. And Lucie read what she had written to me. We were coupled.

The justice of the peace lit his cigar and took credit for a simple, lovely ceremony. Our parents gave us good wishes and went to their respective corners, waiting for the gong to ring. Each family took stock of how well they raised these new soulmates, and our friends wondered how long it would last. *If* it would last. "I give it six months." "How about six weeks?" My parents wondered what the Holy Mother Church would think of this triply illicit union—two divorces, an unwed mother, a civil ceremony (meaningless). Lucie knew her mother didn't love this marriage and didn't think much of me. I was older. I had two kids. Her daughter would now have to help raise them—exhausting! And what would that do to her career chances? What was wrong with her daughter? What was she thinking?

Never mind all that. We were truly mated. How often does that happen? We were determined to make it work.

It was a wonderful day. Fun and relaxed and genuine. A host of happy theater folk sat and ate beneath the apple blossoms, and a cadre of black flies arrived—uninvited—to enjoy the fallen fruit and the fun interplay buzzing between the humans.

Henry Grossman, my good friend and a photographer in demand, photographed the event for *People* magazine.

When we boarded the bus back to the city, Desi sat in the front with the concertina player and sang, and we laughed and felt the bubbles of champagne ascend. Once in New York, my children returned to their mother. What must that homecoming have been like for them?

Lucie and I went to my apartment for the night. In the early morning, we flew to Maui. Mimosas in the early afternoon. After the first-class passengers drifted into their after-dinner doze, we joined the Mile High Club. Only one flight attendant noticed the double occupancy of the restroom, and she smiled at us. We were 37,000 feet high and heading toward a rocky, reef-challenged honeymoon.

Hawaii smells like heaven must. The Maui airport in 1980 was not yet a busy beehive. There was a feeling of coming home to human proportion and scale. The lei-bearers were genuine in their welcome. Lucie got plumeria and gardenias, and I got green maile leaves. "Aloha"—hello and goodbye. Hello to new self, goodbye to old self.

Most people live on a lonely island
Lost in the middle of a foggy sea
Most people long for another island
One where they know they will like to be . . .

Bali Ha'i will whisper
On the wind of the sea
Here am I, your special island
Come to me, come to me.

—RICHARD RODGERS AND OSCAR HAMMERSTEIN,
"BALI HA'I,"

Hawaii is Bali Ha'i, but it is not magic. It's a place where simple connections with others are authentic and honored. This was a chance to find in ourselves a part of our natures we missed or had forgotten.

We went toward our suite. It was then I found out that Lucie is a mischievous child. In the corridor, on the door handles of all the rooms, breakfast menus were hanging and shoes—men's and women's—were on the floor, waiting to be cleaned and polished for the morning. It was irresistible to her. She said, "Let's change them!"

We exchanged every menu from door to door, a hopeless jumble, and every pair of shoes was switched from the right door to a wrong one. It was *Eloise at the Plaza*. Lucie was giggling, totally turned on by this escapade. I was totally turned on by her. It was a screwball comedy screw up that seemed harmless, like toilet-papering trees, soaping windows, or carrying the outhouse from the back of the barn to the middle of downtown on Halloween. After our mischievous mission, we happily fell into the snow-white sheets and down pillows and made love. Three times.

In the morning, we were renewed—love again, uninhibited, no barriers. Complete. Then we went out to our balcony and watched all the guests on their balconies getting completely different breakfasts than they had ordered and folks holding up to the amazed staff pairs of ladies' pumps instead of their brogans. There was minor chaos and laughter. Only a few sourpusses didn't think it was funny.

We got away with our dastardly crime. Was I too old for such hijinks? Lucie was, I think, testing my capacity for joy.

SCENE: Maui, Hawaii

The Hana drive on Maui. A dotted line on the map means "No Good Road." We had driven our little VW Golf rental halfway around the island to Hana and had eaten barbecue—the best in the Western world—at a roadside restaurant. And we decided to take the "No Road" all the way to its end. We were happy and relaxed. It was an adventure, and so was our marriage going to be.

The first few miles of dirt were okay, but then there were no more houses. At the last one, we saw they were selling leis. We bought two. In the back of nowhere, the dirt road suddenly became a track—gravel, sand, grass. It was late afternoon. Above us loomed Haleakalā, the volcano, hiding the sun from our side of the island.

We drove a few miles when suddenly the track dropped away, caved in, and we were on the edge of a washout. The ocean was flowing in front of us where it had cut the land away. The tide was coming in. A big surf broke outside, and the inflow rushed through the gap where the old road had been. It became ocean. I stopped the car. We got out and looked. What to do?

Suddenly, from the little rise on the far side of the ocean gap, a small car approached and headed toward us. It stopped as we had. A man and a woman got out of the car to look at the challenge the sea had made. They held hands and looked at us. We were mirror images of each other, laughing giddily and waving as the ocean separating us crashed and roared.

We watched the sea for a while. There was a moment—a few seconds—when there was a cessation of the inflow from the surge. A rock-filled land base became visible as the sea rushed past to eat more land. When the flow was fullest, it would have almost submerged our little VW. The people over the way were driving a bigger, more substantial car with four-wheel drive. They got back into their car and waited. The moment came. The sea rushed in about four feet deep, ebbing as the flow rolled inland. A wave built outside at the break. The couple waited indecisively for a second or two as the sea flowed out, and then they went! They rolled down the slope, accelerated, and hit the foaming boulders where the road had been. They bounced and almost lost control. An inexorable wave was now coming, maybe the ninth of the wave cycle, supposedly always the biggest. The guy kept control and righted the trajectory of the car. The woman was looking straight at the scary waves coming at them. The guy floored it, and the big car rocketed through the gap and up the new slope where a road had been, went past us, and away.

Our turn. I was looking at the sea. Yes, that big wave broke, ran back out, and the next one was much smaller. The cycle started again. Lucie decided she ought to cross on foot. She could see a path through the big white stones the sea had brought from some other kingdom. I agreed, because our car was much lighter and had less traction. It wasn't a fast car by any description, and the shock absorbers were nil.

I said, "Go now!" She stepped onto the lip of the broken old road and onto the sea break. A small wave had just broken outside, come in, and subsided. Lucie ran, her long legs flashing in the sun. She's a dancer. She stayed straight up and balanced. The wave had gone out, and the next one was building. She ran across the gap, climbed the opposite bank, turned, and smiled big. Made it! Safe on the other side.

My turn. I listened to the small motor turn over. I figured if I misjudged and the light little car was swamped, it would be carried by the backwash out into the wave break. It would be broadside to the wave with the wheels off the ground. It would be rolled over by the surf. If that happened, I would have to get out of a rolling car fast enough to be away from it as it ceded control of itself to the Pacific Ocean. I figured I could swim out of the situation if I got out. Lucie was watching me worriedly. It had occurred to her that the little car might not make it. I waved—I'm coming!

On the third wave, I gunned the little four-cylinder engine and went. I got some speed down the slope and lofted onto the big stones now foaming over. The car bounced high, skidded sideways, was airborne again, and came down hard. I saw the next wave breaking outside, and it looked huge. There went my ninth-wave theory. My epitaph would memorialize my lack of all mathematical skills: "Good boy. Couldn't count." I jammed the accelerator. The wheels caught. I bounced, jounced, and the bank came up. The little car leaped up, and it was over and back on the track.

This moment was iconic. Lucie and I are two of a kind. We are both daring but not stupid. We could take on a risky project and succeed together. What else is a marriage? We hugged. We kissed. We had taken a road less traveled. We were a couple, and we were *one*. We were sealed!

And yet, the arcane furies we both had—the difficulty of trust, of intimacy, the hidden hurts we both had—were still all there, forgotten in the joy of romance, of finding ourselves soul mates. And so life, our teacher, reminded us it has a sense of humor. It would become a long-running series.

SCENE: Hawaii

Our honeymoon was bathed in salt water and tumbled in rough surf. We played, made love . . . and fought. At that point, neither of us knew how to hold back our tempers when our egos were bruised, and we allayed our hidden hurts by blaming each other. The causes of pain are buried. Marriage digs them up. It's the greatest time to learn how to respond positively to those events.

It's hilarious how fights start: loud, bitter, doors slamming, hot coffee thrown, love and marriage over now! Never existed! Names called straight out of fifth-grade recess fights and much worse. Words from heretofore hidden, perhaps unconscious, memories of parental or other violent disputes, or from bias or bigotry existing in someone that has been suppressed. So, vicious, misery-inducing insults are hurled. The atmosphere was as scary as a Hudson Valley thunderstorm, with sky-spanning lightning, violent wind, deluges of water, mini tornadoes, house- and home-wrecking forces—then, suddenly, as in nature, ending, with the huddled survivors hugging, stunned, and wondering what on earth caused such destruction.

And no one can remember what started it! You said—then I said—and . . . what? That was it? That little, stupid, meaningless thing started all this? Are we nuts?

This is ego's work. Ego makes fear. It's worse if you're in paradise with no work to do, nothing to do but be happy with each other, your choice of the one to "ride the river with," someone to be with forever. But not if you're going to be like this! What was I thinking? I don't believe what I'm seeing! Who the fuck are you?

Then, storm over, we kiss and make up. Chagrined. This isn't the end but the beginning for each of us to find out what is good about the other and to remember when the storm winds begin to blow. Neither one of us is a quitter. That's good to find out. But how is it going to work? There had to be other elements.

We got on the plane, having had a taste of just how tricky this marriage thing can be.

SCENE: New York

Manny Azenberg had given us a wonderful wedding present: a tour of the Brian Clark play he produced in New York, *Whose Life Is It Anyway?* Manny asked us to alternate between the roles of the doctor and the paralyzed sculptor patient fighting to die while the hospital wouldn't let him. I would start as the doctor, and we would switch after three weeks. Lucie was the patient first. She was very pregnant by then, and the baby bump had to be disguised in the hospital bed. One solution was to put a bed table over her belly, but when that didn't work, sleight of hand was involved, with giant pillows and bed sheets to fool the eye.

The play is a melodrama stacked in the patient's favor. The hospital's management is villainous, but the staff is sympathetic. The actors, as in all melodrama, must motivate themselves to do things the characters might not logically do. And so the actors have questions that are not answerable in the text.

I struggled with this in rehearsal, which embarrassed Lucie. It brought from her something I came to call her HF—humiliation factor. As rehearsal progressed, I got frustrated and angry at gaps in the text, and the director thought I was one of *those* actors—a grubby method man.

There could be no questioning of the play. It was a big hit. So, I was the problem, not the words, which to me was actually crazy. Actors can be reduced to indicating—overacting—to try to make the story make sense in some emotional way. Our cast was way better than that, and they were instinctively filling in the logical and emotional gaps in their characters and the melodramatic fakery. The audience intuits some honest feelings through a fog of confusion, which has power but lacks sense.

Actors defend themselves from indicating by using a Stanislavski technique, finding an emotion through an "affective memory" that almost fits the moment. This works to keep a scene going. To the audience it feels almost real, but in their hearts, they feel the fakery. They don't know what to make of it, so they sit there and try to go along with whatever emotion is being expressed. But there is a cognitive dissonance with what they are hearing in the story. Thus, much of the play fails to land right. It's almost-right theater. Actors feel empty when the curtain comes down because the text has not supported what it purports to be about.

I fought this fakery passively, then aggressively.

I accepted the melodrama we had on our hands and relied on my fellow actors' moment-to-moment, "be here now" responses. They understood.

Now, when the director would suddenly demand, "Pace! Speed it up!" for some melodramatic effect, we would nod in assent and continue to go at the pace and speed that seemed right to us. The director gave up. He was a decent fellow out of his depth. The melodrama was a big success on Broadway, so can we just move on?

SCENE: Los Angeles

The play opened at the Wilshire Theater in Los Angeles, and it was packed. We did our best. Afterward, there was a conflagration of paparazzi flashbulbs in the lobby as they took thousands of pictures of Lucy, Gary, Lucie, and me. It was so overboard, so strangely excessive, that I marveled at it as if I were a visitor from another century, like the protagonist in Mark Twain's *A Connecticut Yankee in King Arthur's Court*. Lucie and her mom stuck to the promotion script like troupers. It was a great demonstration of the PR skills of Lucille Ball and Lucie Arnaz in the world they knew.

Before we were married, Lucie and I had been chased in New York and Hollywood by paparazzi from the *National Enquirer* who hoped to grab a picture of any hint of drama or scandal from Lucie. As a young girl, her mother had drilled into her that anything remotely embarrassing that she might do could result in a cover story that would sell out the run of newspapers for a day.

Or a week. This was the source of Lucie's powerful urge to avoid any personal behavior that could cause her mother to be humiliated. Her rehearsal process was to accept any direction she was given—know her lines, be on time, never question the script, and, above all, not fight in public over anything that would cause the HF to kick in. This went against her real questing spirit.

As the play progressed, Lucie began to have trouble living the character truly and simply. She was coming up against illogical gaps in her character and the story. I watched this carefully. In San Francisco, we would switch roles—I would be the patient, and she would be the doctor.

SCENE: San Francisco

I was on stage at the Curran Theatre playing the patient, and Lucie was the doctor trying to persuade me to live. A pregnant doctor. Her condition made our scenes especially poignant. A woman carrying a new life, and a man determined to quit on his. As the paralyzed patient, I used techniques from the most melodramatic plays I'd played in summer stock and puked at in theaters in New York, London, Rome, and Paris. But in Rome, do as the Romans do—in a melodrama, play the melodrama. Forget reality. Play the hell out of your stereotyped character. Play the sentiment. Build your dialogue like music to cue the audience for the emotional climax. Bombast is good, subtlety bad. It worked. Lucie and I discussed this phenomenon endlessly, as actors do, trying to improve our craft skills.

Whose Life came into the last weeks of its San Francisco run. I had figured out how to play the melodrama for all I could get out of it, and our audiences loved it. It was the right approach for this political tract and the way to make its point: freedom of choice. It celebrated the heroic, unhappy ending of life because the protagonist had asserted individual rights and antiauthoritarian principles against the Man, the powers that be—unsympathetic and fearful hospital administrators insisting on irrational rules dictated by insurance companies, covering their asses, and searching for new ways not to pay off claims. It was the individual against the system, with the right to suicide as the prize.

I played the lights, lifting my eyes to heaven (or the high ceiling of the theater). Cheesy, but it got applause. John of Arc, martyrdom mode. I undercut my adamant public stand that I had the right to kill myself when, alone in the room, I allowed self-doubt to communicate as powerfully as possible by reaching the back wall of the theater with the only thing I could allow to move on my body—my face. It was a new experience for me and one that made me queasy.

The audience got a cheap shot from the teeth-out, indicated performance. Audiences in Los Angeles, where Lucie had played the patient, had sat quietly. In San Francisco, I ad-libbed raucous jokes at the head doctor, and when he left the room, I looked sorry and chagrined and hopeless. Then, I'd smile, glad I had told the old fart off. I did a good imitation of a six-year-old boy sticking out his tongue behind the teacher's back. Shameless. And the audiences loved the bad boy patient who would die to make a point.

Many viewers didn't care. It was what they were used to. Peter Brook calls it the Deadly Theater. It creates deadly plays and audiences who think all theater is like this. And audiences dwindle.

Lucie watched my solution to playing melodrama and, I think, was appalled. She hadn't had the advantage of thinking of it as the only way this play could succeed because she had given a lovely, quiet, real performance that was wasted on a reality unsupported by the playwright.

We closed our run and went back to LA.

SCENE: Los Angeles

Lucie's water broke early on the morning of December 8. We called the doctor, who calmed our eagerness to run to the hospital. He said, "Call when they are ten minutes apart. And don't eat."

Evening: Lucie was starving. I looked for an open restaurant. Only one—a pizza joint—looked good. I arrived home with the pizza. She took a bite. Contractions started.

Near midnight: The contractions were much closer together. The doctor now said, "Come!" We gathered our stuff—focal point picture for the hospital wall, photos of folks who mattered to her, a pillow from our bedroom, and a thermos jug full of hot coffee on which Lucie had made a beautiful collage, her artist's vision of what our lives would be together. In my haste, I dropped the thermos in the driveway. The inner glass chamber shattered. Now it sounded like a cocktail mixer, but with shattered glass, not ice. I still have this lovely gift from my young wife. Forty-four years later, it still moves me. It's Lucie's take on life: a collage of loving, fun things.

We drove to Cedars-Sinai, and we practiced breathing in the Lamaze method all the way. I timed the contractions, which went from mild and fairly widely spaced to more demanding. The kid's entrance cue was coming up. Dilation was slow but moving forward. Lucie described it as a cramping feeling at first, but as it progressed, it became much more. Her body was gripped in an all-encompassing force like an undertow in an out-of-control ocean. She stayed with the powerful current, never losing concentration or heart. We were sure the next cycle would signal the transition we had prepared for.

The process of birth, for a man, is entry into the secret life of women, into a grand existential event and process with its own rules, history, and tradition. If a man is awake to it, he is in the presence of the life force. All women are intimately connected to it, and one day they must answer to it. At that moment, men realize they are incomplete and need women to complete them. Some men walk away from this. But women can never walk away from this essential knowledge.

Our little nation, our new family, had a problem: Maybe our child wasn't ready to come into this world. He was stuck. The remedy: Lucie had to turn her body over to change the baby's path out of the womb and into life on Earth. The trouble was that she had worked with increasing intensity and pain. The contractions were coming faster and were becoming almost intolerable, and she was tired. Her capacity to endure was ebbing. At points, medical people would offer relief with chemicals, shots, and epidurals. As tempting as it must have been, she said no. As did I. She would not quit. It was her show. She did it so our child would have the healthiest birth possible.

The pain became more intense, but turning over seemed impossible. Nurses changed shifts, and a new woman came in. She said, "Turn over!"

Lucie said, "I can't!"—a sure sign she had reached her limit of endurance.

The nurse ordered her, like a sergeant to a green recruit afraid of the shellfire but who would die if he stayed in his hole, "Turn over, Lucie! Like I showed you. Now! Or this kid's never going to make it!"

Lucie turned. Oh, it hurt! The pain got worse. Transition became a storm at sea with forty-foot waves blown by winds of seventy miles per hour, piling upon each other, each obliterating the next, too fast to keep up. I was trying to keep up with the exercises we were taught—breathe out on every contraction, shallow breaths through pursed lips, puff, inhale, puff! I put my fingers up to her tired white face to cue her to the wave motion. She had to count the number of fingers I showed her, but I wasn't fast enough. One-three-five-two. Breathe—out, in, out. Stay with it, honey. You can do it!

She swatted my hand away. No, no! Not like that!

Sergeant Nurse replaced me, counting fast and rapping out orders. "You've got it! You're doing great! All women do this! Go! Yes, go!" It was TLC, military-style.

Turning over freed the baby. No longer stuck, he entered the door, the mysterious egress to this magical place, the world. A little after 10:00 A.M. on December 9, 1980, Simon Thomas Luckinbill was born and placed in his mother's arms, skin to skin, baby to breast. Lucie and her firstborn. Life and the earth turned over, and the heavens celebrated. Silly grins, tears like warm raindrops wiped with the sleeve of a hospital gown, which had probably felt many. It was done.

When I knew they were safe, I ran for the phone. Grandma Lucy had to know! I found one of the last pay phones in the universe one hundred steps down the hall. I grabbed change from my pocket and dialed the number.

Gary answered. I was very excited. I told him the news. He said, in a flat voice, "Uh-huh. Okay." I asked if I might speak to Lucille. A pause, then he said to Lucille, "Lucy, Lucie's had her baby." This he said in a voice devoid of joy or even a frisson of excitement.

Lucille came on the line. I told her the news and how proud she could be of her daughter and her courage. She now had a beautiful grandson. In her deep growly voice, Lucy said something like, "Fine, glad to hear it. Finally." She, too, was flat. No excitement. I thought it was because that's the way she took such news. That was her. I babbled on, inviting them to come and see for themselves. "Well, we'll see," was the response. I had no idea that this moment would become a rift between me and Lucille that would last until she knew she was dying almost ten years later.

I then called my mother, who was very glad indeed.

The almost overwhelming influence of Lucille Ball was due to a reputation earned the old-fashioned way—with dogged determination to be the best. Not for herself, oddly. Not so much an ego trip, but because something implanted in her from earliest childhood made her into someone who needed to be safe. To do that, she had to drive the bus, organize all things and be perfect—a disorder that today we call OCD. Not naturally funny, she drew a sweet, determined, childlike clown from her deepest innermost self. Karma gave her a show and humorous material masterfully written and plotted, and she took the material, the words and situations, to astounding heights of wondrously funny, genius behavior. Lucille Ball was real. Lucy Ricardo was real. And the reward to audiences is that she will never stop giving them life lessons in wit, slapstick, love, and compassion.

But the Lucille Ball who came into my life late in hers was seldom, in my experience, happy or content. And, I think, not for lack of trying. The mystery of our non-relationship remains. I could not do the dance almost everyone did with her—flattery, subservience to her whims, tempers, attitude, and queen-like shadow. I was genuine with her. I liked her. I respected her. But those feelings were not reciprocated. There was nothing I could do. I love her daughter and that is that. Nothing has changed from then to now. Lucille remained distant, not only to me but to our children. It mystified and hurt my wife, but she loved her mother. She could only speculate why the distancing was ever-present. My opinion? Lucille herself didn't know.

I wrote a letter to Simon about what his birth meant to us. I sent a copy to Lucille. There was no response.

I had made a bet with the head waiter at Chasen's restaurant about the time our baby would be born—fifty bucks if I lost, or a steak dinner with all the trimmings, catered to Lucie's hospital room, if I won. I won. That evening, we ate a Chasen's dinner in the maternity ward.

We brought Simon home to Lucie's house on Patricia Avenue. We stayed in LA until he could safely travel by air, then flew to New York. He rode in his little hand-carry baby bucket. He was a good traveler from the start.

SCENE: New York

We went back to NYC with our baby. Our new apartment was being worked on, so we bunked with Lucie's best friend, Judy Gibson, and bathed Simon in her small kitchen sink. We slept on the floor under a wall-sized display of Judy's shoe collection. We had bought an eleven-room apartment on Central Park at Eighty-Seventh Street. It was on the eleventh floor. Eleven plus eleven is twenty-two, a master number. The building was home to many actors and artists.

The home had a good vibe from its previous owner, Judge Nathan, who, we were told, performed many weddings in the living room overlooking New York. The Macy's Thanksgiving Day Parade started a few blocks south of our expansive windows. The children and I would join the parade under the enormous balloons. Hand in hand, we'd walk south for blocks with Santa and Casper the Friendly Ghost. The city fireworks display on the Fourth of July burst into glory from the Sheep Meadow in the park, south of our windows. I built the children's room into a playground, with bunks and overhead boxes at the twelve-foot ceiling height so the boys could climb ladders, sit in the boxes like a tree house, and cross from one box to the other on a beam. I made a chinning bar and hung a rope from the main beam to swing on. The fifth bedroom was my writing room.

I sold a book-length story to CBS for a miniseries with Lucie to star, playing Adah Isaacs Menken. CBS was riding high then and willing to try new, different ideas. But *George Washington*, a miniseries, flopped badly in the ratings, and they ditched all costume dramas. After a year's work, our series was eighty-sixed. My writing partner was young David Rothkopf, who has since made a grand career as a Washington Deputy Under Secretary of Commerce, political analyst, author, and savant.

I had a second project accepted at CBS: my script of *The Desi Arnaz Story* based on my father-in-law's autobiography (written with Bernie Dilbert, a terrific writer from the *M*A*S*H* TV series) about his fascinating life—escaping to Miami to join his father, penniless, kicked out of Cuba by the Batista regime, the takeover by Machado's government. Desi's family homes were destroyed, his father imprisoned for a time, and his mother left behind in Havana until it could be arranged for her to travel to America to join her husband and son. His rise out of this sudden poverty was through his music—his guitar, his voice, his dancing. He brought the conga line to America. Then came his meeting with Lucille Ball at RKO, their monumental love affair and the glittering success they achieved together. His music was the primary reason for his rise.

The film was in its second pass through the development process when the suits—the CBS bosses, the owners—decided that the movie could go ahead, but without Desi's music. I was looking for a *clever* way to get the music back in when the money men at CBS decided the *Movie of the Week* program was too costly and canceled all the projects.

I then wrote a treatment for a TV pilot about my life with Lucie (two people trying love and marriage again after the first ones didn't work). It was called *One More Try*. The script was written by Lynn Grossman. Lucie wrote a great theme song with her composer friend, Madeline Stone. We made the pilot in New York. It was a good show with great potential, but it didn't make the cut. The executive at CBS who canceled us before even trying our show on the air was later canceled himself over a string of poor programming decisions that left CBS in the ratings cellar.

* * *

Our neighbors in the 271 Central Park West apartment building were Mark Hamill, Meryl Streep and Don Gummer, Garry Trudeau and Jane Pauley, and the artist Chuck Close. Francesco Scavullo, the fashion photographer, had a studio in our building lobby. The building south of us on the side street had been George Gershwin's residence. And on the north side street lived writers Elie Wiesel and Murray Schisgal as well as writer/actor couple Joe Bologna and Renée Taylor. Composers, musicians, models, writers, actors, singers, comedians—our neighborhood was a part of the great and enduring New York vibe that I had dreamed I would belong to someday.

Our building was old and neat and kindly. The operator of the brass-gated elevator was Nick, a Greek gentleman as true as a copper Lincoln penny. He loved our kids.

Halloween, Christmas, Thanksgiving, Easter, and birthdays were celebrated happily there for years. I ran in Central Park every day. Rain, sleet, heat, cold, ice, I was there. We could walk to fifty restaurants and stores surrounding us—Columbus, Amsterdam, Broadway, and the Upper West Side. It was a delicious life. There we raised five children: Nick from ten to seventeen, Ben from five to twelve, Simon from one to seven, Joe from one to five, and Kate from one to two.

Lucie and I worked in New York theater and toured shows in the summer. We toured together in *They're Playing Our Song* for producer Bob Young from the Indianapolis Starlight Theatre, and went on to twelve weeks in big summer venues, including the St. Louis Muny—capacity 11,000 and always packed. Bob was a lovely and generous theater-loving man who paid actors handsomely. And we packed houses. It seemed that regional theater was deliciously alive, especially for musicals.

I played Vernon Gersch like the Marvin Hamlisch I knew. Lucie was my tutor in singing and dancing in a musical. I was a gnarly student, as always. I have a decent tenor voice, but I was so scared of singing onstage because I knew nothing about how music works. I couldn't find the cue to get into my songs. I watched the conductor, who was so kind. She had to cue me with a big nod of her head—*now!*—until I could launch in. I finally got it. So simple. Suddenly, Larry was singing in a musical. Thank you, Fran Liebergall.

Another year, we toured for Bob in a wonderful musical, *I Do! I Do!* Because Robert Preston and Mary Martin had actually played instruments in the original Broadway production, I spent the whole summer learning to play the tenor sax for that show, and Lucie learned to play some violin. We didn't know that most other actors who'd played those roles only mimed playing the instruments while the orchestra covered them in the pit. Lucia Victor, Gower Champion's assistant on the original show, directed. I appealed to the playwright, my friend Tom Jones, to be allowed to add lines from the source play, *The Fourposter* (played by Hume Cronyn and Jessica Tandy), and he agreed. We tried the additions in rehearsal just once. Nope! The play's exposition is perfect in the streamlined version—a lesson for me. Less is usually more.

SCENE: New York

One year into our marriage, Lucie was coming upon her thirtieth birthday. She told me no one had ever surprised her—could ever surprise her—on her birthday. What a challenge! We made a show in secret. I wrote a parody rock and roll song lyric and called it *Dirty Thirty*. I enlisted her best friends. Madeline Stone put my words to music, and Judy Gibson, along with practically every other theater friend Lucie had ever made, created a rock-and-roller backup group. On the day of, I took my young wife to Ted Hook's nightclub and walked her into a raucous musical number celebrating her. She was blown away!

* * *

We found a gorgeous weekend and summer cottage on fifteen acres in Katonah, New York, fifty-five minutes from Times Square. This incredible property also cost $365,000. Twenty-four years later, it sold for $3 million. Our property buys helped us to afford our acting work. They also illustrate how it is impossible now for working folks to buy a home.

We borrowed $50,000 from each of our mothers for the down payment. Not a big stretch for Lucille, but it was all the savings my mother had in the world, and she risked it for us. We gave her generous interest and paid them both back within a year. Lucie told Neil Simon about our new home—fifty-five minutes door-to-door. He quipped, "Big house."

SCENE: New York

I rang the doorbell at the townhouse on East Forty-Ninth Street in New York. It was another in a row of such dwellings typical of an era of graceful mansions built in the early twentieth century. This one was once white but was now a used gray. I'm nothing special, it seemed to say, just a sturdy structure well-built for a long, distinguished, and innately stylish life.

Katharine Hepburn opened her door suddenly, looked me up and down, and said brusquely, "Well, come in. Let's get on with it!"

It was late fall and quite cold in the damp breeze off the East River. I followed Ms. Hepburn up the steep stairs from the small foyer to the first-floor parlor. A fire was struggling in the grate. I was shown to a comfortable couch facing an easy chair on the opposite side of the hearth.

Before I sat, I said, "Let me put more logs on the fire and kick it awake." I started to the wood hod where the tongs and poker were leaning.

She said immediately, "Nope! That's my job." And she bent to the firewood, picked up two of the largest pieces, and knelt to arrange them manually in crisscross fashion atop the embers. They took fire instantly. She was clearly an expert.

I just stood, watching an extraordinary woman do her chores. "That's exactly how I would do it," I said.

"Well then, you know something about it. Sit, sit!"

I sat. Ms. Hepburn took the easy chair. She wore tan bell-bottom pants slightly dusted with ash and pine bark, an old charcoal gray turtleneck sweater, a well-used green cardigan, and scuffed Oxford shoes.

I had sent her my screenplay of John Updike's novella *Of the Farm* by mail and received back an invitation to visit her. I was excited. I knew she was no-nonsense, so I figured an invitation to discuss the film was good news.

"Well," she said abruptly, "the son is awfully weak. I prefer to work with strong men."

A challenge! The story is about the conflict between a New York advertising man—newly married, with a stepson—and his widowed mother, who has dominated everyone in her life with her acerbic persona. But now, in the film's first scene, she has fallen off the tractor as she cut the overgrown fields of the huge Pennsylvania farm where her son grew up. Now she needs help. Her old dog drags her home. She calls her son.

Now a grown man, he has cut physical ties with his mother, but the psychological damage done to his ego growing up is still very strong. His mother demands he leave his job in New York and return to take care of the farm. She knows her heart is damaged. Government regulations are that uncultivated farms must be mowed and maintained.

The son takes his new wife and stepson to Pennsylvania to sort this out, fully intending to return to his job in advertising. His wife is very discomfited by this sudden change in her husband's life and fears what will happen to him if his mother makes demands he will have to fight. She's uncertain who will win. So is he. Life has set up a challenge he must take.

The story struck a chord with me. I had written it as a role I knew how to play. And as I wrote, I kept seeing Hepburn as the mother.

"That's the point," I said instantly. "And, as you saw, the son takes on the challenge his powerful mother has posed to him just as he has begun to imagine that, with marriage and a stepchild, he has overcome his mother's domination of him. But now he must defend that belief."

"The woman is too rough," she said.

I answered, "She's afraid for the first time. She's controlled life, but now life is changing for both mother and son. And the farm is the key. The boy hates the farm. Or does he? The mother has made the farm into a symbol of her own strength and her son's weakness. The story is about how each of these people discovers what real strength is. They fight to the end, and both of them win."

"How?" asked Ms. Hepburn.

"The mother comes to learn her son's real strengths as she watches him deal with her demands and the needs of his wife and stepson. The son discovers the source of his mother's need to control everything and learns to see her very differently."

"Who'll care about this story?" she demanded.

"With you as the mother, they will see the depth of this woman's goodness as she begins to see into her life differently because her son stands up to her differently. He's not the feckless boy she has imagined for too long. He becomes a man before her eyes. Their strengths become different but equal. It's a story that everybody—mother, father, son, daughter—can understand and feel."

"Well, who will play the son?"

I laughed. "Naturally, I wrote it for myself. I understand strong women. My mother was one. In a way, I lived this story. But I'm not insisting I play it."

"Why me?"

"I saw you in *West Side Waltz*. I had just finished a long run in *Chapter Two*, and I went to the Barrymore to see you. I played that theater with *Poor Murderer* in 1976. You are the only person who can play this woman and give her the humanity without the sentimentality. This is the real thing."

"Well," she said—every one of her *well*s was different. This one said, *skip the blather. I'll tell you if I'm right or not. And even if I am, I'll tell you what I'll do and what I won't!*

A pause. A log collapsed in the fireplace. Sparks flew. The lovely smell of New England autumn filled the room. A smile curled on her beautiful lips. A secret one meant not for me but for some thought that was hers alone.

She said, "Would you like a cup of tea?"

I said yes.

She fetched it, a proper tea set. Her own style.

The late shadows began to creep up the staircase from the foyer.

She said, "Spence used to be that way. Knew what he wanted. And said so!"

And we talked a while longer about her life with Spencer Tracy. It was on her mind, but she didn't do anything more than muse with a softness in her voice that had not existed before.

I listened.

Suddenly, she said, "Use my name. I'll write you a letter saying I will take this on. Good luck!"

I went downstairs, filled with a deep softness in my heart for this woman. Alone now and living as she always had—briskly, with a plan—something in her understood the mother character in *Of the Farm*. The loneliness, the fear, the anger that control was seeping away from her life. A time to open to love. To give it. Briskly!

I tried for two years to sell this movie with Ms. Hepburn as the star. I tried film studios and television people. They all said unanimously, "Hepburn? No way, she's box office poison. Everybody knows it."

Fucking Hollywood!

SCENE: New York

From Fifth Avenue to Central Park South, where the cobblestones are worn down by a hundred and fifty years of aching feet, stand tables and kiosks of used books. I can never walk past books. If I picked one up from the table—tended by a ubiquitous immigrant in a knit cap and ragged overcoat, hunched over as if it were cold—and if I was transfixed by a title and read a sentence that somehow reminded me that I was meant to fly, not sleepwalk, through life, in an instant, I was seven years old again with the powerful faith of a child. I was surprised and delighted by my existence in a world where I could be lifted up and soar through the air—by a book! In the absence of a mentor, a book was a window through which I could pass instantly into a state of inspiration, of becoming, of nascence, almost regardless of the story. Words were magic, and if they were ennobling in any way, if they promised to show me things—a hero perhaps, someone just naturally better than me, heroic, honorable, manly—then I was, in a trice, in the wind, gliding and soaring on wings of words, following the leader of the flock as he aimed for a land ten thousand words away, a place of nourishment and hope for a hungry boy.

And that day, my eye caught the title *My Mind on Trial*. I picked up the book and opened it. Inside the cover was a pencil scribble—*.25 cents*. I laughed. What author would want to think this is what it comes down to? On the facing page was a simple dedication: *To Ivan*. The author, Eugen Loebl, was foreign and unknown to me. And who was Ivan?

The story, apparent on the first page, was political economics—communism versus capitalism. I knew nothing of these subjects. Did I want to? I didn't know. It was a personal story. I put a quarter down on the table. The hunched-over guy didn't look up, just extended a hand, brown with old dirt, and slid the coin into his hand and into a coat pocket. Mr. Loebl will never see that coin or any fraction of it. The book is in free flight. It's mine, for now.

I walked into Central Park, already reading, hoping a free bench would appear. Ah! This was serious business.

Eugen Loebl was an economist by education and a communist by conviction and faith. As a boy in Czechoslovakia, he saw the corruption of the autocracy of the old Austro-Hungarian Empire. He was hungry for social justice. He studied

Karl Marx and believed with him that the only way to have social justice was through a worldwide revolution. "Workers of the world, unite! You have nothing to lose but your chains!" The source of all wealth came from manual labor.

He dedicated his life to serving his country after the Czech Communist Party seized power in 1948. He was given a Soviet Order of the Red Star medal for his work on behalf of state socialism. Then in 1949, he was arrested along with thirteen other men, mostly Jews high in the Czech government. The charge was treason, and the penalty, death. There would be a show trial in so the world could see these "traitors" confess their "crimes." It was a Russian massacre of all Jews in their subject countries.

Loebl endured years of mental and physical torture before finally confessing to nonexistent crimes. Eleven of his fellow prisoners were hanged—murdered. Inexplicably, he was not. In 1968, the Prague Spring uprising against Soviet rule succeeded. Overnight, the Soviets invaded his country.

Loebl escaped. He met his ex-wife and Ivan, his son, in Vienna and asked Ivan to go with him to America. Ivan had not known his father through his crucial growing-up years, so he refused. He had become a dedicated communist, as his father had been at his age. Eugen had lost his only son forever.

In prison, he had written a book without pen or paper. He composed it in his mind and memorized its content. It was the book I now held in my hand. In it, he described his complete rethinking and rejection of Marx.

* * *

I met with Eugen in his small apartment close to the Hudson River. He was a quiet, professorial gentleman with a devotion to truth, which underlay his peaceful persona with a seam of iron. This kind gentleman gave me the right to make a play of his book—for nothing. I had found a mentor.

I was compelled by Eugen's story of a horrifying time that is still the daily lot of anyone trapped in Russian, Chinese, and other politically orthodox hells on earth.

The play took two years to write and was called *My Mind on Trial, or Torture and Execution, the Musical.*

George Orwell wrote, "One can write nothing readable unless one constantly struggles to efface one's personality." But I could not efface my personality.

My play morphed into a story of two men who struggle to tell the same story in an opposing way. Two egos fighting for dominance. An unknown immigrant pitches a true, political, human story to a television mogul with the power to give the story wings but who insists on turning it into a clichéd prison story with a happy ending, which is a lie. Eugen fights for the truth of his story, the horrible, hard to bear facts.

I was focused on Loebl's loss of his son. I asked my sons how they felt about the scary stuff people with power do and how they would improve the world. Ben's thoughts were especially poetic. They inspired me to make a third main character, a child who appears to express what such a world seems like to him. The heart of Eugen's story. I wrote poems for the son. Music for the poems was provided by Harold Farberman.

The play had grown like Jack's beanstalk with its brutal comic threat of giants awaiting the hero. I just kept climbing, curious to see what was up there in the attic of my imagination.

I was a member of The Actors Studio Playwrights group, which included Norman Mailer. Norman loved the play. The Studio greenlit a staged reading of it.

The best actors I knew—David Margulies, Richard Zavaglia, Steven Joyce, Lucie, and Walter Willison—agreed to do it. The audience included Harold Clurman, Lee and Paula Strasberg, Elia Kazan, Brother Jonathan (a Catholic playwright), and various Broadway producers who attended these events hoping to find new material.

It was a raw, wild, surreal performance. The actors were fabulous. They charmed and interested the most demanding audience in New York City. And the play even got the respect of Cheryl Crawford, a notoriously tough producer who, along with Clurman, Kazan, and Strasberg, had led the iconic Group Theater, the company of artists I took as my daily inspiration for the theatre life I tried to lead.

Eugen and his wife Greta, an artist, attended. Afterward, I asked Eugen what he thought. He said, "Let us meet and talk."

The play was funny, which I did not expect. And another character is in the play—me, my spirit of fun, of play. My dark sense of the absurd took over. For the first time, I thought, *I'm proud of my writing.* The focus of the story remained an ego fight between truth purified in years of torture and resistance and transactional, amoral disregard of facts that might hinder success.

I called Eugen. He said, "Meet me on the bench in Central Park just south of the Eighty-Sixth Street transverse."

I arrived to find him already sitting on the bench. I sat down and looked at this man I had come to love, whose face I had memorized. His breath, as mine, came out in white vapor-condensed feelings and thoughts. He looked at me for a long time.

Then he said, "I think, Layh-ry,"—he always pronounced my name with a long *a* so it came out softer than Lar-ry—"I think it is your mind that is on trial." He looked at me kindly. There was no criticism in his face or voice, nor any commendation. He had given in good faith. I had taken it in good faith. This was the result.

So be it.

We talked a while more. It was clear he couldn't or wouldn't comment further. It was definitely not out of pique, disappointment, or anger of any kind. I think he didn't get what I'd done with his story. But I think he accepted it. It was 1984—not 1949 or 1968.

We remained friends as I tried to find a company, producer, or director to take the play and get it done on stage. People looked at the length, maybe felt the weight, of the manuscript and said, "Thanks, but no."

Eugen died in 1987. Eugen, I'm sorry I let you down. I did the best I could with your story. I love you.

Here is one of the poems inspired by my sons and my thoughts on Eugen's son, Ivan:

> It's not our world
> This world you've made
> It's dark and we're afraid
> We are your clean, blank bits of paper
> We give you back the words you write
> We are your pure, translucent candles
> We are your only source of light.
>
> What you teach us we will learn
> Whether it's to build or burn
> You're the grown-ups—you are wise
> When will you come to realize
> We'll be like you when we're your size?
> How can you tell us to be truthful
> When you tell lies?
> We see that when you kill a man
> He dies.
>
> You murmur peace and love
> In soothing childish tones
> We see hungry, bloody people
> Standing in a pit of bones.

The play is in the trunk reserved for works whose truth has gone no further. It's a heavy trunk. Heavy with love and aspiration, not with failure. It may all be headed to the shredder after I'm gone. I keep these works around as friends who've grown old with me and of whom memories are comforting.

SCENE: New York

On New Year's Eve 1982, Joseph Henry Luckinbill was born by a cesarean section made necessary by an infection. Lucie had done so well with natural birth, and we had paid close attention to all the proper procedures—no drugs, coffee, or alcohol whatsoever. It looked as though Joe would be born normally, but a last-minute infection diagnosis told us it was too risky, so they gave Lucie anesthetic and prepared to do the surgery.

I threw on a surgical gown, mask, cap, and gloves and started into the delivery operating room. Lucie was already asleep. I was stopped by a nurse telling me no can do. She was called to the surgery, and as I had a foot in the door and was determined to be there for Lucie and Joe, I followed her in. No one paid me any attention.

The surgery goes quickly. Everyone knows their skill. I stood by the wall as they cut the small aperture for this large baby. Joe was out and in the world in seconds. The nurse saw me as she held him for his cleanup. I held out my arms, and she handed me this precious package. I talked to him while they cleaned up the room posthaste and then came to take him for ID and tests. I felt so privileged to have held this boy in the immediate absence of his mother.

In the recovery room, they handed Lucie a slip of paper when she awoke. It said, "Congratulations, you have a son!" Yes, but where is he? And then they came in with a hungry baby. I followed the nurses in and saw my son already at lunch.

SCENE: New York

Katharine Desirée Luckinbill was a surprise. We had gotten pregnant after a sea and sky sojourn at the home Lucie's father had built in Baja Sur, California. Now in New York, Lucille was visiting us. We watched some of the movie *The African Queen* starring Katharine Hepburn and Humphrey Bogart. Suddenly, the slow-moving contractions sped up. The baby was on its way. It would be another boy. I made only boys. This would be the fifth.

On January 11, 1985, we raced to the hospital in an icy blizzard, transported in Big Blue, my twelve-passenger van, driven by the wonderful Kieth Dodge, Lucie's assistant, amanuensis, and best friend. Skidding around the icy city streets, I held Lucie, doing her Lamaze breathing, safe in the back.

We entered the hospital at a run. Things were happening fast. We barely got Lucie onto a gurney before it turned into a race to the OR between the baby and the intern and nurse pushing the wagon so fast I had to run to keep up.

The doctor was ready. Lucie was shifted onto the table in a flash. The baby had already crowned. Lucie was doing the big push. I had a camera and was taking pictures at the side.

The doctor said, "Congratulations, you have a baby girl!"

"What?!" I yelled. "Are you *sure*?"

He stepped back. I looked. Oh my God! A *girl*! And what a girl. Everyone in the room was smiling. I couldn't stop, either.

SCENE: Snapshots of Raising Kids

It all passed like a speedboat ride in a choppy sea. Holding on for dear life, buckets of icy water thrown in our faces, wondering if we are seasick or if we would survive the ride. And exhilarating—laughing like loons, leaning into each other, fighting to hold onto our precarious seats, drenched, seeing together the stunning evanescence of sea and sky and each other's faces, happy and so sad that the ride has to end. We drift to a dock, pile into a road, and suddenly they are all off on separate paths. And we two, mother and father, are alone, together again. Alone as we have not been for three decades—actually, as we have never been.

* * *

I remember Nick in the ocean, competing for a title in a boogie board contest. He and the others spread out along the beach, taking their best shots in the big surf coming in. The short boards are deep in the waves as the riders grab the crests and spin in prescribed maneuvers. Nick exits the water. He's wearing a brightly colored wet suit. He's beautifully muscled, in the prime. He sits on the hard sand next to me and breaks down crying. He thinks he didn't do well. I wonder at his spirit. He is a solo competitor, as I was, and wants badly to win a victory over himself. I recognize this trait—it was the way I taught myself to be a man. Losing is heartache, but it doesn't stop you.

He won, received an elusive and brief *Best* in the sport, then moved on to basketball.

Nick graduated from college with a small stipend I saved for him to organize a band. Bands, of course, are the thing. Rock star—it's what young kids see as a way up and out of their circumstances, the same way I saw the theater.

After college, Nick progressed from producing raves in San Diego to owning his own studio in LA and producing his own percussion albums, winning second place in a huge contest against thousands of contestants. He produced rap and rock albums for new and well-known talent who heard of him through the music underground.

Nick was successful. He is now making huge EDM dance parties with Insomniac in connection with Live Nation. He is Executive Producer for Marketing and Art.

* * *

Ben did very well in high school with the children of Hollywood machers. The interesting thing about him is the depth and breadth of his talents. He moves along at his own deliberate pace from one art form to another, creating something extraordinary in each and moving on. He's a scientist searching for a miracle drug that will save the world—or at least engage his full attention until he finds a superior version that delights him. Visual Arts: painting, collage, cartoons (political and other), anime. Music: white rap and percussion. Performance Art: acting, directing, designing (sets, lights, sound). Writing: plays, essays, poetry, song lyrics, graphic novels (story and pictures).

Beyond that, Ben has made a good living as a first-rate bartender—a cocktail wizard and creator of fine liqueurs. He is investigating life and his place in it. Where will he decide to land?

Ben has written a powerful story—*Factory*—that tells the gripping tale of orphaned street kids in New York City at the beginning of the twentieth century. He is a supremely talented man and a hard worker.

* * *

It was Christmas time. Looking for something to do, Joe found an abandoned ukulele in our basement. It had only two strings. He began to improvise. Could anything come of two loose strings on a moldy uke? On that day, Joe surprised us all by playing and singing Christmas songs on this instrument. We had no idea he could do this. He had taught himself the ABCs of music from a book he found with the orphaned gadget.

At the end of high school, Joe suddenly became aware that his future life was his to make. His sister Kate had been offered a place as a student at the Shenandoah Conservatory in Virginia. Joe had nothing in his future. Now, on his own, he made an appointment with the Music Conservatory at Shenandoah.

June 22, 1980. Kingston, New York. Lucie and Larry wedding day.
The clan gathers. L to R Desi Arnaz, Sr., Edie (his wife), my father,
my mother, me, Lucie, Lucy, Desi, Jr. and his then wife, Linda Purl,
Gary Morton (Lucy's husband). Photo Credit: Henry Grossman.

The Luckinbill heirs. L to R: Nick, Joe, Ben, Simon, Kate. Katonah,
New York.

Joe was a beginner. He had never had an instructor. I thought he would be humiliated trying to match himself against students with years of musical study. But he was like a commando on a mission, determined to win.

At Shenandoah, Joe was ushered into a solo rehearsal room. He took his battered guitar out of its well-used case and began to rehearse, bent over so that I couldn't see his face. I walked away, down the hall, and out the door.

An hour passed, and I went back. Joe was in the room with two musicians. They turned and strode toward me fast. Busy, serious men. They stopped in front of me. "Mr. Luckinbill?"

"Yes," I answered.

"He passed. Joe passed our audition," he said.

"Why?" I demanded. My fear, programmed by my disappointments in the harsh world I was used to, blew out of me like a wordless upchuck.

They both simply smiled. The pianist spoke kindly. "Did you know Joe had made his own CD of his compositions? And we played it. It's good stuff. Original." The guy went on. "Joe was able to reproduce a musical line I hummed for him—exactly. On pitch and melody."

The bassist said, "I hummed a complex bass line to him, and he reproduced it exactly, on pitch and in rhythm."

"But," I said, "he's untrained, can't read music, has never had a lesson . . ."

They looked at each other. "What do you think we do here, Mr. Luckinbill?" And they smiled. No blame. Maybe they were used to this crap as teachers.

"Your son is very intuitive. Very talented, Mr. Luckinbill. You're a lucky man." And they walked on, fast. They had more great, meaningful work to do.

Joe finished Shenandoah Conservatory with a degree in commercial music and set out to make his mark in the music world and as a recording engineer.

Now Joe, who calls his music persona Lugenbühl, has many albums to his credit, writing music, lyrics, arrangements, playing, singing, recording, and sound engineering. All solo. He is a musician's musician, all while trying to be the best father to two fascinating young children.

* * *

Kate is a beautiful woman. At seventeen, she was elected Queen of the Apple Blossom Festival in Shenandoah, Virginia. It's a big deal and a tremendous honor. It urges early aplomb and self-possession together with gratitude and humility. One past queen was Luci Baines Johnson, the president's daughter, and that same year, the Grand Marshall of the event had been Kate's famous grandmother. The press events are professional and grueling. The spotlight is on the young woman—too young to have made her own way yet, so there is an ambiguity.

The person being feted is chosen for her progenitor's achievements. The name value is not her own. This has an effect. Fame is often toxic. Certainly, the good people of Shenandoah and Winchester, Virginia, meant no harm, but in America today, the spotlight harms. It puts an onus on the spotlit person and demands of them a grace that must come from great maturity. Kate, "Lucy's granddaughter," was a great queen. She presented herself with sterling elegance and poise. She charmed everyone with decency and decorum.

Kate nurtures a strong need for self-expression. Melody springs from her effortlessly. As a young adult, she made her own way, acting, singing, writing her own one-woman cabaret show, being a party clown and yoga adept, and working solo shifts in a nursery school as the favorite teacher of kids whose parents are the upwardly mobile, career-obsessed big city folks who want their children but find they haven't time for them, so they farm out their raising. The children are often difficult because their radars are so penetrating. They know something is wrong with the picture, but not what. Kate realized this and did all she could to be a surrogate parent.

Now, she has her own child, and he has not fallen between the cracks. Kate has a sought-after career searching out the apex-performing designers for companies like Microsoft, which she suspended for two years to participate fully as a mother to her wonderful son, while balancing her role as curator of licensing for Desilu, too—which manages the estates of her grandparents.

* * *

Simon is curious about life but still searching out its direction and purpose. He went to three colleges to find it, then began a process of self-education. He has done a great job of it, like a young Torah scholar studying religion and philosophy. Right and wrong. *Tikkun Olam*—"Repair the world." Social justice.

He is, like his brother Ben, an autodidact. Both men were in the vanguard of the generation that discovered better education possibilities than the upscale university diploma mill. Both are better schooled than students who have spent millions of their parents' gelt or taken onerous and sometimes fake loans they will spend their lifetime paying off, to be educated to live in a cubicle, bent over a computer, "plowing back their lives into an occupation as ephemeral as making plastic candy for display purposes only." Humbly, I quote myself— irony is not dead yet.

Simon discovered painting, art, in his thirties. He blossomed. His paintings are brilliant, full of mystery, sweetness, and fantastic color. He has found a new mountain to climb and is intent on conquering it.

* * *

Our children, all of them, had various encounters with fame unsought. The ordinary folks admired the grandparents and were envious of those who presumed to have close acquaintance with the most famous woman in the world. Lucie was hit over the head in grade school by—of all people—the nuns, who had caught a dose of the fame clap. They sneered at her, mistakenly accusing her of thinking herself special. Nothing was further from the truth.

Celebrity is a disease—often fatal.

SCENE: Snapshots of Hollywood

I got to work with Charles Bronson in one of his series of hard man detective movies. It was a potboiler, as everyone involved in it knew. But it was great working with Bronson. I was the villain.

In his trailer, Charley told me a very sad story. His wife, Jill Ireland, was fighting the cancer that eventually took her away. He loved her deeply, and he loved his brother, an alcoholic living on Skid Row in Los Angeles. I had enormous respect for Charles Bronson.

* * *

Buddy Ebsen was a marvelous character-lead kind of actor. He treated me to shots of vodka in his trailer between scenes—every scene. I was, of course, the bad guy.

* * *

I was a good guy who turned crazy and tried to kill my wife—Cloris Leachman—in a TV movie. I didn't get away with it. But she tried to screw up my close-up by reaching into the shot and removing my glasses. She didn't get away with it, either.

* * *

I was Mary Tyler Moore's TV boyfriend very briefly. My TV son didn't like her pizza. Neither did I.

* * *

With Shirley Jones, I was a perfect, long-suffering husband who endured her gambling habit. Who couldn't like Shirley?

* * *

I had the good karma to be invited to appear on Angela Lansbury's long running show, *Murder She Wrote*, four times. I was a bad guy twice and a police detective twice. I could have arrested myself.

Angela was a class act. She had proven herself in every medium of theater, movies, and television. She was a charming and genuine actress with a great comic sense, a singer, a dancer, and a serious artist. I always tried to give depth, intelligence, and sincerity to an outing made so thoroughly pleasurable because of Angela.

She loved actors and acting. Working with her was an acting lesson. To maintain a character and deepen it, playing a formula detective show over many years, is challenging. To deepen the work, you need good writers. To hold on to your character, you can't let down. You must keep asking questions of motivation and factual sense. Angela did that.

She required hip replacement surgery toward the end of the show's run, but she returned to her show and to Broadway. Some performers never let you down.

* * *

Tom Cruise is another class act. I joined the cast of *Cocktail* at the film's first—and only—rehearsal in New York. My part as the girl's father was four intense scenes with my daughter and the boy—Tom—she was in love with, a mere bartender. When the company moved to Toronto to shoot, my part was cut to two scenes. Then to one. That was okay. My character was intended as an obstacle for the boy to overcome. The one scene left was enough for the story. I understood. I played it very strongly. I was a real obstacle. Tom was impressive in his determination to get all he could out of his part.

When I got to the set on the first day, the makeup trailer was already rocking, at 6:00 A.M., very loud music. I needed no makeup, so I waited. Suddenly, the drape separating the room was swept wide. Out came Tom, ready for action. He said in an urgent and dead-serious voice, "I've got a movie to make!" and vanished to the set.

I had to laugh. I understood the passion, if not the expression of it. Between takes on the set, he jumped rope furiously to stay pumped. Whatever it took, he was up for it.

I was paid a good chunk of dough for my one appearance and, unbelievably, the residuals kept coming in at full force until I had made five times my initial fee. Tom is so popular worldwide that he creates a downstream money flow. If anyone deserves Hollywood stardom, it's Tom Cruise. Thanks, Disney. Thanks, Tom.

* * *

I stepped into a TV pilot at the last minute because the producer contacted me when they fired the first guy. The show was with Jonathan Winters and Randy Quaid, and I played Randy's boss, the principal of the school where he taught.

After one scene, I was in the dressing room and heard the loudspeaker: "Actors to the rail!"

A command from Big Brother? I didn't have a clue what it meant. What rail? Why the command?

The other actors were scurrying out of the dressing area, so I stopped one. "What's going on?"

"Show notes. The suits," one yelled over his should while he ran. "Everybody!"

I had never been summoned like that. I didn't go. Finally, the AD came around, knocked, and said politely, "Larry? They're giving notes on your scene."

"Who?" I asked.

"Well, uh, the network execs."

"What? Since when? I like notes—from the director. Not from business-men with MBAs from Harvard."

"Well, it would make my job easier if you . . ." He trailed off.

I saw his problem and was furious. "They come down on you?"

"Well, yeah . . ."

It was a dilemma I didn't want. I was a cooperative actor. One director told me, "You are the most obedient actor I've worked with." I wanted to say, "You should be around when I work on a play. You'd not say that!"

And now, here was this poor guy standing in front of me asking me to help him perpetuate a system in which "actors to the rail" was reasonable.

I didn't argue.

So, this was my moment at the rail. I didn't light the firecracker. The suits needed to be forgiven for trying to keep their jobs by putting in their two cents. I stood at the rail listening to useless blather from decent, well-educated lawyers and accountants who tried to explain to actors how to do their jobs. I knew they, too, were knuckling to others who knew even less about the art of comedy than they, but who had the "arrogance of power" and the need to use it to justify themselves.

It's the world we've knuckled to that's nuts.

Me. Hollywood. Older.
My "Trustworthy Doctor, Judge or
President" headshot.

The real me.
Photo credit: Lucie Arnaz.

One of the many memorable photos taken over the years by our friend, the remarkable, Marc Raboy.

SCENE: *Star Trek V*

I drove up to the Paramount Studios gate right on time. I was expecting to be waved onto the lot, find a parking space, and walk to the appointment in whatever bungalow office it was. A golf cart glided up to me as I went through the gate. The driver said, "Mr. Luckinbill, please come with me. We will park your car for you and bring the keys to you in Mr. Bennett's office."

This was highly unusual for me. The standard operating procedure for an audition was to find the right office, get the sides (miniaturized copies of scenes), study them, wait in the anteroom, take your turn in the line of actors, and, when called, go inside, say a quick hello to the casting folks, read the part, and be politely shown the door. Almost ten times out of ten that would be the scenario.

The auditions for movies were almost perfunctory. The directors knew who they wanted, but per Screen Actors Guild rules, they saw a bunch of actors from stars to well-knowns to long shots with aggressive agents. I was well-known enough to get a few minutes of chitchat and maybe a director's comments about what he or she was looking for, but they had the essential parts cast before the wannabe folks showed up.

I was ushered into an office, and, to my complete surprise, Harve Bennett, the writer and producer, and Bill Shatner, the director and star, got up from their chairs and walked to meet me. We shook hands all around, and I sat down in the circle of deciders facing me. There were no sides, no script to read from. I thought, *Ah, they just want a look at me to see if they even want to make an appointment for me to read.*

I knew almost nothing about *Star Trek* except that its existence was credited to my mother-in-law's defense of it. After their 1960 divorce, Desi and Lucy ran Desilu together for a time, but in 1962, she bought Desi out of his share of the studio and became its sole owner and CEO. As the reluctant "most powerful woman of television," she needed to produce product. Gene Roddenberry brought the pilot idea for *Star Trek* to Desilu to produce, hoping CBS would buy it. CBS passed—too expensive, and sci-fi was too far out. Roddenberry took it to NBC. Lucy thought the show was about a traveling USO show, but Roddenberry nailed the action-adventure-entertainment pitch with six words: "a *Wagon Train* to the stars." Brilliant.

The Board of Directors at Desilu also thought the show would be too expensive, but Lucy overruled them and agreed to produce a pilot, which failed. A second pilot, "Where No Man Has Gone Before," was written, and because Lucille Ball had gone where no woman in Hollywood had gone before, she took financial responsibility in a very bold move, following her superb show business and entertainment intuition, informed by decades of struggle up from nowhere. The pilot succeeded in getting on the air.

And there I was, sitting in front of the inheritors of that decision, waiting for them to say, "Well, thanks for coming in, Larry. We'll be in touch after we see a few other people for this role." And if that were all there was, I'd be disappointed and sad, but I'd swallow it and go over to Nickodell and grab breakfast, saying, "So long."

Harve Bennett, a lovely and tough old-timer, said, "We are very glad to meet you. Bill thought we should."

And Shatner said, "I saw your *Lyndon Johnson* on PBS one night in some hotel room, and I thought you were very impressive. I want you to play Sybok for me."

Bennett said, "Sybok is Spock's brother. He is the other half, the human half. Spock is reason, Sybok is emotion."

"He's an evangelist, a radical who has the power to heal," Shatner said. "I loved the passion you showed me in *Lyndon*. I want you to read the script."

"Sybok steals the *Enterprise* and takes the ship to a planet beyond the Great Barrier, where he believes God lives," said Bennett.

Shatner said, "God has told him to do this. He's a believer, a pirate, a cult leader—a bandit and a healer."

Bennett must have seen the light come into my eyes. He said, "Sybok is a hero and a villain."

"We'll send you home with a script," Shatner said. "I—we—want you to play this part."

And we all shook hands again.

"Read it," Bennett said. "If you want it, let us know tomorrow. Welcome to *Star Trek*."

I read the script. The Sybok story was powerful. I thought I could give the character an inner life, a subtext to help an audience—even the old *Star Trek* cast and their fans—believe in Sybok's quest.

The next morning, I made the call. I said I was very excited to do it. I was in!

SCENE: Preparation

I called Tom Cruise's office and told him I would like to take him up on his offer to use his trainer to prepare myself for filming *Star Trek*. I got word back that the trainer, David, would call me. David was an Oklahoma man who had played for the great Oklahoma Sooners team. I hired him to get me into the best shape of my life. I was fifty-four years old and was already in pretty decent shape. I had never stopped running, swimming, lifting weights, and doing isometrics since Jack LaLanne had changed my physiognomy years before. I looked younger than I was, which never meant anything to me. I had a malleable pudding face that always looked youngish. If I got my weight down to 175 or less, my face found a few planes, bones, and angles that looked more like the leading men I had admired in the movies I grew up wanting to be like. David worked me over. He was a gentle tyrant. I could see how he had gotten Tom into such great shape and kept him there. Tom was obsessive about exercise. I don't think it was vanity as much as a way of life. If you want to be a star, fulfill the requirements.

David showed up at my house in Brentwood (formerly Robert De Niro's house), and we went to the gym and sauna Robert had built in the garage to prepare for the film *Raging Bull*. The speed bag was still there. When we bought the house from his ex-wife, I had put new equipment in the space and used it daily. But with David, the gym was only the first part of the regimen. I did push-ups, sit-ups, and yoga stretches and used the weights for an hour. Then we went to the pool. It was already late September and chilly. I pulled on a wet suit top and did another forty-five minutes of water exercises in the deep end. Then we drove out on Sunset to Will Rogers Park in Pacific Palisades. I ran the polo field with David—two miles—then we went straight uphill a mile, came down, stretched, and headed home. A three-hour workout. I did this every day until the film started shooting.

The next day, I drove forty-five minutes to Trancas, a beach near Malibu, to ride a horse. Shatner is a horse lover and dressage trainer. Sybok's entrance in the movie was to be me riding from far out in the desert on an alien planet, through distorting, mirage-like desert heat waves, toward a starving denizen of the planet, racing mysteriously, ominously at him. Jerry Goldstein's great music would cue the audience that it would be explosive when the rider reached the man now fumbling with his rock gun—don't ask, there always has to be a gun.

I rode around in a circle for two hours. My horse jumped over a stick on the ground. Hi-Yo, Silver!

Cut to me, Sybok, in hood and robes and Vulcan ears, getting off the horse, walking toward the alien, putting my hand on his head gently, and "taking away his pain." Great scene. I was making a convert in my quest to build an army to go to God. First convert, then steal a starship, then cross the uncrossable Great Barrier and say hi to God. Piece of cake. With faith, all things are possible.

I loved everything about Sybok. I was ready when Bill invited me to have a meal and discuss the role. The "meal" occurred at a stand-up table outside a juice bar at 7:30 A.M., us sipping smoothies. Hollywood. In New York, that would have been a dark bar in the theater district, dim with cigarette smoke, and crowded with theater folk contemplating shots of Irish whiskey with feet up on the brass rail.

Shatner: How do you see Sybok?

Me: He's Lenin. Not John—Vladimir Ilyich.

Shatner (squinting): Really?

Me: Yes. Here's why: Lenin started out to make the revolution in Russia for the right reasons—to restore justice to the people after the abuses of the Czars. But he got twisted somehow and ended up becoming a dangerous tyrant. That's the potential arc for Sybok—best of intentions, bad outcome. He resorts to threats and theft but ultimately can't avoid violence, although I believe he is a compassionate Vulcan who will never use weapons himself.

Shatner: But there's the scene where we fight and you have a rock gun.

Me: I would like to fix that. Sybok is Spock's brother. He's basically good. He wants his revolution to succeed without violence. But he's human, too.

Shatner: He doesn't succeed in that.

Me: Yes, but if the audience loves him, he will make the story better, don't you think?

Shatner: Interesting, very interesting. I like your ideas—it's why I wanted you. But Lenin . . . we just don't mention it, you know. We're not making "I Love a Commie" here, so we'll see.

That was our last conversation until Bill called, "That's a wrap!" about ten weeks later.

I played Sybok with that subtext. No one knew. So, his disappointment with himself and the God he conjured up at the end is more poignant. It makes his love for his brother all the more moving. And Leonard Nimoy came through on that. It was our good moment together.

I loved all the guys, especially DeForest Kelley. He was ill with the disease that would take him to heaven, but he never once complained. A brave man. Southern, like me. We shared that. After our big scene, he took me aside and said, "You are going to get an Academy Award someday."

I was stunned. I did not think in those terms, ever. But DeForest saw something in me and wanted me to believe in myself. He and George Takei were my special connections. George had a wild, loud laugh and thought I was funny. Shatner, working a scene, offered to throw him off the set if he laughed again. And that set off another cackle. DeForest would only smile at our tomfoolery.

S C E N E : Search for God

The dark before the dawn. The atmosphere was thick, an embalming sheet wrapped around my face. As we descended into the suffocating caldron below, I chanced uttering a few words in my language in the direction of the alien. I sensed he understood me, but I got only a perfunctory grunt in return. Maybe he knows of my intent to take over his planet to wipe away all the misery of these poor creatures trying to survive in an inhospitable biome that could clearly support only little life as we knew it then. Only the predatory birds circling above gave any hint of life. An indomitable sun was just below the horizon, presaging the pink and orange dawn of another empty, hungry day like the millions before it since the birth of this universe. In the age just past, life had gotten worse for the doomed inhabitants of this god-mocked, unfortunate place. I will now conquer them with love. I will take away their pain. They will follow me in my quest to find the true God.

The alien and I descend from the great vehicle that has transported us to the desolate place—his home, and my chosen place to begin my benign conquest for the good of the universe.

The fire planet rose like a rocket, burning all things beneath it. I was struck by its heat as if by a meteorite traveling from the back of beyond. I looked at the horizon. The reflection of gigantic volcanic peaks in the waters of a soda-saline lake lay before me, still as death itself. Closer were strange, towering structures rising from the lake, wet, sand-dribbled castles made by giants. In the harsh light of another day in this hellish landscape, even the birds suddenly stopped in flight, folded their wings, and sat like avian statues.

Silence . . .

At the side of the vehicle, the alien poured out the bitter coffee from his Styrofoam cup. It sizzled in the already overheated alkali dust at his feet.

I said, "See you on the set."

He said, "Yup," and walked away.

S C E N E : Mono Lake, California

The Paramount Studios van did a U-ey and headed back up the hill to pick up the next cadre of actors. I looked up the hill. The line of horse trailers was maybe a mile long. I saw people gathered around the camera in the distance. Tethered next to them was a horse. A blue horse!

Bill Shatner was giving instructions to the camera crew for the first shot of the film, soon to be *Star Trek V: The Final Frontier.*

I walked up to the group and said a cheery hello. Bill looked up. I found out later that he was under enormous pressure at the studio. They had drastically cut production work time for our film and given the time to the new *Batman* movie that everyone was excited about. This was Bill's first film directing job, and he was overwhelmed. Just seeing all the horse and equipment trailers overwhelmed me. This was a big, important movie for the *Star Trek* franchise. That the Paramount brass had undercut prep time was enough to give a director the willies, and to think his work had been given second-class status must have been a knife in his back.

Bill has always had a healthy ego, shall we say. I thought he wore it well, although I was at the point in my life when I was beginning to believe that my own ego was a hindrance and a distraction. I still followed it like Little Bo-Peep's sheep, but now I was aware of it. I liked Bill very much, and I saw beyond his own self-regard.

But at that moment, he snapped. "No more motivation talk!"

I laughed. I hadn't come here to get motivated. I was ready to fulfill Sybok with every bit of power I saw in him.

Bill backed off. "Good morning," he said. "You're in the first shot. You're going to ride in from the desert, long shot. We'll stay on you all the way. There's a sandbag out there"—he pointed—"which is your mark to pull up. We've already tried the shot, and it's good. Get into wardrobe and get aboard."

The wrangler held the blue horse's bridle. I put a tentative hand on the horse's nose. "Let's be friends" was the idea. The horse shook her head and pulled away with a jerk. "Hah!" I said. *Hates me already*, I thought. I hate riding. I don't like horses, and they return the favor.

The wrangler patted the horse's nose. He said, "She's just a little POed with us. She doesn't like being blue."

"Who does?" I said.

"Her name's Dolly," he said. "Wouldn't hurt a flea. Give her another little pat."

I reached out and touched her neck. She shied away like a debutante with a full dance card.

I was fully kitted up in Sybok drag with a makeup invented and glued on by one of Jack Dawn's longtime Hollywood genius family of artists, with a splendid set of flesh-colored Vulcan ears, a full head of disheveled hair, and my own rich beard.

I sat on Dolly, holding the reins gingerly. The wrangler, also on a horse, led me and Dolly out to the start mark for the shot. I was to ride in at an easy canter à la Omar Sharif's entrance in *Lawrence of Arabia*.

I was very uneasy. The wrangler turned his horse in a jump and rode back at a beautiful gallop, just like in all the cowboy movies I'd ever seen. "Well, hello, Dolly," I said to my equine friend who wouldn't hurt a fly. "You're a professional movie horse. You'll know what to do, like canter, right?"

The horn sounded. Not like at a foxhunt, which is a nice sound. No, this was a raucous, unmusical cross between the protestation of a steer being led to the slaughter and the warning alarm of a sudden gas line break in a factory.

Dolly lurched forward in an uneven half walk, half hurry-up gait. I was swaying side to side and up and down. "Canter, Dolly," I said. She didn't.

What to do? What was my strange inability to love these great, (generally) peaceful beasts that serve man so dutifully?

We were now waddling toward our distant goal. Ahead was an alien farmer scrabbling with a stick in the poisonous dust of this alien planet. At this pace, it would take us about a half hour to get to that farmer.

I nudged Dolly a little, rocking in my seat. She strode forward cow-fully. How the hell do I get his thing to go faster? I wondered.

Then I did something obvious that I didn't like doing—I kicked her in her sides. She woke up with the irritation of someone who had just gotten to sleep and said, "Wha'? Huh? What ya want?"

I kicked again, and she began to move. We shifted gears like my aunt's antique '39 Chevy—with a juddering clutch slip in the wrong gear.

I couldn't blame my ride. I woke up that way often and forgot where I was for a bit. Dolly's dreams were being rudely interrupted. But, as long as I kicked a bit and said, "Come on, girl!" she kept moving. She transitioned to what I guess was a trot. I was bouncing up and down. I remembered posting, a trick riders use to ease the bouncing both for their own and their steed's sakes, and got into the rhythm.

This was not the mastery of the Arabian camel that Sharif had exhibited in his movie.

We got to the mark and the farmer. Bill yelled faintly, "Cut, medium shot!"

The crew trundled all the equipment to where we stood. Bill was exasperated. "Did you do those riding lessons I asked you to?"

Yes, I had. Religiously. And I forgot them as easily as one forgets prayers after church.

He said, "Okay, Larry, get down from the horse and walk to the farmer. Let's get that, fellas."

"I am boldly going where no Luckinbill has ever gone before."

"I *am* Sybok!"

Sybok, the human side.

I knew he wasn't happy about the somewhat casual ride in. Neither was I. Dolly seemed unfazed by Bill's mood. She was an old hand at dealing with showbiz folk. I admired her.

As I approached, the alien farmer grabbed his strange weapon and fumbled to load it. It was an invention of the prop department, a gun that shot rocks as ammo, powered by an unseen force. Why not? Mono Lake had trillions of them. I came close, reached out, placed my open hand on his forehead, and said my first words of the story, "Let me take your pain."

His face changed from fear and agitation to an expression of incredible, unbelieving gratitude. He sank to his knees and converted instantly—the first of my followers.

This was the alien I had ridden with in the van. Then, I had thought he was just surly and uncommunicative, but now I realized he was an excellent actor. He was in character in the van while I was also pondering mine.

I had, by then, done a score or more films, feature and television. But all of a sudden, I found myself fitting in in a new way. I began to be the Sybok obsessed with helping others. My own fears flew away and have never returned. I was free and flying in *Star Trek*!

Later, I found out Bill had reshot the entry scene. Unrecognizable at a distance, he had worn my large riding cape and ridden in through the heat waves rising from the prehistoric landscape that was left of ancient Mono Lake. In the finished film, it was Bill, a superbly skilled rider, on dear old Dolly. *Good,* I thought. He makes me look good!

I also noted he had dubbed one of my lines. It sounded almost like me, but he wanted a different line reading. Okay. Why didn't he just tell me? This is what I hate about movies. Your work is messed with in every direction. Sometimes, even for the better. And . . . amen!

I came to *Star Trek* not knowing anything about it or its fans, who have distinct rankings for all the iterations of the marvelous old stories, and they had strong opinions about the actors who inhabited them. They liked Sybok. I became a fan of Gene Roddenberry's original mind and spirit.

I was invited to two *Star Trek* conventions. I went to the first one to see what they were about. It was in New Jersey. I drove there with one of my children and arrived early in the morning. The hotel was in the middle of highway interchanges—easy on, easy off. The cold morning mist was rising and surrounded the hotel, which looked sort of like a UFO disk vibrating for liftoff. We walked into a strange lobby full of strange people garbed like characters in the *Star Trek* films.

I was asked to make a little speech at this convention, and I described the hotel in the mist outside and wondered if the aliens assembled there were prepared for the takeoff. They didn't get it. Was I making fun of them? I made my amends and left, thinking, this is too strange—absent a sense of humor.

Next I was offered to do a meeting in Las Vegas. My reticence had made Sybok a sort of Garbo figure, famous for my absence. But I didn't "vant to be alone" because by then I had met so many great people who loved *Star Trek* and Sybok.

This convention was much more structured. My visit was planned to the minute. I would appear at a Sybok costume contest, give a talk on stage for the five hundred participants, and then sign almost as many photos and mementos.

At the costume contest, a guy walked out, tall, full head of disheveled hair, and a full beard. He was as tall as me but thinner and wore his Sybok costume very well. He modeled the outfit to applause and walked over to me. We stood side by side, and I said, "You look better than I ever did. This is a great costume you put together!"

He said, "It's your costume. I bought it from the costume warehouse."

There was an ovation for both of us. So far, so good. That afternoon, I went down to get a bite to eat at the lobby diner and sat at the counter next to a young woman. She was wearing a sort of red top garment and black trousers. She was very friendly and attractive. We talked a bit, and I asked her what she did in life. She said, "I teach astrophysics at Harvard."

"Wow," I said. "What are you doing here?"

She said, "I'm here for the convention," and smiled. "I know you're Sybok."

She stood up to pay her check, and I saw that her black and red outfit was that of a *Star Trek* officer of the *Enterprise*. Amazing! The idea of what human-kind might find in exploring the universe and the moral and ethical issues that might create for our civilization to deal with—Roddenberry's invention—was now an iconic part of American entertainment history, and this young person was the proof.

I sat at a table with a handler. People of every description eagerly brought me a photo or artifact to sign. As always, I spoke with each one and asked them questions. I love to make conversation and really find out something about every stranger I meet. The people were surprised at my friendliness and responded in kind. This made my handlers very nervous. Apparently there was a time problem. The older I get, the less time is a problem for me.

I was friendly to all five hundred fans and came away with a new and genuine respect for their warmth, intelligence, and knowledge of themselves and why *Star Trek* is important. Some folks offered me stacks and reams of material to sign. I would have, but Mr. Handler said sternly, "No—only one piece allowed!"

I got that conventions are a business built around fans' desires. When I arrived, I had been given a check in the amount my agent had negotiated. I discovered that the old favorites, Kirk, Spock, and Bones, were paid enormous sums to participate. I was not, but I didn't care. They could have had my signature for nothing. The way I see it, Sybok was a missionary from space. He took the pain of life away for nothing. Sybok was a free Vulcan and a free human man. I, too, was trying to become a free man who could take away pain from those I loved.

Star Trek allowed me to explore real madness, and I learned to think like an alien on camera. That is, to think and act as if walking and chewing gum or rubbing my belly and patting my head at the same time were normal. The essence of good movie acting is thinking—being—as in life, but at the same time thinking only as your character, whether you're speaking, doing complicated business, or in full action. But especially in your close-ups, where the camera eye meshes exactly with the audience's eyes and sees into you, you have nailed it if you can think, actually think, not act-thinking.

I nailed many scenes in *Star Trek*, especially one in which DeForest accepts my offer to take his pain and when Kirk says to me, "You are mad." And I answer, "Am I? We'll see." I was Sybok then, not Larry in any way. And I nailed it.

* * *

Star Trek V and *The Boys in the Band* are the only two of my movies I can watch, and I've made twenty-six movies and a myriad of TV episodes and theater plays. In the theater, I was in charge. No one would yell *Cut!* to stop the action and then edit out my best moments from the final story. In the theater, you sink into the character and sustain it until the final curtain. The character you create is yours. First learn to act in the theater, then try movies. The thinking is the same. The difference is instead of luring a thousand sets of eyes to your story's truth, you are encountering only one eye, the camera. The camera is also an audience. It's a friend willing to believe you—if you believe.

SCENE: The Last Picture Show

I'm sitting before the director of a big-time blockbuster action-adventure film. I have a bit of heat from my last movie. I've had some good parts in five Hollywood features up to now, and the one I just finished is an action-adventure sci-fi in which I was the costar. Word of mouth about my performance is good and from credible sources. I probably have a good shot at moving a little higher up the ladder. "This new one will be *huge*." But I've read it. It's *The Perils of Pauline* redux, brought up-to-date by Freud, Mickey Spillane, de Sade, Masoch, Batman, and Spiderman.

The director wastes no time. "What did you think of the role we sent you to look at?"

Suddenly, a quandary. I have to jump on this, so I tell him, "I love it. The guy is fantastic. The story is great. I know everything you've done, and I love your work. I'd be lucky to get to do my best stuff for you."

But I don't say any of that. I'm here because my agent thinks this is the next step up the Hollywood ladder for me.

I'm regretting being here now. I've been uneasy for weeks for many reasons. Mainly a growing discomfort with living in this untethered place where my children are learning the wrong stuff—that things are more important than people, status is what counts—and my own certainty that violence in entertainment is getting worse, and by acting it, I endorse it. And I hated that my children would come to believe that it was okay.

I want to do honest pictures about real people.

I realize now that I should not be here and that I'm here for the weakest of wrong reasons: I want to please my agent. That's pathetic. And I forgot my kids. That's terrible. Our kids should go to public schools where they'll be with normal kids and ordinary families. I had a lot to learn yet.

I fumble an answer to the director. I stupidly imagine I can propose that he change the role to something less fun-psychotic, to something I could feel was acceptable.

I come up with, "I transform my roles . . . I'm a transformer."

This weak nonsense causes confusion at first, then his eyes glaze over with ice. The room grows instantly cold, extinguishing any "heat" I may have brought in with me.

"Interesting," he says. "Thanks for coming in." Suddenly discovering he has work to do, he stands and calls to his secretary.

I make my way back to the parking lot and my circa 1972 Ford Maverick. The Green Bean, my kids called it. No air, roll-down windows, six cylinders. As I drive off the lot, I feel something strange. My feet weren't hitting the ground! I wasn't trudging home a failure, I was walking on air. Not quite flying, but definitely off the ground. No cape for full liftoff, but Captain Marvel was close by, grinning his goofy grin. I was free!

I heard the voice of Jo Davidson (Gordon's dad), his sweet, leprechaun's voice saying, "*Kvell*, Larry. Happiness is here, all around you. It's yours, son."

Hooray! I would never again play senselessly murderous villains. I had just taken flight far from *The Perils of Pauline*.

If you want to make movies or theater you like and believe in, find or write those stories and make them yourself.

SCENE: GREAT AMERICANS

Lyndon Johnson, President of the United States

Christmastime 1986. I was given a gift. It came at a low point in my working life and coincided with the holy holiday. It scared the heck out of me. It was a major challenge to stand up to my dream and become a hero to myself.

I was given a karmic call to move beyond my myopic focus on the next job, the next character—the "careen" wheel I was on—and return to the simple belief I had in the parables I was taught as a seven-year-old innocent: "With faith all things are possible."

Carl Jung wrote, "Synchronicity: An incident of spiritual significance that asks us to dampen our self-obsession and consider the possibility of the divine." My inner world had found a way to communicate with my outer world.

Lucie and I were in our Just Arluck Productions office in the Actors' Equity building on Forty-Sixth Street in New York City. It was cold, gloomy. Trying to snow. I was staring through the grimy steam rising from the street and obscuring the rooftop of the next building, thinking about our five children and Christmas and money.

I was unemployed. The phone wasn't ringing. I was having one of those low-grade anxiety attacks that all actors have when they have been unengaged for a few months, weeks, or days. I had just finished a Tony-worthy rant to Lucie about "the business" and how terrible it was. How I couldn't take it anymore. And this was it. *It!* I am quitting acting! I don't want to be an actor anymore. I'm done!

The phone rang. It was David Susskind, a brilliant producer and friend who had always understood and supported me. Out of the blue, he informed me that I would play Lyndon Johnson for him in a one-man show for a public television production to be shot in Canada. The script was on its way by messenger. I should read it, say yes, and make plans to be in Toronto over Christmas and New Year's.

I was stunned. "Who else is in it?" I asked, as if that made any difference.

"No one else, just you. It's a one-man show."

My mind raced. The start date was a week away. It was crazy. "Who dropped out?" I asked.

"None of your fucking business. It's you. You're Lyndon. Read the script!" Click. Dial tone.

A messenger banged on the door. A script was dropped on my desk—a draft of a teleplay titled *Lyndon* written by my friend, James Prideaux. I opened the script. It was sixty-nine pages long, single-spaced. Lyndon talking directly to us, whoever we are. I read a few pages and thought, *No! I can't do it.* Sixty-nine pages? Single-spaced! Thousands of words. Why would anyone want to take that on? Start in a week? No! I can't!

I put the script on Lucie's desk. "Read some of this monster, will you?"

Ten minutes later, she dropped the script back on my desk. She said, "If you don't do this, then I guess you really *don't* want to be an actor anymore."

I read some more. Sixty-nine pages of dialogue. Alone in front of a camera. Starting next week. Lyndon Johnson—a gigantic, iconic figure still huge in the public consciousness decades after his presidency ended. Still blamed and hated by a large percentage of Americans for our involvement in the Vietnam War. I was terrified.

I called Susskind and turned it down.

"Why?" he asked. "You're unemployed, aren't you?"

I yelled at him "I'm not six-foot-five, I'm not some corrupt Southern pol, and I'm *not* from goddamned Texas!"

"Aren't you from Arkansas?" he asked mildly.

"Yes, but it's not the same thing. And Johnson? I demonstrated against him in '68. I stood with thousands in front of the Capitol Building and tried to levitate it. I hated Lyndon Johnson!"

A pause. Then David said, "Larry, that will change."

I said, "I'm headed to your office right now to sit knee to knee with you and prove I'm not right for this part."

He said, "Come!"

I went. Jean Kennedy, his wonderful associate, let me in. "He's waiting for you inside. We're *so* glad you're going to do this." And she smiled mischievously.

Inside, I pulled a chair up, sat knee to knee in front of David, and began to read aloud to him.

An amazing thing happened.

As I spoke Lyndon's words, I heard my father's voice coming through mine. His Oklahoma/Texas intonations came softly first, then stronger. As I spoke, he spoke, and I heard that hardscrabble lonesome cowboy sound coming back to my mouth and into my heart. That Bible-inflected and informed way of talking that poured weight and strength onto the simplest words. And I remembered my deeply conflicted relationship with my father. A tear or two came. Slowly I stopped talking and just looked at David.

He smiled at me. The kind smile that hides a hint of the old fox inside.

And Br'er Rabbit came out of the briar patch and said, "Yes."

That *yes* unlocked the door and, eventually, each in their own time, four great Americans came to visit and stayed to remake me.

SCENE: Toronto, Canada

Lyndon on PBS was made in an incredibly short time. It was an unlikely show with a man a majority of Americans professed to hate talking to his audience for two hours, unstopped and unstoppable. A show critical not only of the American military and the military-industrial complex but also of its sway over political decisions. It was underwritten—paid for—by General Dynamics, a prominent member of that complex, and by public television, dependent for its license on the beneficence of the government being challenged.

It got made despite the principal and only actor, me, who from the beginning was reluctant and fearful to take this challenge, not knowing where it would end. For me, it was a road never traveled.

It got made with new and untested makeup techniques and materials that could transform my face and still feel and work like my own flesh. Each day required a five-hour session.

It got made in just a few days. Days that began at 3:30 A.M. and ended at 10:30 P.M. But there was no fatigue, just exhilaration and endless patience for me, the makeup and camera crews, and the director, Charles Jarrott, Golden Globe winner for *Anne of the Thousand Days*.

David always pushed for more speed and more truth. Charles and I were rehearsing in an empty dance studio in Michael Bennett's theater workplace at 890 Broadway in New York, just the two of us, me talking, walking through the set (then just white, bare tape on the floor), as Charley walked backward in front of me as the cameraman would be doing. We would be shooting the show in Toronto in only one more week.

I had researched Lyndon for days at the Paley Center, listening to recordings and looking at film. In rehearsal, I learned that a two-hour solo show can be no more than forty-two pages max. David and I both realized that the script was far too long for the PBS television show we were prepping. He told me, "Cut it yourself." As we got deeper into it, I knew that the opening and closing scenes needed to be rediscovered. He said, "Do it." I went to the source, Merle Miller's book of Lyndon's own words, and found humor and a fuller ending. I edited it down to forty-two pages.

* * *

David came into the studio and sat on a bench against the wall to watch. After a while, I saw that he was getting agitated and antsy, so, I stopped.

"What's wrong, David?" I asked.

He screwed up his face and burst out, "Lyndon would *eat this room!*"

Charley looked at me. I looked at him. I said to David mildly, "You want it bigger?"

David sat back, said nothing. Charley and I started again, and this time, I let the spirit seize me. Lines be damned, I'll make it up! I ate the fucking room! I roared, sped up, and moved at Charley—the camera—so fast that he stumbled backward, but we kept going. We finished the scene.

David said, "Let me tell you my story. Other producers and I were in the hall outside the Oval Office. We were waiting to see the president on some errand for our business. Suddenly, the Oval Office door was flung open and banged against the wall. Lyndon came out so fast we couldn't get out of his way. He shoved me so hard that I slammed against the wall, but he didn't notice. I don't think he saw us. He saw his objective—something he was after, had to fix, to solve, something urgent—and he just blew past us. And down the hall, he started roaring, like you were just now."

"So, have I got it?" I asked.

He sat back, breathed, and said very quietly, "You've got it."

The next day they brought in a makeup man, a kid they found in some theater. They told me we were going to do a makeup test. I said no. I told David I could inhabit Lyndon Johnson now. I could make my face his.

He said, "I believe you could, Larry, but I want you to sit down and let this guy do his stuff. Give it a try."

I sat for four hours. When the guy was done, they turned the chair around to face the mirror.

I saw Lyndon Johnson.

I stood up. I felt six feet, five inches tall. (I am six foot one.)

Something, I believe, entered me then. Something, or someone, whispered to me. Maybe it was the God of All the Arts giving me a glimpse of heavenly life, saying, *you can do this, you can be someone you're not—a hero.* And shazam! I knew I could be Lyndon.

I learned a lesson that day and every day since. You have to have faith. And then you have to walk on water. And so, the collaboration began, one that changed my working life and my soul. Forever.

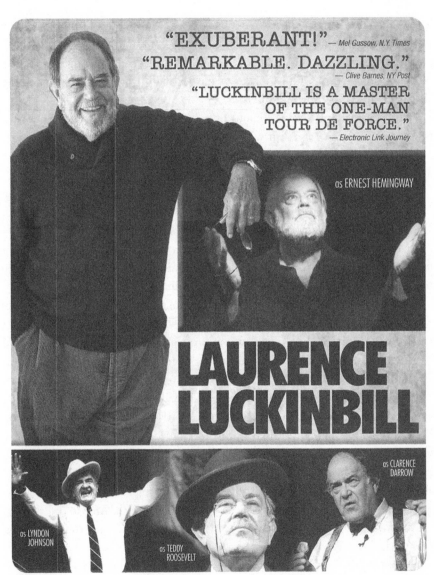

"If you want to make movies or theater you like and believe in, find or write those stories and make them yourself." —Laurence Luckinbill

S C E N E : New York

The *Lyndon* production company returned to New York after filming the show in a Toronto television studio. I was invited to see a rough cut. David Susskind reminded me it was rough and not to be commented on. I knew that, of course. Nothing can destroy a film quicker or nastier than hearing backstage sniping about it before it is shown publicly.

Still, I asked Susskind if I could invite my mother to see it, as she was in town from Arkansas for a visit with us. He was dubious.

I said, "David, the only person my mother knows in show business is me. She likes me, so she will like *Lyndon*." He said okay.

We sat in a small viewing room in his offices on Madison Avenue. After the film ran, David turned the lights back on and looked at my mother. He asked, "How did you like your boy's performance, Mrs. Luckinbill?"

My mother, as always, gave the question serious thought. Then she said, "I liked him fine, Mr. Susskind. I think your wonderful show tells how very, very hard it is to be president. I hope all schoolchildren will see it."

David smiled like the cat that ate the cream. He had done good work. He was proud of the work, of me, and of himself. He had delivered. Then he did an amazing thing: He began to dance a hora, arms up, stepping sideways, and singing, "We're going to win an Emmy, we're going to win an Emmy!" It was astounding. His emotion was real, and it was pure delight, pure joy.

I saw then his greatness and how he had made his reputation for wheeling and dealing and making shows that were essentially artifacts of social justice. He had done his share of ordinary stuff, too, but he never quit trying to make something of importance, and this film was that. I was proud of my mother, too. She was not someone awed by reputation or eminence. She was herself, always. She accepted all people as they came, as people. Her answer to David's question was from the heart, and he knew it. He had faith. And so did she.

Unfortunately, David never knew what a success it was. He died just a few months later at age sixty-six.

I was nominated for the Emmy. David was not. I didn't win.

I have always run away from funerals, but I went to a memorial for David. His son, Andrew, gave a magnificent speech in his honor. It was simply a reading of his credits. Powerful. Moving. It reminded me of my own goals: to matter, to stand tall, to reach for something higher, something finer than we are. To be worthy, to find real love. Thank you, David Susskind, for choosing me.

SCENE: *Lyndon* in Texas

Lucie and I were chosen to star in the first national tour of *Social Security*, Mike Nichols's production of a Broadway hit comedy by Andrew Bergman. The chance to work with Mike was a good thing, so we took the job. It would be a whole season of work, ending in Los Angeles at the Ahmanson.

It was summer. We moved our family to Del Mar, on the beach in California. Lucie's father had passed the year before, and the house would be sold. Lucie and her brother had agreed not to keep it. The kids begged them not to sell it, and they were right. It was on two lots, right on one of the best beaches in the state.

I got a call from a man in Texas who had seen *Lyndon* on PBS. He wanted to know if I was available to bring the play to the stage in a benefit performance for a politician seeking an important state office. I had never done the show on stage.

I knew I would have to reinvent it as a stage vehicle, and I knew I could do it. I said yes. I called my friend, Broadway director Jack O'Brien, who was then running the Old Globe, a theater company in Balboa Park, San Diego. I asked him if he had a spare stage where I could relearn and stage *Lyndon* for the Texas date. He did.

I commuted there for two weeks. I staged it myself and imagined a setting that would work. The story needed a podium in the houses of Congress, a desk and other furniture for the Oval Office (including a rocking chair à la JFK), and a hotel room in the Driskill Hotel in Austin, where Lyndon always went for the election returns.

Meanwhile, I was trying to relearn the show.

The gentleman in Austin planning this enormous gig was Don Buford, a grand and canny guy who was reinventing himself from political candidate and operative to theatrical show producer. He told me, "Politics is just show business for ugly people."

Don had provided me with the exact set I requested. I had one afternoon of rehearsal on the day of the show and then went into makeup with the same man who had done the makeup for the PBS show. Don had arranged that.

I walked out on the stage of the still-unfinished Wortham Theater Center in Houston in the same suit and tie I had worn on TV. *Lyndon*'s audience was eleven hundred Democrats, all standing, talking and laughing, bourbon glasses sloshing, exchanging local political gossip. It was a political convention, not a play.

In my solo show as Lyndon Baines Johnson. "Bobby, your brother told me to tell you that he's offered and I've accepted the candidacy for vice president. Apparently, somebody in your normally efficient organization . . . screwwwwwwwwwed up!"

"The Secret Service brought Mrs. Johnson into a small, little hallway . . . and there set Jackie . . . all alone. Bird said she never saw anyone so alone in her whole life."

"Hey hey, LBJ, how many kids did you kill today?"

I knew if I didn't turn this into a theater event right now, I'd never get control of this event that required sober attention.

Lyndon took charge: He ate the room!

Instantly, the tribal instinct kicked in. Bourbons were downed, seats occupied, and Lyndon got his first story-directed laugh—a joke on the Republicans!

SCENE: Los Angeles to New York

We were still living in Hollywood when, on April 26, 1989, Lucille Ball died at seventy-seven years of age.

Lucie was shattered. This was a life-changing event in multiple ways—sorrow, regret, the final abandonment, the *who am I now*? Their relationship had been in crisis when Lucy passed. Truncated. Her mother had been unhappy before it happened. She said that she didn't want to live five more years. And so, she didn't.

We were just about to return then to New York to try to restore our family to more stable values, to get away from Hollywood's narcissism and transactional caste-system culture. But Lucie was suddenly saddled with disposing of her mother's entire estate.

* * *

I hadn't arrived at parenthood with a plan for raising children. I believed I had grown up almost wild. My working parents could not be present during the day. I walked to school from the first day. I rode my bike or the public bus in high school and junior college. The kids' world was fairly safe. No drugs. Reefer madness was still in the obscure distance. We were in a dream state. Oblivious white privilege ran our world, and we were tiny cogs in it. Just keep turning and no one will notice.

I had chores after school, mainly cleaning the house, making beds, and clearing trash. And in the summer, mowing the lawn, trimming hedges, and feeding the chickens (and on Sunday, wringing the neck of one and boiling the feathers off it for dinner). My younger sister and I shared the housework. Schoolwork was up to us.

So, my idea of raising my own kids was basically, "Leave 'em alone and they'll come home wagging their tails behind them." I figured ours would negotiate school okay because I did. I made their lunches and put them in brown paper bags on which I drew pictures and wrote stuff to amuse them and let them know I was thinking of them.

Lucie and I showed up at the school meetings but didn't oversee their school days like some parents. We showed up for the sports they played but didn't get in their faces about their relationships or try to mold them into super students. I figured they would discover who they were and what they wanted to do with their lives on their own. I had forgotten my own miseries in that painful process. I got through it. Why wouldn't they?

SCENE: Hollywood

In our ninth year of marriage, I wanted to surprise Lucie as I had on her thirtieth birthday. It was a celebration of our tenth year together, a year early—that was the surprise. I made a show for her with Judy and backup. I hired a hall at the Hollywood Roosevelt Hotel, did a couple of secret rehearsals with Lucie's musical director and the ladies, and invited our Los Angeles theater friends. And this time, I was in the show.

I performed a few of her father's most beloved love songs. I gave myself a glitzy club singer's costume and did my act. It was well-intentioned but under-rehearsed. My nerves grabbed me. The pitch wobbled. Not the best audition I've ever offered. But I got through it, a lover's tremulous serenade under the balcony.

She was surprised, but the effect was weird. She seemed embarrassed, unsettled, and ill at ease. I thought it was me. Was she humiliated by my inexpert renditions of Desi's songs? The folks I invited were an enthusiastic audience. I wasn't a flop, just okay, and everyone got the point: I Love Lucie.

We flew to Hawaii as we had on our honeymoon to be alone together and reconnect to our first days. But she didn't want that. She seemed bored with the big island in a quiet hotel. She wanted to be in Oahu. She had lots of club friends there—Jimmy Borges, Don Ho, pianist Betty Loo Taylor ("Lady Fingers"), Patti Swallie (Don's companion who was featured in his act), and others of Oahu's night people. We spent our time with these folks. Hardly alone.

There was something distant about Lucie this time. On the flight over, I asked the flight attendant to hide in her salad a diamond ring I had designed and had made. But I was afraid she would swallow it by mistake, so when lunch came, I said, "Careful eating that salad. You never know what might be in it." Of course, she found the ring. It's a spectacular ring, but again her reaction seemed muted, flat. Not at all ungrateful, just preoccupied.

I wondered what was on her mind. Had something changed between us? Our Hawaii trip did not bring back the exhilaration of our honeymoon. It was crowded with other people.

On the day we left, she gave me a beautiful bamboo briefcase she had bought in the hotel store. The card said *To the Big Kahuna*. I didn't feel like the Big Kahuna.

It was my turn to be uneasy. Our lovemaking was no longer open, free, and fun. Something was definitely different. The preceding nine years had been fabulously intense. We were now the parents of five children. New York is a challenging but wondrous place to raise children. We had smart, kind, honest people to help us. Jean Ferguson, our chief care helper and housekeeper, kept the house in order. She was so loving that our kids relied on her as family. So did we.

During that time, I did four Broadway shows. Lucie did her own TV series, *The Lucie Arnaz Show*. She built her own nightclub act, playing in Vegas, Reno, Atlantic City, and regional venues. She had embarked on a most satisfying new strand of her long working life. She was recreating herself with more control over her working life. She was taking charge.

* * *

Actors are patient. We wait to be wanted. We try for things we don't get, mourn them a little, and go back to waiting with purpose, hope, and a willingness to endure. We endure rejection, the worry over money, and the mix of panic, hope, desire, and determination to stick it out. And the intensity builds. In the end, it can define you. You get used to it. It's the salient fact of your life—you have *no* control. You have become intense ambition. The dénouement of such a life ought not to be an increase in this intensity but a resolution of it.

And then to discover that what may have appeared as a detour in a career, in the urgent need to place yourself in the world and the work you've chosen to represent who you are, to be who you are, is not a detour. It's what you were always meant to be. And you grab it as a piece of flotsam floating past that can save your life. You hang on for dear life. Your attention is riveted on the life-saving thing. Things like mundane life, relationships, love and what you thought it meant, and the result of that love—a partner, children—can recede in your view and become part of the rear horizon while your grip on the driftwood becomes your primary need. You are self-absorbed and don't know it. You are on the "No Road" past Hana, and you don't know where you're going, but suddenly, it's not an adventure anymore. It's an obsession.

It was a time of Lucie beginning to define herself as separate from her parents, to get out from under the great, bright cloud of their magnificent achievements that had inevitably cast shade on their two children.

And, in this decade, Lucie actually lost them all: In 1985, her stepmother, Edie, whom she adored and who had taught her so much. A year later, her beloved father died in his home as Lucie held him in her arms. Then, in 1989, her mother. Lucie's paternal grandmother had also just died after years of dementia. And then, the final blow—Willie Mae Barker, the wonderful woman who had raised Lucie while her parents worked.

Like all deaths in the immediate family, so much is left unsaid and even unknown. Do we ever know our parents? We think we do, and it's only when they must depart from us that we realize how much of their lives we never knew and now will remain a mystery to us. The *who am I?* question becomes inevitable. If you believe in spirit, it helps. But even then, its utterness must be survived. Life—its cruelty and kindness—goes on, and the survivor now knows, for sure, that she, too, will follow into that "undiscovered country" and life after her will go on.

Lucie was devastated by all these primary losses and each time had to overcome her feelings in order to deal with the public demand to mourn with her—the demand for information about how it all happened, how she felt, and what she would do now.

She mastered the test with great strength of mind and will, with poise and class. She represented her parents as any daughter of royalty would. And she did it alone. The long process distracted her from her feelings and gave her no way to deal with them or even to feel them.

My older sister and my father had both gone into that good night a little before this, and I had felt all these things. I was there for my wife to help in every way I could. And yet, neither of us had the best psychological or spiritual knowledge that could give us answers, however unsatisfactory, about coping with such things. My way was to tough it out, to compartmentalize the pain. Lucie's was to plunge into the good daughter role and serve others, not herself. I admired her, held her when she wept, walked with her through her fury at life and all the inexplicable misery and unfairness that death brings, and tried to take on as much of her pain as possible.

How can anyone be ready is the question. When someone's grief seems so insurmountable, words don't help much. So I could really only hold her. And I did. And all our children, young as they were, held her. They saw and felt her pain. Did it help? Yes, up to a point. Change must come from so many fundamental connections shattered, so many earthquakes and aftershocks to endure. And it did.

* * *

INFIDELITY.

Lucie swore, "It was just erotic wrestling."

* * *

What do you do when someone you love . . . what is the right word? Trespasses? To use another's property without permission, to miss the mark, to grab the nearest standing object for support, to seize the illusory need of the now and disbelieve the reality of the eternal.

I had to hear again and believe the most ancient plea to love, to guide us to peace and compassion: "Forgive us our trespasses, as we forgive those who trespass against us."

What must be done depends not on the trespasser but on the trespassed against. But what if the trespasser has not just sneaked onto your back forty to bow hunt deer offseason but is instead walking across your heart wearing sharp spikes and punching a thousand little holes, which bleed trust, love, contentment, humor, and the belief that love has ever existed? What if then all possibility flees, leaving two sudden strangers at the dinner table, talking past each other at the children while something, someone, waits in the shadows to destroy your life, all your lives? What if you go blind and deaf to spirit, and red rage tries to stop your heart to kill the pain? And the gates of Hell swing open and you want to run through them to destruction?

I had a double-barreled, twelve-gauge Parker shotgun, last manufactured the year I was born. It was elegant, heavy, and loaded with sabot slugs for coyotes. Perfect. Safety on, I laid it carefully in the front seat of my car and drove. It was a moonless night. I parked and saw a shadow get out of a car and walk toward a house. I stepped out, walked forward, and pointed my protector, my avenger, at the shadow, which suddenly stopped moving—paralyzed. I was ten yards away. He was playing dead like a rabbit. I couldn't miss.

But I couldn't do it. I had run through the gates and down into the nine circles of Hell. I saw Hell. So, I left the frozen shadow in place, got back in my car, and drove home to my life. I wish it had all been a dream.

* * *

> In the middle of the way of my life I found myself in a dark wood.
> The straightforward path was lost. It is hard even to speak of this
> savage place, which the very thought of renews the fear. So bitter is
> it, that death is little more, so, I will speak of the good, which there
> I found.
>
> —DANTE, THE INFERNO (JOHN CIARDI, TRANSLATOR)

> Let me not to the marriage of true minds
> Admit impediment. Love is not love

Which alters when it alteration finds . . .
But bears it out even to the edge of doom.
—WILLIAM SHAKESPEARE, "SONNET 116"

Great poetry and the distillation of great wisdom into great music don't help unless you believe in it. Love doesn't help when you believe it's lost. Dante found good in Hell, Shakespeare in the act of steadfastness, of staying true to even altered love.

I'm here to swear to another kind of love—the one I ran into like a crash test dummy. Fidelity. Constancy. Loyalty.

Hamlet tells Polonius that the actors should be treated better than they deserve, because, "If you use every man after his own desert, who shall 'scape whipping? Use them after your own honor and dignity. The less they deserve, the more merit is in your bounty."

I deserved whipping, if any player ever did, for the mess I had made of my first marriage and the hurt I had put upon Robin and our two sons. "So bitter is it, that death is little more."

I had blamed myself and thought my life was over, nothing but broken promises and betrayals ahead. Then came Lucie. She resurrected me.

Now, I could hate her. But I could not *not* love her. She had lived so long with loss, and had filled the darkness with distraction trying to find out who she was. "I'm dancing as fast as I can," she had said.

I had wandered much longer and had been shipwrecked before I knew how to assess my own worth. Dante, guided into Hell by Virgil the poet, fainted twice when he saw the punishments reserved for lust and wrath, his own sins—and mine. I never had a chance to visit Hell with a cool poet, so I just drank and screwed around until Hell visited me and showed me the same ugly scene of a marriage I had unwittingly destroyed.

Then Lucie and I found each other. Karma is a good thing.

But karma is a credit card. It must be paid in full at some point, or the interest will kill you. Amid our struggle together to learn that lesson, we raised five children. It has taken a lifetime.

And as Paul said to the Corinthians, and now to me and to Lucie . . . *love never fails*. For me, to bring myself to trust again. For Lucie, to abandon a neediness she couldn't see into. It was opaque. A dark mirror wherein she tried to see herself, but saw someone else she didn't quite recognize but tried to believe was her.

SCENE: New York to Hollywood to New York

Things break, and the process of rebuilding—with broken bricks—begins.

I insisted we move our growing brood out of Hollywood to the Westchester County woods in Katonah, New York. We owned a little cottage as a getaway, a Cape Cod-style farmhouse with a well and a cellar, a pond, a hill for sledding, a waterfall, and a swamp. Kid heaven. We renovated the structure with ancient beams and joists from a 300-year-old Dutch barn. We lived there for twenty-six years.

We left Hollywood to step back from its craziness and raise our children in good public schools in the country, away from showbiz. A place for them to learn to fly.

But how could we escape our theater destiny? We were an acting family. Lucie and I worked together in film and TV, on tours of musicals and plays. The plays were my bailiwick. We took our children with us on every tour we did together, without much thought as to how they would respond. They were hotel kids. We moved between LA and New York, the two grazing pastures for the theatrical nomads we were.

Actors go where the work seems fruitful. New York had theater, media, and some television and film production (since vastly increased). LA had media and lots of TV and film, but not much theater.

Oddly, when we moved to one coast, we got calls to work on the other. But with each move we made to one or the other, we put down roots, bought a house, renovated it, found schools for the children, and then, four or five years in, work would get scarce on one coast and we would move to the other.

Lucie was a name but not in any way a captive of her family's fame. It was the opposite. She was her own woman. We were both determined to make a career in the theater. She went to musicals. I went to *Macbeth*. I was different. The only name I had was won by my work in the theater. As I became slightly more well-known, I could move into television and movies, but I had to prove myself for each new job and show. That was the life we were born to live, each of us trying to find a hold that was a little more secure on the icy mountain of show business, like all actors.

We had committed to living in Katonah, away from the gravitational pull of both New York City and Los Angeles. Work in both places waned and became occasional. Rather than the mad race to auditions and the wait for the phone to ring, we made our own lives professionally and raised our family.

It was a decade of tension as we struggled to repair and reconstruct our marriage, which undoubtedly bled onto our children, who could not understand the stress between their parents. It was intermittent but occasionally ferocious. Doors slammed. Silences. Cars stopped on busy highways for one person to get out and insist on walking twenty miles from nowhere.

Neither of us had the necessary psychological tools to help us grow into adults in charge of ourselves, our careers, and, most importantly, our roles as parents. We were making it up as we went, and neither of us knew what a functioning family looked or felt like. I tortured her and myself with jealousy. Images I made up and even partially knew came and went in my brain like strobe lights, blinding, hurtful, and with crazy-making intensity. She responded like an addict in first stage withdrawal.

But the ultimate truth that we both knew—always knew, even when we hurt each other the most—was that there was no one in this world for either of us but the other. I never once doubted that. That's why it hurt so much. She may have had her doubts, but I don't think so. This was real, whatever it was. We were real. The kids were real.

We were both in the soup. After a long time, we realized we were not in separate bowls but in the same one together. The predicament, the fact, was still there like an old road sign reading STOP with a lot of bullet holes in it, but none in the heart of hearts—none fatal.

Finally, the day came when we could laugh at each other's lousy shooting skills, and that laughter made a new kind of friend. We were newly made.

SCENE: *Lyndon*

I got a call from the Lyndon Baines Johnson Presidential Library in Austin, Texas. The call was from the director of the library, Harry Middleton. The word had spread about the *Lyndon* show on stage. Harry invited me to perform the show at the library.

We were having a tour of the library when, around the corner, down the hall, came a small female person. She was wearing an apron and was barefoot. Her shoes were tucked into the apron pockets. A cleaning woman maybe. She walked directly up to us, and I saw who it was.

Involuntarily, I blurted out, "You look just like my mother!"

And Lady Bird Johnson replied, in a honey-soft, East Texas–accented, musical voice, "Why thank you! I believe that is the best compliment I have *evah* had."

Lady Bird Johnson was a queen in my view. An American queen—a woman of unquestioned dignity, honor, patience, and kindness. She was her husband's best and wisest advisor and canniest critic. She loved him devotedly, and, to my surprise, I came to believe he returned her love fully and with respect.

I performed *Lyndon* at the library, and Lady Bird sat in the third row, her preferred seat. The play was a success.

Don Buford wrassled up three cowboy TV crews, and we filmed the show at the beautiful Paramount Theatre in Austin, just blocks from the Texas State Capitol.

SCENE: Texas Tour

Don expanded that one performance into a tour of the show in Texas. The day before leaving Los Angeles to start the tour, I slipped on an oil slick on Wilshire Boulevard and tore what was left of my right meniscus. I had a soft cast put on and flew to Texas. Don rented a van, got me a cane, and I sat in the back lengthwise, stretching out my leg on pillows. We drove across Texas, a painful trip for me.

I played the Opera House with a cane and a severe limp. Afterward, there was a reception, as happened after every show in Texas. People are courteous and want to connect with a performer. It's old-style and feels like a frontier holdover from the time when any new visitor bringing a show or a cultural event to a small cow town was eagerly awaited and welcomed. After the show, I gimped my way around. I quickly ripped off my rubber face and stood painfully while the entire audience filed by and shook my hand. A lean, tough old cowboy shook my hand, leaned toward me, and quietly said, "I hated LBJ. He was an SOB. Seeing this show tonight changed my mind. He was alright, but you know"—he was leaning in, whispering—"I never knew the man was a cripple!"

We played the show at San Marcos State Teachers College, where Lyndon went to college. At lunch, I was introduced to Robert Oswald, the older brother of Lee Harvey. Naturally, talk turned to the question of *did he do it and did he do it alone?* A highly intelligent, articulate businessman, Robert strongly believed his brother killed Kennedy. When he spoke to Lee before he was killed by Jack Ruby, Lee had said, "Don't believe everything you're going to hear about this." Robert was certain Lee had done it, and alone.

At another small college. On the day, a professor asked me, out of the blue, if I would address his history class before the show. I had a three-hour makeup session in an hour or so, but I went. The classroom was full. I started discussing

Lyndon's presidency, voting rights, Medicare, etc. I noticed many glassy-eyed stares on the faces of the students. I asked, "You know LBJ, don't you?" No, they didn't. What? This is a college history class in Texas. I looked at the professor. His look said, *this is what I have to work with*. I told the class, "Well, I expect you do know JFK." Silence. Finally, a hand went up. "Yes?" The student said in a slow drawl, "It's an airport in New York City."

That night, the show was played, as we say, "to an oil painting of an audience." Dead. Frozen. We no longer teach civics as a vital—or any kind—of subject. No democracy can survive without an informed population. Why don't we know this?

I played the show in Marshall, East Texas, where Lady Bird grew up. And just as I had cried reading the script to David when I heard my father's Arky/Tex accent coming out of me, when I heard the people Claudia Alta Johnson grew up with speaking in that same soft, unassuming, modest lilt, I felt at home.

S C E N E : Mayflower Hotel, Washington, DC

President Lyndon Johnson stepped into an eighth-floor elevator with two Secret Service agents and an official. The elevator stopped at each floor and took on people on its way to the lobby. The passengers were dressed formally for an event. They knew each other and were excited, chattering and laughing as they walked into the elevator. But when they saw that their fellow passenger was the president, the talk trailed off into quiet and odd looks to each other. After only one glance at Johnson, they did not look at him or the Secret Service men again. The elevator doors opened into a crowded and lively atmosphere. There was a festivity about to begin in the hotel.

Lyndon and his cohort stepped into the lobby. As the crowd noticed the president and slowed down for a look, so did a group of Secret Service officers, who immediately stopped the president's party. It appeared that they intended to arrest the Secret Service personnel accompanying the president. The official with Johnson took charge. He spoke to the group of new Secret Service operatives quietly. People continued to gape at the president as if they didn't believe their own eyes. By now, the new Secret Service men were laughing and joking with the men in the president's party. Finally, they stepped aside to let Laurence Luckinbill, as Johnson, and the strapping young actors from Catholic University's Drama Department (very convincing as serious members of the Secret Service) proceed immediately toward the hotel's kitchen. The "official," Texan Don Buford, had explained that Lyndon was about to make a surprise

"Landslide! I carried forty four states and the District of Columbia and I tell you, lookin' at those returns, I was in *hog heaven!*"

Lady Bird Johnson and me after a performance of *LYNDON* at the LBJ Library in Austin, Texas.

appearance at tonight's celebration of the twenty-fifth anniversary of his inauguration. And it would be a surprise—Lyndon Johnson had died some seventeen years past.

Showtime! I burst out of the kitchen door and traversed the ballroom at a run. Lyndon was in a rage at the slow pace of progress on his initiatives to eliminate ignorance, poverty, want, prejudice, and inequality in the country he loved. Time was short and it was being wasted. There was not a second to lose. The goddamned Republicans were resisting change! The goddamned war was in the way! He wanted Americans to transform into a Great Society, and he wanted it *now!*

I had come from behind the audience on one side of our stage, and they had to turn in their seats to see as I walked up the narrow corridor between the rows of seats. At the far side of our platform, they stood up to be able to catch sight of Lyndon. I was like an express train roaring forth. The surprise worked—people were shocked and delighted to see the man most of them knew so well back on his high horse, charging into battle. His biblically cadenced phrases and his salty, fearless ripping into what their country lacked and needed and must get were exactly what they knew and loved about him. He was rude, stubborn, determined, pissed off, brilliant, and funny all at once. He was furious at them, but they knew he never held a grudge. He was Texas at its most raw and its best.

I climbed to the temporary stage and stopped center. The audience was Lyndon's Cabinet members, the folks who had paid big for Democratic causes, Lady Bird, and the members of her family. "Lyndon" gave them forty-five minutes of himself.

The end of the show came. I said, almost sang, "America, America, God shed his grace on thee and crown thy good with brotherhood from sea to shining sea."

Then I turned and took the steps down toward Lyndon's actual family. I had one more line, my finisher, a rousing yell Lyndon had done when he won his 1964 election by a staggering landslide. But as I reached the bottom of the steps, Lady Bird was up from her seat and coming toward me, arms wide, an enormous smile of congratulations on her face.

And I . . . stiff-armed her, rushed past her to the exit, turned, and gave my last line. It was a great, rousing ending! The audience exploded. Leaped to their feet. Applause. Cheers. And I was offstage . . .

. . . But I had left Lady Bird standing there alone like a debutante abandoned by a rude, ungentlemanly dance partner. Oh my God. What had I done?

I've gone over and over that moment of shame ever since. Even now that she's gone—they're all gone—and it's been thirty-three years, I cannot forget or forgive my idiotic actor need to say all my lines and leave the lady in the lurch. I had let the queen down.

I apologized. Lady Bird said, "That's alright, honey. Lyndon would have done the same."

Lynda Bird Robb, her eldest daughter, said, "I wish my two children had been here. They didn't know their grandfather very well."

Mrs. Johnson invited me to dinner at the ranch in Johnson City. I accepted. She sent me an armful of Texas wildflowers from her garden. I pressed and framed them, and they hang on the wall in my home today. Over the years, she and I exchanged letters from time to time. My notes were always of gratitude, hers always giving and motherly, in the restrained way of a Texan frontier woman, which was her heritage.

SCENE: Austin

I was in the dressing room at the LBJ Library theater trying to tie my tie. It was almost showtime. I was in full LBJ makeup—the nose, the upper lip and chin, the sides of the face, the ear appendages, and the close-fitting gray and black hairpiece.

There was a sharp knock at the door. "Who the hell is it?" I yelled. I was extremely nervous. Lady Bird would be in the audience again, along with friends and close associates who had known the president very well.

The knock came again, louder. I yelled, "What?!"

"Mrs. Johnson would like to see you," said a stern male voice. Oh shit! My tie still undone; I opened the door. A Secret Service stalwart stood there. He stepped aside, and Lady Bird, in evening dress, came forward. She saw my untied presidential cravat—the same black and silver striped tie I had worn in the television show—and noticed my nerves.

She stepped up to me, reached up, took the ends of my tie, and began to tie it. She said, "I always tied Lyndon's tie, too."

I have no idea what I said. I was stunned. Expertly, she drew the tie up and stepped back. The Secret Service guy said briskly, "They would like a photo of you and Mrs. Johnson together."

She took my arm and we walked into the large room. The staff photographers were there, set up for the picture. They guided us to a spot in the center of a long flat-white wall. The lights were already flooding the area and the wall. We were arranged facing each other. She looked very pretty. Cruel people denigrated her looks, especially when comparing her to Jackie Kennedy. That time was long gone. I had never judged her and never would. I always thought her true beauty could be found in her grace, humanity, and kindness. It always shone through for me.

She looked up at me. I looked down at her. I was considerably taller, but I knew she was used to looking up. The photo was fired off in several iterations. Later, copies were sent to me from the library. There we were, in the foreground, looking at each other, and behind us, on the white wall, was an enormous shadow, looming benignly over us in sharp and indelible profile. It was Lyndon Johnson.

I had rewritten the show from top to bottom by then, adding Lyndon's sharp, always pointed, and always very funny jokes. I had cut and shaped it to fit audiences at West Point Military Academy, at the Air Force Academy, for Democratic and Republican party groups, and at universities, colleges, and regional theaters all over the US. I had kibitzed with local audiences about local political issues, adding Lyndon's advice to solve their problems.

One night as I was standing in the wings waiting to go on, I was prompted from somewhere to look toward the stage as I had set it up, podium with the presidential seal, state flag on one side, American flag on the other. I focused on the Stars and Stripes. I have the same child's reverence for that bit of cloth as I've always had, while also understanding how distant our country is from fulfilling its stated ideals. A thought bloomed in me like a flower. A number seemed to be imprinted on the folds of the flag. 58,000. Fifty-eight thousand. A number like a still-bleeding wound. I thought I was getting a message.

This is the number of soldiers the US sacrificed to try to solve a theory—the Domino Theory that if Vietnam fell, we would be inundated by communism taking over Asia and the world. The theory, as it turned out, was false. The lies told to defend it were many. The military lied to Lyndon, Lyndon lied to us, diplomats lied to each other, and the body bags kept arriving en masse at Andrews Air Force Base. And Lyndon was responsible—and took responsibility and left office. Then, Nixon kept the lies going, starting with making a deal with the North Vietnamese to cause them to refuse Lyndon's offer to stop the bombing and the war if they wished to negotiate peace. Nixon's scheme worked. He betrayed us and lied to Lyndon about it so that he would be elected. Nixon beat Hubert Humphrey, a decent man, by an indecent act.

I asked Lady Bird how her husband had taken all the deaths of his soldiers. "Oh honey," she said. "I would get up in the night, three in the morning, and he'd not be in bed beside me. And I'd hear moaning, moaning coming from the hall, and I'd open the door just a little, and there he'd be, in his pajamas, and in his hand was the Situation Report with the casualty list, the deaths, you know, from the actions the day before. And he would be weeping, honey, with tears dripping down his face. He hated that war." She said that last sentence quietly but with such power, such quiet vehemence. It was the power of a woman who stood by her man, who was forced into making decisions that killed people. She was now his widow. Too soon.

And as I waited to go on stage, that memory flooded my thoughts until I could think of nothing else. Fifty-eight thousand boys. American boys. God keep them. Don't let it be in vain.

And the lights rose onstage, and I walked out to face America with that one thought in my mind, a mantra given to me by Lyndon. His burden. Now my burden. And America's.

* * *

Lyndon:

"I did not want to be the president who built empires, sought grandeur, or extended dominion. I wanted to be the president who educated children, who helped to feed the hungry, who helped the poor to find their way and protected the right of every citizen to vote in every election. I wanted to be the president who ended war among the brothers of this earth. I hope you will remember what I've done. I hope I haven't exaggerated. I may have.

We had a little boy down in our hill country who ran in one day and said, 'Momma, Momma, come quick! I just saw a big lion in our backyard!" His mother went running out, and there stood the old family dog. And she said, 'That's not a lion, that's Rover. Now you told me a story. You go up to your room. You stay an hour. You turn out the light, and go down on your knees and beg the Lord to forgive you for telling stories.'

After about an hour, she went up to his room, and she says, 'Did you pray to the Lord?'

'Yes,' he says.

'Did you ask him to forgive you?'

'Yes,' he says.

'Well, what did the Lord say?'

And the boy says, 'Momma, the Lord said he thought it was a lion, too.'

I don't know if you see all these problems that face America—the priorities, the tinderboxes: poverty, filth, education, disease,

isolationism, narrow nationalism, protectionism. I don't know if
you see all these lions or not, but I hope you do. And I hope that
the Lord thinks they're lions, too."

—LYNDON BAINES JOHNSON 1908—1973

SCENE: GREAT AMERICANS

Clarence Darrow, "The Defender of the Damned"

I was to play *Lyndon* in Boulder, Colorado, at a festival honoring former senator
and 1968 presidential candidate Eugene McCarthy. I had been a McCarthy
supporter and had manned a storefront campaign office for him. I worried
that McCarthy, who had vigorously opposed Lyndon and the war in that race,
would hate the entertainment—a play about his political foe.

Instead, I offered to do another play featuring a strong, liberal American
political figure I thought would make McCarthy comfortable. The Boulder
folks didn't go along. *Lyndon* was just fine, they said. But it was a weekend
of events, and they still had one open night. "I'll do *Lyndon*," I said, "and I'll
give you a second show for free, but the new show will have views opposing
Lyndon's—and be more in line with McCarthy's liberalism." The promoters
were interested, but who did I have in mind?

Don Buford and I thought of Clarence Darrow, the greatest criminal defense lawyer in American history. Famous, controversial, had a crisis-filled life,
great climactic trials, associated with socialists, anarchists, commies and radicals
of all kinds—perfect for the senator's interests.

The Republic of Boulder agreed. The fact was, although I had revised and
reshaped the Lyndon play and had written several plays of my own, the time
was too short to think of writing this one. So I settled for a one-man play about
Darrow that had been done on Broadway by Henry Fonda. I had seen the
play, loved Fonda, and talked to him about it several times. I thought the play
was a skim job and hadn't told the real story of Darrow. But, it would serve
the occasion of entertaining my political idol, Senator McCarthy. I did not
anticipate the lesson in Washington's political ways that the master was about to
teach. Nor did I know then that my choice to do a play I didn't love would lead
me deep into Darrow's life and work, and compel me to undertake the most
thorough character study of the man I could make.

When you walk out alone on stage to be someone else for a lifetime of two
hours, you need all the help you can get. For the Boulder *Darrow*, with a play

that felt unfinished and the memory of the great Fonda and even the sound of his voice to obliterate before I could begin to work, I needed to feel right for the part. The look was essential.

I was rehearsing in Los Angeles. I found a white linen suit at the Mark Taper Forum theater at the Music Center. My old friend, Gordon Davidson, the genius guru who ran that theater, made sure the wardrobe door was open. The suit was marked "For Chris Reeve" inside, and although I was not built like Chris, it fit very well. So far, so good.

So, I played Clarence Darrow in Superman's white linen suit from a Mark Taper Forum production of Tennessee Williams' *Summer and Smoke*. The night I did the show, I was challenged by a 100-year-old gentleman in the audience who had been a spectator at the Ludlow Mine Strikers trial in Pueblo, Colorado, where Darrow was a witness.

"How did you like the show?" I asked.

"It was alright," he snapped, "but Darrow never wore a white suit!"

A day later, after both shows were over, McCarthy strolled back to his hotel with me. He was followed by a bevy of beautiful women, all of a certain age, like an aging rock star from the '60s with his aging groupies, all eager for a word, a photo, a smile, a touch from the master. He took it all with charming equanimity, seemingly unengaged with the adulation.

Over drinks, I asked him what he thought of the two men I had played for him. "Oh, well," he said, "Clarence Darrow is interesting, but Lyndon! That was him up there, all right!"

I was shocked. "You liked him?"

"Oh yes," he said with a smile. "I liked Lyndon. He was wrong about the war, that's all, but we believed alike on almost everything else. The Beltway, Washington, and the press made us out to be enemies, but we weren't." He looked at me kindly and laughed. "That's the thing about Washington. Forget the drama, and don't believe everything you read."

The play I had used that night was one only Henry Fonda's authenticity could make work. The owners of the rights to that play mistook Fonda's brilliance for the play itself, which wasn't. I began to study Darrow. I suggested changes to strengthen the play where Darrow himself was strong. The play's owners said, "If it ain't broke, don't fix it!" But it was only light entertainment, not the story of the man.

I had to do my own play. I immediately got the theatrical rights to Darrow's autobiography and other writings from the Darrow estate and wrote my own play. The owners of the other play tried to stop me. But I was determined that the real story of Darrow be told, so after more threats and legal posturing, they gave up. I opened my play, *Clarence Darrow Tonight!*, in New York at the Ensemble Studio Theater. It was a success.

I played theaters across the country, at ABA events and Continuing Legal Education conferences, and at State Bar meetings where I moderated panel discussions on the unfinished issues of justice in America and the bloody battles fought over them. Today, the moral and ethical evolution of our country clearly continues. People want to understand how to change this circular, self-defeating social reality. I've had to learn what I stand for. I offered the evidence—one show at a time.

I played to one of the most dedicated audiences I have experienced in seventy years in the theater. It was arranged by our financial advisor and my mentor, Albert Horowitz, one of the wisest, most just, kindest humans I have ever known. In a tiny former factory in Teaneck, New Jersey, now a dedicated arts center, one hundred people sat in rapt attention for two hours in ninety-five-degree heat due to a temporarily out-of-commission AC system, as Darrow strove to answer the question of his story: What is justice? At the end, they leaped to their feet and cheered Darrow and then kept me another hour and a half to talk about local and world issues of justice that were important to them. One elderly man stood up and told us he had known Darrow's mentor, Eugene Debs. This gentleman had been inspired to commit to a life as a pro bono public defender.

In 1996, the play won the American Bar Association's Silver Gavel Award for "Outstanding efforts to foster public understanding of the law." It was nominated for a Dramatist's Guild Award for Best Play that same year. I went alone to the ceremony and sat in the back row. I didn't want a repeat of the seat-changing caper at the 1978 Tony Awards. I did not win. This time, I took the loss philosophically. I had ceased to believe in awards or compare myself to others long before that. I had done the work and was happy. "Nuff said," as we Arkansawyers tell it.

Elaine Fauria, a family member, asked me to play *Darrow*. She taught at a school in Queens that had a reputation for educational innovation and excellence. The trouble was I was to perform for fifth graders. I almost said no. How on earth, I wondered, would fifth graders know about justice, labor struggles, capital punishment, pacifism, socialism, and the intricacies and gnarly parts of the law, which seem to have nothing to do with justice? Elaine told me not to worry. Her students would be up to it.

I dressed in my *Darrow* suit in the principal's office and went to the auditorium. The school was old and elegant in architecture and reflected the social respect education was given in the 1930s. I entered the auditorium, full of fresh-faced, noisy ten-year-olds. They were a portrait of New York, where

ARLUCK ENTERTAINMENT
Presents
LAURENCE LUCKINBILL
in
Clarence Darrow Tonight!
A New One-man Play by
Laurence Luckinbill
Based on the autobiography "The Story Of My Life"
by Clarence Darrow

"I don't know what attracted me to the study of the law. I know I didn't want to work." —Clarence Darrow

"Listen! The first shots you fire at the people gathered here today will be the signal for a civil war."

almost every country in the world is represented. These children were stewing in a very juicy melting pot.

To my absolute surprise and delight, these kids settled down to this difficult soliloquy and gave it their total concentration. They got most of it.

I finished. Instantly, five teachers with handheld mics were racing through the aisles, singling out students, shoving the mics in their faces, and telling them to ask me questions. The questions came, and they were informed and legitimate. A Continuing Law Education for fifth graders! The questions were set up by teachers who had read the play well and informed their students well. And the questions were rocketing toward the stage.

One hand in the front row had gone up each time but was not seen by the teachers. A bell rang, and students began grabbing their book bags when the hand went up again in the front row. I said, "Wait a minute, someone here has a question. I want to give him a chance."

The principal gave the nod to proceed. The questioner stood up.

I asked, "What's your name?"

He piped up, "José."

I said, "Okay, José, what's your question?"

He said, "When did you die?"

Everyone laughed. The boy shrank back as if he had committed a crime.

I yelled, "Just a minute! That is a very good question." They became quiet. "What that question means is that what José saw up here, he believed was real. That Clarence Darrow is real, and all the stuff he told you that explains what justice is and isn't, is real, too! Right, José?" José nodded vigorously.

"I'll answer the question," I said. "Clarence Darrow was born in 1857 and died in 1938." I was looking at each of the faces in the front row and seeing Black, brown, white, Asian, Israeli, Pacific Islander, Arab, Nordic, Native American, and East Indian faces, expectant.

I said, "So when Darrow was a little kid about your age, his home was a station on the Underground Railroad, which was one way slaves escaped to freedom from the South of our country. They were smuggled to Canada, where slavery was illegal. So, a young Darrow saw Black people being made free by Black and white folks even before the Civil War. Have you heard of the Civil War?" Heads nodded solemnly. "And," I went on, "he died in 1938, just before the Nazis in Germany started the Second World War. Have you heard of that?"

Heads nodded yes. I saw a student in the front row wearing a yarmulke, his hair in long *pais* strands on either side of his pale, thin face. I spoke directly to him. "And before Darrow died, the Nazis had already started their plan to kill all the Jews they could catch, and that horrible act was called . . ." I looked at the Jewish kid. He piped up, "The Holocaust!"

"Yes," I said. "So, you can see, each of our lives holds in the parentheses of our own life and death the past, present, and future of the human race."

The second bell rang more insistently. My audience evaporated. Elaine was right. It's never too early to tell children the great things about America.

* * *

Darrow:

"What is justice? It doesn't mean power or cunning or greed. It doesn't mean following old precedents or accepted rules of the past. It doesn't mean producing more wealth while the great mass of humanity is never very far removed from want. It's not logic, fine distinctions, or lofty ideals. Maybe it doesn't mean anything. Maybe justice doesn't exist. And maybe it doesn't matter. Maybe the only thing that matters is that if we realize our common suffering and our common need, it will create in us not a desire for justice, but only a desire to help in this world, in proportion to our strength."

—CLARENCE SEWARD DARROW 1857–1938

SCENE: New York, *Cabaret*, Studio 54

My last Broadway flight.

I walked into a small rehearsal room in the theater district. I knew some of the people there. I was there as a candidate to play Herr Schultz in Sam Mendes' revival of *Cabaret*. I was given a few pages to read—a scene.

I didn't give the scene any thought. I just read it as I always do, searchingly in wonder at the words, sentiments, and desires of the character. When I finished my reading, I could feel something unusual in such an audition room—a sense of unanimity. A palpable warmth enveloped me from the folks in charge of the show. They liked what they heard. Then, somewhat tentatively, someone asked me if I would sing for them. I do not consider myself a singer, even though I can carry a tune and even harmonize a bit. I had done only a few leading roles in musicals, so I was uncomfortable presenting myself as a singer. And I said so.

A man stood up, smiling, and said, "You can do this. Let me help." And he handed me music and lyrics for one of the few songs Herr Schultz sings in the show. I looked at John Kander and Fred Ebb's simple, beautiful sentiments in the song called "Married." It is a very moving little poem to love.

> How the world can change,
> It can change like that!
> Due to one little word,
> Married.
>
> See a palace rise
> From a two-room flat
> Due to one little word,
> Married.
>
> And the old despair
> That was often there
> Suddenly ceases to be,
> For you wake one day
> Look around and say,
> Somebody wonderful
> Married me!
>
> —Kander and Ebb, "Married," Cabaret

Patrick Vacariello, the musical director and conductor of the onstage Kit Kat Club Band, sat at the piano and played the simple melody. And I sang "Married." I did it my way, thinking through it, taking my time, and phrasing the lyric to allow my immediate love for the song to bloom. Patrick followed my lead. Then, as I finished, he began to play again, this time in the gentle swing of waltz time, which is what the song is, ending with Schultz and Frau Schneider dancing together as they are beguiled by love. It's a moment in a relationship that cannot last—Schultz is a Jew, Schneider an Aryan, and the Nazis have taken over in Germany. This relationship hasn't a chance, but these two elderly last-chance lovers embrace it wholly anyway. It's a very high moment in the play.

Patrick played the last notes and I finished, this time attempting the waltz tempo while interpreting the song as I felt it. He supported my over the bar singing but kept me to the tempo by gently emphasizing the *one-two-three* beat of the waltz. Thus, I was encouraged, taught, and mentored to believe that I could not only sing but also maintain a tempo. And dance, which I did, alone in the middle of the room. There was applause, and I was made a member of the *Cabaret* company on the spot!

Now came rehearsals. Five of us were new, replacing five original cast members. Me, Carol Shelley for Fraulein Schneider, Michael Stuhlbarg for the young Nazi, Victoria Clark for Fraulein Kost, and Susan Egan for Sally Bowles. We would get two weeks of rehearsal, one dress rehearsal at the put-in with the existing cast, and off we'd go. Some reviewers would be there looking at the new kids, so it would be an opening night for the five of us. I was back on Broadway! In a musical!

I saw something powerful in the character that appealed to me—the simplicity that life could be good if you had faith that people were essentially good, as Anne Frank expressed. Almost all Jewish people in Germany believed that their assimilation into the culture and their profound contributions to it had been so thorough that what was coming for them was improbable, actually impossible.

So, Schultz was a true man—delighted with life but aware of its impermanence. His delight in a pineapple, his pleasure in running his simple shop, and his courting of Frau Schneider were a real backdrop for the murderous nightmare looming up for them.

My good fortune was that a mentor gave me a book by a German Jew, Victor Klemperer. It is called *I Will Bear Witness*. Klemperer was a professor of romance languages, a writer and critic for cultural events, a member of the establishment who had fought for Germany in WWI, and was married to a well-connected Aryan woman. The book, secretly begun in Berlin in 1933, describes in horrific detail exactly how the National Socialist government proceeded methodically to destroy Jewish people in Germany. In Klemperer's case, his Aryan wife and cultural eminence protected him for a while, but, as the Final Solution drew nearer, his existence was challenged hourly. The couple survived but had been reduced to penury and almost starved. The wife went mad from stress. His faith in humanity was a life-or-death challenge. I made my Schultz out of Klemperer. He was my nightly guide, his wise words in my ear before going on stage made sweeter by Schultz's faith.

I loved my time in the show. Mendes' take on it was darker and more anarchic than the original Hal Prince version or even Bob Fosse's film. My Schultz was framed against that, but I decided to give a true counterweight to anarchy.

The real depth of my version of the character was grounded in my love for Lucie. Our relationship had been extremely stressed, but both of us had been tempered in the fire, and both had chosen to see our marriage through all of its mountains and valleys, ice storms and wildfires.

At the end of the play, as I stepped onto the steel platform and looked directly at the audience, headed for extinction by an insane human—Nazism—tears came down my cheeks. I was not weeping for Schultz. He knew, as Klemperer believed, that he would become an artifact of history and a footnote, but his natural joy in mankind, life, and love was still his. No one and nothing, certainly not cruel and pointless death in a gas chamber, could take that away. My struggle has been not to lose affective memory, my belief that the arc of history bends toward justice. Even now, that art aimed to counter hate and cynicism may yet help stem what could be an inevitable slide of America into the same chaos, tyranny, and terror that destroyed so much of the world before it could be stopped by America's "better angels."

But, now we need "Flights of Angels."

SCENE: GREAT AMERICANS

Theodore Roosevelt, President of the United States

At the turn of the millennium, there was a revival of interest in Theodore Roosevelt. It had been a century since Teddy had become president after McKinley's assassination. The US had returned to Panama the canal we had built. We were ramping up to a war with Saddam Hussein over mythical weapons of mass destruction. America's war on Iraq was not exactly "The War to End All Wars," nor did it "make the world safe for democracy." In fact, it shook the world's trust in American truth and honor and democracy's check on injustice, even theft. Were we just after the oil? Was it twenty-first century colonialism? It was an illustration of George Washington's 1796 farewell address warning against foreign entanglements, which make us slaves to the "effects, and lead us astray from our duty and self-interest" (see J. William Fulbright's *The Arrogance of Power*). The stage was set for a millennial version of a warrior president.

The vision of American troops entering Damascus (Paris, 1944?) to a shower of flowers and kisses by damsels wearing burkas with only their eyes showing was the depth of ignorance from a self-regarding nation and government. George W. Bush was no Washington or Lincoln. He was a mild and decent man, in one sense a reincarnation of Theodore Roosevelt, although an ill-informed and rash "warrior president." Full disclosure: I wasn't ignorant, but I believed the dangerous hype myself, hoping vainly (and stupidly) that we could create democracy in an ancient tyrannical patriarchy with "shock and awe." I voted for Bush. My children, more informed than I, have never let me forget my momentary lapse into Republican madness.

Harry Middleton called and asked if I had a play on Teddy Roosevelt. There were a couple of pieces in circulation, but none were satisfactory. I said I would write one. It was late September. The show would be at the LBJ Library in mid-January. Time was running fast. I was determined the piece would have a real story with a plot, not just be a chronology of "and then I was elected to . . ." listings like the other stuff out there. I went to my friends, the librarians at the South Salem Library in Westchester County, New York where we lived. The staff there was very pleased with my work, and that they had played a major part in supplying the research.

At that point, the only thing I knew about Teddy was that my father had been born the first year of his presidency and was seventeen the year he died. Soon I had thirty-five books arrayed on my worktable. They looked like cartoon porcupines full of color-coded Post-its stuck in places where a thought, fact, or word seemed to demand to be a part of the mosaic of Teddy I was building.

A month passed, and I had promised to read my *Teddy* play to friends, but I had no play yet. Lucie had come to the office from the house several times to ask me to help her with our 250 Christmas cards. Each time I had put her off. I was obsessed with the deadline, and I had nothing but a pile of facts. Teddy, the man, had not appeared yet. Finally, Lucie came up to the office again around midnight. Exasperated, she said, "I've done all the cards for my friends. Now do yours!" And she tossed two greeting cards on my desk. I signed them. For my two friends.

Maybe that sparked something: family! Duty! I pulled Teddy's sister Corinne's book out of the pack. I scanned it and quickly judged that it was worshipful sibling treacle, pet names they called each other and all. But this night, I was up against it. I had about six weeks left to create, rehearse, and perform a new one-man show. And my wife was ticked off. I signed the two Christmas cards to do my family duty. Feeling sheepish, I opened Corinne's book and shortly came upon the paragraph that ignited the engine, the motor, of the play that quickly became *Teddy Tonight!*

In July 1918, Corinne had asked her brother, age sixty and a decade out of office, to speak to a political meeting in Saratoga, New York, on behalf of her husband, who was running for a New York state office on the Republican ticket. Teddy agreed, but a day before the event, his youngest son, Quentin, was shot down in aerial combat with a German air ace over no-man's-land at the German–French border. The initial hope was that Quentin had survived, but increasingly, certainty became that he had not. Corinne telephoned her brother in Oyster Bay, New York, to say that, under the circumstances, he didn't need to travel upstate. Teddy replied, "Under the circumstances, it is my simple duty." He left his wife, Edith, in Oyster Bay and went to Saratoga.

He spoke as always from copious notes, but then, suddenly, put away his prepared remarks and commented emotionally on the boys who were giving their lives for their country at the crest of their young manhood and who surely deserved—those who lived—to come home to a country that was worthy of their sacrifice. He never mentioned his own son.

This was the moment I had searched for. A public speech for duty that inescapably turns to private emotion. I wrote the play in the following three weeks, built a mosaic of hundreds of pieces, and immediately began learning the forty-one pages, finding Teddy's thoughts and moves, the right wardrobe, the correct mustache (a saga in its own right), and dreaming up a simple set that could be mounted in the 1,100 seat theater at the LBJ Library. It played very well, and again, Lady Bird Johnson was there, third row center.

SCENE: Midland, Texas

In Midland, TX, touring *Teddy, Tonight!*, I arrived at a university to find the theater and was directed to the gym. I walked into the gorgeous 6,000-seat athletic facility where six or eight volleyball nets were set up and a women's volleyball championship was being played. I asked the manager where the theater was. He said, "Here." He saw my face and said, "Don't worry, we have curtains!"

"Curtains?"

"Yep. A whole system. See 'em up there? Million dollar system! They draw right in for a more intimate theater space."

Intimate? The bare ceiling was fifty feet up, the bleacher seats vast. I said, "Draw the curtains tight. I need a theater with about five hundred seats." This was my high estimate of the size of the audience I would draw in an oil town.

The guy laughed. "We've sold 5,300 tickets, friend. Extra foldout chairs are on call for tomorrow."

Oh my God! My immediate thought was, *Get out your script!* I went to the hotel. A call was waiting. The management asked if I would like to escort First Lady Laura Bush's mother, Jenna Welch, to the reception after the show. Of course.

I worked on the show. Late afternoon, my actor buddy Richie Zavaglia and his partner Marilyn arrived from Dallas. They were having trouble getting tickets, telling me, "Your show is sold out!"

Touring the US is hit-or-miss. Theaters are mostly old, dusty, and ill-equipped. Or they are resplendent with all the equipment better and newer than Broadway theaters. My aim was always to play for all who wanted *Great Americans* in their town. I felt like a missionary, a combination performer and civics teacher. I have always said my shows were edge-of-the-seat shows in which the *e poi?* question is paramount—what will happen next? They were hit shows constructed to make the most dramatic stories from the lives of the men I represented and loved.

That night in Midland was a revelation. The enormous gym was curtained tightly, and the set the management had recreated to a T on the stage was exactly right. The bench with the teddy bear sitting quietly on it stage left, the podium with the presidential seal up center, and a single Victorian table and easy chair stage right, with a background of palms and ferns representing Cuba, all bathed in exactly the warm glow described in our contract rider. And extra rows of foldout chairs crowded the stage. Almost six thousand people in Midland, Texas, had turned out to hear Teddy Roosevelt's story.

The audience was enthusiastic, eager to applaud and highly attentive. When there's an audience so involved, the actor feels protected by belief and urged to take chances. I tried to give them the best Teddy ever.

Afterward, I escorted Mrs. Welch to the party where we were both overwhelmed with well-wishers. The lady was super intelligent, calm, kind, and down-to-earth. A lovely companion at age eighty-three. She left us at ninety-nine.

SCENE: New York

I opened for a New York run in a lovely new off-Broadway theater. *Teddy Tonight!* was the inaugural production in the new Abingdon Theatre complex at Thirty-Sixth Street and Eighth Avenue. The show opened in the brand-new June Havoc Theatre there.

Between her concerts, Lucie had jumped in to help as always. On opening night, she was still sweeping construction detritus off the floors and cleaning the communal toilets as I got ready in the dressing room, which was in a corner of the backstage behind a curtain.

The show worked. Ms. Nancy Jackson, one of Teddy's grandchildren, attended the performance and spoke about her father Archibald Roosevelt, the gentle Archie. She was touched that I had put her father in the play both as a child and as a severely wounded captain and recipient of the Silver Star.

And Theodore Roosevelt IV, a look-alike for his great-grandfather, showed up unannounced one night and afterward commented that the show was "Very good, fine, alright, alright" but lacked one thing: a proper acknowledgment of Teddy's role in the conservation of our wild lands. He told me a story of a grand moment at the end of Teddy's presidency that I had missed. The following night, I put it in the show as a permanent part of the story.

Theodore Roosevelt. *TEDDY, TONIGHT!* "Just Bully!" Photo credit: Simon Luckinbill.

Teddy spins a tall tale of shooting the giant grizzly bear for his five beloved children.

Teddy still inspires by his devotion to his family and deep love of service to his fellows on earth. "All in all, he was a man" (William Shakespeare, *Julius Caesar*).

The story of my solo presentation of *Teddy Tonight!* was capped by the 2021 release of a graphic novel of the play text by publisher Dead Reckoning, and further honored by the 2022 Theodore Roosevelt Children's Book Prize from the Theodore Roosevelt Association.

* * *

Teddy:

> "No country is worth living in unless you're willing to die for it. And no country is worth dying for unless you're willing to live in it unselfishly, to do service, to be a torchbearer content to run with the torch as far as you can, then hand it to another runner before you fall . . . so, there are two things I want you to make up your mind to: first, that you are going to have a good time as long as you live, and next, that you're going to do something worthwhile, that you are going to do all the things you set out to do, because life and death are both part of the same great adventure, and the worst of all fears is the fear of living."
>
> —THEODORE ROOSEVELT 1858–1919

SCENE: New York

I am driving on the Saw Mill River Parkway from the city back to our Westchester house. Magnificently colored leaves detach themselves from the trees, floating, whirling, and dropping to earth. My hands are on the wheel at ten and two. I look at them. Strong and steady, as always. My mind is racing. I have just been told I have prostate cancer. The doctor at New York Hospital, head of his department, steady, calm, kind, with a warm Virginia accent, has just explained what has happened and what will happen in various scenarios depending on my decisions. My front seat is stacked with books I bought at Barnes & Noble. I will research the shit out of this situation. Suddenly, I feel like I am looking at my hands for the last time. I—this person, this persona, this flesh—will die, and I will be gone from the earth. Who will mourn? Do I want anybody to mourn?

Suddenly, I see myself down, flat on the pavement in the city, on Broadway at Forty-Fifth Street in front of the Brill building. I have fallen, and people, rushing, as always, are stepping over me with their New York take-care-of-business walk. Leaning forward, careful not to step on the obstruction they sense on the sidewalk, but not looking down, vaguely aware it's a body—me.

I glance in the rearview mirror. I look pretty good for a guy who just heard a potential death sentence. I smile at my little mental drama. Then, I laugh. I had told my wife the situation before leaving the city, called her in London where she's rehearsing a big new musical. I am in New York rehearsing my Teddy Roosevelt show.

She hears the news: Cancer. Prostate. The best choice of three possibilities is to remove the cancer along with the prostate—a radical surgery. Prostatectomy. I have just learned to pronounce this new word. If they don't miss even one of the cancer cells, there's a reasonable recovery prognosis. I'll live, but unless there is successful nerve-sparing surgery, there's a high probability of not only incontinence but also permanent damage to the ability to get an erection or ever have normal sex again. As a sidebar, I will never have another ejaculation of semen. No more normal coming, no more easy sex.

Silence on the phone. In the background, I hear Lucie's stage manager calling the cast to the stage. Finally, she says, "Well, the good news is they're not cutting out your tongue."

I know my wife. She has to defuse her deep fears. This is the perfect way, her way, to make light of it while also commenting on our sex life. I laugh again. It is a wonderful wisecrack.

Then I feel alone. Sad. Wow. Tough comment. Doesn't she care? What about my feelings? Well, what about them? Life is tough. Death is tough. Sex is good any way you make it. We will make it, if the operation works. If it's in time. If there's not even one cell . . .

It's an absolutely gorgeous fall day in upstate New York. This is a place I will love until my dying day, which ain't yet! We will make it. The bright leaves swirl and lift in the breeze but keep falling. They will come to earth . . . when their work is done.

SCENE: New York

Lucie was in London, struggling through a rehearsal process with a demanding producer and the British theater's way of working. I was in New York and had been told by my doctor that I should take all the time I needed to decide which treatment would best deal with my prostate cancer. It was, so far, contained in one half of the prostate. I had read everything I could find. The choice came down to seed radiation to target each cancer cell in the affected part of the organ or a complete surgical removal. General radiation was ruled out as too much, with the nasty side effect of burning parts of the body. The side effects of seed radiation were considered acceptable. The one option—radical prostatectomy—was offered with a ninety-five percent rate of cure, or as close as medicine at that time (only a couple of decades ago) could offer. Seed radiation's history gave it a sixty to seventy percent chance of eliminating every cancer cell. Without that, there was a thirty to forty percent chance some cells would escape and eventually develop into a killing cancer.

The possible side effects of the total surgery were permanent incontinence and complete loss of my sexual capacity. I was between a rock and a no-hard-on place. I needed mentors. I needed to talk to someone who had recovered from prostate cancer. Someone recommended that I call Buddy Hackett, the comedian. I did. In his distinctive, funny Brooklyn way, he answered, saying, "I noo you would cuall. I'm psychic. Did you know that?" I didn't know Buddy, but we had many friends in common, including my wife and her mother. Buddy listened to my story and immediately said, "Cuall Sidney Poitier, he knows everything about prostate cancer. Cuall him at the Hillcrest Country Club. He plays dere. You gonna be alright. I'm psychic, and I know!"

What are the odds? I was given the next move for my life by a sweet guy I had watched in *The Music Man* on TV.

I called Hillcrest, identified myself, and asked if I could speak with Sidney Poitier. There was no hesitancy. "He's on the links, sir, but I'll give him the message when he is done playing."

An hour passed. The phone rang. "This is Sidney Poitier."

I said, "This is Laurence Luckinbill, and you don't know me but . . ."

"Of course I do," he answered in his unmistakable warm and open way.

I don't remember what I felt, but it was so surprising and so together, so down to earth and so powerful. I knew this man instantly. The real thing. Big star? Yes, but possessing compassion, humility, and mastery all at once.

I told him my story as briefly as possible. There was intense listening at the other end of the line. I felt totally understood as by an old friend. Then he said, "My father died of prostate cancer. My uncles died of it, and my brother. I am not going to die from prostate cancer. I have had it. I did the radical surgery. I recommend you do it, and as soon as possible. If my father had done it, he would be alive now."

He was emphatic and very personal. I felt I had not been preached at but rather seriously advised exactly what to do by one of my closest friends who had nothing but my survival in mind.

I went back to New York Hospital to talk to my doctor, the head of urology. I said nothing about my conversation with Sidney, but it had a powerful effect on me. I told my doctor I was close to making a decision but wanted to hear again why he was for the surgery. He said, "It's because I believe you will survive this operation and live a longer life. The worst possible thing would be if the cancer escapes the lobe, enters the other one, and moves into your body, organs, and bones. So, tomorrow morning, give me your answer."

I said, "Let's do it."

"You will not regret it. I will be very careful to spare the nerves relating to sexual function and incontinence," he said.

"How many of these have you done?" I asked.

"Thousands," he said. "Let's get started. I'll need your blood. I'll make an appointment for you to donate right away."

I had the operation. Lynne and Leo came to New York to be with me. I was scared, but I took their strength as mine. A few weeks later, the catheter was removed (oh my God, the relief!), as well as the urine bag (yay!).

I called Sidney at his home and told him how it went. He said, "You'll not regret it. Are you traveling soon?"

"Yes," I said, "I have to go to London to see Lucie's opening."

"My advice," he said, "is to fly first class. Sit near the bathroom, and you have ten seconds!"

I laughed and said goodbye to this great man, a mentor who had saved my life. As he said, I had to stay by a bathroom for a few weeks. The sexual function side was more complicated and took more time to evolve into what it would become.

I have learned how good life is no matter what. And how good people are, strangers who become saviors. Samaritans who stop for you, not to get anything from you or for their own egos, but just to give to others freely.

Both Buddy and Sidney have returned to spirit. Sidney could not save those of his family who may not have listened, but he saved my life. I will never forget it, and I have passed his salvation message on to many others. I hope he was met at the gate by his father.

SCENE: GREAT AMERICANS

Ernest Hemingway, Writer

Harry Middleton called. Again. The University of Texas had acquired some papers from Ernest Hemingway's estate. They were planning a press rollout.

Could I possibly have a Hemingway play for three performances at the LBJ Library and UT? The occasion was about three months away.

As an adolescent, I had read all of Hemingway's writings in my local library. My literary high school best friend and I had traded notes about the great Hemingway as we rode the buses to and from school. He was our mentor to manhood. I loved him.

Then, in 1961, Hemingway committed suicide and I dropped him. We weren't friends anymore. The reason? Catholicism. I was Catholic and rigidly so. Following my family's and church's extreme orthodoxy, I condemned Hemingway to Hell for committing the mortal sin of offing himself. I knew nothing of the circumstances and I didn't look into it. He did a bad thing and was now in Hell where he belonged. I had no mercy for the man. I was done with him, and he was done with me, too.

I was tempted to say no to Harry. But very recently, something odd had happened that gave me pause. My friend, Isaiah Scheffer, had called me in a panic. He had created a winter program, American Writers in Paris, at the Symphony Space, a grand old movie theater at Ninety-Fifth and Broadway in New York.

Isaiah asked me to read a story the following night for the event. A new young writer had written a book of stories about Paris. He would read and talk. Fritz Weaver, a wonderful old-school actor and longtime friend, would read a Henry James story about Paris. And James Naughton, another marvelous actor and friend, was set to read a Hemingway in Paris piece from *A Moveable Feast*. But Naughton was suddenly unavailable, and could I fill in?

My first thought was, *No, I can't,* but because of my relationship with Scheffer, my "I can't" turned to "yes." And now I was in the dark theater in a single spotlight, standing behind a podium on a freezing February night, reading to a packed house Hemingway's tale of riding the train back to Schruns in Austria, to Hadley and their young son, John (Bumby), after his first and fatal tryst with Pauline in Paris. He felt the guilt that any young husband and father would at his betrayal of wife and son, but faced it so intensely and painfully and with the icy clarity and deep self-condemnation with which Hemingway experienced everything.

I had decided to read the story simply, in my own voice, not to reach for any emotions that were not my own. To do nothing that forced the words into any simulacrum of a Hemingway style. Just be myself. So, I read my own feelings. The audience demanded eight curtain calls from Hemingway that night. Isaiah came smiling up to me on stage and yelled in my ear over the roar of applause, "There's your next one-man show!"

I said something rude back. But divine synchronicity—mentorship—came from Isaiah's words. I was seventy-one, ten years older than Hemingway when he killed himself. What if he had lived to be my age? What great works might he have produced? Wasn't it time for me to at least look into the circumstances of his mental state at the time of his death?

What I found was horrifying. The mental torture of a man, a writer, in such physical and psychic distress that he submitted to the brutal electroshock therapy of the time, hoping for relief from his suicidal depression, which was made so much worse by erasing his short-term memory and making it impossible for him to be—that is, to write. What is a writer without a memory? Nothing.

I called Harry Middleton at the LBJ Library, said I would have a play for him on time, and got to work.

The next two months were a deep blur. I constructed a theater piece from Hemingway's fiction in a way that focused on the extreme vulnerability of the man and proved the greatness of his art by the way he transformed himself through it. It was about seventy-five minutes long. Short, but perfect for Texas needs. I tried it out in a benefit reading for the South Salem Library, as I did with all my shows. They were moved by Hemingway's struggle.

Two weeks before the performance, I wrote to the Hemingway estate requesting permission to do the reading for this one occasion. I still wasn't convinced there was a one-man show to be made. I was getting ready to fly to Texas when I got an ominous-looking letter from the New York lawyer representing Hemingway's remaining son Patrick, in Idaho.

I called the lawyer who had represented me in my legal battle over the right to write a Clarence Darrow play. He said, "Don't open the letter yet. There's no urgency. Go, do the show. It's a one-shot. Then see what they want to do."

The show in Texas went okay. In the dressing room afterward, I opened the letter from the Hemingway estate. I read a total rejection of me—a dismissal of any possibility of me, personally, ever being allowed to interpret Hemingway. For some reason, I seemed to be persona non grata. The letter was unnecessarily harsh, and I wondered what fear Patrick Hemingway, by then quite old, must live in. I was stunned.

There was a sharp knock at the door. On the other side stood a well-dressed gentleman who looked at me curiously for a moment and said, "I liked what you did very much. Do you have permission from the estate to do it?"

This was it. Cheese it, the estate cops! For some reason, I laughed. I said, "Am I busted? No, I don't have permission, and I have a letter to prove it, but this was the sole and final performance of this little show anywhere on planet Earth, I assure you."

"Had a little difficulty getting cooperation from the owners, I imagine," the gentleman inquired, raising his eyebrows slightly.

"Well, yes," I said. "Are you here to read me my rights and cuff me?"

He smiled. "I was very moved but suspected you would never get any help from the family. We have had some difficulty there, too. But what you have managed to do with the material is very enlightening. Can we have breakfast tomorrow morning?"

"Well . . . sure." What was going on?

"It'll have to be way early, say, 6:00 A.M.? I have to be back in Baton Rouge for the game."

"Oh. Sure." *The game*, I thought. What game?

I met with the gentleman, a professor at LSU and a delightful and cultured man who was deep in scholarly work of his own, as well as acting as the administrator of The Hemingway Foundation, which held rights to and responsibility for Hemingway's letters, a gift from Mary Hemingway, Ernest's widow. The letters were separate from the works of fiction. The foundation had heard that an actor was interpreting Hemingway in performances in Texas and wanted to check it out. He was impressed by what he saw, and at breakfast, he asked if I would be interested in putting together a Hemingway play with the letters as the sole source. Amazing!

I said I would read the materials the foundation had and see if I thought a theater piece could be made. There was precedence—Oscar Wilde, George Bernard Shaw, and others had been the subjects of successful shows constructed from their letters. I said I would get back to him as soon as possible.

"I'll wait to hear," he said and left. He had to get back to see the Bayou Bengals play that day. This man took everything seriously—teaching, scholarship, writing, Hemingway, and football. I was encouraged.

I read all the letters and started to work. I immediately realized that here was a very different man from the Hemingway of his fiction and the popular conception of the macho he-man. His self-cultivated public persona had done him perhaps more harm than good. What was that about? I was fascinated, riveted. Who was this man? This was a man who loved his work. Who had studied Cézanne's paintings and been dazzled by what he omitted from those paintings, hungry to know how to make something beautiful and true for the world. "One simple sentence to make you feel something more than you understood. Something beyond attainment, like looking into the source of life. I *had* to write. To endure and not be forgotten."

The boy from the Ozarks understood him. Emotional, vulnerable, hurt, mean as hell, sweet, a great friend, a bitter enemy, intractable, moody, reflective, rash, loving. This was beyond anything I had dreamed. He seemed to be a man

As Ernest Hemingway. "One sentence . . . just . . . ONE sentence . . . !"

without a skin, sensitive to every touch the universe threw at him. Hurting all the time, fascinated by the toreros who faced death in the bullring as a necessity of the gift of life. When he was hanging out with friends and laughing, or fighting a big fish, or risking his life to kill a leopard in the bush, he was aware of every conceivable side of existence—as predator, prey, observer, the observed, the criticized, the one who failed and succeeded simultaneously.

So, the riptide of synchronicity grabbed me again, and I was drawn deeper into the Hemingway persona and struggle for life and art. I had to make my own mosaic portrait of the man without a skin, working solely from his extraordinary and terrifying letters. The foundation was free to seek some kind of furtherance of the truth about the man. To the scholars, he was not preserved in amber and was not a purely commercial package to be offered like a product. He was a living entity still to be researched and discovered. Still totally alive. The whole truth was still waiting out there to be known.

I wrote an interior monologue from the letters, powered by Hemingway's inability to write even one good, coherent sentence. It was what it was—excruciating. It was all there in his letters and the published known facts about his suicide on July 2, 1961.

Now, I came face to face with my own former prejudices and limitations and began to see into the white heat at the core of a human being. Judgment became impossible, a violation. Understanding was all. I wished he could have forgiven himself.

In writing a play based on the work and words of another, the surprising thing is the amount of transitional material you have to create. I never make a conscious effort to write like someone else to make it fit in, it just happens. Working on Hemingway, I created connective tissue that even the foundation scholars had to ask, "Is that him or you?" And by that time, I wasn't sure. The subject and his words remain inviolate, and yet the structure, the plot, demands a creation equal at least to the subject's life.

I built a ninety-minute theater piece, an interior monologue articulated only to himself, only his thoughts, in the pre-dawn darkness of the last two minutes of his life as he stepped from his bed to the basement gun cabinet, to the foyer, and into eternity. I titled the show simply *Hemingway*. I played it first for the foundation at their meeting in Key West, only blocks from Hemingway's house and almost within view of his beloved home in Cuba just over the horizon. Meeting scholars, writers, and professors who spoke in seminars that focused light on so much of Hemingway's life, work, and times was very satisfying. My theatrical interpretation was embraced as a worthy part of the search for the truth of Ernest.

In 2005, I premiered the play at the Abingdon Theatre. My son, Ben, directed the show and did the lights and sound. I chose not to have critics in because I still wasn't sure of what I had and first wanted to know what Abingdon's theatrically hip audience would make of it. The acting challenge was that, in Ernest's mind, there is no audience. He is totally in his own mind. The actor cannot contact the watchers in any way. I was alone, isolated, lost, as Ernest was that morning.

There is no respite for the audience. I was asking them to go through the terror, sorrow, and heart-tearing flashes of gallant and savage self-deprecating humor that was this man. In the end, the audience sat silent. Then they slowly began to applaud. And applaud. A reverence for a great and fallen "man without a skin." To know that there is nothing left to being but mercy and love. I believe that Hemingway discovered that in the end. He belongs in the pantheon of great Americans. In 1954, he was awarded the Nobel Prize in Literature.

* * *

Hemingway:
> "*Toro*! *Recibiendo*! Await the charge without moving your feet once the charge has started, not moving until the sword has gone in, all the way to the knuckles of the right hand. I understand, Maera. We can meet only in death. And if the courage to die equals the ability to kill, then the meeting might be pure enough to last forever. Endure or be forgotten!

Dad, I loved the poem you wrote to me in your last letter.

I can't seem to think of a way
To say what I'd most like to say
To my very dear son
Whose book is just done
Except give my love—hooray!

> You're here, Pop, aren't you? Hiding in the sun, in the cheap seats where I can't see you, wearing your dirty fishing clothes, back from "yon Great Smokies!" Oh, I hope you are. Can we please chum together now?

[He loads the gun, snaps it shut.]

Will this end the silence between us?

"Pop, can we please chum together now?"

[He places the shotgun butt down and leans forward, in an attitude of devout prayer, with his forehead on the muzzle of the gun. He reaches for the trigger.]

Toro! Recibiendo!"

[The sun rises, filling the room with dazzling summer light, into which he disappears.]

—ERNEST MILLER HEMINGWAY 1899–1961

SCENE: Coda for Great Americans

For thirty-five years, I have traveled our country and the world, telling the stories of four great Americans who let me stand in their shoes on stage for a time.

I made plays of their lives and learned to act them. But it wasn't acting. It was, finally, just being. I had been invited—chosen—to do this work for them. And that kid in the Ozark mountains, who longed to matter, who had hoped for some other higher, finer life than the one he saw, was, at age fifty-five, thrown in with companions engaged in the urgent task of all American lives, transforming the mad idealism and canny practicality of our Founders into an actual American dream. Not one made of material things but of truth and spirit. These men were willing to do the hard labor of making real the promise of equality, liberty, and law that offered a chance of justice and mercy. They had taken on this mission and drew me into it with them. Could they make a silk purse out of a razorback pig's ear?

They were what I was not—brave, eloquent, hardheaded, daring. And they had humor and wit when the chips were down. They were all flawed men. But good men. Mentors. Fathers. They showed me again what many of us strangely forget. Those musty quill-scratched parchments are America's secular bible, not to be worshipped as sacred writ, but as detailed instructions to be rediscovered and reinterpreted as time changes life. A comprehensive field guide to making the best life man can have on this earth. They reminded me, with harsh facts, that our ideals are carriers of disease, racism and a craze for power to spread it. And that those infected hate all others who dare to disagree with their insane obsession that white is the only color God made to run the world.

In 2022, a white mob, sick with fear and ready to murder if democracy denied them their fevered dream of a new, white, Hitler-esque thousand-year

Reich in America, attacked our Capitol hoping to kill equality and justice without mercy. Great Americans had long sounded the alarm for this. They offered the only defense there is.

"We the people" must rise up. Democracy is ours to lose. Democracy is America. Without it, it's nothing. My mentors knew this. All of them hated war. They were not killers. They fought with words and acts to save us from ourselves. And then they passed on.

Standing in their shoes, I was taller. I was not a hero. But I could go on stage with the words I'd been given and be here, now, to revive the old wisdom and the power of common sense. To tell the truth and to trust the people to bring democracy back to life.

Words in a theater had saved me. Words matter. They are all I have. I'm a missionary. "Do what you can, with what you have, with where you are," said Teddy. If we speak now, "we shall nobly save or meanly lose the last, best hope of earth," according to Lincoln.

This is the choice.

It's urgent.

Endure or be forgotten.

SCENE: Miami, Florida

To be or not.

What I've learned: you spend a very short time as a studly fellow in full possession of your powers, and a very long time as an old man watching your powers dwindle. Not one by one, but in droves, scads, stacks, all at once. First it's a knee, then an Achilles tendon, then your atria bubble into dysfunction, then you go deaf, you pee a little all the time, short of breath and of stature, you lose inches of height and erection and gain inches in your belly, your hips, and your ass. You can't open a jar or carry a twenty-pound bag of birdseed twenty feet.

Case in point: I'm on the phone in our waterfront Coconut Grove condo trying to find a doctor. The rigging of the sailboats in the slips below the balcony clank and whistle in the errant ocean breeze and distract me from my pain. The pain is severe. I bend at the waist, press against the wall, wipe my sweat and tears, and lean over the wastebasket in case I projectile vomit everything in my stomach, which isn't much. This abdominal fury has been getting worse since we got to Florida this morning from New York.

We're in Florida to see our daughter act in a show at the University of Miami. And now, I have to find a doctor because I think I'm dying. I can't walk, sit, or stand. I can't lie down. The pain has moved from my abdomen to my lower back, right hip, and leg. Two thoughts rage through my mind: I'm going to die now, and in Florida for God's sake!

We race to Mercy Hospital, Miami. Mercy is exactly the wrong word—there's no mercy in this emergency room where next to me sits an aged, elegant Cuban gentleman whose entire scalp is split open and caked with dried blood. He sits upright as a grandee in his bloody white shirt. He has no English, and I have no Spanish. His daughter translates that they are immigrants. We are citizens with connections. Neither of us can get help. The staff are primarily Spanish speakers but are as disorganized as a preschool class. There is one, count her, *one* doctor on duty. She is Asian and young and seems panicked as she races back and forth among us, giving instructions to people in an incomprehensible dialect of English.

The Cuban gent has been here, his daughter tells me, since he fell on the stair in the middle of the previous night. He is still waiting for his interview. I am sitting crouched in agony in every direction.

I've told them my pain level is ten. When I first went in, I tried to be accurate and picked five or six, although I could barely get the words out. The person checking me in said, "Say ten or they won't pay attention." Now it *is* ten. It's *twenty*. I've been here almost five hours, and no doctor has spoken to me. Now, I fear I won't be able to stand or walk when they call my name. And I fear being a public spectacle of unendurable pain: "Sissy Actor Makes Spectacle of Self in ER." Now, I am just trying to survive a neurological disaster.

I waited thirteen hours before getting an X-ray, blood test, and a Band-Aid for the fingertip they drew blood from. No diagnosis. The ER bill came back at $13,000—a thousand dollars an hour to sit on a gurney in a hallway. Thank God for Medicare. And the Screen Actors Guild—they paid the bill, having decided that the service I got was worth $378. And Mercy accepted it! Are we a country with a screwed-up health care system or what? You be the judge.

I am still hobbling and in horrible pain. I am told there's a miracle cure place in Miami Beach. I will have to drive there. My wife and daughter are rehearsing a play at Coconut Grove Playhouse, our daughter's first Equity job and she's still a student! The next morning, I manage to get into the rental car and drive to Miami Beach. My foot is on fire, my hip is distorted in the bucket seat, and my T-shirt is soaking wet from perspiration even though the car AC is on max. It takes me five minutes to get out of the car and to the door of the athletic studio.

There is nothing to the place, just a receptionist who accepts my pain as nothing worth writing home about. Everyone has pain seems to be her immature, cheerful assessment. I don't have to wait; I'm taken right to a small room with a table made up with a white sheet with another folded neatly on top. The attendant asks me to strip naked and get under the sheet. I'm happy to oblige until I try to get up on the table and pull the sheet over me without screaming. After a time, an elf comes in, a small, plump, cheerful elf whose name is Andrew and who looks at my medical rap sheet, asks me a few questions—history of the pain, etc.—and then puts his hand on my belly and presses lightly, then stronger. His hand is cool, but it seems to emanate a power. I ask where he was trained. He says, "The Swedish Institute in New York. We're going to work on your Chi." What's a Chi? The elf is intent, staring at his hand, exerting power without pressure. I am feeling the energy, the heat of his hand, in my lower back. My legs start vibrating. He lets up. The sensation stops.

"Have you done acupuncture?" he asks.

"On my knee when I had a torn meniscus," I answer. "And it didn't help."

"Ah," he responds. He is painting my body with alcohol swabs—groin, stomach, knees, thighs, feet, upper chest, arms, neck, face, and head. From somewhere, he produces little . . . things that appear in his hand briefly and which, one by one, very swiftly, he jabs into my skin. Needles. And they hurt when they're inserted and continue to hurt. A lot. They seem to draw pain to them. He pulls the sheet over me and says, "Rest. Don't roll over. This treatment is going to lower your blood pressure. Don't try to get up. I'll be back." It's all prestidigitation. Magic. I lie there like a skeptical puffer fish sitting at the bottom of a reef.

I'm pissed off and hurting and full of doubt and wondering why the price for this session is so high. My mind is filled with my usual dark clouds of suspicion, irritation, and unfocused discomfort from being stuck with so many needles. I don't look at them. They feel enormous, thick, long, and stuck deep into my body. My back is killing me. I make up my mind to endure this. As time passes, I begin to feel better. Pain and irritation are replaced by a sensation that something is happening at the needle sites, some transaction happening in me but without me, without my having any way to input my usual physical or mental self into the process. Twitches and tics and itches and scratches subside. A warmth suffuses me. Naked, alone under a cool sheet, in a dark room, my body is changing. I've known vaguely about chakras, the centers of nerve activity, the points and pathways through which Chi works creating and maintaining flowing energy. I begin to imagine this happening. It's a new kind of arousal. I'm feeling alive, buzzing with energy. Is my pain all mine? Yes. But it's different now!

The elf returns. It seems like hours have passed. The day had begun to expand. I realized I had been drawn into a different time continuum by the needles, in the enforced hiatus from my usual frets and furies and weariness and the concentration on the consistent, irritating pain of needle pricks instead of on the grand dramatic pain of back and legs and my life, my mistakes, and fuckups.

I try to get off the table but roll to the floor. The elf helps me down. I'm a very strong guy, but how strong is jelly? I walk on my own to another room. No pain, or no thought of it. I'm placed on my back on a Korean invention, a bed of nails, or so it seems. They start to glow purple and ripple. Each "nail" works separately. I ride this machine as best I can. The purpose is to stimulate my entire nervous system, and again I'm so occupied with sensation I can't think about pain.

I climb into the car and drive back down Route 95 to Coconut Grove. My pain comes back on that crazy highway because Florida drivers think they're in a bumper car game. It's irrational and highly dangerous. I get home and climb into bed. I take an antispasm pill and go to sleep.

This became my routine for months. I didn't go back to New York. I stayed in Florida because I must get well. One day the elf says, "We're done with acupuncture. Tomorrow we're starting you on tai chi."

I had stopped using the opioid painkillers and could move without pain. I walked next door to a gym and dance space. The main room had a wall-length mirror and a long bench on the opposite wall. I sat on the bench, avoiding, as always, the mirror. An ebony apparition appeared in the doorway haloed by the morning Florida sun. It was sudden, like a panther becoming visible through jungle leaves. The elf had told me about this extraordinary man who had cured himself of AIDS. Naturally, I disbelieved. Why did I doubt? We had lost almost fifty friends to the disease, starting with our friend Richard in the very early onset of the outbreak in New York, when it was feared so much that Richard's roommates forced him out of the apartment they shared for fear of contagion. It was the medieval plague. Much more has been learned since, but it was obviously, clearly impossible to cure yourself. That much I was sure of.

And I'm here to learn tai chi from this man? I eyed him dubiously. I said, "I was told you cured yourself of AIDS. How did you do it?"

He just looked at me for a long time. Finally, the Black Panther spoke quietly. "Stand up," he said.

I stood, not knowing why I obeyed. He said, "Step forward."

I looked at him. He was not ordering me, just assuming I would do as he asked. I took a step, looking at him. What the hell.

He watched me without judgment or attitude. A silence. Then he said mildly, "Who are you going to fight?"

"What?"

"Your right foot is planted, and your left is cocked forward, ready to leap. Your hands are coiled, fingers tucked, almost fists. Your shoulders are hunched, and your head is thrust forward. Look at yourself."

I didn't look. I looked at him. I thought, *Fuck this!* but didn't say it.

"Look in the mirror," he said again, kindly, calmly.

I lifted my head and looked at the man in the mirror on the far wall. He was as described—someone crouched for a fight. Someone hostile. Someone . . . afraid. I saw a seventy-three-year-old man, hunched over, his face lined, his eyes squinting, his moves set, his lower body crouching, but without strength. The portrait of a man trying to project strength, trying to act aggressive, in control, on alert, prepared—but actually projecting weakness. Sadness. Loss. Of what? I was not flying, for sure. I was stuck. On the ground. In the mud. Done.

I looked at myself in the ballet mirror. Not a dancer from *Chorus Line*. Not a kid riding a stick pretending it's a horse. Not Mercutio discovering it's a play in a theater, where I'm safe in my feelings. Not even a *Great Americans* pretender, but a prisoner. Was I still longing for escape? *Volare*—to fly, *cantare*—to sing. Had I given up? Was it too late? I turned away.

The ebony statue said again, "Look in the mirror."

I looked, and something started to dissolve. I tried to look away.

He said, "Say to the mirror, 'I am a noble man. I have done many noble things. I will do many more.'"

And I started to weep. Tears ran into my mouth. Unashamed, I cried. I wiped my face with my bare arm. I stood there.

He said, "We will continue this on Monday—maybe."

As I stood, frozen in place, the panther glided through the sunlit door and became the light. I stood there. I wondered if he had even been there. Something was. Someone. I never saw this teacher again. I've never forgotten what I was given. A gift for the rest of my life. How have I used it?

I am a noble man. I have done many noble things. I will do many more.

SCENE: Stepping Off the Samsara Wheel

I wake up in the morning. It is freezing in the east. The bare trees outside the window are black gravestones with silver tears running down their faces and icicles dripping from witchy branches clutching at icy air.

Even the trees are cold! I go downstairs. The pale sun will not dispel the heavy clouds full of snow today. It feels like forever that it's been this way. A few

Lucie and I, a fine romance.

"Look Ma, I 'got my chance'! An EMMY award for *Lucy and Desi: A Home Movie*."

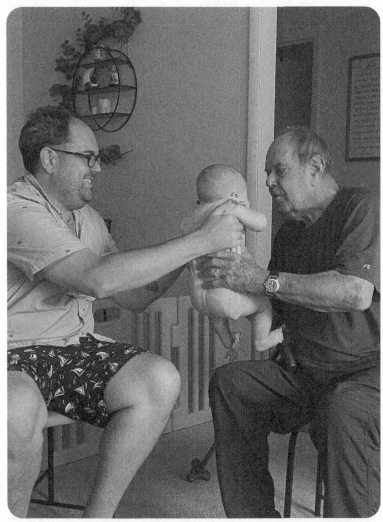

Our second child, Joe Luckinbill, presenting the award for best third grandchild, *The Georgie*.

days of spring and summer, and then years of winter. I get why the Pilgrims and Puritans marched south down the valley of the Connecticut River. They wanted to get warm. They were depressed and pissed off. But did those lily-white trespassers really have to massacre the local indigenous owners of the land?

I could understand their bad humor. After living next to the Sound, I, too, was depressed and pissed off. But didn't the invaders have a scrap of humor, courage, or a smidgen of negotiating skill left to work out peace with their neighbors? Did they regard the Wampanoag, the Mohegan, and the Pequot as illegal aliens? "Go back to where you came from?" What's the word for alien in Algonquin, I wonder?

I build a fire. My wife comes in. I say, "If I don't go someplace warm, I will die soon." That got her attention. I was turning eighty and didn't know why life had no taste or juice anymore, other than with my family. New York seemed done with me, my "careen," my one-man shows. They had Disney and actor-acrobats with implanted kneepads, and everybody was a 'tween.

Lucie said, "And go where?"

I thought. "Warm," I said. "Dry. With sunlight."

We looked at each other and said, "Not fucking Florida!"

SCENE: (Another) New Chance

We had smart, knowledgeable, literate friends living in Palm Springs, California. Theater folk. They urged us to visit. Lucie had childhood roots there. We set aside time, found a short-term rental, and flew west to California.

The approach over jagged mountains into Palm Springs can be rough, even in a large jet. We dropped and pitched and yawed all the way and landed hard, a sign that the winds had been very strong coming through the mountain passes surrounding Palm Springs like a giant cupped hand. But once here, the mountains exude restoration, repair, goodness. They are high and rough but not foreboding. They promise peace.

We landed here in 2013 thinking we would stay a month. Our New York pals warned, "Everybody in Palm Springs is *old!*"

The first mentoring I got from an "old guy" was, "Move here and you'll get ten more years on your life."

I laughed and said, "Yeah? How old are you?"

He said, "Guess."

I guessed eighty.

He laughed. "Eighty-nine," he said. Lenny Green became a good friend. He died, content to go, at ninety-nine, a day short of one hundred.

In the desert, the mountains say, "Look up. See all of your life, your history, see it whole, see it real, see it in spirit. The errors, the blind spots, the dark alleys your troubled soul wandered into, the pain you caused, the pain you took on, the comedy mask you wore locked onto your face, the tragedy mask you never deserved. See all of it now and know peace with it. All of it. Here things seem clearer."

Lucie has loved me. Finally, I believe it. What a shock! To know how long it takes to dissolve old festering fear and to accept that you are good. She has taught me the way. We may have taught each other.

Aware of the impermanence of all things, I no longer assume anything. I own nothing and no one—never have and never will, never could and never can. If nothing is permanent, do we have any obligations to anyone else? Yes! With impermanence comes responsibility to everyone, to everything, to the earth. To my friends, helpers, and mentors, especially to the woman who opened her soul in trust to me.

We are residents here now. Sunshine. Heat for your bones. The calm mountains to look up to every morning. It's a town full of joggers, swimmers, bicyclists, walkers, and doers. We reciprocate by donating our services to perform for many needy organizations. We are here permanently. Lucie said, "This is my *last* house." I said, "Uh-huh, okay."

Here, Lucie and I finally became one entity, a partnership that has endured formidable challenges but has finally become an absolute reality. Here, for the first time in my life, I have found peace and have begun to love myself.

SCENE: The End and the Beginning

I have now lived eighty-nine years. I have written my affective memories.

The task I set out upon was to write what I know, to explain myself to myself. To find out, in fact, who I am. The longer it took to write, the more truth appeared. And the deeper I dug, the clearer my distortions came to light. I became the observer in this science fair experiment, tweaking the dials of the microscope infinitesimally tighter to focus on my activities, couplings, dreams, entanglements, fantasies, struggles, successes, and failures. As they came to the foreground, my life became relative, not special. Am I uniquely ordinary? Or am I ordinarily unique?

I am a hologram wherein each pixel replicates the complete me. And so are you. Now I wonder if all the beings created since sapiens stood up and said to the world *I am*, if all of us together, actually make one single human

Lucie and me. Baja, Mexico. Forty four years of marriage . . . and counting. And they said it wouldn't last.

being. Male, female, all the variations, the colors, the beliefs, all the ages of our existence are really all one, all longing to return to the Creator of all.

I have seen much of life and not enough.

I am at my desk on a cold, slicing, rainy day. I've written too much of my life and not enough. I'm feeling old for a change. I've got to finish this odyssey from then to now. It's driving me nuts. I've written everything I can tell, but not everything I have learned in the telling.

But who will read it? My family. Maybe. Or have I worn out my welcome even there?

Shall I stop? Write *The End* and go to dinner now? Writers I revere say every book is a mountain gratuitously climbed. Am I a writer? I don't know. Will piling up words and events and scenes that seem to me to explain my existence on this planet ever make a book? Is it funny? Is it dramatic? Is it important? Tomorrow I'll start again to end it with a fresh yellow pad and a new pen. I will jump-cut to the last chapter, the resolution I seek. Maybe there is an epiphany. Maybe more than one.

SCENE: Arkansas

I am standing on the high wooden back porch of our original home in Fort Smith, Arkansas, 416 North Nineteeth Street, to be exact.

I look down. My sister Lynne is there in the early morning sunlight, looking up. Happy for me.

Behind her, gathered in shadow where there would be no shadow, are others—an audience. Mother, Father, Sally, Leo, Doctor Kernodle and his wife Portia, my Aunt Annie, Cecil Smith and Cleo, and many others I remember, all the mentors, all those who helped me, all who cared what happened to this kid who stands on the platform, now ready to try to fly one more time.

To you, Pop: *Volare . . . cantare . . .* sing a song to the blue sky, to love. *Ciao, ci vediamo.*

To Mom: No more worrying. Your kidlets are waiting for you at the dance. Wear the black velvet pantsuit you wore at that last Christmas. It was the best. I've got some work to finish, and I'll be right along to join you.

From the side, all in light, come others: the living—Lucie, my children, my own family, my siblings' progeny, all who have held me up and propped me up and challenged and forgiven every stupid, crass, selfish thing I've ever done or said or thought. They are all here, looking at me. Hoping for me. Willing me to do what I said I'd do, what I was meant to do from the first day of my life to now.

To my wife: I've learned to fly. Our way. Joy. Peace. Ease. Don't be afraid, my dearest friend, my partner. I'll be waiting for you in the cool shade. It's not far, just . . . right over there . . .

I check my cape. It's pinned to my T-shirt better now. I'm pretty sure it will work this time. This time I'll fly. I'll get across the weedy yard, past the chicken coop and the barn, and into the place that waits on the other side of the fence, just beyond where I can see. But I know what's out there is all good.

Those who have arrived look up at me on my little stage. They have all loved me more than I've ever deserved. They deserve a better show now than I've ever done before. They are encouraging, smiling.

I look at them standing in the sunlight—Lucie, Nick, Ben, Simon, Joe, Kate, and my grandchildren, JD, Eliza, and George.

I give my cape a last flip. It's perfect. I step out into the air . . . and . . .

THE END

ABOUT THE AUTHOR

LAURENCE LUCKINBILL awoke in 1934, as he had planned, on planet earth, in a place called Arkansas, the town of Fort Smith, near the legendary Ozark Mountains. It was a dark and stormy night.

What to do?

His parents decreed: Catholic School. He was fine there as self-appointed class clown and self-styled slacker. Then the University of Arkansas, where he failed pre-med spectacularly. The U.S. Army and Catholic University of America followed as the night the day.

Obviously, there was nothing to do but become an actor.

Five beans in his jeans, he hit New York to seek his fortune. At the foot of a skyscraping

Photo credit: Lucie Arnaz.

beanstalk, like Jack, he climbed. What giants did he find?

Tee-Vee, The-ater, Picture Shows. From soap opera to *Boys In The Band* to *Star Trek V*.

Climbed higher. Built and performed four solo plays of Great Americans: Lyndon Johnson, Clarence Darrow, Teddy Roosevelt, Ernest Hemingway.

A sixty-three year climb for a harvest of beautiful beans:

> New York Critics Circle Award
> Tony Nomination
> Emmy Award
> ABA Silver Gavel Award
> Dramatists Guild Nomination
> Children's Book Award
> Arkansas Entertainers Hall Of Fame

Meanwhile, back on earth, love and marriage with Lucie Arnaz. She, 28. He, 45. They worked it out. Happily. Raised five children. Now three grandchildren. Learn more at www.laurenceluckinbill.com.

Vita Bona Est. Don't let anybody tell you different.